International Economics

3rd Edition

L. Alan Winters

Based on S. J. Wells' original

London
GEORGE ALLEN & UNWIN
Boston   Sydney

© George Allen and Unwin (Publishers) Ltd 1969, 1973 and 1985

George Allen & Unwin (Publishers) Ltd,
40 Museum Street, London WC1A 1LU, UK

George Allen & Unwin (Publishers) Ltd,
Park Lane, Hemel Hempstead, Herts HP2 4TE, UK

Allen & Unwin, Inc.,
Fifty Cross Street, Winchester, Mass. 01890, USA

George Allen & Unwin Australia Pty Ltd,
8 Napier Street, North Sydney, NSW 2060, Australia

First published in 1969 and written by Sidney J. Wells
Second edition published in 1973 and revised by E. W. Brassloff
Third edition published in 1985 and rewritten by L. Alan Winters

British Library Cataloguing in Publication Data

Winters, L. Alan
    International economics. – 3rd ed.
1. International economic relations
I. Title   II. Wells, Sidney J.
337   HF1411
ISBN 0-04-330349-8
ISBN 0-04-330350-1 Pbk

Library of Congress Cataloging in Publication Data

Winters L. Alan
    International economics
Rev. ed. of: International economics/by Sidney J. Wells; revised by E. W.
Brassloff. 1973.
Bibliography: p.
Includes index
1. International economic relations.   2. Commerce.
I. Wells, Sidney J. (Sidney John). International economics.   II. Title
HF1411.W57 1985   337   84-28284
ISBN 0-04-330349-8
ISBN 0-04-330350-1 (pbk.)

Set in 10 on 11 point Baskerville by Fotographics (Bedford) Ltd
Printed and bound in Great Britain by
Anchor Brendon Ltd, Tiptree, Essex

Contents

PART III

Contents

TO JACKIE
PAUL AND PHILIP
and
TO MEG
VICKI AND CATEY

Preface to the First Edition

This book aims at meeting the oft-repeated demand by teachers and students for a modern textbook to cover the elements of modern international economics at a level appropriate to a second or third year undergraduate course, in which the student might or might not wish to specialize intensively in international economics. My object is to produce a book containing the body of knowledge with which every aspiring graduate in economics ought to be familiar, and which will at the same time provide a groundwork text upon which those who wish to specialize in international economics at postgraduate level might be able to build. For the benefit of the latter, I have indicated throughout the text the lines along which the advanced student should develop his more specialized reading – although I hope that *all* students will refuse to be content with reading this one book.

I also have in mind that a large number of intelligent people, whether university students or not, are seriously interested in a wide range of problems in international economics. In my work as an occasional extra-mural lecturer I have been most impressed by the keen desire of many people in all walks of life to become more fully acquainted with problems of the world economy. Accordingly I have tried to write this book in such a way that intelligent laymen, who have little grounding in formal economic analysis, will find their way about it without undue difficulty.

In writing a textbook it is difficult to make full acknowledgement to all the people who have played a part, directly or otherwise, in its writing. As an economist who has always been especially interested in international economic problems, I owe a debt to a large number of scholars who have influenced my thinking; notably Professors James Meade and Harry Johnson, and Dr W. M. Corden. On particular points I have tried to make full acknowledgement in text and notes; if there has been any omission, I trust the oversight will be forgiven. I feel that it is also appropriate to place on record the enormous debt (intellectual and personal) which I owe to Professor James Meade. My debt to James Meade as a scholar should be apparent from the following pages. My debt to him as a teacher and one-time supervisor is even more profound.

Part of the pleasure I have derived from writing this book has been due to the help received from a large number of people. Indeed it has seemed at times a truly co-operative endeavour. I am especially grateful to those who read through and commented upon the first draft, either in whole or in part. I would like to record my thanks to my colleagues at the University of Salford, Dr Wolfgang Brassloff and Mr Peter Lomas. With Dr Brassloff I spent many hours discussing the basic framework of the book, as well as the final draft. For penetrating criticism on content I am especially indebted to Dr W. M. Corden, Nuffield Reader in International Economics at the University of Oxford, Mr Dudley Peake of the University College of North Wales, Bangor, Professor D. J. Coppock of the University of Manchester, and Mr David Robertson of the University of Reading. I also showed the draft to one of my ex-students at Salford, Miss Margaret Smith. As representing the consumer interest, Margaret Smith's comments were invaluable and, I hope, have made the book a little more acceptable to the undergraduate reader. My Secretary Miss Margaret Parker has typed and retyped seemingly endless drafts with fortitude and patience; in the closing stages of the work she has

Preface to the First Edition

been helped by Miss Pauline Bolger of Salford University and also by Mrs Callaghan and Mrs Parker. I am grateful to Mr Reginald Oliver, who prepared the diagrams for the press. As with every piece of work I have attempted I owe a great debt to my wife, Margaret, and family who not only helped in drawing up the tables and checking facts and figures, but also provided the encouragement which every writer requires. Finally, I must thank Mr Charles A. Furth, of Allen and Unwin, who not only suggested that I should write this book but who has been a model of patience and kindliness in seeing this work completed.

SIDNEY WELLS

University of Salford
November 1968

Preface to the Revised Edition

Few textbooks stand the test of time as well as Sidney Wells' *International Economics* has. First published in 1969, and slightly revised by Dr E. W. Brassloff in 1973, it has been a leading introduction to international economics for fifteen years. Much has changed over these years, however, both in international economics and in the international economy, and it has now become necessary to make further and more drastic revisions. It has been my honour and pleasure to carry out this task.

The present edition has been completely rewritten in the course of revision. In some places this was quite inevitable, because the nature of the analysis has changed since the late 1960s. Thus, for example, the discussion of flexible exchange rates, macro-economic policy, the oil price and developments in the International Monetary Fund could not have been other than entirely new. In other instances I have chosen to rewrite the original text to take account of more recent analytical research and changes in emphasis. Thus, I adopt a different approach to the Heckscher–Ohlin theory of trade, and devote a chapter to modern theories of trade based on technology and on imperfect competition. Finally, I have increased the emphasis on testing economic hypotheses. In part this reflects my own interests, but mainly it arises from changes in the general approach to economics over the last decade.

Such drastic revision has, inevitably, had some cost – especially as the new edition is no longer than the original. First, some of the controversies of the 1960s have died a natural death; for example, the problem of sterling features only briefly, and then as an issue of recent economic history. Second, there is somewhat less space devoted to institutional matters than previously. Third, the discussion of international economic integration has been shortened, as have, fourth, certain issues in development economics. These contractions have been made reluctantly, but given the availability of alternative textbooks and the size constraints on the present edition I hope they do not do too much violence to Wells' original intentions. While the differences just noted are considerable, the new edition is still a direct descendant of Wells' *International Economics*. It bears the same overall structure, it fulfils the same purposes, it presents many of the same arguments and it has the same flavour of applied, as opposed to purely abstract, economics.

In preparing this edition, I have drawn extensively on the goodwill of my friends. Among those to whom I am most grateful for advice are Alan Armstrong, John Beath, David Demery and Partha Sen of the University of Bristol and Oli Havrylyshyn of George Washington University, who read and commented upon various draft chapters, and William Shaw of the World Bank, and John Black of the University of Exeter who read and commented on the complete draft. To the last, in particular, I owe a great debt. His help covered every aspect of the book, from its structure to its preparation for printing, and that his advice was not always taken is due only to my own stubbornness and indolence. The burdens of typing were shared by Karen Adams, Mary Harthan, Vicky Sugui and Janet Wright, with super-human patience and efficiency, while the figures were excellently traced by Carrie Pharoah. I am most grateful to all of them. The proposal that I should make this revision came from Nicholas Brealey of George Allen & Unwin, who has been helpful and patient throughout its gestation. Naturally none of these people, nor my employers, bears any responsibility for the book's views or shortcomings.

My final debt of gratitude is to my family. My daughters, Vicki and Catey, have always been solicitous as to the book's progress, and have been very tolerant of the absences and preoccupations that authorship seems to involve. My wife, Meg, has been all these things, as well as a willing partner in proof reading and preparing the manuscript. She has been sympathetic and supportive throughout the endeavour, and without her I doubt that it would have been completed.

The University of Bristol
and
The World Bank

L. ALAN WINTERS
March 1984

Acknowledgements

I am grateful to the following for permission to reproduce their copyright material:

The American Economic Association and Professor P. Isard (Figure 19.2)

Cambridge University Press (Table 18.3)

Chapman and Hall Publishing Co. (Table 18.2)

Gower Publishing Co. Ltd (Table 15.1)

Heinemann Educational Books Ltd (Table 7.1)

The International Monetary Fund (Tables 18.4, 24.1 and 24.2)

The Editor of *The Journal of Common Market Studies* (Table 7.1)

Lloyds Bank Ltd (Table 17.2)

The Morgan Bank (Table 28.2)

North Holland Publishing Co. (Tables 17.3 and 18.1)

The Editor of *The Observer*

The Organization for Economic Co-operation and Development (Tables 17.1 and 18.5)

The Editor of the *Southern Economic Journal* (Table 6.3)

The Trade Policy Research Centre (Table 6.1 – extracted from Table 1 of an article by Hugh Corbet, 'The Importance of Being Earnest about Further GATT Negotiations', which appeared in the September 1979 number of *The World Economy*, the quarterly journal of the Trade Policy Research Centre, London – and Table 6.2 – extracted from Tables 3.1 and 3.7 of Nicholas Oulton, 'Effective Protection of British Industry', in W. M. Corden and Gerhard Fels, *Public Assistance to Industry: Protection and Subsidies in Britain and Germany*, London: Macmillan, for the Trade Policy Research Centre, London, and Institut für Weltwirtschaft, Kiel, 1976; and Boulder, Colorado: Westview Press, 1976.

1 Introduction – Why, What and How

1.1 WHY INTERNATIONAL ECONOMICS?

Why do we need textbooks on international economics? What indeed differentiates economic transactions between countries from those that take place within a country? Are economic principles relating to the international economy different from those appropriate to a single country? What is special about international economics to justify separate textbooks, courses and, in some places of learning, separate examination papers?

In many ways it is neither necessary nor desirable for the student to make a hard and fast distinction in his/her mind between problems in general economics and those in international economics. Indeed, the greater the number of links that s/he can find between general economic theory and the special field of international economics, the better will s/he understand both. My hope is that as s/he works through this book the reader will constantly relate what s/he learns to the broad body of general economic theory with which s/he is already familiar – or becoming familiar.

There are nevertheless several reasons for the development of a distinctive branch of economics dealing with problems of the international economy. Some of these reasons are practical, some pedagogic. Perhaps the most obvious justification for a separate study arises from the barriers between countries that prevent the completely free movement of goods, persons and capital. These barriers may be political, social or linguistic, as well as economic. Barriers that are primarily economic take the form of customs duties, direct trade restrictions or exchange controls. Sometimes the impediments are more subtle, taking the form of elaborate customs procedures, packaging requirements, health regulations and 'mixing' regulations that require the use of a given minimum quantity of a domestically produced raw material in conjunction with an imported product. Such trade barriers are rarely important enough to impede the flow of trade *within* a country; but, to the extent that they are important *between* countries, they give rise to a number of problems that form part of the study of international economics.

The nineteenth-century classical economist believed that the immobility of factors of production between countries, as contrasted with their mobility within a country, was the most important distinguishing feature of international trade. This view is now outmoded and it is widely realised that factors do move extensively between countries (and sometimes sluggishly within a country). None the less, it still remains true that restrictions, legal or otherwise, on inter-country factor movements are much more widespread than internal barriers and that the prevalence of these restrictions has important economic consequences.

Another justification for a special book on international economics is that there are differences between countries in their currency systems. The mere existence of different currencies is in itself of minor significance. For example, if the value of one currency in terms of another is rigidly fixed and a citizen of one country can freely convert his currency into that of any other country, the fact that one country uses pounds while another uses dollars matters little. In reality, however, differences in currencies often reflect more fundamental differences in economic

1

systems and policies. In the world in which we live, the value of one currency in terms of another does change – in some cases frequently, in others only at rare intervals. Every time a change takes place, or indeed looks as if it *might* take place, a number of economic (and sometimes political) problems arise. Nor are all currencies equally acceptable: some are widely used in international trade, others are virtually inconvertible into any other currency. This consideration itself gives rise to a further set of economic problems.

Another factor – perhaps the most significant one that distinguishes inter-national from internal economic transactions – is that economic conditions and policies are likely to differ more markedly between countries than within a country. For example, demand may be high in Britain when incomes are rising rapidly; as a result Britons are likely to purchase more goods from France – or perhaps take more and longer holidays in that country. This will be reflected either in a depreciation of sterling, as Britons sell sterling to obtain the francs with which to buy French goods, or in a British balance of payments deficit, as existing British stocks of francs are run down by expenditure in France. Each of these outcomes has further consequences and each, at times, has been considered a major economic problem to be solved by policy-makers.

Such questions do not arise within a country. The residents of a *region* might very well 'import' more from other regions than they 'export' to them, but no balance of payments problem would become apparent. This is because all regions use the same currency and, as they share a common banking system, the flow of funds from the deficit to the surplus region takes the form of a transfer of balances between banks of the same country, or even between branches of the same bank. Accordingly there is little danger of a region losing all its means of payments; wealth is merely transferred from one region to the other.

This is not to deny that differences in income employment and economic activity can grow up between regions of one country – compare, for example, North-East and South-East England – but just to argue that the symptoms are different. So too, however, are the cures. The regions of any one country face pretty much the same monetary and fiscal policies. Slight differences may exist in micro-economic incentives – for example, development grants to stimulate investment in depressed regions – but broadly they inhabit the same economic environment. Between countries, on the other hand, policies can vary immensely: the relative prices of two countries' monies (and outputs) can vary through exchange rate changes; interest rates can vary; the balance between private and public provision of services can vary; and so on.

These different 'menus' of policy really stem from a further fundamental difference between international and inter-regional trade. The former involves partners from different *sovereign* states; the latter does not. The central govern-ment typically determines regional policy for its regions and does so with a view to the national, rather than the strictly regional, interest. In international trade, two national governments are potentially involved, each defining policy in terms of the welfare of its own residents rather than those of the world as a whole. Most prominent among the results of this difference in policy environments is the ability to make income transfers between two transactors. Inter-regional transfers occur all the time and are frequently not even explicitly measured; for example, Londoners' tax bills finance Ulster's unemployment benefit with little or no political problem. International transfers are politically almost impossible to effect – witness the unpopularity of foreign aid flows and the constant squabbling over Britain's contribution to the European Community's budget. Thus not only do policies vary more between countries than within them, but their fundamental

2

directions differ: inter-regional trade falls within one jurisdiction, international trade falls under two.

Finally, geographical considerations also give rise to a number of special economic problems best dealt with under the umbrella of international trade theory. Countries differ in size and resource endowment. They often have their own transport systems with differences in transport, tariffs, and freight regulations.

1.2   ISSUES IN INTERNATIONAL ECONOMICS

Having argued why international economics should be treated as a separate subject, we now briefly identify some of the issues it considers. Figure 1.1(A), which describes the patterns of world trade, defines several of them:

- Why has the value of world trade increased fifteen-fold over twenty years?
- How much is due to changes in prices and how much to changes in quantities?
- Why has the share of fuels risen by two and a half times?
- What are the consequences of such large changes?
- Why have the shares of other primary goods fallen so much?

Figures 1.1(B) and (C), which refer to British trade, define several more, most of which could as easily be posed about any individual country:

- Why does Britain export relatively more and import relatively less machinery than the world as a whole?
- Why has the discrepancy narrowed since 1960?
- Why have manufacturers displaced primary goods as Britain's main imports?

These figures consider only one dimension of international trade – its commodity composition. Beyond that there are many more questions to be posed:

- What has allowed countries like Singapore, Korea and Taiwan to double their shares of world manufactured trade since 1963?
- Why has the share of world output traded internationally increased from $8\frac{1}{2}$ per cent in 1950 to 16 per cent in 1980?
- Why do some countries have surpluses of exports over imports and others the reverse? Does this matter, and can anything be done about it?
- Why do some firms build factories abroad?
- How does one country's macro-economic policy affect another's economic performance?
- Why do exchange rates fluctuate so much; or rather, do exchange rates fluctuate 'so much'?
- Why do countries hold reserves of foreign currencies?
- What constitutes international money?
- What are Euro-dollars?

If these questions seem rather dry and academic, international economics also has its quota of policy problems. For example:

3

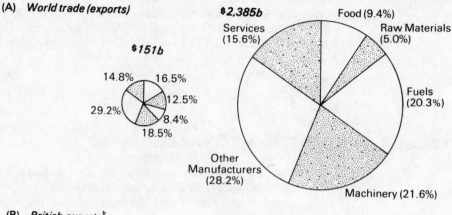

(A) *World trade (exports)*

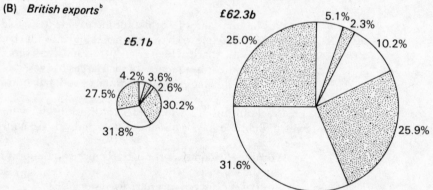

(B) *British exports*[b]

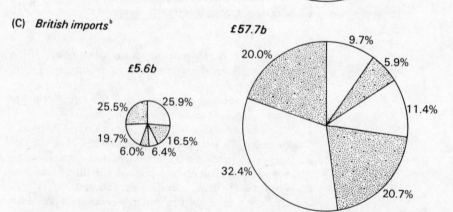

(C) *British imports*[b]

Notes:
[a] The segments are in the same order in all diagrams; they are defined on the diagram for world exports, 1980.
[b] The scale for the British data is sixteen times larger than for the world data.
Sources: United Nations Conference on Trade and Development, *Handbook of International Trade and Development Statistics* (1983); Central Statistical Office, *United Kingdom Balance of Payments* (1969, 1983); and the World Bank Databank.

Figure 1.1.   *Trading patterns, 1960 and 1980. (A) World Trade (exports). (B) British exports. (C) British imports.*

- Should Britain curtail her imports of clothes from Asia, or of cars from Japan?
- Does Britain gain economically from membership of the EEC?
- Should international migration be encouraged or discouraged?
- Should the multinationals be controlled?
- Should short-term capital flows ('hot money') be taxed or banned?
- Should exchange rates be fixed?
- Should the International Monetary Fund be strengthened?
- Should developing countries' debts be re-scheduled or written off?
- Would it pay such countries to repudiate their debts?

All of these questions and many more are the subject matter of international economics. Some have straightforward answers, some are controversial, and some seem, frankly, quite intractable. The purpose of this book is not so much to present a list of answers as to introduce the student to the ways and means by which economists analyse these questions. Plenty of them will be resolved in this process, but, more importantly, at the end of the course the student will be equipped to pose and answer new questions for him or herself.

1.3   ON STUDYING INTERNATIONAL ECONOMICS

Having treated the 'why' and 'what' of international economics, we now consider the 'how'. This section is not an essay in economic method, but it does introduce certain important ideas that will clarify the nature of the arguments made below.

**Positive and
normative
economics**

First, we distinguish throughout the book between *positive* and *normative* economics. The former deals with how the world is, the latter with how it ought to be. Statements of positive economics are, at least in principle, susceptible to test, by confronting them with 'the facts'. Normative statements, on the other hand, while obviously having factual dimensions, also add value judgements. Ultimately, disagreements over normative issues cannot be settled by fact alone, for it is possible for people to agree entirely about the facts of two situations but still to differ as to which is preferable.

International economics encompasses both the positive and normative approaches – often, in the past, without separating the two very clearly. For example, Ricardo's comparative advantage theory of international trade serves both to predict patterns of trade (a positive aspect) and to show the benefits of free trade over protection (a normative aspect). Below, however, we aim to keep the distinction clear, and also to resolve positive (testable) issues before letting normative or judgemental factors loose on a question.

**Theory
and
refutation**

The purposes of positive economics are to understand and predict economic phenomena. In order to do this, we generally need to organise our information according to some guiding principle – what we might loosely call a theory. Typically, theories are rather abstract and unrealistic, but by concentrating on one crucial aspect of the question in hand they shed light on practical issues. The role of assumption in economic theorising is to allow this concentration on crucial aspects in a rigorous fashion by stripping away distracting details. To be useful, however, a theory must bear some relation to known facts. Thus the phenomenon being explained must be real and observable, and the predictions made by the theory broadly correct. Unfortunately in economics many more theories exist than have been adequately tested; we shall frequently encounter cases below where many

5

possible explanations exist for a phenomenon but where the empirical job of deciding how well each describes the world has not yet been completed.

In devising an economic theory, we presuppose that certain assumed features of the world are true, and from these deduce predictions about economic behaviour. The assumptions really define the theory. They come in two basic types: assumptions about unobservables (e.g. that consumers maximise utility), and strategic simplifications, which, while not literally true, facilitate analysis without fundamentally altering the predictions. The latter obviously depend on the circumstances, but a typical example would be assuming perfect competition. Neither type of assumption is open to direct testing – the first for obvious reasons and the second because it cannot be known beforehand whether a particular simplification will make a theory's predictions unrealistic or not. Thus, in order to see whether a theory is likely to be useful, we have to test its predictions.

The procedure is as follows. A specific hypothesis is formed; it makes specific assumptions (A) and from them logically deduces predictions about observable phenomena (P). Provided the assumptions (A) are sufficient to guarantee the outcome (P), A can be tested by observing whether or not P occurs. Observation can only *reject* A with certainty, however; it can never prove beyond doubt that assumptions A *are* true (justified), because one can never exclude the possibility that some other set of circumstances might actually have given rise to P. Thus, observing 'not-P' tells us that 'not-A' is true, but observing P tells us only that A *could be* true. We should proceed, therefore, by a series of hypotheses and rejections, the body of theory extant at any time being merely those assumptions that appear useful and that have not yet been rejected. Theory is just the best tool kit we happen to have at any point of time; there is nothing absolute, or even provenly 'true', about it.

Indeed, economists frequently have to use theory that they know does not predict certain phenomena well, but if it is the best available it may survive even though various refutations of its predictions exist. It is in these circumstances that disagreements arise and normative considerations slip in. Without universal agreement on what constitutes sufficient grounds for rejecting a theory, or on what the trade-off between 'usefulness' and 'refutation' should be, economists tend to favour those positive theories that best fit their normative preconceptions. (This is not unique to economics, or even to social science. For example, witness the way scientific groups lined up over the issue of whether or not lead in petrol was a serious health hazard: those with broader 'environmental interests' said it was; those concerned with industrial growth said it was not.)

Statistical testing

Nearly all testing of predictions in economics involves the use of statistics, and this further complicates matters. Nothing can be measured with perfect accuracy and, in economics, variables are always subject to shocks and changes other than those of interest to a particular theory. Thus, for instance, while theory might suggest that a particular parameter, say $ß$, should have the value zero, an estimate of $ß$, say $\hat{ß}$, 'close to' zero would not be sufficient grounds for rejecting that view. The crucial question, of course, is what constitutes 'close to'.

Imagine that we could conduct hundreds of independent tests of the hypothesis that $ß = 0$, under circumstances in which $ß = 0$ were actually true. We could then work out a range within which, say, 95 per cent of the estimates of $ß$ would fall under these circumstances. (All this can be done theoretically – we do not actually have to do the tests.) Now consider the one test we actually have conducted, which has produced the estimate $\hat{ß}$. If $\hat{ß}$ falls inside the 95 per cent range we have just calculated, we accept (do not reject) the hypothesis that $ß = 0$, whereas if it falls outside the range we reject the hypothesis. Clearly in the latter case we have a 5 per cent chance of rejecting the hypothesis when it is actually true, because 5 per cent of the estimates will lie outside the range even when $ß = 0$. Thus we say that we are '95 per cent confident' that $ß \neq 0$, or alternatively that we have rejected the hypothesis $ß = 0$ 'at 5 per cent significance'. Clearly, the chances of mistakenly rejecting $ß = 0$ could be reduced to 1 per cent by calculating the range to include 99 per cent of the estimates when the hypothesis is true; this would be referred to as testing 'at 1 per cent significance'.

The range that includes 99 per cent of the estimates obviously exceeds that including 95 per cent, and sometimes these ranges can be so large as to be almost useless. For example, a test of a price elasticity with critical range -10 to $+10$ would not be useful, because we rarely expect to find price elasticities exceeding 5, even when they are most definitely not zero. Consequently, such a test would be almost powerless to reject the hypothesis that the elasticity is zero. Thus the range and the level of significance of a test have to be chosen carefully to balance the chances of wrongly rejecting the hypothesis against those of failing correctly to identify cases where it does not hold.

Economists frequently report estimates of parameters of interest along with their 'standard errors'. The latter are used in constructing the critical ranges for conducting hypothesis tests. Suppose we wish to test whether parameter $ß$ takes the value m; let $\hat{ß}$ be our estimate and s its standard error. At 5 per cent significance, the acceptance range is $(m \pm 1.96s)$ and at 1 per cent $(m \pm 2.58s)$. If $\hat{ß}$ lies outside these ranges we reject the hypotheses at 5 per cent and 1 per cent significance, respectively. Sometimes we talk of a parameter 'being significant at 5 per cent'; this means that it is significantly different from zero at 5 per cent significance, namely that $\hat{ß}$ lies outside the range $\pm 1.96s$.[1]

Conclusion on method

Thus we see that positive economics should ideally proceed by a series of hypotheses and refutations. A suggestion (hypothesis) is advanced that relates particular observable phenomena to unobservable assumptions in a logically water-tight fashion. Assuming the hypothesis is true, we ask what range the observables would have in the real world, given our imperfect methods of measurement and the presence of other shocks. If our actual observations fall within this range, the hypothesis is tentatively accepted, whereas if they fall outside it is rejected. After several such tests, and with a view to the usefulness (power) of the hypothesis and the available alternatives, the hypothesis is incorporated into the body of theory or rejected completely.

There is room for ambiguity and disagreement about what constitutes sufficient grounds for rejection of a hypothesis, but otherwise the procedure outlined seems fairly objective and straightforward. This is not to claim, however, that positive economics is entirely 'value-free'. Unfortunately, normative considerations do sometimes influence the strength of the rejection criteria applied. More importantly, they also influence the set of questions asked and the hypotheses tested in the first place. The latter is quite unavoidable and all that one can hope is that, given the hypotheses, objective and scientific procedures are used to evaluate them, and that value judgements are consciously made and explicitly reported.

Some terminology

Below we shall frequently talk of a *model* of some economic process. A model is really no more than a theory: it is a simplified and small-scale replica of reality – the nature of the simplification being dictated by the theory and made concrete in the model by assumptions about economic behaviour.

Another term frequently encountered is *regression equation* or *regression*. This is a technique econometricians use to measure the relationship between certain economic variables and another, particular variable of interest: thus, to explain the demand for shoes, we might regress the quantity sold on incomes and the relative prices of shoes and other goods. Regression coefficients record the effect that a determining variable (e.g. income) has on the variable of interest (demand); there is typically one coefficient per determining variable. Interest is focused on the regression coefficients first as a measure of the quantitative effect that one variable has on another, and second to test whether or not that effect could reasonably be supposed to be zero. For the latter task, we use the estimate of the regression coefficient ($\hat{\beta}$) and its standard error (s) in the way just described, and test whether or not β (the 'true' effect of the determining variable) could be zero.

1.4 ABOUT THIS BOOK

The approach

This book provides an introduction to the main aspects of international economics. It presents the theory in an accessible form and tries wherever possible to provide empirical evidence and applications to back up that theory. Compared to the first edition, less space is devoted to institutional details – describing how things work – and more to the testing and evaluation of alternative theoretical approaches. Thus the emphasis is shifted somewhat towards international economics as an intellectual discipline, and away from the international economy as a phenomenon. The reader will none the less, still find much on the latter to interest him / her.

A corollary of including more empirical work is that there is a greater air of uncertainty about this book than in most others. Economic theory appears very confident in its descriptions of causes and consequences, and a theoretical explanation can always be found for any casual observation we happen to make. When we systematically confront theory with data, however, its shortcomings are clearly visible, and it becomes obvious that we should, in fact, be rather tentative about most of our claims, both positive and normative. This does not mean that economics is not useful (after all, the errors in weather forecasts do not lead us to reject meteorology as a useful discipline), but it does call for a certain modesty and caution on the part of economists. By illustrating this fact, this book is merely being realistic.

The use of mathematics in the text is very slight. Mathematical symbols are occasionally useful as a form of notational shorthand, but very rarely is there any manipulation. The predominant mode of argument is verbal, supported and illustrated by graphs. This tends to make the analysis slightly less precise than mathematics would allow, but it certainly does not make it simple-minded. Several of the arguments presented are quite sophisticated and need to be read slowly and several times over. This almost certainly applies to section 1.3, which you have just read, and which is among the most difficult of the book.

Each chapter ends with a selected and annotated Further Reading. The references given will allow you to follow up various points from the text more deeply or in different directions. Except in the few cases noted, the arguments should be accessible to the student who has successfully worked through the relevant chapter of this book, although for the empirical papers further study may be required to master the econometric techniques used. The latter, however, are not essential in order to understand the main economic content of the results. It is not necessary to read every reference; rather you should be guided by the notes provided.

The plan The book is organised along the lines of Marshall's distinction between the 'pure' and the 'monetary' branches of international trade theory. As an expository device this distinction has much to commend it, for it helps in relating international trade to other fields of economics. Pure theory is concerned with real as opposed to monetary magnitudes, its subject matter being the theory of value or price in an international context. Tariff theory, and such questions as the determination of the pattern of international trade and the effects of economic growth, fall within its purview. International monetary economics, on the other hand, is concerned with the theory of money and employment in an international setting; it deals with such problems as balance of payments equilibria, exchange rates, the transmission of business fluctuations between countries, the demand for international reserves and the Euro-dollar market.

Part I of this book deals with pure theory. It starts with the positive theory of international trade, examining various explanations for the existence and the pattern of trade. Chapters 2, 3 and 4 take us from Ricardo's theory of comparative advantage through to modern theories based on technological mastery and differentiated products. In the course of these chapters the benefits of international trade are introduced, but these are not treated formally until Chapter 5. Chapters 6 and 7 introduce tariffs and non-tariff restrictions on international trade. They deal with positive aspects of these questions, including, in the latter case, a description of many of the interferences to international trade that are possible. Chapters 8 and 9 consider the normative arguments for and against protection in both industrial and developing economies, and Chapter 10 examines how tariffs are actually set in the real world. Chapter 11 deals with the formation of customs unions, in which groups of countries abolish tariffs on their mutual trade and harmonise their other economic policies. This is illustrated in Chapter 12, which discusses the European Economic Community (the EEC). Chapters 13 and 15 switch from considering the movement of goods between countries to the movement of factors of production: Chapter 13 considers the parallels between goods and factor movements, while Chapter 15 deals with the particular case of multinational companies. Between them lies Chapter 14, which considers the interaction of international trade and economic growth.

Monetary aspects of the international economy are the subject of Parts II and III. Part II deals basically with a single country in a monetary world. Chapter 16 introduces the concepts of the balance of payments and the exchange rate. Chapters 17 and 18 deal with the effects of national income and prices on the balance of payments, while Chapters 19 and 20 integrate international and domestic aspects of macro-economics. Chapter 21 is devoted to the determinants of exchange rates – an area of very rapid development in contemporary international economics. Chapter 22 asks how macro-economic policy should be conducted in an open economy and Chapter 24 whether, all things considered, fixed or floating exchange rates are preferable. Chapter 23 pulls these various analyses together into a study of the effects of the discovery of the North Sea oil on British international trade.

Part III shifts attention to global monetary issues. Chapter 25 deals with the demand for reserves of international money, while Chapters 26 and 27 consider the supply. The latter pair take a historical perspective, taking us from a discussion of the nineteenth-century gold standard through the era of fixed exchange rates to the present 'non-system' of floating rates and potential debt crises. The role of institutions such as the International Monetary Fund and Special Drawing Rights (SDRs) is considered closely. Chapter 28 concludes the book with an analysis of the Euro-dollar market.

It is hoped that the reader who perseveres through this book will feel at the end that, although s/he has learnt something, s/he has still a vast amount more to learn. At best a textbook should be like an iceberg, showing but a fraction of the vast bulk of material that makes up the whole study. If, after working through it, the student comes to regard this book as an introduction to an exciting field of economic science, and feels moved to acquaint him/herself at first hand with some of the more detailed and more distinguished texts, then its writing will have been abundantly worthwhile.

FURTHER READING

For more details of the patterns of world and British trade introduced in section 1.2, see *Winters* (1984c) and *Mansell* (1980) respectively. A useful introduction to economic methodology is *Blaug* (1980), while the use of statistics for hypothesis testing and estimation will be covered by any elementary statistics textbook; see, for example, *Yeomans* (1968).

NOTES

1 These are the values for large samples. Where only small samples of data are available the ranges are somewhat larger. They also refer to tests of the hypothesis $ß = 0$ against the alternative $ß \neq 0$. Where we wish to test it against, say $ß > m$, the acceptance region is below $(m + 1.64s)$ at 5 per cent and below $(m + 2.33s)$ at 1 per cent. That is, we do not reject $ß = m$ in favour of $ß > m$, if $ß$ is positive and below $(m + 1.64s)$ or if it takes any negative value.

Part I

2 Comparative Costs and International Trade

The pure theory of international trade encompasses the determinants of trade and its consequences, the methods of controlling trade and their consequences, and the interaction between international trade and other real aspects of the economy. Our first three chapters deal almost exclusively with the positive analysis of the causes of trade. The principal question posed is why country A exports good X while country B exports good Y. Or to be more concrete: why have Japanese electronic goods swept the world; why must India import food; why has Britain switched from being a net exporter of manufactures to being a net importer?

The chapters start with the earliest and simplest of trade theories – the classical or Ricardian theory – and progress through neoclassical analysis to recent work. Ricardo, writing in 1817, attributed trade to differences in countries' ability to produce different goods: one produced one good relatively cheaply, the other another good. The differences arose from differences in labour productivity but were not otherwise explained; presumably they lay in variations in countries' natural environments or available technologies. Although Ricardo's is a positive theory of trade (an explanation), he was arguably more interested in normative issues. The theory emerged from his battle to repeal the Corn Laws, and he used it to demonstrate the superiority of free trade over autarchy (no trade). This chapter also examines this aspect of Ricardo's writing, although a full treatment of trade and economic welfare is postponed until Chapter 5.

Chapter 3 presents the neoclassical theory of international trade. This is primarily incorporated in the Heckscher–Ohlin theory, which explains countries' differing abilities in different goods by reference to differences in their endowments of factors of production. Thus it offers some justification for Ricardo's differing labour productivities, because in different countries labour has different quantities of other factors with which to combine. The Heckscher–Ohlin theory is still the dominant mode of thought within international trade theory and it underlies much of the normative analysis and extensions of later chapters.

The next chapter deals with modern trade theory. On the one hand this re-emphasises technology, but seeks to explain it further than Ricardo did, and on the other it stresses the role of product differentiation in international trade. The latter is a new, and apparently fruitful, area of research that incorporates imperfect competition into international trade theory and offers some explanation for 'intra-industry' trade. This phenomenon – of countries simultaneously both importing and exporting very similar goods – is virtually impossible to explain with earlier trade theory, which depends only on differences in costs of production to generate trade.

2.1 SOME TOOLS OF ANALYSIS

Before embarking on the Ricardian model, we need to explore a few basic tools of analysis. International economics is not a separate subject but a single branch of the general subject of economics. Thus the international economist uses the same tools of analysis and terminology as other economists. In particular, for questions of international trade we use techniques familiar from micro-economics, welfare economics and general equilibrium analysis. The brief introduction that follows may be pursued in any micro-economics textbook – for example, Lancaster (1969), or Russell and Wilkinson (1979). Throughout this chapter we shall assume that perfect competition and perfect information rule in all markets. We shall also generally limit ourselves to considering just two goods.

Consumption

We start by considering a single consumer, assuming that his preferences over the goods he consumes can be represented by a series of *indifference curves*, as in Figure 2.1. The slope of an indifference curve, which is always negative, is known as the *marginal rate of substitution* (MRS) between the two goods (X and Y). It tells us how much Y the consumer must be offered in return for a unit of X if his welfare is to remain unchanged.

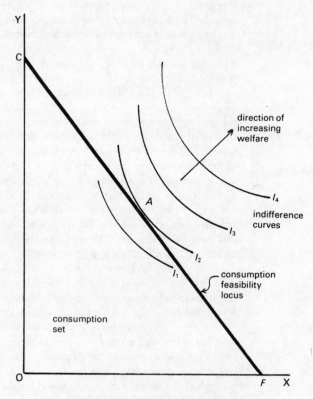

Figure 2.1   *Consumer equilibrium*

The consumer makes his choices over a set of possible consumption choices defined by his income and the prices of the goods. This set is known as the *consumption set* and its outermost frontier as the *consumption feasibility locus*. The latter shows the maximum of X available for any consumption of Y, and vice versa. Suppose the consumer has income 20 and that the prices of X and Y are 2 and 1 per unit respectively. He can buy 10X or 20Y or any mixture just exhausting his income. These mixtures are shown by line *CF* in Figure 2.1 – hence area O*CF* is the consumption set and *CF* the consumption feasibility locus. The slope of *CF* is given by the price ratio, because it shows how much Y could be added to consumption in return for one X.

14

The consumer will always aim to be on his highest indifference curve. This will be where an indifference curve just touches the consumption feasibility set – such as at A in Figure 2.1. Note how the marginal rate of substitution equals the price ratio ($MRS = P$). This is necessary if the consumer is actually maximising welfare. (Imagine a position where $MRS = 3$ and $P = 2$. How could we raise welfare?)

Production

We assume that a country's stock of factors of production is fixed, but that all can be used in producing either X or Y; we also assume that firms maximise their profits, which implies minimising costs for any level of production. The *marginal cost* of X is the (minimum) cost of producing an additional unit of X, and similarly for Y. The *marginal rate of transformation (MRT)* is the rate at which the marginal unit of X can be transformed into Y. This is merely the ratio of their marginal costs. It may also be thought of as the marginal opportunity cost of Y in terms of X – i.e. how much X has to be forgone in order to raise Y-output by one unit.

Given the factors of production, technology and the assumptions of efficiency and full employment, we can calculate the whole range of possible combinations of output. This is known as the *production set*, and its frontier is the *production possibility frontier* or the *transformation frontier*. The latter shows the maximum X available given output of Y, and vice versa. The *MRT* is the slope of the transformation frontier – check that you know why. If firms are maximising profits, the equilibrium values of *MRT* and the price ratio (Y per X) must be equal. (If $MRT = 3$ and $P = 2$ producers would seek to transform X into Y, obtaining 3Y per X, and then sell these at 2Y for 1X to obtain a profit of $\frac{1}{2}$X. Such a position cannot be an equilibrium since there is an incentive to increase Y-output.) The only exception to this equality is where one good is not being produced. Y will not be produced whenever $MRT < P$, because then producing a unit of Y uses up more resources (X) than can be purchased by selling it.

Equilibrium

For a closed economy – one that undertakes no international trade – consumption is limited to what can be produced locally: thus the production set becomes the consumption set. Hence Figure 2.1 could be reinterpreted to represent the equilibrium of a closed economy with preferences I (we ignore the problems of adding different people's preferences, for now) and production possibility frontier CF. Since, from above, $MRS = P$ and $MRT = P$, the marginal rate of substitution, the marginal rate of transformation and the price ratio will all be equal in full equilibrium.

2.2 ABSOLUTE AND COMPARATIVE COSTS

Absolute advantage

The seed of modern international trade theory comes from Adam Smith (1776). His concern with the division of labour as a means of increasing efficiency is well known and he generalised this to specialisation between trades and between countries:

> It is the maxim of every prudent master of a family, never to attempt to make at home what it will cost him more to make than buy. The tailor does not attempt to make his own shoes, but buys them from the shoemaker. The shoemaker does not attempt to make his own clothes but employs a tailor. The farmer attempts to make neither the one nor the other, but employs those different artificers. All of them find it for their interest to employ their whole industry in a way in which they have some advantage over their neighbours, and to purchase

with a part of its produce, or what is the same thing, with the price of part of it, whatever else they have occasion for.

What is prudence in the conduct of every private family, can scarce be folly in that of a great kingdom. If a foreign country can supply us with a commodity cheaper than we ourselves can make it, better buy of them with some part of the produce of own industry, employed in a way in which we have some advantage. (1961 reprint, p. 424)

Thus countries trade, and should trade, in order to acquire their consumption more cheaply. They buy abroad when foreign prices are below domestic ones. Prices are the immediate determinant of trade, and, although much of what follows below delves behind relative prices, this basic fact should never be forgotten.

Smith also argued that, by extending the market, international trade allows greater specialisation and division of labour than would otherwise be possible. It therefore offers scope for additional gain by reducing costs below their autarchy levels. This is a separate argument from the pure trade argument of the quotation, and is held over until Chapter 4 below.

To make the pure trade example more concrete, suppose we have only two goods (food and cloth) and two countries (Britain and America). Further assume that transport is costless and that labour, which is mobile between industries, is the only factor of production. Assume that the labour requirements for each good and country are as follows:

Labour per unit of output in	Britain	America
Food	5	3
Cloth	2	6

In the absence of trade – that is, under *autarchy* – prices will reflect labour requirements. So, if wages are the same in the two countries, Britain will be the cheaper source of cloth and America cheaper for food. Hence, when trade first opens, Britain will export cloth and import food.

Trade can increase economic welfare in both countries. Suppose that under autarchy each country has 60 units of labour in each industry. Britain's production (and, under autarchy, consumption) is 12 of food and 30 of cloth – write this as (12,30) – whilst America's is (20,10). World production is (32,40). Now redistribute labour such that America has 120 workers in food and Britain has 120 in cloth. World production becomes (40,60), so that, by specialising and trading, each country can consume its autarchy bundle and there is still some of each product left over. Each country could thus raise its consumption of each good, and, assuming more of each good is better than less, the trading outcome *could* allow both countries to increase their welfare. Thus, not only can *absolute advantage* describe international trade patterns, but it can also provide the rationale to prescribe their implementation as a means to raising economic welfare.

Comparative advantage

The example above worked very conveniently. Britain was the least-cost producer of cloth and America the least-cost producer of food, and the opportunities for trade were obvious enough. What, however, if one country – Britain, say – were more efficient in the production of both goods? Absolute advantage would suggest that both goods should be purchased from Britain, but this could not be a long-term solution, because Britain would not wish to buy anything from America in return. Writing some forty years after Smith, Ricardo (1817) was the first economist to analyse this situation formally, with his justly famous law of comparative advantage.

16

Suppose our matrix of labour requirements were:

Labour per unit of output in	Britain	America
Food	5	6
Cloth	2	12

Although Britain now requires less labour than America in both industries, this does not preclude profitable trade. Previously we used money prices and wage rates to compare the efficiencies of the two economies; now we use relative prices and barter. In Britain under autarchy 1 unit of food trades for $2\frac{1}{2}$ units of cloth – each is equivalent to five men's output. (The *relative price* of food and cloth depends only on the relative labour inputs provided that (i) both goods are produced and (ii) labour productivity is independent of the level of output in each industry. We assume the former, and the latter is implied by our simple numbers above.) Similarly, in America 1 unit of food trades for a $\frac{1}{2}$ unit of cloth – both the product of six men.

When we open trade between America and Britain, the different relative prices provide scope for profitable trade. For example, if American relative prices prevailed in the trading world, a Briton owning 1 unit of food could swap it in Britain for $2\frac{1}{2}$ units of cloth and then, selling these in America, realise 5 units of food – an overall profit of 4 units of food. Similarly, if British prices prevailed, an American entrepreneur initially employing twelve men to produce 1 unit of cloth could switch to producing 2 units of food, and, selling these in Britain, receive 5 units of cloth – again a profitable trade. At intermediate relative prices, both countries would gain, although not by as much as in the examples given.

An alternative view of international trade is as a form of technical innovation. By increasing the choice of methods for transforming food and cloth, it cannot harm society (the new method need not be used), and may benefit it if the new method is an improvement on the old. Clearly for Britain, international trade offering 2 food for 1 cloth is a substantial improvement over the autarchic possibility of 2/5 food for 1 cloth. Hence Britons will seek to obtain food by switching factors of production from food to cloth and then transforming the resulting cloth into food through international trade, rather than by using the factors directly in food production. For Americans, the opposite incentive would apply. Thus, each country shifts towards the good in which it has a *comparative advantage*. Britain is comparatively more efficient in cloth than in food, whereas America is more efficient (less inefficient) in food: Britain requires 5/6th of the American inputs in food but only 1/6th in cloth.

In this simple example, the law of comparative advantage states that country A will export good F if and only if

$$\frac{l_F^A}{l_F^B} < \frac{l_C^A}{l_C^B} \tag{2.1}$$

where l_j^i is the input requirement for good j in country i. In the 'two-by-two' model, (2.1) may also be expressed as

$$\frac{l_F^A}{l_C^A} < \frac{l_F^B}{l_C^B} \tag{2.2}$$

which implies that A exports the good for which its input requirements are relatively lower compared with those of country B.

We shall illustrate the gains from trade geometrically in this case. The left panel of Figure 2.2(A) shows Britain's production possibility frontier assuming she has, as before, 120 labourers (*DH*). If all produce cloth, 60 units are available. As they are switched from cloth to food, 5 cloth are lost for each 2 food gained, until ultimately just 24 food are available. Under autarchy the production set is also the consumption set, so consumers as a group will choose some point on *DH* as the final consumption and production equilibrium, say *J*. The corresponding production possibility frontier (*GC*) for America is shown on the right, also assuming 120 labourers. It is smaller than Britain's because America is absolutely less efficient than Britain.

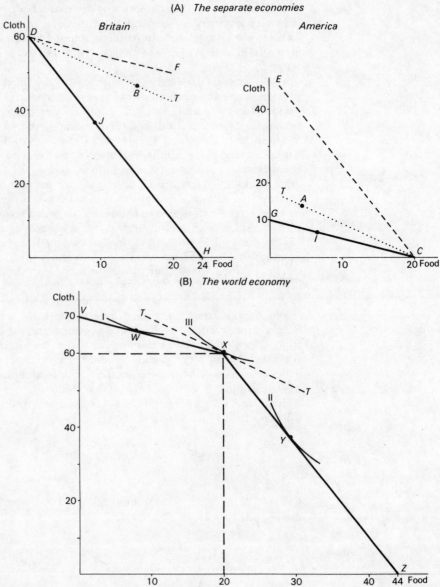

Figure 2.2 *Two trading economies – constant costs. (A) The separate economies. (B) The world economy.*

18

Now open trade: Britain concentrates on cloth production and America on food. Suppose, for now, that each specialises entirely, so that British production shifts to *D* and American to *C*. For Britain, *DF* shows the consumption possibilities of production at *D* if she can trade at America's autarchic prices. Its slope is one-half, indicating America's willingness to transform any 1/2 cloth into 1 food. Thus it would be possible for Britain to consume anywhere along *DF*, which clearly dominates its autarchy consumption locus. Correspondingly, if America specialises and can still trade at British autarchy prices, she has a 'trading' consumption feasibility locus of *EC*, which again dominates her autarchy possibilities.

Observe how the possibility of gains from trade depends on trade occurring at a price ratio other than the country's own autarchy ratio. This is obvious enough: if foreigners transformed goods at the same rate as locals, there would be no reason to trade abroad rather than at home. None the less it is important. Note also that it would not be possible simultaneously for Britain to trade at American prices and for America to trade at British prices. In full equilibrium, the two trading price ratios must be the same, because the two countries are at opposite ends of the same transaction. The determination of this common trading price and of the final production and consumption points are considered in the next section.

2.3   SPECIALISATION AND THE TERMS OF TRADE

The building blocks

While Figure 2.2(A) illustrates the potential for welfare gains from trade, it does not fully define the final trading equilibrium in terms of either the final price ratio or the final production and consumption points. To examine these questions we shall assume that all people in both countries have identical, homothetic, preferences.[1] This allows us to aggregate preferences in each country into a single 'national social welfare function' and then to combine these into a single world welfare function. These functions may be represented by families of indifference curves, which behave just like individual preferences, and we assume that society, like individuals, seeks to attain the highest indifference curve possible. (Further details of the aggregation of preferences appear in Chapter 5 below.)

We shall also combine the individual country production structures to describe a single (world) economy with two techniques for transforming food into cloth – one British and one American. Combining the two transformation curves in Figure 2.2(A), we can construct the world transformation curve in part (B) of the figure. If both countries produce only cloth, total output is 0 food and 70 cloth: (0,70). If both countries produce only food, output is (44,0). These are shown as points *V* and *Z*. Now suppose that, starting from *V*, some food is desired: if it is produced in Britain $2\frac{1}{2}$ cloth must be surrendered, whereas in America the price is only $\frac{1}{2}$ cloth. Hence, moving from *V*, world output is maximised if America switches from cloth to its comparative advantage good, food. This continues until America is entirely specialised in food. World production is then given by point *X*, i.e. (20,60). If still more food is required, we must then use the less efficient technique – Britain – surrendering $2\frac{1}{2}$ cloth per food unit: this takes us along *XZ* towards *Z*. Hence *VXZ* represents the *world transformation schedule* of food for cloth, *assuming that the most efficient techniques are used*.

The terms of trade

The 'terms of trade' is just another expression for the relative price of one good in terms of another, although it is usually reserved for cases where the two goods originate from different countries. As before, prices are determined by the

19

maximisation of welfare over the feasible consumption set. Here this exercise is conducted on a world scale, confronting the world transformation function with the world preference function.

We consider three alternative positions for the world indifference curves. If demand is strongly oriented towards cloth – giving indifference curves of family I – equilibrium occurs at W. Here, Britain is entirely specialised in cloth but America produces both goods. The world price ratio is determined by the slope of the social indifference curve at equilibrium, and at W this equals the American rate of transformation, because America is the marginal producer. That is, to obtain 1 extra unit of cloth, 2 units of American food must be surrendered, because Britain has no resources not already devoted to cloth. In this circumstance, the world price ratio equals the American autarchy price ratio. Britain gains from trade (she can trade along DF in Figure 2.2(A)) but America on the other hand gains nothing, since both foreign trade and switching factors between industries offer the same rate of transformation of food for cloth. Clearly this would apply wherever the tangency between the indifference curve and transformation surface occurred between V and X.

An equivalent case is social indifference curve II – which produces equilibrium Y. Here, America specialises and gains, but, with the terms of trade at Britain's autarchy price ratio, Britain does not.

The more interesting case is indifference curve III. Here, both countries specialise and the world terms of trade are determined by the slope of the indifference curve at point X (the slope of TT). It is clear that this could lie anywhere between the slope of VX (America's autarchy price ratio) and XZ (Britain's autarchy price ratio). Within these limits, the terms of trade are determined solely by the shape of the indifference curve – i.e. the pattern of demand.

Assuming equilibrium at X, and terms of trade TT, British and American consumption possibilities are shown in Figure 2.2(A) as DT and CT respectively (DT, CT and TT are all parallel). The final terms of trade differ from both autarchy price ratios and hence both countries benefit from trade. The final consumption baskets for each country lie along DT and CT respectively and, given our assumption of identical homothetic preferences, they must contain goods in the same proportions as the world equilibrium X. They are thus points A and B. Britain produces at D and consumes at B, selling cloth for food, while America produces at C and consumes at A, trading from C to A, which precisely matches Britain's trade from D to B.

The world production point X arises at any terms of trade between the two autarchy price ratios. This does not mean that the terms of trade are irrelevant however, for they determine the distribution of the gains from trade. Suppose that tastes change from our previous equilibrium so that food becomes more highly valued. People will surrender more cloth per unit of food, so the terms of trade line becomes steeper. Hence both DT and CT become steeper: the former, pivoting on D, leads to a contraction of the British consumption set, while the latter, pivoting on C, expands the American consumption set. Thus a shift in a country's terms of trade in favour of its exports (i.e. a rising relative price of exports) increases its economic welfare.

Specialisation

Let us summarise these results. In the simple Ricardian two-by-two model either:

(i) just one country specialises and gains from trade. The terms of trade settle at the other (non-specialising) country's autarchy price ratio and that country gains nothing by trade; or

(ii)   both countries specialise and both gain by trade. The terms of trade depend
       on demand patterns, but must lie between the two autarchy price ratios.

Which of these outcomes occurs depends on both the size and efficiency of the
countries and on demand patterns. Given the latter, the smaller a country's output
the greater the probability that it specialises. (In Figure 2.2, the smaller America's
output, the closer would X be to the upright axis and the greater the chance that
the highest of any family of indifference curves would be tangent to XZ rather than
to VX). Thus it seems that large or efficient countries have less to gain through
trade than small countries, since trade is less likely to expand their consumption
sets.[2]

If this seems somewhat counter-intuitive, it is because the model does not fully
reflect reality. In order to produce the outcomes described, we must have perfectly
competitive good and factor markets and the government must not intervene at
all in international trade. Large countries, however, are often felt to gain from
trade because they have market power: by threatening to withdraw from or hinder
trade they (or their large companies) can threaten to damage small partners, and
hence appropriate some of the latter's gains to themselves.

**Money and
prices**   Most international trade theory uses barter theory as we have just done, but before
proceeding we should at least assure ourselves that there is a consistent story of
money and absolute prices to accompany it. Return to the table of labour requirements on p. 17 above. If both British and American workers earn 1 unit of local
currency per day, that table also represents *local currency* prices under autarchy.
Suppose initially that when trade is opened the exchange rate is £1 = $1. No one
would wish to buy American goods, so there would be no demand for dollars, but
everyone would be trying to get pounds in order to buy British goods. Hence the
pound would tend to rise in value – say to £1 = $2. At this price America is the
cheaper source of food and Britain the cheaper source of cloth, and, by following
absolute prices, trade would also fall into the comparative advantage pattern.

The equilibrium exchange rate will be determined so that, given local currency
wages, each country is absolutely the cheaper for its comparative advantage good
and there is only one price for each good. This, in fact, amounts to determining the
terms of trade, because once the terms of trade are set, as in Figure 2.2(B), so too is
the exchange rate. At X, for example, terms of trade of 1 food to $1\frac{1}{2}$ cloth imply an
exchange rate of £1 = $2. (American food costs $6, or £3, per unit; British cloth £2.)
At equibilibrium W, however, the terms of trade are 1 food to $\frac{1}{2}$ cloth – the
American autarchy ratio. This requires an exchange rate of £1 = £6 so that British
and American cloth are both £2 per unit and food is £1 per unit.

Hence, underlying the comparative advantage analysis is a monetary analysis
that shows how, with people buying from the cheapest source and with the
exchange rate flexible, the required trade patterns come about. Note in passing
that in this model wages differ between countries: labour in the more efficient
country receives higher wages and consumption.

2.4   FURTHER ANALYSIS OF THE RICARDIAN MODEL

The previous two sections have sketched a complete model of world trade based
on Ricardo's seminal law of comparative advantage. This analysis underlies nearly
all later trade theory, and to facilitate our study of this we now look more deeply at
the model, in terms other than Ricardo's.

The assumptions

International trade takes place because goods are available more cheaply from abroad than at home. Ricardo's model explains the pattern of trade by relating prices to certain fundamental features of the economies concerned. This requires several assumptions:

(i)   There is only one factor of production – labour.

(ii)   Its productivity – i.e. the production technology – differs between countries, but no explanation is made of these technological differences.

(iii) Labour is perfectly mobile between industries within a country but perfectly immobile between countries.

(iv)   There are constant returns to scale in each industry – i.e. unit costs are independent of the level of output.

(v)   There are no impediments to trade such as tariffs or transport costs.

Assumptions (iii) and (iv) ensure that each country's transformation curve between cloth and food is a straight line. The rate of transformation is quite independent of the composition of output – e.g. it is always 1 food for $\frac{1}{2}$ cloth for America. Hence there is only one price ratio consistent with the production of both goods – in America this is 2 cloth for 1 food; any other price ratio causes producers to specialise, because then 1 unit of labour can earn more money in one branch than the other. Thus, labour productivities determine costs (rates of transformation), which determine the direction of trade when it occurs. In Ricardo's model, therefore, the assumptions ensure that the direction of trade is determined solely by comparative labour productivities.

As with nearly all trade theory, the immediate cause of the direction of trade is relative prices. Ricardo's assumptions determine relative prices by relative labour productivities; other theories postulate other determinants, but the basic approach remains the same. This section and the next chapters now consider relaxing Ricardo's assumptions and extending his model.

Opportunity costs

Ricardo expressed his theory in terms of the labour theory of value – labour was the only factor of production. This was an expositional convenience rather than a statement of fact, but it nevertheless took many years for trade theory to escape from this strait-jacket. The latter was accomplished by Haberler (1936), who re-expressed the theory in terms of *opportunity costs*. The opportunity cost of good X is the amount of good Y that has to be surrendered in order to obtain a unit of X. In Ricardo's theory this transformation occurs by shifting labour from one industry to another, so opportunity costs are naturally defined in terms of relative labour productivities. However, it is obvious that a similar concept would apply even when there were several factors of production. Provided that these general opportunity costs were constant, the whole of the above theory would follow without change. We need merely treat the labour requirements on p. 17 above as being requirements for general bundles of factors, with lower requirements indicating greater efficiency. However, with more factors, costs are unlikely to be constant, and we shall see in Chapter 3 how this affects trade theory.

Demand

The Ricardian theory is a supply theory of international trade: it is differences in supply conditions that give rise to the possibilities of trade, and trade occurs even when, as above, demand conditions are identical across countries. This is not to dismiss demand, however, for it explains much of the detail of the final outcome. In any case, the analysis may be completed without the assumption of identical demand without any fundamental differences (see, for example, our first edition, Chapter 4, or Chacholiades, 1981).

22

Many goods and countries

One obvious shortcoming of our theory is its unrealistic two-by-two nature. This might be justified on pedagogic grounds, but in fact multi-dimensional trade theory is much more complex and ambiguous in its results than the simple models. This book will not present any such analysis, leaving it to more advanced texts, but we shall summarise some of the results and point out – where necessary – the dangers of simply extrapolating from the two-by-two case.

Consider first a model with two countries but many goods. We can establish a chain of comparative advantage, similar to equation (2.1), that ranks goods ($i = 1 \ldots n$) by country A's comparative advantage. Thus

$$\frac{l_1^A}{l_1^B} \leq \frac{l_2^A}{l_2^B} \leq \ldots \frac{l_i^A}{l_i^B} \leq \ldots \leq \frac{l_n^A}{l_n^B}, \tag{2.3}$$

which states that, of all goods, good 1 requires the least inputs in A relative to B, and so on. The two-by-two theory generalises in an obvious fashion here: A will produce and export goods to the left (where its advantage is greatest) and B will export those to the right. At most, one good could be produced in both countries – where the labour input ratio equals the terms of trade. The precise point at which the chain is 'broken', whether there is a common good, and the terms of trade all depend, as before, on the structure of demand as well as of productivities.

Next consider many countries ($j = 1 \ldots m$) but only two goods. Again a chain exists, but now like (2.2):

$$\frac{l_F^1}{l_C^1} \leq \frac{l_F^2}{l_C^2} \leq \ldots \leq \frac{l_F^j}{l_C^j} \leq \ldots \frac{l_F^m}{l_C^m}. \tag{2.4}$$

This states that country 1 has the greatest comparative advantage (efficiency) in food relative to cloth, etc. The chain will again be broken by demand, but if country j exports food so too will every country to the left of it in (2.4). At most, one country produces both goods, and, if it does, the world terms of trade equal its autarchy ratio and it gains nothing by trade. Note also that nothing here determines bilateral trade links (i.e. who exports to whom); only total exports are determined. This case can be analysed geometrically as in Figure 2.2(B). The only difference is that the world transformation surface has a face (straight section) for each country, with faces (countries) ordered as in (2.4).

The generalisation to many countries *and* many goods is more complex, but roughly speaking the chain concept persists. Each country will tend to specialise, producing several goods only if world relative prices equal its autarchy price ratio. Similarly there will be only a limited number of cases of two countries producing the same good. In this particular case, then, multi-dimensional trade theory does bear a strong resemblance to the simple model.

Trade impediments

In a two-country model, trade impediments that involve only extra costs – for example, tariffs and transport costs as opposed to subsidies – can change the point at which the chain of comparative advantage is broken, but not reverse the ordering of goods within it. For example, B's tariffs may prevent A from exporting good 1 in chain (2.3), and thereby oblige it to export good i, where in the absence of tariffs i would have been imported. However, they cannot change the fact that all A's imports must lie to the right of its exports in chain (2.3); in the example quoted, good 1 would merely become non-traded. Similarly, transport costs can insert a band of non-traded goods into chain (2.3) but again not mix up the ordering of imports and exports: if a round-trip costs 10 per cent of the value of trade (that is, swapping £100 of exports for £100 of imports costs £10), there will be a band of goods covering a 10 per cent range of relative productivities in (2.3) that will be non-traded. However, A will still export from the goods to the left of the band and import from those to the right. Thus, while with only two countries trade impediments might complicate the results, they do not fundamentally reverse them.

Once the model is generalised to many countries and many goods, however, or to allow for traded intermediate goods (inputs into the production of other goods), trade impediments can destroy the chains of comparative advantage. Hence, while the basic notions of comparative advantage certainly still help to explain trade patterns in these more realistic cases, totally specific and unambiguous predictions about who exports what are not always possible.

2.5   TESTING RICARDIAN THEORY

We have spent much effort exploring the implications of various assumptions in the Ricardian model. In the end this is helpful only if it enhances our understanding of the world we inhabit: ultimately our models must have some link with reality. The intuitive connection is clear enough, but to be confident of the model's usefulness we need the firmer evidence of proper econometric studies. The Ricardian theory was first formally tested by MacDougall (1951) – 134 years after its inception!

MacDougall considered the UK's and the USA's trade in 1937. Since UK–US bilateral trade was distorted by tariffs and was small relative to their total trade, he generalised the Ricardian theory to argue that a country with a comparative advantage in some good would have a relatively large share of third-country markets in that good. Strictly, the theory states that generally only one country will export any good, so that comparative advantage will be associated with 100 per cent shares and disadvantage with 0 per cent shares. However, if we allow for transport costs, differences in quality, etc., MacDougall's assertion seems reasonable. (Nevertheless, observe that having several exporters for any good is already sufficient to refute simple Ricardian trade theory!)

Using data for twenty-five manufactured products, MacDougall found that the UK/US export ratio to third markets was strongly negatively related to both the ratio of UK to US physical labour requirements and the ratio of UK to US labour costs. This seems to confirm the basic thrust of the theory: where productivity is comparatively high so too are exports. Interestingly, however, MacDougall found that, where UK and US labour costs were roughly equal, exports were not equal but rather the UK's were more than twice the USA's. This he attributed to the UK's reputation for high quality and to Imperial Preference.

These results have been broadly corroborated on many different industries and years (see Bhagwati, 1964), although through time the extent of the UK's advantage in the equal-cost case has been declining. In fact, MacDougall's basic results have never really been challenged. Bhagwati (1964) has, however, seriously challenged their interpretation on theoretical and empirical grounds.

Theoretically he objected (a) that Ricardo said nothing about third-country markets (we have dismissed this above), and (b) that, while for any one good a relative cheapening of UK supplies by 10 per cent may increase the UK share by, say, x per cent, it does not follow, when comparing two goods one of which has a lower UK/US cost relative by 10 per cent, that the relatively less costly good will have an x per cent higher market share. That depends on the goods' demand curves. Nevertheless, by lumping all goods into the same cross-section regression equation, MacDougall is implicitly assuming that a given cost advantage translates into the same market share benefit for all goods. This is plainly not precisely true and can only be countered by observing that, theory notwithstanding, the results have received sufficient support for us to accept the approach as a reasonable approximation.

On empirical grounds, Bhagwati's criticism is also interesting. The causal chain of the Ricardian theory runs from labour costs to autarchy prices to the direction of trade. Given the imperfections in trade that we postulated above, however, *post-trade* prices in each country should partly reflect autarchy prices (imperfections prevent US and UK prices being wholly equalised). Hence we would expect correlations between relative (post-trade) export prices and export shares – which MacDougall found – and also between relative costs and relative prices. Bhagwati, however, could find no evidence of the latter and therefore argued that, since the causal chain could not be established, the Ricardian theory should be rejected even though its ultimate prediction appeared to be corroborated. Certainly we must suspect predictions whose mechanisms are not explicable, but in this case the bulk of the Ricardian theory may be salvaged.

Schematically the argument may be represented thus:

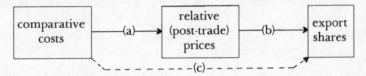

The solid lines represent the 'traditional' causal chain. Link (a) could not be established empirically, but links (b) and (c) were empirically justified. So, to justify the Ricardian theory, we need essentially to establish a causal explanation for (c) that does not depend on (a). Suppose different industries earn different rates of profit – owing possibly to different degrees of monopoly or capital costs. Prices may then be independent of labour costs, but costs are still important because the lower are costs the higher are export profits and hence the greater is the incentive to export. Thus, with independent prices, industries with comparative cost advantages will still export relatively more owing to the stronger incentives to supply exports. This breaks with the Ricardian model discussed above by introducing an additional element of costs, but in Ricardo's other writing profits are fully recognised and may differ between industries except in the very longest of runs.

To conclude, therefore, while the specific predictions of Ricardian trade theory are not supported by the data – especially the prediction of almost complete specialisation – the general tenor of the results is that comparative advantage can explain broad trade patterns and that relating comparative advantage to relative labour requirements (or costs) is not grossly misleading.

FURTHER READING

Our first edition gives a brief historical sketch of classical trade theory (Chapter 2): the classic reference is *Viner* (1937). Among alternative textbook introductions to trade theory the best are *Caves and Jones* (1981) and *Lindert and Kindleberger* (1982), who follow a similar scheme to ourselves, and *Findlay* (1970a), who is rather different. *Bhagwati* (1964) is authoritative and also very interesting (although not entirely correct) on empirical testing, whilst *MacDougall* (1951) is a magnificent example of applied economics. *Jones* (1976) considers expanding the two-by-two model. Most of these references will be more accessible after you have read Chapter 3 below.

Among more advanced treatments of the subjects of this chapter are *Chipman* (1966), and also *Dixit and Norman* (1980) and *Deardorff* (1979, 1980) who make use of the techniques of revealed preference and duality in considering multi-dimensional trade theory. Duality is introduced by *Mussa* (1979) as well as by Dixit and Norman.

NOTES

1 Homotheticity implies that the proportions in which people consume the two goods do not vary with total consumption expenditure.
2 This conclusion is reinforced if market size influences efficiency (by allowing more internal specialisation), because then large countries have less need of trade to reap economies of scale than do smaller countries.

3 Neo-Classical Trade Theory

This chapter develops the analysis of Chapter 2 along neo-classical lines. First, it relaxes the assumption of constant costs, showing how international trade under increasing costs will rarely involve complete specialisation. Second, it develops a rationale for increasing costs and for differences in comparative productivity in terms of countries' differing endowments of factors of production. This is the Heckscher–Ohlin model of trade, and it is examined in some detail, both theoretically and empirically. The final section considers factor supplies in the very long run and in the short run; the latter gives rise to an interesting model of international trade that will be used in several later chapters.

3.1 INTERNATIONAL TRADE WITH INCREASING COSTS

Section 2.1 introduced the tools required for exploring neo-classical trade theory, but one vital extension is required. Our discussion of the transformation function was predicated upon constant relative labour costs: labour requirements per unit of output were fixed and constant in each industry and consequently the marginal rate of transformation of food for cloth was constant regardless of the pattern of production. Thus the transformation curve was a straight line. In section 2.4 we reinterpreted the transformation curve in terms of opportunity costs, allowing for many factors of production, but we still clung to constant costs. We now relax that assumption.

Increasing costs

In this and most subsequent chapters we shall assume that industries face increasing costs: as the output of cloth rises, successive units cost more to produce. In opportunity cost terms, as cloth (food) output increases, successive increments require the surrender of increasing amounts of food (cloth); the marginal rate of transformation of cloth into food falls as cloth output rises. This implies that the transformation curve is bowed outwards away from the origin. The slope will still be negative – implying that more food always entails less cloth – but it will change from being relatively shallow at high cloth outputs (low MRT) to being relatively steep at low cloth outputs. Figure 3.1 below shows a typical example.

Before we discuss possible causes of increasing costs we must define some terminology. We use decreasing, constant or increasing *returns to scale* to describe how costs change when *all* factors of production are increased proportionately – that is, when the technique of production (the relative inputs of the factors) is unchanged but the scale of the enterprise is increased. On the other hand we use diminishing, constant or increasing *marginal returns* to refer to the increase in output available by adding an extra unit of just one factor. In this case technique does change, because the relative factor inputs have altered. In neo-classical trade theory we usually assume *constant returns to scale* but *diminishing marginal returns to each factor*.

We mention three possible causes of increasing costs. First, some factors may be better suited to cloth production and others to food: as we shift more from food to cloth, we increasingly move factors with a high output of food into cloth where they have low productivity. Second, there may be some wholly specific factors of

27

production, limited to particular industries: for example, coal mines are limited to coal production. If these are fixed in supply, as we draft more of the mobile factors into an industry, these factors encounter diminishing marginal returns, and hence cannot match their productivity in other industries. Third, industries may require homogeneous and mobile factors in different proportions. Thus, when both goods are produced in quantity, factors can be allocated between industries to exploit their different requirements of different factors, but under complete specialisation the producing industry must accept the factor proportions endowed on the country. However, this is the crux of the Heckscher–Ohlin theorem, and so discussion is postponed until the next section.

International equilibrium

With the exception of the curved transformation curve, the analysis of international trade proceeds precisely as in Chapter 2; it is summarised in Figure 3.1. The two national transformation frontiers are shown as DH and GC and the autarchic equilibria as J and I respectively. Note that in autarchy, Britain, which still has a comparative advantage in cloth, has a relatively lower price for cloth than America. This is evident from the slope of the transformation curve ($MRT = P$), which is steeper at J than at I.

In part (B) of the figure, the world transformation curve is constructed by adding the outputs of the two countries, assuming that both face the same price ratio and therefore that both have the same marginal rate of transformation. (This is clearly a condition for maximising world output. If America's MRT exceeded Britain's, say $3C = 1F$ and $2C = 1F$ respectively, it would pay to switch a unit of American food output to cloth, yielding 3 cloth, while increasing British food output by 1 unit, sacrificing only 2 cloth.) The addition of transformation curves is effected practically by inverting one of the national curves and sliding it along the other, keeping the two sets of axes parallel. The origin of the former then traces out the world transformation curve. (Because the two curves are just touching at their point of contact, they have there the same slopes or MRTs.) This operation is sketched in Figure 3.1(B).

If the MRT takes a common value for both America and Britain, that same value must also apply to the world as a whole, for transformation must occur in either America or Britain. Hence the slope of the world transformation curve at any point equals the slopes of the national curves at the points that just add up to give that world point. This is illustrated in Figure 3.1(B). World preferences define X as the maximum welfare point on the world transformation curve VXZ, and the terms of trade as TT. Production at X requires the national curves to be positioned as shown and national production to be at point L for Britain and K for America. The national curves at these points both have slope $T'T'$, which is the same as slope TT.

With production at L and K and terms of trade $T'T'$, each country can consume anywhere along the lines $T'T'$ in Figure 3.1(A); but, given our assumption of identical preferences, the shares of the goods in total consumption must be identical and hence the final outcomes are given by A and B respectively. Clearly these outcomes dominate the autarchy points. Britain trades cloth for food to get from production point L to consumption point B, while America makes the precisely opposite trade to get from K to A.

International trade has two effects on each economy: it increases the output of one good (the comparative advantage good) and increases consumption of the other. This reflects the price changes induced by trade. In Britain, the relative price of cloth rises, which encourages production and diverts consumption: with a higher price producers can afford to produce more cloth despite the fact that this

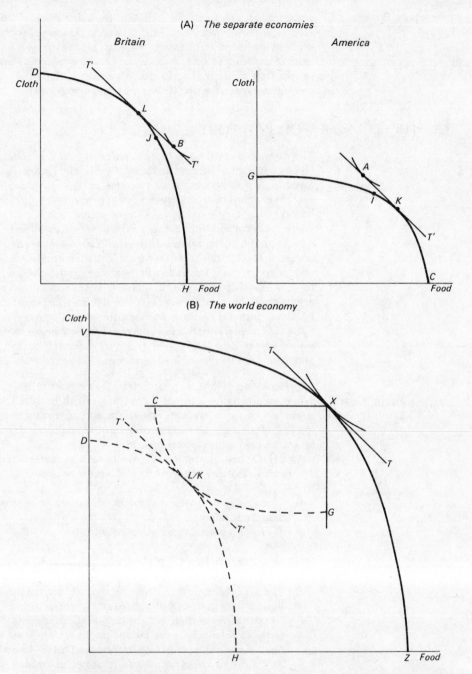

Figure 3.1 *Two trading economies. (A) The separate economies. (B) The World economy.*

raises opportunity costs, while the lower relative price for food forces food production to be cut back in order to reduce opportunity costs in line with prices.

The most important difference between this model and the Ricardian outcome is that here we no longer have complete specialisation. With increasing costs

America can produce a little cloth at the same price as Britain can produce a lot. Hence both American and British cloth producers can coexist; there will just be more of the latter. The cause of trade then is not merely costs, but that, at any given level of cost (price), one country can produce relatively more of a good than the other. That is, their transformation curves differ in shape. This recognition of incomplete specialisation is clearly a big gain in realism.

3.2 THE HECKSCHER–OHLIN THEORY

The neo-classical theory of international trade reaches its apotheosis in the Heckscher–Ohlin theory. Initiated by Eli Heckscher in 1919 in an article in Swedish, it first became widely recognised with the publication of Ohlin (1933). Since then it has been massively researched, refined and formalised, probably way beyond what its original authors would accept.

Heckscher and Ohlin asked *why* productivities differed across countries; why transformation possibilities differed. Ricardo said technology differed, but they argued that countries' abilities varied with their endowments of different factors of production. Hence America, with her huge prairies, was well equipped to produce food, while Britain, with abundant labour, was better at manufacturing. This argument has great intuitive force – and it is a short step from production to trade. Provided demand patterns do not differ much between countries, the *Heckscher–Ohlin theorem* of trade states: *countries will export those goods whose production is relatively intensive in the factors with which they are well endowed*. The rest of this chapter explores and formalises this sensible observation.

The assumptions

The Heckscher–Ohlin approach (H–O) stresses the role of factor endowments. When we formalise it into a theorem, we wish to isolate this feature as the only possible cause of international trade and to examine its consequences. This implies not that it is *actually* the only cause of trade, but that it is interesting to know how the world would look if it were.

The H–O theorem may be shown to be true under a set of seven assumptions. The first two isolate endowments as the cause of trade:

(i) Consumption is determined by identical, homothetic, preferences (as we assumed above).

(ii) Technology is identical across countries.

The next two restrict the technology in important respects:

(iii) The production functions for each good exhibit constant returns to scale but diminishing marginal returns to any single factor.

(iv) Goods differ in their requirements of different factor inputs. If one good requires relatively more labour than another at one set of factor prices, it does so at all sets of factor prices. This is known as the exclusion of 'factor-intensity reversals' and it allows us to identify the labour-intensive product unambiguously.

The next two assumptions describe economic behaviour:

(v) Perfect competition exists in all factor and product markets.

(vi) There are no impediments to trade, such as tariffs or transport costs, but the migration of factors of production is quite impossible.

The final assumption imposes restrictions on the world:

(vii)   There are just two factors, two goods and two countries. The factors are homogeneous within countries, identical between them, and fixed in supply.

The role that these assumptions play will become clearer as the proof proceeds, but we can note here that they have different status. Assumptions (i) and (ii) are necessary to pose the question 'what does factor-endowment-related trade look like?' Assumptions (vi) and (vii) are mainly for convenience and can be partially relaxed. Assumptions (iii)–(v) are critical: (v) ensures the equality of prices and costs, and of prices and marginal utilities in consumption; (iv) allows us to identify *the* labour-intensive good technically, i.e. regardless of any economic phenomenon; and (iii) is central to the translation of price signals into quantity changes – its absence would not necessarily reverse the pattern of trade but it would make it impossible to prove that the H–O result always rules.

Commodity and factor prices

We start our proof by introducing a new tool of analysis – the *isoquant*. An isoquant is drawn on a graph with quantities of factors on the axes; it connects all combinations of the two factors that could produce a given output of a particular good. There is a separate isoquant for each level of output. Figure 3.2 shows isoquants for two goods. Their shape – convex to the origin – derives from the assumption of diminishing marginal returns: as labour replaces capital, increasing amounts are required to substitute for successive units of capital.

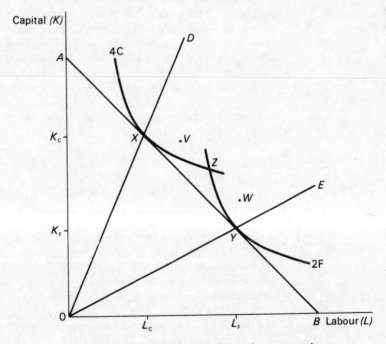

Figure 3.2   *Production conditions for two goods*

Constant returns to scale defines the relationship between isoquants. It implies that doubling all inputs doubles outputs with no change in technique. Hence the isoquant for 2 units of output is just an expanded version of that for 1 unit. An

31

important feature of the expansion is that, as we move out along any ray from the origin (like OD in Figure 3.2), each successive isoquant has the same slope as we cross it; the isoquant for 1 million units, say, looks just like that for 1 unit with the scale on the axes multiplied by 1 million. Hence the whole of the production technology for a good can be summarised by the shape of a single isoquant.

Figure 3.2 shows representatives of two sets of isoquants: for cloth (C) – the more capital-intensive – and for food (F). It also shows a budget-line for firms buying factors in the factor markets. Given factor prices, line AB represents all the bundles of factors purchasable for, say, £1. Clearly its slope is the factor price ratio: it shows how much extra capital could be bought by purchasing 1 less unit of labour. Profit-maximising firms will always produce the maximum possible for £1 and hence will produce on the isoquant that is just tangential to the budget line. This defines the factor intensities of their production methods. Thus cloth producers will produce 4 cloth for £1 using K_C of capital and L_C of labour, while food producers will produce 2 food using K_F and L_F.

Under perfect competition, costs equal prices. If we know that the cost of producing 4C equals that of producing 2F, we also know that their prices must be equal (£1), and hence we know the commodity price ratio – 2 cloth per 1 unit food. Thus Figure 3.2 shows how we can move from a given factor price ratio (the slope of AB) to a unique commodity price ratio. In fact, we can also work backwards. If the commodity price ratio were given, such that 2 cloth traded for 1 food, we know from the competitiveness assumptions that both must cost the same. The isoquants 4C and 2F must therefore be tangential to the same budget-line, and a little experimentation will show that AB is the only possible line that is tangential to both. Once AB is drawn, however, the factor price ratio is known from its slope. Hence, under the assumptions given, there is a unique one-for-one relationship between factor prices and commodity prices. Any lowering of the relative price of labour lowers the relative price of the labour-intensive good. (Check this by flattening AB in Figure 3.2. If the new line is still tangential to 2F, it must be tangential to a cloth isoquant below 4, and 1 food would now trade for less than 2 cloth.)

We can see these links algebraically as follows. Perfect competition ensures that prices equal costs: hence

$$P_F = \theta_{FL} w + \theta_{FK} r$$

$$P_C = \theta_{CL} w + \theta_{CK} r$$

(3.1)

where P_F and P_C are food and cloth prices, w and r are wages and capital rentals, and θ_{ij} (i = F,C; j = L,K) are the shares of factor j in the costs for good i. These equations define the factor price to commodity price link. Clearly, however, (3.1) may be rewritten to show w and r as functions of P_F, P_C and the θ_{ij}, and this defines the reverse link. Provided the θ_{ij} satisfy certain conditions (derived from the H–O assumptions), the latter is unique.

International trade

Suppose the world comprised two identical countries. In autarchy each would have the same equilibrium – say that in Figure 3.2. There would be no scope for trade between them since commodity prices would be identical. Now grant one country – America (A) – an increased supply of labour, holding (for now) everything else constant. With constant commodity prices, factor prices are constant, and constant factor prices imply unchanged techniques of production (points X and Y in Figure 3.2). So how could the extra labour be absorbed into the American economy? Not by giving a little to each industry, because that would change their techniques of production, but by increasing the output of food and decreasing that of cloth. Reducing cloth output releases factors in bundles of K_C capital and L_C labour (remember the technique of production is given); however, food will absorb them in proportions K_F and L_F. Hence, for every K_C of capital taken on by food producers, considerably more than L_C of labour will be required and these workers will be found from the pool of 'new' labour.

This argument is due to Rybczynski (1955) and may be summarised as saying that, under the assumptions enumerated above (including frozen commodity prices), the country better endowed with labour will produce absolutely more food (the labour-intensive good) and absolutely less cloth (capital-intensive).

We assumed identical preferences across countries. Thus the extra food will be consumed only if its price falls relative to cloth. This in turn reduces the relative price of labour, as we saw above; so, with extra labour, complete equilibrium in America actually requires relatively lower wages, lower food prices and greater food output than in Britain. Obversely, of course, Britain is now capital-abundant relative to America and she will have relatively low capital rentals, low cloth prices and high cloth output.

Finally, suppose we now open trade between America and Britain. With different relative prices there is now scope for profitable trade, and it takes the form predicted by the H–O theorem: Britain, which is capital-abundant, exports cloth (the capital-intensive good) and America (labour-abundant) exports food (labour-intensive).

To explore the final world equilibrium we note that the H–O assumptions guarantee that transformation curves are bowed outwards and that they differ between countries (see Appendix). The capital-abundant country's curve is biased towards cloth production and, at any commodity price ratio, entails its producing a higher ratio of cloth to food than the other country. Thus the world and national equilibria are just as in Figure 3.1, and all the previous conclusions follow.

Further notes on Heckscher–Ohlin

International trade results in both countries facing the same (world) commodity price ratio. By our previous result on the unique relationship between factor and commodity prices, therefore, we conclude that trade also equalises factor prices. This is an important and empirically verifiable conclusion of the H–O theorem, and we shall return to it in Chapter 13 below, where an alternative proof is also given.

The validity of Heckscher–Ohlin depends crucially on the absence of factor-intensity reversals. Figure 3.3 illustrates how the theorem breaks down if this is violated. Suppose food technology gives much greater opportunities for the substitution of labour for capital than cloth technology. The food isoquants will be relatively straight (indicating a wide range of possible input bundles), those for cloth strongly curved. The difficulty is that under these circumstances there are two factor price ratios (represented by AB and DE) consistent with a single commodity price ratio (4C:2F). Furthermore, at one ratio cloth is capital-intensive (DE), whereas at the other ratio food is. If America's trading equilibrium is DE and Britain's AB, Heckscher–Ohlin trade is impossible, because America's labour-intensive good and Britain's capital-intensive good are the same!

Our proof of the Heckscher–Ohlin theorem also depended on both goods actually being produced (if not, the factor budget line AB could not be drawn). This is not strictly required for the trade theorem, but it is necessary for the factor price equalisation result just outlined.

We held demand patterns constant over countries to emphasise the role of factor endowment differences. Although this is not entirely necessary, the H–O theorem can in fact be overturned if demand patterns differ substantially. If the capital-abundant country's demand is sufficiently strongly biased towards capital-intensive goods, it will have higher autarchy prices for both capital and the capital-intensive good than the other country. Hence it will import them when trade occurs. This has led some economists to define a country's abundant factor as that for which its autarchy price is relatively lower, rather than our physical definition, and, in this form, demand cannot upset the theorem for it has already been taken into account.

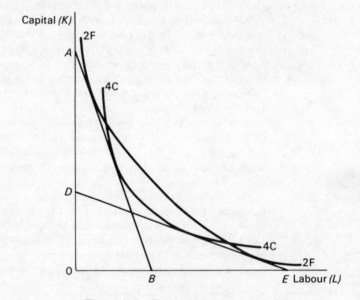

Figure 3.3   *Factor-intensity reversals*

We should also note that all the results here are of a comparative static nature. We have compared the full equilibria of the world economy under trade and autarchy. We have done nothing to discuss the actual transition from autarchy to trade or the effects of the growth in the supply of one of the factors.

Multi-dimensional Heckscher–Ohlin

Generalising the Heckscher–Ohlin model beyond two dimensions has proved very tricky, although recently some results have emerged. Jones (1974) considered a small trading economy in a multi-good, two-factor world. (A small country has no influence over world prices.) The country imports most goods, producing just the one or two that maximise the value of its national output at the given world prices. With many goods, the ones produced will frequently lie in the middle of the list of goods ordered by capital intensity, hence the country will import goods both more and less capital-intensive than its exports. Jones showed that, the greater the small country's capital abundance, the more capital-intensive will be the goods it actually produces. Clearly such complete specialisation is unrealistic, but this result does warn us that exports will not always be uniformly either more or less capital-intensive than its imports.

Returning to a multi-country model with large countries, the following results have been obtained:

34

- A country's net exports of a good (exports *minus* imports) are negatively correlated with the difference between its autarchy price and the world price for that good. That is, on average countries export those goods that they produce relatively cheaply, but not necessarily every one of them.
- If differences in countries' factor endowments are small, each country will export goods intensive in its relatively abundant factors, provided 'intensive' and 'abundant' are defined in a particular fashion. For large endowment differences, however, the most that can be said is that, if factor prices are not equalised across countries, there will be a correlation between net exports and the intensive use of abundant factors. The 'small' difference case is a precise, but not very relevant generalisation of H–O; the latter 'statistical' result is weaker but potentially more useful.

3.3   TESTING THE HECKSCHER–OHLIN THEOREM

In its simple form, Heckscher–Ohlin gives one easily tested prediction: factor prices will be equalised across countries. This is manifestly false, so the simple version must immediately be rejected. It is possible, however, that factor prices have been moved towards equality (this is difficult to test, for we cannot observe autarchy prices), and that trade satisfies the H–O pattern. Economists have therefore subjected H–O to a series of direct tests. These have usually involved comparing the factor contents of a bundle of imports and a bundle of exports. This is a slightly weaker form of the theorem than we examined, but it is more easily generalisable to many dimensions. Our results above clearly entail that the capital-abundant country's exports will embody more capital than its imports.

The Leontief paradox

The first thorough test of the Heckscher–Ohlin theory was Leontief (1954), which considered US trade in 1947. Leontief used an input–output table (which shows the inputs required in producing a unit of each output in the economy) to calculate the factor inputs for a typical $1m. of US exports and for a typical $1m. of local substitutes for US imports. The input–output tables allowed him to include not only labour and capital at the last stage of production, but also that embodied in inputs to that stage, and in inputs to inputs, etc. For example, the labour input to cars included not only assembly workers, but also workers who produced the glass and the steel used, and those who produced the coal to make the steel, and so on. Assuming that the USA was the most capital-abundant country in 1947, H–O predicts that US exports should embody relatively more capital to labour than import substitutes. In fact his results showed the opposite:

	Requirements per typical $1m. worth of:		
	Exports	Import substitutes	Import/export ratio
Capital ($,000, 1947 prices)	2,551	3,091	1.212
Labour (man-years)	182	170	0.932
Capital/labour ratio	13.99	18.18	

Responses to Leontief

Leontief's findings were catalytic. They generated huge volumes of research aimed variously at undermining their statistical basis, at modifying H–O to 'dissolve' the paradox, and at seeking further explanations of trade. Chapter 4 deals with the last category as well as presenting some further empirical results; here we briefly consider the other responses and their consequences for the theory itself.

Leontief's reaction to his results was that American labour was more efficient than world labour – by a factor of three – and hence that the USA was labour-abundant in terms of 'efficiency units' if not in actual workers. Therefore, perhaps there was no paradox at all. This is entirely *ad hoc*. There is no reason to suppose that higher US efficiency resides only or even mainly in labour rather than capital, or that a factor of three was justified. It is hardly a satisfactory explanation, although it would save H–O intact.

A related explanation, of which we shall see more below, is that by merely counting heads Leontief ignored workers' skills – their *human capital*. If this were added to physical capital, US exports would probably prove to be capital-intensive. However, theorists have questioned whether the two forms of capital are really perfectly substitutable, and statistical tests have suggested that human capital is better treated as a third factor determining trade. In fact, human capital appears to be the USA's relatively abundant factor and is prominent in her export composition. That labour and human capital were joint inputs (complements) in production could explain Leontief's results, although only at the expense of introducing extra factors into H–O.

Another factor that similarly helps explain the paradox is natural resources. Vanek (1959) showed that US imports were much more natural-resource-intense than her exports, suggesting that the USA is short of such resources. Further, he suggested, capital and natural resources are complementary, so that importing resources necessarily entails importing capital. Several researchers have repeated Leontief's exercise excluding resource-based industries and found that the paradox disappears. This appears to reconcile H–O and the Leontief paradox, although the treatment of natural resources as factors of production usable in any industry (as H–O factors are) is very unrealistic. This result is therefore better interpreted as saying that certain obvious commodities fall outside the H–O framework.

A more threatening explanation of the paradox was that factor-intensity reversals were prevalent. This would just destroy the H–O theory. Minhas (1963) found different degrees of substitutability between labour and capital in different industries, which shows that reversals must occur at some point. However, Bhagwati (1969b, ch. 1, Addendum) showed that, of 210 possible reversals, only 18 occurred between the US and India's factor price ratios, where the USA has approximately the highest wage/rental ratio and India the lowest. Hence, as a practical explanation, factor-intensity reversals are probably not important, which is fortunate for H–O.

A telling statistical point has recently been made by Leamer (1980). He showed that, even when H–O holds for balanced trade, we cannot say for unbalanced trade which factor will be relatively stronger in imports or exports. However, even for unbalanced trade the production basket of goods will always use more of the abundant factor than the consumption basket. Re-examining US trade for 1947 (when the USA had a large export surplus) Leamer found production more capital-intensive than consumption, and hence concluded that there is no paradox.

Various other explanations for the Leontief paradox have been suggested, although subsequent research has not supported them. They include: that US consumption is biased towards capital-intensive goods – the evidence, if anything suggests an opposite bias; that trade impediments distort trade – but Deardorff

(1982) showed that, provided subsidies are not dominant, distortions cannot reverse trade patterns; that Leontief should have considered only immediate (direct) factor inputs rather than total inputs via the input–output table – again Deardorff (1983) has shown the opposite; and that Leontief should have considered not capital stock but the flow of capital services used, i.e. taking into account the rate of capacity utilisation – this is wrong because the rate of utilisation is an endogenous economic variable and thus cannot be the fundamental determinant of trade. The stock of capital, on the other hand, is assumed quite exogenous.

Recent tests – extending Heckscher–Ohlin

Of the explanations offered above for Leontief's paradox, the most promising are natural resources and human capital. Natural resources cannot really be fitted into the Heckscher–Ohlin framework because they are not transferable between industries; resource–based industries have, therefore, usually been omitted in later exercises. Human capital may be treated either as affecting technology or as an additional factor within a known and common technology. The former view, which is explored in Chapter 4, holds that technology is basically 'embodied' in the skills of its designers and controllers; here we briefly examine the latter view, despite our opinion that it is the inferior interpretation.

Baldwin (1971) considered the factor content of US trade in 1962 for a large range of factors, including many different levels and types of human capital. He found that US exports were intensive relative to imports in: labour measured in man-years (confirming Leontief), more highly educated labour, more highly paid labour (pay and skills are positively related), and particularly engineers and scientists. Excluding natural resource industries nearly eliminates the paradox in man-years, and emphasises the differences between exports and imports for the other measures. This suggests that H–O has some role in non-resource-based trade.

Stern and Maskus (1981) also extended Leontief, but using a single measure of human capital based on rates of pay – assuming the higher the wage the more skilled the employee. For 1958 they confirmed the paradox, but found that imports embodied only 80 per cent of the human capital of exports, the figure falling to 66 per cent if resource industries were excluded. For 1972, however, the paradox disappeared – imports appearing to be relatively labour-intensive compared with exports – but simultaneously the net export of human capital declined sharply, with imports and exports being roughly similar in their intensities. This could be reconciled with H–O if in 1958 the USA were relatively well endowed with skilled labour, but less so in 1972. This accords with casual observation – Japan and Western Europe have caught up rapidly in education and technology over the period – but of course it would have to be confirmed by careful measurement before these results could constitute a full test of H–O. Stern and Maskus also estimated the factor content of production and consumption, as recommended by Leamer, and found them almost identical for all three factors. This removes the paradox, but at the expense of leaving H–O explaining virtually nothing at all.

Usually more favourable to H–O are tests of less developed countries' trade. Havrylyshyn (1984), for example, showed that for a sample of LDCs both the physical and human capital intensities of imports exceeded those of production, which, in turn, exceeded those of exports. He attributed the clearer results here to the greater differences between LDCs and their major markets (the industrial countries) than between different industrial countries in their mutual trade. As we shall see, however, not all LDC–industrial country trade displays H–O features.

More direct than the factor content of trade, we could just examine whether the commodities exported by a capital-abundant country are capital-intensive. This is normally done by regressing trade flows or net exports (exports minus imports) for each good on various measures of the good's factor intensity. We would expect US net trade to be positively correlated with capital intensity (i.e. she exports more of the capital-intensive commodities).

Multiple regression allows us to consider many factors simultaneously, so these regression tests generally consider several different trade theories at once. We shall examine them in Chapter 4, but note here that they do shed some light on Heckscher–Ohlin. In a series of regressions, Baldwin (1971) found US net exports negatively related to capital intensity – thus confirming the Leontief paradox by a quite different route. He also found some evidence of the positive role of human skills. This was strongly confirmed by Stern and Maskus (1981), who found net exports related positively to human capital inputs and negatively to crude labour and physical capital inputs in every year from 1958 to 1976.

UK trade

The attraction of testing trade theories on early US data is that the USA could be presumed to be at the extreme of factor endowments, being more capital-abundant (physical and human) than any other country. Hence her exports to any and all countries would, in theory, be capital-intensive. For intermediate countries, however, the position is less clear, as we saw above: exports are concentrated in one area of the factor-intensity spectrum, and imports will normally lie on either side of that area. Hence total export *versus* total import tests are unlikely to be fruitful. This probably accounts for the growing agnosticism of US tests (other countries now have similar endowments), and for the lack of factor-based tests for other countries.

Baldwin (1979) calculated the factor content for many countries' total trade in the early 1960s. He found UK imports embodying much more capital than exports and the opposite for many developing countries. Katrak (1982) considered the years 1968, 1972 and 1978, finding that exports and imports had similar capital intensities at first but that by 1978 exports were 4 per cent more intense. This was accompanied by a slight fall between 1968 and 1972 in their skill intensity, although Britain still appeared to be a substantial net exporter of inputs of skilled labour.

More detailed results for the 1970s are found in Smith *et al.* (1983). This regression study included many variables, but UK trade performance was persistently related negatively to capital/labour ratios and positively to human capital intensity (in which professional and technical manpower were the dominant aspect). These results applied strongly to UK trade with developing countries (the UK imported capital-intensive goods, confirming Baldwin's view) but less so to trade with the EEC. The latter appears to be largely independent of factor considerations, probably because UK and European factor endowments are so similar.

None of the tests described here is a full test of Heckscher–Ohlin, for none simultaneously and formally considers the three interrelated components: factor endowments, factor intensity and the pattern of trade. On the other hand, we have enough informal feel for the first to conclude from these tests (and the many others available) that factor proportions cannot explain the pattern of international trade unaided. US trade certainly did not conform to the simple H–O predictions and, while the introduction of human capital as a third factor does help to resolve some of the empirical difficulties, it is not clear that it can be made entirely consistent with the factor proportions theory. Stern (1975) concluded that 'the simple Heckscher–Ohlin model does not rest on strong empirical foundations'. This is certainly true for developed countries' mutual trade, although it is possibly overstated for the (smaller) trade flows between developed and less developed countries.

3.4 HECKSCHER–OHLIN IN THE LONG AND SHORT RUNS

Heckscher–Ohlin is a comparative static theory. It compares two worlds each with two countries. In one the countries are (and always have been and will be) under autarchy, whereas in the other they trade. The theory describes the equilibrium in the latter, using data from the former. Unfortunately, the real world is not like this, and to be useful we have to be sure that H–O will translate into real time. This is far from certain and is actually very complex, but we consider here two minor aspects, both relating to capital. Heckscher–Ohlin assumes that factors of production are homogeneous, identical across countries, fixed in supply and applicable in both (all) industries. This section considers the last two assumptions.

**The very
long run**

For periods of five–ten years it may be reasonable to assume that countries' relative rankings in capital abundance do not change. For longer periods, however, this is not realistic. Both population and capital stocks are then subject to change, and, if they change in response to other economic phenomena, these phenomena will ultimately determine international trade patterns, via their effects on factor supplies.

We can illustrate this with respect to capital. The capital stock changes through investment, and, in the long run, investment equals savings. Thus the ultimate determinant of capital abundance, and hence of trade, is differences in the level of savings. If we have two countries identical except for their propensity to save (reflecting their desire to postpone consumption for the future), eventually the higher saver will become relatively capital-abundant and export the capital-intensive good.

The short run

We now focus on the applicability of capital in both industries. If this is to occur in real time, capital must be immediately and costlessly transferable between industries. This is plainly untrue – buses cannot change into computers over-night – and so we now look at a model in which capital is specific to the industry in which it was first installed.

Our model has three factors of production – food capital (K_F), cloth capital (K_C) and labour. This makes it extremely unlikely that factor prices and commodity prices will be uniquely linked, because the equations corresponding to (3.1) are

$$P_F = \theta_{FL}w + \theta_{FK}r_K$$
$$P_C = \theta_{CL}w + \theta_{CK}r_C$$

(3.2)

where r_K and r_C are the rentals of the specific capitals. These two equations cannot be rearranged to express the three factor prices as functions of the commodity prices and θ_{ij} alone. This means we cannot determine the direction of trade in the same way as we did above.

In fact it is rather complex to predict trade patterns unambiguously. At a simple level, however, imagine the two countries have equal amounts of labour and food capital. Trade will then be determined by endowments of cloth capital, with the better-endowed country exporting cloth. Clearly a similar argument could be made for food capital. Now suppose capital endowments are equal but labour endowments unequal. The labour-abundant country will then use more labour in both industries, but, relatively speaking, labour will be concentrated in the labour-intensive industry, because this industry can absorb more labour without dramatic declines in its productivity. Since both countries have identical capital stocks, the labour-abundant country produces relatively more of the labour-intensive good and hence exports it when trade occurs. The difficulties in predicting trade patterns arise when endowments differ in more complex ways: for example, if one country has relatively more labour (tending to raise food output) and relatively little food capital (tending to reduce it). Here the outcome depends on the precise shapes of the production functions and we cannot make any generalisations.

This specific factor model may be taken in its own right or as a short-run version of the Heckscher–Ohlin model, referring to periods over which capital cannot be reallocated. In longer runs, capital moves by having net depreciation or scrapping in one industry and net investment in the other. In this case, H–O considerations determine full equilibria, as above, and this model differs from H–O only when something changes. Consider briefly the transition from autarchy to free trade for a small country. The world price ratio (which is unaffected by whether a small country trades) is shown as *TT* or *T'T'* in Figure 3.4. The country's long-run transformation curve is given by *AB*; but in the short run, given the capital allocation, it is less easy to transform cloth into food, so the short-run curve (*DE*) lies inside *AB* except at *J*, the autarchic equilibrium. The two curves correspond at *J* because there the short-term, fixed allocation of capital is just that required for long-run maximum output. When trade is opened, labour is reallocated, moving production from *J* to *K*. Then, through time, as capital gradually moves, *DE* expands out to *AB* and production expands out to *L*. As this occurs, consumption jumps from *J* to *M* and then expands gradually to *N*.

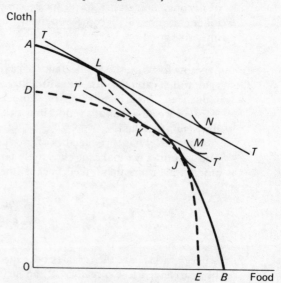

Figure 3.4 *Adjustment from autarchy to free trade.*

This model, as well as spelling out some elementary dynamics, also has interesting implications for factor prices and economic growth, to which we return below.

FURTHER READING

The analysis of general transformation curves was introduced by *Haberler* (1936). It, and the basic Heckscher–Ohlin model, may be pursued in the texts recommended for Chapter 2. Additional references on the latter include *Samuelson* (1949), *Jones* (1956–7) and *Lancaster* (1957); *Ohlin* (1933) – the classic reference – is also stimulating. On multi-dimensional versions, *Deardorff* (1982) and *Dixit and Woodland* (1982) are excellent although difficult, whilst Jones' results are best described in *Caves and Jones* (1981).

The Leontief paradox is admirably surveyed by *Bhagwati* (1964, 1969a), *Findlay* (1970a) and *Baldwin* (1971), and at a higher level by *Stern* (1975) and *Deardorff* (1983). The empirical references of the text and also *Leamer* (1974) should be consulted, and more empirical works on various countries may be located in the surveys. All these references, however, will be more accessible when you have read Chapter 4.

The specific factors model is introduced in *Caves and Jones* (1981). We shall give further references in Chapter 5 below. *Findlay* (1970b) considers the very long run.

APPENDIX: THE SHAPE OF THE TRANSFORMATION CURVE

Imagine our economy is endowed with 200 units of capital (200K) and 100 of labour (100L), and that the maximum possible output of food is 100F and of cloth 100C. The straight-line transformation curve of Chapter 2 showed that, if labour (then the only factor) were split equally between industries, output would be (50F, 50C). We can replicate that outcome now by always keeping our two factors in fixed proportion: allocating (100K, 50L) to each industry would produce (50F, 50C), because constant returns to scale ensures that halving *all* factors just halves output. However, we can actually do better than this. So far, both industries have the same capital/labour ratio, so we are operating at some point like Z in Figure 3.2. Inspection of Figure 3.2, however, shows that, by shifting a little labour from cloth to food and a little capital from food to cloth (to reach points V and W, say), we can actually increase output of both goods. At its middle the transformation curve allows more of each output than the straight line – hence it is bowed outwards.

The bias of the capital-abundant country's transformation curve towards the capital-intensive good is obvious enough. In Figure 3.2, a country with endowment X could produce 4C but less than 2F, whereas one with endowment Y could produce 2F but less than 4C.

4 Modern Trade Theory

The Leontief paradox generated several responses among trade economists. We have examined above the statistical arguments and the minor modifications to Heckscher–Ohlin. We now consider the most constructive response – the development of new theories. These primarily hinge around technology, and are treated in section 4.1. Section 4.2 briefly considers how economies of scale and the degree of monopoly influence trade patterns, and section 4.3 develops them further into theories of differentiated trade. The latter explain the phenomenon of 'intra-industry' trade – the simultaneous import and export of the same good – which is quite beyond traditional theory. Finally, section 4.4 summarises the current position of positive international trade theory, and asks why, despite its poor empirical showing, the Heckscher–Ohlin theory is still so influential.

4.1 TECHNOLOGY THEORIES OF INTERNATIONAL TRADE

The theories of this section return to Ricardo's basic approach, but pay more attention to the factors determining technology. Basically it is *changing* technology that determines trade, so we are moving from equilibrium to disequilibrium theories.

The imitation gap

In Ricardo's static model, technology differed between countries for ever. In Posner's (1961) imitation gap theory, technological differences are seen as temporary and part of a dynamic process, with technology constantly evolving through a series of inventions and innovations. Immediately after inventing a new good, a country has a comparative advantage in, and hence exports, that good. Its advantage persists until its partners have, by one means or another, acquired the new technology themselves, at which time trade will no longer be necessary. Trade occurs to the extent that the *imitation gap* exceeds the *demand gap*. The *demand gap* is the time taken for a good invented in one country to be demanded in others, while the *imitation gap* is the time required for one country's invention to become producible elsewhere. Clearly these gaps depend on many factors and will differ between commodities.

This technology theory could give rise to two sorts of trade. Even if both countries A and B are equally adept at making inventions, there is likely to be trade between them, for invention is partly a random process. A's lead in one field will be balanced by B's in another, possibly closely related, field. Trade between richer countries often takes this form, and only if technological advance were to stop entirely would it disappear.

The alternative trade pattern arises if A is persistently more dynamic than B. Then A always exports modern or advanced goods and B pays for them with (lower-priced) standard goods. As time progresses, modern goods become standard (e.g. motor cars), but A is always technically in advance of B and earning monopoly rents on its new products. Country A may be the more dynamic for a number of reasons, which we discuss below, but technological leads, once gained, can be self-perpetuating. This is likely if the development of technology is linear, in that one must have mastered the use of one level of technology before one can

42

invent the next. This seems plausible for many goods, especially if the pressure for, and basic germ of, innovation comes from the users rather than the designers of technology, as Rothwell (1980) suggested.

Failure can also be self-reinforcing. For example, B's disadvantage in high-value modern goods is likely to result in persistent balance of payments crises and lower incomes, and, if this discourages investment in research and development and in high technology industries, B becomes caught in a vicious circle of failure and (relative) decline. Britain is sometimes held to be in this position relative to West Germany and Japan, and something of this nature clearly characterises trade between rich countries ('the North') and poor ('the South') (Balogh, 1963).

Economic dynamism

Crucial to the technology approach to trade is the question of what causes innovation. Obviously luck has some role, but there must also be systematic factors. Since technological advances have to be sought rather than merely falling from the sky, we are basically asking why some countries undertake more (or better) research and development (R&D) than others.

First, institutions may differ: for example, strong patent laws may encourage R&D (because one can reap the benefits of an innovation oneself), and so too may favourable tax laws.

Second, a country may be well endowed with the factors required for R&D. These include scientists and engineers and their equipment and, since R&D is an investment, sufficient savings to finance their activities. (Very poor countries may be unable to afford to divert people from immediate production into uncertain investment tasks like R&D.) The supply of skilled manpower depends on earlier decisions about educational investment and is clearly related to the supply of human capital in general that we discussed in section 3.3.

Third, innovators need a market for their output. They need to know what the market wants and the institutional arrangements for supplying and selling those things. The market also needs to be large and rich, since new goods are frequently costly, and the innovators need to be assured of access to it before beginning their research projects. All these reasons suggest that rich countries will be the principal sources of innovation.

The product cycle

Innovation may occur in the rich OECD countries, but this does not explain why production should. Could not innovators set up their factories in the countries where conditions – e.g. resources, factors of production – are best suited to producing their goods? Posner did not answer this question, but Hirsch (1967) and Vernon (1966) did. They argued that the factors required for a good vary through its life-time. Initially, as new goods are being developed and first sold, there is considerable uncertainty over both their production and marketability. This must be met by flexibility, which requires considerable inputs of skilled labour (Hirsch) and proximity to the market in order to receive and respond to customer reactions (Vernon). Since these are the same factors as stimulate innovation, there is a locational link between innovation and production: new goods will be produced and exported by the rich and large economies.

As the product matures, its basic technology and functional specification become standardised (although peripheral product differentiation may still be rife), making flexibility less important. World demand grows, making large-scale production feasible, and production costs become significant – especially if, as is usual, other, similarly endowed, countries are able to imitate the innovation. These changes tend to shift comparative advantage away from innovating countries, which are typically high-cost locations, towards other relatively wealthy,

43

capital-abundant, countries. Hence physical capital replaces human capital as the intensive factor, and the innovating country may well switch from exporting to importing the good.

The final stage occurs when (if) technology and specification become wholly standardised and universally known. This often allows production to be broken down into a number of relatively unskilled tasks, and certainly stimulates competition and pressure to reduce costs. Thus comparative advantage finally shifts to the low-wage, labour-abundant developing countries, which eventually become net exporters.

The last two stages of this cycle are less clearly defined than the first in practice, but it is clear that the cycle could help to explain the pattern of US trade, since the USA was, during the 1950s and 1960s, the archetypal innovator. Note that with international investment the whole of the cycle could take place under the auspices of a single firm. Note also that, whereas in Posner's theory countries' endowments (of knowledge) changed, in the product cycle it is the good that changes its input requirements. The later stages of the cycle correspond closely to the Heckscher–Ohlin theory, and, in the absence of innovation, trade would settle down to a Heckscher–Ohlin pattern.

Testing the technology theories

Although one would not expect technology to explain all international trade, the theories of this section have a strong intuitive appeal. Empirical evidence backs this up in an informal way, but the difficulties of actually measuring technological advantage are likely always to preclude convincing results. The most direct evidence comes from case studies of particular industries. Wells (1969) provided several examples of innovations in consumers' durable goods (TVs, washing machines, etc.) spreading outwards from the USA, with the subsequent reversal of US trade patterns. But perhaps most striking is the semi-conductor, or transistor, industry (Tilton, 1971, especially ch. 2). Invented in the USA, semi-conductor production spread to Western Europe and Japan over the 1950s and 1960s. Since then, while production has spread more slowly, the use of semi-conductors in consumer goods has very largely shifted from the West to the rapidly developing nations of South-East Asia. A similar process now appears to be affecting silicon-chip technology, which was initiated by the USA but has been rapidly taken over in commercial use by the Far East. In this case, however, current developments and applications are as advanced in Japan as in the USA, which suggests that leadership can change hands over time. How far these results generalise – or rather, what proportion of goods actually exhibit product cycle developments – is not clear, but it is probably not very great.

More formal econometric evidence on technology theories requires proxies for technological leadership. Two main ones exist: research and development effort (input into technology) and patents (part of the output). These are usually included in regression equations (along with a number of other variables) to explain the country composition of trade in particular goods or the commodity composition of a particular country's trade.

Of the former type is Soete (1981). For each of forty product groups he related OECD countries' export performance to their shares of patents in the industry, population, distance from world markets and capital abundance. The last factor appeared unimportant, but the others were generally significant. For about three-quarters of Soete's groups, a country's export performance was positively related to its share of patents. Those goods where patents did not affect trade were standardised goods such as textiles, basic chemicals and food, while those where

44

they had strongest effects were the technological industries such as aircraft, weapons, office equipment and scientific instruments.

Country studies include Stern and Maskus (1981), who found US industries' net exports positively related to both their ratio of R&D to value-added (R&D intensity) and the share of scientists and engineers in total employment, and Baldwin (1971), who also found the latter useful.

R&D as a factor of production

A distinction should be made between two different approaches to technology and innovativeness. Ignoring certain conceptual problems, we might treat innovativeness, or R&D, as akin to a factor of production. A country cannot, for example, expect to achieve long-run success in electrical engineering except through a series of innovations and developments. Hence countries well endowed with R&D inputs have a comparative advantage in this industry and the analysis of Chapter 3 carries through. In this view, given their endowments, countries have no discretion over their comparative advantage. Posner's approach, however, implies no such restriction: what matters is being more advanced than your competitors; implicitly, countries can specialise in any industry provided they generate sufficient innovations. In the former case, trade responds to the R&D intensity of particular goods (R&D-abundant countries export R&D-intensive goods). In the latter case, it is the gap between countries in any particular good that is important; although equal amounts of R&D by two partners will generate trade – because the countries will discover different things – the greater one country's lead in R&D the greater its net exports.

Hughes (1983) attempted to separate these two causal chains by relating UK export performance by industry to both the industry's R&D intensity and the gap between UK and competitors' R&D in that industry. Both hypotheses received some support, but the 'factor' approach appeared to be the stronger. A similar test is found in Katrak (1973). He related US/UK relative exports to human capital intensity and the US/UK R&D gap; again human capital seemed more important. In a further development of this test, Katrak (1982) examined the factor content of UK trade, treating scientists in R&D and scientists in other activities as separate factors. Neither really reflected technological gaps, but the former emphasised innovation whereas the latter emphasised skilled production. In the event, UK exports in 1972 contained 20 per cent more of each factor than UK imports, which is consistent with the UK's relatively skill-abundant position, but does not identify whether UK advantage lies in skilled production or in innovation.

Summary

Technological differences and changes can explain much international trade in manufactured goods. While goods are relatively young we expect them to be exported by the country of innovation. Thereafter trade may cease as knowledge is diffused, or reverse as knowledge is replaced by factor endowments as the principal determinant of trade. The fact that one innovation frequently leads to another means that innovations tend to originate in just a few countries, but, as Western Europe and Japan gradually gain on the USA, we see that changes in relative dynamism can occur. There are at least two channels through which research and development is translated into export advantage and it is not yet clear which, if either, is dominant. Nor is it really clear why some countries seem to be so much more dynamic than others. Thus, we are not yet in a position to develop very formal models of technology akin to the Heckscher–Ohlin theory.

45

4.2   ECONOMIES OF SCALE

An obvious motive for international trade is the exploitation of economies of scale. Trade opens up the prospect of larger markets and hence reduces unit costs. If we have two countries and two industries each with economies of scale there are clearly profits and social benefits to be earned by specialisation. If the scale economies are strong, the transformation curve will actually curve inwards, and the analysis is just an extreme version of that of Figure 2.2.

As before, trade patterns will be determined by relative prices. If trade is opened from a position of autarchy, each country exports its relatively cheap good and, by thus increasing output, further reduces its relative price of that good. If demand is identical between countries, pre-trade prices reflect comparative advantage and specialisation follows the obvious pattern. If, however, demand is biased strongly enough to give countries relatively low prices in their 'non-advantage' goods, each will specialise in the 'wrong' good. Trade will still be preferable to autarchy, but not as beneficial as if comparative advantage determined specialisation.

A similar case can arise if countries differ in size and industries differ in the extent of their economies of scale. Here the larger country will have a relatively lower autarchic price for the 'scale-good' regardless of comparative advantage, and so specialisation could again be incorrect. Under completely free trade, however, the smaller country, observing that it could now capture the whole of the world market in the scale-good, would have an incentive to switch to that good wholesale. Whether this actually occurs depends on the precise working of the price mechanism, but if we introduce transport costs and trade impediments it seems unlikely. Hence we are left with a presumption that large economies will specialise in goods with greater economies of scale.

This argument has received some empirical support. Katrak (1973) found the USA specialised in scale-goods relative to the UK, and Hufbauer (1970) found countries' exports of scale-goods positively correlated with their size. On the other hand, Baldwin (1971) found no role for scale in the US trade figures, and Smith *et al.* (1983) found only dubious evidence for the UK. Note, however, that as a middle-sized market among OECD countries it is not clear whether to expect a positive or negative relationship for the UK.

A possible confounding variable on these results is industrial concentration – the degree of monopoly. Industries with high economies of scale tend to be very concentrated and there is some reason to expect this to harm trade performance. Basically a monopolist tries to exploit his home market by forcing up price; this increases the likelihood of imports coming in. Similarly, if he is obliged (legally) to charge the same at home and abroad, he may choose not to sell on the (competitive) world market because that would force him to charge less in his monopolistic market at home. Furthermore, monopoly is often associated with general inefficiency – X-inefficiency – which harms trade performance. All these arguments suggest that net exports will be lower for monopolised industries. Against them must be set the facts that exporting involves fixed costs (setting up dealerships, etc.) and also greater risks than home sales, both of which tend to preclude small firms from exporting. However, in most industries firms reach an efficient exporting size well before they attain very high concentration.

Evidence on concentration is mixed, but Utton and Morgan (1983) suggest some support for views expressed above, at least for labour-intensive industries.

Empirically there are two separate elements to the measurement of economies of scale. First the extent to which scale reduces costs and second whether or not the minimum efficient scale (MES) for a firm is large or small relative to the market size. For example, that costs halve as firm size doubles is of hardly any consequence if there is room for, say, 1,000 firms at MES. Pratten (1971) estimated that, from a sample of twenty-seven industries in the 1960s, MES exceeded half the British market for nine: dyes, rolled steel products, cars, aircraft, machine tools, turbo generators, electric motors, electronic capital goods and plastics. However, of these only dyes, aircraft, electric motors and plastics had cost increases of over 10 per cent by operating at half MES. At the other extreme, costs at half MES were higher by 15 per cent and 25 per cent in bread and cement respectively, but there was room for at least 100 and 200 MES firms respectively. Other evidence – e.g. Hufbauer (1970) – broadly confirms these results on wider samples, so we must conclude that economies of scale are likely to be a significant factor in the determination of international trade.

4.3 DEMAND THEORIES AND INTRA-INDUSTRY TRADE

It is clear from the previous chapters that differences in demand could entail different autarchy prices and hence produce international trade. Countries with relatively high demand for food, say, would import it from those with relatively low demand. We shall not pursue this avenue further, although it is not unimportant, but rather attend to a different aspect of demand: the demand for variety. If there is a demand for different varieties of a particular good, a completely new form of trade can emerge – *intra-industry trade* (IIT). In all our previous theories, trade in any good flowed only one way – that is, a country either exported or imported that good, but not both.

Intra-industry trade

Intra-industry trade is the simultaneous export and import of basically the same good – for example, Britain and Germany trading Mercedes and Jaguars with each other. It is usually measured as the proportion of total trade accounted for by 'overlapping' exports and imports. Hence if exports are £100 and imports £60, £120 of trade 'overlaps' (£60 of imports and £60 of exports) and £40 does not: IIT would thus be 75 per cent. Formally, the most common measure of IIT for any good i is:

$$B_i = \frac{(X_i + M_i) - |X_i - M_i|}{(X_i + M_i)} \cdot 100\% \qquad (4.1)$$

where X and M are exports and imports, and $|x|$ is the absolute value of x. $(X + M)$ is total trade, while $|X - M|$ is the degree of non-overlap, i.e. the extent that trade is unbalanced. Observe that the measure does not depend on the sign of the trade imbalance, just its size.

For perfect *inter-industry trade*, where trade flows just one way, $B = 0\%$. For example, if we only export a good, $X + M = |X - M| = X$, so the top of (4.1) is zero. For perfect *intra-industry trade*, $B = 100\%$: trade is balanced, $X = M$, so $|X - M| = 0$. Between these extremes, high Bs indicate a greater degree of IIT. Observe that B is a relative measure: we could double both X and M without altering it.

Aggregation

So far we have avoided defining good i or, equivalently, saying how similar items must be to be treated as varieties of the same good rather than separate goods. This is an arbitrary and largely unresolved issue. Clearly if we define goods so precisely that any good can be produced in only one country (e.g. German lager is a different good from Dutch lager), IIT is impossible, which is not helpful. But

47

neither should we go to the other extreme and, say, define manufactures as a single good, for then exporting aircraft in return for rubber ducks would look like IIT, which is just as silly.

As disaggregation proceeds to finer levels, measured IIT declines, because surpluses on one good will no longer be offset by deficits on another. For example, suppose we have two types of car, 1 and 2; let $X_1 = 100$, $M_1 = 60$, $X_2 = 60$ and $M_2 = 100$. The separate IIT measures are both 75 per cent, suggesting the car industry has 75 per cent IIT. However, if we combine the two types into a single aggregate called 'cars', $X_c = 160$ and $M_c = 160$, and the industry now appears to have 100 per cent intra-industry trade.

Official classifications of international trade are based on the Standard International Trade Classification (SITC), now in its second revision, SITC (R2). The classification is numerical, with more digits indicating greater detail: this is evident in Table 4.1, which describes part of the UK classification. Even at its finest level the SITC does not define homogeneous groups, but data are rarely analysed at this level. More common are data at the '3' or '4-digit level', which roughly accord with industries.

Table 4.1 An example of the UK international trade classification

		Number of categories at this level in SITC (R2)
SECTION 7	MACHINERY AND TRANSPORT EQUIPMENT	10
Division 71	Power Generating Machinery and Equipment	63
Group 713	Internal combustion piston engines, and parts thereof	233
Sub-group 713.3	Internal combustion engines, marine propulsion	786
Heading 713.31	– outboard	1,832[a]
Code[b] 84061000	of cylinder capacity 325 cm^3 or less	
84061200	of cylinder capacity more than 325 cm^3	c. 10,000

Sources: United Nations (1981); Customs and Excise, *Guide to the Classification for Overseas Trade Statistics* (1983).
Notes:
[a] Total of all 5-digit and undivided 4-digit sub-groups.
[b] This level is specific to UK statistics.

Grubel and Lloyd (1975), in a pioneering book, examined the effect of aggregation on Australia's measured IIT in 1968–9. Averaging over all trade flows, they found it fell from 43 per cent at 1-digit level, through 20 per cent (3-digits), 15 per cent (4-digits) to 6 per cent at 7-digit level. Greenaway and Milner (1983), examining UK trade in 1977, found average IIT of 69 per cent for chemicals at the 3-digit level, declining to 67 per cent (4-digits) to 53 per cent at 5-digits. Similar patterns emerged for other UK manufacturing groups. IIT has grown over recent years: Grubel and Lloyd found the average of 3-digit measures for OECD countries rising from 36 per cent in 1959 to 48 per cent by 1967. It also shows considerable variation over countries: 69 per cent for the UK, 65 per cent for France, 46 per cent

48

for Germany, 49 per cent for the USA, and 21 per cent for Japan in 1967 at the 3-digit level (Grubel and Lloyd, 1975).

Although there clearly are measurement problems, these figures all suggest that intra-industry trade is not a mere statistical artefact. We therefore now turn to the economics of it.

Homogeneous goods

Intra-industry trade is possible in perfectly homogeneous goods in a few minor cases. First *entrepôt* trade: when goods are shipped in bulk to Rotterdam, and then re-shipped to Germany or Switzerland, this appears as Dutch IIT if the goods pass through Dutch customs. This is especially likely if, for example, Dutch industry repacks the goods into retail sizes in the process. Second *seasonality*: Britain imports apples in January and exports them in September; hence over a year IIT appears. This is a problem of temporal, rather than commodity, aggregation. Similarly, *transport costs* can produce IIT along extended national boundaries. For instance, if masons buy stone from the nearest quarry, it may be that at the southern end of the Franco-German border a French firm serves parts of both countries, whereas in the north a German firm does.

Differential goods

These arguments cannot explain the recorded quantities of IIT, however. For this we must turn to the theory of differentiated products. Within what we commonly define as a good there will be scope for minor variations, which differentiate one variety of the good from another without going beyond the bounds of the same basic good. Differentiation may be largely cosmetic, relying on brand images (e.g. soap powder), or functional, where specifications differ (e.g. pocket calculators). Either way, we merely assume – entirely realistically – that different varieties are demanded by consumers. This may be because all of them like some variety (e.g. theatre tickets), or because individuals differ in their requirements (e.g. the demand for cars).

There are two ways that demand for variety can generate international trade. The first, and less realistic, assumes that different varieties require different factor proportions in production (Finger, 1975; Falvey, 1981). Hence the whole exercise becomes like Heckscher–Ohlin, each country producing the varieties most suiting its endowments. This amounts to arguing that IIT is just an aggregation problem with varieties incorrectly grouped into goods so that 'the same good' seems to have several production technologies. Apart from its intuitive implausibility, this approach cannot account for the strong growth of IIT over time.

The second approach appeals to economies of scale in the production of varieties. Thus the most efficient way of supplying the varieties demanded in a trading world is by specialisation in varieties and subsequent two-way trade. There have been several recent formalisations of this approach, but all make the two crucial assumptions that demand exists for many varieties and that this cannot be efficiently met locally because of economies of scale. In all these models, product differentiation leads to imperfect competition among producers – usually monopolistic competition where firms face downward-sloping demand curves but free entry to the industry competes profits down to normal levels.

In any such economy, variety must be traded off against cost. Not every conceivable variety can be produced, because that would involve too great a loss of economies of scale,[1] whereas producing just one variety at huge scale would do too much violence to tastes. Imagine that this trade-off has been made in each of America and Britain, resulting in n_A and n_B varieties respectively. Now open trade

49

(ignoring transport costs). If the American and British varieties are identical, there is an immediate gain by pooling the production of each at one site and reaping the scale economies. If none of the varieties is identical, consumers in each country now have $(n_A + n_B)$ varieties to choose from, which also raises welfare. In fact, the final equilibrium will probably be somewhere in between. Some varieties will be displaced by very similar foreign rivals, but the final number will exceed n_A and n_B. Foreign trade, therefore, is likely to raise welfare by both increasing choice and reducing costs.

This approach can easily be integrated with the earlier supply models of trade to explain both inter- and intra-industry trade. Suppose food production is subject to constant returns to scale, while cloth has both economies of scale and product differentiation. Factor endowments determine the basic food/cloth specialisation, but within cloth there may be IIT. If factor endowments are very different, Heckscher–Ohlin inter-industry trade will predominate, with the world consuming only those varieties of cloth that Britain produces. If they are similar, however, IIT dominates, with America exporting food and some varieties of cloth in return for many other varieties of cloth from Britain. IIT in cloth will thus exist, but net trade (exports minus imports) will reflect traditional comparative advantage. The extent of IIT in cloth clearly depends on the similarity of factor endowments.

Another possible determinant of IIT is per capita income. So far the varieties of a good that a country produces have been assumed to be purely random. However this is not very plausible. Domestic producers have a competitive edge in their own markets because they avoid transport costs and tariffs, and they will maximise the benefits of this by producing those varieties that have the largest domestic markets. Hence, assuming production conditions are identical across the world, countries will produce to satisfy local tastes, and have large shares of their home markets. A major determinant of tastes is income: the rich demand (and can pay for) better goods. When we allow trade, therefore, it is likely that rich consumers will buy more varieties imported from other rich countries than of those from poor countries. The more similar two countries' per capita incomes, the more, *ceteris paribus*, they will trade varieties with each other (Linder, 1961).

The last two paragraphs suggest why virtually all intra-industry trade occurs between the rich OECD countries, and also, since these economies appear to have converged since 1950, why such trade has grown in importance. A further explanation of the latter comes from Barker's (1977) *variety hypothesis*. Roughly speaking, foreign varieties are available to consumers only if they pay the premium due to transport costs, etc. At relatively low incomes they choose to avoid this, making do with local varieties, but, as incomes rise, increasing numbers can afford to pay the premium to obtain the (imported) varieties that suit them best. The ratio of imported units to domestic units consumed thus rises with income. This offers one explanation of why the income elasticity of demand for imports exceeds unity; that is, why imports typically grow faster than income.

Yet a further reason advanced for the growth of IIT is the dismantling of tariff barriers. Industrial adjustment is probably easier with intra- rather than inter-industry specialisation, because shifts within an industry probably involve smaller changes in factor demands. Hence Hufbauer and Chilas (1974) suggest that governments have deliberately biased tariff reductions towards IIT, which has involved reducing tariffs mainly on the goods traded between rich countries. A striking example of the potency of mutual tariff reductions between rich countries was the huge growth of mutual IIT following the formation of the European Economic Community.

50

Empirical evidence on intra-industry trade

Intra-industry trade generated considerable activity among applied economists in the 1970s, mostly devoted to explaining industries' differences in IIT in terms of industry characteristics. Two major problems existed. First, there was little theoretical guidance on what to expect, although this is gradually being resolved, as we saw above. Second, many of the causes thought to be important are poorly, if at all, measurable. Consequently, results have varied according to the proxies chosen for the various effects. We briefly examine two major studies.

Caves (1981), examined IIT among thirteen OECD nations in 1970, on ninety-four SITC 3-digit goods. He related it to measures of product heterogeneity, product differentiation, scale economies, integrated production, foreign direct investment and trade barriers. The first three have been justified above as necessary conditions for intra-industry trade. However, Caves introduced some interesting refinements to those arguments. First he argued that, while 'technical' product differentiation will stimulate intra-industry trade (as above), 'brand-image' differentiation may hinder it because brand images do not travel. This is supported by his data: factors like R&D that suggest technical differentiation had positive influence, while factors like advertising expenditure reduced IIT. Second, while some economies of scale are necessary for IIT, greater rather than lesser economies hinder IIT because they confine production to a few countries. Product heterogeneity, on the other hand, clearly stimulates trade. Foreign direct investment is the ownership of factories in one country by firms in another. This is a substitute for trade, especially if trade is determined by technology, because it takes production rather than goods to the market. It is countered, however, by the international integration of production, which causes multinational companies to shift semi-finished goods between factories, and possibly to produce different varieties of output in different countries. The negative influence appears to dominate. Trade barriers might be expected to hinder trade, but overall little evidence emerges of this.

At a broader level, Havrylyshyn and Civan (1983) found strong evidence that across countries the extent of IIT increases with per capita income. In particular, it is low for LDCs – even the relatively industrialised ones.

Conclusion

Intra-industry trade is a relatively new phenomenon – at least its current predominance is new – and an even newer research area. We have suggested several reasons for its existence, but all hinge around a desire for variety and economies of scale. Clearly, then, it is more likely to appear in manufactured trade than other trade, and especially in moderately sophisticated goods. Current theory has explained it and started to explore its welfare implications, but there remains much to be done. In particular, the question of which varieties a country should produce is to be formalised, as are the reasons for the rapid growth of intra-industry trade. Although empirical studies have suggested some support for existing theory, there is certainly not yet a universally accepted view of the position.

4.4 TRADE THEORY: A CONCLUSION

We have examined four broad theories of the pattern of international trade: three based on supply conditions – the Ricardian, Heckscher–Ohlin and technology theories – and one on demand. They clearly have different implications, and so we should briefly try to reconcile them. Two approaches are possible.

First, we could seek a general theory for all trade either based on a combination

51

of the theories, or using just the one that best fits the evidence. This is an empirical question, and it underlies several of the regression studies already mentioned. Leamer (1974) distinguished three groups of variables determining trade performance:

- 'state of development' variables – GDP and population;
- 'resistance' variables – tariffs, distance from markets; and
- 'resource' variables – capital intensity, R&D, education levels and electricity use (a proxy for industrial sophistication).

Using a sample of many countries and industries, he found that trade dependence (the ratio of imports to GDP) is best explained by the development variables, with resource explanations coming a poor third. This, of course, refers to the amount of trade and not its composition, but it lends support to the economies of scale / Linder approach to trade. Among the (insignificant) resource effects, R&D coupled with the factor-intensity variables perform best. Looking at net exports, however, resources (especially R&D) become the predominant factor. These results tend to emphasise the more recent explanations explored in this chapter at the expense of the factor endowments approach. Hirsch (1975) and Aquino (1981) reach similar conclusions.

A second approach is more catholic. It recognises the strengths of each theory within its own sphere of influence, allowing each to explain the direction of trade of certain goods. This is potentially fruitful provided two puzzles are solved: first, how are goods allocated to theories – intuition is probably sufficient in most cases; and, second, which theories dominate in cases of conflict – this is largely unresolved, but we return to it below.

Following Hufbauer (1970) and Hirsch (1974) we might identify three classes of goods – each with a different source of comparative advantage:

- *Ricardo* goods are allocated over countries on the basis of production conditions. They include natural resource industries – oil, coal, wheat – and simple processing industries based on materials – e.g. food processing and non-ferrous metal refining. Comparative advantage generally lies with developing countries because they are at less disadvantage in this sphere than in other types of trade.
- *Heckscher–Ohlin* goods comprise mainly 'foot-loose' manufactures. These have well-established technologies and no essential specific factors; they are free to migrate around the world in search of ideal factor endowments. Examples include: textiles, ferrous metals and building materials. Comparative advantage goes with factor endowments, as we saw in Chapter 3, and we may expect such trade to be relatively important between developing and developed countries.
- *Technological goods* emanate from the most developed nations. Their production is characterized by sophisticated, rapidly developing, non-transferable technologies, and, in the product cycle view, by proximity to large and affluent markets. Obvious examples include aircraft and computers. In some cases they will mature in Heckscher–Ohlin goods, but some are likely to remain constantly in this category.

Within the last two categories we might also distinguish sub-groups of goods where product variety is particularly important, and thus where intra-industry

52

trade may be expected. Motor vehicles would be a Heckscher–Ohlin example of this, and photographic equipment a technological-trade example.

Table 4.2 classifies various countries' trade into these groups. It illustrates developed countries' comparative advantage in technological products and developing countries' advantage in Ricardian goods. The Heckscher–Ohlin category is equally represented in both groups' trade, and in UK exports and imports, but of course, within the category, labour- and capital-intensive goods will figure differently. In the UK case, at least, exports and imports appear to be roughly equal in the 'variety' sub-categories.

Table 4.2 Patterns of trade, 1980 (percentages[a])

Region	Ricardo goods	Class of goods[b] Heckscher–Ohlin goods Standard	Differentiated	Technological goods Standard	Differentiated
World exports	39	22	8	22	3
Industrial countries' exports	23	24	12	31	4
Developing countries' exports	60	25	1	7	1
UK exports	25	22	8	34	5
UK imports	41	21	8	24	4

Notes:
[a] Percentages do not sum to 100 because certain categories of trade are excluded from the classification.
[b] Classification derived from Hufbauer and Chilas (1974).
Source: World Bank Databank.

Hirsch (1974) conducted a similar analysis on a country level. For 1968–71 he found the USA very strong in technology goods (even labour-intensive ones), and fairly strong in Ricardian goods; the EEC weak in Ricardian goods but moderately strong in the others; and Japan very weak in Ricardian goods but very strong in Heckscher–Ohlin goods. Evidence since then in Heller (1976) and Katrak (1982) suggests that Japan is moving into technological goods while Britain is, relatively, moving out of them into capital-intensive Heckscher–Olin goods.

An interesting contrast to these results is found in Hufbauer and Chilas (1974). They examined inter-regional trade and specialisation within the USA, which, they argued, is similar to world trade but without any artificial barriers. There they found Heckscher–Ohlin specialisation the greatest; they argued that this is not repeated in world trade because trade barriers have been erected especially to avoid the rigours of free inter-industry trade.

Trade in services

A greatly under-researched aspect of international trade is trade in services. In principle, this is not different from merchandise trade, but owing to the difficulties of measuring service flows it has been largely neglected. Shipping and air transport would be classified as capital-intensive Heckscher–Ohlin trade, (provided one looks behind flags of convenience to the real owners of ships), while banking and financial services clearly have technological and economies of scale components. Tourism could fall into any category: Ricardian if people travel for ski-ing, beaches, etc.; Heckscher–Ohlin if the attractions are based on levels of personal service; and technological if visitors seek specialist conference centres or skills like theatre or concerts. Some confirmation of these views may be found in Sapir and Lutz (1981).

The persistence of Heckscher–Ohlin

Science proceeds by refutation. Theories make assumptions and develop from them logically necessary predictions. If these predictions are correct, the theory is not proven, because there may have been other causes; if they are wrong, however, the theory is refuted, because if the conclusion must follow from the assumptions, the absence of the conclusion must indicate the inapplicability of at least one assumption. Obviously one does not throw away theories after just one refutation, but one might ask why, after so many refutations (see especially section 3.3), Heckscher–Ohlin will not lie down and die, at least in its role as 'the' theory of trade.

First, H–O has a great intuitive appeal: 'surely', its proponents say, 'trade must tend to make use of "surplus" factors, and import the fruits of scarce ones. Hence, even if we cannot go all the way to Samuelson's factor-price equalisation, there must be some tendency towards it.'

Second, H–O is magnificently powerful; it is one of the most powerful theories of all economics. With 'a few assumptions' it takes us from observations of factor endowments, through to the structure of production and trade, factor prices, commodity prices, the effects of factor growth (see Chapter 14 below), and the distribution of income. Compare this with the limited scope of the other theories. H–O thus provides a much more fertile field for exploring the effects of tariffs, etc.

Third, if we wish to have a general theory of trade (as opposed to several), H–O is still a good candidate, at least if we admit human capital, as for example Leamer (1974) and Baldwin (1971) have shown. Certainly the product cycle and Ricardian approaches seem no stronger as *universal* theories.

Fourth, there is continuing argument about the validity of the refutations. We saw in section 3.3 that the most likely explanations of Leontief's paradox did not strike at the very heart of H–O. Moreover, proponents have argued that existing tests are so distorted by trade barriers, changing conditions and imperfect information that they do not constitute a fair test of a static theory of free trade. Deardorff (1982) has dismissed the first of these complaints, and the last two amount to complaining that 'the world doesn't fit our theory'. Change and imperfections are a fact of life and, if a theory cannot function, even as a broad tendency, in their presence, one can question its worth.

The fifth reason for H–O's survival concerns economics in general. Neo-classical general equilibrium economics concentrates on the question of efficient allocation in a static framework with basically free markets. H–O fits happily into this framework, so it benefits from being part of a larger 'research programme', receiving results from elsewhere in the programme and proceeding within a received framework. This framework defines the 'permissible' questions and, by precluding awkward questions, speeds progress on less awkward ones. For instance, it is entirely within the mainstream to try to extend the dimensionality of H–O, but not to question whether it makes sense to aggregate capital into a single unit. Hence H–O is really the international trade manifestation of a broader programme, and lives and dies with that programme. What factors control the growth of programmes is a complex and contentious issue, but one cannot help observing that neo-classical economic theory runs very close to the West's prevailing political orthodoxy.

Where does all this leave us? Heckscher–Ohlin is a useful tool for international economists, and it provides considerable insight into the workings of market economies. It should, however, be handled with care. It does not directly explain

54

much of the world around us and it is not applicable to all components of trade. Hence, although we shall make some use of it below, we should beware of taking its predictions too literally or of being drawn into the minutiae of what is at best only a broad brush approximation to the real world.

FURTHER READING

The technology theories of trade are expounded well in the original references given in the text. An excellent reference for early work is *Vernon* (1970), especially the seminal empirical paper by *Hufbauer* (1970), which has underlain so much later research. Subsequent results are summarised by *Deardorff* (1983). Additional useful references include *Hirsch* (1975), *Walker* (1979) and *Aquino* (1981). The economies of scale argument is presented more fully by *Grubel* (1981). Full general equilibrium analyses of trade under economies of scale are difficult: they include *Melvin* (1969), *Panagariya* (1980) and *Markusen and Melvin* (1981).

Intra-industry trade is analysed empirically by *Hesse* (1974), *Grubel and Lloyd* (1975), *Loertscher and Wolter* (1980), *Caves* (1981) and *Havrylyshyn and Civan* (forthcoming). The theoretical underpinnings start with *Barker* (1977), and include *Krugman* (1979, 1981) (which are fairly easy), *Dixit and Norman* (1980), *Lancaster* (1980) and *Helpman* (1981). Krugman and Dixit and Norman assume everyone demands variety, while Lancaster and Helpman consider specific demand varying over consumers. The contrast is neatly made in *Lancaster* (1982). An interesting application of the theory to trade in cars is *Hocking* (1980).

On comparing the theories, see the references of the text – especially *Hirsch* (1974). On Heckscher–Ohlin's survival, see *Blaug* (1980) and *de Marchi* (1976).

NOTE

1 Strictly, this is inevitable only if (i) there are very many varieties for which some demand exists, and (ii) the economies of scale arise at least partly from fixed costs associated with producing any single variety.

5 International Trade and Welfare

The previous chapters dealt with the causes of international trade, and also touched briefly upon its consequences for welfare: because trade increased the set of consumption possibilities, it was held to be beneficial. This chapter formalises this argument a little further. It considers the conditions that must be met to ensure beneficial trade and introduces some tools for the analysis of economic welfare. These tools include community indifference curves – which summarise society's preferences – and the general theory of second best – which cautions us against applying our simple models to the real world too glibly. These are issues of *normative* or *prescriptive* economics, rather than of positive analysis such as has occupied us so far. The chapter concludes, however, with the positive analysis of the effects of trade on income distribution.

The results of this chapter are put to use in the next seven chapters as we examine the impact of commercial policy. For centuries, economists have been asked whether protecting domestic industry from foreign competition is economically advantageous. Chapters 6 and 7 introduce the simple analysis of tariffs and non-tariff barriers respectively, while Chapters 8 and 9 further develop the welfare implications of protection. Finally, Chapters 10–12 consider tariffs in the real world and the economics of customs unions such as the European Economic Community.

5.1   THE CASE FOR FREE TRADE

We saw above how free trade (trade with no impediments) enlarged the feasible consumption set for a community; from that, we concluded that free trade was beneficial. The gains from trade contained both a *production* component – which increased world output through greater specialisation – and a *consumption* component – which arose because consumption and production points could differ. For a single country (say, Britain in Figure 3.1), trade changes production in order to maximise the value of output at world prices (at prices $T'T'$, L represents the maximum value of any production combination). Consumption changes in order to take advantage of the new relative prices offered by trade (with budget-line $T'T'$, B maximises utility). We now briefly re-examine the assumptions underlying this argument.

Production   Consider the maximisation of the value of output. The mechanism presupposed perfect competition (very many small producers) and perfect information. Each producer took the price (P) he faced as exogenously given – nothing he could do individually could affect the price – and maximised his profits by producing at a level where marginal costs (MC) equalled price. Since for each good $P_i = MC_i$ ($i = X, Y$), overall we have

$$P = \frac{P_X}{P_Y} = \frac{MC_X}{MC_Y} = MRT \tag{5.1}$$

where P is the relative price of X in terms of Y and MRT the marginal rate of

56

transformation of Y into X. This is the condition from section 2.1 for maximising the value of output.

There are two areas where this chain might break down. First, the costs faced by producers may not accurately reflect the costs faced by society. This may be because of ignorance (producers do not know their own costs accurately) or taxes and subsidies on factors of production. It may also be because of *externalities* – costs or benefits that one economic activity imposes on another, other than via the price mechanism. For instance, cloth production may involve pumping soot into the atmosphere, the costs of which fall on everyone, not just cloth producers. Hence the social *MC* of cloth will exceed private *MC* and private decisions will not ensure that (5.1) holds for social costs. A positive externality might be that, in producing food, farmers cultivate the countryside in a way that pleases the community at large by providing pleasant country walks. In this case private *MC* exceeds social *MC*.

The second possible break-down concerns the failure of price to equal marginal costs. The most obvious example is of a *monopoly* that exploits its market power by restricting output so that marginal revenue (which is below price) equals marginal costs. Second, taxes on output drive a wedge between price and marginal costs. Third, in increasing returns industries, marginal costs are below average costs (*AC*) because each additional unit reduces the cost of all previous units. Hence $P = MC$ will not cover costs, so, unless the government supports such firms, the market must set $P \geqslant AC > MC$.

If free trade is to maximise the value of output, none of these problems, which are known as *distortions*, must arise: a fairly tall order for the real world.

All this analysis assumes that firms carefully and informedly minimise costs. It is often suggested, however, that in the absence of foreign competition firms become lazy and do not actually operate on their production frontiers. This seems particularly likely for monopolists, and has been called *X-inefficiency* by Leibenstein (1966). In this case, opening free trade will raise the value of output not only through specialisation, but also by pushing the transformation curve outwards. This 'salutary jolt' was frequently advanced as a reason for Britain joining the EEC. It also characterised much of the official reaction to complaints that the high value of sterling stimulated foreign competition over the early 1980s.

Consumption

A similar set of arguments applies to consumption. Taking prices as given, consumers consume until their marginal utility from a good is proportional to its price, with the same factor of proportionality for each good. Hence

$$P = \frac{P_X}{P_Y} = \frac{MU_X}{MU_Y} = MRS \tag{5.2}$$

where *MRS* is the marginal rate of substitution. We saw in Chapter 2 how (5.2) maximised welfare for an individual. Just as before, externalities can separate private and social utility, and taxes and monopsony (market power for buyers) can separate prices and marginal utilities.

A further benefit of free trade concerns uncertainty. International trade breaks the dependence of consumption on local production. Hence, if food output is uncertain – because the weather varies – one can compensate somewhat by importing in times of shortage and exporting in times of plenty. Clearly one cannot avoid all the consequences of output fluctuations, because income fluctuates with output, but some smoothing is possible. This assumes, of course, that world output does not fluctuate as much as domestic output, but this seems reasonable given that for most commodities the world comprises many producers operating under varying conditions. It is improbable that all will, say, suffer drought at the same time.

This sort of 'smoothing trade' represents a rescheduling of food consumption relative to production. Trade provides the means both of swapping cloth for food, and thus of spreading a shortfall of food over the whole basket of consumption, and also of converting food today into food tomorrow, so that shortfalls may be spread out over a number of years. All that is required for the latter is that countries be able to have an excess of imports over exports in some periods and the opposite in others; that is, that trade can be temporarily unbalanced. Although most of our pure theory in Part I of this book concerns balanced trade, this ability to reschedule consumption should not be ignored as a source of gain.

Pareto efficiency

So far we have not asked in what sense – if any – free trade maximises world welfare. It seems obvious enough from Figure 3.1, but that case is restricted by having identical tastes in both countries. We therefore now consider a broader case and show that free trade (under all the foregoing assumptions) is *Pareto optimal*. A division of welfare between countries is Pareto optimal if one country can be made better off only by making at least one other worse off. In other words: there is no way of making every country better off, or of raising one's welfare, holding all the others' constant. This is clearly agnostic on the question of distribution; writing W_i for i's welfare ($W_A = 60$, $W_B = 60$) and ($W_A = 1$, $W_B = 119$) could both be Pareto optimal distributions. However, it does seem to provide a reasonable *minimum* condition for the allocation of income to maximise world welfare.

The necessary conditions for Pareto optimality between countries are easily established. First, no rearrangement of production among countries must be able to produce more of one good without resulting in less of the other. Otherwise, additional output could be 'freely' produced, potentially raising every country's welfare. As we saw in section 3.1, this entails the equality of MRTs across countries. (If Britain's MRT were 3Y:2X and America's 3Y:1X, we could increase X-output by letting America produce 1 unit less and letting Britain convert the resulting 3Y into 2X. The only limit to this is that both countries produce both goods.) Similarly with consumption: assuming each country has a national welfare function (see section 5.2), output can only be optimally allocated if the MRSs for each country are identical. (Check this by an analogy to the production case.) Finally, again as we saw above, these (common) MRSs and MRTs must be equal.

Free trade is able to meet these conditions simply, because under utility and profit maximisation MRSs and MRTs are set equal to the price ratio, and with free trade there is just one world price ratio. Hence free trade is Pareto optimal: no country could be made better off under free trade without some other country suffering. Note, however, that this says nothing about the distribution of welfare between countries, and neither does it imply that free trade is necessarily optimal for any single country. The latter is the subject of the next few chapters.

A *Pareto improvement* is any change that benefits one party without harming any other. From the definition of optimality, it is always possible to make a Pareto improvement from any point that is not Pareto optimal.

5.2 COMMUNITY INDIFFERENCE AND SOCIAL WELFARE

Identical preferences

So far we have assumed that all members of a community have identical and homothetic utility functions. Homotheticity implies that the shares of different goods in consumption expenditure are determined only by relative prices and not by income; thus, as income changes (holding prices constant), expenditure on each good changes by the same proportion. Now, since everyone in the country faces the same prices, they all consume goods in the same proportion. Total consumption of each good is, therefore, just its proportion times total expenditure. Under these circumstances we can combine individual preferences into a single set of *community indifference curves* that summarises the choices society will make between goods when faced with any (social) consumption set. These are drawn with goods on the axes, and will look just like an individual's indifferences curves; in particular, they will not intersect.

Such community indifference curves will not, however, tell us how well off each member of society is. Shifting £100 from man A to man B leaves society at the same point on the same indifference curve because, by assumption A and B will spend the £100 identically. (This is the reason that the aggregation is possible.) Thus, while international trade may be socially desirable, it need not necessarily benefit every member of society. With the present assumptions, however, we know that if trade puts society onto a higher community indifference curve, everybody *could* be made better off if income were suitably redistributed. (For example, give each person the same proportion of national income before and after trade.) Hence trade is *potentially* Pareto improving and is actually Pareto improving if the redistributions are made. Of course, redistribution has to be done in such a way as to maintain the crucial equalities $MRT = P = MRS$, which rules out commodity and factor taxes, and also, if we consider the trade-off between work and leisure, income taxes. (Income tax reduces the return to working – money – relative to leisure – watching TV, say.) This leaves us with so-called 'lump-sum taxes', which shift income between individuals independently of how they earn or spend it. These, of course, are virtually unknown in the real world and they are a slender reed on which to proclaim the optimality of free trade. None the less, that is what economists tend to do.[1]

Now suppose that preferences differ between individuals: community indifference curves can still be drawn, but they may intersect. The reason is that society's 'preferences', as exhibited in its behaviour, reflect the distribution of income. If people who like claret receive most of the national income, claret is 'highly valued' by society in the sense that, at any price ratio, relatively much will be bought. On the other hand, if beer drinkers receive most income, claret will be relatively less highly valued. Given a particular endowment of beer and claret, more beer is required to compensate for the loss of one bottle of claret under the first distribution of income than under the second. At that point, the slopes of the two community indifference curves differ, and so they intersect.

Intersecting indifference curves make welfare comparisons virtually impossible. Preferring A to B on one set of curves is quite consistent with preferring B to A on another. (Try this in a diagram yourself.) Since opening trade shifts the distribution of income, it is possible that, whereas opening trade looks beneficial with pre-trade distribution, autarchy looks preferable with post-trade distribution. This arises because some people gain from trade while others lose. However, it may be proved that (under all the assumptions of section 5.1) free trade is *potentially* preferable to autarchy in the sense that there is some distribution of income under free trade that leaves everyone at least as well off as under autarchy (Samuelson, 1962). This is because free trade allows society to reach a point where more of *every* good is available than under autarchy (see Figure 3.1). Then everyone can be made better off regardless of preferences, for they can be offered their autarchy bundle plus something extra. Society may not actually choose such a point in the absence of government intervention, but its existence is sufficient to show that trade could be beneficial. (In normative economics, the ability to get more of every good is frequently used as the sufficient criterion for defining a potentially beneficial change.)

The social welfare function

We have shown that free trade is potentially Pareto improving, and can always be made actually so by the requisite redistribution. If we stick rigidly to Pareto criteria, we can recommend free trade only if that redistribution is made. This is too restrictive, however, because such redistribution is rare, and yet countries constantly make economic decisions on trade *vs.* autarchy. They do so by means of their governments' views about income distribution, and, provided these views are stable, we can use them to choose, as it were, between different families of community indifference curves. Either we can assume that the government always acts to keep income distribution in its favoured form and hence that only one family of community indifference curves ever applies, or we can assume that it evaluates all individuals' baskets of consumption in terms of a single *social welfare function* that uniquely orders all possible outcomes. The social welfare function reflects both efficiency – for example, to maximise welfare everybody's MRSs must be the same – and distribution – for example, more equality is preferable to less. Stringent conditions must be satisfied if the social welfare function is to be 'well behaved' and reflect individual welfare (by well-behaved we mean that it behaves like an individual utility function). It nevertheless provides the best, albeit inadequate, means of representing the collective welfare judgements that are necessary for normative trade theory. Henceforth we shall assume that each country has a well-behaved social welfare function and that societies, through their governments, act to maximise this.

5.3   SECOND BEST

Some people – for reasons entirely beyond the author's ken – enjoy drinking tomato juice with Worcester sauce and a glacé cherry. If they find, however, that one day no tomato juice is available, we would not expect them to drink just Worcester sauce with a cherry! So it is in economics. If conditions x, y and z must be satisfied to obtain full optimality, it does not follow that, given the absence of x, achieving y and z will still take us closest to optimality. This conclusion is known as the general theory of second best.

Consider the argument for free trade in section 5.1. The *first-best* solution (the full optimum) involved having no externalities, taxes or monopoly. But suppose there were an externality leading to the over-production of good X. The *second-best* solution, assuming that the externality could not be removed, would, fairly obviously, be to impose a tax on X to cut its production back a little. Another example concerns establishing free trade areas between a few nations. Suppose country A's imports from a low-cost producer, B, face tariffs, whereas those from a high-cost source, C, face none, and that consequently A imports only from C. First best would be to abolish all tariffs, but, if that were impossible, a uniform tariff on all imports might be preferable to the supposed situation, for it would allow A to benefit from B's comparative advantage, which had previously been hidden by the tariff.

Observe carefully that we say 'might'. Second best merely states that achieving $(n - 1)$ of the optimality conditions *may not* be the best possible position in the absence of the nth. Nor does it state that, in the absence of one optimality condition, we cannot rank positions with respect to the remainder; in general we can (see especially Chapter 8). It merely says that we must examine each case on its merits, and not necessarily expect one optimality condition to be unaffected by the failure of another.

Given the obvious prevalence of distortions and market imperfections in the real world, one might ask why so much attention is paid to the conditions of the first-best position of free trade. First, free trade is the easiest case to analyse and it provides a useful theoretical benchmark. Second, and less important, it provides, given its assumptions, an ideal – a clear position relative to which everything else is second best. Third, the existence of distortions does not automatically invalidate the free-trade prescriptions. We still have to identify the areas where policy will actually be beneficial in countering unavoidable distortions, and then to administer it efficiently. Thus, free trade may, in fact, prove quite a robust policy prescription for an open economy.

5.4 TRADE AND THE DISTRIBUTION OF INCOME

International trade is clearly likely to affect the distribution of real income, because some people are better placed than others to benefit from it. Intuitively one would expect the main beneficiaries to be the consumers of foreign goods and producers of export goods. The latter benefit, however, only for factors specific to that industry. Mobile factors are paid the same in every industry, so that those that happen to be employed in the export industry have no advantage over identical factors employed elsewhere. It is true, however, that the real income gain experienced by (all units of) a factor of production is related to its importance in producing exports. In our simple two-by-two Heckscher–Ohlin model above, with incomplete specialisation, the factor intensively used in exports gains absolutely from the opening of trade, while the other factor loses absolutely (Stolper and Samuelson, 1941), despite the fact that trading increases total national income.

**The marginal
productivity
theory of wages**

To prove the Stolper–Samuelson result we first need to consider the determinants of wages and capital rentals. Firms demand factors in order to produce goods and sell them. If they maximise profits, they will go on purchasing labour so long as the cost per unit – i.e. the wage – is below the revenue earned by selling that unit's produce. This revenue comprises the physical output derived by employing the extra unit of labour – its marginal physical productivity (MPP_L) – multiplied by the price of output. Hence, in equilibrium, the wage equals the marginal revenue productivity, or, in symbols, for labour in industry i:

$$w_L = p_i MPP_L^i. \tag{5.3}$$

Alternatively (5.3) can be written as

$$\frac{w_L}{p_i} = MPP_L^i, \tag{5.4}$$

which states that the real wage in terms of output i is just labour's marginal physical productivity in that industry.

Analogous reasoning can show that capital (or any other factor) will be paid its marginal product. A convenient feature of constant returns to scale technologies is that, if every factor is paid its marginal product, output is just exhausted. Given that

61

assumption, the marginal productivity theory entirely explains income distribution between factors. Diminishing marginal returns – another of Heckscher–Ohlin's assumptions – implies that, as more of a factor is used relative to other factors, its MPP falls. This proves very important below.

The Stolper–Samuelson theorem

The Stolper–Samuelson theorem states that under the two-by-two Heckscher–Ohlin assumptions, and with incomplete specialisation, a rise in the relative price of one good benefits (absolutely) that good's intensive factor and harms (absolutely) the other factor. For concreteness, assume that the price of the labour-intensive good, X rises.[2] This increases the output of X and decreases that of Y, and both labour and capital move from Y to X. Imagine initially that factor prices do not change; neither industry then changes its factor proportions, so Y would shed factors in ratio 1L:1K, say, while X (the labour-intensive industry) would recruit them in ratio 2L:1K, say. Clearly this would generate an excess demand for labour, raising its relative price. This in turn encourages *both* industries to economise on labour, hence *in both industries* the labour/capital ratio falls. Now, given diminishing marginal returns, this raises labour's MPP and reduces capital's. (Each unit of capital has less labour to work with.) However, from (5.4) we know that, with rising MPP_L in each industry, labour's wage in terms of each good must have risen. Hence, no matter what combination of X and Y labour buys, the real wage must be higher than previously. The opposite applies to capital: a falling MPP_K reduces the rental in terms of each good and hence also in terms of any conceivable consumption basket.

If the real wage increases in terms of both goods, its proportionate rise in money terms must exceed that of either price. Conversely, the rise in the capital's money rental (a fall is just a negative rise) must be less than either price change. Using ^ to denote proportionate changes, we have the ordering:

$$\hat{r} < \hat{p}_Y < \hat{p}_X < \hat{w}. \tag{5.5}$$

Trade changes relative prices and hence absolute factor rewards. Under H–O, opening trade raises the relative price of the good intensive in the abundant factor and thus benefits that factor and harms the other. Intuitively, under autarchy the unabundant factor can reap the rewards of its scarcity, but trade allows the country to circumvent that scarcity by importing the factor's services from abroad (albeit already embodied in goods). Thus, trade erodes that factor's scarcity rents. Notice that in this analysis labour and capital have opposing interests in the opening and closing of trade, but all labour has identical interests, as does all capital.

The specific factors case

We can extend this analysis to the specific factor model of section 3.4, with mobile labour but two immobile capitals K_X and K_Y with returns r_x and r_Y respectively. Imagine that, as before, p_X rises relative to p_Y. At constant factor prices, X now becomes relatively more profitable than Y, so output of X tends to rise. Now, however, only labour can shift. In the X-industry, therefore, MPP_L falls and MPP_K rises, because each unit of X-capital has more labour to work with, while in the Y-industry MPP_L rises but MPP_K falls. Consider the capital rentals: MPP_K^X rises, and so, by the equivalent of (5.4), does K_X's rental relative to the price of X, that is $\hat{r}_X > \hat{p}_X$. Similarly, $\hat{r}_Y < \hat{p}_Y$, since MPP_K^Y falls. The wage on the other hand must fall relative to p_X (MPP_L^X falls) and rise relative to p_Y. Hence overall we have

$$\hat{r}_Y < \hat{p}_Y < \hat{w} < \hat{p}_X < \hat{r}_X. \tag{5.6}$$

The specific factor in the industry whose price has risen gains absolutely: its money return rises more than any price. The other specific capital loses absolutely. The wage change is intermediate, however, and the real wage change could go either way. If labour consumes mostly Y, real wages rise, whereas if it consumes mostly X they fall.

In both (5.5) and (5.6) the change in the price of a good is sandwiched between the changes in the prices of the factors it uses. This is because costs are a mixture of both factor prices (both factors are used in positive amounts), and prices equal costs. Hence at either end of chains like these a factor price change must be found. It also implies that specific factors will tend to change more in price than mobile factors.

A test of Heckscher–Ohlin

Unlike the H–O case, the specific factors model allows labour and capital in an industry to have similar interests in the opening of trade while capitals in different industries have different interests. Suppose p_Y does not change: $\hat{p}_Y = 0$, so $\hat{r}_X > \hat{w} > 0$ and both factors gain from the price rise of X. Hence both labour and capital would be likely to support protection for the X-industry, whereas Y capitalists would oppose it. Magee (1980) considered the attitudes of US labour and capital towards protection in their own industries. Of twenty-one industries, he found nineteen had labour and capital displaying the same preferences over protection; he also found that labour split 3:1 in favour of protection and capital 2:1 in favour. Both results tend to support the specific factor model over H–O, although with the proviso that both labour and capital are industry specific.

Many factors and goods

The basic observation that some factor must be at the extremes of the list of price changes such as (5.6) generalises to any dimensionality. For any single price change, at least one factor must gain and another lose, and completely specific factors will be so affected by changes in the price of 'their' good. Beyond that, however, the strongest available result is that with the same number of (non-specific) factors as commodities, each factor has at least one 'enemy good' – a good whose price rise is harmful to it – but not necessarily any 'friend good' – whose price rise is beneficial.

FURTHER READING

The best introduction to the welfare analysis of trade is *Findlay* (1970a, chs 2 and 6), who builds on *Samuelson's* (1962) classic paper. *Bhagwati* (1964) provides an excellent survey and summary. More detailed treatments of welfare economics in general include *de V. Graaf* (1957), *Little* (1957) or *Winch* (1971) – which are welfare texts – or *Meade* (1951), *Bator* (1957) or *Layard and Walters* (1978, chs 1 and 2). The classic references on second best are *Meade* (1951) and *Lipsey and Lancaster* (1956–7). *Stolper and Samuelson* (1941) is useful for the result that bears its name, but among textbook expositions *Caves and Jones* (1981) is probably best. The specific factor model is also covered there, as well as in *Jones* (1971), *Mayer* (1974) and *Neary* (1978). The multi-dimensional results are summarised in *Jones* (1976).

Recent analysis eschewing community indifference maps includes *Dixit and Norman* (1980), who cover all the topics of this chapter, and *Smith* (1982), who is excellent on the gains from trade.

NOTES

1 Even lump-sum taxes will distort economic behaviour if they apply any systematic criterion in determining tax rates. Thus, even with them, it is difficult to see how systematic redistribution is

possible. In fact, Smith (1982) has shown that much trade theory can be conducted without lump-sum taxes, provided that other taxes are suitably chosen. Although they are clearly not so determined in fact, this possibility brings trade results nearer to actual application.

2 We talk loosely of prices rising. In fact we are strictly comparing two economies identical in every respect except in that one has a higher price for one good than the other.

6 Methods of Protection: (A) The Tariff

This chapter analyses tariffs as a tool of economic policy. It starts by considering a tariff on a single good, tracing both its positive and normative (welfare) effects. It then considers a special variable tariff used by the EEC countries for agricultural protection, and extends the earlier analysis to a general equilibrium framework. Section 6.2 shows how a tariff is equivalent to the joint imposition of a consumption tax and a production subsidy. Section 6.3 distinguishes between *nominal* protection – the extent to which a tariff raises the price of a final good – and *effective* protection – the extent to which the tariff structure raises the returns to the factors producing a good. The final section, considers the measurement and history of tariffs and their effects. It presents detailed data on UK protection via tariffs and taxes and also assesses certain estimates of the welfare effects of protection.

6.1 TARIFFS – A SIMPLE ANALYSIS

A tariff is an amount of money paid by an importer to the government to allow him to bring goods into the country. It may be levied in two different ways. A *specific duty or tariff* is levied per unit quantity of imports: e.g. £1 per gallon of whisky. It is independent of the price of the initial import, although of course the final (imported) price will include the tariff. An *ad valorem tariff*, on the other hand, is levied per unit value of imports: e.g. 65 per cent on chewing tobacco. This clearly depends on both the quantity and price of imports. Administratively this is a great advantage in times of inflation, because it is 'inflation-linked'. For most purposes, the two are equivalent, although specific duties provide the importer some incentive to import dearer but better goods, because then the duty represents a smaller percentage of the final value.

A single good
We start by analysing the impact of a tariff on a single good, holding everything else constant. We assume that the good accounts for only a minute proportion of total expenditure, so that any change in its price has a negligible effect on the general purchasing power of money or real income. Suppose good X is produced domestically by a competitive industry with supply curve S_hS_h in Figure 6.1. Assume that an identical good may be imported, also with a rising supply curve. The latter is not shown in the figure, but combined with home supply let it imply a total supply curve of SS: this shows the price required to bring forth any particular overall supply. With demand curve DD and free trade, price is p_f and total quantity q_f; local supplies are h_f (the value of S_hS_h at p_f) and imports are $(q_f - h_f)$.

Now introduce a specific tariff t. To bring forth any level of imports, the landed (tariff-inclusive) price must rise by t, allowing the price indicated by SS to be paid to the foreign seller and t to the government. Thus the 'effective' foreign supply curve will rise by t and, adding S_hS_h for domestic supplies, will produce a new total supply curve $S_hS'S'$. The new equilibrium has internal price p_t and, total quantity q_t, comprising h_t domestic supplies and $(q_t - h_t)$ of imports. Imports fall because both total consumption has fallen and local output has increased. Consumers pay p_t for every unit bought – but, whereas for domestic sales all this accrues to the producer,

65

for imported sales only p_m accrues to the producer while t accrues to the govern-ment. The import price is lower than under free trade, because, with a rising supply curve for imports, the reduced quantity of imports can be called forth at a lower price.

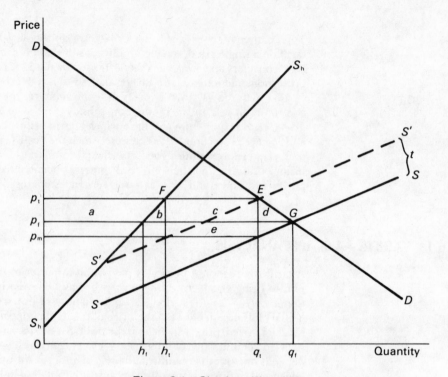

Figure 6.1 *Simple tariff analysis*

Welfare analysis

The welfare effects of the tariff may be calculated by means of consumer and producer surplus.

Consumer surplus represents the utility that consumers get from consuming a good over and above what they surrendered to get it. If the marginal utility of money is constant, both can be measured in money terms – hence our earlier assumption that X is too insignificant to affect the purchasing power of money. Consider the demand curve in Figure 6.1. For the first unit a buyer is willing to pay just £D, hence £D is the utility he gains from it. For the next unit someone is willing to pay slightly below £D; hence the value of two units is this amount plus £D. We can similarly calculate the total value of n units by adding up the prices at which each would be the marginal unit sold. This amounts to calculating the area under the demand curve between the axis and the last unit. Thus the utility derived from the consumption of q_t units of X is the area DEq_tO in Figure 6.1. The consumer surplus of selling q_t at the unit price of p_t is therefore area DEp_t – i.e. total utility less total expenditure, which is price × quantity, or area Op_tEq_t.

Producer surplus is similar: roughly speaking, it represents profits. For a competitive industry, the supply curve shows what each successive unit costs (supply price = marginal cost) and producer surplus is the difference between this and total revenue. Thus, for domestic sales of h_t, producer surplus is area p_tFS_h ($= Op_tFh_t$ less OS_hFh_t).

66

We now consider moving from the free-trade equilibrium G to the tariff equilibrium E. Consumption falls to q_t, and consumers' surplus falls by area $a+b+c+d$ $(Dp_fG - Dp_tE)$. Production on the other hand rises to h_t, increasing producer surplus by a. Government revenue also increases, because the remaining $(q_t - h_t)$ of imports pay $(p_t - p_m)$ in tariffs, generating revenue $c + e$. Hence the total loss of welfare at E relative to G is $a+b+c+d-a-(c+e) = b+d-e$. This could be either positive or negative. Area b represents a producer loss, area d a consumer loss and area e the gain from the reduction in the price of imports. The areas a and c are consumer surpluses redistributed towards producers and government respectively.

The small country

In this simple model, any gain from tariffs arises from the fall in the price of imports. This occurs because falling demand for imports cuts the supply price. If our country is very small, however, such market power will not exist. If any unit not sold to us can be sold elsewhere in the world for p_f, the price we face will never fall below p_f. Figure 6.2 illustrates this special case using the previous notation. The foreign supply curve is horizontal at p_f and is raised to $p_t (= p_f + t)$ by the tariff.

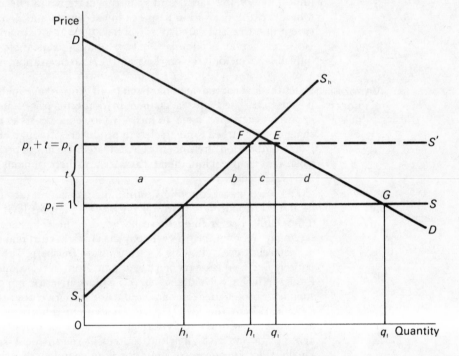

Figure 6.2   *The tariff in a small country*

Clearly the tariff is now harmful, because b and d remain while e has disappeared. In fact, the free-trade point G is the welfare-maximising point. Consumers consume X until the marginal utility of the last unit (the height of the demand curve) just equals the marginal cost of producing it (the height of the supply, or marginal cost curve). Any further units would involve costs above marginal utility, while any fewer units would involve losing the excess of utility over costs at consumption below q_f. The two sources of X – home production and imports – both have the same marginal costs. Hence no rearrangement of sources could reduce the overall cost of consuming q_f of X.

67

Measuring the welfare effects

Figure 6.2 illustrates an approximate method of measuring the loss of welfare from the tariff. The area of triangle b is measured by $\frac{1}{2}t\,(h_t - h_f)$ and the area of d by $\frac{1}{2}t\,(q_f - q_t)$. Hence welfare loss $(\triangle W)$ is

$$\triangle W = \tfrac{1}{2}t\,(h_t - h_f) + \tfrac{1}{2}t\,(q_f - q_t) = \tfrac{1}{2}t\triangle m \qquad (6.1)$$

where $\triangle m$ is the change in imports (m), which is $(q_f - h_f) - (q_t - h_t)$. Now, if we measure X in units such that its free-trade price (p_f) is 1, the change in imports equals $m.\epsilon_m.t$, where ϵ_m is the price elasticity of demand for imports and t, the tariff, represents the proportionate price change between free trade and tariffs. Hence

$$\triangle W = \tfrac{1}{2}m.\epsilon_m.t^2. \qquad (6.2)$$

This formula, which is due to Meade (1951), is quite widely applied. Strictly it is applicable only to small markets and in the absence of other tariff changes, in order to be sure that the supply and demand curves do not shift with the imposition of the tariff, and that the marginal utility of money is constant. Moreover, the derivation assumes linear supply and demand schedules; to the extent that this is violated, (6.2) will be a poor approximation to the welfare loss. However, some economists believe that it is possible to correct for these difficulties even for large markets, and (6.2) has been applied to total imports.

Variable import levies

So far the level of the tariff has been fixed. Any change in the foreign supply curve is thus translated into a change in domestic prices and quantities. Foreign exporters therefore, have an incentive to reduce costs in order to increase their share of our market. Conversely, our producers, although offered some protection from competition, are not entirely insulated. Technical progress abroad will, with a constant tariff, eat into their local sales, and there remains some uncertainty over the local price.

The European Economic Community has counteracted these 'problems' for local food producers by introducing variable import levies on food. A domestic (European) price is fixed for each good – the reference price at Duisberg in Germany – and imports have to pay the tariff that just makes their net price equal the reference price allowing for transport to Duisberg. The European price is thus entirely fixed; consumers can never gain from, nor producers be threatened by, foreign efficiency. Neither is there any incentive for importers to seek low-cost supplies abroad, because any reduction in price they can negotiate merely disappears into the levy. Hence what might otherwise be tariff revenue can actually be appropriated by foreign producers, or by EEC importers, who could agree to buy from high-priced sources in return for a 'kickback' of some sort. Finally, since European consumption is independent of world prices and supplies, any fluctuations in these fall disproportionately more heavily on other markets: fixing the European price makes prices elsewhere in the world more prone to fluctuation. Variable levies (tariffs) are thus substantially less efficient than exogenous tariffs from every country's point of view.

General equilibrium

The assumption above that our industry was small allowed us to ignore any effects that protection of X had on any other industry. We now correct that by examining tariffs in a two-good general equilibrium model, assuming for convenience that we are still dealing with a small country.

Figure 6.3 summarises the analysis. FF is the transformation frontier and slope TT is the world terms of trade (exogenous to our country). By previous analysis, production takes place at *P*, maximising the value of domestic output, and consumption at *C*, maximising welfare along the consumption possibility locus *TT*. Trade is shown by triangle *PHC* – exporting *PH* of Y and importing *HC* of X. Suppose a tariff is levied on imports of X. The world price is unaffected, but residents now have to surrender more Y per unit X than previously. Suppose the tariff converts the world price ratio *TT* into an internal price ratio *II*. Producers now maximise the value of output at those prices (setting *MRT* = slope *II*) and choose point *P'*. Given *P'* and world prices *TT*, the consumption locus is *T'T'*; consumers also face internal prices *II*, and so choose the point along *T'T'* where *MRS* = slope *II*; that is, point *C'*. Tariff-ridden trade involves exchanging *P'H'* of Y for *H'C'* of X, although, of the latter, only *H'D'* goes directly to local residents, *D'C'* being tariff revenue.

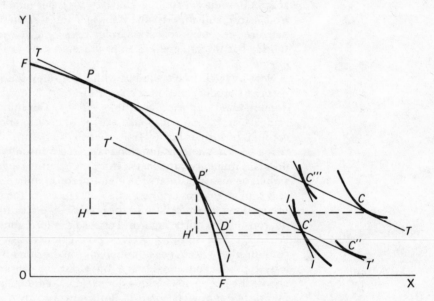

Figure 6.3 *Tariff in a small country: general equilibrium*

Note how domestic *MRT* and *MRS* are equal, but, because of the tariff, they do not equal the rate at which goods can be transformed through trade (slope *TT*). Observe also how, given the full optimality of free trade, the tariff equilibrium must be sub-optimal. As before, the difference comprises a production and a consumption component. The former is the loss in the value of national output at world prices between *P* and *P'*. (World prices represent the 'true worth' of goods, since X and Y can always be converted at that rate through trade.) The latter arises because the social indifference curve at *C'* is not the highest possible, even given consumption locus *T'T'*.

An implicit assumption in all this is that the government spends its revenue just as the private sector would. This is necessary in order that we have the same community indifference map before and after the tariff change, and it is usually excused by assuming that the revenue is returned to consumers by means of non-distortionary lump-sum transfers. It does not, in fact, matter whether the tariff is paid in good X or Y, so long as the revenue is returned in this manner. Perhaps more remarkable, however, is that neither does it matter whether exports or imports are subject to the tariff. It is the act of trading that is taxed, in effect; any effort to convert surplus Y into X through trade results in the loss of some goods, which means that less X is available to the private transactor per unit Y than is offered by foreigners. This equivalence between export and import taxes is known as *Lerner's symmetry theorem* (Lerner, 1936).

6.2   TAXES AND SUBSIDIES

We digress from tariffs briefly to note the effects of taxes and subsidies on production and consumption. Return to Figure 6.2 and suppose that producers are offered a subsidy of t. The domestic price is still determined by the import price p_f (no one will pay more if X is available from abroad at p_f), so consumption remains at q_f, but producers are now paid $(p_f + t) = p_t$ per unit. Hence domestic output rises from h_f to h_t, and imports fall by $(h_t - h_f)$. The government loses area $a + b$ in terms of net revenue, but producers' surplus rises by a. A net loss of b is recorded. The subsidy has the same effect on producers as the tariff, but has no consumption effect.

Now imagine free trade but with a consumption tax of t. Again imports still occur, so producers cannot charge above p_f, but the consumers' price on both domestic and imported units if $(p_f + t) = p_t$. Consumption falls to q_t, production remains at h_f, and imports make up the difference. Area $a+b+c+d$ is lost to consumers' surplus but $a+b+c$ accrues to the government as tax revenue. The net cost is thus d. The consumption tax affects consumers just as the tariff does, but does not influence producers. Thus, the tariff is equivalent in all respects to the simultaneous application of an identical consumption tax and production subsidy.

A similar analysis can be made for Figure 6.3, the general equilibrium case. A production subsidy for X shifts the producers' price ratio to *II*, and production to *P'*, but consumers, still facing world prices *TT* (= *T'T'*), consume where *MRS* = slope *TT*, i.e. at *C"*. The subsidy involves production costs, as with the tariff, but no consumption costs. A consumption tax, on the other hand, involves no production loss, so production remains at *P*, but along the consumption locus *TT* consumers choose the point where *MRS* = slope *II* (the tax-ridden price ratio). This is *C'''*, which may be better or worse than *C"*. Both, however, are dominated by *C* and dominate *C'*.

For both tariffs and taxes and for subsidies it is relative prices that are important, as is obvious from the general equilibrium model. Hence *relative* not absolute protection matters: a tax of 100 per cent on X is equivalent to a 50 per cent tax on X plus a 25 per cent subsidy on Y:

$$\frac{2.0p_X}{p_Y} = \frac{1.5p_X}{0.75p_Y},$$

where p_X and p_Y are the pre-tax prices of X and Y respectively. Clearly, both policies double the relative price of X.

6.3   EFFECTIVE PROTECTION

So far we have assumed that industries are completely vertically integrated: they take primary factors of production and transform them into goods for final consumption, without any intervening market transactions. This is plainly untrue – intermediate goods obviously exist, and, more important, are obviously traded internationally (e.g. car engines). The theory of effective protection – 'discovered' by economists in the 1960s, but well known by every Victorian businessman – attempts to allow for this. Crudely, if tariffs or taxes are levied on an industry's inputs, profits are likely to fall – the industry is 'dis-protected' – and factors will tend to move out of it.

A definition

If an industry can buy any amount of intermediate goods and services at fixed prices on the world market, its output is determined by its supply of primary factors of production. This in turn is determined largely by the rewards that those factors receive. Hence to relate an industry's output to its protection we must find the effect of protection on factor rewards. The sum of all factor rewards in an industry is known as its *value-added*. An industry takes physical inputs worth, say, £x, adds value from primary factors worth £V, to produce gross output of £z = £(x + V). Value-added equals the value of gross output less the value of physical inputs. An industry's effective protection (g) is the extent to which taxes and tariffs raise its value-added. Denote value-added under free trade by V and with protection by V', then for industry i

$$g_i = \frac{V_i' - V_i}{V_i}. \tag{6.3}$$

Effective protection depends not only on an industry's own tariff, but also on those on all its inputs.

Measurement

Imagine starting from free trade and imposing tariffs, at differing rates, on all the various goods (final and intermediate) that are traded. One would expect this to affect industries' values-added in a very complex fashion: demand would change if relative prices did, cheaper inputs would be substituted for dearer ones, and the amount (or even direction) of foreign trade may be changed, thus altering the terms of trade. This would make measuring effective protection very difficult. Economists have, therefore, sought to restrict their measurements to much simpler circumstances, hoping that, although their assumptions may not be literally true, they will be sufficiently robust for the measurements still to have some value.

In the simplest case five assumptions are made:

(i) the country is small, i.e. world prices are fixed;
(ii) every good traded without tariffs remains traded with tariffs;
(iii) the inputs required for producing a unit of each output are rigidly fixed in physical terms;
(iv) there are no non-traded inputs other than primary factors;
(v) there are no other taxes or distortions in the system.

Value-added per unit of output is the price of a unit less the value of intermediate inputs. Under free trade,

$$V_i = p_i - \sum_j a_{ij} p_j, \tag{6.4}$$

where V_i is value-added per unit of i, p_i is the (world) price of i, and a_{ij} are the inputs of j required per unit output of i. Assumptions (i) and (ii) ensure that the post-tariff price of every good, p_i', is given by

$$p_i' = (1 + t_i) p_i. \tag{6.5}$$

Hence post-tax value-added is

$$V_i' = p_i' - \sum_j a_{ij} p_j'$$

$$= (1 + t_i) p_i - \sum_j a_{ij} (1 + t_j) p_j. \tag{6.6}$$

Now, measuring all goods in units such that $p_i = 1$ and substituting (6.5) and (6.6) into (6.3) yields:

$$g_i = \frac{t_i - \sum_j a_{ij} t_j}{1 - \sum_j a_{ij}} \tag{6.7}$$

The last step depends crucially on (6.5) and (6.6) having the same a_{ij}, i.e. on protection not altering input–output coefficients (assumption (iii)). This assumption also ensures that g_i reflects factor rewards, because, if factor values rise without factor quantities changing, rewards must have risen.

For students who find it useful, a numerical example of effective protection is given in the Appendix to this chapter.

It may seem surprising that demand figures nowhere in this formula. This is because assumptions (i) and (ii) divorce supply from demand. Any difference (positive or negative) between local supply and demand can always be made up at the ruling world price. Local producers produce until marginal cost equals price; hence, since demand does not affect price (which is the world price plus the tariff), neither can it affect local output. It may also appear surprising that, while tariffs on inputs are important, tariffs on inputs into inputs are not. The reason again is the small country assumption. This fixes the local price of inputs quite independently of their local costs of production, provided, of course, that they remain traded (assumption (ii)). Thus, it is of no interest to car producers whether steel producers pay taxes on their coal, so long as steel is always available at a fixed price.

If i's tariff is low but its inputs' tariffs are high, g_i could be negative, meaning that the tariff structure discourages production. If all tariffs are equal $t_i = t_j = \bar{t}$, g_i also equals t for every industry. If, however, tariff structures are escalating – i.e. they increase with the degree of processing – outputs will tend to be higher rated than inputs and g_i will exceed t_i: effective protection will exceed nominal protection.

Some refinements   Various refinements are possible to the basic formula.

First, *other taxes and subsidies* can be incorporated: taxes raise internal prices like tariffs; subsidies reduce them. Hence, for example, a coal tax will reduce value-added in the iron and steel industry.

Second, *non-tradable inputs* can be handled in two possible ways. If they are supplied at constant cost, they can be treated just like traded goods but with zero tariffs. If, alternatively, they are wholly fixed in supply, they can be treated as factors of production. Then g_i measures the change in the sum of value-added plus expenditure on non-traded inputs; but, of course, its implications for the industry are then less clear, because it is not known whether factors or non-traded industries will collect any additional rewards. Between these extremes, and also if they have traded inputs themselves, non-traded inputs are difficult to incorporate into effective protection calculations.

Third, some *factors* may not have the rigidly fixed supply generally assumed in trade theory. If a factor has perfectly elastic supply (e.g. capital if it may be imported, or labour if there is a reserve army of unemployed), then its reward (price) will not change, and all the extra value-added will accrue to the other factors, with proportionately larger effects.

Fourth, some *substitution* between physical inputs can be handled, although substitution between physical inputs and primary factors is much more complex.

Fifth, the tariff structure may unbalance trade; assuming this is corrected by an *exchange rate* change, this too must be incorporated into the formula. An *x* per cent depreciation is equivalent to an *x* per cent import tariff and export subsidy. It raises the prices of all traded goods by *x* per cent, and hence affects protective levels. This stresses the relativeness of protection. At the old exchange rate it is possible for all tradable industries to have positive effective protection. This, however, will generate a balance of payments surplus, which will appreciate the exchange rate and so dis-protect tradable relative to non-tradable industries. The net result will be that some tradables will be protected and others dis-protected relative to non-tradables. Non-tradables may or may not gain relative to their former position.

In practice, only the first two of these refinements are regularly made. The remainder are more complex and are more usually handled by means of an econometric model. Rather than solve the model analytically as in equation (6.7), this approach involves solving a model of the economy numerically, once with tariffs and once without. Value-added in each industry is then compared between solutions. Such models can be generalised in many other ways, but of course their requirements in terms of information and computing resources frequently exceed those available to researchers – especially for LDCs. Hence the imperfect measures introduced here are still commonly used.

Rates of effective protection give information about the impact of protection on production. (Consumers react to the level of prices, not value-added, and hence are affected by nominal protection.) For example, an industry with a 50 per cent effective rate of protection can afford to be 50 per cent less efficient (use 50 per cent more labour and capital) than its foreign rivals, and still maintain its domestic sales. Thus, to break into an industrial country market where the local industry has high effective rates of protection, a developing country must really be very efficient indeed (or highly subsidised). Effective protection studies of developing countries' own protection frequently reveal huge production distortions – effective rates of 200 per cent and above – and occasionally even negative value-added at world prices. (This arises when domestic taxes and subsidies conceal the fact that the physical inputs alone cost more than the value of the final output.) Although the effective rate calculations have been subject to many reservations above, very high rates of protection certainly indicate major distortions requiring some policy response.

6.4 TARIFFS IN FACT

Measurement Before we can discuss tariffs we need a measure of them. For precisely defined goods this is easy, but for aggregates substantial difficulties emerge. How does one aggregate high tariffs on apples with low ones on bananas to get a single figure for fruit? If we take a simple unweighted mean, tariffs on minor items of trade figure too strongly. If, on the other hand, we weight tariffs by the share of total imports they cover, high tariffs are under-represented, for high tariffs, *ceteris paribus*, reduce imports. Popular among the latter style of measure is dividing total tariff revenue by total import value – this generates a Paasche (current weighted) index of tariffs. Possibly more convincing is to weight tariffs together by local consumption or production (which respectively under- and over-represent high tariffs – check that you see why) or by hypothesised free-trade levels of trade. These, however, are all much more difficult to apply, and consequently the simple averages are used more frequently. However, one should always ask the nature of the tariff measure before making use of it.

History

Tariffs are as old as international trade itself, and, however we measure them, there have been considerable fluctuations in their levels over time. For example, the mid-nineteenth century is usually thought of as a period of relatively free trade, whereas the latter part was relatively protectionist. Similarly Britain has been mainly a free trader since 1850, whereas America has a more protectionist tradition. However, as Capie (1983) has shown, these generalities can be overstated. In the 1870s, for example, 'free-trade' Britain had average tariffs (duties ÷ imports) of 5 per cent, while allegedly protectionist France and Germany had averages of 7 per cent and 8 per cent respectively. America and Russia, however, were more protectionist, with average tariff rates of about 30 per cent over most of the period 1850–1910.

By the First World War, British tariffs were fairly low; furthermore they were balanced by excise taxes on competing domestic goods and hence offered virtually no protection to British industry. In 1915, the McKenna Duties changed this, imposing $33\frac{1}{3}$ per cent duties on cars, instruments and time-pieces. The next large increase came in 1921 with a more widespread tariff of 30 per cent. These and the McKenna tariffs were renewed and gradually extended until the Import Duties Act of 1932 instituted a general tariff of at least 10 per cent, from which only Commonwealth and Empire countries were exempt, under the Imperial Preference system. This protectionist stance persisted until the Second World War.

The GATT

The General Agreement on Tariffs and Trade was established after the Second World War in an attempt to liberalise trade from its pre-war restrictions. Initially it had been hoped to establish an international trading organisation with considerable powers to free international trade, but when this failed for political reasons the major countries designed a looser framework of de-restriction – the GATT.

The core of the GATT is an undertaking by the Contracting Parties to engage in mutual tariff reductions, and to extend to all other Contracting Parties any reductions made in favour of any one participating country. This is known as the 'most favoured nation' clause. The essence of the GATT is non-discrimination and reciprocity: hence the Contracting Parties undertook not to extend new *preferences*, although existing preferential arrangements, e.g. British Commonwealth Preferences, were allowed to continue. Customs unions and free trade areas are permitted, however, provided they satisfy certain requirements.

Negotiation takes the form of 'Rounds', the first of which was in 1947. The latest two – the Kennedy Round (1964–7) and the Tokyo Round (1973–9) – have been the most extensive, with tariffs cut on most manufactured goods. In each case, the average decrease was by about a third, to be implemented over the five years following the Round. As may be seen from Table 6.1, tariffs are now, on average, pretty low in the developed world, especially on raw materials.

Unfortunately, the GATT has not been at all successful in securing a reduction in the level of agricultural protection among the Contracting Parties. Neither has it fully satisfied the aspirations of the less developed countries – mainly on account of its impotence in face of protective farm policies in Western industrialised countries, and the continuing protectionism in simple manufactures such as textiles and clothing. Frequently, while tariffs on these goods are low, non-tariff protection is very high, and here GATT has failed to make any progress (see Chapter 7).

Table 6.1 Tariffs and the Tokyo Round

(A) *By product:*		Tariff averages		Rate of reduction %
		Pre-Tokyo	Post-Tokyo	
Total industrial products	W[a]	7.2	4.9	33
	S[a]	10.6	6.5	38
Raw materials	W	0.8	0.4	52
	S	2.6	1.7	36
Semi-manufactures	W	5.8	4.1	30
	S	9.7	6.2	36
Finished manufacturers	W	10.3	6.9	33
	S	12.2	7.4	39
(B) *By country:*				
United States	W	6.2	4.4	30
	S	12.1	7.0	42
EEC[b]	W	6.6	4.8	27
	S	8.1	5.6	31
Japan	W	5.2	2.6	49
	S	10.2	6.0	41

Notes:
[a] W denotes weighted average (by imports), S simple average.
[b] Separate UK figures are unavailable because all EEC countries negotiated together.
Sources: (A) General Agreement on Tariffs and Trade (1979); (B) Corbet (1979).

Current British tariffs

The most recent complete study of British protection is by Oulton (1976). Some of his results are quoted in Table 6.2. They refer to 1968 (before the Kennedy Round and accession to the EEC) so current rates are almost certainly lower and rather different in structure. Tariff protection is probably around 50 per cent lower, but 'total' protection, which includes other taxes and subsidies, has not fallen so far. The 'effective rate on exportables' is calculated on the assumption that those parts of domestic industry that export receive no benefit from tariffs. They pay taxes on inputs but have to sell at world prices (there are virtually no export subsidies proper). Hence, import-competing branches of firms in the grain industry have value-added 156 per cent higher than would be possible under free trade, while exporting branches have value-added 15 per cent lower. Resources are therefore likely to move out of exporting into import-competing activities, a typical consequence of tariff protection.

Broadly speaking, the nominal tariff rates in Table 6.2 increase as the degree of processing rises. Such escalation causes effective rates to exceed nominal rates. In particular, manufacturing industry is protected relative to primary goods. LDCs frequently complain that this feature of developed country protection prevents their breaking out of primary production into even the simplest of processing. Effective rates show greater dispersion than nominal rates and can clearly be very high in particular instances. The sample in the table shows many of the more extreme commodities, but certain general comments are worth recording. Grain milling is highly protected, as is agriculture in general when taxes and subsidies are included. The highest nominal and effective rates are found on relatively simple, capital-intensive manufactures, e.g. iron castings and motor vehicles, but, despite their low tariffs, textiles and clothing are more heavily protected given their non-tariff barriers. Sophisticated sectors – e.g. aerospace – probably need less protection because they are under less threat from abroad. Besides, government purchasing policy can greatly help these industries in much less obvious ways. Non-tradables like transport have negative tariff protection, although operating subsidies can reverse this, as for railways.

Table 6.2   British tariffs, 1968[a]

	Nominal tariff on total imports %	Effective tariff on importables %	'Total' effective protection for importables %	Effective tariff on exportables %
(A) Summary by commodity groups				
Primary products	1.5	3.6	9.1	−3.6
Intermediate products (1)[b]	6.7	14.9	8.9	−7.3
Intermediate products (2)[b]	5.6	12.5	9.5	−5.4
Investment goods	10.4	18.9	16.8	−11.9
Consumer goods	8.4	17.0	12.8	−8.1
Construction and services	0.0	−1.3	−7.9	−1.3
TOTAL MANUFACTURING	7.8	15.8	12.2	−8.4
TOTAL INDUSTRIES	2.8	4.9	0.6	−3.9
(B) Detail by commodity:				
Agriculture	2.1	3.4	28.4	−2.6
Grain milling	14.9	171.2	156.0	−15.1
Other cereal foodstuffs	0.3	−8.0	−18.2	−9.0
Sugar	0.1	−2.2	−7.7	−2.8
Pharmaceutical chemicals and preparations	2.6	2.6	−0.8	−4.0
Toilet preparations	13.2	41.1	37.2	−9.6
Paint	0.0	−5.0	−10.1	−5.0
Iron castings	23.9	57.3	53.5	−9.9
Agricultural machinery	10.7	21.2	17.0	−9.5
Textile machinery	21.9	48.5	46.2	−8.7
Instrument engineering	12.4	17.7	15.1	−8.6
Electrical machinery	22.6	46.1	44.3	−9.7
Motor vehicles	17.8	41.5	36.3	−30.0
Aerospace equipment	0.8	−2.6	−3.3	−4.4
Cotton, spinning and weaving	5.6	6.0	4.3	−14.3
Woollen and worsted	4.5	8.7	5.9	−9.2
Hosiery and knitted goods	8.6	15.8	14.0	−8.9
Construction	0.0	−3.1	−11.3	−3.1
Gas	0.0	−1.4	−6.6	−1.4
Railways	0.0	−2.6	36.8	−2.6
Road transport	0.0	−0.7	−12.9	−0.7

Notes:
[a] Tariff averages are calculated as total duties as a percentage of imports.
[b] Intermediate products (2) embody a higher degree of processing than Intermediate products (1).
Source: Oulton (1976).

Many attempts have been made to calculate the effects of tariff structures on production, trade and welfare. The major empirical problem is estimating the relevant price elasticities of demand – the slopes of the supply and demand schedules in the figures we drew above. This is discussed in Chapter 18 below, where we conclude that, although figures are estimable, they are subject to considerable margins of error. Once the elasticity is 'known' (or assumed), formula (6.2) can be simply applied. It merely remains to decide whether or not its assumptions are sufficiently well satisfied for us to believe the result.

An excellent study, which carefully lays out the underlying analysis and data, is Magee (1972) on the US economy in 1971. For imports not subject to quotas but where local substitutes existed, Magee assumed price elasticities of demand and supply of -0.75 and 1.50 respectively. The average tariff was 7.9 per cent and, with local production of $45b. ($= h_t$ in Figure 6.2) and consumption of $57b. ($q_t$), Magee calculated a producers' surplus loss (area b) of $177m. and consumers' surplus loss of $114m. Thus, tariffs imposed a loss equivalent to 2.4 per cent of such imports. For non-competitive imports (where US supply was very small), tariffs cost about $202m. or 0.8 per cent of imports. Import quotas, on the other hand, were significantly more costly: welfare costs amounted to $3.6b. or 40 per cent of imports, of which about $2.4b. were losses equivalent to the tariff losses and $1.2b. resulted from quotas' inability to raise revenue. (This is discussed in Chapter 7.) Magee also considered US exports, concluding that foreign tariffs did not greatly affect US welfare from manufacturing, but that on agricultural exports they cost up to $5b. p.a.

The overall estimate is that in 1971 import restrictions cost the US economy $3–5b. in lost welfare – about 0.3–0.5 per cent of national income – mostly arising from quotas. This is based on the small country assumption and would be reduced if we relaxed it to allow the terms of trade to change. Moreover, if trade restrictions were abolished, considerable adjustment costs would arise in the short term. Against this we should recognise that, as the economy grows, so do these costs, and that protection might reduce efficiency and/or the rate of economic growth in a way that these simple static calculations can not capture.

Table 6.3 The effects of the Tokyo Round on trade and welfare[a]

	Exports $b.	Changes in Imports $b.	Welfare % of GDP
All countries[a]	13.2	13.7	0.10
Industrialised countries	13.4	14.1	0.11
UK	1.2	1.2	0.18
France	1.5	1.5	0.05
Sweden	0.4	0.8	0.98
Japan	0.4	0.6	0.08
USA	3.3	2.3	0.03
Developing countries	–0.2	–0.3	0.00

Notes:
[a] Based on economies as in 1976 – i.e. applying the changes to 1976 economies.
[b] The changes in total exports and imports are not equal because certain countries are omitted from the analysis.
Source: Deardorff and Stern (1983b).

A much more sophisticated, model-based, estimate of welfare effects comes from Deardorff and Stern (1983b). They roughly repeated Magee's exercise but allowed for terms of trade effects, exchange rate adjustment, changes in consumption and production, and substitution between factors of production. They considered the changes negotiated in the Tokyo Round – including certain minor non-tariff agreements – and their results appear in Table 6.3.

The negotiations brought the developing countries negligible or negative gains. This is probably because general reductions in tariffs reduce the advantages they reap from their tariff concessions (see Chapter 10), while the non-tariff barriers they face are not being altered. Among the industrialised countries, the gains from the Tokyo Round do not appear to be evenly shared. Sweden is a strong beneficiary, whereas larger countries like the USA appear to gain less. These results are clearly no better than the model they derive from. They should be treated with caution, and the interested reader should consult the original source for details. They are also subject to the caveats listed above. Nevertheless, both this and the Magee analysis leave a strong impression that tariffs do not matter much so far as static efficiency is concerned. This is not to deny that protection might affect economic growth or X-efficiency, but just to note that the static analysis of this chapter, although a useful benchmark, is not empirically very significant in present circumstances.

FURTHER READING

Possibly the best supplement to our treatment of tariffs is *Magee* (1972). The variable import levy is analysed, with very interesting data, by *Sampson and Snape* (1980). Effective protection was introduced by *Corden* (1966) and is most thoroughly discussed in *Corden* (1971). *Oulton* (1976) is a detailed study of the UK, while *Little, Scitovsky and Scott* (1970) and *Balassa* (1971) provide data on developing countries. Quantitative estimates of protection include *Baldwin* (1976), *Batchelor and Minford* (1977) – which is too uncritical in its application of the assumptions, but does apply to the UK – and *Cline et al.* (1978), as well as those in the text. The GATT is described by *MacBean and Snowden* (1981), while *Preeg* (1970) discusses tariff averages and the political stories behind the Kennedy Round. Useful textbook alternatives to this chapter are *Yeats* (1979) and *Greenaway* (1983).

APPENDIX: EFFECTIVE PROTECTION – AN EXAMPLE

Table 6.A.1

| | Parameters | | Free trade | | Tariff-ridden Internal | |
	Quantities (tons)	World price per ton (£) (p_i)	Trade value (£)	Tariff (%) (t_i)	price per ton (£) (p_i')	Value (£)
Iron ore	2	100	200	25	125	250
Coal	1	300	300	$16\frac{2}{3}$	350	350
Value-added[a]	—	—	(500)	—	—	(700)
Pig iron	1	1,000	1,000	30	1,300	1,300

Note:
[a] Derived from the other rows.

Imagine a very simple pig iron industry, which produces pig iron from iron ore and coal. The first three columns of Table 6.A.1 summarise its technology and the world prices it faces. Thus, 1 ton of pig iron requires 2 tons of ore and 1 of coal. At world prices the iron ore costs £200 and the coal £300, and so, with pig iron worth £1,000 per ton, value-added amounts to £500. Now suppose we impose tariffs of 25 per cent, 16.67 per cent and 30 per cent on ore, coal and pig iron, respectively (column 4). The internal price structure changes (column 5) and, given fixed physical input–output coefficients, the relative values of the inputs and outputs change (column 6). Thus, for 1 ton of output, ore input now costs £250 and coal input £350, but, with the output now worth £1,300, value-added has risen to £700. This is an increase of 40 per cent over free-trade value-added, so the rate of effective protection on pig iron production is 40 per cent.

Now recast the exercise in terms of the formulae in the text. First, all physical units are re-defined so that free-trade prices are unity. Thus, column 2 of Table 6.A.2 contains only ones. In column 1 we show how many new units of iron ore (one hundredth of a ton) are required to make one new unit of pig iron (one thousandth of a ton): if 2 tons of ore go into 1 ton of pig iron, then 0.2 one hundredths of ore enter 1 thousandth of pig iron. The coal coefficient is calculated similarly. This column defines the input–output coefficients a_{ij}. Column 3 now shows the free-trade value of inputs required for £1 worth of output; £0.5 of the input is value-added, which equals $1 - \Sigma a_{ij}$. Column 4 expresses the tariffs as proportions, column 5 defines the new, tariff-ridden, prices and column 6 gives the same physical inputs and outputs valued at the new prices. Value-added is now 0.7, which is $p_i' - \sum_j a_{ij} p_j'$, in the terms of equation (6.6). Clearly, effective protection is again calculated as $(0.7 - 0.5)/0.5$ expressed as a percentage, and this can immediately be verified as the result of formula (6.7).

Table 6.A.2

	Parameters		Free trade value (£)	Tariff (t_i)	Tariff-ridden Internal price (p_i')	Value (£)
	Quantities (a_{ij})	World price (p_i)				
Iron ore	0.2	1	0.2	0.25	1.25	0.25
Coal	0.3	1	0.3	0.1667	1.1667	0.35
Value-added[a]	—	—	(0.5)	—	—	(0.7)
Pig iron	1	1	1.0	0.30	1.3	1.3

Note:
[a] Derived from the other rows.

7 Methods of Protection: (B) Non-Tariff Barriers

Trade can be restricted by a large range of measures other than tariffs, ranging from import prohibition to the vague wording of customs instructions. These are called non-tariff barriers (NTBs). This chapter starts with the simplest NTB – a simple import quota, examining its effects and comparing them with those of the tariff. We then consider a recent variant – the voluntary export restraint, whereby exporters 'voluntarily' restrict their exports. The next section introduces NTBs in all their variety, and attempts a formal definition. Finally, section 7.3 considers the prevalence of non-tariff barriers and tries to gauge their economic costs. General studies are hard to find, but we examine two specific sectors that are heavily restricted by NTBs: agriculture, and textiles and clothing.

7.1 QUANTITATIVE RESTRICTIONS

The archetypal NTB is the import quota. This fixes a maximum level (quantity or value) for imports, allowing free access up to the quota but complete prohibition beyond it. Quotas seem attractive to both governments and domestic industry by virtue of their certainty. The effect of a tariff on local output or on expenditure on imports can be 'undermined' by reductions in the supply price of imports. With a quota, however, maximum import penetration and expenditure are fixed. Of course, consumers have different interests: with a tariff they can benefit from import price reductions; with a quota they cannot.

The effects of a quota   Figure 7.1 illustrates the effect of a quota in the simplest case: a small country facing competitive suppliers and with a competitive local industry. Under free trade at the world price p_w, consumption of X would be q_f and domestic supply, according to supply curve SS, h_f; imports would be $(q_f - h_f)$. Now suppose imports are restricted by a physical quota to $(q_q - h_f)$. The overall supply schedule of X to the home market is now $SHGS'$: at prices below p_w, only domestic supplies are available, at p_w imports up to $(q_q - h_f)$ are available, but beyond quantity q_q marginal units are available only from domestic sources, so the supply curve slopes upward again. With this supply curve and the original demand curve, equilibrium obtains at E, with price p_r, consumption q_r, output h_r and imports $(q_r - h_r) = (q_q - h_f)$.

The welfare effects may be calculated in the way used for tariffs in Chapter 6. Area a is transferred from consumers to producers, rectangle c from consumers to importers (who buy abroad at p_w and sell at home at p_r), and triangles b and d from consumers to nobody. These last represent the deadweight loss of the quota. Area c represents the rents accruing on the artificially scarce imports – often referred to as the 'quota rents'.

The equivalence of tariffs and quotas   Comparing Figures 6.2 and 7.1 reveals that, if the government could gain area c to compensate for the revenue it took under tariffs, tariffs and quotas would be precisely equivalent. (Imagine imposing a tariff of $(p_r - p_w)$ in Figure 7.1.) Equivalence means that the explicit tariff required to reduce imports to $(q_r - h_r)$ equals the 'implicit tariff' – i.e. the difference between local and world prices – that results from a quota of $(q_r - h_r)$. In these circumstances, the effects of quotas can be fitted into our earlier analyses by converting them into their tariff equivalents and proceeding as before.

Unfortunately this equivalence is not a robust result. It generalises to the case of a large country (where the foreign supply curve slopes upwards), but not any further. Bhagwati (1969a, ch. 9) showed that any one of monopoly in domestic production, monopoly in foreign supply or monopoly among quota holders is sufficient to destroy the equivalence, and later research has shown that it also breaks down in the presence of uncertainty (Pelcovits, 1976) and under retaliation (Rodriguez, 1974).

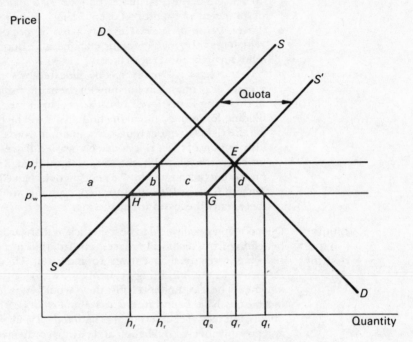

Figure 7.1 *Quotas and tariffs under competition*

The intuition of the first case is quite straightforward. Imagine a domestic monopolist protected by a tariff: a rise in his price would both cut demand and increase imports, cutting his sales by two routes. Now imagine exactly the same starting point, but brought about by a quota: the same rise in price would cut demand but *not* increase imports. Thus raising prices under a quota carries less penalty than under a tariff. In other words, because imports do not respond to internal price changes under quotas, quotas grant the local monopolist more monopoly power than he has under tariffs. Hence, for a given level of imports, the implicit tariff under quotas exceeds the explicit tariff.

The case of a monopoly importer is also straightforward. Under the quota nothing can increase the importer's supply of goods, whereas under a tariff a higher price generates higher supplies. Clearly, then, the importer is likely to behave differently under the two systems. Perhaps more important, however, is that quotas often *create* importing monopolies. Whereas under tariffs anyone may import, under quotas only quota holders may, and great care must be taken in distributing quotas if this is not to induce monopoly.

81

Distributing quotas

Several methods are available for distributing quotas, and they have rather different economic effects:

- *First come first served.* This entails allowing imports from 1 January until the quota is exhausted and then just closing the border. It imposes huge uncertainty on buyers and exporters, and grants the quota rents to people with storage facilities.
- *Auction.* The government sells quotas to the highest bidders. This grants the quota rent to the government, but may involve creating monopoly if the highest bidder is willing to take on the whole quota. If buyers are limited to, say, 10 per cent of the total quota, monopoly is avoided, but possibly at the expense of some rent and at the cost of enforcing laws against trading quotas.
- *Administrative allocation.* This may avoid monopoly, but quota holders get the rent. It may also involve inefficiency, because quotas may not be issued to those who can make most use of them.
- *Non-price bidding.* Quotas may be allocated by some non-price, resource-using method, e.g. physically queuing for them, or, for industrial inputs, on the basis of the using firms' levels of capacity. These methods tie up real resources in bidding for quotas, and in the limit firms will be prepared to spend up to £c to get the rights to quota rents of £c. In other words, rather than worry about the distribution of area c, it is merely wasted by resource-using bidding. This is probably the least efficient allocation method. Krueger (1974) estimated that quota rents accounted for 7.3 per cent of Indian GDP in 1964 and 15 per cent of Turkish GDP in 1968. If equivalent amounts were wasted in competition for these rents, the losses are staggering.

Voluntary export restraint

Quotas are generally held to be less efficient than tariffs. They preclude an importer benefiting from technical progress abroad, thus increasing instability abroad and reducing foreigners' incentives to innovate. They also become increasingly restrictive as the importing economy grows, because imports cannot grow with income, whereas under tariffs they would. For these reasons international institutions have been rather strict about quotas. The GATT allows emergency quotas, but they are subject to international surveillance, cannot be discriminatory and possibly involve retaliation and paying compensation. Countries have, therefore, been hesitant about introducing them, and recently they have been displaced by voluntary export restraints (VERs).

Under a VER, the importing country 'persuades' an exporter or group of exporters 'voluntarily' to restrain their exports. It is usually signed in the face of threatened action by the importer, being accepted by the exporter as the lesser of two evils. A VER is basically a quota administered by the exporter. It differs from import quotas in that the quota rent definitely accrues to the exporters (rather than to importing agencies), but also in that it is probably more sympathetically (and laxly?) administered. Moreover, because they have to be negotiated periodically, VERs have a higher political profile than quotas, and so may well be less long-lived or restrictive.[1]

The attractions of VERs to importers are less obvious. By granting the rents to the exporters, VERs worsen the terms of trade, and, by forgoing the administration, the government loses some control over its details. Furthermore, the need to allocate the permitted trade over suppliers may cartelise a previously competitive foreign supply, thus worsening the importer's terms of trade even more. Against this, VERs fall outside the GATT system, bind exporters into complicity in controlling trade and can be applied discriminatorily. In short, VERs appear to trade political gains against economic losses.

82

7.2 OTHER NON-TARIFF BARRIERS

A definition   Non-tariff barriers to international trade (NTBs) strictly comprise any measures, other than tariffs, that affect trade. Such a definition is too broad to be practically useful, however, because it could include policies ranging from the restriction of textile imports – which we would wish to include – to the provision of public fire services – which we presumably would not. The distinction between the two examples is one of *intent*: the former policy is clearly intended to affect trade, whereas any consequences of the latter for trade are coincidental. With this in mind, UNCTAD (the United Nations Conference on Trade and Development) has proposed a three-fold classification of NTBs. Within each class of NTB, they distinguish Group A measures, which operate primarily through quantitative restrictions on trade, from Group B measures, which operate through prices and costs. The three classes are:

- *Type I*: commercial policies designed primarily to protect import-competing sectors or to promote exporting sectors; e.g.

  Group A (quantitative measures): import quotas, restrictions of public purchases to domestic goods, export restraints.
  Group B (price–cost measures): variable levies, production subsidies, income tax concessions on export profits, advanced deposit schemes for imports, different exchange rates for different transactions (multiple exchange rates).

- *Type II*: measures not primarily associated with commercial policy, but that have occasionally been used for protective purposes; e.g.

  Group A: excess trade documentation, delays in customs procedures, advertising restrictions.
  Group B: customs valuation procedures, health requirements, labelling requirements, sales and excise taxes, selective employment taxes.

- *Type III*: measures applied with no intent of protection, but that may have spill-over effects on trade; e.g.

  Group A: government spending plans,[2] restrictions on toxic materials.
  Group B: regional subsidies, monopoly policy, variations in national insurance provisions, national weights and measures.

The limit on class IIIB is rather contentious. Even factors such as the public provision of education and roads and the relief from local rates for industry could affect the prices of tradable goods, and hence could arguably be included. We feel, however, that to include such measures among NTBs is to raise the free market on to too high a pedestal. Their inclusion would imply that any deviation from the free market is a 'barrier' or 'distortion' from the 'proper' state of affairs, whereas in fact economists have long recognised that governments have a legitimate role in the provision of certain goods and services. For example, defence and judicial services must be publicly provided because they are collectively consumed (they are 'public goods' in the technical sense – see Winch, 1971); water and electricity must be publicly controlled as natural monopolies; roads are most efficiently provided publicly because of the huge transactions costs of a wholly private system; and education and health may be more efficiently and equitably supplied centrally. (Equity is a legitimate political objective of government; economics is concerned only with the *means* of achieving it, e.g. whether or not the provision of services or income supplements is a more efficient way to achieve equity, not with the *end* itself.) Such items as these should be excluded from the realms of NTBs because they correct, rather than introduce, deficiencies in the free market.

A similar argument affects some of the measures in other lists. For example, not all health regulations should be regarded as potential NTBs. The illegality of the non-medical use of heroin in Britain must affect heroin growers abroad, but it is hardly an NTB, and similarly for the Saudi Arabian ban on alcohol. More difficult to judge are circumstances where, say, milk has to be of a particular standard before being sold in Britain. Basic health requirements such as being free from tuberculosis seem uncontentious; if potential exporters cannot meet that standard it is just unfortunate for them. On the other hand, the British government's decision in early 1983 that UHT milk, sold all over France and subject to rigorous French health regulations, might be dangerous for Britons is, *prima facie*, an NTB (see *The Times* of 9 February and 18 March 1983 for a history of this decision).

A further possible consideration in defining NTBs is *differential incidence*. To be classed as an NTB, a measure should affect domestic and foreign suppliers or buyers differently. Measures do not have to be explicitly discriminatory to have differential incidence, however. For example, a banana tax in Britain might notionally be levied on both British and foreign banana supplies, but the non-existence of British supplies would render the tax *de facto* differential.

The definition of NTBs has important political implications. By so categorising a measure we are implying that it constitutes a legitimate area of international concern over national economic policy, and, indeed, that ultimately it should be removed. Our definition should include both intent and differential incidence as criteria: whereas Type I and II measures are NTBs, we doubt the case for including Type III in the class. Only where the declared objective of a Type III measure could be achieved more efficiently in some less trade-distorting way would we recommend calling the measure an NTB. This does not remove such measures from economists' scrutiny, because spill-over effects can be very important, but it does limit the extent to which international views on health, safety, distribution, etc., can implicitly be forced on an independent country.

The effects of NTBs

We examined the effects of taxes and subsidies and of variable levies in Chapter 6 because they are closely related to tariffs. Most other Group B NTBs can be similarly treated. For example, an import deposit scheme is basically a tariff on imports. Before receiving customs clearance, importers have to deposit at the central bank some fraction or multiple of the value of their imports. This deposit receives no interest, so the importer is making an interest-free loan to the authorities, the interest forgone representing the implicit tariff. Similarly, requiring excessive health and safety tests on imports raises their prices like a tariff, although here resources may be wasted in the protection, and the revenue may accrue to private firms if they undertake the tests on behalf of the government.

The effects of Group B NTBs may thus be calculated, at least roughly, by converting them into tariff or tax/subsidy equivalents and examining the welfare triangles and revenue effects discussed in Chapter 6. Group A NTBs, however, are generally more difficult to assess. The archetype – the quota – was discussed in section 7.1. Some other NTBs are similar. For example, public purchasing policies are *de facto* quotas: if only the government buys artillery and it buys only locally, imports are effectively banned. Similarly, in late 1982 the French government insisted that all imports of video tape-recorders be made through the tiny customs post at Poitiers. This limited imports to Poitiers' small capacity to process them.

84

Many economists convert such quotas and 'pseudo-quotas' into tariff equivalents in order to assess their consequences, but, as we saw above, this is strictly legitimate only in very special circumstances.

Many other NTBs defy quantification. For example, the impact of regular changes in health and safety standards is impossible to assess, particularly as such changes affect trade mainly by increasing uncertainty. (Exporters cannot be sure that their goods will meet current or future standards.) Such measures have been noted in the literature, but are rarely measured.

7.3 NON-TARIFF BARRIERS IN PRACTICE

Quantitative restrictions on trade originated during the First World War, and although they were reduced at the Armistice they never entirely disappeared. The late 1920s and 1930s saw their re-emergence – especially in the planned economy of Germany – as a supplement to tariff protection. The Second World War exacerbated the position, as did the post-war dollar shortage and huge structural readjustment required in Europe. Between about 1960 and 1975 the European countries sought to reduce their barriers in most areas of trade – agricultural support policies and textile industries being the main exceptions. Since then, however, there seems to have been some drift back towards increased protection.

Between 1950 and 1973 the GATT sponsored a substantial reduction in tariffs. In some cases these were immediately replaced by NTBs, but, even if they were not, NTBs became relatively more important and, of course, visible. The Tokyo Round explicitly considered the problem and made modest progress in the codification and limitation of NTBs on developed countries' mutual trade. Simultaneously, however, barriers were being raised on 'sensitive' manufactures, where developing countries – especially those of South-East Asia – and Japan were competing effectively, and on agricultural goods.

Levels of NTBs

The recent growth of NTBs has been documented by Page (1979, 1981). She calculated the proportion of trade in 1974 that would have been subject to at least one NTB under the regimes operating in 1974, 1979 and 1980. She included as NTBs only measures directly affecting trade – roughly Type I NTBs from above – and excluded measures such as health restrictions, customs hindrances, etc. None the less, the figures show a quite obvious increase in the extent of intervention, especially for manufactures (see Table 7.1). The increase has been concentrated in the recession-hit OECD economies, being noticeably absent in Japan, which weathered the 1970s more successfully than most. (This may, however, reflect Page's inability to record the subtler NTBs.) By commodity, we observe the already high level of NTBs in agriculture, contrasted with the huge rise from a low base for most manufactures. Textiles and clothing were already subject to significant control by 1974.

Despite their startling nature, Page's results are probably underestimates of the rise in NTB protection. First, several NTBs are omitted. Second, no allowance is made for the restrictiveness of those included. The measure reflects only presence vs. absence, and it is difficult to believe that NTBs existing in 1974 have not been subsequently tightened, given the growth of the new ones. Third, NTBs tend to be concentrated within product groups onto particular sensitive items. For example, the 66 per cent recorded for iron and steel may reflect 100 per cent control of standard items and none on specialist steels not produced outside OECD. Fourth, existing NTBs in 1974 tended to reduce imports, thus reducing the weight that afflicted commodities received in Page's statistic.

Table 7.1 Trade subject to NTBs, 1974–80 (%)

(A) *By country:*	Manufactures			All trade		
	1974	*1979*	*1980*	*1974*	*1979*	*1980*
France	0	16.0	16.2	32.8	42.6	42.7
Germany	0	17.9	18.3	37.3	47.1	47.3
UK	0.2	17.0	17.4	38.5	47.4	47.9
USA	5.6	18.4	21.0	36.2	44.4	45.8
Japan	0	4.3	4.3	56.1	59.4	59.4
EEC(9)	0.1	15.7	16.1	35.8	44.5	44.8
OECD	4.0	16.8	17.4	36.3	43.8	44.3
Oil exporters	45.8	59.8	59.8	54.0	65.3	65.3
Non-oil LDCs	25.0	22.7	22.8	49.8	46.8	46.9
World	12.9	23.0	23.6	40.1	47.5	47.8

(B) *By commodity:*	*1974*	*1979*
Cereals	76	76
Fruit and vegetables	70	78
Silk fibres	6	71
Textiles	21	35
Iron and steel	16	66
Aircraft	12	83
Clothing	20	48
Footwear	1	32

Sources: (A) Page (1981); (B) Page (1979).

An alternative approach to NTBs is to estimate their effects in terms of the price differential they induce between local and world prices. Roningen and Yeats (1976) did this for a sample of six goods and four developed countries. The results are variable but, on average, prices in Sweden and Japan exceeded world prices by 50–60 per cent, while for the USA and France the excess was about 30 per cent. Around 10 per cent was due to transport, and, for agricultural goods in France and Sweden, most of the remainder to variable levies (which we consider a tariff barrier). None the less, the residual attributed to NTBs can be up to 90 per cent (Japanese food) and 110 per cent (Swedish drugs), and although their sample is small and non-random Roningen and Yeats must have identified a significant problem in international trade. A worrying additional feature of their study is that their 'residual price differentials' appear to be uncorrelated with frequency measures of NTBs of the sort used by Page.

Tariffs and NTBs We have rather implied that tariffs and NTBs are substitutes, reductions in the former being compensated for by rises in the latter. There is some truth in this so far as changes are concerned, but in terms of levels of protection the two approaches seem to be complementary. The relative importance of the two measures is difficult to assess because of the absence of many comprehensive studies of NTBs. However, Magee (1972) suggested that US quotas are far more costly than tariffs – largely, however, because he assumed that the quota rents accrue overseas (see pp. 77-8 above). Baldwin (1970), in a classic study, found that NTBs contributed only about 30 per cent of the USA's effective protection in 1958, as did Oulton (1976) for the UK in 1968. However, they both included only a very limited menu of NTBs. Coupled with subsequent changes in protection, this must suggest at least parity of effect between NTBs and tariffs by now. Yeats (1979) quoted studies by UNCTAD suggesting considerably larger effects for NTBs, especially when considering restrictions on LDC's trade.

There can be little doubt, therefore, that NTBs currently represent a greater threat to world trade than tariffs. They are inherently less visible than tariffs, but even the visible parts are now reckoned more restrictive and costly than tariffs. They are also a greater obstacle to economic development, because they are much more concentrated than tariffs onto sensitive industries and products. We now conclude this chapter by briefly considering the barriers in two particular sectors: agriculture, and textiles and clothing.

Agricultural protection

We have already described the EEC's variable levy system as a form of tariff protection (see p. 68 above). It fixes the internal price of agricultural imports regardless of the world price. Internal prices are substantially above world prices, which results in grossly inflated European output of temperate food-stuffs, and requires levies of up to 300 per cent on certain goods at particular times. The levies are also supplemented by ordinary tariffs (which are paid regardless of the relationship between the internal and world prices) and a range of Group A NTBs such as quotas, discretionary import licensing, state trading and seasonal prohibitions. Yeats (1979) quoted average nominal protection of 18 per cent via tariffs and 56 per cent via levies, and effective rates of 49 per cent and 134 per cent respectively. Cline *et al.* (1978) suggested that a 60 per cent cut in the tariff equivalent of EEC agricultural NTBs would boost imports by about $\frac{1}{2}$b. and welfare by about $1b. p.a. at 1971 prices. At today's prices this would be at least doubled.

On a world scale, Yeats (1979) states that UNCTAD has estimated that in 1971 developing countries' exports would have risen by $17b. had developed countries' agriculture not been protected. Developed country food producers – especially those of North America and Australasia – would also have increased their output. World GNP would have risen by around $84b., or 2 per cent, with welfare gains of at least the same order of magnitude. At today's prices and incomes these figures should again be doubled.

Clothing and textiles

After agriculture, textiles and clothing are probably the most contentious industries in terms of trade policy. They comprise mostly standardised labour-intensive processes applied to widely available raw materials, and hence are ideally suited to LDCs' early stages of industrialisation. Unfortunately they also still comprise a substantial part of developed countries' industrial output, frequently employing relatively elderly workers and being highly concentrated geographically. They have thus become a battleground for trade diplomacy and a hunting ground for trade economists seeking evidence.

The market for textiles has grown less rapidly than the markets for other goods since at least 1900. In the early twentieth century, established producers were already being squeezed between new suppliers and a static demand; by the 1930s the USA had deemed textiles worthy of special treatment and the UK had arranged preferential treatment of her textiles throughout the Empire. In the early GATT rounds, textiles received special treatment, but this could not reverse the decline of traditional producers in the face of expansion by LDCs and Japan, and in the late 1950s Britain concluded VERs with Hong Kong, Japan and India.

Britain was not alone in feeling the pinch. In 1961, multilateral controls were introduced under the auspices of the GATT. Designed to avoid 'serious damage' to developed country producers, these provisions were contrary to several GATT

87

principles (unilateral and discriminatory quotas being forbidden). In allowing them, the GATT was just recognising, and seeking to contain, their grave threat to the emerging liberal trading order. The restrictions initially formed a 'Short-Term Arrangement on Cotton Textiles', but within a year were encompassed by a stronger 'Long-Term Arrangement Regarding International Trade in Cotton Textiles' (LTA). The LTA applied for five years at first, but was then extended until 1970 and then 1973. It covered twenty-nine countries and provided for only a limited growth in quotas over the period (5 per cent per annum). This permitted European output to expand rather than contract in an orderly way (although employment fell), which suggests that its intent was protectionist rather than merely to smooth adjustment.

The LTA was superseded by the MFA (the Multi-Fibre Agreement), which covered more textile fibres and more countries. Its provisions were originally somewhat more liberal over the nature and extent of quotas, but its renewals and re-negotiation in 1979 and 1982 have, particularly at the EEC's insistence, allowed ever fiercer controls.

Behind these international controls, Britain has sought to stimulate some adjustment in the textile industry. Incentives have been offered to rationalise the industry – replacing old plant with new, and moving into new lines. Indeed, the improvement in productivity has outweighed import penetration as the immediate cause of job losses. Output and employment are nevertheless still much higher than can be justified by any notion of comparative advantage.

The net effect of the MFA has been to raise textile and clothing prices by 5–10 per cent (this is the 'quota effect', in addition to that of tariffs) and to induce exporters to diversify into non-protected and higher-quality lines of produce. In the longer run, this has exacerbated the pressure on domestic producers and has probably stimulated the development of the South-East Asian producers from simple to sophisticated goods and processes.

The Consumers' Association (1979) reached similar conclusions for UK clothing imports. They claimed that prices were around 18–40 per cent higher because of the MFA, and that exporters had 'traded up' to higher-value lines very considerably. This had both reduced the supply of cheaper clothes and stored up trouble for British producers in future. Further, they argued, British firms had not stepped into the markets freed from imports, so the employment effects of the MFA had been negligible.

The welfare effects are hard to gauge. Keesing and Wolf (1980) quoted US welfare losses of up to 10 per cent of the expenditure on clothing and textiles, and of up to $81,000 per annum per American textile job preserved. Hamilton (1981) suggested that liberalising Swedish VERs against LDCs enough to raise imports by 50 per cent would have raised Swedish real income by $21 per capita in 1981. He estimated that existing VERs cost $41,000 per annum per job saved in welfare terms. Hamilton also calculated, however, that production subsidies to Swedish textile firms cost only around $8,000 per annum per job saved, which suggests that some short-term adjustment assistance may be 'affordable' on social grounds.

FURTHER READING

The theoretical analysis of quotas is best accomplished by *Bhagwati* (1969b, ch. 9), who covers the basic case and the (non-) equivalence with tariffs. *Corden* (1971) also provides useful insight, and *Krueger* (1974) is the classic reference on rent-seeking. Voluntary export restraints are introduced by *Takacs* (1978) and *Hindley* (1980). *Baldwin* (1970) provides a thorough and classic early survey of non-tariff barriers in general, attempting some quantification. Other briefer general coverage comes from *Yeats* (1979), which is excellent, and *Greenaway* (1983). The former covers several attempts at measurement and should be supplemented by *Roningen and Yeats* (1976), *Cline et al.* (1978), *Page* (1979, 1981) and *Gard and Riedel* (1980). The case of textiles is extensively documented: *Keesing and Wolf* (1980) provide an excellent survey, while *Corden and Fels* (1976) consider domestic policies, *Hamilton* (1981) attempts quantification, and *Dore* (1982) discusses various sociological aspects of decline. Agriculture is dealt with by *Cline et al.* (1978) and *Yeats* (1979).

NOTES

1   VERs and quotas also differ in circumstances of monopoly and where they are applied discriminatorily – see Takacs (1978).
2   For example, a non-nuclear electricity generating programme limits other countries' exports of reactors.

8 Arguments for Protection in Equilibrium

This chapter and the next examine the arguments for protection and also the form that protection should take. Protection is justified economically when the conditions for the optimality of free trade are violated, but different violations entail different solutions. This chapter considers equilibrium arguments – conditions that would entail protection forever – while the next considers disequilibrium cases. Frequently the case for protection is political or strategic: e.g. the desire for a domestic steel industry in case of war. These are perfectly legitimate objectives, but the strategic gains should be weighed against the economic losses that they entail. These vary with the form that protection takes.

Before commencing, let us dispose of one entirely spurious argument for protection: that free trade exposes our producers to 'unfair' competition from cheaper factors of production abroad. This implies that all cheap imports from abroad should be discouraged, which clearly undermines the whole of international trade based on comparative advantage. Closely related is the view that by importing the products of under-paid 'sweated labour' elsewhere in the world we are conniving at these peoples' exploitation. To substantiate this we should need to show that, when 'sweated labourers' are offered the choice of producing for export or not at all, they mistake their own interests in choosing the former. This is possible, but it is not an easy proposition to uphold. On a more practical level, even if it were the case, we should still need to be sure that a trade embargo would improve their lot.

8.1 DOMESTIC DISTORTIONS

Conditions for optimality

We have seen above (section 5.1) that a necessary condition for the maximisation of welfare in an open economy is

$$MRTT_S = MRT_S = MRS_S \tag{8.1}$$

where *MRTT* is the marginal rate of transformation through trade, *MRT* is the marginal rate of transformation (through production), and *MRS* is the marginal rate of substitution (in consumption). All refer to social and not private marginal rates, and are thus subscripted S. The equality of the two marginal rates of transformation ensures that no increase in output is achievable by switching between domestic production and trade as a means of transformation. The equality of the marginal rate of substitution and the (common) marginal rate of transformation ensures that no increase in welfare is achievable by altering the bundle of goods made available by production and trade.

This section considers an economy where (8.1) does not apply, and asks (i) how the equalities can be achieved, i.e. how optimality can be brought about, and (ii) whether, failing that, some second-best improvement may be made. At the same time, it considers the opposite question: if we have an economy satisfying (8.1), but wish for some *non-economic* reason to alter the resulting equilibrium, what is the least-cost method of doing so? The answers are intimately related.

It does not matter whether (8.1) is brought about by prices or by planning, but we shall concentrate on the price mechanism. Under the latter, agents set their marginal rates equal to prices, which they take as given. The economic links in that process are shown in Figure 8.1. In the absence of any distortions, the consumer price ratio (P_C) determines the private marginal rate of substitution (MRS_P), which in turn determines the social rate (MRS_S); similarly for the production and trade sectors. In the perfect economy, all links are characterised by equality.

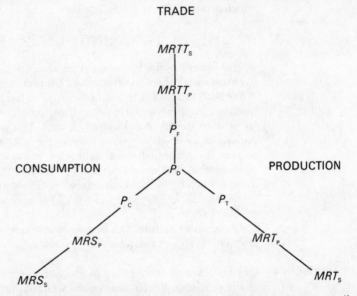

P_C, P_T and P_F are consumers', producers' and world relative prices, respectively.
P_D is domestic tax-exclusive prices.
MRS is the marginal rate of substitution (in consumption).
MRT is the marginal rate of transformation (in production).
$MRTT$ is the marginal rate of transformation through trade.
Subscript S denotes social values and subscript P denotes private values.

Figure 8.1 *Price signals in the market economy*

Distortions

Two basic sets of distortions can corrupt (8.1): (a) market imperfections, which cause private and social marginal rates to differ, and (b) taxes, which cause the prices that agents face to differ from domestic tax-exclusive prices. (We include in the concept 'taxes' subsidies, which are merely negative taxes.) Group (a) distortions are autonomous, but group (b) are policy variables.

Suppose we have an economy with perfect markets everywhere except in consumption, where an autonomous externality causes private and social rates of transformation to diverge. Assume

$$MRS_P = Z . MRS_S \qquad (8.2)$$

where $Z \neq 1$. Overall we have

$$MRTT_S = MRT_S = P_D = P_C = MRS_P \neq MRS_S. \qquad (8.3)$$

91

To restore full optimality we could manipulate $MRTT$ and MRT, but a simpler procedure would be to operate directly on consumption. We require a policy such that when private consumers set $MRS_P = P_C$ they also produce $MRS_S = P_D$. An obvious candidate is a consumption tax that sets

$$P_C = \mathcal{Z}.P_D, \tag{8.4}$$

which produces the required equality

$$MRTT_S = MRT_S = P_D = P_C/\mathcal{Z} = MRS_P/\mathcal{Z} = MRS_S. \tag{8.5}$$

This illustrates the following general rule: if there is a distortion in any sector of the economy, it is optimally met by a countervailing distortion *in the same sector*.

We shall look at some detailed examples later, but we now consider the related question. Suppose we have an undistorted economy but that for strategic reasons we wish to stimulate the output of steel. This means that, relative to the market equilibrium, we wish to allow a rise in the MRT of steel, because if output is to rise so too, in increasing costs industries, must marginal costs. Again Figure 8.1 suggests that, if we use a production subsidy that raises P_T relative to P_D we can avoid disturbing the equalities elsewhere in the system. In general, to impose some non-economic change on a sector of the economy, the optimal policy is applied only in that sector.

These rules define first-best policies, but even among other, second-best, alternatives some ranking is usually possible.

Production

Our first example concerns a production externality in an otherwise perfect small trading economy. To maximise welfare, the general rules suggest that a production tax is the first-best response. Second best is a tariff because, although the tariff introduces distortions to the consumption sector, it does at least have some effect on production. Third best is free trade, and last a consumption tax (which merely introduces further distortions without touching the original one).

Figure 8.2(A) summarises the analysis. Let the externality cause the social costs of Y to exceed the private costs. The relationship between the two is shown at the top right of the figure. More X has to be surrendered socially per unit of Y than privately, hence relative social costs exceed (are less steep than) relative private costs, the difference in slope representing the extent of the externality. The free-trade equilibrium is given by points P and C. The terms of trade are given by slope TT and these determine domestic prices (P_D in the general notation). Producers set $MRT_P = P_T = P_D$, which given the externality implies that $MRT_S =$ slope II. Thus, with transformation frontier FF, production takes place at P. This is non-optimal, however, because $MRT_S | \neq P_F = MRTT_S$; private decisions do not maximise the social value of output. *Given production*, however, consumption is undistorted and so reaches the maximal position along the ruling consumption locus TT – that is, point C.

Now suppose we subsidise X to just offset the externality. At the prevailing prices – defined by slope TT – producers' returns on X rise; they thus switch from Y to X, moving round the transformation frontier to P'. Internal prices (P_D) still equal slope TT, but private producer prices (P_T) equal slope $J'J'$ (steeper, because X is subsidised); private MRT_P is set to P_T, and, accounting for the externality, $MRT_S = P_D$. Thus at prices P_D, P' maximises the social value of output. Given P', undistorted trade and consumption allow consumption to settle at C', which is plainly the optimum. Thus a production tax is first best.

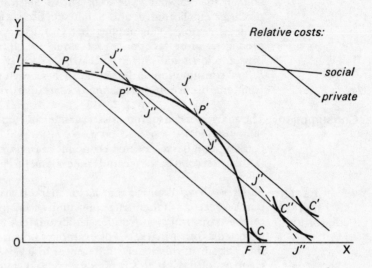

(A) *A production externality*

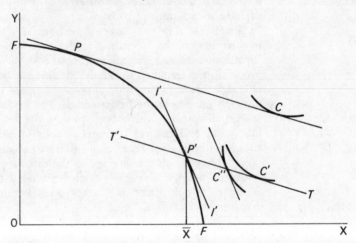

(B) *A production objective*

Figure 8.2   *Trade policy and distortions. (A) A production externality.
(B) A production objective*

The figure also illustrates the consequences of imposing a tariff on X at a rate
below that of the optimum production subsidy. This moves production from *P* to
P", not so far round as *P*' because the tariff does not fully off-set the externality. The
tariff-ridden private costs are shown by *J*"*J*" both at *P*" and also at *C*", the
consumption point. The consumption distortion inherent in the tariff means that
the improved production allocation is now partly off-set by a new consumption
misallocation. However, it may be shown that a tariff can always be found to
improve on *laissez-faire*. Thus, in the presence of a production externality, a
production tax/subsidy is optimal, but a tariff is second best. The second-best tariff
will be at a rate below the first-best production subsidy.

The related question is how best to shift production away from the free-trade point if that is what is desired. This is illustrated in Figure 8.2(B). Free trade produces equilibrium P and C, but suppose society requires at least $\bar{X}$ of X for strategic reasons. This implies that production must shift to P', at which point producers must face prices of slope $I'T'$. If a production subsidy is used, consumption is undistorted and can be at C', but if a tariff is used $MRS = MRT = P_D \neq P_F$, and consumption settles at C'', which is clearly inferior. The tariff introduces an additional distortion (on consumption) relative to the production tax.

Consumption The analysis of consumption externalities and external objectives is very similar to that just carried out. To cure a consumption distortion, or to change the consumption basket for non-economic reasons, consumption taxes are first best, tariffs are second best, free trade is next, and production taxes are last.

Factor market distortions So far we have assumed that factor markets are perfect, so that industries can purchase factors at their true opportunity cost, and production always takes place on the transformation frontier. Unfortunately, factor markets are as frequently distorted as other markets. For example, industries tend to pay different wages to their labour. If this reflects differences in levels of skill or in the non-pecuniary elements of the job, this is not distortionary, but if it arises from the industries' different monopsony power, or from any monopoly powers of the trades unions, or from social legislation, it is distortionary and imposes economic costs. Similarly, differential labour taxes or differential institutional hindrances on borrowing capital also constitute distortions.

The effects of factor market distortions are, first, to shrink the transformation frontier inwards and, second, to distort relative costs so that, even along the shrunken-in frontier, private and social costs differ. The latter is equivalent to the production externality just analysed and may be treated accordingly. However, although this finds the optimal point along the ruling transformation frontier, it does nothing about the frontier itself. The first-best solution is to cure the factor market distortion, which both pushes the transformation frontier out to its maximum and ensures a tangency solution along it. This cure could involve countervailing factor taxes or institutional changes. Either way the moral is the same: policy should be directed at the distorted sector – in this case the factor markets. The general rule also carries through to the reverse question: to stimulate factor use (employment, say) factor taxes are first best, followed by production taxes and then tariffs.

Conclusion This analysis is a fine example of the theory of second best. It shows that, in the presence of one distortion, applying the usual optimality conditions to the other sectors (i.e. free trade) is not optimal. It also shows, however, that this does not leave us powerless; we can still make rather strong orderings among the remaining second-best policies.

The practical conclusion of the analysis is that incurable distortions should be treated in the sector in which they occur, and not by more general policies. Thus, while domestic distortions constitute a valid case for protection via taxes or subsidies, they do not constitute a case for tariffs or quotas.

The empirical application of the results of this section is unusual, for governments do not usually justify protection in terms of distortions within their own economies. None the less, the prevalence of domestic distortions suggests that there is considerable scope for application. An interesting example of the use of the non-economic objective argument is the case of agricultural protection. Nearly every country seeks to maintain agriculture for political and strategic reasons. Prior to acceding to the EEC, Britain used a system of deficiency payments – income subsidies – but on accession she adopted the less efficient approach of tariff protection. The result was a large rise in British food prices, because, whereas under the former system consumers faced world prices, under the latter they faced the same (distorted) prices as farmers received. The loss of consumers' surplus was considerable. Miller (1971) quoted *predicted* welfare losses from the switch in protective methods as £200–500m. per annum at 1969 prices. This is about 3–8 per cent of food consumption or about $\frac{1}{2}$–$1\frac{1}{4}$ per cent of national income in 1969.

Johnson (1967a), following Snape (1963), explored this issue more fully in the case of the sugar market. Most Western nations protect their domestic sugar-beet producers from competition from tropical cane producers, but use tariffs rather than deficiency payments. He suggested that using the inappropriate policy to support output cost the protecting nations about $200m. in lost welfare and the efficient world producers about another $200m. in lost producer surpluses. These figures refer to 1959 (before the EEC was effective) and together accounted for approaching 50 per cent of the value of world sugar trade! It is unlikely that the situation has improved.

8.2 THE OPTIMUM TARIFF

A general
analysis

Figure 8.1 suggests that there is scope for the private and social marginal rates of transformation through trade to differ. Furthermore, the general rules suggest that, if this is so, it should be met by a countervailing policy distortion in the trade sector; one such is a tariff.

The cause of any discrepancy between private and social MRTT is market power in international trade. Suppose Britain were the only market for tea, and that tea were produced abroad under conditions of increasing costs. A reduction in Britain's demand for tea would thus cut the world price and improve Britain's terms of trade. However, to exploit this market power Britons must act in concert. Each individual takes the price of tea as given: his own influence on the price is negligible and hence the cost of his marginal unit is just the ruling world price. In general equilibrium notation, $MRTT_P = P_F$. For Britain as a whole, however, the marginal cost exceeds the price, because purchasing an extra unit not only costs the ruling price but also drives up the price on all previous units. The latter element is ignored by individuals because it is borne by other people (it is a sort of externality), but socially it should be taken into account. Hence socially we have, say,

$$MRTT_S = Z.P_F = Z.MRTT_P, \qquad (8.6)$$

with $Z > 1$. Overall the situation is

$$MRTT_S \neq MRTT_P = P_F = P_D = MRS_S = MRT_S. \qquad (8.7)$$

Our general rule suggests meeting this with a tariff that drives a wedge between P_F and P_D such that $P_D = Z.P_F$. This implies:

$$MRTT_S = Z.MRTT_P = Z.P_F = P_D = MRS_S = MRT_S. \qquad (8.8)$$

This tariff, which maximises welfare, is known as the optimum tariff.

We saw in section 6.2 that a tariff is equivalent to a production subsidy plus a consumption tax. Figure 8.1 confirms this. A production subsidy such that $P_T = Z.P_D$ and a consumption tax such that $P_C = Z.P_D$ would have the following effects:

$$MRTT_S = Z.MRTT_P = Z.P_F = Z.P_D = P_C = MRS_S$$
$$= P_T = MRT_S \qquad (8.9)$$

Equation (8.9) shows that neither a production tax nor a consumption tax alone could produce optimality; however, it may be shown that either (at the right rate) is superior to free trade. For non-economic objectives a tariff is first best only if the objective is defined in terms of trade rather than output or consumption.

A partial equilibrium illustration

The optimum tariff has a long history in international economics – Mill and Marshall were quite aware of the argument – and so we now analyse it more explicitly. The essence of the case for the tariff is that, acting individually, residents fail to take account of their collective market power, and hence fail to reap the benefits that it would accord. A single monopsonist would realise that each unit bought forced up the price on all units and would exploit this to maximise his welfare (profits) from importing. The tariff works by inducing the many individuals acting separately to behave as if they were a single monopsonist.

The position of the profit-maximising monopsonist is illustrated in Figure 8.3. He buys imports until the marginal cost (*MC*) just equals the price at which he can resell them domestically, as shown by the demand curve. Thus he chooses equilibrium *B*. The individuals, on the other hand, do not recognise (or care about) the effect that they have on each other's prices, and thus buy for as long as their demand price exceeds the supply price (as shown by the supply curve). Thus they choose equilibrium *A*. The tariff essentially taxes them for the extent to which they harm each other. Thus an *ad valorem* tariff of t would raise the import supply curve *to residents* up to *MC* in the figure: q_m costs p_t per unit paid to the exporter and $t.p_t$ to the government. The new competitive equilibrium becomes *B*. The supply curve to the country as a whole, however, is unchanged, and the fall in the price paid abroad $(p_f - p_t)$ represents the terms of trade gain.

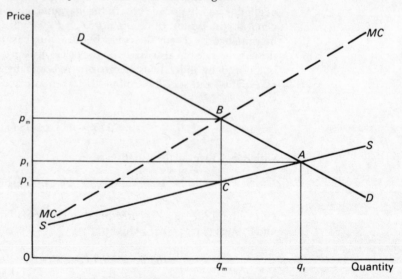

Figure 8.3   *The optimum tariff: partial equilibrium*

The size of the optimum tariff is easily calculable in this case. Write the import supply curve as $p = p(q)$, where p, the price necessary to call forth supply q, is a function of q. Then the total cost of q is $p.q$ and marginal cost is

$$MC = p + \frac{\mathrm{d}p}{\mathrm{d}q} \cdot q \qquad (8.10)$$

$$= (1 + \frac{1}{\epsilon})p$$

where ϵ is the price elasticity of supply of imports $(\mathrm{d}q/\mathrm{d}p)\,(p/q)$. Hence the tariff necessary to shift the private supply price up to (social) marginal cost at any given quantity is given by $(1+t)p = MC$. Thus

$$t = MC/p - 1 \qquad (8.11)$$

$$t = 1/\epsilon$$

The optimum tariff is just the reciprocal of the elasticity of supply. Observe how if supply is perfectly elastic ($\epsilon = \infty$) the optimum tariff is zero, which is just the small country case.

General equilibrium

We now consider the general equilibrium analysis of the optimum tariff in Figure 8.4. Part (A) of the figure displays the foreign offer curve facing a country with some market power (GG): it shows all the combinations of X and Y that the rest of the world is prepared to trade with us. Our imports are shown with a + and exports with a −. GG's curvative indicates that more imports are available only at the cost of raising their price in terms of X. The terms of trade (price) are indicated by the slope of the line from the origin to the trade point (e.g. OC), while the $MRTT$ is given by the offer curve's slope at the trade point.

Figure 8.4(B) shows the free-trade equilibrium. FF is the transformation frontier. Given any production point, P, the consumption possibilities are defined by the foreign offer curve with its origin positioned at P; the consumption point must lie on such a locus. Under free trade, producers set $MRT_p = P_T = P_F$ and consumers $MRS_p = P_C = P_F$. Hence at equilibrium the terms of trade line CP is tangent to FF at the production point P, and tangent to the social indifference curve at the consumption point C. C is clearly sub-optimal, because even with production fixed at P we could reach a higher indifference curve along GG, and once we let production shift we can do even better.

In Figure 8.4(C) we have constructed the so-called 'Baldwin-envelope', the broken line BF. This represents the consumption possibility locus allowing both production and the amount of foreign trade to change. It is constructed by drawing in the consumption locus for each production point in turn (that is, sketching in the foreign offer curve with its origin at every point along FF in turn), and then joining up the outermost points of these loci. The resulting curve envelopes all the consumption possibilities − hence its name. The envelope has one very special property: at any point, the envelope's slope, the slope of GG at that point and the slope of FF at the relevant production point are all equal. The tangency of GG and BF is obvious; if it were not so, GG would cross BF, and BF would not be the outer locus. The result with FF may be seen as follows: suppose GG and FF had different slopes at the relevant points, say 2X:1Y and 3X:1Y respectively; if we produced one unit less Y we would gain 3X, and trading these gain $1\frac{1}{2}$Y – a net gain of $\frac{1}{2}$Y; hence if the slopes differ, a net gain in consumption is possible, which shows that consumption was not being maximised at such a position.

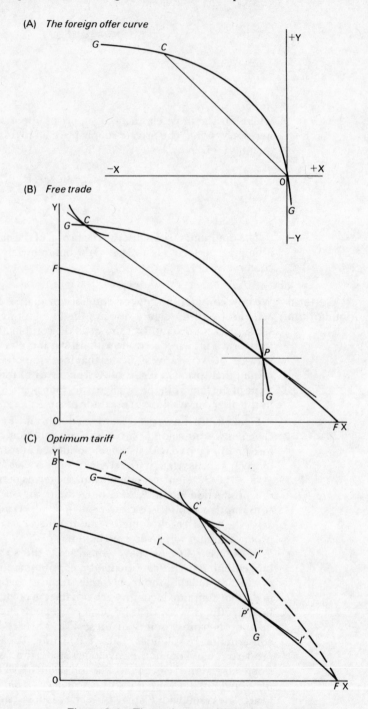

Figure 8.4   *The optimum tariff: general equilibrium*

Since the Baldwin envelope shows the maximal consumption possibilities, the welfare maximum must be where it is tangent to a social indifference curve – that is, point C' in the figure. Tracing back along the foreign offer curve tangent at C' defines production point P', and the terms of trade – slope $P'C'$. To achieve P', producers must set their MRT to slope $I'I'$ and with terms of trade $P'C'$ this involves a production subsidy on Y. Similarly, given P', if consumers are to achieve C', they must pay a tax on Y to convert trade prices $P'C'$ into internal prices $I''I''$, which equal MRS at C'. Now, by the envelope theorem, we know that the slopes of BF and GG at C' and of FF at P' are equal. Hence consumers' and producers' price ratios are equal, but not equal to the terms of trade; i.e. $P_C = P_T \neq P_F$. This, of course, is the hallmark of a tariff. Hence a tariff enables us to reach the maximum welfare point C'. Finally, the envelope theorem immediately provides our optimality conditions.

$$MRTT_s \quad = \quad MRS_s \quad = \quad MRT_s \qquad (8.12)$$
$$\text{(slope GG)} \qquad \text{(slope BF)} \qquad \text{(slope FF)}$$

All this analysis can be combined with the domestic distortions cases to examine distortions in large countries. It is rather messy, but the basic result is that two policies are required: the optimum tariff to maximise the benefit from changing the terms of trade, and a domestic policy to counteract the other distortion.

Export taxes

In general equilibrium, export and import taxes are equivalent (see section 6.1 above), so all the previous analysis could be applied to export taxes: by surcharging exports the final price asked of foreigners is driven up, provided of course that the price elasticity of demand is not infinite. In fact there is probably more scope for export taxes than for optimal tariffs, because exports are usually more specialised than imports and hence are more likely to permit market power.

Retaliation

The optimum tariff improves the tariff-imposing country's welfare, but only at the expense of the rest of the world, which suffers a deterioration in its terms of trade as well as the inefficiencies associated with reduced specialisation. This has led economists to ask what happens if the rest of the world retaliates. Johnson (1953–4) analysed this case, assuming that two countries take it in turns to impose the optimum tariff against each other on the (mistaken) assumption that the other country will not retaliate. His conclusions were:

(i) Several 'rounds' will be required, because by imposing a tariff a country alters its own offer curve. Hence, retaliation would shift GG in our Figure 8.4, making our previously optimum tariff no longer optimal.
(ii) Equilibrium would, however, eventually be achieved before trade was entirely eliminated. This is because the gain from the optimum tariff arises solely from changes in the terms of trade; thus no trade implies no gain, but merely the loss of specialisation. Hence each party has an interest in stopping short of eliminating trade.
(iii) One or other country *could* remain better off after the tariff war than under free trade, but since free trade is Pareto optimal it is not possible for both to gain from a trade war.

Applications

The optimum tariff is a wholly selfish piece of economic policy: it raises A's welfare at the expense of B's. Thus governments do not readily admit to using it. None the less it is empirically quite important. Nearly all developed countries have some market power over their exports, at least in the short run, as witnessed by the non-

99

infinite price elasticities of demand that they face (see Chapter 18). There is thus scope for optimum tariffs. Furthermore, the benefits claimed by advocates of protectionism frequently stem largely from the terms of trade effects – e.g. Cambridge Economic Policy Group (*Cambridge Economic Policy Review*, 1979), where import controls raise the terms of trade by about 20 per cent, which accounts for around half the perceived benefits of protection. Despite their small size, LDCs also frequently have market power in their export markets. This is not often manifest in export taxes, but the use of tariffs is common and clearly has some terms of trade objectives. (Note, however, that, where market power covers only part of exports, tariffs and export taxes are not wholly equivalent.)

8.3   THE REVENUE TARIFF

All the previous analysis assumes that governments can raise or distribute revenues costlessly and without distortion. Hence the most obvious difference between tariffs and subsidies – that one earns and the other absorbs revenue – is quite irrelevant. Once we recognise the falsity of this premise, however, we have another element of second best to consider. The preference for subsidies for stimulating output, for example, may be entirely outweighed by the distortions entailed, and the resources absorbed, in raising the cash to fund them.

This problem is particularly acute for developing countries, where the information necessary for levying taxes on incomes or domestic transactions frequently does not exist, at least not without a huge expenditure of resources. Foreign trade, on the other hand, is eminently taxable: it is always monetised (unlike many domestic transactions); it is conducted by sophisticated agents; it is extensively documented for non-fiscal reasons; it is geographically concentrated at the main ports; and it is frequently concentrated in terms of products and traders. For these countries, then, the major considerations in favour of tariffs are their efficient revenue-raising effects and their ease of administration.

FURTHER READING

Much of this chapter is based on *Corden's* excellent article (1957). Domestic distortions are discussed in *Haberler* (1950), *Bhagwati and Ramaswami* (1963) and *Johnson* (1965a); *Bhagwati, Ramaswami and Srinivasan* (1969) provides a simple mathematical summary, while *Bhagwati* (1971) offers a general theory of distortions, economic growth and welfare. Greater detail on factor market distortions may be found in *Magee* (1973a), while *Johnson* (1971) also covers some useful ground.

Bhagwati (1968) and *Corden* (1974) cover all the issues in this chapter as well as broader questions of commercial policy. The latter contains much detail but works almost entirely in a partial equilibrium framework. *Bhagwati* (1981, part IV) covers several related topics, although not all the essays are easy.

9 Arguments for Protection in Disequilibrium

This chapter shifts attention to protection under circumstances of disequilibrium. Disequilibrium is interpreted broadly to include not only situations of change, but also circumstances where although the economy is stationary its position does not satisfy the neo-classical condition of full employment. The topics considered are dumping, the infant industry and infant country arguments, and protection as a means to full employment.

9.1 DUMPING

Dumping is, broadly speaking, selling goods abroad at unrealistically low prices. In legal terms, 'unrealistically low' is usually interpreted as below the home price of identical items after allowing for transport costs, etc. Discriminating monopoly, whereby a firm exports at the world price but exploits its monopoly power at home to raise domestic prices, is included in the definition. In this case, of course, any harm done is entirely borne by the domestic economy and dumping constitutes no case at all for protection by the importer.

Economically more interesting is where exports are sold at below cost (including some minimal profit margin). In this case the importer suffers a distortion, and policy may be justified. Clearly such dumping is possible in the long run only if government or some other branch of the firm subsidises the loss-making exports. Also, there are practical difficulties in defining the relevant costs. For example, should we consider short-run marginal cost (SRMC) or long-run average costs, which allow for capacity costs? During a slump, when spare capacity exists, SRMC is often very low in capital-intensive industries and economic theory suggests that any exports at prices above that level should be sought. Import-competing producers facing such competition, however, argue that long-run costs are relevant and that such exports constitute dumping. The steel industry is often held to be prone to such 'counter-cyclical' dumping, but Tarr (1979), in a detailed study, could not detect it.

One might wonder why countries should object to being offered imports at below their 'realistic' price, because such an offer increases their welfare. The reason lies in the disequilibrium nature of the situation. If cheap imports were guaranteed to eternity, that would be fine, but the worry is that once the dumping firm has eliminated domestic competition it will exploit its (new-found) monopoly position to the detriment of the importer. Since it is costly to re-establish industries once they have closed down, it sometimes pays to keep them going even though, pro tem, imports undercut local prices. Thus, the crux of the argument lies in the prospect of dumping being stopped at some time in the future, and in the costs of closing down and starting up industries as the import price varies.

Dumping is outlawed under the GATT: dumped goods may be subjected to countervailing duties, and export subsidies are firmly forbidden. One of the countries most concerned with dumping is the USA, where the President is obliged to impose countervailing duties on any dumped imports. During the 1970s, several such actions were threatened and the arguments hinged mainly on the role of various non-tariff measures in the exporting countries. These investigations

101

tended to define any government policy as a non-tariff distortion: for example, railway subsidies and local rates relief were both considered as sources of support for UK industries alleged to be dumping in the USA. (Both proved infinitesimal in their effects in fact.)

From Chapter 8 we should note that the correct response to dumping is a production subsidy rather than a tariff. This is because it protects producers while still allowing consumers to benefit from the exporter's generosity.

9.2   INFANT INDUSTRY PROTECTION

The basic argument

The infant industry argument is perhaps the most widely quoted justification for protection. Suppose that country A has a potential comparative advantage in an industry, but that because of an earlier start country B has established that industry to such an extent that A's producers cannot compete in the short run. If the infant industry were protected over this vital stage, eventually the world would be better off from the more appropriate exploitation of comparative advantage in the long run.

This argument is not as persuasive as it first seems, but let us accept its basic case for now. As with several other arguments, however, it is more a case for a subsidy than for a tariff. The objective concerns production – production must be stimulated in order that the industry mature – and thus the consumption restriction stemming from the tariff is an unwanted distortion. Indeed, curtailing domestic consumption of a good whose output is being stimulated seems particularly perverse.

If the current costs of protection are to be adequately repaid, the industry will have to earn above-normal profits in its later years. In technical terms, protection will be justified only if the discounted value of all future profits exceeds the discounted value of all the costs incurred. By itself, however, this is not sufficient to justify protection, because, if private profits cover private costs, the industry should be established without any public intervention at all. Every private investment involves forgoing current consumption (i.e. making 'losses') in return for higher future consumption. Thus, in order to justify protection we have also to show either that the private sector is unable to undertake some (privately) profitable investment, or that a privately unprofitable industry is none the less socially desirable, i.e. that there is an externality.

Private market failure

We now consider the circumstances that may lead to a new industry suffering short-term losses despite being potentially profitable in the long run. First, with imports still entering, the domestic industry may be unable to achieve sufficient economies of scale. Second, the industry may be subject to 'learning by doing': either labour or management may reach maximum productivity only after a prolonged period of experience with production, so the early (learning) units will be relatively costly.

These two factors, however, do not separate private and social costs; to justify protection they need to be supplemented by reasons for the failure of the private sector to undertake the required investment. First the private sector may have worse *information* than the government: although the government may not have superior knowledge about particular cost structures or market prospects, it may well be better informed about future macro-economic conditions, infrastructure investment, education, factor market conditions and so on. Thus what seems privately unprofitable may actually be profitable on the government's

102

information. Of course, the first-best solution to this situation is to stimulate the information flow, but given governments' credibility problems this may not be easy.

The second private market failure concerns *capital market imperfections*: it may be that private capital markets are unwilling to finance the infant industry even though it is expected to yield at least market rates of return. This may be because of an unwillingness to

- finance investment in 'human capital' (the learned skills of the workers), because they offer no saleable collateral if the loan is not repaid;
- make very large loans – this is particularly relevant to the economies of scale case;
- finance new (unknown) entrepreneurs and products; or
- make long illiquid investments – that is particularly relevant to the learning by doing case.

The last three stem partly from a difference in private and social attitudes to risk. Private risk exceeds social risk because, if a loan is repudiated or has to be liquidated quickly at a low price, there is private loss but no social loss since the lender's loss is balanced by someone else's gain. This difference is likely to be greatest for long, large and inherently risky loans, especially in LDCs where capital markets are thin.

Capital market imperfections have considerable relevance, even in developed countries so far as research and development based industries are concerned. However, yet again the first-best solution is to overcome the imperfection rather than restrict international trade. For example, the government might issue its own debt and re-lend to new industries at 'correct' rates – 'development banks', both national and international, essentially do this.

Externalities

A third cause of infant industries' falling costs through time concerns the *training of labour*. If labour must be trained to undertake manufacturing tasks, someone must bear the cost. If the first firm or industry in the field does so, however, the workers, once trained, can leave to work for other firms, which, because they do not bear the training costs, can pay higher wages. In other words, an individual firm cannot always appropriate the benefits of its training programme, and this discourages it from starting such a programme. Thus industry never gets off the ground. This is a classic externality – in the factor markets – and should accordingly be met by subsidies to industrial training or the provision of free technical education. Again, tariffs are only third best.

Another externality that reduces social costs for an established industry concerns *external economies of scale*. As it grows, an industry may stimulate facilities that benefit other industries, e.g. research institutions, infrastructure and specialist suppliers. The economy-wide benefits that these institutions confer should be set against the original industry's costs. Yet again, however, first best would be for the government to support these institutions directly rather than offer tariff protection. More difficult to subsidise directly, however, is any change in the atmosphere or attitude towards industrialisation that the growth of a new industry engenders; such externalities are best met by production subsidies.

Practical difficulties

Even if the arguments above apply in theory, there still remains the question of whether protection will actually allow the benefits to be reaped. Young protected industries are frequently rather concentrated on this often hinders efficiency. For

103

example, several authors have found profits to be abnormally high in industries that are both protected *and* concentrated (e.g. Lyons, 1981). Others have found that costs are not minimised in such cases – e.g. Leibenstein's (1966) X-inefficiency, Bloch's (1974) finding that costs rise with protection, or Caves *et al.*'s (1980) finding that economies of scale are *not* properly exploited behind tariff barriers.

The question must also be faced of how and when to remove infant protection. The industry can frequently claim that a few more years will 'do the trick', and no government likes to admit defeat by abandoning an industry formerly favoured in the 'national interest'.

The infant industry argument was first stated by Alexander Hamilton (1790), advocating protection in the newly formed USA, and it has figured strongly in American commercial policy ever since. List (1841) also developed it in the German context, although his approach is more infant country than infant industry – see section 9.3 below.

A recent empirical examination of infant industry protection is Krueger and Tuncer (1982). This examined the *necessary (but not sufficient)* condition for successful infant protection that costs in the protected industry should fall through time. Judging what would have happened without protection by cost changes elsewhere in the economy, Krueger and Tuncer interpreted this to mean that protected infants' costs should fall faster than costs elsewhere. Using data on Turkish industry, they found that neither industry nor firm improvements in productivity bore any relationship to the amount of protection offered to an industry. Hence, they argued, the infant industry case is lost because one of the necessary conditions for its success is violated. This is slightly overstated because the analysis ignores external effects outside the protected industry and, of course, it refers to only one country, but it is certainly salutary.

Conclusion

We have seen that the infant industry case for protection rests on two tenets: first, that *through time* the social costs of production will fall, and, second, that some of the benefits of this are not appropriated by the private sector, either because they are external to the firm (industry) or because the private sector is unable to exploit the opportunities offered. Although the infant industry case is frequently citied to justify tariffs, we have seen that tariffs are not first best even under the postulated conditions. Tariffs can really only be justified on administrative or revenue-raising grounds. Furthermore, there are some reasons to doubt the empirical success of infant industry protection, although further research is necessary to be sure.

The senescent industry

Closely related to the infant industry case is an argument for protecting senescent (senile) industries. This is frequently advanced in the UK context (e.g. Trades Union Congress, 1983): British industry is old and has suffered years of neglect and mismanagement, runs the argument, but behind a temporary tariff wall it could re-equip and emerge lean and competitive. This argument is subject to all the caveats stated above plus the additional question of whether such an industry could actually be saved given that its initial comparative advantage has clearly been eroded. One should also ask what will be changed so dramatically that an industry, whose management and labour have let it decline so far already, could be regenerated. Only in very specific cases, e.g. of dramatically new technology or new lines of production, does success seem plausible.

More convincing is the argument that for social reasons, or to avoid the adjustment costs of contracting and then expanding industries when demand changes, threatened industries should be temporarily protected to allow an orderly contraction. The European textile industries provide good examples of this.

Declining for sixty years, the UK cotton industry has received both protection and adjustment assistance to encourage rationalisation, new processes, and so on. This has not saved the industry, except in a few specialist lines, but it has eased adjustment in Lancashire. The human costs of adjustment, however, hardly constitute a case for spreading adjustment over several generations and one must wonder whether in the long run such a policy has proved worthwhile.

9.3 THE 'INFANT COUNTRY' CASE

The 'infant country' case is merely the infant industry case on a large scale. Clearly one cannot protect every economic activity, because protection is merely relative (see p. 70 above), but one could protect broad sectors, such as industry. Some of the externalities listed in the previous section spread across all industry, and this suggests that widespread protection might cause a general take-off into industrial growth. In particular, it is argued, most countries have started their industrialisation behind protective barriers, and many have become quite advanced under such conditions (e.g. Germany and the USA). There have, however, been less successful efforts at protection (e.g. the Latin American economies), and highly successful countries operating with relatively free trade (e.g. the East Asian economies), so such casual evidence is far from conclusive.

*The desire
for
industrialisation*

Before asking how to industrialise, however, we should ask why. The following arguments have been advanced for the promotion of industrial activity. First, primary prices are much more variable than manufactures' prices; this is held to be detrimental to economic growth, although empirical work by MacBean (1966) and Lim (1976) tends to deny this. Second, over the long run, primary prices are falling relative to manufactures' prices, which is clearly to the detriment of non-industrial countries. This proposition bears some truth for non-oil primaries recently, but it is far from established that it is either necessarily true or quantitatively significant (see Spraos, 1980). Third, manufacturing offers more scope for improvements in productivity than does agriculture. For example, technology advances faster, economies of scale are more common and external benefits are greater. Fourth, marginal productivity in manufacturing exceeds that in agriculture – especially subsistence agriculture – and hence transferring labour into manufacturing will increase total output. Some economists, e.g. Lewis (1954), have argued that the marginal product of agricultural workers can be zero or negative. This seems rather exaggerated, but productivity is probably lower in agriculture than elsewhere. Fifth, employment in industry affects attitudes in matters such as punctuality, the precision of work, and so on, and this has general economic benefits. Sixth, in the very long run, the world as a whole will probably become more industrialised because, as per capita incomes grow, the demand for manufactures tends to grow faster than that for primaries. Thus industrialisation appears desirable in a dynamic sense.

Against all these arguments we should observe that, if every country switched into manufacturing, the relative price of manufactures would fall, negating the purpose of switching. Many economists feel that LDCs would do better to improve their agriculture rather than switch out of it. Others have observed that industry tends to accumulate in the towns and its growth is associated with high urban unemployment. People migrate to the towns hoping to obtain industrial jobs (which are relatively well paid), but are frustrated. This is harmful both socially and economically – at least if the marginal product of agricultural workers exceeds zero. To some extent it may be alleviated, however, by encouraging small-scale, 'intermediate technology' rural industry.

Overall there is probably some case for industrialisation by LDCs, although it is far from the universal panacea that is sometimes assumed. We therefore now consider how industrialisation may be encouraged, assuming that, without policy, the 'infant' problems identified above would preclude it.

Import substitution vs. export promotion

The policy of industrialisation behind protective barriers is known as import substitution (IS). Essentially the government seeks gradually to replace imported manufactures by indigenous output; this is contrasted with a policy of export promotion (EP), which seeks to boost manufactured exports. Either can be achieved by trade taxes (tariffs) or by production taxes, and we now know how the choice should be made. In the past, IS has been more popular, but much recent research has suggested that EP is better. They are, however, in no sense equivalent: one curtails international trade, while the other encourages it.

The factors that might encourage IS relative to EP are:

- *The terms of trade effects*: if the country is large in any of its markets, EP would worsen its terms of trade, whereas IS would improve them. This is just the optimum tariff argument and is logically separate from IS or EP: the country should impose the optimum tariff and then decide whether to pursue EP or IS *from there.*
- *Information*: EP requires knowledge of world markets, whereas for IS the government need look only at actual imports to gauge demand.
- *Certainty*: the major problem with EP is that if it is successful the importing countries tend to get resentful. For example, the huge export successes of the East Asian countries – e.g. Japan, Taiwan, Korea – have been met by increasing restrictions in the West. Even ignoring this, EP involves greater specialisation and hence greater risks if market conditions change.
- *Insulation*: if the rest of the world economy is unstable, EP is likely to involve greater domestic shocks than IS. It is also often felt that EP increases economic dependency, which can be harmful both politically and economically (e.g. in bargaining situations).

In favour of EP over IS are:

- *Comparative advantage*: EP allows one to exploit comparative advantage rather than frustrate it.
- *Specialisation*: exports are generally more concentrated than imports, so concentrating on them involves greater specialisation, which lowers costs via economies of scale and comparative advantage.
- *Transparency*: to the extent that EP requires subsidies, the costs are obvious and this probably leads to regular policy assessments. To the extent that IS relies on tariffs and quotas, its costs are largely hidden.
- *Administration*: EP is as often pursued by fixing a realistic exchange rate as by explicit subsidies. This is very cheap to administer compared with the quotas and production subsidies of IS.
- *Long-run structure*: if the belief is that eventually policy will not be necessary – i.e. that IS and EP are temporary phases – the ultimate shape of the economy must be considered. More often than not this will involve significant export industries, hence EP is moving in the right direction.

- *Flexibility*: although there is not yet much theoretical explanation for it, there is some evidence that more outward-oriented economies adjusted better to the oil price shocks of the mid-1970s. This is despite the fact that such economies suffered proportionately greater shocks by virtue of their being more open (Balassa, 1981).

Experiences with IS and EP

Over the 1950s and 1960s IS was tried extensively both in Latin America and in newly independent countries around the world. Studies of these episodes are in general rather discouraging. Partly this reflects poorly designed IS policies: the strength of protection rarely seemed to reflect the externalities stemming from industries, barriers tended to proliferate, bureaucracies grew, and new industries were discouraged (protection tending to go to existing ones). Partly, however, the problems of IS are inherent: industries are limited to small scale; exports fall as they are starved of resources; foreign exchange shortages emerge that curtail imports of essential raw materials and capital goods; and income is redistributed towards scarce factors – e.g. capital.

IS regimes tend to follow a fairly regular pattern. The early stages appear to be quite successful in reducing imports and foreign exchange outgoings as imported consumer goods are displaced. This is an 'easy' stage, for such goods are usually well suited to LDCs' productive abilities. Such growth, however, eventually runs out, because in most LDCs the consumer market is relatively small. Then follows a more difficult stage as intermediate and capital goods fall under the controls. This tends to generate bureaucracy, as the controls are fashioned to allow essential imports and exclude others. Increasingly the private sector has to devote resources to dealing with the bureaucrats and winning the right to import – the rent-seeking behaviour discussed in section 7.1. Thus ultimately IS is usually disappointing.

The alternative of EP appears generally more successful. For example, Krueger (1983a) examined twenty policy episodes, covering ten LDCs, since 1953. In the EP episodes, the average rate of GDP growth was $8\frac{1}{2}$ per cent, whereas in four moderate IS cases growth averaged $7\frac{3}{4}$ per cent and in ten full IS cases $4\frac{1}{4}$ per cent. Similarly the prodigious growth of countries such as Korea, Taiwan and Hong Kong testifies to the success of their export-oriented policies. Of course, GDP growth is not an end in itself, but such growth rates must ultimately boost consumption. We should note, however, that there may be an element of reverse causation in these figures: rapidly expanding economies may feel more able to dismantle protection than stagnant ones. Also they refer to EP only over a period of trade liberalisation; recent Western protectionism may dull its gloss. At present, however, the evidence seems to indicate that outward- rather than inward-looking industrialisation policies are to be preferred in the long run.

9.4 FULL EMPLOYMENT ARGUMENTS

The basic argument

Another common argument for tariffs is to boost employment. Generalising (incorrectly) from partial equilibrium analysis, people argue that, since tariffs increase the demand for domestic output, they will surely draw resources out of the pool of unemployed. This presupposes that the pool has the right skills and location, and even then tariffs are only second best.

At a subtler level, however, we should note that, in the simple first-best market economy normally assumed by trade theorists, unemployment is impossible. Some sort of market failure is necessary to generate it, and rigidities in prices and wages are the most usual candidates. If wages do not adjust to changes in the demand for labour, recession is met by laying off labour rather than by reducing its wage. (This is not necessarily irrational – see section 19.3.) This is essentially the Keynesian world, in which any increase in demand leads to increased output and income rather than to rising prices.

Let us assume we are in such a world, and that nothing can be done about money wages. Assume also that we have a fixed exchange rate. Any attempt to expand the domestic economy by monetary or fiscal means is likely to cause a balance of payments crisis by dragging in imports. To cure this, we require an expenditure-switching policy, to switch demand from foreign to domestic goods. (This is explained in detail in Chapter 19 below.) Compare two such policies: a devaluation of the exchange rate and a tariff. The former raises import prices at home and lowers export prices abroad, stimulating the demand for domestic goods in both markets; the latter only raises import prices at home, putting all the strain on that side of the market, and stimulating import-competing industries relative to export industries. This sacrifices the benefits of specialisation and may involve considerable welfare loss. (It has also been argued that tariffs are likely to entail retaliation by trading partners, thus further penalising export industries, whereas devaluations will not. This is not empirically well supported, however; competitive devaluations are not at all unknown.)

The assumption of the fixed exchange rate is necessary for tariffs to have much effect at all. Suppose the exchange rate were flexible and we imposed a tariff from a position of equilibrium. This would induce a tendency towards balance of payments surplus, which would be offset by an appreciation of the exchange rate. The net result would be virtually no change in the net demand for domestic output, and hence no employment benefit, but a continuing distortion towards import-competing industries.

Thus, any case for tariffs to stimulate employment rests on the need to permit domestic expansion without balance of payments crises and the rigidity of both money wages and the exchange rate.

Keynes and the tariff

An excellent exposition of this argument is Keynes (1931). Accepting the impossibility of devaluing sterling in the early 1930s, Keynes suggested a uniform tariff on imports and, if possible, an equal subsidy on exports. This, he argued, would be equivalent to a devaluation and could provide a screen behind which expansionary domestic policies could be pursued. Retaliation would not follow because the level of imports would not be reduced by the tariff; it was just that a given level of imports would be consistent with a higher level of national income. Indeed, he said, if partners were more liberal or expansionary, and hence bought more British exports, the British tariff would not be necessary at all! The second-best nature of the argument was fully recognised by Keynes, and when sterling was eventually devalued he immediately repudiated his protectionist stance.

Cambridge and the tariff

More recently, similar arguments have been advanced in the UK by the Cambridge Economic Policy Group (*Cambridge Economic Policy Review*, especially 1978). They advocate tariffs on imports of manufactures and semi-manufactures high enough to offset the increase in imports arising from a domestic expansion necessary to remove unemployment. This would involve tariffs of around 50–100 per cent. They argue that any distortions these tariffs would entail would be of secondary welfare significance relative to the increase in output that the extra employment would permit. They also dismiss as unimportant any consumer losses arising from having to consume British variants of goods rather than the foreign varieties that consumers manifestly prefer.

The novel part of their argument is to say that devaluation, even though possible today, will not work. Their reason is that devaluation raises import prices and, by thus cutting real wages and raising the cost of imported materials, stimulates domestic inflation to such an extent that the devaluation is offset and British goods end up relatively no cheaper. Tariffs, on the other hand, do not stimulate inflation: first, because although they raise import prices this can be offset by redistributing the tariff revenue to the workers and thus maintaining real wages; and, second, because provided only finished manufactures are taxed the prices of industrial materials do not rise. This, they say, will allow the domestic expansion to proceed and, by increasing output, actually raise wages. The different between devaluation and tariffs derives from two crucial assumptions: first, that real wages are rigid (and thus that labour bids up money wages to compensate for any real income loss due to inflation), and, second, that domestic prices are fixed as a constant mark-up over costs. The former means that devaluation is inflated away, while the latter prevents inflation in response to tariffs.

There are several strong objections to the Cambridge argument. First, wages are protected at the expense of profits, and one must fear for the future of investment. Second, there is no evidence that protection will not worsen Britain's productivity record by removing the pressure from manufacturers. Third, the loss of desired foreign varieties of goods represents a real income loss as surely as do rising prices. Hence wage pressure could occur under tariffs. Fourth, there is no evidence that, despite tariffs of over 50 per cent and huge rises in demand, domestic manufacturers will not raise their prices! The evidence adduced by CEPG themselves is quite inappropriate. Fifth, there is very little evidence that real wages would not be somewhat reduced by devaluation.

Liberalisation and employment

The fact that tariffs are not a good policy for ensuring long-run employment does not mean that, in the short run, tariffs should be abolished. The success of trade liberalisation depends on resources being able to move between industries according to comparative advantage, and this requires both mobility and wage flexibility. If these are missing in the short run, the resources released by the contraction of formerly protected industries will not all be re-absorbed elsewhere, and unemployment will result. There is therefore a reasonable case to be made for not exacerbating short-term cyclical unemployment by cutting tariffs or subsidies during a slump. This does not weaken the long-run case for freer trade, nor does it apply if the unemployment is long run or structural; it merely recognises that adjustment costs can be high and that choosing the 'right' time for adjustment can be beneficial. Adjustment should not be postponed forever on these grounds, however.

The balance of payments tariff

A corollary of the 'employment tariff' is the balance of payments tariff. The former is introduced to permit domestic expansion without balance of payments crises, whereas the latter is introduced during the crisis to avoid the need for domestic contraction or devaluation. It is subject to all the above objections, but, balance of payments crises are none the less accepted by the GATT as a legitimate reason for (temporary) protection. Among protective devices, however, the tariff is the best, because, unlike the full employment case, the objective here is clearly defined in terms of foreign trade rather than employment. Examples of crisis protection are the UK import surcharge of 15 per cent introduced in 1964 and the USA's 10 per cent surcharge introduced in August 1971. The USA additionally tried to use its tariff as a bargaining counter in the restructuring of the international monetary system, agreeing to remove it only if Europe and Japan agreed to revalue their currencies (see section 26.3).

FURTHER READING

The best overall reference on the arguments in this chapter is *Corden* (1974). The infant industry case is explored further by *Johnson* (1965a) and *Baldwin* (1969). The import substitution vs. export promotion debate has been extensively researched. *Krueger* (1983a) provides a recent short summary, while *Little, Scitovsky and Scott* (1970), *Bhagwati* (1978) and *Krueger* (1978) provide great detail. Empirical evidence may be found in *Diaz Alejandro* (1975). *Keynes* (1931) is well worth reading in the original. The CEPG position is best advocated in *Cambridge Economic Policy Review* (1978), to which *Hindley* (1983) provides an excellent counter.

10 Tariffs in the Real World

We have now encountered the main arguments for protection in general and for tariffs in particular. The only first-best case for tariffs is the optimum tariff or terms of trade argument, which was seen to be definitely anti-social. Among second-best arguments perhaps the most persuasive is the revenue argument – that, among protective policies, tariffs are the least distortionary in terms of their collection, and that this might outweigh any allocative disadvantages they have. The arguments for protection in general – and thus for tariffs if these fiscal considerations apply – include domestic distortions (including the infant industry case), employment objectives, industrialisation policy and anti-dumping policy. For most countries, the first is probably the most relevant.

Many economists feel that the case for protection rests on so many particular assumptions that the presumption of free trade is theoretically overwhelming. This is too simplistic, however. Although there is much that can go wrong with protective policies – such as inefficiencies and rent-seeking – economic distortions are so prevalent that there are many circumstances where protection would be beneficial. However, before protection can be confidently recommended the economist should be able to pinpoint precisely which distortions he is trying to counteract. It is not legitimate to jump from observing distortions in general to recommending protection in general.

In fact, tariffs are rarely, if ever, justified directly in terms of distortions, and the evidence suggests that neither are they determined by such criteria. Although governments may decide their general attitude towards protection on the basis of a broad economic philosophy, the details of protection under either relatively liberal or relatively protectionist regimes owe more to politics than to economics. This chapter starts by examining the determination of tariff structures in the real world.

10.1 TARIFF SETTING IN DEVELOPED COUNTRIES

Even if we accept all the second-best arguments for intervening in trade – those where intervention is beneficial but not optimal – there are far more tariffs and quotas in the world than our theory would lead us to expect. This means that some – possibly most – are economically harmful, at least by the criteria we have applied so far. This may, of course, be mere ignorance on the part of policy-makers: they may be either unable to observe the consequences of tariffs or unable to interpret their observations. More likely, however, is that protection is actually determined in ways other than to maximise national income in the way we have assumed.

Costs and benefits

Before examining the evidence on tariff structure we should perhaps emphasise two costs and benefits that have been largely ignored in our previous analysis of protection and national welfare. In practice they are probably the two most important influences on private perceptions of the case for protection.

Distribution
We implicitly ignored this by assuming that the benefits of trade or of optimal

111

protective policies could always be redistributed so that everybody benefited. In the usual situation of no redistribution, however, some people may lose when society gains and vice versa. For the interested parties, distributive factors frequently outweigh their share of any communal costs or benefits.

Adjustment costs

Most of our theory was of a comparative static nature – comparing equilibria with and without protection. It did not explore how the shift from one to another was made. If the *transition costs* of such a shift are high, it may not be worth making the change, even though doing so eventually yields higher welfare. This is particularly so if society has a strong preference for current over future consumption (a characteristic of poor people), because the transition costs are immediate whereas the benefits may be distant.

Policy-makers' goals

Commercial policy is determined not by popular vote but by politicians and officials. While these will have some regard for national economic welfare, they have, unlike our theory, other aims as well. Generally speaking, politicians wish to be re-elected, although a general and independent wish 'to do good' may also exist. Officials, on the other hand, obviously have to offer some support to their political masters, but beyond that they also appear to be sensitive to outside pressure in terms of lobbying, especially if it comes from the sector they are most concerned with. (Thus the Steel Section of the Department of Industry tends to reflect British Steel's views; the Department of Energy tends to support oil industry interests, and so on.) To explain tariffs, therefore, we have to see how they impinge on these various aims.

The need for re-election in a popular vote might suggest that tariff policy would be used to benefit the greatest possible number of voters – what Caves (1976) has called the 'adding-machine' approach. This would tend to promote free trade, which favours the myriad consumers over the few producers who might be protected under the alternative. Among protected industries it would appear to favour those with large labour forces (labour-intensive industries) and decentralised structures, so that the benefit is widespread over constituencies. In fact, this view is too simplistic, especially vis-à-vis consumers. To attract votes, the benefits conferred must be visible and large enough to outweigh other factors. While general protection policy may have large effects (e.g. Britain's cheap food policy in the late 1940s was popular), any particular tariff will have only a small effect on consumers because it covers only small proportions of their budgets. Thus piece-meal changes in tariffs may be the critical election issue for workers in the affected industries, but will rarely be so for the mass of consumers.

Lobbying

By presenting their case strongly and persistently, by acquiring publicity and by making political contributions, well-organised lobbies can bring great pressure to bear on both politicians and officials. This may be direct – for example, by force of argument or threatening to absorb disproportionate amounts of time – or indirect, by influencing public opinion. Thus, where lobbying is easy we would expect to find more successful bids for protection.

Lobbying is a public good in the technical sense that if, say, one steel producer 'buys' protection for steel, all other producers benefit from it, even though they have not contributed to the costs. Thus there is a 'free rider' problem: each producer is inclined to wait for others to do the lobbying. This is most easily overcome where there are few producers to coordinate, where there is already a producers' organisation providing other services, and where some sanction exists

112

against free riders. These conditions are most closely met by concentrated industries and least of all by consumers.

Lobbying is also apparently more successful if it aims to prevent declines in welfare – avert crises – than if it is designed to improve upon an already stable or acceptable position. It is also likely to be stronger the greater the hardship it seeks to avert. Hence we expect to find protection being introduced for ailing industries with immobile factors – especially labour, where immobility is associated with elderly, geographically concentrated and traditionally skilled work forces. It is also more likely in industries intensive in a country's scarce factors, which helps to explain why lobbying is usually for the protection of import-competing industries rather than for the promotion of export industries.

Finger (1981) argued that government institutions are set up in such a way as to make lobbying essential. Protection redistributes income from one section of society to another, a process sufficiently dangerous politically for administrations to be almost unable to undertake it frankly. Thus, Finger argued, commissions, boards of experts, courts of inquiry, etc., are established, ostensibly to collect information on the costs and benefits of protection but actually to obsfucate, cloud and slow down the whole process. Lobbyists can then become effective by influencing and manipulating this bureaucracy. Thus the decision-taking process is biased towards business, which has the resources for lobbying, while appearing to be apolitical, even-handed and objective; by this means redistributional choices can be made without serious political consequences.

Empirical evidence

An early example of empirical work on tariff formation was Caves (1976). He tested three models on Canadian nominal and effective protection in 1963: the adding-machine model, the interest group model (based on lobbying), and the 'national interest' model, which assumes that infant industry protection is offered to sectors where it is likely to be effective (i.e. those offering high wages, rapid growth and balanced development). He found no evidence for the first and only weak evidence for the third. The interest group theory performed fairly well, however, and explained about half of the variation of tariff rates between different industries.

A more recent exercise along similar lines is Ray (1981), although this included fewer explanatory variables. Ray found US tariffs by industry positively related to concentration (supporting the lobbying hypothesis), negatively related to skill intensity and positively related to labour intensity. The latter two suggest Stolper–Samuelson considerations, since the USA has abundant skills but relatively scarce simple labour. Ray also considered US non-tariff barriers: these appear to complement tariffs, but to be relatively more important in physical-capital-intensive industries producing homogeneous goods. (Possibly in such industries, tariffs alone are insufficiently protective because competitors are so much more efficient than the USA.) There is also some evidence that the USA's NTBs are used in retaliation for foreign NTBs.

Turning to protection in seven major US competitors, Ray again found skilled labour dis-protected. This probably reflects skilled labour's importance in export industries relative to import-competing industries, which might arise either from Heckscher–Ohlin considerations (assuming the countries covered are all skill-abundant), or from the role of skill in manufactured exports as outlined in the modern trade theories of Chapter 4.

An alternative approach to tariff formation is to look at voting patterns on protection issues. Baldwin (1976) found that congressmen tended to support protective measures the greater the proportion of import-competing industries in

113

their constituencies and the greater the contribution that the three major trades unions in favour of the measure had made to their campaign funds. The former suggests that import-competing industries tend to form a single protectionist lobby: industry X supports industry Y's protection, even though it harms factors in X, in return for Y's support for X's protection. The latter result emphasises the role of labour in calling for protection in the USA.

A final approach considers tariff negotiations. The Kennedy Round of the GATT negotiations produced universal tariff reductions among major trading nations except on particular, specified, goods. Cheh (1974) examined the exceptions made by the USA. Apart from the obvious strategic goods and those – mainly textiles – where GATT escape clauses were already operative, the exceptions appeared to be aimed at reducing short-term labour adjustment costs. This was manifest by efforts to maintain tariffs on industries that were (i) labour-intensive (especially in unskilled or older workers), (ii) geographically concentrated (which would reduce the chances of re-employing displaced workers), and/or (iii) slow growing or declining. Riedel (1977) repeated Cheh's exercise on West German data. He found similar results when he considered effective total protection (including NTBs) but not for nominal tariffs alone.

Conclusion Tariffs are apparently primarily determined by issues of distribution – at least in North America to which most of the research applies. The distributional interests of concentrated import-competing industries are best represented, while governments appear to be most concerned to avoid imposing (additional) adjustment costs on weak sections of the labour force – the old, the unskilled, and where alternative jobs are few. The high protection offered to textiles illustrates these points. Additionally, consumers' interests carry much less weight than industries'. For example, among primary and simple manufactured goods, consumer goods – especially agricultural ones – are highly protected, but industrial raw materials nearly all enter duty free. The discrepancy between the two groups' influence probably reflects their different abilities to organise effective lobbies.

10.2 TARIFF NEGOTIATION AND THE LDCs

LDCs and the GATT We briefly described the GATT in Chapter 6. We now consider in more detail the process by which trade liberalisation is negotiated under the GATT, and its impact on LDCs.

From 1948 to 1963, liberalisation proceeded by means of bilateral tariff reductions on particular items, subsequently extended to all other GATT members under the most favoured nation (MFN) clause. Such bilateralism proved necessary because, while governments may possibly have accepted the case for universal free trade, they certainly did not accept that for unilateral free trade. (This again illustrates the emphasis of industrial over consumer interests.) Thus, before reducing their tariffs – 'making a concession' – governments believed that they should receive a compensating reciprocal concession from their trading partners.

The main theoretical argument for demanding a reciprocal reduction is that it will improve the terms of trade, which implies that the partner (or partners together) constitute a large country whose tariff initially worsened the terms of trade. If the partner is small, the benefits of its liberalisation must be sought in terms of the extra exports generating infant industry and full employment effects. In practice, one suspects, just as governments tend to overemphasise the adjustment costs of contracting existing import-competing industries (see section 10.1), they also overemphasise the benefits of expanding existing export industries.

Such bilateral negotiations can lead to substantial biases in the pattern of trade liberalisation. For instance, when Britain seeks tariff reductions by her partners, she will aim to negotiate about an industry in which she believes she has a comparative advantage, in order that when the reduction is extended to competing exporters by the MFN clause she will be able to capture much of the newly opened market. She will also negotiate with other developed countries, because their markets, being larger, offer greater returns to liberalisation. These countries in turn will seek reciprocal concessions from Britain in areas of their comparative advantage. They will also offer concessions in Britain's area of comparative advantage in order that, of their extra imports, the greatest share possible comes from Britain, thus encouraging her to make greater reciprocal concessions. For example, Britain and France might find considerable mutual benefits in swapping tariff reductions on beer and claret – much of the French concession on beer would benefit Britain, while Britain's claret concession would benefit France. They would find little gain, however, from negotiating reductions on tea and coffee because all the extra trade would accrue to other producers.

Thus, under this old system, tariff reductions became heavily concentrated on goods of interest to the developed markets. The LDCs, having little to offer by way of markets, could gain no reductions in their areas of interest. This was exacerbated by the fact that, as we saw in Chapter 4, expanding intra-industry trade is probably less painful than expanding inter-industry trade, since it involves lower adjustment costs and less likelihood of any factor actually suffering from liberalisation. There was therefore an additional incentive towards freeing intra-OECD trade rather than OECD–LDC trade, since the former is mainly intra-industry and the latter inter-industry.[1]

By 1963, however, the 'easy' tariff reductions obtainable by bilateral means had been largely exhausted and a more sweeping approach was required. Thus, in the Kennedy and Tokyo Rounds, general formulas were negotiated subject only to specified exceptions. Unfortunately, this did not greatly improve the LDCs' position because they had insufficient power to affect either the formulas or the exceptions. As we have seen, the principal exceptions were agricultural goods, textiles, other manufactures already subject to GATT 'escape clauses' (i.e. where developed countries had already imposed restrictions) and goods intensive in unskilled labour (where the LDCs have a comparative advantage). Also, of course, neither Round made much progress on non-tariff barriers, which probably fall disproportionately on LDCs' manufactured exports.

The Theory

Disenchantment over the tariff negotiations and the alleged secular decline in the relative price of primary exports led to the formation of the United Nations Conference on Trade and Development (UNCTAD) in 1964. UNCTAD has functioned in parallel with the GATT and has witnessed many of the most bitter North–South arguments. One of its early apparent successes was the Generalised System of Preferences (GSP). The LDCs had always been treated preferentially under the GATT in that they were not required to reciprocate developed countries' tariff concessions. The GSP extended their preference by allowing the OECD ('donor') countries to reduce tariff levels on LDC manufactured exports below their MFN rates. The European countries and Japan introduced GSP schemes in 1971–2, and renewed and reformulated them in 1981. Canada and the USA introduced their schemes in 1974 and 1976 respectively.

115

The benefits of the GSP were seen primarily in terms of the infant industry/ country case: the additional demand for exports would stimulate economies of scale and externalities such that eventually world income would rise. Additionally, even if the quantities traded did not change (because donors' internal prices did not change), the existing LDC exporters would earn higher revenue, for they would receive themselves what was formerly paid in MFN tariffs. This was seen as an acceptable redistribution. There was some possibility of trade diversion (see section 11.1) whereby the donor's demand for imports was diverted from efficient OECD suppliers paying the full tariff to LDC suppliers whose real costs exceeded OECD's, but who could undercut the latter because they were paying only reduced tariffs. This would be a real cost to the world, but was expected to be relatively small and easily outweighed by the benefits from stimulating trade.

The Outcome

In fact, the GSP has been disappointing for a number of reasons. First, nearly all the included products are subject to quotas on preferential imports; beyond the quota, MFN tariffs are payable. Second, many goods are excluded entirely or subject to very restrictive quotas; these are the usual set of labour-intensive low-technology goods that LDCs can produce effectively – textiles, leather, clothing, and processed agricultural goods. Third, the GSP contains escape clauses, allowing concessions to be withdrawn if 'market disruption' occurs. All these factors discourage LDCs from investing in extra capacity in response to the GSP, because they make preferential treatment uncertain. Indeed, they make its removal certain if the LDCs are too successful!

The actual benefits rely, therefore, mainly on the revenue effects to existing exporters. However, LDC manufactured exports are relatively small and, more importantly, are concentrated among a few relatively advanced 'newly industrialising countries' (NICs), which could probably manage well enough without preferences. Furthermore, MFN tariffs are mostly low anyway, so preferences offer little revenue or competitive advantage, especially since the Tokyo Round. Finally, the EEC offers greater preferences to its 'associated states' than under the GSP (see section 12.1), so the little preference that exists is 'undercut' as well.

Murray (1977) quantified these factors starkly. In 1976, GSP 'donors' imported goods worth nearly $36b. from GSP beneficiaries: of these, 58 per cent faced zero MFN tariffs; 15 per cent were agricultural goods excluded from the GSP; 14 per cent were industrial goods excluded from the GSP to protect domestic producers; and just 13 per cent fell under the GSP! Furthermore, among the $3.6b. of industrialised imports that did receive concessions, 47 per cent came from four countries – Taiwan (15 per cent), Mexico (12 per cent), Yugoslavia (11 per cent) and South Korea (9 per cent).

Murray estimated that the net increase in trade due to the GSP was about $0.4b. (at 1970 prices) and that the scheme could have displaced up to 25,000 jobs in donor countries. This is clearly very small. MacBean and Snowden (1981), on the other hand, argued that the GSP had been more beneficial than these figures suggest, first because significant dynamic and external effects would eventually emerge in the major LDC beneficiaries, and second because the GSP encouraged LDCs to maintain outward- rather than inward-looking strategies. Appealing to the evidence presented in the last chapter, they argued that this represents a useful contribution.

The EEC's new GSP attempts to meet some of the criticisms voiced above. In particular, certain NICs receive little or no preference, and quotas on preferential imports are now country-specific. This gives poorer countries a chance to benefit and offers them some certainty over how much they will be able to sell. In addition, imports from the world's poorest nations are guaranteed duty-free access in any event.

FURTHER READING

Tariff determination is a new and booming research sector. *Lindert and Kindleberger* (1982) introduce the field, while *Baldwin* (1982) gives a fuller survey. The early articles – *Cheh* (1974) and *Caves* (1976) – are well worth reading, as is *Pincus* (1975) on the US 1824 Tariff Act. *Helleiner* (1977) shows how multinationals can influence tariff policy even in large countries like the USA. Further interesting references include *Brock and Magee* (1978) on lobbying and politicians, *Takacs* (1981) on the demand for protection, and *Finger, Hall and Nelson* (1982) on the political processes of winning protection.

The mechanics of bilateral tariff negotiation are discussed by *Johnson* (1965a, 1967a) and also by *Caves and Jones* (1981). The GSP is briefly discussed by *Morton and Tulloch* (1977) and *MacBean and Snowden* (1981). Greater detail is to be found in *Murray* (1977), *Weston* (1981) and United Nations Conference on Trade and Development, *General Report on the Implementation of the Generalized System of Preferences. Baldwin and Murray* (1977) and *Ahmed* (1978) present empirical estimates of the effects of the GSP.

NOTE

1   The LDCs did, to some extent, prejudge this question of what they could gain from the GATT, because they explicitly rejected the principle of reciprocity. None the less, it is unlikely that they would have fared much better even if they had sought full participation.

117

11 Customs Unions

International trade is still subject to many restrictions. In this chapter, therefore, we examine attempts by groups of countries to integrate their economies to a greater extent than ordinary trade permits, by arranging some sort of preferential trading system. Perhaps the most visible of such attempts is the European Economic Community (EEC) formed by ten West European states. This is described in the next chapter. The present chapter deals with the theory of international economic integration.

Degress of integration

International economic integration takes many forms. In order of increasing strength of preference and commitment the main types are:

Preference areas, whereby certain countries agree to levy reduced, or preferential, tariffs on their mutual trade. These are outlawed under the GATT except for those already in existence when the GATT was signed in 1947. Most prominent among the latter were Britain's Commonwealth Preference System, and similar arrangements between France and Belgium and their overseas possessions, which have been perpetuated by means of the EEC's Association Convention. The GSP (see Chapter 10) is also a form of non-reciprocal preference area.

Free trade areas, whereby partners abolish tariffs on mutual trade, but each partner determines its own tariff on extra-area trade. A potential problem here is that traders will try to import into the partner with the lowest external tariff and then re-export to the others tariff-free from there. To avoid this, complex rules of origin tend to govern intra-area trade to ensure that free trade refers only to partners' produce and not their imports. EFTA and LAFTA (respectively the European and Latin American Free Trade Associations) are examples.

Customs unions involve intra-union free trade but also a common external tariff.

Common markets are customs unions with additional provisions to encourage trade through the free mobility of factors of production and the harmonisation of trading standards and practices.

Economic union adds further harmonisation in the areas of general economic, legal and social policies, and the development of union-wide policies. This was the expressed goal of the EEC, although in many respects progress has ceased in the Common Market phase. Economic union may be supplemented by *monetary union*, which would greatly ease the process of coordination.

Political union is the ultimate form of economic integration. It involves the submersion of all separate national institutions. Even within this category, however, several degrees of integration exist. For example, in the USA the states have substantial powers of taxation, whereas in the UK local government has few such powers.

Despite the GATT's code of non-discrimination, it does permit free trade areas and fuller schemes of integration, provided that they (i) cover nearly all partners' mutual trade, (ii) have a definite timetable for the elimination of intra-area tariffs, and (iii) do not increase the average restrictiveness of the partners' external tariffs.

11.1 TRADE CREATION AND TRADE DIVERSION

In this section we examine the simple analytics of preferential tariff reductions. We assume that tariffs are abolished on imports from some subset of exporters

118

(the 'partners') but not on those from others; we examine both the positive and normative consequences of this situation.

Second best

Before 1950, economists tended to assume that, since free trade was preferable to restricted trade, partially free trade would also be preferable since it represented a step in the right direction. As we saw in Chapter 5, however, this is fallacious as a general rule: the general theory of second best states that, unless all the conditions necessary for optimality can be achieved, it may not be desirable to achieve just some of them. Hence, unless every country's exports to Britain enter free from restriction, it may not be desirable to allow exports from France to do so. This was first formally demonstrated for customs unions by Viner (1950).

Trade creation and trade diversion

Viner coined the phrases 'trade creation' and 'trade diversion' to cover the two *production* effects of a customs union. Consider country A's welfare when it forms a customs union with B; let C represent the rest of the world. Consider only a single good and assume that A, B and C can supply it at prices (opportunity costs) of £5, £4 and £3 respectively. That is, C is the cheapest source. Before union, both B and C face the same tariff; after union B faces no tariffs, but C, we shall assume, faces the same rate as before.

If the initial tariff were 100 per cent, A would undercut both B and C (with tariff-inclusive prices of £8 and £6 respectively) and hence supply its own market. Forming a customs union would lead to *trade creation*, because B's post-union price would fall to £4 and so it would capture A's market. Imports would replace home sales and A would gain because supplies would now be available from a lower-cost source than previously.

Alternatively, assume the tariff were only 50 per cent. Now the pre-union position would entail A's importing from C, for C's net price would be only £4.50. The post-union position, however, would be as before, with imports from B at price £4. This is *trade diversion* (existing imports are diverted to new partner sources) and it involves a social loss, because imports previously costing £3 (with the government collecting the remaining £1.50) are displaced by those costing £4.

A slightly more complex case is illustrated in Figure 11.1. Here A's domestic supply curve (*SS*) exhibits increasing costs, and we also introduce a demand curve (*DD*). We persist with partial equilibrium and with fixed prices for B and C, however. (Both these assumptions may be easily relaxed.) The case illustrated involves elements of both diversion and creation. The pre-union equilibrium involves imports from C, since $p_C (1 + t) < p_B (1 + t)$, domestic output h_t, and consumption q_t. The tariff revenue on the imports is given by area $c + e$. The post-union equilibrium has imports from B, since $p_B < p_C (1 + t)$, domestic output h_u and consumption q_u. Trade creation has occurred, in that imports have displaced home output by $(h_t - h_u)$, and trade diversion in that the imports have switched from C to B. There is also an increase in consumption as the internal (tariff-inclusive) price falls, which Viner did not take into account.

The welfare effects are easily calculated. Consumer surplus rises by $a + b + c + d$ as consumption expands from q_t to q_u. Of this, a is gained from producers, whose surplus falls with their output, and c is gained from the government, since the latter has lost its tariff revenue. Areas b and d are pure gain: d from the better allocation of consumption expenditures and b from the resources released as the (inefficient) domestic industry contracts. This represents the gain from trade creation. There is one further component, however: area e. This was initially part of tariff revenue (imports cost society only p_C) but, post-union, it is lost to B's producers. This represents the loss due to trade diversion. The net effect of the customs union is,

119

therefore, $b + d - e$, which may take either sign. Note, in particular, that even with no trade creation ($b = 0$) the customs union could still be beneficial if the consumption effects (d) outweighed the diversion effects (e). This result, contrary to Viner's view, is due to Lipsey (1960).

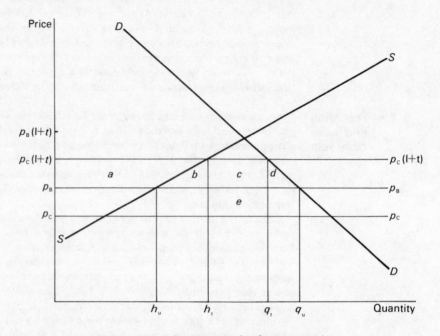

Figure 11.1   *A customs union for one country*

Desirable unions

It is possible to generalise these results somewhat to cover more complex cost conditions, general equilibrium and many goods, but the analysis is messy and the results increasingly ambiguous. Nevertheless, trade creation is generally found to be preferable to trade diversion, and on this basis economists have attempted to identify the conditions under which a given union is likely to be beneficial. A customs union will tend to be more beneficial:

- the larger the union, because then there is more chance of including the least-cost producer; in the limit, the world is the optimal customs union;
- the higher pre-union tariffs, because the pre-union position then involves greater production and consumption distortions;
- the lower post-union external tariffs, because this reduces the scope for diversion;
- the greater the overlap between partners' production bundles, because no overlap would entail no scope for trade creation on the production side; and
- given the degree of overlap, the greater the cost differences between partners, in order to increase the benefits of specialisation.

So far we have considered only the country granting the preferences. The benefits its partners receive may be in the terms of trade (see section 11.2), through infant industry or export promotion considerations, or from easing their balance of payments constraints (assuming that for some reason they cannot cure their

120

deficits any other way). For example, in Figure 11.1, area e was lost to country A but, to the extent that B's producers earned producers' surplus on their extra output, it would not be lost to the union as a whole. Thus, even if one member of a union loses, the union as a whole may gain. Indeed, as with so many trade policies, it is likely that the benefits will not be evenly spread, and that some redistribution will be necessary to persuade certain countries to partake. Newlyn (1965) argued that, among LDCs, distributional issues are the most important and that failure to solve them led, for example, to the demise of the East African Common Market. Even within the EEC, one cannot be unaware of the constant debate over distribution rather than over issues of efficiency.

Once we admit the possibility of costless redistribution between partners, however, we can elegantly prove that customs unions need never harm any country. Suppose the world is in full (tariff-ridden) equilibrium before union. After union, a particular common external tariff structure could be found that made the union's net trade with C precisely equal the sum of A's and B's pre-union net trade with C. This would leave C quite unaffected by the union. Now consider A and B. Their original consumption bundles would still be available, because their combined production possibilities and net trade with C would be unchanged. Hence, at worst the union need have no effect on them and in all probability production and consumption could be rearranged to make both A and B better off.

This argument (due to Kemp and Wan, 1976) is, of course, wholly unrealistic, but it does serve an analytic purpose. It shows that any harmful effects of customs unions stem from the absence of optimal policy and redistribution, features whose presence is frequently assumed in other areas of trade theory (e.g. the benefits of free trade, and the literature on domestic distortions). It also shows that, under the assumptions, it is possible to shift the world economy from tariff-ridden trade to free trade in a series of Pareto-improving customs unions, which lends some support to the pre-Vinerian view that customs unions are a step in the right direction.

The rest of the world

In our simple model, trade diversion reduced the rest of the world's sales in country A. This could have negative effects along infant industry or balance of payments lines, or by reducing specialisation. It could also worsen the terms of trade, if C's supply curve sloped upwards, because lower sales would then entail lower prices. Hence, despite Kemp and Wan's conclusion that it need not happen, a customs union will probably harm the rest of the world. It was partly in fear of such adverse effects from the formation of the EEC that the USA initiated the Kennedy Round of tariff negotiations in 1963, aiming to reduce the degree of members' preference by reducing MFN tariffs.

Occasionally, a customs union may generate 'external trade creation' whereby trade with the rest of the world is increased. This occurs if C's goods are complementary to goods whose internal consumption is increased by the union. There is some evidence that British and American exports of capital goods rose after the formation of the EEC in response to the investment boom that the latter produced in member countries.

11.2 THE MOTIVES FOR CUSTOMS UNIONS

The previous section asked the question 'if, starting from tariff-ridden trade, we were to form a particular customs union, what would be the effects?' This begs the question of why trade was tariff-ridden in the first place when we know that free trade is (Pareto) optimal. It compares customs unions with a non-optional starting point, rather than with the outcome of optimal economic policy.

This is illustrated by treating customs union formation as the result of two separate steps: first, the reduction of tariffs on all imports, to generate the post-union internal price (p_B in Figure 11.1) but with imports still coming from C; and, second, the subsequent switching of imports from C to B. The first step is unambiguously beneficial – generating all the trade creation we found above – while the second – whose sole effect is to give away customs revenue – is unambiguously harmful. Thus, the real question is why countries choose to implement both steps when just one would yield higher welfare: why prefer customs unions to unilateral trade liberalisation?

This is another aspect of the reciprocity question. Above we suggested that countries seek reciprocal tariff concessions instead of unilateral free trade for terms of trade reasons, infant industry and country reasons, domestic political reasons and, occasionally (and usually misguidedly) balance of payments reasons. The last tended to dominate Britain's consideration of entry to the EEC, but, especially given today's floating exchange rates, the first two are more interesting.

The terms of trade

If the partners in a customs union have some market power, the union may provide a means of exploiting this. Mundell (1964) explored the terms of trade consequences of A's preferential tariff reduction in favour of B. He examined the changes in the value of trade that would result if prices were constant, and then asked how prices would have to change to restore equilibrium. We would expect A's discrimination to raise the demand for B's goods and reduce that for the rest of the world's (C's). Hence, we would expect B's terms of trade to improve (B's prices rise) while C's worsen. A's terms of trade may go either way depending on whether it trades more heavily with B or C, and on the extent of the trade creation. Symmetrically, B's discrimination in favour of A will generally improve A's terms of trade and worsen C's. Combining these to consider mutual preferences between A and B – i.e. a customs union – we see that C's terms of trade will worsen, while those of A and B are indeterminate. However, the union as a whole experiences an improvement because the rest of the world suffers; thus at least one of A or B must gain, and it is always possible to arrange things so that both do.

It is the partner's discrimination that yields a country's welfare gains, and in general such discrimination is not in the partner's best interests. Thus the role of the customs union is the trading of discrimination, which, at the expense of the rest of the world, can benefit both partners relative to free trade. There are two attractions to achieving these terms of trade gains through customs union rather than by A and B individually imposing (non-discriminatory) optimum tariffs. First, the trade diversion deriving from the preferential tariff cuts improves the union's terms of trade by cutting trade with C. Second, to maximise A and B's joint welfare, each has to impose tariffs beyond the level that would maximise its own welfare given the tariff imposed by the other. Thus, without the strict institutional control of a customs union, neither country can be entirely confident that its partner would fully cooperate in restricting trade.

Infant industry considerations

If for some strategic or infant industry reason countries wish to have more industry than free trade would permit, a customs union can achieve this at a lower cost than can non-discriminatory tariff reductions. Thus, provided that the initial decision to sponsor industry was well founded, the customs union represents an improvement over free trade. The gains are analogous to those of opening trade in our simple models above – namely, increased specialisation and economies of scale.

122

Suppose A and B are concerned only about having industry in general, and not about the particular manufactured products that are produced. Before integration each may, for example, have sufficient protection to ensure that it has both a hat and a coat industry. The customs union permits the mutual penetration of partners' markets, and so, for example, after integration A could supply all the union's hats and B all its coats. This would be beneficial either if A had comparative advantage in hats and B in coats or if the industries had economies of scale such that concentrating production reduced costs regardless of location. It seems that much of this sort of readjustment followed from the formation of the EEC; specialisation took place at a very specific level of product design, and resulted in increased intra-industry rather than inter-industry trade.

Dynamic effects

In discussing Britain's entry to the EEC much was made of possibly 'dynamic' effects. These were essentially the infant industry benefits that we discussed above: larger markets would generate economies of scale, external benefits, reinvestment in modern plant, and so on. There was also talk about the benefits of the 'cold winds of competition' increasing efficiency – the X-efficiency argument of section 5.1 above. These benefits would probably have been available from an export-oriented non-discriminatory policy; but it is possible that, because of political factors, they could stem only from EEC markets. By joining the EEC, British exporters received a firm commitment of duty-free access to EEC markets, much firmer than could ever have been given (or believed) for markets where no political link existed. Thus the political dimension of the EEC increased exporters' confidence (certainty) and may consequently have led to stronger investment and external effects than free trade.

Political factors

Many commentators view customs unions as the first step towards political cooperation and unification between nations. Certainly the EEC was seen by some as a way of ensuring that France and Germany never had the means to fight each other again. Also, political arguments were prominent in Britain's desire to join the EEC: it was felt that she would have more influence as a leading member of a powerful bloc than as a medium-sized individual nation. Such objectives are perfectly legitimate and all that economists can do is to note that political aims sometimes have economic costs.

FURTHER READING

The best introduction to the theory and measurement of customs unions is *Robson* (1984), while *Robson* (1971) presents an interesting selection of essays.

Early theoretical developments are surveyed by *Lipsey* (1960) and more recently by *Krause* (1972) and *Lloyd* (1982), although the latter is rather hard work. The arguments for the formation of customs unions (the subject of section 11.2) were initiated by *Mundell* (1964), *Cooper and Massel* (1965a, b), *Johnson* (1965b) and *Corden* (1972a). *Wonnacott and Wonnacott* (1981) also contribute to this literature, showing how the rest of the world's tariffs and transport costs may encourage union formation.

12 The European Economic Community

To most readers of this book, the best-known example of international economic integration will be the European Economic Community (EEC). It would be inappropriate in a book such as this to devote much space to its institutional structure and detailed history, but we stop briefly to consider these matters.

Section 12.1 outlines the history of Western European integration and describes the EEC as presently constituted. Section 12.2 then deals with empirical attempts to assess the effects of such integration.

12.1 ECONOMIC INTEGRATION IN WESTERN EUROPE

Modern economic integration in Western Europe began in 1948 with the formation of Benelux – a customs union comprising Belgium and Luxembourg (which already had some links) and the Netherlands. This took several years to become fully operational because, although internal tariffs were abolished, NTBs persisted into the 1950s. The Netherlands in particular had to undertake substantial adjustment as it reduced the extent to which trade and internal economic activity were controlled. Nevertheless, the union became well established and the economies are now very highly integrated.

The European Coal and Steel Community

The European Coal and Steel Community (ECSC) represented the first major step towards the EEC. Its origins were as much political as economic, its purpose being to stimulate the recovery of heavy industries in (West) Germany while making it impossible for their output ever to be used to wage war again. The proposal – due to Jean Monnet and Robert Schuman – was that, by establishing a truly common European market in coal, iron and steel, countries would become so inter-dependent that war would be not only 'unthinkable, but materially impossible'. The customs union was to be supplemented by a 'High Authority', which had the power to dictate national output quotas, establish maximum and minimum prices, and enforce the laws of free competition (which outlawed subsidies, etc.). The High Authority was an administrative body, controlled in policy but not day-to-day matters by a Council of the Community on which the separate governments were represented, and also by a European Parliament. A Court of Justice was also established to oversee the legal aspects of the Community.

The ECSC was born in 1951 by the Treaty of Paris. The members were 'the Six' – Belgium, France, West Germany, Italy, Luxembourg and the Netherlands. The UK was invited to join but declined – ostensibly fearing to grant power over vital industries to a non-elected extra-parliamentary body like the High Authority. In fact, Britain resisted any measures of integration that contained elements of federalism, parliamentary or otherwise. The ECSC was a qualified success. The coordination of investment improved and tariffs were abolished, but frequently national NTBs were permitted, such as subsidies to Belgian coal producers.

The Treaty of Rome

Subsequent to the ECSC, attempts were made to establish further supra-national European organisations. A defence community (the EDC) and a political community (the EPC) were negotiated between 'the Six' but foundered mainly on

124

the rocks of French politics. Then in 1955 plans were made for the formation of a general common market or economic community (the EEC) and an atomic energy community (Euratom). These came to fruition in the Treaties of Rome in 1957, after a period of intense negotiation. Again, although taking part in the early negotiations, Britain remained aloof from the final agreements. At first, the EEC and Euratom existed separately but parallel to the ECSC, but in 1967 the three bodies were merged, with one Commission (successor to the High Authority – the 'European executive'), one Council, one Parliament and one Court.

The EEC provided a general common market among 'the Six'. The customs union covered trade in all goods; internal tariffs were reduced in stages so that by 1968 all intra-EEC trade was duty free. Eventually, it was hoped, legal and administrative harmonisation would allow the abolition of internal customs posts, but this has yet to occur. The common external tariff was set at the average of the rates in the partner countries. This involved tariff increases for West Germany and Benelux and decreases for France and Italy.

For most goods the EEC promoted competition and the free market, but for agriculture considerable intervention was envisaged. In all members, agriculture provided a substantial part of income and employment, and in all it was strongly protected. Among the initial administrative and political successes of the EEC was the establishment of a Common Agricultural Policy (CAP), which treated all community farms equally. As we saw above, this involves high and guaranteed domestic prices, variable import levies and considerable surpluses of certain goods; it is a costly and inefficient policy. Nevertheless, it was a political necessity – particularly so far as France was concerned – if the Community was to be established.

The Treaty of Rome envisaged common policies in many other areas too: for example, transport, fiscal structure, general macro-economic policy, competition policy, standards and measures and social policy. These have been achieved with varying degrees of success. For example, Commission rulings on aspects of competition are frequent and powerful, whereas virtually nothing has happened in the transport sector. It was also intended that both labour and capital should be freely mobile within the EEC, and this has now largely been achieved.

Britain and European integration

Britain did nothing to hinder integration among 'the Six', but she was shy of joining anything smacking of supra-nationality or federalism. She felt herself different from the other European countries, with stronger ties with America and the rest of the world and also with a much smaller and more efficient agricultural sector. (Recall that Britain supported farmers by deficiency payments – essentially income supplements – which kept food prices low and avoided surpluses, unlike 'the Six's' tariff-based policies.) Hence, although Britain favoured intra-European free trade, she resisted the administrative and political structures of the EEC. The Scandinavian countries held similar suspicions, while the Swiss constitution explicitly forbade any international political associations. Thus, these countries excluded themselves from the EEC and, fearful that they would suffer as the EEC stimulated 'the Six's' economic growth, formed a looser association in 1960 – the European Free Trade Association (EFTA). The members were Austria, Denmark, Norway, Portugal, Sweden, Switzerland and the UK, of which the last was entirely dominant.

EFTA provided for mutual free trade in manufactured goods and some primaries between members. It made no effort to establish common external tariffs, however, or to coordinate any other aspect of economic life. The absence of a common external tariff meant that elaborate rules of origin were necessary to

125

prevent non-EFTA goods from entering via the lowest tariff country and then moving freely from there. This required a secretariat, but beyond that EFTA had no administrative structure.

Very soon after EFTA was initiated, the UK changed her mind and sought full membership of the EEC. She sought many concessions from the Treaty of Rome, however, especially over agricultural protection and the rights to continue some form of Commonwealth Preference; consequently in 1962 negotiations closed without reaching a conclusion. A further, and less combative, application was made in 1967, but this too failed, largely because of French fears of the political consequences of expanding the Community. Finally in late 1968 the issue was revived again, and agreement was reached in 1971 for accessions on 1 January 1973. Ireland, Denmark and Norway reached similar agreements, although at the last moment Norway withdrew her application after she had voted to stay out in a referendum.

The terms reached for British accession were very complex, but broadly speaking they were not very favourable to the new member. The CAP was hardly changed at all, and Britain assumed a substantial part of its financing costs – she was expected to provide about 19 per cent of the EEC's total budget. The provisions for Commonwealth sugar and New Zealand dairy products and meat were not generous to the suppliers, although long transitional periods were allowed to permit them to diversify away from the British market. The transitional period for industrial tariffs and the agricultural system was set at five years. A number of problems, such as the role of sterling, were left entirely undecided.

The Labour Party (in opposition in 1971) argued that these terms were not acceptable and promised to re-negotiate them and put the result to the people in a referendum. Re-negotiation during 1974 led to some improvements – Britain's long-run budget share was reduced and the rate of increase of agricultural prices slowed – and on the (Labour) government's recommendation the new terms were accepted in the referendum of 1976. Political opposition to membership still smoulders on, however, with the Labour Party fighting (and losing) the 1983 general election on a secessionist ticket. The issues dominating the negotiations also still persist. Every year sees an argument over agricultural prices between Britain (with some West German support) favouring lower prices and the rest favouring higher prices, at least for their surplus products. Similarly, frequent attempts to reform – or at least to reconsider – the CAP fail in the face of French, Irish and Danish opposition; and the allocation of fishery rights brought gunboats into the North Sea in 1983. Recent years have also produced acrimonious debates as Britain seeks to draw back some of her 'excessive' budget contributions. Overall, the political development of the Community has been slow and fitful.

The Community today

The EEC currently comprises ten European states: 'the Six' (Belgium, France, West Germany, Italy, Luxembourg and the Netherlands), Britain, Denmark and Ireland – who acceded in 1973 – and Greece – who acceded in 1980. Spain and Portugal are pursuing full membership. Free-trade agreements for manufactures exist with Austria, Finland, Iceland, Norway, Portugal, Sweden and Switzerland – the rump of EFTA. Thus the EEC offers its members a large and affluent market, unimpeded by tariffs. In 1979, the nine full members plus Greece accounted for about 29 per cent of market economies' total GDP – $2,406b. compared with the USA's $2,377b. and Japan's $1,000b. – while GDP per head was $9,060 compared with $10,777 and $8,627 respectively. Of members' total international trade, around half is conducted with other members – rather more for the smaller continental countries and rather less for Britain. If we include such intra-EEC trade as 'foreign trade' the EEC accounts for 29 per cent of world trade (USA $11\frac{1}{2}$ per cent), whereas if we treat it as internal trade the EEC's world share is $17\frac{1}{2}$ per cent (USA's $13\frac{1}{2}$ per cent). Europe's greater dependence on external trade might suggest that European integration does not yet rival American integration, which has, after all, been under way for 200 years.

Although the countries of the EEC form a single large bloc, they are not entirely alike. Incomes vary from $4,647 per capita for Greece to $10,254 for Luxembourg and $9,590 for West Germany (1981, at purchasing power parities). The sources of income also vary. For example, Ireland derives 13 per cent of GDP from agriculture, followed by Italy (6.3 per cent), Denmark (5.9 per cent) and France (4.3 per cent), whereas West Germany and the UK derive only 2.1 per cent and 1.9 per cent respectively from that source.

Related to per capita incomes and agricultural shares are the costs and benefits of the Community budget. Almost 75 per cent of expenditure is devoted to agriculture (70 per cent on supporting prices), while a substantial portion of income comes from the levies on agricultural imports. Thus, countries with large agricultural sectors tend to benefit relative to those with smaller output and greater imports. Social and regional policies, which are oriented more towards ailing industrial areas, each account for only $4\frac{1}{2}$ per cent of the budget. Thus, in 1979 Britain contributed 21.1 per cent of the budget compared with receipts of just 12.6 per cent. Only West Germany showed a similar deficit (29.5 per cent compared with 21.4 per cent); other countries were net gainers. Britain has consistently pleaded the injustice of this situation as she is one of the poorer members (sixth in the list by per capital income, with income 91 per cent of the average), and consequently since 1979 she has received a rebate, bringing her contribution down to around 17.5 per cent. No long-term solution to this problem has yet emerged, however.

The associated states

The EEC has special relations with two other broad groups of countries. First, the African, Carribean and Pacific (ACP) States: these forty-seven developing countries receive tariff-free access to EEC markets for nearly all their exports, as well as significant aid flows and an export earnings guarantee scheme that guarantees concessionary loans from the EEC if export earnings decline seriously. In return, they offer EEC members certain concessions in their own markets, but stop short of tariff-free access.

The association is governed by the Lomé Convention of 1975. Its origins lay in France's insistence that her overseas territories be included within the EEC structure, since they were formally considered as part of France herself. Full membership was not appropriate, so associateship was developed, which had the added attraction to the French that other members bore some of the costs of aid and support. Certain other countries were brought into the association – defined at first by the Youndé Convention – including former possessions of other members.

When Britain acceded she wished her developing partners in the Common-wealth and Empire to be granted association. This was allowed except for the Asian states, which, the French argued, were qualitatively different from existing associates. Although separate, but less favourable, agreements have been negotiated with most of the excluded states, in general British accession required a considerable reorientation of their trade. Winters (1984b) has shown, for example, that India and Sri Lanka's share of Britain's tea imports fell from 57 per cent to 35 per cent between 1971 and 1979.

The second type of association is with certain Mediterranean countries. These

127

associates receive tariff-free access for industrial goods and certain concessions, subject to quota, on agricultural goods; in return they have to grant almost full reciprocity. They also receive some aid flows and technical cooperation.

The Commission comprises fourteen commissioners appointed by member states for four-year terms: two from each of the larger members and one from the others. It initiates Community policy and executes it, but it cannot actually make policy – that falls to the *Council*. The Commission is explicitly supra-national, and represents the EEC as a body in world negotiations, such as at the GATT.

The Council formally comprises the heads of government from all member states, although most business is, of course, conducted by deputies – either the ministers concerned with specific issues (e.g. agriculture ministers discuss the CAP, and finance ministers the budget), or, for day-to-day matters, permanent officials. The Council shares executive power with the Commission. It may adopt the latter's policy proposals, in which case they become law, but it may not generally amend them. Decisions are theoretically taken by majority vote, but a country's right of veto on important issues of national interest is recognised. In practice, most decisions are reached by trading compromises on (often unrelated) issues to obtain a unanimously acceptable package.

The Court of Justice interprets Community law. Its findings are binding even on member governments. The judges are appointed by member states, but they are required to be quite independent of national interests and cannot be removed by member governments.

The European Parliament has a small but growing role in the Community. It must be consulted by the Commission and the Council before they decide many issues, and it has some power over the Community budget. Its greatest power is to dismiss the Commission *en masse*, although this is such an unwieldy weapon that it is of little practical use.

12.2 THE EVIDENCE ON CUSTOMS UNIONS

Considerable effort has been devoted to estimating the effects of international economic integration both *ex ante* (before the event) and *ex post* (afterwards). Some studies have concentrated merely on trade flows, while others have made welfare comparisons. This section samples the literature on European integration – especially Britain's position – starting with simple trade effects.

To measure the effect of integration on international trade flows we need estimates of trade both with and without integration. In the simplest case – an *ex post* study – the former is directly observable, but trade under identical conditions except for integration has to be hypothesised. This hypothesis has come to be known as the *anti-monde*, and its construction is clearly the critical task in assessing integration effects. Economists generally assume that, in the absence of integration, trade patterns between partners would either have followed pre-integration trends (a time-series approach) or have been determined by the same factors as determine trade between non-partners (a cross-section approach). The former presupposes constancy of behaviour through time, but not across countries, whereas the latter assumes the opposite.

Table 12.1 presents some impression of the potency of integration in Europe. Intra-bloc trade – i.e. trade between members – grew substantially as a share of total trade in the early years of the EEC and EFTA, and after the realignment of

128

1973 the new EEC members switched away from their former EFTA partners
towards their new EEC partners. (The EEC–EFTA trade share fell between 1973
and 1975, but this is not reported in the table.)

Table 12.1   Intra-block trade in Europe, 1960–81

	Intra-bloc exports as percentage of total exports			
	1960	1970	1975	1981
'The Six'	34.6	48.9	—	—
'The Nine'[a]	—	—	49.4	51.5
EFTA	15.7	21.8	—	—
'Residual EFTA'[bd]	—	—	16.1	12.2
'The Nine' and 'residual EFTA'[cd]	—	—	12.9	12.6

Notes:
[a] Excludes Greece.
[b] EFTA less countries acceding to the EEC in 1973.
[c] Inter-bloc trade covered by free-trade agreement.
[d] Manufactures only.
Source: United Nations Conference on Trade and Development, *Handbook of
International Trade and Development Statistics* (1983).

Of the many studies of European integration in the 1960s we shall consider just
two. Truman (1975) examined nineteen goods in ten European markets. For each
he looked at the shares of partner countries, of non-partner countries and of
domestic suppliers in total absorption of the good. He compared observed shares
under integration with *anti-monde* shares evolving along their pre-integration
trends, interpreting differences as in column 3 of Table 12.2.

Table 12.2   Trade creation and diversion in Europe

			Estimates ($b.) 1968	
Share	Movement	Interpretation	EEC	EFTA
Domestic share	lower	trade creation	7.2	0.9
	higher	trade erosion[a]	0.4	0.8
Partner share	higher	trade creation plus diversion	8.2	1.2
Non-partner share	lower	trade diversion	1.0	0.3
	higher	external trade creation	2.4	3.0

Note:
[a] Trade erosion occurs where domestic producers increased their share of the
market at the expense of either partners or non-partners. It could arise from
changes in X-efficiency or economies of scale, and was first identified by Corden
(1972a).
Source: Truman (1975), Table 1.4.

Over half his cases exhibit internal and external trade creation, and in half the
cases where non-partners suffer it is partly as a result of rising domestic shares.
This might reflect integration-induced economies of scale or, for the EEC, that the
common external tariff exceeded the pre-integration national tariff. The
magnitudes of the effects are also shown in Table 12.2. Total trade creation
amounts to 8.6 per cent of the change in demand between the pre- and post-

integration years – a relatively modest amount. Obviously, the welfare effects will fall short of the gross trade effects, but some gains are likely given the excess of creation over diversion.

A second study of European integration is Aitken (1973). Aitken considered only the origin of imports and so could not separate creation and diversion. He explained trade flows between European countries in terms of their GNPs, populations and locations. Prior to integration, all countries' trade flows appear to derive from the same explanation, whereas after integration intra-EEC and intra-EFTA trade became relatively more important than trade between unrelated countries. He suggested that in 1967 integration increased intra-EEC trade by $9–11b. and intra-EFTA trade by between $1.3–2.4b. Exports from EFTA to EEC fell by about $0.6b. and those from EEC to EFTA by $0.2b. The latter figures represent only part of the diversion induced by integration, of course, since they cover only a subset of non-partner countries.

In a similar study, Aitken and Obutelewicz (1976) examined the impact that association has had on trade between the EEC and the original associated states. The results are startling, suggesting that up to 95 per cent of the relevant trade flows can be explained by the institutional links! This is probably over-estimated, but it cannot be denied that association has significant effects.

UK accession to the EEC

UK accession to the EEC was the subject of many *ex ante* studies during the 1960s. Methodologies varied greatly, as did the results, but the basic conclusion was that in *static* terms accession would impose a small cost on the economy, worsening both the balance of payments and economic welfare. The losses were predicted to arise primarily from food imports and budget transfers. The effects on net manufactured trade (exports minus imports) were expected to be small, but several economists expected significant increases in both exports and imports.

Much more contentious were estimates of the dynamic effects of entry. Dynamic benefits were forecast to arise from greater specialisation (and hence economies of scale); re-equipping with modern plant to exploit new markets; inflows of foreign investment from EEC partners and from US firms using Britain as a platform for serving Europe; and gains in efficiency induced by the 'cold winds of competition'. Professor Nicholas Kaldor, on the other hand, predicted dynamic losses as weak British industries collapsed under fierce European competition.

Table 12.3 Shares in the UK visible trade (percentages)

	EEC 'The Six'	EFTA and Irish Republic	Other developed countries	Developing countries
Exports:				
1962	19.8	15.7	34.4[a]	30.1
1970–2	21.8	18.6	32.8	26.8
1979–81	34.0	17.9	22.5	25.6
Imports:				
1962	15.8	13.4	36.0[a]	34.8
1970–2	22.3	18.8	32.3	26.6
1979–81	36.6	17.1	25.4	20.9

Note:
[a]Estimate.
Source: Department of Trade and Industry (1983).

Despite ten years' experience, these predictions have not yet been properly tested – not least because none of them allowed for the economic turmoil of the 1970s. Thus, disentangling integration effects from those of the oil price rise, high inflation and floating exchange rates has proved very complex.

Some simple figures are reported in Table 12.3. They show how, over the 1960s, Britain's international trade – both exports and imports – was slowly gravitating towards EEC countries – not least because they were among the most dynamic in the developed world. A stronger shift towards EFTA is also evident, doubtless stimulated by the free-trade arrangements. After accession to the EEC, however, a dramatic realignment is evident. Britain's trade with 'the Six' increased its share at the expense of both 'other developed countries' and her former partners in EFTA. On the export side, this corresponded to an increase in Britain's share of EEC imports, reversing many years of decline and despite continuing decline in Britain's share of other markets (see Winters, 1983b; 1984b). Mere trade shares do not prove causation, but it is difficult to avoid the conclusion that integration has had a substantial effect.

There are also a few formal *ex post* studies of Britain's accession. For example, Bacon, Godley and McFarquhar (1978) estimated that in 1977 British food imports cost £300m. more than they need have done, while Bale and Lutz (1981) suggested welfare losses of around £50m. stemming from CAP protection in just five commodities in 1976. Winters (1984a) presented estimates for UK manufactured imports: by 1979, he suggested, trade creation could have been as great as £12b. (£10b. internal and £2b. external), and certainly exceeded £6b. Total sales of manufacturing were around £104b. in 1979, which represents a significant shift from UK to EEC sources of supply. Unfortunately, it is not clear that the full benefits of trade creation that we identified above have yet been felt, because it is not obvious that the resources displaced by EEC imports have yet been fully utilised elsewhere. For other elements of trade, Winters (1983b, 1984b) identified considerable reorientation of agricultural trade (including substantial trade erosion as domestic output grows) and some expansion of manufactured exports – by about £3b. in 1978. The latter suggests that accession has worsened the UK's trade balance in manufactures – and probably by rather more than most commentators predicted.

FURTHER READING

The best single introduction to the European Economic Community is *Swann* (1978). Brief introductions to empirical work are given by *Mayes* (1978), *Robson* (1984) and *Winters* (1984b). The references in the text might be supplemented by *Williamson and Bottrill* (1969) and *Balassa* (1975) for estimates concerning 'the Six' and EFTA, and by *Miller* (1971), *National Institute* (1971), *Williamson* (1971) and *Miller and Spencer* (1977) on predictions of the UK's accession (the last with an elegant general equilibrium welfare model). *Fukuda* (1973) is interesting on the effects of the UK's access on the third world.

13 Factor Prices and Factor Mobility

So far, all our theory has assumed that goods are perfectly mobile between countries but that factors of production, although mobile between industries, are perfectly immobile between countries. The slightest acquaintance with reality suggests that this is too extreme, if not totally incorrect, and so this chapter considers the incentives for and consequences of factor mobility. Chapter 15 below also treats this issue but in the specific context of multi-national companies. Both this and the next chapter – on economic growth – build on the positive analysis of the Heckscher–Ohlin model in Chapter 3. A brief review of that chapter would provide a useful introduction.

13.1 FACTOR MOBILITY AND WORLD WELFARE

We saw above (Chapters 3 and 5) that, if the value of world output is to be maximised, each factor of production must be distributed among industries and countries such that its marginal social product is identical in all uses. If this were not the case, output could be raised by shifting factors from low to high marginal product activities. Thus international factor mobility is required to maximise world output if, without it, marginal products would differ between countries. If, on the other hand, marginal products were equalised across the world, no such mobility would be necessary.

Let us take the argument one step further. If we assume perfect competition, full information, costless adjustment and no externalities or economies of scale, factors' rewards (prices) will equal their marginal social products (see Chapter 5). Under these circumstances, differing factor prices across countries will signal the need for factor mobility, and, equally important, any international migration that equalised factor prices would maximise world output. In general, migration will tend to equalise rewards: as, say, labour leaves low-wage areas for high-wage areas the supply of labour falls in the former, raising wages, and rises in the latter, reducing them. Thus, just as international trade, which shifts goods from areas of low prices to areas of high prices, is beneficial, so too is international migration, which shifts factors from areas of low rewards to areas of high rewards.

Of course, in comparing factor rewards over countries, care must be taken to compare like with like. Differences between average wages in, say, Britain and Burundi would not prescribe mobility if they arose from Britons' greater skills or compensated for the non-pecuniary disadvantages of living in an industrial country. They would, however, indicate gains to mobility if they stemmed from the greater amounts of physical capital or better technology available to *any* worker, either Briton or Burundian, working in Britain.

13.2 THE FACTOR PRICE EQUALISATION THEOREM

We have seen that if factor prices are equalised across countries there is no need for, nor any incentive for, international factor mobility. It is pertinent to ask, therefore, whether international trade alone could generate such an outcome.

132

Recalling Chapters 2 and 3, it seems unlikely within the Ricardian framework, which treats wages exogenously, but possible within the Heckscher–Ohlin model, at least with sufficient assumptions. Indeed this question has been a central theme of the development of the latter model. Heckscher argued informally that trade would equalise factor prices, but under very restrictive technology assumptions, while Ohlin argued only that it would tend to do so. The first systematic treatment was due to Samuelson (1948, 1949) and, although we examined his analysis in Chapter 3, we shall recapitulate it here.

The Samuelson theorem

Samuelson showed that, under a set of fairly strict assumptions, free trade would equalise factor prices. The assumptions are broadly those that were made in Chapter 3 to derive the Heckscher–Ohlin theorem of trade, and we start by rehearsing them:

(i) Consumption patterns are homothethic and identical between countries.
(ii) Technology is identical across countries.
(iii) Production functions display constant returns to scale and diminishing marginal returns to each factor.
(iv) There are no factor-intensity reversals.
(v) Perfect competition rules in all markets.
(vi) There are no impediments to trade.
(vii) There are just two goods, two factors and two countries. Goods and factors are identical over countries.

In order to ensure factor price equalisation (FPE), we do not need assumption (i), but we must add

(viii) Incomplete specialisation.

Using these assumptions, we show first that FPE is consistent with international equilibrium, which requires equal goods prices in the two countries – from assumption (vi) – and thus equal costs of production. Assumption (v) ensures prices equal costs, while assumption (viii) ensures that both goods are produced at finite cost in both countries. If factor prices are identical, so too will be techniques of production, because technique depends only on the factor price ratio – assumptions (ii)–(v). Thus, with equal factor prices and identical techniques, costs of production will be equalised, and the proposition is established.

We now show that international equilibrium cannot exist without FPE. Starting from the equilibrium just defined, let us slightly increase wages in country A. This will raise the costs of the labour-intensive product more than the other, and thus increase A's relative price of the former. But with B's prices unchanged this would not be consistent with international equilibrium. This argument generalises to other factor price differences between countries, and so we have established that factor price equalisation is necessary for full equilibrium.

We can give more flesh to this argument using Samuelson's own geometric analysis. Figure 13.1(A) shows the relationships between relative factor rewards (wages and rentals), factor intensities and relative goods prices. The lower quadrant shows for each good the optimum capital/labour ratio (k) for any given factor price ratio. Assumptions (iii) and (v) ensure that each factor price ratio is associated with a unique factor input ratio in each industry: assumption (v) ensures that factors are paid their marginal products, while, in assumption (iii), constant returns to scale ensure that the size of the industry does not affect input proportions, and diminishing marginal returns ensure that, as the input of one factor rises, its marginal product (and reward) falls while that of the other factor rises. Thus each input ratio is associated with a unique ratio of marginal products and thus of factor rewards. Assumption (ii) means that these relationships hold in both countries. As drawn, good X is the more capital-intensive at each factor price ratio – satisfying assumption (iv).

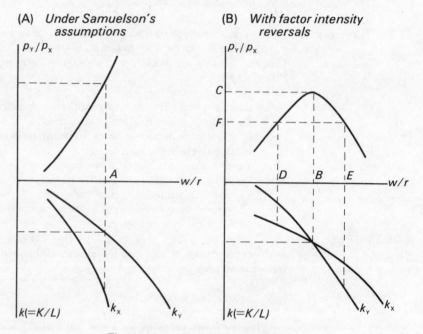

Figure 13.1 *Factor price equalisation*

The upper quadrant plots relative goods prices. At factor prices A, techniques of production are determined in the lower quadrant, and thus relative goods prices may be determined. Now suppose wages were slightly higher than at A. Industry Y, employing relatively more labour, will suffer more than industry X and thus the price ratio p_Y/p_X will increase as shown. Similar arguments plot out the whole of the function between relative good and factor prices, and hence, as we saw in Chapter 3, the relationship is monotonic and single-valued.[1] Thus common prices under international trade entail common factor prices.

Specialisation and factor-intensity reversals

Figure 13.1 also illustrates how factor-intensity reversals can upset factor price equalisation. In part (B), Y is labour-intensive at low wage–rental ratios but capital-intensive at high ratios. (Y shows greater substitution between factors than X.) At factor price ratio B, factor intensities are identical between industries and the goods price ratio is given by C. Now consider a lower factor price ratio (D). Industry Y uses relatively more of the cheaper factor than X and thus must have a relatively lower price than at C. Similarly, however, at a higher factor price ratio (E): Y also uses more of the relatively cheaper factor and thus has a lower price here as well. Hence, with factor-intensity reversals, a given goods price ratio (F) may be consistent with two different factor price ratios. Thus FPE is not assured, although neither is it ruled out.

The assumption of non-specialisation also plays a crucial role in the FPE argument. In Chapter 3 we saw how two goods' prices (costs of production) are required to determine two factor prices uniquely, and we can see it here also. Suppose country A specialised in commodity X; industry X would be required to employ A's total endowment of labour and capital: its factor intensity would be fixed exogenously by A's endowments. Given our technology assumptions, however, a given factor intensity is uniquely linked to a particular factor price ratio, and so A's factor price ratio would be determined also. Now suppose the price of X rose relatively. Country B may respond as in our analysis above, with rewards to X's intensive factor rising, but A cannot do so. It earns more for its export good, to be sure, but its factor price *ratio* cannot change, because industry X still uses exactly the same combination of factors as before. Obviously, whether or not specialisation actually occurs is determined by endowments and demand throughout the world, but, without it FPE is no longer assured.

It may seem strange that, in discussing factor prices, factor supplies (endowments) have been hardly mentioned. They enter indirectly, however, because, through their influence on the countries' transformation frontiers, they determine both the world prices of goods and each country's degree of specialisation. The only circumstance where endowments do not matter is for a non-specialised small country: with fixed world prices, the country's factor price ratio is entirely insensitive to endowment changes, unless the latter are so great as to induce specialisation.

Generalisations

Factor price equalisation is one of the hallmarks of the Heckscher–Ohlin model and has thus been one of the first issues to be investigated in any attempted generalisation. One such is the specific factors model – whereby each good uses a specific factor in addition to any mobile factors. FPE is unlikely in this case because the number of factors exceeds the number of goods, so the latter's prices will generally be insufficient to determine the former's.

We can illustrate this by considering a small country again. Previously, endowments did not affect the country's factor prices (given non-specialisation), so differently endowed countries would have equal prices. Now, however, endowments do matter, because X-capital cannot shift to industry Y and vice versa. Thus if the supply of X-capital is raised it must all be used in X-production. If labour does not shift from Y to X, this alters factor proportions in X and thus marginal productivities and factor rewards in X production. If, on the other hand, labour does shift, factor proportions in Y are disturbed with consequent changes in rewards there. Thus, with factor prices sensitive to endowments, equalisation over different countries is unlikely. Interestingly, however, it may be shown that, if the factor used by both industries is internationally mobile, FPE does result, even if the other factors are immobile.

Multi-dimensional factor price equalisation theorems also exist. With more factors than goods (as in the previous paragraph), equalisation is unlikely. With equal numbers, or more goods than factors, FPE must occur except when specialisation intervenes, and even then it is possible. With more goods than factors there would seem to be a greater chance of some goods not being produced in some countries – see Jones' model (p. 34), where each country produces only two out of many goods – but Dixit and Norman (1980) show that, in general, increasing the number of goods neither necessarily increases nor necessarily decreases the chances of *FPE*.

135

The assumptions necessary to prove the inevitability of factor price equalisation are very strict. Indeed, many economists treat Samuelson's work as showing the practical impossibility of FPE, but since his assumptions are sufficient rather than necessary for the result this is a misinterpretation. Nevertheless, that factor prices are not equalised around the world is entirely obvious, and this section briefly summarises some possible reasons for this.

We have already seen how *complete specialisation* and *factor-intensity reversals* can upset the equalisation result. The latter is probably not of great significance practically (see p. 36 above), but the former may be. Clearly some countries do not produce some goods and this may lead to differences in rewards and to migration. For example, computer engineers tend to migrate from poor to rich countries, presumably because they are unable to earn sufficient at home where computers are not produced.

A further cause of factor price differences is trade impediments, which preclude the complete equality of goods prices across the world. *Transport costs* affect all trade while *tariffs* and *non-tariff barriers* affect most. Together they raise the relative price of a country's importable good and thus raise its intensive factor's reward relative to Samuelson's no impediment case.

The area probably responsible for most of the observed differences in factor rewards is the technology assumptions. Different countries appear to have '*differences in atmosphere*' that affect the productivity of their industries independently of factor inputs. For example, Pratten (1976) reported that German firms commonly obtain 25 per cent per worker more than British firms from identical machines. Similarly, part of the higher productivity of American managers over most others probably stems as much from the social conventions militating towards working hard and succeeding as from other factor inputs. Whatever their cause, and whether they affect particular industries or factors, or whole economies, differences in atmosphere will generally prevent FPE and will make migration necessary if world output is to be maximised.

A further technological cause of factor price differences may be *economies of scale*. If different countries are reaping differing economies of scale, they may have identical prices (average costs) but different marginal productivities and thence different factor prices. An interesting feature of this case is that even if factor prices are equal there may be gains to migration, because concentrating production geographically may reduce costs below free-trade levels.

Trade vs. factor mobility

The simple Heckscher–Ohlin model predicts that trade and factor migration can be substitutes: either alone is sufficient to induce the international equality of factor and good prices. This does not necessarily mean, however, that with perfect factor mobility there will be no trade. Suppose that trade has brought the factor price ratios of two countries to within 5 per cent of each other, but that full equality is frustrated by specialisation. If we now allow mobility, factors will move, but only sufficiently to take up the 5 per cent disparity. Their doing so will somewhat alter the size of trade flows; it need not change the fact or the pattern of trade, however. The final equilibrium will involve both trade and (the results of) factor mobility.

A counter-example to this occurs if the inequality of factor prices is due to tariffs. Tariffs mean that, for so long as any trade exists, the goods price ratios in the two countries must differ by the amount of the tariff. Thus trade *prevents* FPE and will eventually be displaced by factor mobility: if mobility is possible, even the smallest tariff eventually becomes prohibitive of international trade!

FURTHER READING

The classic references on factor price equalisation are *Samuelson* (1948, and, especially, 1949). *Dixit and Norman* (1980) treat the issue excellently, including multi-dimensional cases, but they concentrate on necessary rather than sufficient conditions for equalisation, and their treatment is rather technical. *Samuelson* (1981) offers a fascinating overview of the question, including discussion of Heckscher's and Ohlin's views.

On mobility itself *Mundell* (1957) is the classic reference, while the *Journal of International Economics* (vol. 14, no. 3/4, 1983) prints a symposium of recent work, not all of which is difficult.

NOTE

1   An alternative proof of this proposition is given in section 3.2.

14 International Trade and Economic Growth

The ultimate purpose of economics is to increase economic welfare. So far we have concentrated almost entirely on the optimal allocation of a given bundle of resources, but it is obvious that welfare may also be improved either by increasing the quantity of resources available or by learning to do more with a given bundle. Both of these possibilities represent economic growth – the first through factor augmentation and the second through technical progress. Some economists feel that conventional measures of economic growth based on the output of goods and services (gross national product) do not satisfactorily reflect economic welfare, arguing that they ignore factors such as pollution and the negative externalities from congestion (see Mishan, 1967, and a reply by Beckerman, 1974). We shall ignore this controversy here, however, and assume that increased productive capabilities represent improved opportunities for economic welfare. We shall, however, encounter one instance where growth may be harmful – in section 14.2.

In many respects, then, the subject of this chapter is among the most important treated in the whole book. Unfortunately, it is also among the least satisfactory. We have seen already how international trade theory possesses its share of ambiguities and conundrums, and growth theory is just as bad. In combination they conspire to make economic theorising a most frustrating activity.

14.1 THE RYBCZYNSKI THEOREM

The Heckscher–Ohlin case

We start by recapitulating one of the fundamental components of the Heckscher–Ohlin trade model: the Rybczynski theorem. This comparative static theorem states that comparing two small, open economies, identical in every respect except their factor endowments, the economy better endowed with capital will produce *absolutely* more of the capital-intensive good and *absolutely* less of the labour-intensive good than the other economy. Ignoring the dynamics of transition from one equilibrium to another, this translates into the following theorem of growth: *if a small trading country's endowment of one factor increases, its output of the good using that factor intensively will rise and output of the other good fall.*

A proof of the Rybczynski Theorem was presented in Chapter 3, but we will briefly repeat it here. Adopting all the Heckscher–Ohlin assumptions plus non-specialisation and the small country assumption, let us assume that our country has attained a full trading equilibrium. Now assume that it receives a grant of real capital from abroad. How is the extra capital to be used? With fixed goods and factor prices (deriving from the small country assumption and factor price equalisation), factor proportions in each industry will be fixed. Thus the only way of absorbing capital is to increase output in the capital-intensive sector (say, X) and reduce it in the other (Y). As Y-output is reduced, factors are released in ratio $K_Y:L_Y$; if X takes on all the labour released, it will require more than K_Y of capital, by virtue of its being the capital intensive sector, and this extra capital can be obtained only from the capital grant. The only limit to this process is if specialisation occurs before the capital is fully absorbed. In this case, the remaining capital is absorbed by X (as its price falls), but, of course, Y-output cannot fall any further.

Notice that nothing has been said about imports or exports. The increased endowment may entail higher output of either importables or exportables; excepting extreme demand conditions, the former change will reduce international trade while the latter will increase it. Notice also that the theorem referred to a small country. A large country would experience similar pressures but its changes in output would affect world prices and the results would no longer be unambiguous.

The specific factors case

A development of the standard Heckscher–Ohlin model is the specific factors case. Suppose now a small country receives an increment of one sector-specific capital – say, K_X. This raises output in industry X by two mechanisms: first because capital has a positive marginal product, holding labour input constant; and second because, by raising the capital/labour ratio, it increases labour's marginal revenue product in X, which raises wages and bids labour away from Y. With no increment in its own capital, therefore, industry Y loses output as it loses labour. Thus, in this respect factor growth has similar effects to those in the Heckscher–Ohlin model: one industry increases output absolutely while the other reduces it absolutely.

The specific factors model differs from Heckscher–Ohlin, however, in one important respect. Heckscher–Ohlin maintained constant factor prices, at least in the absence of specialisation, but with specific factors they vary. We saw in the previous paragraph how industry X's capital/labour ratio rose, and how by bidding labour from Y it caused Y's to do likewise. Thus labour's marginal revenue product (given prices) rose in both industries, raising wages, while capital's fell in both, reducing capital rentals. Thus, an increment of one sort of capital reduced returns not only to existing holders of that capital, but also to holders of the other capital.

Long-run growth

We have treated changes in factor supplies as exogenously given data, but this is not realistic. Both population growth and the capital stock are affected by economic growth. We shall not consider the former, but two observations may be made on the latter. First, the capital stock is incremented by investment, and, since, in the long run, investment equals saving, the ultimate determinant of the supply of capital is the propensity to save. Countries more willing to save will generally increase their relative capital abundance.

Second, the process of economic growth tends to generate changes in factor endowments. Poor countries are less able than richer countries to generate surplus income to save, and are thus most unlikely to be relatively capital-abundant. Similarly, at the top end of the income scale there appears to be a tendency for endowments to shift from physical to human capital abundance as growth occurs. Thus we expect to find dynamic countries changing their patterns of trade relatively rapidly: Japan, a prime example, moved rapidly from exporting labour-intensive goods (e.g. textiles and toys), through physical–capital-intensive goods (e.g. ships and steel) into skill- and technology-intensive sectors (e.g. electronics). A more recent instance is South Korea, which seems to have reached the physical capital stage recently, often displacing Japan from her former markets.

Observe that these stages of comparative advantage may allow us to make predictions about unusually dynamic or stagnant economies, but not about changes in the general pattern of trade in response to general economic growth. This is because trade is determined by *relative* factor abundance and, if all countries evolve roughly together, relativities are not easily predictable.

Technical progress

The previous analysis referred to factor accumulation, but technological advance is probably a more important source of economic growth. Frequently, however,

139

we can treat the latter as being factor augmenting, and thus apply the earlier analysis anyway. For example, progress may have the result of increasing the productivity of all units of capital by x per cent; we can then analyse the economy as if it were applying x per cent more capital to a given technology, rather than an unchanged capital stock to a new technology.

If this 'dodge' does not work – because, for example, technical progress is restricted to one industry – matters become much more complex. In general, we would expect output of the good experiencing technical progress to rise, since its costs fall below the given world price at unchanged output. This may or may not reduce output of the other good, however, depending on how many (and which) factors the advancing technology releases or absorbs.

14.2 IMMISERISING GROWTH

Growth and trade

The previous section considered the consequences of economic growth on production and on factor rewards, but not on the direction of trade. The reason is that trade results from differences between countries, and growth in any country might either increase or decrease these. Thus, for example, a country experiencing capital augmentation will switch production from labour- to capital-intensive goods; this will increase trade if the country previously exported capital-intensive goods or reduce it if it exported labour-intensive goods. Similarly, technical progress may boost either export or import-competing sectors and so increase or decrease trade.

A further complication arises from demand. If demand is not homothetic – i.e. if goods have different income elasticities – economic growth changes the pattern of demand. Thus a country suddenly becoming very rich may increase its demand for Rolls Royces disproportionately, and this will be reflected in its international trade. Such demand factors will be experienced even if growth leaves the pattern of production quite unchanged.

If our country is small, it is not of great consequence whether growth stimulates or reduces world trade, because a small country can conduct any amount (or direction) of trade at fixed world prices. This allows us to assert that economic growth should always be beneficial. By definition, economic growth will allow a country to produce its pre-growth bundle of goods plus some output in addition. The country can thus reach its pre-growth consumption bundle (trading as before), and then have some further consumption as it trades or consumes the additional output. Of course, it may not actually choose to determine its consumption along these lines: it may, for example, consume less X after growth than before. Nevertheless, provided that all the price signals are correct – i.e. that they maintain the marginal equalities MRS = MRT = MRTT – we know that the chosen position is preferred to the one with consumption of more of both goods and that this, in turn, is preferred to the pre-growth position.

The terms of trade

Now consider a large country, whose terms of trade vary with the amount of trade. If economic growth increases the supply of exports, and the world's demand for those exports is inelastic, it is possible that the export price falls so far that the country is actually worse off for growing! This possibility, known as *immiserising growth*, is illustrated in Figure 14.1. The pre-growth position has transformation frontier *FF*, production at *P*, consumption at *C*, and terms of trade *TT*. Both *P* and *C* lie on the foreign offer curve, which is not drawn, but which would be curved to reflect the dependence of prices on the amounts traded. (Figure 8.4(B) illustrates

equilibrium for a large country in this type of diagram.) After growth, the transformation frontier shifts out to $F'F'$ and, although nothing else changes, a
completely new equilibrium arises, with consumption at C'. The foreign offer
curve linking P' and C' is the same as that linking P and C, but with its origin shifted
from P to P'. Its curvature means that the country is unable to convert its additional
output into consumption at so favourable a rate. Thus, the extra supply of exports
of X (up from JP to $J'P'$) brings forth virtually no extra Y from the rest of the world.

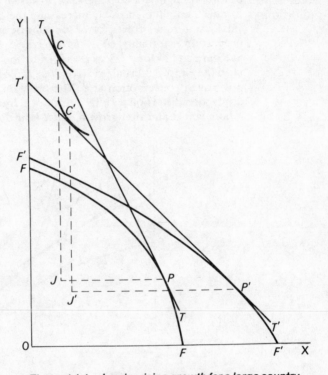

Figure 14.1 *Immiserising growth for a large country*

Certain primary commodity producers may find themselves with something
approaching immiserising growth. The price elasticities of demand for food and
raw materials are low, at least in the short run, and so bumper harvests are met by
falling world prices. This leads certain major producers to curtail output with a
view to supporting the price. For example, the USA pays farmers not to produce
wheat, Saudi Arabia controls oil production and Brazil controls coffee sales. All this
suggests that economic growth based on these sectors may not be viewed as a
blessing.

The difficulty faced by the large country is that, as it pushes out the transformation frontier, economic growth also, in some sense, exacerbates the (large
country) distortion of the marginal conditions. Thus, the additional utility
obtainable from the former is outweighed by the additional loss from the latter.
This suggests a cure: the optimal tariff. The optimal tariff corrects the marginal
trade distortion and ensures that consumption occurs at the optimal point on the
consumption possibility locus (the Baldwin envelope). The post-growth transformation frontier lies everywhere outside (strictly speaking: not inside) the
pre-growth one; hence, with an unchanged foreign offer curve, the post-growth

141

consumption possibility locus also lies everywhere outside its pre-growth equivalent. Thus, if, by means of optimal tariffs, the optimum points are chosen both before and after growth, welfare will certainly be increased by growth, since, for any point on the pre-growth consumption possibility locus, some point on the post-growth locus allows more of both goods.

Growth and domestic distortions

A similar analysis in fact applies to all distortions. Growth in the presence of any distortion might not be beneficial, because it both pushes out the transformation frontier and alters (possibly increasing) the degree of distortion. Thus, even for small countries, growth could be immiserising in the presence of a tariff, a production externality, consumption taxes, etc. The first mentioned is illustrated in Figure 14.2. World prices are given by the slope of PC or $P'C'$, and with a fixed tariff they imply internal prices of slope II. Post-growth consumption at C' is below pre-growth consumption at C. The problem is that growth enlarges the tariff's production distortionary effect. As drawn, free trade would entail specialisation in X both before and after growth, and P' is further from that position than is P.

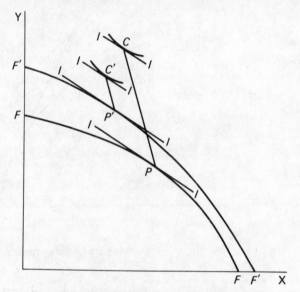

Figure 14.2   *Immiserising growth with a tariff*

These results generalise to multi-commodity and multi-factor settings, and given the prevalence of distortions one might expect them to have a wide applicability. To our knowledge, however, no empirical study exists that considers whether economic growth has actually been harmful by virtue of increasing distortions. Returning to the large country case, multi-dimensionality introduces the possibility of a fate worse than immiserising growth. If a country has the same trade pattern as a growing economy but without the growth, it suffers the terms of trade deterioration without any counteracting quantity effects.

14.3   THE TRANSFER PROBLEM

The previous section considered the consequences of one country's economic growth on world equilibrium. We noted that in extreme cases growth could actually be harmful because it exacerbated an existing market distortion. We now examine the related issue of one country giving or transferring income to another, and ask a similar set of questions. History has produced several instances of such pure transfers – most notably German reparations paid to the Allies after World War I and the USA's grants of Marshall Aid to Europe after World War II. Currently, the analysis applies to donations of foreign aid and also, if we ignore the subsequent repayments, to flows of international investment.

The issue we shall address is whether a transfer affects the terms of trade between the two countries, and if so, how. In particular, we ask whether it is possible for the donor to gain more through terms of trade changes than it loses through the initial transfer, and, correspondingly, whether the recipient could suffer a net loss.

The terms of trade

We start with a simple two-country model, assuming that the transfer shifts purchasing power from A to B but does not affect the distribution of productive resources at all. We ask how the demand for each good would be affected at unchanged world prices (terms of trade), and from this deduce how prices must change in order to re-establish equilibrium. Notice that we are dealing here with the large country case again.

Suppose that, starting from full equilibrium, the transfer from A to B is of £T. Of this additional income, B will spend $m^B T$ on imports, where m^B is B's marginal propensity to import, and the remainder, $(1 - m^B)T$, on B's exportable good.[1] Correspondingly, A will allocate her income change of $-£T$ as $-m^A T$ on imports and $-(1-m^A)T$ on exportables. Now, B's imports and A's exportable are the same good; hence, at unchanged terms of trade, world demand for that good changes by

$$\triangle D = m^B T - (1 - m^A)T = (m^A + m^B - 1)T. \tag{14.1}$$

Thus, the transfer increases demand for A's exportable good if

$$m^A + m^B > 1. \tag{14.2}$$

If this is so, A's terms of trade would have to improve (i.e. her export price rise) in order to bring post-transfer demands back into line with unchanged supplies. (Exactly the same conclusion would arise if we examined demand for B's exportable.)

Thus we see that the donor's terms of trade will improve if, on average, countries' marginal consumption is biased towards foreign goods – i.e. towards each other's goods. Given the existence of transport costs and non-tradable services, this seems unlikely, although Jones (1975) argued to the contrary.

Immiserising transfers?

Changes in the terms of trade affect real incomes in the two countries on top of the direct effects of the transfer. These effects are known as the 'secondary burden' or 'secondary gain', according to sign. The question then arises whether the donor's secondary gain could offset its primary loss from the initial transfer. The answer is generally 'no' – at least provided markets are stable. Suppose for a moment that the primary and secondary changes just balance – i.e. that the terms of trade changed by just enough to leave both donor and recipient at their pre-transfer levels of income. Could this represent a final equilibrium? With incomes unchanged, only prices differ between the pre- and post-transfer equilibria. However, provided markets are stable, the higher price of A's exportable will boost supply and cut demand for it; thus, at the assumed terms of trade, there

143

would be an excess supply of A's exportable, which would serve to reduce its price. Hence, a completely offsetting terms of trade change could not be an equilibrium; that could only exist with a lower price for A's export, i.e. with a smaller terms of trade change.

As might be guessed from previous sections, these results are not particularly robust to changes in assumptions. Immiserising transfers are possible for large countries in a multi-country world, and in the presence of domestic distortions. Unlike the immiserising growth case, however, the circumstances necessary to produce immiserising transfers are sufficiently strict and unlikely for us to ignore such transfers as a practical possibility.

An early debate on the transfer problem was between Keynes (1929) and Ohlin (1929). Keynes argued that post-war reparations would greatly reduce Germany's export prices as she sought to earn a sufficient export surplus to pay the transfer to the Allies. This assumed that the price mechanism had to bear all the burden of adjustment. Ohlin, on the other hand, pointed out that, since transfers affected incomes, income effects could generate Germany's required surplus, with the richer Allies importing more and the poorer Germans importing less, thus entailing a much smaller terms of trade change than Keynes allowed. It is clear that modern treatments run much closer to Ohlin's view than to Keynes'.

14.4   EXPORTS AND GROWTH

We turn now very briefly from pure theory to an empirical approach to the question of international trade and growth. Both through history and across countries, economic growth appears to be correlated with higher levels of international trade. This is far from inevitable from the preceding analysis, however. One explanation might be that countries are actually rather specialised – in particular varieties of goods, if not in particular goods (see Chapter 4). If so, domestic growth increases the supply of rather few of the items consumed, and so, almost inevitably, it must be accompanied by additional trade to convert its fruits into a consumable bundle of goods. Coupled with this is the fact that, as incomes rise, consumers are likely to increase their demand for foreign varieties of goods (they are more able to pay the additional costs that importing involves, see p. 50 above). Thus growth is likely to increase trade from the import side as well. This effect will be supplemented if countries that are growing fast also tend to reduce their trade barriers more rapidly.

Export-led growth An entirely different approach is to argue that, if exports grow for some exogenous reason, this actually stimulates growth. Several possible analyses of this exist. First, there is the straightforward Keynesian notion that exports are injections into the circular flow of income and that they boost income and output via the multiplier. (This is explained further in Chapter 17.) This is fine as far as it goes, but, if injections are all that is required, would not increasing government expenditure do as well?

Part of the answer to this comes from the second analysis of export-led growth. By increasing foreign exchange receipts, exports permit a higher level of imports. This could stimulate growth if these imports comprise essential raw materials or capital equipment – an argument relevant to development economics. It may also *allow* more domestically generated growth if this has been constrained by the need to keep import demand below a certain level. This argument applies to many developed and developing countries: growth is curtailed in order that import payments do not exceed export revenues – thus more exports allow more imports and thus more growth. This approach was expounded by Thirlwall (1980). It seems to have much truth in it, but it is more an 'import' or 'foreign exchange' theory of growth than an 'export' theory, because anything that raises imports (e.g. an export price rise or a transfer) stimulates growth.

A third view is that exposure to international competition helps to remove allocative inefficiencies that may build up in relatively closed economies. Thus an increasing rate of exporting does not cause a country's transformation frontier to shift outwards any faster, but it does allow the actual production point to approach any given frontier more closely. During the transitional stage, as misallocations are removed, the economy will thus grow faster than usual, since both 'natural growth' and 'reallocative growth' will be combined. In the long run, however, when maximum allocative efficiency has been achieved, growth rates will slip back to normal rates, although, of course, at a higher *level* of income than would have been achieved without the external stimulus.

Part of this argument is that resources have higher productivity in export industries than elsewhere. Thus, shifting them into export processes raises output independent of any dynamic considerations. Gains may arise from any of the following. Greater capacity utilisation and economies of scale may be possible because industries are no longer constrained by the domestic economy. Rent-seeking in the import-competing sector may fall as resources leave for the export sector; i.e. there is less competition for import-related rents as the attractions of exporting increase. Similarly, other misallocations associated with too much concentration on the home market may evaporate: e.g. excessive capital intensity. New technologies may be available from foreign rivals, or have emerged locally in response to greater competition in exporting. Management may be better for similar reasons.

Closely related but logically different are two further factors. First, the export sector may be more dynamic than the rest of the economy for similar reasons to those outlined above. Thus, increasing its size will raise overall growth rates without any change in individual sectors' growth rates. Second, as the export sector grows it may create ever more positive externalities for the rest of the economy, thereby raising the latter's levels or growth rates of productivity. Among the relevant externalities may be training labour and management, spin-offs from research, and new investment opportunities (see Chapter 9).

Empirical results

Many studies exist of the exports–growth relationship. They are hindered by the simultaneous causation that inevitably exists: exports may stimulate growth, but growth also stimulates exports by increasing supply. Furthermore, since exports comprise part of GDP, export and GDP growth must inevitably be somewhat related. Thus, finding a positive correlation between export and GDP growth does not constitute a thorough test of the export-led growth hypothesis. However, little other evidence exists.

Among the most convincing of such studies is Feder (1983). Feder decomposed the export effect into a part due to differences in productivity between export and non-export sectors and a part due to positive externalities between sectors. He found, in a cross-section of thirty-one LDCs' growth over 1964–73, that a 1 per cent increase in export growth was associated with a 0.08 per cent per annum increase in GDP growth via productivity differences, and a 0.13 per cent increase via externalities. Decomposing actual growth over the decade into its causes, he found that, of mean growth of 6.5 per cent per annum, investment explained 2.5 per cent per annum, labour-force growth 1.6 per cent per annum, productivity differences between exports and other sectors 0.7 per cent per annum, externalities 1.1 per cent per annum, and other trends 0.6 per cent per annum.

FURTHER READING

The standard results on the Rybczynski theorem may be pursued in the references given for Chapter 3. *Smallwood* (1975) approaches the subject by adding international trade to standard growth theory (rather than vice versa) and generates some interesting insights. *Balassa* (1979) explores the changing stages of economic development with respect to trade patterns. On immiserising growth, *Bhagwati* (1971) provides the most useful reference, integrating the subject with the theory of distortions. For multi-dimensional generalisations, see *Eaton and Panagariya* (1982) and *Smith* (1982).

Classic references on the transfer problem are *Samuelson* (1952, 1954) and *Mundell* (1960). *Caves and Jones* (1981) offer an alternative elementary treatment, while *Brecher and Bhagwati* (1981, 1982) analyse immiserising transfers under various conditions.

Export-led growth is considered by *Cornwall* (1977) and *Thirlwall* (1980), for developed countries, and by *Balassa* (1979) and *Tyler* (1981), among others, for developing countries.

NOTE

1   The marginal propensity to import records the proportion of an additional unit of income that is spent on imports.

15 Capital Movements and the Multinationals

Everybody has heard of the multinationals, and nearly everybody has a view about them. This chapter looks beyond the rhetoric and asks, first, why multinationals have come about and, second, in precisely what ways they affect economic welfare. We discover that the predominant feature of multi-nationality is market failure. The chapter starts by briefly describing the extent of multinational activity and concludes by seeing how they affect the theory of the preceding chapters.

15.1 INTRODUCTION

Portfolio vs. direct investment

Portfolio investment overseas is investment in the bonds or securities of organisations in one country by residents of another. It confers no special rights on the investor; in particular he has no more control over the borrowing firm than any other shareholder does. Firms and individuals undertake portfolio investment for financial reasons: for example, foreign firms may offer particularly high or secure rates of return, or variations in their returns may tend to cancel out variations in domestic returns, if foreign and domestic returns are negatively correlated.

Foreign direct investment (FDI), on the other hand, is the purchase *and control* of an entity in one country by residents of another. A transaction falls into this class if it grants the lender 'significant influence' over the foreign entity or increases his stake in any such entity (Central Statistical Office, *United Kingdom Balance of Payments*). The important distinction between direct and portfolio investment lies in control, and explanations for FDI must reflect this.

The result of FDI is a multinational, or transnational, enterprise (MNE) – a company that owns or controls significant activities in at least two countries. Each MNE has a parent company or head office situated in its 'home' country, and subsidiaries situated abroad in 'host' countries. The precise relationship between parent and subsidiaries varies between companies, but we shall not investigate this. We merely assume that the parent exercises significant control over each subsidiary.

Some history

Foreign investment was prominent in the nineteenth century, but it mainly involved portfolio lending to developing countries for railway or municipal development. Britain was the major creditor and London the predominant centre; however, except indirectly through her political power, Britain exercised no control over the borrowers of funds. This lending reached its zenith around 1913. Between the wars, foreign investment declined: direct investment grew to about one-quarter of the total and the USA became a principal creditor. Although the Second World War caused very substantial losses of foreign assets, the climate that followed it – especially after 1958 – proved highly conducive to foreign investment. Post-war investment, however, has been primarily direct rather than portfolio.

The growth of FDI owed much to the improvements in transport and communications since 1945, which made it feasible to exercise control from a distance. It also stemmed from the economic need for the USA to export capital to the rest of the world – both to stimulate recovery and to keep the international financial system functioning (see Chapter 26) – and from the US tax laws, which favoured

147

FDI. By the 1960s these factors were weakening, and resistance emerged around the world to US control of local industry. The US outflow eased and other countries started FDI in the USA. The 1970s have generally seen less FDI than the 1960s, although for Britain the oil surpluses and the removal of foreign currency controls in 1979 generated a large outflow.

MNEs today

Past investment has bequeathed us a very substantial amount of multi-nationality. In 1976, the developed economies owned an outstanding stock of FDI of about $276b. – equivalent to $5\frac{1}{2}$ per cent of world GDP excluding the centrally planned economies. Of this, 47 per cent was American owned, with the UK (11.2 per cent) and West Germany (6.9 per cent) coming next (Organization for Economic Co-operation and Development, 1981). Canada was host to the largest proportion of this (15 per cent), followed by the USA (11 per cent) and the UK (9 per cent); developing countries received 33 per cent in all (United Nations, 1978). While the location of FDI is more dispersed than the ownership, MNE subsidiaries still account for formidable proportions of their hosts' economic activity. For example, they provide over half of Canadian manufacturing output, with corresponding figures of 21 per cent for the UK, 29 per cent for Australia, 28 per cent for France and 22 per cent for West Germany. Japan, however, has pursued an anti-FDI policy and has only 4 per cent of manufacturing due to MNEs.

Not all MNEs are large, but they are larger than domestic firms on average and some are truly immense. The turnover of the largest exceeds the GNP of certain OECD and most developing countries. In 1973, 12 per cent of total OECD employment was due to just 260 MNEs. Nearly half of MNEs have interests in only one country other than their base country, but 11 per cent have interests in ten or more countries. Recent years have seen considerable increases in geographical diversification.

MNE activity is not spread evenly over industries. Indeed, it is differences between industries that offer most opportunities for identifying the causes of FDI. MNEs tend to predominate in technological sectors – (e.g. chemicals and electrical engineering), but also to be strong where brand images are important (e.g. food and tobacco) and where economies of scale require huge levels of output (e.g. petrol refining and motor vehicles). For example, in Britain in 1968 MNE subsidiaries accounted for 0 per cent of the output of metal furniture and 1 per cent of industrial fans, but 48 per cent of pharmaceuticals, 69 per cent of office machinery, 74 per cent of tractors, and 82 per cent of soups (Business Statistics Office, *Report on the Census of Production*, 1968, vol. 158).

Theoretically more interesting are the data in Table 15.1, which show the breakdown between FDI and exports as a means of serving foreign markets. Column 3 shows that technological industries tend to be more open than others (as we would expect from Chapter 4); but, within that, FDI and exporting appear to be substitutes. Office equipment, chemicals, rubber, vehicles and tobacco stress FDI, whereas aerospace, shipbuilding, metals and textiles favour exporting. The next section seeks explanations of these differences.

15.2 THE CAUSES OF FOREIGN DIRECT INVESTMENT

In asking why FDI takes place we are essentially asking the following two questions. First, if there is a demand for good X in country A, why is it not met either by (a) local firms in A, or (b) exports from country B. Second, suppose a firm in country B wishes to expand; why does it not do so by (a) producing more X in B and exporting, (b) expanding into some other line within B, (c) buying shares (portfolio investment) in A, or (d) licensing some firm in A to use its technology to produce X. The answers, of course, are, first, that a B-owned subsidiary in A can out-compete other potential suppliers, and, second, that the profits from FDI appear to exceed those from the alternative means of expansion. But why?

Table 15.1   Foreign involvement of 866 largest industrial firms, 1977[a]

Industry	Foreign involvement[b]			
	Overseas production ratio	Parent export ratio	Overseas sales ratio	Overseas market sourcing ratio
	$\dfrac{F}{P+F}$	$\dfrac{X}{P}$	$\dfrac{F+X}{P+F}$	$\dfrac{F}{F+X}$
High research intensity:				
Aerospace	7.5	33.8	38.7	19.3
Office equipment (incl. computers)	41.5	8.2	46.3	89.6
Petroleum	42.7	17.9	53.0	80.6
Measurement, scientific and photographic equipment	33.1	19.3	46.0	72.0
Electronics and electrical appliances	20.5	22.8	38.6	53.2
Chemicals and pharmaceuticals (incl. soap and cosmetics)	29.0	20.3	43.4	66.8
Total	33.5	20.2	47.0	71.3
Medium research intensity:				
Industrial and farm equipment	22.9	28.3	44.7	51.2
Shipbuilding, railroad and transportation equipment	8.8	32.2	38.2	23.1
Rubber	34.2	7.0	38.8	88.1
Motor vehicles (incl. components)	20.6	20.7	37.0	55.7
Metal manufacturing and products	13.5	23.2	33.5	40.3
Total	18.4	22.7	36.9	49.8
Low research intensity:				
Building materials	27.9	8.3	33.9	82.3
Tobacco	40.8	5.9	44.3	92.1
Beverages	17.4	3.8	20.5	84.7
Food	28.8	5.1	32.5	88.8
Paper and wood products	18.1	15.9	31.1	58.1
Textiles, apparel, leather goods	15.5	15.1	28.3	54.8
Publishing and printing	9.2	2.7	11.6	78.9
Total	25.0	8.3	31.2	80.2
Other manufacturing	5.8	14.8	19.7	29.6
TOTAL	26.6	18.8	40.4	65.9

Notes:
[a] Although the data refer only to the largest firms they are probably not unrepresentative of all firms.
[b] In symbols, F is sales by subsidiaries outside parent's home country; P is parent's total sales; and X is parent's exports.
Source: Dunning and Pearce (1981), Table 6.6.

We shall answer these questions using Dunning's (1979, 1982) *Eclectic theory* of FDI. This incorporates a wide range of possible causes without being too precise about how they interrelate. Other theorists have been more definite but, as yet, simpler more powerful theories have not proved universally successful.

The eclectic theory of FDI

Dunning distinguished three groups of 'advantages' that determine the propensity of a firm, industry or country to be a net recipient or exporter of FDI:

- *Ownership advantages* – factors that enable a particular firm to expand at all, e.g. rights to particular technologies or supplies of factors.
- *Internalisation advantages* – whether expansion is best accomplished within the firm, or by selling the rights to the means of expansion to other firms.
- *Locational advantages* – whether expansion is best achieved at home or abroad (regardless of who undertakes it). This is essentially a question of comparative advantage.

We shall examine the determinants of these advantages later, but first we see how they fit together to influence FDI, as a form of foreign involvement. Suppose there is a foreign demand for X and that a particular domestic firm has an ownership advantage in X. Table 15.2 relates this firm's approach to expansion to its other advantages. If there is no internalisation gain, the firm may as well license its ownership advantage to another firm; this is especially so if locational factors indicate expansion abroad, because foreign firms will normally be better attuned to local conditions and hence better able to manage such expansion than our own firm. If, on the other hand, there are internalisation gains, our firm should undertake the expansion itself; if locational factors favour home expansion it expands at home and exports, whereas if they favour foreign expansion FDI occurs and an MNE is born. Observe how all three advantages are necessary to induce multinational activity.

Table 15.2 The foreign involvement decision

Internalisation advantage	Locational advantage	
	Abroad	Home
Yes	MNE	export
No	license, abroad	license, home?

An alternative formalisation of the export/FDI decision is due to Hirsch (1976). Again assume demand exists in country A, and that a firm in country B is deciding its policy. It considers four groups of costs:

P_A, P_B production costs in A and B respectively – the *locational variables*;
K the cost to *other firms* of matching our firm's knowledge and intangible assets; i.e. our firm's *ownership advantages*;
M the additional cost of exporting to A rather than selling local produce (e.g. transport, tariffs, etc.); and
C the additional cost of controlling a plant abroad rather than at home.

M and C are elements of the *internalisation advantages*.
These costs identify three alternatives for serving A:

150

(i)   a local firm sets up in A, with costs $(P_A + K)$, i.e. it has to overcome our owner-
       ship advantages;
(ii)   our firm exports, with costs $(P_B + M)$; and
(iii) our firm establishes a foreign plant, with costs $(P_A + C)$.

Assuming that the good produced is identical under all three outcomes, and that
there are no further complications such as dynamic or strategic factors to consider,
the least-cost choice will be made.

If the foreign firm's costs $(P_A + K)$ are least, there is perhaps also scope for
licensing to occur: if A is going to erode B's ownership advantages anyway, B may
as well benefit from that by selling them to A at slightly under K.

This example is grossly over-simplified, because many different considerations
enter the simple costs K, M and C (as we shall see below), but it does provide a
framework on which to hang a more realistic analysis. It also stresses that it is
relative, not absolute, advantages that are important in determining FDI.

Ownership advantages

Ownership advantages are advantages specific to the expanding firm relative to its
competitors overseas. They are a necessary condition for FDI and stem from
various market imperfections. (Under perfect competition firms are identical.)
They may already exist within a firm, or alternatively arise only through the act of
FDI. We consider the former category first.

Technology. The expanding firm may have superior products, processes, management techniques or marketing skills. Such factors are *public goods* within the firm,
because their use in one area does not reduce the amount usable elsewhere. They
therefore provide an ideal base for expansion. Such advantages are frequently
embodied within an existing skilled labour force.

Industrial organisation and size. Large and diversified firms are generally better
equipped for innovation and have more resources to fight price wars or legal suits
over patents. Monopolies have excess profits and less concern over technology
leaking out to rivals. Large firms are more likely to have reaped firm-level
economies of scale, for instance in marketing, research and finance.

Access. Access to raw materials may be embodied in property rights, while access
to markets may arise from government action. Companies backed by large and
powerful governments may derive advantages in other markets through their
governments' political influence.

Finance. Large and diverse firms are frequently able to raise money more
cheaply than others, largely because their profits show less variability. This may
apply to a firm with several interests in a single country, but is more likely to apply
once a firm has become multi-national. Operating and selling in several countries
stabilises profits because problems in one country are normally offset by success in
another. Since investors desire stability they are willing to buy MNE shares at
relatively high prices. This argument is frequently rejected by arguing that, rather
than buy equity in a single firm operating in many countries, investors could get
equal stability but more flexibility by buying equity in separate firms in each
country. This, however, ignores the transaction costs, exchange restrictions and
imperfect knowledge that would blight such an alternative. MNEs therefore offer
investors a cheap and simple method of geographical diversification.

Ownership advantages also arise directly from multi-nationality itself via MNEs'
access to many capital markets, their ability to deal freely in many currencies, the
ease with which they can shift activity in response to changing factor endowments
and government policy, and their freedom from dependence on a single
government.

151

Many economists feel that internalisation is the key condition for FDI. Internalisation gains arise if market imperfections prevent the effective sale of ownership advantages to other firms, thus making their exploitation by their original owner the only possibility. The role of internalisation was first identified in a classic article by Coase (1937). Coase asked why the market ruled for transactions *between* firms, but not for transactions *within* firms. The reason is that in the latter case transactions costs outweigh any efficiency gains that the market may have over administrative allocation. He further suggested that any transactions subject to such market costs would eventually be internalised – that is, brought under one administrative head to eliminate the market.

The nature of the market failures giving rise to FDI clearly depend on the ownership advantage whose sale is impeded, but we give here some examples.

Costs of negotiation. If legal charges or stamp duty are very high for example contract-making may be discouraged. Closely related is the impossibility of transferring some things to other firms – e.g. the ingenuity of a particular personnel manager.

Opportunism. Suppose I have a simple idea for making £1m. How can I persuade you to pay £$\frac{1}{2}$m. for it without revealing so much that you discover it for nothing? Conversely, unless you see it first, how can you know it is worth anything? This problem blights technological and managerial innovations, especially where patent control is weak. Related to this is

Uncertainty. Suppose we can fix the sale somehow; neither of us can be sure it will work until afterwards, and this uncertainty is likely to reduce your offer price.

Control over the use of the advantage. For example, if the advantage resides in brand loyalty, the production of poor goods under a brand-mark damages all users of that mark, not just the offending licensee. Alternatively, selling your latest technology to rivals increases the probability that they will improve on it and overtake you in future.

Unexploited economies of scale. These are frequently argued to apply to under-utilised managerial capacity: a firm cannot generally hire out 20 per cent of its management capacity, and so to use it the firm must expand itself. Relatedly, the acquisition of *monopoly power* through expansion is also a (private) internalisation gain, as is any *financial benefit* from foreign diversification.

Taxes and tariffs. By manipulating the prices of *intra-firm* sales of parts or services, a firm may be able to reduce the taxes or tariffs that would hit market transactions. This is known as *transfer pricing*. Although it is illegal in nearly all countries, it is probably widespread because it is almost impossible for the authorities to know what the 'correct' price should be. This is especially so for transfers of technical or managerial services from HQ to subsidiaries. Kopits (1976) suggested that MNE subsidiaries in the UK probably pay 30–50 per cent more than they should for such services.

Internalisation advantages all arise from market imperfections. Their precise nature depends on the ownership advantage whose transfer is blocked: some give rise to huge internalisation gains (e.g. management capacity), others very few (e.g. mining rights, which can easily be let).

Locational advantages provide the international element of multi-nationality. They derive from the mainstream of international economics, essentially reflecting comparative advantage or distortions of it. Obvious contributors are: the *relative transportation costs* of raw materials and finished goods; the *locations* of materials and markets; the *cultural similarities* between an MNE's home and potential host countries; *unexploited economies of scale* at plant level; *factor endowments*; government *tax concessions, tariff rates, investment grants, etc.*, and *risks* of expropriation.

Under this heading we should perhaps note a factor that apparently does not explain FDI: relative rates of return. If different countries have different rates of return on capital, simple theory would lead us to expect a migration of capital towards the higher returns. While this explains some of the American outflow of investment since 1950, it cannot explain the preference for direct over portfolio investment, or why the outflow of FDI was partly balanced by a portfolio inflow.

Empirical evidence

There is much descriptive empirical work on MNEs, but less formal hypothesis testing; this is because of the formidable difficulties of measuring the various effects just described – especially those pertaining to internalisation. As with intra-industry trade – to which FDI research is often linked – conclusions tend to vary according to which proxies are used for immeasurable effects.

Caves (1974a) considered the shares of US subsidiaries in the output of cross-sections of UK and Canadian industries, relating them to 'intangible assets', the propensity to multi-plant production at home, entrepreneurial capacity and locational factors. 'Intangibles' included research effort, advertising intensity, size and economies of scale. These all represent ownership advantages, and they proved, especially the first two, significant explanations for both Canadian and UK samples. Multi-plant activity basically reflects internalisation: the MNE is, after all, just a special form of multi-plant operation. It proved important for the US share of Canadian industry, but not for the UK. The entrepreneurial hypotheses (either ownership or internalisation) received no support, while locational factors (relative wages) helped explain US penetration of UK industry.

Caves found little role for firm size in explaining FDI. Horst (1972) replicated this result in an industry cross-section of US investment in Canada, finding only the extent of the Canadian market and the level of protection significant; however *within* an industry he concluded that *only* size distinguishes MNEs from single-country firms. That is, size captures all the firm-specific ownership and internalisation advantages such as innovativeness, bargaining power and spreading fixed costs.

Further evidence on size comes from Wolf (1977). He compared three modes of expansion – diversification at home, exporting and FDI – and related them, across US industries, to average firm size and technological level (the proportion of scientists and engineers in total employment). He found domestic diversification more closely related to size, and foreign involvement (exports plus FDI) more closely related to technology. Within the latter, however, industries with large firms showed more bias towards FDI than others. Hence, while technological leadership helps foreign involvement (ownership advantages), large firm sizes appear to relate to multi-plant expansion at home and abroad.

A refinement of the eclectic theory investigated by Lall (1980) concerns the transferability of ownership advantages. We have so far implicitly considered them costlessly transferable public goods within the MNE, but this is too simple. Lall examined various ownership advantages and argued that those most easily transferable geographically will give rise to most FDI. American MNEs' advantages will be non-transferable if they are tied either to the firms' HQs or to the US economy. He argued that new technology falls into the former class (cf. the product cycle), whereas plant economies of scale and skilled manual labour fall into the latter. All these variables stimulate exports relative to FDI, although technology and plant economies do affect FDI positively to some extent. Among transferable ownership advantages, which boost FDI as a share of foreign involvement, are product differentiation (advertising) and managerial inputs.

Conclusion

FDI is related to three groups of 'advantages': ownership, internalisation and location. Internalisation has proved difficult to pin down empirically, although theoretically it is crucial. The other two have received empirical support. The most important ownership advantages for FDI appear to be technological sophistication, advertising intensity and economies of scale on an industry level, and size at a firm level. The role of technology is plainly visible from column 1 of Table 15.1.

15.3 MULTINATIONALS AND WELFARE

Multinationals affect the welfare of both their home and host countries. This section concentrates mainly on the latter, but some comments are passed on the former. MNEs maximise profits on a world scale – shifting resources to areas where their returns are highest and buying inputs where their prices are lowest. Such efficiency would seem sure to increase world welfare; however, because MNEs exist primarily because of market imperfections, this is not necessarily so. As we saw above, unless all markets are perfect, growth in one sector need not be beneficial: improved resource allocation has to be traded against (possible) increases in market imperfections.

Pure capital flows

We start by considering a pure capital flow between countries, devoid of any of the special advantages listed above. Assume two countries, a single good and a fixed world stock of capital. In Figure 15.1, MPK_A represents the marginal product of capital in country A, which, assuming perfect markets and constant returns to scale, equals capital's return (rent) in A. More capital involves lower rents by diminishing marginal returns. MPK_B is the corresponding schedule for B, but measured from origin O_B rather than O_A. In the absence of capital mobility, let A have $O_A K$ of capital and B, $O_B K$. Assuming no factor price equalisation, rentals are r_A and r_B respectively.

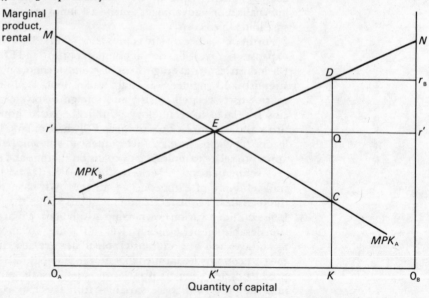

Figure 15.1 *The effects of international capital flow.*

154

If capital were now allowed to move (costlessly), it would flow from A to B in search of higher rewards. Rentals in A would rise and those in B fall, until ultimately both would equal r' and the world stock of capital would be allocated $O_A K'$ and $O_B K'$. This involves a gain in world output. When the first unit of capital is shifted, country A's output falls by KC $(= MPK_A)$ but B's rises by KD $(= MPK_B)$. Repeating this analysis for every unit, world output increases by area CED.

The flow also has implications for the distribution of income. Without mobility, capitalists in A earn area $O_A KCr_A$, i.e. capital stock multiplied by rental. The remainder of A's output, MCr_A, accrues to labour. (A's output is the area under MPK_A: the first unit of capital produces $O_A M$, the second slightly less, until the last produces KC; the total is the sum of these amounts, namely area $O_A MCK$). After the switch, labour's returns fall to MEr'. Labour in B, on the other hand, increases its earnings from NDr_B to NEr' because it has more capital to work with. A's capitalists gain from the change (assuming they still own the capital switched to B), because their returns rise with no change in quantity owned, while B's capitalists suffer. Taking countries as a whole, capital mobility means that income and output now differ. For example, after the switch, A produces $O_A MEK'$, but earns $(MEr' + O_A KQr')$; B produces $O_B NEK'$, but earns $(NEr' + O_B KQr')$. Note that, although A loses output by exporting capital, it gains income (by amount EQC). B gains both output and income.

Thus we see that pure capital mobility with perfect markets raises both countries' incomes – and hence world income. Even in this simple case, however, complex distributional changes occur. In particular, if no redistribution occurs, labour in the exporting country and capitalists in the importing country lose from capital mobility.

Generalising, now, to several goods we can develop some further results. For example, the Rybczynski theorem (or its specific factor analogue) states that, for a small country, a capital inflow absolutely reduces output (specific factor rewards) in the labour-intensive industry. Similarly, for a large country, immiserising growth is possible if FDI substantially reduces the relative price of an inelastically demanded export. In both these cases, the costs to local residents are greater than in the standard cases in Chapter 14 because the returns to the 'new' capital accrue abroad.

We now look at MNEs in a less rigorous but more realistic fashion. Following Hood and Young (1979) we consider their effects under three headings: resource transfer effects, balance of payments effects, and sovereignty.

Resource transfer effects

MNEs transfer to their hosts bundles of resources comprising different proportions of technology, management, sales ability and capital. If capital alone is required, it is much more cheaply available through other borrowing, so FDI should not be viewed simply as a source of capital. Furthermore, MNEs often raise local funds and, if through their market power they can do so cheaply, their presence could crowd out other socially desirable activities.

Technology is the most significant component of the package – at least to LDCs, which have no alternative sources for it. Any problems arise from the terms on which it is bought. MNEs are very skilled negotiators (see below) and in a bilateral negotiation with the government of a poor country are likely to be able to strike a very favourable bargain. This is particularly so over technology where the buyer has so little information. Hence royalties are often high, and licences to use technology restricted in terms of servicing, the provision of parts, the extent of development permitted, etc. There is also complaint about the appropriateness of technology. MNEs frequently pass old techniques from the developed countries on

155

to LDCs without any adaptation. These can be too capital-intensive for the local economy, resulting in a 'dualistic' structure: a small advanced industrial sector linked to the outside world surrounded by a large, capital-starved poor sector. For developed hosts, however, the opposite complaint is often heard: MNEs' technology is too unsophisticated, and local R&D is reduced in favour of R&D at head office.

The effect of the management component on economic welfare is two-edged. MNEs may train local management who then move into local business to its benefit. Britain is often thought to have benefited from such a flow from US subsidiaries, and also from local managers emulating their MNE colleagues. Alternatively, by paying relatively well and conferring great status, MNEs may absorb entrepreneurial talents from local enterprise.

Overall, MNEs probably raise their hosts' efficiency. They tend to improve allocation by (a) concentrating on a country's comparative advantage goods (the locational advantage), (b) stimulating competition, (c) demonstrating better techniques, and (d) introducing technology. Caves (1974b), for example, reported that in Australian industries the share of MNEs in output is positively related to productivity and negatively to profits. It is not clear, however, either that this is always the case, or that, even when efficiency does improve, most or even any of the gains accrue locally. The cases where efficiency does not improve arise where the MNEs introduce more distortions into the economy.

Balance of payments effects

MNEs are often blamed for their balance of payments effects: the capital-exporting country faces a large sudden deficit when the FDI occurs, while the host faces a small perpetual deficit as profits are repatriated. The corresponding benefits are usually forgotten. The exporter's deficit can be troublesome if it pushes the balance of payments into crisis, stimulating harsh corrective measures. In theory, if the investment is sound, the country should be able to borrow abroad to finance it, for a sound investment will generate the wherewithall to service the debt (and more). In practice, however, this is not always the case because, unless the investing company undertakes the borrowing itself (which it might not wish to do, if, say, it had large domestic cash balances), the potential lenders may not know about the direct investment or be able to assess its viability. To them, it may merely look like capital flight, which will not encourage them to lend. Thus, on occasion, a temporary ban on FDI may be desirable, although only as a cure for short-term liquidity problems rather than as a long-run balance of payments policy.

The host country's perpetual deficit will also be problematic if the investment is unsound, because then it will not generate the income for its own service. A sound investment should not produce such difficulties, although it may imply a change in the relative price of tradable and non-tradable goods if the FDI is in a non-tradable sector, since profit repatriation must eventually be paid for in tradable goods. This may involve some costly restructuring elsewhere in the economy and/or make economic policy more difficult to conduct; however, it seems unlikely to make a sound investment harmful absolutely.

Hence the basic problem seems to be one of unsound investment; as we saw before, only market imperfections can make socially unsound projects privately profitable. A related, but conceptually different, problem concerning uncertainty should also be mentioned here. A change in the environment could render an initially sound project unprofitable, both socially and privately. FDI clearly affects the exposure of the economy to different exogenous shocks, but this observation justifies intervention only if the government has better information than private agents about future shocks (or if shocks have different private and social impacts).

156

The host's perpetual deficit can be serious if the investment does not generate the income to cover the repatriation; but, again, a sound investment will do so. Hence the basic problem is unsound investment and, as before, only market imperfections can make socially unsound projects privately profitable.

Concern has also been expressed over the effects of MNEs on trade flows. MNEs are often thought to be more trade-intensive than other companies, but this reflects the industries they inhabit more than their own behaviour. In Britain, for example, Solomon and Ingham (1977) suggested that MNEs export less than home firms in engineering industries, while Panić and Joyce (1980) suggested that their exports were stagnant relative to other firms' over the 1970s. On the other hand, there is evidence that subsidiaries tend to import parts and capital equipment from the home country, and also finished goods for models not made locally. For example, Ford (UK) claims to be both the largest exporter and the largest importer of vehicles in Britain. The use of imported components absorbs foreign exchange and reduces MNEs' stimulus to the local economy. Governments can sometimes circumvent this by insisting on 'local content' agreements. None the less, this lack of 'linkage' is a cause for concern.

Sovereignty

Sovereignty lies at the heart of many of the concerns voiced so far. MNEs are less dependent on their host countries, or countries of origin, than domestic companies, and are consequently more difficult to control. This is particularly the case for subsidiaries in LDCs, which are often implicitly protected by the political power of their home country. It is not at all unknown for MNEs to pursue covert political objectives in their host countries – for example, ITT's resistance to Allende's regime in Chile in the early 1970s.

By means of their internationality, MNEs are frequently able to circumvent local economic policies, for example by frustrating credit squeezes or avoiding exchange restrictions by transferring money from abroad. They are also, by means of their political and economic power, more able to confront local policy directly. For example, when Ford (UK) broke the British government's pay policy in 1978 the government proved quite powerless.

Possibly even more disturbing, MNEs are able to influence government policy, especially when they are selecting a site for expansion. This can lead to distortions and loss. Host governments are keen to attract investment, and MNEs, with their large resources and experience, are able to dominate local governments in negotiations. In particular, host governments lack the information needed to assess what incentives have to be offered to secure the investment. The result is that MNEs are often able to obtain investment grants, tax holidays, protection, etc., in excess of their needs and sometimes in excess of the benefits they bring to the host nation. The countries of the Andean Pact (in northern Latin America) have sought quite successfully to overcome this by pooling information on MNEs (Vaitsos, 1976), and similar efforts have been made in the EEC. Nevertheless, when in the late 1970s Ford planned to build a new engine plant in Europe they played one country against another (notably Spain, Belgium and the UK), to the extent of persuading the UK, the final choice, to pay nearly half the capital costs of the project.

Less dramatically, the restrictions that MNEs impose on their subsidiaries frequently prevent the subsidiaries from behaving optimally. For example, Hood and Young (1979) reported that 75 per cent of subsidiaries in Scotland carried out no R&D at all, and that 81 per cent of Andean subsidiaries were subject to restrictions on their exports; Steuer (1973) reported that 30 per cent of UK

157

subsidiaries had their exports controlled by their head office. These restrictions can clearly be harmful to the host nation.

Conclusion

It is difficult to generalise about MNEs because their behaviour and circumstances are so varied. Their success at becoming multi-national suggests some degree of efficiency, and their movement of resources to areas of highest return suggests that they improve resource allocation. The competition of hosts for their presence also suggests that they are felt to be beneficial, because they boost output, offer employment, pay taxes and stimulate competition. Against this we must note that their *raison d'être* is market imperfections and that their existence and growth may strengthen such distortions in the ways we have just discussed. In summary, MNEs probably increase world income, but given their distributional effects their growth may not be Pareto improving. The cases where they are not beneficial arise from economic distortions; if the distortions are of the MNEs' making, there is a case for corrective action against them but, if they are merely exploiting existing distortions (e.g. existing investment grants, etc.), it is the distortions that are at fault. Given some measure of control, the MNEs are probably a benign economic force.

The capital exporter

We have already sketched some welfare and balance of payments effects on the capital exporter and we now consider them slightly more thoroughly. The important question for the exporter is: what is the alternative to FDI? Three possibilities exist: (i) no investment occurs, (ii) the investing country invests at home, or (iii) some foreign firm makes the (foreign) investment. Presumably the firm will not undertake FDI unless it thinks it privately profitable, so our question is whether the investment is *socially* desirable.

Under alternatives (i) and (iii) – i.e. when there is no alternative home investment – the main wedge between private and social gains concerns the balance of payments. If the investment would cause a balance of payments crisis, maybe it should be financed from abroad. However, as we noted above, if the investment is sound it is not obvious why it should cause a crisis. Under (i) one might also consider that FDI raises the world capital stock in the industry concerned and hence reduces the rate of return. If much of the existing stock is owned by our nationals, this reduction in their earnings must be balanced against the increase in the earnings of the investing company.

Alternative (ii) assumes an equivalent home investment is feasible. This introduces several other possible private–social wedges. First, *taxation*: the private company looks at profits net of tax, caring not to whom the tax is paid. Socially, however, we would prefer taxes to be paid to us rather than to foreigners. Second, *default risk*: investors make allowance for the default or confiscation of their investment. If default occurs abroad, both private and social losses occur, but, if it occurs at home, the same private loss occurs but no social loss, because the investment remains with our nationals. Third, *externalities*: if the domestic economy suffers unemployment, domestic investment will reduce it via the multiplier. Similarly Balogh and Streeten (1960) argued that the economy is in perpetual disequilibrium, so that one investment creates scope for another: e.g. a shoe factory generates opportunities for a new tannery, which generates demand for hides, etc. With domestic investment, most of this dynamic linkage occurs at home; with foreign investment, abroad.

All these arguments suggest that, if there is a genuine choice between equivalent domestic and overseas investments, private criteria will overemphasise the latter. Much of the agitation against FDI presupposes this choice exists, but we

158

suspect that this is not so. Domestic investment may be available, but only for lower social returns than FDI. Hence this sub-section suggests reasons for being careful over FDI, not for automatically restricting it.

15.4 MULTINATIONALS AND INTERNATIONAL TRADE THEORY

The gap between the analysis of this chapter, relying on imperfect competition, and the bulk of international trade theory, relying on perfect competition, is obvious. The Ricardian theory of trade can incorporate capital flows but not direct investment. With Heckscher–Ohlin, trade and factor movements are entirely substitutable: trade equalises factor prices, eliminating any need for factor mobility, whereas, if factor mobility equalised factor prices, commodity prices would be equalised, thus eliminating trade. Only the modern theories of Chapter 4 are compatible with FDI, and they relate trade and investment to the same stimuli. This, and the extent to which MNEs shift components and finished goods between branches (intra-firm trade), suggest that trade and FDI may well be complementary.

Trade theory is not well developed for imperfect competition, so that aspect of FDI presents considerable analytical difficulties. If, however, we ignore this, the foreign ownership aspect presents few problems. MNEs respond to comparative advantage (their locational decisions), and, given their lack of dependence on any one country, are possibly more sensitive to changes in comparative advantage than are national firms. We saw above how trade and growth theory could handle capital flows once we allow for production in one country to be income in another. Finally, although MNEs might influence the pattern of commercial policy, or reduce its effectiveness, they do not affect the fundamental analysis. Thus, while MNEs are an important topic for further research, their existence does not demolish international trade theory, as has sometimes been claimed.

FURTHER READING

Among textbooks *Grubel* (1981) and *Lindert and Kindleberger* (1982) offer some detail on this topic, but the best introductions are two book-length surveys: *Hood and Young* (1979) and *Caves* (1983). Two useful collections of essays are *Dunning* (1972, 1974); see especially *Horst and Streeten* in the latter. On the causes of FDI, *Caves* (1974a), *Dunning* (1979) and *Lall* (1980) are important, while *Hymer* (1979) is a classic reference. *Steuer* (1973) examines MNEs in Britain but is rather complacent; *Panić and Joyce* (1980) are more critical. *Lipsey and Weiss* (1981) examine exports and FDI empirically, while *Reddaway* (1968) provides a wealth of data on balance of payments effects. *Lall* (1973) examines transfer pricing in detail. For the role of MNEs in LDCs, *Lall and Streeten* (1977) is an excellent study of both theory and empirical evidence, and *Vaitsos* (1974, 1976) provides a strong critique. *Helleiner* (1973) provides evidence on the question of trade.

Part II

16 The Balance of Payments

Part I of this book dealt with the causes and effects of international trade in a barter economy. Every transaction involved the exchange of one good for another. We now add an element of realism by introducing money. In the real world, virtually every transaction involves swapping goods (or assets) for money. This, of course, is much more efficient than barter: it removes the need for the double coincidence of wants and it allows one to sell in one period and buy in another. However, it also introduces additional analytical problems: we have to consider the causes and consequences of imbalance between sales and purchases, we have to recognise that money and financial assets may cross international borders, and we have to handle additional relative prices – in particular the price of one country's money in terms of another's. Adding money also allows us more easily to aggregate trade flows in the many different goods that exist, and takes us naturally into the macroeconomics of the international economy.

Part II of this book tackles these problems. It considers the determinants of the level of exports and imports – prices, incomes and various non-price factors – and examines the interaction of international trade and national income. It looks at the foreign exchange market and seeks explanations of the movements in exchange rates. It considers how exchange rates affect the macro-economic control of an economy and its insulation from economic shocks abroad, and it also discusses the pros and cons of the floating exchange rate regime of the 1970s. Finally, combining all this analysis it considers the impact of the oil price rises and the discovery of North Sea oil on the British economy.

This chapter sets the scene for these analyses by introducing two important concepts. Before we can discuss international transactions meaningfully, we must measure them. This is done in section 16.1, where the balance of payments accounts are described. Section 16.2 offers a very brief description of the main British international transactions. Section 16.3 then introduces the exchange rate, defining various concepts and briefly surveying recent experience. Finally, section 16.4 summarises the remaining chapters of Part II.

16.1 BALANCE OF PAYMENTS CONCEPTS

The principles The balance of payments accounts record all economic transactions between a country's residents and the rest of the world. These include not only buying and selling goods and assets, but also, for example, gifts, and transfers within companies when no money changes hands. Residents include individuals who live permanently within the country, government agencies and companies, although not their overseas subsidiaries.

In theory, the accounts are drawn up by double-entry bookkeeping methods, by which every transaction appears twice, once as a credit and once as a debit; that is, broadly speaking, once as the object bought or sold is transferred, and once as payment is made for it. We define a credit (recorded with a + sign) as any transaction notionally giving rise to an inflow of cash, and a debit (–) as any transaction notionally causing an outflow of cash. Consider the following simple examples, which are recorded in Table 16.1.

(i) An export worth £5 bartered for an import worth £5. We record +£5 for the export (notional cash inflow) and –£5 for imports (cash outflow).

(ii) An export worth £10 paid for by the (foreign) importer running down his bank balance in London. We record +£10 for the export and –£10 for the reduction in foreign holdings of sterling.

(iii) An export worth £10 paid for in foreign currency. We record +£10 for the export and –£10 for the increase in domestic holdings of foreign cash. (Holding foreign cash amounts to making a deposit in a foreign central bank, and this requires an outflow of cash.)

(iv) The purchase, for £100, of a foreign subsidiary by a British firm, financed by borrowing abroad. We record –£100 for the purchase, and +£100 for the increase in foreign holdings of sterling.

(v) The repayment of the debt incurred in (iv) from the subsidiary's earnings. We record +£100 for the inflow of profits and –£100 for the reduction in foreign claims.

Table 16.1 A specimen balance of payments account

Credits (+)			Debits (–)		
Exports	£25	(i+ii+iii)	Imports	£5	(i)
Profits from abroad	£100	(v)			
			Investment abroad	£100	(iv)
			Reduction in foreign holdings of £	£10	(ii)
			Increase in holdings of foreign currency	£10	(iii)
Increase in claims by foreigners	£100	(iv)	Reduction in claims by foreigners	£100	(v)

Observe that, although we define our signs by reference to notional cash flow, no flow need actually occur. For example, transaction (i) involved no cash at all, and transactions (iv) and (v) could be effected entirely abroad, with no money crossing the British border. In Table 16.1 we recorded separately both an increase and a decrease in claims by foreigners; in all actual accounts, however, these are combined to yield a single figure for changes in net liabilities, rises in which are recorded as a credit.

Two transactions do not fall happily into this system. First, gifts. A gift of sterling to a foreigner is recorded as a debit under transfers, and the corresponding credit is, say, the increase in claims by foreigners as the recipient banks his gift in London. Gifts of goods are recorded as exports of goods with the debit item recorded as a transfer, just as if we made a gift of money that was immediately spent on British exports. The second difficulty concerns the foreign exchange reserves. The government holds a stock of foreign currency, and when this is reduced it is recorded in the balance of payments accounts as a credit (+). Think of the reserves as comprising stocks of gold (as they used to), which can only be sold abroad. A reduction in the stock involves exporting and hence receives a + sign.

Balance of payments disequilibrium

Since every transaction enters the balance of payments account twice (with opposite signs), the sum of the account must be zero. What, then, constitutes balance of payments disequilibrium? Disequilibrium is when some crucial subset of the accounts fails to sum to zero. What is crucial depends on the question being asked, and we shall discover below that there are several subsets, or balances, of interest. Economists refer to the selection of the 'crucial' subset as 'drawing the line'. If we imagine all transactions listed in a column, we put the ones of interest 'above the line' and the rest 'below the line'. Clearly, if the whole column sums to zero, the sum (balance) above the line must be equal and opposite to the sum below the line. Equilibrium requires that both be zero.

Normally we are interested in having balance over *autonomous transactions*. These are transactions that occur regardless of the size of other items in the balance of payments – i.e. transactions undertaken in their own right. The remaining transactions, called *accommodating transactions*, occur only to complete some other foreign transaction. For example, exporting goods is autonomous, but the resulting increase in balances of foreign currencies is accommodating. It is obviously impossible to discover the motive of every transactor, or to classify all motives unambiguously as either autonomous or accommodating. We therefore adopt various conventions of classification, and different conventions give rise to different balance of payments concepts.

The UK balance of payments accounts

We now illustrate the principles of balance of payments accounting by looking at the layout of the UK accounts. These are summarised in Table 16.2.

Table 16.2 The UK balance of payments, 1980[a]

		£ million	
CURRENT ACCOUNT			
	Visible balance	+1,185	
+	Services	+4,060	
	= *Trade balance*		*+5,245*
+	Interest, profits and dividends	−273	
+	Transfers	−2,107	
	= *Current balance*		*+2,865*
LONG-TERM CAPITAL			
+	Direct investment (excl. oil companies)	−915	
+	Portfolio investments	−2,294	
+	Other long-term capital	+157	
	= *Basic balance*		*−187*
SHORT-TERM CAPITAL			
+	Trade credit	−1,170	
+	UK banks' dealings	−482	
+	Exchange reserves in sterling	+1,262	
+	Other external liabilities	+2,558	
+	Other short-term capital	−980	
+	Balancing item	+191	
	= *Balance for official financing*		*1,192*
OFFICIAL FINANCING			
+	Reductions in official reserves	−291	
+	Other official finance	−901	
	= *Sum*		*0*

Note:
[a] All figures are net – that is, credits less debits.
Source: Central Statistical Office, *United Kingdom Balance of Payments* (1982).

The current account
The main element of the current account is visible trade – imports and exports of

tangible, or visible, goods, the net balance of which is referred to as the *visible balance*. The remainder are invisibles, which comprise: trade in services – such as earnings from providing sea and air transport to foreigners and commissions on insurance deals; interest, profits and dividends earned and paid abroad; and transfers. Service trade is conceptually identical to visible trade: the items traded have to be produced and enter the production side of the national accounts. The balances on service and visible trade comprise the *trade balance*, which shows the net claim on the country's resources that international trade imposes. Earnings from abroad record Britain's earnings from foreign production, while earnings paid abroad show the part of the incomes derived from British production that accrues to foreigners. Net earnings from abroad reflect the difference between domestic product (output produced in Britain) and national product (output owned by Britons). Finally, transfers have no direct effect on production. They merely reflect one use that income is put to, and their net value is recorded in the national accounts as an item of expenditure.

The sum of all current transactions is the *current balance*. It measures the difference between national income and national expenditure.

Let Y be national income (output plus income from abroad),
    A be national expenditure,
    N be sales by residents to residents,
    X be sales abroad plus income earned abroad (i.e. total credits), and
    M be purchases from and income paid abroad.

Now, expenditure not spent abroad must go on local goods, and similarly income not earned abroad must come from local sales. Hence:

$$Y - X = N = A - M \qquad (16.1)$$

from which

$$\text{current balance} = X - M = Y - A. \qquad (16.2)$$

We shall return to this fundamental equation of balance of payments theory below. Now we move down the accounts to look at capital transactions.

The capital accounts

Apart from occasional capital transfers, the first component of the capital account is investment, which includes direct investment, portfolio investment and certain long-term official flows. Direct investment abroad occurs when a British resident acquires direct ownership of real assets abroad, while an inflow of direct investment represents the purchase of British assets by foreigners. Portfolio investment, on the other hand, arises from dealings in long-term financial instruments such as shares and government stock. Clearly there are arbitrary elements in these definitions: for instance, how many shares in a foreign company must a resident buy before acquiring control; what constitutes a long-term instrument? You should, therefore, check your national definitions before using published figures.

The sum of the current and long-term capital balances constitutes the *basic balance*. This was once considered very important – indeed, it was identified as 'the' balance of payments – because, with strong controls on short-term capital flows, it was felt possible to define 'basic' transactions as autonomous and all the rest as accommodating. This is no longer so, but basic balance is still significant for a country's liquidity (the amount of immediately accessible funds it has). 'Basic' deficits require financing from stocks of short-term liquid assets; and if these are scarce (as in Britain in 1976), the basic balance is important.

The remainder of the capital account considers short-term capital flows. These range from trade credits, through private loans and bank lending, to changes in foreign central banks' holdings of sterling and government stocks. Monetary transactions such as these are carried out mainly by telephone and computer links, and huge amounts of money can flow backwards and forwards during an hour. Hence, unlike the transactions above, it is impossible to record gross flows. Rather, statisticians record net flows over a period of time (e.g. a day) by comparing the stocks of assets at the beginning and end of the period. Thus, despite the relatively modest net figures, massive gross flows can occur on particular occasions.

Official financing

The final major element of the accounts is official financing. This records only accommodating transactions undertaken by official institutions. The main elements are transactions between monetary authorities (loans to or from the International Monetary Fund, or other central banks), government borrowing on foreign money markets, and changes in the UK foreign exchange reserves.

These transactions form the basis of another attempt to separate autonomous from accommodating transactions, captured in the *balance for official financing*. All private transactions and all government transactions except those explicitly aimed at managing the exchange rate are treated as autonomous. This balance therefore reflects the extent to which the monetary authorities have to intervene in the market to take up the imbalance in total private and government non-monetary transactions. It is of interest in that it summarises the pressure on the foreign exchange reserves and also the extent to which foreign transactions inject money into, or withdraw it from, the domestic economy.

By including the whole of the current and capital balances, the official financing balance clearly defines too much as autonomous – for example, many changes in private bank balances are accommodating. However, with the current high degree of international capital mobility, it is probably a more relevant summary than the basic balance, which includes too little.

The balancing item

One final component remains in Table 16.2: the balancing item. If accounting methods were perfect, double-entry accounts would always sum to zero because every transaction would appear twice – once positively and once negatively. In practice, however, we cannot simultaneously observe both sides of every trans-action. We may observe you importing £100 worth of goods, but we cannot at that precise time observe whether you pay by borrowing abroad or by running down your balance of foreign exchange. All we can do is to look, at the end of the day, at how overall borrowing and cash positions have changed. Hence, for most transactions the two sides are measured independently, and, since different components of the accounts are measured with different degrees of accuracy and with slightly different timing conventions, it is no longer guaranteed that they will sum to zero. The balancing item is introduced as an extra item to ensure that, in the end, they do so. The government may be assumed to know its own transactions perfectly, so the balancing item is best thought of as a component of the current and capital balances, introduced to ensure that their sum is equal and opposite to the official financing balance.

The balancing item can be very significant in particular years, but, over the course of several years, positive and negative entries tend to cancel out, leaving a very small unexplained residual.

The current account again

We have seen that the current account measures the difference between national income and expenditure. We can now see that this involves net investment abroad. Drawing the line below the current account means that (ignoring the balancing item) the current balance must be equal and opposite to the sum of the capital and official financing balances. These explicitly involve dealings in foreign assets, with net acquisitions appearing with a negative sign because they involve an outflow of cash. Now suppose that we have a current surplus; the other accounts must be equally in deficit. Thus, we acquire net foreign assets, i.e. increase our wealth, by the extent of the current surplus. This is so whether the surplus is spent redeeming foreign debts, adding to the reserves or buying new foreign assets. This is, of course, precisely analogous to our personal finances. If you have a grant of £1,500 and spend only £1,400 over the year, your current assets (wealth) rise by £100.

To summarise, the current balance measures the excess of our receipts from abroad over our expenditure abroad. By definition this equals, *ex post*, the difference between national income and expenditure, and also the national net acquisition of foreign assets.

16.2   UK FOREIGN TRANSACTIONS

We now turn from the form to the content of the balance of payments accounts, and consider briefly the nature and size of the UK's various foreign transactions. These are described in figures and tables that you should look at carefully. The text outlines only the most obvious features. We do not consider the measurement of the various series. For anyone wishing to use these data, this essential question should be pursued in the official literature – e.g. Central Statistical Office, *United Kingdom Balance of Payments* (annual) and *Economic Trends* (monthly); Department of Trade and Industry, *British Business* (weekly).

Visible trade

Visibles account for the bulk of Britain's current transactions. Their pattern in 1980 is summarised in Figure 16.1 (lower part) and Table 16.3. Table 16.3 shows the huge extent to which British trade has become concentrated on the EEC. It also clearly shows that EEC links have primarily displaced links with the Commonwealth countries – Britain's traditional markets. The surplus with the EEC in 1980 was the first since accession in 1973, and reflects mainly sales of oil; in other goods, the EEC countries export more to Britain than they import from her. North Sea oil is also evident in the recent switch from deficit to surplus with oil-exporting countries.

Possibly the most striking feature of the commodity composition of visible trade is the similarity of exports and imports in the major groups. It is no longer true that the UK exports manufactures to pay for food and raw materials. Figure 16.1 shows near balance in manufactured trade in 1980; by 1983 the UK had a deficit in this trade. The growth of manufactured imports has occurred fairly steadily, from 18 per cent of total imports in 1950, to 33 per cent in 1960, 53 per cent in 1970 and 63 per cent in 1980, but there has been strong recent growth in finished manufactures, with shares of 4 per cent, 11 per cent, 24 per cent and 36 per cent respectively. Coupled with relatively stagnant home demand, this expansion has

The Balance of
Payments

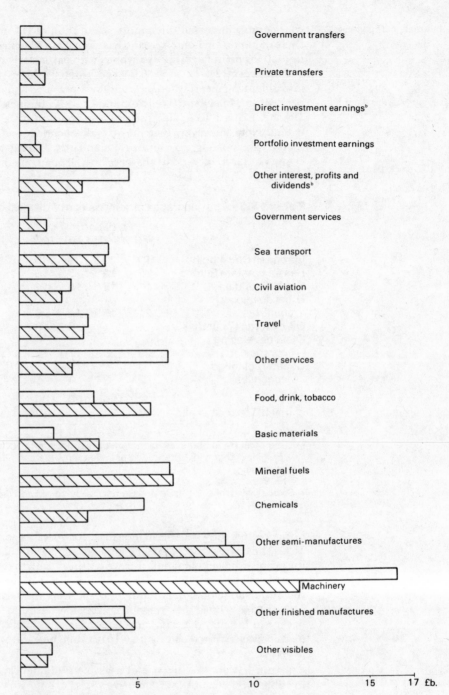

Government transfers

Private transfers

Direct investment earnings[b]

Portfolio investment earnings

Other interest, profits and
dividends[b]

Government services

Sea transport

Civil aviation

Travel

Other services

Food, drink, tobacco

Basic materials

Mineral fuels

Chemicals

Other semi-manufactures

Machinery

Other finished manufactures

Other visibles

5   10   15   17 £b.

Notes:
[a] Credits (exports) unshaded; debits (imports) shaded.
[b] Profits accruing to oil companies appear under 'direct investment earnings' for debits,
but under 'other interest, profits and dividends' for credits.
Sources: Central Statistical Office, *United Kingdom Balance of Payments* (1982) and
Economic Trends (November 1982).

Figure 16.1   *United Kingdom current transactions, 1980*

169

considerably increased the import penetration of UK markets. For instance, the share of imports in home demand has risen from 17 per cent in 1968 to 25 per cent in 1980 for manufacturing as a whole, with particularly strong growth in clothing and footwear (12 per cent to 30 per cent), motor vehicles (5 per cent to 46 per cent), instrument engineering (30 per cent to 61 per cent) and electrical engineering (14 per cent to 37 per cent) (Wells and Imber, 1977; Business Statistics Office, *Business Monitor*). Exports have also risen as a proportion of sales, but not to the same extent. Note, however, that the overall openness and penetration of the UK market are not high by historical standards. During much of the nineteenth century, total credits and debits were both around one-third of GNP – above their share today.

Table 16.3 The geographical composition of UK visible trade[a] (percentages)

	Exports				Imports			
	1950	1960	1970	1980	1950	1960	1970	1980
European Community[b]	19	22	29	43	19	20	27	41
Rest of Western Europe	12	12	17	15	8	11	14	15
North America	11	16	15	11	15	20	21	15
Other developed countries	21	15	12	6	16	12	9	7
Oil-exporting countries	6	7	6	10	9	11	9	9
Other developing countries	29	25	17	12	30	22	15	11
Centrally planned economies	2	3	4	3	3	4	4	2
Total	100	100	100	100	100	100	100	100
of which Commonwealth	38	34	20	12[c]	40	31	23	11[c]

Notes:
[a] Overseas Trade Statistics Basis; figures may not sum to 100 because of rounding.
[b] Belgium, Denmark, France, West Germany, Ireland, Italy, Luxembourg and the Netherlands.
[c] 1979.
Sources: Mansell (1980); Central Statistical Office, *Monthly Digest of Statistics* (November 1982).

Figure 16.2 shows shares in industrial countries' exports of manufactures since 1899. The obvious message is the gradual, and natural, displacement of the UK as the prime exporter of manufactures over the twentieth century (in fact, the process started well before 1899). It also shows the effects of the world wars. The first hit the European nations very hard, and, following the second, West Germany and Japan had to rebuild their trade from very low bases. At least part of the post-war decline in Britain's share has arisen because of its artificial inflation in 1950. This decline was arrested during the 1970s, but now shows signs of resuming its progress.

Britain has almost always had a visible trade deficit, financing it through an invisible surplus. Since 1825, only five years have shown visible surpluses – in each case associated with a severe squeeze of the domestic economy: 1956, 1958, 1971, 1980 and 1981.

Invisible trade

Invisible or service trade, is described in the middle part of Figure 16.1. The amounts are quite significant – invisible exports amount to one-third of visible exports – but it should never be believed that they could in any sense replace visible exports. Among the various headings, shipping, civil aviation and tourism are roughly in balance. Years ago, Britain was a net exporter of shipping services; however, with the growth of other fleets, the decline of Commonwealth links and the increasing insistence by nations that they carry their own trade, she is now usually in deficit. Civil aviation, on the other hand, has shown consistent surpluses since 1960, amounting to 20–25 per cent of debits; but since it is a relatively small industry its overall contribution is fairly small.

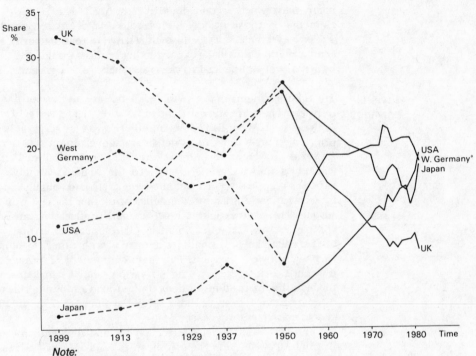

Note:
a West Germany estimated until 1937.
Sources: Maizels (1965); Mansell (1980); *National Institute Economic Review* (December 1982).

Figure 16.2 *Shares in industrial countries' exports of manufactures*

Travel expenditure comprises about 20–25 per cent business travel and the remainder leisure travel or tourism. The former records a modest surplus every year and is relatively insensitive to economic conditions. The latter is volatile, responding to prices and incomes as well as to non-economic factors such as the Olympic Games; it has also been subject to fierce legal restrictions in the past. Until 1967, tourism showed a deficit; the next six years were roughly balanced, followed by six of strong surplus. The last were probably due to the relative cheapness of Britain following the depreciations of sterling in 1972/3 and 1976, with the peak surplus coinciding with the Royal Jubilee in 1977. Since 1979, appreciation has cut receipts and boosted debits, resulting in deficits since 1981. The principal source of travel receipts is the EEC, followed by North America (reversing their positions in 1970), while debits accrue mostly to the EEC and the rest of Western Europe.

The government service account has always shown a substantial deficit. About half the credits (£201m. in 1980) accrue through military expenditure – e.g. the US

171

hiring of military bases in the UK – and a further quarter comprise receipts for services provided to EEC institutions. Of the debits, 15 per cent is diplomatic and administrative expenditure abroad and the rest (£1,021m.) is military expenditure, two-thirds of which is in West Germany. The final element of the account is 'other services', which is in substantial surplus. These include commissions on foreign trade, consultancy fees, royalties, telecommunications and postal fees, and expenditure by foreign students and journalists in the UK. The main credit item, however, is the earnings of financial institutions, such as banks and insurance companies, which account for £1,601m. in all. This is one of the most buoyant elements of British trade – both credits and debits increased five-fold over the 1970s. Nevertheless, it is still small relative to manufacturing: to balance a 1 per cent fall in manufacturing exports, other services would have to raise their exports by $5\frac{1}{2}$ per cent, or financial services raise theirs by 22 per cent!

Invisible earnings

The other elements of the invisible balance are interest, profits and dividends and transfers. These are shown in the top section of Figure 16.1 for 1980: total credits of these items were £10,055m. and there was an overall deficit of £2,380m. The principal contributor to this deficit was government transfers abroad, totalling £1,832m., of which net contributions to EEC institutions of £825m. and foreign aid (excluding military) of £649m. were the main identifiable components. The earnings on portfolio investments were small and roughly balanced, while direct investment earnings showed a deficit and other interest profits and dividends a surplus. The last two figures, however, partly reflect the statistical treatment of oil companies: their debits (£2,965m. in 1980) appear under 'direct investment', while their credits (probably small) are lumped in with 'other'. Non-oil direct investment earnings showed a surplus. The main component of 'other interest, profits and dividends' is interest accruing on various short-term loans, mostly channelled through the financial institutions of the City. Combining this with their fees, it is estimated that City institutions earned around £2,275m. in 1980 – about $6\frac{1}{2}$ per cent of manufacturing's earnings.

The overall deficit on interest, profits and dividends in 1980 was unique in British history since the Napoleonic wars. Data are obviously not perfect but, over the nineteenth century, net invisible earnings appear to have grown steadily until, in 1910–13, they alone paid for 25 per cent of visible imports. The slump of the 1930s reduced earnings substantially but, since import prices also fell, earnings still financed about 20 per cent of imports. The Second World War substantially reduced Britain's overseas assets: many were sold and many destroyed or neglected. By 1946–8 net earnings covered only 10 per cent of visible imports. This improved over 1949–52 – probably because of the boom in primary commodity prices – but thereafter gradually declined to the deficit of 1980. This decline partly reflected Britain's loss of political and industrial power: foreign assets were not maintained, further investment was increasingly restricted, and the government took on increasing amounts of debt to support the value of sterling. It also reflected growing investment in Britain by American multinational companies; this grew rapidly in the 1970s as the North Sea was developed. Since 1980, Britain has run current account surpluses, and investing these at the high nominal rates of interest available has turned interest, profits and dividends back into surplus.

Investment transactions

Investment flows show much greater volatility than trade flows; hence our discussion ranges more widely than the single year's figures given in Table 16.2. Over the 1970s there was a fairly steady inflow of direct investment – especially from the oil companies – and periods of strong portfolio investment coinciding with high rates of interest. Outflows were fairly modest at first, but grew as economic growth seemed less secure in Britain and, after 1979, as exchange controls on investment were removed. Recently, massive outflows of both direct and portfolio investment have occurred. The largest single source of direct investment abroad is the unremitted profits of foreign subsidiaries. These profits are treated as if they were paid to the British parent company – showing up as invisible earnings – and then reinvested – showing up as direct investment. In fact, of course, no explicit transfer occurs. The main inflows of portfolio investment are purchases of government stock. There is no information on the assets purchased by outgoing portfolio investment, but it is known that over half of such investment is undertaken by pension funds, investment trusts and insurance companies.

There is nothing new in these flows of international investment. Britain's high invisible earnings of the nineteenth century reflected earlier investment, mostly in mines and plantations and in social investment in developing areas. The former constituted direct investment, but the latter should be classed as portfolio investment, as British residents took up the stock of foreign governments. Post Second World War investment has been concentrated in manufacturing, and, until the 1970s, conducted principally with the USA. During the 1970s, investment was of more general origin and the phenomenon of 'cross-hauling' – two countries investing in each other – has grown. In 1980, however, over 60 per cent of UK inward and outward direct investment was still with North America.

Turning to short-term capital movements, there are four main elements to consider. First, trade credit, which is basically an accommodating flow lubricating the machinery of international trade in goods. Second, UK banks' overseas transactions, which were legally restricted until 1979 but have since expanded rapidly. Third, 'exchange reserves in sterling', which are other countries' official holdings of sterling – the 'sterling balances'. In 1971, an inflow in this category reflected confidence in Britain's 'sound money' policy; this was gradually eroded, however, by the Heath–Barber boom of 1972–3 and the difficulties of 1974–5, culminating in a huge outflow in 1976. The process was interrupted in 1974 because many of the oil producers of OPEC kept their reserves in sterling. Hence, until they had adjusted to their new wealth, much of it was placed short term in London. Indeed, it was fears that an OPEC member, Nigeria, was about to move out of sterling that finally precipitated the crisis in July 1976. The final component is 'other external liabilities', which are short-term sterling debts held privately abroad. These were not encouraged over the early 1970s, but as the British economy stabilised in 1977 they began to reappear, ending with a stampede into sterling over 1979–81. These last two elements are the main components of 'hot money', movements of which are generally large and volatile.

Official financing

This component summarises the behaviour of the monetary authorities, showing how they meet the surplus or deficit of the other accounts. The main element is changes in the level of the reserves, with drawings on the reserves recorded as positive elements. Overall, the reserves increased over the 1970s, hardly falling even in the sterling crisis of 1976. The latter was, in fact, met mainly by foreign currency borrowing undertaken by public corporations and local authorities. This is included under official finance, however, because its motivation was so obviously official finance, and because the central government underwrote any losses that these bodies made by borrowing abroad in foreign currency terms rather than at home in sterling. The other element of official finance is transactions with other monetary authorities – mainly the IMF – which was also exploited during 1976–7.

173

Foreign assets and liabilities

So far we have considered the flows of investment; we now turn to the stocks of assets and liabilities – i.e. to Britain's net worth in foreign assets. Table 16.4 summarises the position (although we should note that data are very imprecise in this area). Direct investment accounts for about 40 per cent of the UK's gross assets abroad, and these considerably outweigh foreign-owned assets in the UK. Portfolio assets are absolutely smaller, but also show a considerable positive net worth. Liabilities exceed assets in short-term capital, however, illustrating the scope for the liquidity problems that have periodically beset the UK (e.g. 1967, 1972, 1976). However, by 1981, the ample surplus of official finance assets went some way towards alleviating these dangers.

Table 16.4 Balance sheet of UK foreign assets and liabilities (£m.)

	1970		1981	
	Assets	Liabilities	Assets	Liabilities
Private sector:				
Direct investment	8,800	4,885	41,660	26,525
Portfolio investment	5,600	2,075	23,120[a]	5,800
Trade credit and advance				
payments	2,704	818	12,769	4,955
Other short–term	677	3,217	12,372	26,538
Public sector:				
Public corporations and				
local authorities[b]	—	124	—	1,122
Central government				
Long term	1,359	2,160	3,415	1,649
Short term[b]	153	2,467	852	7,423
Official finance	1,178	1,136	11,960	4,263
Total	20,471	16,882	106,148	78,275

Notes:
[a] Including £1,120m. 'miscellaneous' investment.
[b] Excluding official finance.
Source: Central Statistical Office, *United Kingdom Balance of Payments* (1982), Tables 11.1 and 11.2.

To put these figures in perspective, note that in 1981 net worth would finance visible and invisible imports for only four–five months, while gross assets would last only seventeen months. Also, the total worth of the domestic capital stock in 1981 was about £1,200b. About 6 per cent of this was foreign-owned, while UK assets abroad added about 8.5 per cent to the domestic stock.

16.3 THE FOREIGN EXCHANGE RATE

One of the most obvious features of most international trade is that the partners wish to work in different currencies. A British manufacturer buys most of his inputs and consumes his profits in Britain – paying in terms of sterling. If he sells his wares in France, however, his purchasers will normally have only francs to offer. Some exchange is therefore necessary between sterling and francs, and this defines the rate of exchange or exchange rate. Quite simply, the exchange rate is the price of one money in terms of another, and, like other prices, it is determined by supply and demand in the market. We shall examine the determinants of these in Chapter 21 below; here we need merely note that they may arise from current or capital transactions and from private or official sources.

Some terminology

The exchange rate may be expressed in two ways: $2.00 per £1.00 or, equivalently, £0.50 per $1.00. The former – the foreign currency price of one unit of domestic currency – is the UK's convention, and will be used throughout this book. Most countries, however, use the latter – the local currency price of one unit of foreign currency.

Changes in the exchange rate are known as *appreciations* and *depreciations*, or, if they occur under a fixed exchange rate regime (see below), as *revaluations* and *devaluations*. An appreciation (revaluation) indicates an increase in value: e.g. for sterling, a rise from $2.00:£1.00 to $2.50:£1.00, or, in the other convention, a fall from £0.50:$1.00 to £0.40:$1.00. (Observe, it is beneficial to hold an appreciating currency.) Obviously, if the pound appreciates relative to the dollar, the dollar depreciates relative to the pound – not, however, by the same percentage! A move from $2.00 to $2.50 represents a 25 per cent appreciation of sterling, but only a 20 per cent depreciation of the dollar, £0.50 to £0.40. The $ per £ rate is multiplied by 5/4, while the £ per $ rate is divided by 5/4.

With many currencies in the world, there must be many exchange rates, e.g. $:£, $:DM, DM:£, etc. We refer to each individual rate as a *nominal exchange rate*. Often, however, it is useful to have a summary measure of, say, the value of sterling relative to the value of all other currencies. This is particularly so when exchange rates are flexible, because sterling may appreciate relative to some and depreciate relative to others. This summary measure is known as the *effective exchange rate*. It is really no more than an index number, and the only problem about it is the weights with which to combine the rates against each currency. If we were interested in imports, we might use weights based on the value of imports denominated in each currency. Obviously depreciation relative to the US dollar (supplying at least 10 per cent of UK imports) is more important than depreciation relative to the Swedish krona (3 per cent of imports), so the dollar gets more weight.

Generally, however, we are interested in both exports and imports and the weights are based on both. They take account not only of bilateral trade, i.e. trade flowing directly between two countries, but also of the extent to which the countries compete in third markets. For example, Japan and Italy have very little mutual trade, but, because they sell in the same third markets, a change in the yen exchange rate impinges on Italian competitiveness, and hence affects the lira effective exchange rate. The weight of the yen in the lira effective rate shows the amount that the lira would have to depreciate (relative to all currencies) to just offset the balance of trade effects on Italy of a 1 per cent depreciation of the yen (relative to all currencies), taking account of world trade patterns and the responsiveness of trade flows to relative prices.

Economists have recently started referring to the *'real exchange rate'*. This measures not the price of two monies, but the relative prices of two nations' bundles of output. It is no use being able to buy more dollars per pound if each dollar now buys fewer goods. If we express things relative to some base date, and if the nominal $:£ exchange rate is r and the USA and UK price indices p_s and p_k respectively, the 'real sterling exchange rate' is rp_k/p_s. A 'real' appreciation occurs either through a nominal appreciation (rising r), or through a relative rise in UK local currency prices (a rise in p_k/p_s). The 'real exchange rate' is no more than the ratio of UK to USA prices measured in dollars – the sterling value of p_k is converted to dollars by means of r – and hence it reflects relative UK:US competitiveness.

175

Clearly, by simultaneously considering many exchange rates and price levels, one could construct real effective exchange rates.

Exchange rate regimes

The exchange rate – the price of foreign currency – is determined by supply and demand. The demand for foreign currency arises from debit items on the balance of payments, i.e. from spending abroad; the supply arises from credit items. Any tendency towards surplus on the balance of payments creates an excess supply of foreign currency, driving down its price in terms of domestic currency or driving up (appreciating) the value of domestic currency in terms of foreign currency. Hence if, at any given exchange rate, credits exceed debits, the exchange rate is forced above that level. Equilibrium can occur only where excess supply is zero, i.e. where credits equal debits, and the exchange rate must move to bring this about.

There are two polar ways of bringing about this equality. First, under a system of *perfectly flexible exchange rates* (or *'clean floating'*), the monetary authorities keep out of the foreign exchange market entirely. Official finance is thus set to zero, and the balance of the remaining accounts must also be zero, since total credit and debits are equalised. For such a market to be useful it must be stable: the excess supply of foreign currency must be eliminated by the appreciation that it induces. In the long run this occurs through items in the basic balance. An appreciation of sterling raises the dollar price of goods and assets priced in sterling (a good worth £1.00 sells for $2.00 before appreciation and for $2.50 afterwards). Hence British goods and assets lose competitiveness abroad and net credits fall, so reducing the excess supply of foreign currency. These processes take time, however, and so, in the short run, stability depends on the short-term capital account. The main mechanism assumed is as follows: if people have some expected level of the exchange rate in mind, rises above that level are expected to be followed by falls. To hold sterling while expecting a fall is to expect losses, so, once the rate has risen above your expected level, it pays to sell and move your capital into foreign currency. If everyone does so, however, the excess supply of foreign currency disappears (because demand for it has risen), and the rise in sterling stops or reverses itself. These processes are explored in Chapters 18, 19 and 21 below.

The second polar approach to equalising total credits and debits is a system of *fixed exchange rates*. Here the authorities are committed to maintaining a particular exchange rate – or rather a narrow band of exchange rates, e.g. from $2.38 to $2.42 per £1.00. They do this by being always prepared to buy pounds for dollars at $2.38 and sell them at $2.42. Their purchases and sales show up as official finance. Disequilibrium now appears as movements in the reserves rather than as changes in the exchange rate. In other words, whereas previously price bore the adjustment in the exchange market, here quantity does. The only limits to this process are the extent of the official finance available, and the ability of the economy to balance the current and capital accounts in the long run without exchange rate changes. This is explored below in Chapters 17, 19 and 20.

Between these polar cases lie a number of exchange rate regimes that try to combine the advantages of both systems. Under the *adjustable-peg* system – or *Bretton Woods* system (named after the international conference at which it was devised) – countries generally maintain fixed rates, but at times of 'fundamental disequilibrium' the parity, or peg rate, may be altered. This system was used from 1945 to 1971. Although it was basically successful, it broke down because countries were reluctant to make parity changes and because, since all countries pegged their currencies to the dollar, there was nothing the USA could do about its exchange rate. This is discussed in Chapter 26 below.

A variant of the adjustable-peg is the *crawling-peg*. The problem of the former is that parity changes are traumatic events that give rise to huge volumes of speculation because the direction of the impending change is obvious to everyone. The crawling-peg replaces one large change with a continuous series of changes small enough to make speculation not worthwhile. It has been adopted by several inflation-prone middle-income countries, but has not proved popular in the developed world.

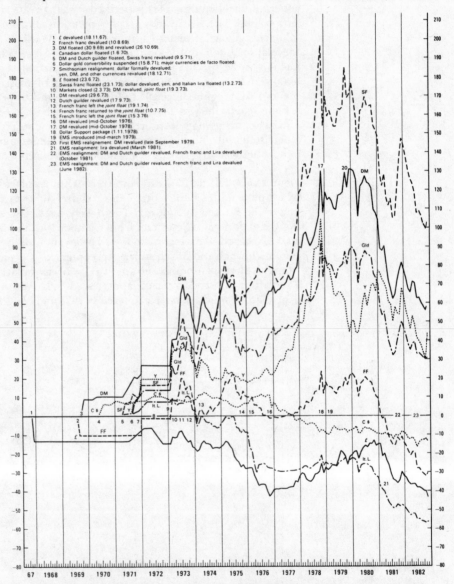

1 £ devalued (18.11.67).
2 French franc devalued (10.8.69).
3 DM floated (30.9.69) and revalued (26.10.69).
4 Canadian dollar floated (1.6.70).
5 DM and Dutch guilder floated, Swiss franc revalued (9.5.71).
6 Dollar gold convertibility suspended (15.8.71), major currencies de facto floated.
7 Smithsonian realignment: dollar formally devalued,
   yen, DM, and other currencies revalued (18.12.71).
8 £ floated (23.6.72).
9 Swiss franc floated (23.1.73); dollar devalued, yen, and Italian lira floated (13.2.73).
10 Markets closed (2.3.73); DM revalued, joint float (19.3.73).
11 DM revalued (29.6.73).
13 Dutch guilder revalued (17.9.73).
14 French franc left the joint float (19.1.74).
14 French franc returned to the joint float (10.7.75).
15 French franc left the joint float (15.3.76).
16 DM revalued (mid-October 1976).
17 DM revalued (mid-October 1978).
18 Dollar Support package (1.11.1978).
19 EMS introduced (mid-march 1979).
20 First EMS realignment: DM revalued (late September 1979).
21 EMS realignment: lira devalued (March 1981).
22 EMS realignment: DM and Dutch guilder revalued, French franc and Lira devalued
   (October 1981).
23 EMS realignment: DM and Dutch guilder revalued, French franc and Lira devalued
   (June 1982).

Source: Organization for Economic Co-operation and Development, *Economic Outlook.*
Currencies: £ – sterling; C $ – Canadian dollar; DM – Deutsche mark; FF – French franc;
SF – Swiss franc; Y – Yen; It. L – Italian lira; and Gld – gold.

Figure 16.3   *Exchange rates of major currencies against the dollar (percentage deviations with respect to dollar parities of October 1967, end of month figures – US$ per unit)*

177

At the other extreme, perfect flexibility was felt to encourage volatility when it was tried briefly in late 1973. It was therefore adapted into *managed floating*. This permits some official activity, but in a basically floating exchange rate market. Least interventionist is *leaning-against-the-wind* – aimed at smoothing out day-to-day fluctuations in the exchange rate without trying to influence its longer-run trends. More interventionist is the so-called *'dirty' float*, which involves the government pursuing some unspecified exchange rate target. The essence is in the 'unspecified' part, because by keeping their intentions secret the authorities hope to avoid giving speculators information on which to act. This may curb speculation, but it may also merely give rise to large volumes of uninformed and highly volatile speculation. The role of speculation is discussed in section 24.2. Managed floating – with different amounts of management – has been the predominant regime since 1973. Governments mostly protest that they are merely leaning against the wind, but the persistence, in both extent and direction, of much official financing suggests more than that. (A persistent official surplus must reflect a persistent current and capital deficit; since under pure floating this would be impossible, it is hard to believe it actually arises purely from day-to-day smoothing.)

Some data

Figures 16.3 and 16.4 illustrate some recent history of exchange rates. Figure 16.3 – which plots nominal exchange rates – shows the comparative tranquillity of the end of the Bretton Woods era. There were a few discrete changes in par values, but the majority were constant from October 1967 to May 1971. The latter half of 1971 saw a period of floating followed by an attempt to restore the adjustable-peg system through the Smithsonian Agreement of December 1971. Britain broke from this after six months, and after twelve it was replaced by generalised floating. Thereafter, most currencies appreciated relative to the dollar (the dollar depreciated), although not steadily: early 1974 and late 1975 were periods of dollar

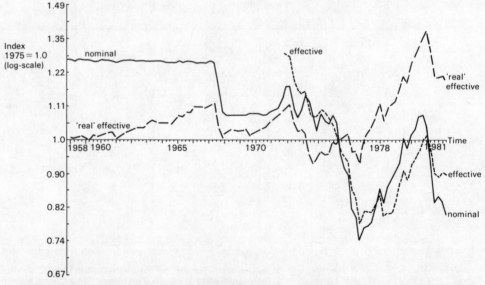

Sources: International Monetary Fund, *International Financial Statistics* for nominal; Winters (1983a) for 'real' effective (relative manufactured export prices); Central Statistical Office, *Economic Trends*, for effective.
[a] All rates are measured in dollars per pound and as index numbers (1975 = 1.0).

Figure 16.4   *United Kingdom exchange rates, 1958–82*

strength – all currencies falling relative to the dollar – whereas 1978 was a year of deep crisis for the dollar. Exchange rates also showed considerable volatility: in the first year of floating, the Deutsche Mark rose by 20 per cent and then fell back again, repeating the process over the following eighteen months.

Figure 16.4 shows the British history in more detail. The nominal exchange rate series shows clearly the periods of fixity, the crises of 1976, and the subsequent rise and fall of sterling. The effective exchange rate differs from this series by the extent to which the dollar moved against other currencies; it tells much the same story. The 'real' effective exchange rate series used here refers to UK export prices for manufactures relative to competing exporters' prices, and uses total manufactured exports as weights, but other 'real' exchange rates would tell roughly the same story. Over 1960–72, Britain suffered greater inflation than her competitors, and, although the 1967 devaluation improved competitiveness, it did not cure the basic problem: with fixed exchange rates, higher inflation eventually results in uncompetitiveness. The float downwards over 1972–3 greatly improved competitiveness – i.e. reduced the 'real' exchange rate – but over 1974–6 the real and nominal rates bore little relation to each other. The nominal depreciation just balanced higher inflation. This coincided with a period of great monetary expansion. Once the monetary position began to be brought under control, however, the real and nominal exchange rates linked up again, and the subsequent appreciation of sterling made British industry hugely uncompetitive. Fortunately, this position is now beginning to reverse.

16.4 A SUMMARY OF PART II

This chapter has introduced the balance of payments and the exchange rate. The rest of Part II analyses them – their behaviour under particular circumstances, their causes and their effects. We start in Chapter 17 with the simplest, but empirically most important, determinant of the level of international trade – national income. We show how income and trade interact and also how incomes in different countries are connected through international trade. We next consider how prices affect trade in Chapter 18, taking the principal determinant of relative prices to be the exchange rate. A section is devoted to measuring price elasticities in international trade, and another to elements of non-price competitiveness such as design and quality.

Chapter 19 broadens the discussion to examine how trade fits into the macro-economic balance of an economy. In particular we observe that any change in trade performance must have concomitant changes somewhere else in the economy. Only by recognising these changes can satisfactory policy be devised for controlling the current account. This chapter considers the 'small, open economy' – an economy that has no influence over the prices at which it trades with the rest of the world – and also the importance of wage rigidity in balance of payments theory.

Chapter 20 introduces a further macro-economic approach to the balance of payments – the monetary approach, comparing it with the results and models of the previous chapters. We then leave the fixed exchange rate world and consider the determination of exchange rates under a flexible system in Chapter 21. After examining various transactions in foreign exchange, we consider the simple purchasing power parity theory of exchange rates and find it deficient. Next we examine recent work on exchange rates and financial assets – viewing the

179

exchange rate as a means of equating the supply of and demand for world stocks of various assets. The chapter concludes with a discussion of recent exchange rate behaviour.

The exchange rate regime – fixed or floating – turns out to be an important influence on the effectiveness of macro-economic policy. After a brief discussion of the theory of economic policy in general, Chapter 22 considers this issue. It starts with a simple analysis due to Mundell and Fleming, and develops it in several directions. It concludes with some evidence on the degree of financial integration in the world economy. This discussion is extended into a general discussion of the pros and cons of floating exchange rates in Chapter 24. Particular attention is paid to the ability of flexible rates to insulate an economy from external shocks and to the form and role of speculation. Finally there is a brief discussion of optimum currency areas, during which the European Monetary System is described.

The intervening chapter (Chapter 23) is devoted to the analysis of the oil shocks of the 1970s. We start with the effects of the oil price rise – falling income but increased manufactured output in the West – and then consider the effects of an oil discovery such as in the North Sea – which involves some de-industrialisation, but none the less raises national income. Finally, the two shocks are combined in a study of the UK economy over the 1970s.

FURTHER READING

The conceptual problems of the balance of payments are explored in *Meade* (1951) and *Machlup* (1966). *Cohen* (1969) gives a useful alternative textbook treatment, and the introduction of Central Statistical Office, *United Kingdom Balance of Payments* (annual) provides a useful official summary. The latter also, of course, provides data on the UK position and also detailed explanatory notes. The US accounts appear in *Department of Commerce, Survey of Current Business* (monthly) and are discussed by *Stern et al.* (1977). For the history of the UK balance of payments, see *Thirlwall* (1980), ch. 7, *Mansell* (1980), *Imlah* (1958) – on the nineteenth century – and *Dornbusch and Fischer* (1980) – on the last decade. Effective exchange rates were introduced in *Artus and Rhomberg* (1973) and recent UK practice is described in Central Statistical Office, *Economic Trends* (March 1981).

17 National Income and the Trade Balance

We start our explanation of the macro-economics of the open economy with the simplest of aggregate models. For this chapter we shall assume fixed exchange rates and fixed prices throughout the world economy and, ignoring all assets and income from abroad, focus solely on the trade balance. The first two assumptions place us in a Keynesian world where income can settle, at least temporarily, at a level insufficient to generate full employment. Below full employment, income is determined by the level of demand because, with fixed prices and spare resources, supply can expand to meet any rise in demand, whereas, if demand fell further, supply would fall with it as there would be no virtue in producing goods that could not be sold. In this world there is no guarantee that the balance of trade will be in equilibrium either. As we shall discover, there is a relationship between the balance of trade and income (via the demand for domestic output), but in the absence of price flexibility and/or changes in stocks of assets this is not sufficient to ensure balance.

We would not wish to pretend that this model provides a complete or realistic view of the economy. We introduce these simplifications to enable us to concentrate on the relationship between trade and the national income. On the other hand, plenty of econometric evidence suggests that over the short run, when prices *are* sticky and asset stocks *are* fairly constant, income is a major determinant of trade movements and vice versa. Hence even the simple analysis provided here gives us considerable insight into the real world.

The chapter starts by modifying the well-known closed-economy multiplier to take account of imports. It then goes on to a two-country model in which one country's imports are recognised as the other's exports. This further modifies the multiplier, and also illustrates the interdependence of the world economy. Section 17.3 introduces two econometric models of the international multiplier. The first shows the effects of each OECD country's growth on its neighbours and is used to assess the 'locomotive' and 'convoy' approaches to world growth that were current in the mid-1970s. The second modifies the basic theory to take account of balance of payments constraints. The last section presents some evidence on the relationship between incomes and international trade in the real world.

17.1 FOREIGN TRADE AND THE MULTIPLIER

The concept of the multiplier is familiar to any student of economics. (If it is not, consult an elementary book on macro-economics, such as Brooman, 1970.) Briefly, the multiplier records the extent to which national income rises in response to the injection of one unit of extra expenditure. It is derived from the circular flow of income by noting that if income is to be in equilibrium (i.e. at the same level at every point in the circular flow) total injections must equal total withdrawals. In a simple closed-economy model with no government, the multiplier takes the value of $1/s$, where s is the marginal propensity to save.

We now generalise the multiplier to take account of international trade. We start with an economy small enough that its actions have no perceptible effect on incomes in the rest of the world. International trade introduces a new injection to the circular flow – namely exports, which provide demand for our output independent of our level of income – and a new withdrawal – imports. Like savings, imports absorb expenditure without generating any corresponding demand for local goods. Continuing with the assumption of no government, and adopting the simplest linear equations, we describe this situation algebraically as follows:

$$S = a + sY,\tag{17.1}$$

where savings (S) is a function of income (Y), with s being the marginal propensity to save and a a constant amount of savings independent of income.

$$M = b + mY,\tag{17.2}$$

where imports (M) are also related to income, with m being the marginal propensity to import.

$$I + X = S + M,\tag{17.3}$$

where total injections (investment, I, plus exports, X) equal total withdrawals, which is the equilibrium condition. Substituting (17.1) and (17.2) into (17.3) and regrouping yields

$$Y = \frac{-(a+b)}{(s+m)} + \frac{1}{(s+m)}(I+X).\tag{17.4}$$

Hence the multiplier, the increment in Y per unit increment in I, is $1/(s+m)$. Mathematically:

$$\frac{dY}{dI} = \frac{1}{s+m}.\tag{17.5}$$

Since m is positive – imports rise with income – the open-economy multiplier $1/(s+m)$ is less than the closed-economy multiplier $1/s$. In other words, the more open the economy, in the sense of the higher the *marginal* propensity to import, the less sensitive is national income to changes in injections, because more of the effect seeps away overseas.

The multiplier applies to increases in exports as well as in investment. Starting from equilibrium, suppose exports rise by a small increment ΔX. Equation (17.4) shows that income rises by $\Delta Y = \Delta X/(s+m)$ and substituting this into (17.1) shows that imports rise by $\Delta M = m\Delta X/(s+m)$. Now, if there were no domestic savings, $s=0$, $\Delta M = \Delta X$, so the trade balance would be unaffected by the increase in exports. However, if $s > 0$, the fraction $m/(s+m)$ is less than 1, and so $\Delta M < \Delta X$; that is, imports rise but not sufficiently to offset the rise in exports. Hence, even when we allow for the multiplier, an increase in exports improves the balance of trade:

$$\Delta B = \Delta X - \Delta M = \Delta X - \frac{m}{s+m}\Delta X = \frac{s}{s+m}\Delta X.\tag{17.6}$$

The extent of the improvement depends crucially on the marginal propensity to save. If this is small, although rising exports may boost income substantially, they do little for the balance of payments because imports rise almost in line.

17.2   REPERCUSSION EFFECTS

We now relax the small country assumption. Assume that our economy is large enough to affect incomes abroad. For instance, if our imports account for 10 per cent of the demand for the rest of world's goods, a 20 per cent increase in our imports will immediately raise the demand for their goods by 2 per cent. This, of course, raises their incomes, increasing their demand for goods, some of which is met by exports from our country. Hence in this case not all expenditure on imports is lost to an economy. By boosting incomes abroad, some of it finds its way back via increased exports.

We examine this situation in a model of a world comprising two countries, each satisfying all but the small country assumptions used in the previous section. We denote all foreign variables by an asterisk (*). Individually, both countries will satisfy equations (17.1)–(17.4), but now, instead of exports being an exogenous variable, we recognise that our exports are their imports, i.e. $X = M^*$, and vice versa, $M = X^*$. We now have two equilibrium conditions:

$$I + X = S + M \qquad (17.7)$$

and

$$I^* + X^* = S^* + M^*.$$

Substituting from (17.1) and (17.2) for S, M and X ($\equiv M^*$) and similar equations for S^*, M^* and X^* yields:

$$I + a^* + m^* Y^* = a + sY + b + mY \qquad (17.8)$$

and

$$I^* + a + mY = a^* + s^* Y^* + b^* + m^* Y^*.$$

With I and I^* still exogenous, these two equations in two unknowns (Y and Y^*) may be solved simultaneously to yield:

$$\vee \quad \frac{dY}{dI} = \frac{1}{s + m \left(\dfrac{s^*}{s^* + m^*} \right)} \qquad (17.9)$$

$$\frac{dY}{dI^*} = \frac{m^*}{(s^* + m^*)} \frac{1}{s + m \left(\dfrac{s^*}{s^* + m^*} \right)} \qquad (17.10)$$

Equation (17.9) defines the multiplier effect of our own exogenous expenditure (investment) changes. It is plainly greater than the simple open-economy multiplier of the previous section, because the denominator of the fraction is reduced: $s^*/(s^* + m^*) < 1$. This makes sense intuitively because previously we assumed exports to be fixed, whereas here we assume them to be positively related to our income via our imports and foreign income. There are also, however, multiplier effects from foreign investment, as shown by (17.10). This is the product of two effects: first, the increase in their imports (our exports), ignoring any repercussion effects (see ΔM in (17.6)), and, second, the standard (repercussion) foreign trade multiplier effect on exogenous increases in demand (see (17.9)). Hence, once we allow for repercussion effects, the two economies become strongly interconnected. Each economy is affected by both exogenous changes and the parameters of economic behaviour in each other.

First, we can generalise the results to many countries (Metzler, 1950, 1951). This should be clear intuitively – breaking up the rest of the world into many separate countries changes nothing fundamental – but it is slightly complex

183

mathematically. It may be shown that, as above, the closed-economy multiplier is the largest, the small open-economy multiplier smallest and the (repercussion) foreign trade multiplier in between.

Second, it would be possible – and more realistic – to relate imports not to national income but to national expenditure. This alters the various multipliers in detail and, while possibly significant in some practical applications, is not of great significance theoretically (Meade, 1951; Thirlwall, 1980).

Third, we could use very much more realistic functions for the variables than we have done. It is easy to introduce a government sector with exogenous expenditure and tax revenue a function of income, and it is also simple to allow either investment or exports to vary with income. Further, if one is prepared to solve the model numerically (by computer) rather than analytically (as above), it is possible to break free of the simple linear forms, and to introduce additional explanatory variables into the functions.

17.3 THE TRANSMISSION OF ECONOMIC DISTURBANCES

We have just seen how an economic shock in one country affects other countries' economies via the mechanism of international trade. Hence a government no longer has sole control over its own economy; the economy is affected by other governments, and so economic policy-making exhibits some interdependence. Crudely, the more open an economy, the more it responds to external shocks and hence the greater its dependence on policy-making elsewhere. All of this raises the possibility that a country may raise its own level of income and employment more effectively by persuading other countries to expand than by trying to expand, say by fiscal stimulus, itself. This lay at the heart of many summit meetings in recent years at which the weaker economies tried to persuade their stronger and larger neighbours to pursue more expansionary policies for the common good.

During the latter half of the 1970s, the theory of expansion by selected countries pulling the rest of the world economies out of the slump was graced with the name 'the locomotive theory'. The idea was that, if the United States, West Germany and Japan expanded and therefore imported more, they would increase the demand for goods from other developed countries. This would create income and employment in these countries, and improve their balances of trade. The latter would then allow them to expand their economies in turn, reinforcing their earlier growth and returning some of it to the 'locomotive' economies. To some extent this happened – over 1977 the USA expanded strongly – but overall the policy was not a great success. The extent of the expansion required in the locomotive countries was too great; besides, they had internal reasons – mostly to do with inflation – for not wishing to expand.

The 'locomotive theory' was briefly superseded by the 'convoy theory'. This held that, although it might not be feasible for a few countries to expand sufficiently to pull the remainder along, if all OECD countries expanded together, all would experience rising exports as well as rising imports and hence at least most would avoid balance of payments difficulties. This would allow weaker economies to undertake expansion of an order that they could not contemplate alone. This idea also foundered – again largely because the strong fully employed economies had little interest in expansion whether initiated by themselves or others.

We now look at the feasibility of these policies and the extent of international interdependence, using a simple econometric model designed by the Organization for Economic Co-operation and Development (OECD) for this very purpose.

184

OECD (1979) describes a simple multi-country model of the world economy based almost entirely on the theory of this chapter. For each of twenty-three OECD countries, it has an equation relating income to exogenous injections via the multiplier (like (17.4) above), and an import function (like (17.2)). It also has a world trade segment, which converts imports by OECD and non-OECD countries into exports by the OECD countries. In a multi-country setting, of course, we cannot just equate M^* and X as we did above; we have to build up country j's exports, X_j, as the sum of imports into each market times j's share of that market, i.e. $X_j = \sum_i \alpha_{ij} M_i$.

The market shares α_{ij}, determine the direction of the transmission of economic shocks. For example, suppose West Germany reflates her economy by a fiscal expansion. The resulting imports are then shared out via the α_{ij}s among Germany's trading partners, where, as exports, they set off further multiplier processes. Countries trading very little with Germany (e.g. Portugal) gain little direct benefit from her expansion, whereas those trading a lot (e.g. Austria) gain substantially. Once Germany's partners start to expand, of course, this passes through to their partners, including Germany, in a second round of expansion, and so on.

Table 17.1 reports some results from the OECD model for 1978. The first three rows give various background statistics: GNP, to indicate the size of each economy,

Table 17.1 Results from the OECD linkage model

	USA	Japan	W. Germany	France	UK	Ireland	All OECD
GNP[a] ($USb.)	2,156	963	643	476	316	12	6,775
Multiplier[b]	1.40	1.43	1.19	1.16	1.11	0.91	—
Marginal propensity to import[c]	0.19	0.15	0.48	0.48	0.64	1.01	—
(A) Effect on growth rate of 1% stimulus of country in heading							
USA	1.47	0.04	0.05	0.04	0.04	0.00	1.81
Japan	0.25	1.26	0.06	0.05	0.05	0.00	1.84
W. Germany	0.23	0.05	1.25	0.21	0.11	0.01	2.38
France	0.15	0.04	0.19	1.21	0.09	0.00	2.03
UK	0.28	0.06	0.16	0.14	1.17	0.03	2.32
Ireland	0.38	0.06	0.22	0.17	0.73	0.98	3.07
All OECD	0.74	0.21	0.23	0.18	0.13	0.01	2.04
(B) Effect on balance of trade ($US[b]) of 1% stimulus of country in heading							
USA	−3.35	0.44	0.49	0.41	0.40	0.02	−1.13
Japan	0.93	−1.20	0.27	0.23	0.23	0.01	0.68
W. Germany	0.35	0.10	−2.43	0.37	0.22	0.01	−0.08
France	0.19	0.05	0.26	−2.15	0.14	0.01	−0.81
UK	0.13	0.04	0.09	0.08	−1.91	0.02	−0.55
Ireland	0.00	0.00	0.00	0.00	0.01	−0.12	0.01
All OECD	−0.72	−0.31	−0.42	−0.39	−0.33	−0.02	−1.70

Notes:
[a] 1978 at current prices. *Source*: International Monetary Fund, *International Financial Statistics*, Yearbook, 1981.
[b] Multiplier on exports and government expenditure: average for the year after the stimulus occurs. *Source*: OECD (1979), Table 2, column 1 × [column 2 + column 3]/2.
[c] OECD present income elasticities for imports (ϵ_M). But $\epsilon_M = (dM/dY) \cdot (Y/M)$, hence marginal propensity is $\epsilon_M \cdot (M/Y)$. *Source*: ϵ_M from OECD (1979), Table 3, Y from row 1, and M from International Monetary Fund, *Annual Reports*.
Source: (A) and (B) – Organization for Economic Co-operation and Development (1979).

and estimates of the multiplier and the marginal propensity to import. Each column shows the effect of an increase in government expenditure, equal to 1 per cent of total domestic demand, carried out by the country named at the top of the column. We report in part (A) the percentage increase in each country's GNP over the year of the stimulus, and in part (B) the effect on each country's balance of trade over that year.

Consider, for example, an expansion of government expenditure in the USA by 1 per cent of total demand (this is a large stimulus – around $20b.). In the year after the injection, GNP is 1.47 per cent higher in the USA, 0.38 per cent higher in Ireland and 0.15 per cent higher in France. Similarly, the USA trade balance worsens by $3.35b., while those of her partners improve. For OECD overall, the expansion amounts to 0.74 per cent of total GNP and the balance of payments deterioration to $0.72b.

There are several points to be noted from these results. First, the effects of each country's stimulus on its own GNP, given along the diagonal of part (A) of Table 17.1, show how more open economies benefit less from their own stimuli. (The multiplier of below unity for Ireland stems from the implausible marginal propensity to import of above unity.) Second, the effects on other countries depend partly on the size of the economy undertaking expansion and partly on its openness. For example, the West German economy is 33 per cent smaller than the Japanese economy, but its greater openness makes it a more effective 'locomotive'. (The German influence on total OECD income exceeds that of Japan, 0.23 per cent compared with 0.21 per cent.) Indeed, the pressure on the Japanese over the 1970s was as much to open their economy as to expand it. Third, we can see the importance of the direction of trade. For instance, the USA is the most effective stimulator of the world economy, being both large and, on the margin, fairly open; yet France is more reliant on Germany, which takes 17 per cent of her exports and Ireland on the UK, which takes 46 per cent of hers.

A fourth feature is the strong expansionary effect of 'the convoy'. If all OECD countries expand together (see the last column), total GNP rises by twice the stimulus, even over the first year. Allowing for subsequent effects, the long-run multiplier is around 3. The benefits are not perfectly equally divided, but it is clear that most countries gain significantly from the 'convoy'. In part (B) of the table we see the balance of trade effects of overall expansion. Most countries in the OECD conduct over 60 per cent of their trade with other OECD countries, hence expansion in concert involves less strain on their balances of payments than does expansion alone. For example, expanding alone worsens the UK deficit by $1.91b., whereas in a convoy the decline is only $0.55b. In fact some countries, notably Japan, actually improve their trade balances in the convoy. This reflects Japan's low marginal propensity to import and high *marginal* share of other OECD markets. The net worsening of the OECD's trade balance from concerted expansion is only $1.70b. This reflects the extra imports from outside the group, and is surprisingly small.

Hoarding and finance

It is well known from Keynes that, if income is transferred from people who spend it to people who do not, aggregate demand drops and a multiple contraction can occur. The presence of a banking system helps to avoid this possibility by receiving deposits from people who have spare cash and transferring them, temporarily, to those who are short and who are therefore likely to spend it. The world is just a single large economy, and we can view it too in this way. Any country earning more than it spends is withdrawing demand from the world economy – i.e. it is hoarding – and, unless its surplus spending power is transferred elsewhere by lending, total demand is reduced.

The OECD model assumed that nearly all of any injection of income was passed on as extra demand for goods; that is, that marginal propensities to save were fairly low, and hence multipliers fairly high. But suppose we had a country that did not wish to increase its demand and merely neutralised any injection from increased exports by increasing savings or taxes. Then there would be no multiplier effect and the whole expansionary impulse would cease. Two sets of countries come immediately to mind as candidates for this sort of behaviour: countries that are already satiated with goods and services, and countries that have reached full employment.

At least in the short run, the oil producers found themselves in the former group after the large oil price rises. They received huge transfers of spending power, but were initially just unable to make use of it all. This was a major reason for the mid-1970s depression. In order to pay for their oil, Western nations had to improve their balances of trade in manufactures. Most attempted this by deflating and reducing imports, but, of course, just as expansion gets shared out among the OECD nations so does contraction. Each country found its exports falling as a result of its partners' contraction, and so had to reduce imports further, and so on. The result was a deep slump. Just as a concerted expansion worsens the total OECD trade balance with non-OECD relatively little, so the large suplus required to pay the higher oil prices required a large contraction.

Definitions of full employment differ, but there are certainly times when countries do not welcome extra demand. Frequently in that position over the last thirty years has been West Germany, which, having suffered two hyper-inflations, has been sensitive to any degree of economic overheating. Japan, on the other hand, has had a more pragmatic view of externally generated demand, but seems to have been unable to return much of it to the rest of the world by raising imports. Hence among developed nations, Germany and Japan have been the nearest to being hoarders.

We shall discuss international finance in detail later, but here we should note that, if OPEC and the developed surplus countries like West Germany and Japan lent out their surpluses, world expansion could still proceed, but only within limits. The countries that borrow are running balance of payments deficits and, if their deficits are persistent, questions must eventually arise about their credit-worthiness. Gradually, then, loans will be made only conditionally – usually on condition that the recipient cure its deficit, which usually entails deflation. Hence we could find a world divided into two classes of country: those that could expand but will not, and those that would expand but cannot.

This is the view adopted by the Cambridge Economic Policy Group (CEPG) in a series of reports (*Cambridge Economic Policy Review*, April 1979, December 1980 and December 1981). They distinguish countries constrained from expansion by their balances of payments from those that are unconstrained. The former have some maximum deficit that they can finance, and determine their GNP so as to bring this about. Given a level of exports determined by other countries' behaviour, they know how many imports they can afford; the import function then indicates what level of income this implies and fiscal policy is used to bring it about. The import function (17.2) is being used 'backwards'. These countries welcome any boost to exports because, by relaxing their payments constraint, it permits further growth. Hence, constrained countries pass on their expansionary stimuli and permit the international multiplier to work.

The unconstrained countries, on the other hand, can choose their level of GNP

187

independently of their balance of payments and with regard to other criteria – usually domestic employment and inflation. Assuming these countries have already settled at their desired income level, they will not permit any extra exports to expand the economy. Hence, an increase in their exports generates no feedback effects for other countries' exports. Consequently they represent a block in the multiplier process.

The CEPG use this framework to draw a radical solution. They argue that imports from unconstrained countries are basically wasted, because they increase income in neither the supplying (unconstrained) country nor any other. Hence, if an expansionary stimulus is not to run rapidly into the sand, care must be taken to avoid buying *extra* goods from such countries. For oil this is impossible except to the extent that alternative energy sources are available, but for manufactures they suggest that import controls should be used to direct incremental trade to flow only between constrained countries. By these means, they argue, the multiplier can be kept high and its effects concentrated on those countries that desire growth.

Within the confines of the simple, fixed-price, single-good model these conclusions are correct. When we consider the complexities of the real world, however, they are not very robust. We have already seen that trade controls reduce welfare, and we shall see later that a devaluation by the constrained countries relative to the unconstrained countries should redirect trade in the desired fashion without incurring these losses. There would also clearly be difficulties as countries shifted between being constrained and not. In 1978, the UK was certainly balance of payments constrained (economic policy was heavily focused on the external sector), but by 1981 she was clearly unconstrained (with a substantial current surplus). Hence, in 1978 her partners were to discriminate in Britain's favour, whereas three years later they were to discriminate against her. Pity the diplomats who had to negotiate that!

We have dwelt long on this simple Keynesian model for two reasons. First, it illustrates simply the interdependencies that occur in international economics. International transmission and policy-making encompass much more than simple fiscal stimuli, but the basic notion that countries affect each other is just the same as in our simple model. Second, despite its strong assumptions, this model has actually much to teach us. In the short run (six–nine months) the assumptions of the model are fairly well met, and the simple Keynesian transmission process is dominant. Even in the longer run, with flexible prices and important changes in stocks of assets, the basic income effects still operate, even if we observe them rather less closely.

17.4 INCOME EFFECTS – THE EMPIRICAL EVIDENCE

So far, we have looked at the relationships between income and international trade from a purely theoretical viewpoint. We *assumed* that the import function took the form (17.2) and in the previous section we plugged some *a priori* numbers into it. We now have to complete the picture by asking what evidence there is of a relationship and also what its nature is. We shall ignore the effect of prices and exchange rates by, as above, assuming them constant. This is done in econometrics by estimating multiple regressions relating imports to both prices and incomes (and possibly other effects). We then interpret the regression coefficient on income as showing the effects on imports of a unit change in income holding prices constant.

Imagine an economy in equilibrium; then let us give it an injection of income from abroad holding everything else – prices, output, tastes, etc. – constant. Unless any of the goods it consumes are inferior, consumption of every good will increase. With constant domestic output, this will certainly increase imports. Unfortunately, however, in nearly all circumstances, income increases not in isolation, but in conjunction with output, and this causes complications, because the additional domestic output is likely to displace imports. Hence the net effect of an *income and output* expansion is not certain *a priori*, being comprised of both positive and negative effects. (This, of course, is precisely what we saw in Chapter 14; economic growth may be pro- or anti-import biased.) When economists talk of 'income elasticities of demand for imports' or 'the marginal propensity to import', they are almost invariably referring to this combined effect rather than to that of income alone.

These ideas can be formalised as follows. Assuming for now that we have a single good and that imported and domestically supplied units are perfect substitutes, we can write:

$$M = D - S. \tag{17.11}$$

That is, imports equal the difference between demand and supply. Then, differentiating with respect to income and output (Y), and multiplying by (Y/M) yields

$$\frac{dM}{dY} \cdot \frac{Y}{M} = \frac{dD}{dY} \cdot \frac{Y}{M} - \frac{dS}{dY} \cdot \frac{Y}{M}.$$

If we multiply the first term on the right by (D/D) and the second by (S/S) and substitute for the elasticity terms, we get

$$\epsilon_M = \epsilon_D \cdot \frac{D}{M} - \epsilon_S \cdot \frac{S}{M}. \tag{17.12}$$

That is, the income elasticity of imports depends positively on the demand elasticity and negatively on the supply elasticity. In general we expect both to be positive, and, although for imports $D > S$ (so that ϵ_D receives greater weight), it would be possible for the import elasticity to be negative if ϵ_S were large. This could easily be the case for those goods where the extra output was concentrated.

Equation (17.12) illustrates two other features. If domestic and foreign goods are perfectly substitutable, the import elasticity is merely a derived parameter arising from the basic supply and demand relationships. There is no reason to believe it constant or to use it in economic policy-making (Pearce, 1970). If, on the other hand, goods are strongly differentiated, as Barker (1977) believed, and we are looking at an imported variety, local supply will be zero (or very small), and hence ϵ_M will closely approximate ϵ_D, and will be positive.

Let us now look at some results. The level of imports relative to income (the average propensity to consume) is determined by factors like the size of a country and the extent of specialisation, but by far the most important factor in explaining *changes* in imports, even over fairly long periods, is current changes in income.

A representative set of income elasticities is given in Table 17.2. These are taken from Panić (1975) and come from regressions of imports on income, the extent of capacity working (see below), and prices over the period 1957–72. They therefore reflect the effect of income, holding the other two variables constant. They are

189

reported in elasticity form so they show the percentage change in imports for a 1 per cent change in income. To obtain the marginal propensity to import, we multiply the elasticity by the average propensity.

Table 17.2 Income elasticities of demand for imports

	UK	W. Germany	France
Food, beverages and tobacco	0.35	0.86	0.84
Basic materials	0.66	1.22	0.70
Fuels	2.47	2.66	1.26
Manufactured goods	3.09	2.14	2.19
semi-manufactures	2.37	2.06	n.a.
finished products	4.30	3.52	n.a.
Total imports	1.82	1.31	1.63

Note:
n.a. = not available.
Source: Panić (1975), 1957–72.

There are marked differences between the UK and the other two economies. The UK's imports of food and basic materials have lower income elasticities than the others' because of her high level of imports. More serious is the greater sensitivity of the UK's manufactured imports, especially finished manufactures. The latter have always exhibited higher income elasticities than other imports, partly because they include luxury and durable goods, and partly because, with greater scope for product differentiation, variety considerations have more play. In the 1950s, this hardly mattered, because in 1957 finished manufactures accounted for only 8 per cent of total imports, but by 1980 this had risen to 36 per cent; in 1980, on Panić's figures, for every £1.00 increment of national income, £0.42 would be spent on imports of finished manufactures!

Panić's results may be criticised on a number of grounds. For instance, they ignore tariffs (which fell substantially over his sample period) and his data are now rather dated and are too aggregated. All these points are true but there is little reason to suppose that they substantially change the story. For example, Barker (1977) and Thirlwall (1980) both reported high elasticities from disaggregated data, while Taplin (1973) showed the UK and USA to have the highest elasticities for total manufactures among a sample of twenty-six countries.

Panić's variable on capacity working was intended to capture the possibility that, as British industry approached full capacity, it would be less able to expand – i.e. ϵ_S in (17.12) would fall. Under these circumstances, ϵ_M would reflect ϵ_D more closely and would consequently be greater. In fact, he found no such effect. A more successful separation of the roles ϵ_S and ϵ_D is found in Khan and Ross (1975). They argued that in the long run there will be an equilibrium relationship between imports and income that reflects the adjustment of both domestic supply and demand, and that will be manifest in the relation of trend imports to trend income. In addition, there will be short-run effects that reflect only the demand side of domestic behaviour (because supply is assumed fixed in the short run), which will be reflected in a relationship between the deviations of actual imports from trend and actual income from trend. Combining these components, Khan and Ross estimated cyclical (short-run, demand) elasticities and secular (long-run, equilibrium) elasticities for a sample of fourteen developed countries' visible imports. The former are all positive, but the latter have mixed signs. The more dynamic economies tend to have negative secular income elasticities (e.g. −0.71 for

190

Japan, −0.21 for West Germany), showing that local output can reduce imports in the long run, but the less successful ones have positive elasticities (e.g. 1.91 for the USA, 0.89 for the UK, 0.50 for Belgium); see Table 17.3.

Table 17.3 Income elasticities for various OECD countries' trade

	Total visible imports Khan–Ross (1958–72)		Total visible exports Goldstein–Khan (1955–70)	
	Current[a]	Potential	Current[b]	Secular
Belgium	1.58	0.50	0.98	1.90
France	3.56	−1.71	1.40	1.70
W. Germany	2.23	−0.21	0.40	2.07
Italy	2.13	−0.47	0.95	2.21
Japan	1.94	0.71	1.21	3.64
Netherlands	1.40	0.44	1.02	1.92
United States	0.55	1.91	0.60	1.01
United Kingdom	0.94	0.89	0.90	0.90

Notes:
[a] Current half-year.
[b] Current quarter.
Sources: listed in column headings.

A ratchet effect

These results suggest that rapid increases in demand generate more imports than the same increase spread over a longer period. They also imply, however, that rapid declines cut imports correspondingly quickly. In fact we have little experience of falling imports, so the latter implication is rather weak. It has been challenged by Brechling and Wolfe (1965), who argued that there is a ratchet effect whereby imports sucked in during a boom are not pushed out over the next slump. Hence import penetration rises in a series of steps, each step coinciding with a boom.

The basic idea is that capturing new markets is expensive. Hence, once foreign producers have a share of the British market, they try to maintain it even though it may not be very profitable during a slump. However, if, when the slump ends, they can increase their supplies faster than British producers (perhaps by switching goods from other markets), they can reap the benefits in terms of rapidly rising sales. The evidence for this is weak, but it is an idea worthy of consideration, especially if one is contemplating a dash for growth.

The conclusion must be that, especially for manufactures, but also for imports as a whole, income elasticities exceed 1, often quite substantially. This explains why, as economies have grown over the last thirty years, the average propensity to import (imports/income) has risen, for every 1 per cent in income causes a larger than 1 per cent rise in imports. There is also plenty of evidence that in the UK import elasticities are rather higher than elsewhere in OECD. Of course, as economists we should not stop here; we must ask why the elasticities take these values, but that issue is held over until the end of the next chapter.

Exports and income

Exports from one country are merely the imports for another. Thus, all that we have said above about imports carries over to exports except that exports are determined by foreign rather than domestic incomes. There are, however, two additional factors that warrant consideration. First, the possibility of importers switching their demand between competing exporters and, second, the possibility that exports are affected by domestic as well as foreign incomes.

Above we argued that rising incomes in, say, France would normally stimulate French imports. That raises other countries' exports in total, but it does not necessarily raise British exports, because France need not buy any extra goods from Britain. Thus if we are concerned with British exports we need to consider not only our partners' marginal propensities to import but also how they allocate their imports over competing suppliers. If one supplier is relatively unpopular, or is unable to meet all its demands, imports from that supplier may not keep pace with imports from other sources. This appears to be Britain's position. Even ignoring relative prices, it seems that, as countries' incomes increase, their imports from Britain increase less rapidly than total imports. Considering all importers at once, this means that as world income grows it appears that Britain's share of world trade declines.

We say 'appears' because it is not unambiguously clear that the cause of Britain's declining share of world trade is rising incomes abroad. Over time, Britain's share of world trade has fallen dramatically, and world incomes have risen dramatically, but this does not necessarily add up to a causal relationship. An equally good empirical explanation is that the income elasticity of demand for British exports is the same as for other countries' exports (which would imply a constant share of world trade), but that there is some additional factor that causes Britain's exports to be displaced by others'. It is true that economists have not yet identified that additional factor – it is usually captured as a strong declining trend term in econometric work on exports – but it is well to be aware that it is not yet proven beyond doubt that British exports suffer from an unusually low income elasticity. Functions explaining British exports exhibit either a low income elasticity and no trend, or a normal elasticity and a strong negative trend. There is as yet no way of telling them apart and these two different descriptions must at the moment be taken to be referring to the same phenomenon.

To illustrate the orders of magnitude involved, we consider the work of Goldstein and Khan (1976). These authors estimated both supply and demand functions for total exports for a sample of nine OECD countries over the years 1955–70 (see Table 17.3). Their demand curves contained relative prices and world income and allowed for the effects of these variables to take several quarters to fully affect exports. The long-run income elasticities ranged from 3.64 for Japan and 2.07 for West Germany to 1.01 for the USA and 0.90 for the UK. The elasticity of total world trade with respect to world income is approximately 1.4, so these figures reflect Japan's and Germany's rising shares of world trade and the USA's and the UK's falling shares. Note that no trend or additional factor was included in the demand equations.

A disaggregated study of UK exports from 1955 to 1973 by Winters (1981) showed that considerable variations occur in income effects over destinations and commodities. For British visible exports as a whole Winters found an income elasticity of 1.35 counteracted by a decline of 3.4 per cent per annum due to unspecified trend factors; at a disaggregated level, income elasticities ranged from 0.66 (textiles) to 1.76 (scientific instruments) and trend factors from −12.6 per cent per annum (textile fibres) to +2.7 per cent per annum (drink). Consumer goods and metal-based intermediate goods showed the greatest sensitivity to income, and non-metallic intermediates the least.

This low income elasticity or negative trend result is perhaps the most interesting and crucial of the questions surrounding British trade performance. We shall return to it in section 18.4 below.

Exports and the pressure of demand

The second factor specific to exports is the so-called pressure of demand hypothesis. This suggests that, as the British economy expands, British firms find it easier to sell at home than to export. This is usually supposed to occur through either the physical curtailment of the supply of exports or the worsening of non-price competitiveness. The latter includes factors such as delivery times, after-sales service, design of goods and the willingness to adapt goods to foreign requirements. Some of these factors are fixed in the short run, for instance design, but some, especially delivery delays, are amenable to short-run manipulation.

Before considering the evidence on this hypothesis, we should note that it presumes a different mode of behaviour for exporting firms from that normally assumed. In the simple profit-maximising model of the exporting firm, firms ration exports by price, so in order to justify the pressure of demand hypothesis we need to find some reason why prices are not flexible. This is normally explained in terms of oligopolistic behaviour, where price rigidities tend to be observed. We also, incidentally, need a good explanation of why the home market should be preferred to the export market. This is an issue that is not often confronted in the literature, but the usual reasoning is that export markets are more costly and risky to service and therefore less profitable.

Among empirical studies, Artus (1970) found significant pressure of demand effects on UK exports of motor vehicles and chemicals, while Winters (1974) confirmed that the strength of the effect depended on the relative profitability of home and export markets: the relatively more profitable the export market, the smaller the effect of the pressure of demand on exports. The magnitude of the effects of the pressure of demand is not very large: Winters (1974) found that on average a 1 per cent increase in the pressure of demand reduced manufactured exports by around 0.2 per cent, while in Winters (1981) the corresponding figure for total exports was 0.36 per cent. Looking more directly at one quantifiable dimension of non-price competitiveness, Lund and Miner (1973) found that a 10 per cent increase in waiting times reduced export orders by about 2 per cent, while Artus (1973) estimated that a 10 per cent rise in domestic demand increased the waiting time for machine-tools export orders by around 3 per cent. None of this is very precise, but overall there is a strong impression that exports do suffer somewhat in the face of strong domestic demand.

FURTHER READING

The classic references on international multipliers are *Machlup* (1943, *Meade* (1951) and *Metzler* (1950, 1951). Alternative textbook explanations are *Thirlwall* (1980), *Lindert and Kindleberger* (1982) for a geometric approach, and *Dornbusch* (1980a) for more algebra.

Organization of Economic Co-operation and Development (1979) describes both the OECD model and its use in policy-making, while *OECD Economic Outlook* – especially December 1976 and 1977 – and *Feinstein and Reddaway* (1978) describe economic policy discussions during the 1970s. *Komiya* (1980) discusses interdependence generally.

For evidence on income effects see *Panić* (1975) and *Khan and Ross* (1975), which are straightforward. More complex are *Barker* (1977) and *Magee* (1975). On the pressure of demand effect for imports see *Hughes and Thirlwall* (1977), *Barker* (1979) and *Whitley and Wilson* (1979). For export income elasticities *Goldstein and Khan* (1978) and *Winters* (1981) are accessible if you ignore the technical material.

Exports and the pressure of demand are discussed by *Steuer, Ball and Eaton* (1966), *Artus* (1970), *Winters* (1974) and *Greene* (1975), and by *Henry* (1970), who adopts a different approach. *Thirlwall* (1980) provides a short survey of both export and import elasticities.

18 Prices, Competitiveness and the Current Account

Having considered the way that incomes affect international trade, we now turn to the other major economic variable: prices, including the price of foreign money – the exchange rate. Just as before we sought to isolate the income effects, here we shall try to isolate the price effects. It is not quite as straightforward as before, however, because price changes affect real incomes by changing the relationship between money expenditure and the quantities bought. However, provided we are careful, this complication should not cause too much trouble. We shall assume that the government's fiscal stance is fixed, so that income changes, if at all, only in response to price changes. We shall also for convenience assume that foreign incomes are unchanged. This is the same 'small country' assumption that we used in Chapter 17, and it does not imply that the home economy is necessarily a price-taker. We shall consider only the current account of the balance of payments, and indeed we shall concentrate mainly on the trade balance.

The price we consider in most detail is the exchange rate. We shall not yet ask what determines the exchange rate; rather we shall investigate the effects of its shifting from one exogenous value to another.

The chapter starts with an early analysis of devaluation that concentrates exclusively on price effects – the elasticities approach. This involves deriving the demand curve for imports and the supply curve for exports and then examining the equilibria in these two markets. The results of exchange rate changes depend on the elasticities of demand and supply, hence the name. The approach is subject to some limitations, however, and these are spelt out at the end of section 18.1. Section 18.2 examines the empirical evidence on price elasticities. Most of it refers to visible trade, but price and income elasticities for invisible trade are also reported. As well as reporting numbers, this section also introduces certain methodological points. The final part of the chapter digresses slightly to deal with non-price competitiveness. After offering a definition it discusses various aspects of this phenomenon: supply rigidities, research and development, design, marketing effort and the link between the quality of exports and the exchange rate. These factors are thought to be of considerable significance in the real world, even if they have yet to make much impact on economic theory.

18.1 DEVALUATION: THE ELASTICITIES ANALYSIS

The elasticities approach to devaluation concentrates on the price elasticities of demand and supply for exports and imports. It has a long pedigree, culminating with Robinson (1937), but it is no longer considered a sufficient analysis by itself. We study it in detail partly because price responses are the very essence of contemporary Western economics, but mainly because it analyses the impact effects of devaluation from which all the later developments are born.

The import demand curve

We start with the market for a single imported good – say, oranges. We assume that the UK – the importer – produces some oranges, identical to the imported ones; hence her demand for imports is the difference between local demand in total and local supply. As the price changes, import demand will reflect the changes in both local supply and demand, and, since those are normally in opposite directions, we would expect imports to be relatively sensitive to prices.

We can see this diagrammatically in Figure 18.1. On the left we have the UK's demand (D) and supply (S) schedules for oranges. For any price, we can calculate the residual, which is imports, and transfer this horizontally to the right of the diagram to plot imports against prices. The import demand curve is flatter (more elastic) than either of the two basic relationships. If price exceeds p_0, the supply exceeds demand, and we observe exports rather than imports; our procedure would then yield a supply curve for exports.

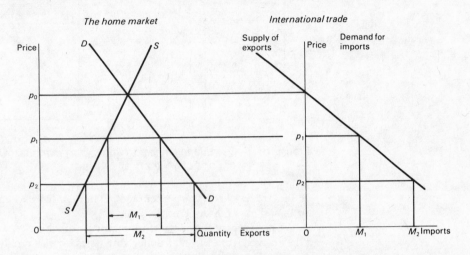

Figure 18.1   *The home market and the demand for imports*

The import
market

We now combine our demand curve for imported oranges with a corresponding supply curve of imported oranges, to explore the market equilibrium. Assuming that the rest of the world conducts all its transactions in dollars, foreign exporters will be interested in their returns in terms of dollars rather than pounds. Hence, in order to plot the demand and supply curves on one diagram, we need to convert the two prices to the same currency. We choose to work in terms of sterling, so we divide the dollar prices in the foreign supply schedule by the exchange rate to get their sterling equivalent. The final outcome is shown in Figure 18.2(A) where we plot the demand for (D) and supply of (S) imported oranges in the UK against the sterling price.

Now suppose the exchange rate is devalued from, say, $2.50:£1.00 to $2.00:£1.00. Assuming other prices and incomes are unchanged, the demand curve does not shift at all. The supply curve, on the other hand, rises by one quarter to S', because the sterling that orange sellers earn is now worth fewer dollars than before: in order to supply the same quantity of oranges they require more pounds. To be specific, suppose the marginal kilo of oranges is worth $1.00 to the foreign producers (that is, the price they can earn by selling elsewhere). Before devaluation they require £0.40 to cover this (= $1 ÷ 2.5), but afterwards they require £0.50 ($1 ÷ 2). With unchanged demand but a higher supply schedule, the market equilibrium moves to give a lower quantity but a higher price. The exact movements in price and quantity depend on both schedules, but the direction of the change in total expenditure on imports depends only on the elasticity of demand.

195

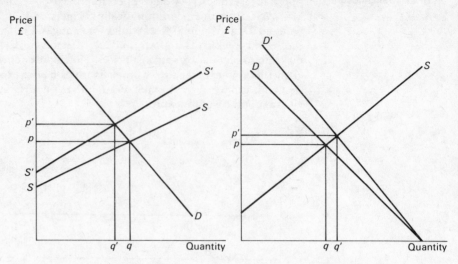

Figure 18.2   *Devaluation in import and export markets. (A) Imports of oranges. (B)
Exports of whisky.*

If demand is elastic, the percentage fall in quantity exceeds the percentage rise in price and expenditure falls.

We now repeat the exercise for exports – of whisky, say. An export supply curve (S) – derived from Britain's underlying demand and supply relationships – and the foreign demand curve (D) are shown in Figure 18.2(B). As before, the figure is fundamentally in terms of dollar prices but has been converted into sterling. Suppose we now devalue; this time the supply curve remains unaffected (assuming incomes and all other prices including factor prices in the UK are unchanged), but the demand curve shifts. A bottle of whisky costing £10.00 originally sold abroad for $25.00, but now it sells for a mere $20.00. Hence, without harming sales, the whisky producers could charge £12.50 a bottle; this is reflected in a rise of the demand curve by one quarter to D'. As before, this produces a new equilibrium, but this time both price and quantity rise, so we know immediately that revenue rises.

The net result of devaluation is that export earnings from whisky certainly rise, while import expenditure on oranges could have risen or fallen. Overall, the balance of these changes could be positive or negative, depending on the elasticities of demand and supply in the two markets.

Some special cases

It is instructive at this point to consider a few particular values of these elasticities. First, suppose that demand in neither market were sensitive to price (because, say, of import quotas). Both demand curves would be vertical. Devaluation would affect neither quantity, but by raising import prices and not changing export prices it would necessarily worsen the trade balance. If supply were completely fixed, on the other hand, unchanged quantities but rising export prices would improve the trade balance. (Draw your own diagrams to confirm this.)

Second, consider a small country proper that faces fixed world prices in dollars for both its exports and imports. At these prices it is assumed to be able to sell and buy unlimited quantities. Hence at any particular exchange rate the supply curve of imports and the demand curve for exports are horizontal – that is, the

196

elasticities of supply of imports and of demand for exports are infinite. The price in Britain is just the sterling equivalent of the fixed world price. A devaluation acts much as before, raising the supply curve of imports by 25 per cent along its length and the demand curve for exports similarly, as is shown in Figure 18.3(A) and (B). Obviously the improvement in the trade balance will be greater the more elastic are import demand (reducing imports) and export supply (expanding exports). Furthermore, we can show that, if devaluation occurs from a point of balanced trade, the trade balance cannot deteriorate. Export and import prices rise equally, hence, even with no quantity changes, trade would remain balanced because the values of exports and imports would be equally affected. But any quantity effects that do exist will improve the balance – hence the result.

(A) *Imports – small country*
($\epsilon_M^S = \infty$)

(B) *Exports – small country*
($\epsilon_X^D = \infty$)

(C) *Exports – Keynsian supply*
($\epsilon_X^S = \infty$)

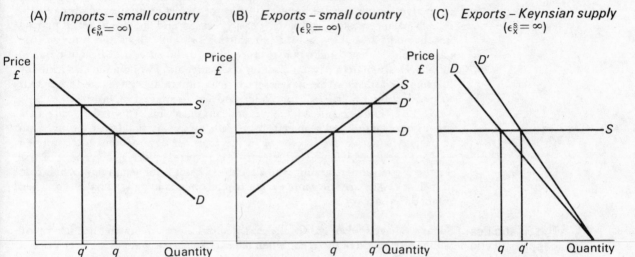

Figure 18.3   *Some special cases. (A) Imports – small country. (B) Exports – small country. (C) Exports – Keynesian supply.*

Finally consider the Keynesian case where the prices of both exports and imports are fixed in the seller's currency and there is, at least around the market equilibrium, unlimited supply at those prices – i.e. infinite supply elasticities. The import market is still as in Figure 18.3(A), but the export market is transformed. Instead of a horizontal demand curve, we have a horizontal supply curve, and we revert to the downward sloping demand curve. Devaluation raises this proportionately – as before – with the result shown in Figure 18.3(C). The extent of the revenue increase depends entirely on how much is sold abroad. Given a fixed sterling price, the devaluation reduces the dollar price of whisky by the full extent (i.e. from \$25.00 to \$20.00 a bottle), so the quantity change depends solely on the foreign elasticity of demand for whisky.

We can formalise this case quite simply. Consider a 1 per cent devaluation. From Figure 18.3(A) we know that import prices rise by 1 per cent and import quantities by ϵ_M^D per cent, where ϵ_M^D is the import demand elasticity ($\epsilon_M^D < 0$). Hence import expenditure rises by $(1 + \epsilon_M^D)$ per cent. From Figure 18.3(C) we also know that (sterling) export prices remain unchanged, but that quantity, and therefore revenue, rise $-\epsilon_X^D$ per cent, where ϵ_X^D is the (negative) foreign elasticity of demand for our exports. Now, if the value of exports and imports are equal, these percentage changes apply to the same base, and so the trade balance will improve if the percentage change in exports exceeds that in imports – that is, if

$$-\epsilon_X^D > (1+\epsilon_M^D) \tag{18.1}$$

or if

$$\epsilon_X^D + \epsilon_M^D < -1. \tag{18.2}$$

In words, a small devaluation will improve the trade balance in the presence of infinite supply elasticities if the sum of the elasticities of demand is less than −1 (i.e. is absolutely greater than 1). This is known as the *Marshall–Lerner* condition and it has figured prominently in the history of international economics. Note its restrictive assumptions: infinite elasticities of supply at home and abroad, and initially balanced trade. The latter is easily relaxed, an initial trade deficit making improvement less likely, but the introduction of supply elasticities is messy. The basic result is that devaluation is more likely to be successful if high demand elasticities are matched by high supply elasticities and low demand elasticities by low supply elasticities. This may be seen by experimenting with Figure 18.2, but for formal details see Stern (1973) or Lindert and Kindleberger (1982).

We have conducted all our analysis in terms of sterling. This makes sense if we are primarily interested in the effects of trade on the internal UK economy. If, on the other hand, we are interested in the effect of devaluation on the foreign exchange reserves, it would be better to work in terms of foreign currency (dollars). To check your understanding, you should work out some examples for this case also. The results are the same except where trade is initially unbalanced, when minor differences occur.

The elasticities approach and its problems

So far we have spoken only of the markets for (imported) oranges and (exported) whisky. We have assumed that, when the exchange rate changes, only the price of the good we are analysing is affected, leaving all other prices and incomes unchanged. In analysing oranges, we implicitly assumed the price of whisky to be constant and vice versa, even though when we added the two markets to calculate the trade balance we knew that this must be false. The elasticities approach to the balance of payments proceeds by treating total imports as we have treated oranges, and total exports as we have treated whisky. And it is precisely these *ceteris paribus* (other things being equal) assumptions that prove its main weakness, for devaluation affects the whole of the economy, not just small sections in isolation.

The elasticities approach deals only with two goods – imports and exports – but it plainly cannot claim to be derived from a two-good model. With only two goods it would be impossible for 'other prices' to remain constant while we considered exports, for 'other' would imply 'import' and we know that import prices change. Similarly, even if we assume that sterling export prices are constant while we consider imports, the extra demand for exports must affect incomes and the factor markets and so affect the production of importable goods. Hence behind the elasticities model there must lie at least one more market – a market for non-traded goods. It is possible that changes in the output of this sector could compensate for changes in the output of the tradable goods, and so allow the latter to move up and down their supply curves without affecting incomes and factor prices. Even then, however, there are complications, because devaluation may disturb the price of non-tradables (see section 19.2). In fact, it requires very restrictive assumptions to justify the elasticities approach in a full economic model (see Dornbusch, 1975a).

198

Why study such an unrealistic model? Partly to introduce tools that will be useful later on, but also because the elasticities approach offers a reasonable approximation to the truth in certain circumstances. The horizontal supply schedules may be realistic if there is unemployment, as may be the fixed non-traded price if domestic markets are oligopolistic. In the short run, therefore, elasticity results may apply. Also, of course, although everything may change in response to devaluation, the impact of devaluation operates through the channels we have just discussed. Thus, while income will be affected ultimately, the stimulus is felt only through the effects analysed in the elasticities approach. Hence this section quantifies the initial impact of devaluation and provides the first step to the analysis of its final incidence.

18.2 PRICE ELASTICITIES IN PRACTICE

Before going on to more complete models of devaluation, we evaluate some of the elasticities that have proved crucial so far. For considerable periods of the past it was felt that international trade elasticities were so low that the Marshall–Lerner conditions would be violated, a view known as elasticity pessimism. This is relatively rare now, mainly because of an influential study by Orcutt (1950), which catalogued several reasons why existing econometric estimates tended to be understatements, and a subsequent series of estimates based on new data and more careful methodology. That said, however, current estimates must still be treated with great caution, and are even now not very high.

Estimating import price elasticities

Given our derivation of the import demand curve as the residual of total domestic demand and domestic supply, the obvious way to calculate the import elasticity would be to estimate the domestic parameters and calculate it from those. In fact this is rarely pursued – especially for manufactures – because it is rare that the perfect substitutability of domestic and foreign supplies actually applies. Most investigators, therefore, work directly on the import market, relating import quantities to import prices. The vast majority also simplify the process further by assuming that the supply elasticity of imports is infinite. This fixes the import price quite independently of the quantity that our country demands. Can we therefore expect that regressing total imports on their average price will give a fair estimate of the elasticity of demand for imports? The answer, following Orcutt (1950), is generally 'no', for the following reasons:

Identification. Suppose the elasticity of supply is not infinite. Then the price and quantity of imports are determined simultaneously by both demand and supply factors, and the observed values reflect both sets of effects. The elasticity that arises from the regression of such data will be a mixture of the (negative) demand elasticity and the (positive) supply elasticity.

Aggregation. If elasticities of supply are not infinite, the effect of supply shifts on prices depends on the elasticity of demand: the lower the elasticity, the greater the price change and the lower the quantity change. When we add many imports together into total imports, the changes in the average price will be dominated by the inelastic goods, and since these will be associated with small quantity changes the overall estimate of the elasticity will be too low. This problem is significant for total imports, but, where basic raw materials and manufactures are separated, it is probably less so.

The quantum effect. Orcutt suggested that small changes in prices (as occur in the absence of exchange rate changes) will have less effect than large (devaluation-

199

induced) changes. In fact, the evidence for this is very weak (Goldstein and Khan, 1976).

Errors of measurement. If the price series are measured with error – that is, if they appear to reflect price changes that did not occur and that therefore have no associated quantity change – then the average response to price changes will be biased towards zero. This is probably rather significant, not least because econometricians are usually forced to use unit value series instead of price indices. Official trade statistics record the value of transactions of a particular sort and also the quantity, but not the price. The only price indicator available is the value divided by the quantity, which is known as the unit value. If the headings under which trade is recorded are homogeneous – e.g. coffee of a particular standard – then the unit value closely approximates the price. But, if the heading is very heterogeneous – e.g. tractors of engine power 25–37 kW – there is room for trouble.

Suppose there are two types of tractor, A and B, which sell for £10,000 and £20,000 respectively. Suppose initially that 100 of each are imported. The unit value of tractor imports is £15,000. Now suppose that sales shift, so that only 50 of A are bought and 150 of B. The quantity is unchanged but the value has increased, hence the unit value has increased despite the fact that no price has changed.

There is only one way to avoid this problem – better data. Some genuine price indices are available for international trade and, in general, using these increases the size of the estimated elasticities (e.g. Kravis and Lipsey, 1971, 1982).

Lags. Orcutt argued that relating the current year's imports to the current year's prices would omit any effect that took longer than a year to appear. This is undoubtedly important. There are five possible reasons why lags may exist: information lags – it takes time to discover that prices have changed, although not in the case of devaluation; technical lags – it is necessary to sell old stock before buying new; adjustment costs – drawing up new contracts and liquidating old ones takes time; order–delivery lags – for most goods there is a significant lag between placing an order and receiving the goods; and expectations – if a price change is believed to be transitory, people will not react until it has proved itself otherwise. Fortunately, given its pervasiveness, this problem is easily overcome: one includes lagged prices in the regression as well as current ones, and this is now almost universal practice.

Table 18.1 Price elasticities for various OECD countries' trade

| | Total visible imports | | Total visible exports Goldstein–Khan (1955–70) | | |
| | Khan–Ross (1958–72)[a] | Taplin (1954–70) | Demand | | Supply |
			Short-run[b]	Long-run	Long-run
Belgium	–0.22	–0.65	–0.04	–0.07	1.6
France	–0.30	–0.39	–1.10	–1.34	1.3
W. Germany	–0.53	–0.61	–0.25	–1.32	1.2
Italy	–1.67	–1.03	–1.02	–2.36	2.0
Japan	0.15	–0.81	0.07	0.20	–0.1
Netherlands	0.38	–0.02	–1.26	–2.39	2.3
USA	–1.00	–1.05	–1.26	–2.12	3.9
UK	0.40	–0.22	–1.17	–1.18	0.8

Notes:
[a] Current half-year only.
[b] Current quarter.
Sources: recorded in column headings together with sample periods.

Some representative estimates of price elasticities of demand for total visible imports appear in Table 18.1. The first set is taken from Khan and Ross (1975). In view of their aggregation and their omission of lagged prices, they are probably biased positively; in particular, the three positive values should not be taken seriously. Probably more reliable are Taplin's (1973) in the second column. These stem from annual data and allow for lags of up to one year on prices. Taplin found negative price elasticities for total imports into twenty-four of the twenty-five countries he studied. He also calculated elasticities for broad groups of goods, finding manufactured imports generally more elastic than basic materials and food.

These results suggest that British imports are relatively insensitive to prices. Disaggregated studies dispute this, however; prominent among them is Barker (1970). Barker examined UK imports disaggregated into eighty-four commodity groups. Using specially constructed unit value series to approximate prices, he searched carefully for price effects. His results are summarised in Table 18.2. As hinted above, elasticities appear to increase with the degree of processing. These results are rather dated now, but subsequent research, although slightly less detailed, suggests that time has not changed the basic conclusions.

Table 18.2 UK import price elasticities[a]

Food, drink and tobacco	−0.31
Raw materials	−0.06
Fuels	−0.56
Semi-manufactures	−1.22
Finished manufactures	−1.62
Total visible imports	−0.65

Note:
[a] Estimated 1955–66; elasticities refer to 1966.
Source: Barker (1970).

Estimating export price elasticities

The formalities of estimating export price elasticities are the same as those for import price elasticities, but some of the practicalities are rather different. First, neither demand nor supply elasticities are infinite, which makes the identification problem more significant. This means that supply and demand factors have to be estimated simultaneously either as two separate equations (Goldstein and Khan, 1978) or combined into a single quantity function derived from the theory of oligopolistic markets (e.g. Winters, 1981).

The second difference concerns the nature of competition in export markets. As we saw above, exports are affected not only by the rate at which partner countries import but also by the extent to which they switch their given level of imports among competing suppliers. If the switching is more price sensitive than the import decision, exports could be substantially more price elastic than imports. Looked at differently, this says that British exports to France compete partly with local French goods (the import dimension) and partly with German and Italian exports to France (the switching dimension). Hence, export equations should include two foreign price terms.

The third practical difference concerns lags. Possibly because of the switching dimension, exports seem to take longer to react than imports. Hence lags of up to five years are not rare in export equations.

Table 18.1 above presents Goldstein and Khan's estimates of elasticities for total visible exports in both the long and short runs. Their results are highly aggregated, and, although they allow for lags, they require both price and income responses to show the same pattern through time. In Chapter 17 we argued that incomes are the main determinant of export behaviour and that they are not subject to long lags; thus Table 18.1 probably overstates the export price elasticity in the short run and understates it in the long run. On the basis of this table, the Marshall–Lerner conditions are satisfied for every country except Japan and Belgium. The Japanese results for both exports and imports are very strange, however, and should not be taken seriously. Both exports and imports for the UK appear to be relatively insensitive to prices.

Table 18.3 UK export price elasticities with respect to different prices[a]

Commodity		Price[b]	
	$\bar{p}^{UK}/p^C$	$\bar{p}^{UK}/p^L$	p^{UK}/p^H
Food	0.0	−0.88	2.23
Drink	−0.93	−0.44	0.69
Textile fibres	0.0	−0.83	0.13
Petroleum products	−2.19	−1.75	0.21
Other non-manufactures	−0.68	−0.29	0.10
Chemicals	−0.31	−0.42	0.57
Textiles	−1.83	−0.34	0.68
Iron and steel	0.0	0.0	0.16
Non-ferrous metals	0.0	−0.62	0.12
Metal manufactures	−2.72	−0.27	0.95
Mechanical engineering	−1.50	0.0	0.15
Electrical engineering	−1.55	−0.30	0.14
Transport equipment	−1.36	−0.33	0.0
Scientific instruments, etc.	−0.71	−0.34	0.14
Clothing, footware, travel goods	−1.37	−1.03	0.17
Other non-manufacturing	−1.76	−0.33	0.61
Total	−1.18	−0.35	0.36

Notes:
[a] Annual data 1958–73.
[b] $\bar{p}^{UK}$ is the UK price in dollars
p^{UK} is the UK price in sterling
p^C is competitors' prices in dollars
p^L is the importers' local prices in dollars
p^H is the UK domestic price in sterling.
Source: Winters (1981).

We have mentioned the Marshall–Lerner condition, but the last column of Table 18.1 shows quite clearly that its assumptions are not satisfied. The elasticities of supply reported there are nowhere near infinity. The UK appears to be relatively insensitive to prices in this respect also, and it is tempting to try to explain her poor trade performance by reference to this feature; however, so far there is no firm evidence to relate the two phenomena. Nevertheless the pervasiveness of relatively low price elasticities for the UK does suggest some degree of inflexibility.

More detailed work is harder to find for exports than for imports, but Winters (1981) provided some evidence for the UK. Disaggregating visible exports by sixteen commodities and ten areas of destination, Winters explained UK exports with reference to three price terms: UK prices (in dollars) relative to competing exporters' prices (the switching dimension); UK prices relative to importers' domestic prices (the importing dimension); and UK export prices (in sterling) relative to UK domestic prices (a supply side variable). The extent and time pattern of responses differ substantially between both areas and commodities. For, example, in Table 18.3 the most price-sensitive goods are seen to be either (a) not highly differentiated (e.g. textiles and petroleum products), or (b) finished manufactures (e.g. metal manufactures and other manufactures).

In general, the longest response lags are on the competitors' prices and the shortest on the importers' own domestic prices. Winters hypothesised that this is due to informational problems: foreign importers of UK goods discover local price trends substantially sooner than they discover price changes in potential alternative suppliers.

The 'J-curve'

These results suggest that, while in the long run elasticities may be sufficient to make devaluation successful, the short-run response may be perverse. This would produce a sort of J-shape in a graph of the balance of trade through time, with the balance worsening before it improved in response to devaluation. A particular factor in the short-run responses is the currency in which trade is invoiced. Most trade in the few months after a devaluation will have been arranged before it. If prices were fixed then in terms of sterling, British traders will receive or pay what they expected regardless of devaluation; if they were fixed in dollars, however, devaluation will raise the sterling value of the transaction. Hence importers of dollar-priced goods will pay out more and exporters receive more than anticipated. Unfortunately, most manufactured trade is invoiced in the exporter's currency – hence devaluation will usually cause an immediate worsening of the trade balance. The duration of this effect depends on the longevity of pre-devaluation contracts; Carse, Williamson and Wood (1980) estimated that a 10 per cent devaluation worsens the British trade balance by about 3 per cent of export value for six months, gradually reducing to 0.5 per cent after two years. Once old contracts have been worked off, the extent of the J-curve depends on how rapidly prices are adjusted to the new exchange rate and how quickly quantities respond to the new prices. Thirlwall (1980) quoted the worsening as lasting about nine months for the 1967 devaluation.

Table 18.4 Some parameters of UK invisible trade[a]

	Exchange rate effects		Activity effects	Short-run elasticity	
	Debits	Credits	Variable	Debits	Credits
Freight transport	0.6	−1.0[b]	UK and world trade	0.68	1.14
Passenger transport and travel	−0.56	−3.25	Permanent income	1.03	0.66[c]
Other services	−1.0[b]	−0.55	GNP	0.30	0.35[c]
Direct investment earnings	0.0[d]	−1.0[b]	Actual output ÷ potential output	−1.02	3.63
Other earnings	0.0[d]	−1.0[b]	None	—	—
Private transfers	0.0[d]	−1.0[b]	GNP	1.73	4.13

Notes:
[a] Sample period 1961–74. All relationships contain effects additional to those listed.
[b] Small country assumption: Britain adopts world price fixed in dollars. Hence sterling payments rise by the proportion of devaluation.
[c] Elasticity of British exports with respect to total world exports of the service concerned.
[d] Flows are insensitive to the exchange rate and are denominated in sterling.
Source: Bond (1979).

Invisibles account for around one-third of British current credits, but nothing like that proportion of the econometric effort devoted to trade. In principle, invisible trade is no different from visible trade, but in practice it has proved hard to estimate its parameters. Since most invisibles are intermediate services – i.e. sold to businesses rather than to final consumers – we often relate sales to the level of activity in the purchasing sector rather than to income. Table 18.4 presents some estimates of income and price elasticities of demand for the UK. The price elasticities are in a form that reports the change in sterling receipts with respect to exchange rate changes. This highlights the role of the currency in which flows are denominated in determining the effect of the exchange rate on the balance of payments. We comment briefly on each type of invisible trade.

Freight transport

This is related to the amount of international trade carried out both by Britain and on routes not passing through Britain but for which Britain provides much shipping. The market for shipping is competitive; prices are set in dollars, and Britain is a small country. With the world demand for shipping fixed, Britain's receipts from shipping increase as the exchange rate falls. Sterling expenditure per unit of imported shipping rises similarly, but the higher cost of shipping relative to domestic services leads to some economies in its use, so total expenditure rises by only 0.6 per cent per 1 per cent depreciation in sterling.

Passenger transport and travel

These are complementary goods and are best considered together. There are two components – business travel, which is inelastic, and personal travel, which is highly elastic with respect to both prices and incomes. The exchange rate elasticities reflect both a substitution effect, as Britain becomes relatively more expensive or cheaper, and, for credits, a valuation effect that foreigners' dollar expenditure is worth more sterling as the exchange rate falls. The high elasticity for credits reflects the ability of cheap countries to capture tourists from dear ones. Not shown here, but also important, are special events like the Olympics and the Royal Jubilee.

Other services

Imports are surprisingly income inelastic and Britain is losing her share of the world market very rapidly: every 1 per cent growth of world exports generates only 0.35 per cent growth in UK exports. The debit exchange rate elasticity of −1.0 again reflects world prices fixed in terms of dollars, coupled with quantities quite insensitive to prices.

Investment earnings

These depend mainly on the stocks of assets held and their rates of return, neither of which is given in the table; however, there is some cyclical fluctuation in profits on direct investments, which explains the activity elasticities given. The exchange rate effects reflect the fact that flows are denominated in the debtor's currency. Hence devaluation raises the sterling value of dollar-denominated earnings from abroad but does not affect sterling-denominated outflows (debits). If, on the other hand, Britain were obliged to make outflows denominated in dollars, we would record −1.0 under debits, which would indicate that devaluation increased the outflow proportionately. In these circumstances, a country that was a net debtor would find that devaluation increased the net outflow of income abroad thus deflating the economy. Cooper (1971) has argued that this is a problem for many developing countries.

Private transfers

These are very income sensitive and are generally denominated in the donor's currency.

18.3 BRITAIN'S TRADE PERFORMANCE AND NON-PRICE COMPETITIVENESS

An overriding feature of British economic history over the last thirty years has been her apparently poor trade performance. We have just examined the price elasticities for British trade and have found them rather low. In the previous chapter we considered income elasticities and found British imports very sensitive to incomes and British exports either insensitive or subject to strong negative trends. Both intellectually and from the point of view of economic policy, these income elasticities or trends present the most crucial and challenging question in this area of economics. In this section we see if economics has anything to contribute in explaining or reversing this dismal performance. First, however, we ask whether it matters that Britain is losing her share of both the domestic and world markets.

Trade performance: does it matter?

The short answer to this question is 'yes, it does matter'. High imports do not matter *per se* – they just show that one is exploiting the gains from specialisation. Neither does a falling share of world trade necessarily matter. Britain's share of world exports of manufactures has fallen from around 33 per cent in 1899 to 30 per cent by 1913, 26 per cent in 1950 and 9.5 per cent in 1980. Britain was the predominant manufacturing nation in the nineteenth century and it would be absurd to hope that, as others emerged, she should still undertake a third or more of world trade. Similarly, as Europe and Japan emerged from the devastation of the Second World War, it was plain that they must take up their shares of world commerce.

The problem is that the UK's trade performance has constrained her economic growth. Low export growth means relatively stagnant injections, while a high marginal propensity means a low multiplier. Furthermore, for most of the post-war period the divergent growth of exports and imports resulted in a balance of payments constraint: the government wished to expand the economy, but was prevented from doing so because the trade accounts would become unbalanced. During the 1950s and 1960s this was manifest by large balance of payments deficits on official settlements. As autonomous expenditure rose above autonomous receipts, there was an excess supply of sterling. Committed to maintaining the exchange rate, the authorities had to spend the foreign exchange reserves to buy up the surplus sterling; when the reserves ran out, economic growth had to stop. During this period the succession of fiscal expansions followed by balance of payments induced contractions became known as 'stop–go'.

After 1972, sterling was floated: the government was no longer committed to maintaining the exchange rate. For a while it believed that this cut it free of the foreign constraint and would permit an almost unlimited 'go'; thus it embarked on the Heath–Barber boom of 1972–3. It rapidly became plain, however, that a poor trade performance was still a constraint – it was just manifest differently. Since floating, 'go's have resulted in rapid inflation coupled with the rapid depreciation of the exchange rate. We shall explore these phenomena in detail later. Here it

205

suffices to say that no amount of floating can break the identity that the value of exports must roughly equal the value of imports; and, if you have some immutable relationship between imports and income, then trade performance largely determines growth.

Even at present, British growth is constrained by her trade performance. Exports have been buoyed up by the huge injection of revenue from North Sea oil, but the very high marginal propensity to import still leaves us with a low multiplier. Any autonomous injection – either from increased investment or from fiscal policy – is mostly leaked straight out of the economy in extra imports. Hence little is left over to boost domestic employment, whilst the rising imports rapidly eat into the oil revenues.

Let us now consider the main question: why is Britain's trade performance so weak? There is a short answer here, too: we just do not know. There are many theories, and there are also some strong indications about what does *not* cause the problems, but as yet there is no generally accepted explanation.

Among the factors that do not explain Britain's trade performance are the following. It is not solely due to prices: Britain lost her share of world trade even over quite long periods when price competitiveness was improving. It is not due to Britain's trade being concentrated on the wrong markets or in the wrong types of goods: demand for the types of good that Britain produces has grown more rapidly than average (Panić and Rajan, 1971). It is not due to weaknesses in particular sectors: there is hardly a single good in which Britain has increased her share of world trade. It is not just due to the loss of her Commonwealth links: it is true that former colonies have moved away from British goods faster than other markets, but again Britain has lost out in all markets.

The answer appears to be, therefore, in non-price competitiveness.

Non-price competitiveness

Non-price competitiveness is a nebulous concept. It covers all aspects of competitiveness excluding price; it therefore helps determine the position of the demand curve in price–quantity space. An improvement in non-price competitiveness shifts the demand curve out – more can be sold at the same price. Actually there is a conceptual difficulty here, which we can mention although not solve. Imagine that there were only two sorts of car: Rolls-Royces, which sell for £50,000 and Mini-Metros that sell for £5,000. Suppose now that British Leyland raised the price of the Metro to £50,000; not many would sell! But would this be because Metros were uncompetitive in the price sense (i.e. just too expensive), or in the non-price sense (not as good as the alternatives)? The answer is either or both. The moral is that almost any degree of non-price uncompetitiveness could be overcome by charging a low enough price. This has led Armington (1977) to argue that non-price competitiveness is an unnecessary and meaningless concept.

In this sub-section we shall assume that there is some meaning to the term non-price competitiveness, and we shall assume that for some reason relative prices cannot be changed very much.

Supply problems

There are three main groups of reasons that have been advanced for Britain's poor trade performance. The first is just straightforward supply inelasticity. Strictly speaking this is not a dimension of non-price competitiveness, but in practice it is difficult to distinguish the two problems. First, if supply cannot expand to keep pace with demand, it may appear that the demand for British goods is growing more slowly than other countries' demand even if it is not. Second, a persistent inability to satisfy demand will eventually lead to its curtailment. In the traditional theory of the firm this occurs through rising prices, but in oligopolistic markets it is likely to occur through non-price rationing, e.g. lengthening delivery lags, reduced sales efforts, etc. Hence, supply difficulties will eventually lead to shifting demand curves anyway.

Goldstein and Khan (1978) found Britain's price elasticity of supply rather low, which is perhaps indicative of supply problems, but they found nothing exceptional about her elasticity of supply with respect to the level of productive capacity. Of course, we should also ask what determines capacity and this is more contentious. 'Supply-side' economists hold that economic conditions in Britain are not conducive to investment, especially of a risky nature, because of high personal tax rates and the antipathy between management and labour. The objective indicators of labour relations, such as days lost to strikes, do not support the latter view: Britain has many strike-free industries and is overall around the average for OECD (*Department of Employment Gazette*, November 1980). However, a general mistrust of labour could easily lead to lower investment in Britain (especially among multinational companies), quite independent of such indicators. (Indeed, the infrequency of strikes could just indicate that management always gives in to labour!) Similarly, the evidence is far from obvious that Britain's tax system imposes higher burdens on entrepreneurs than that in most other countries (e.g. Central Statistical Office, *Economic Trends*, December issues, especially 1979).

Finally, of course, Britain has now experienced several years of 'supply-side' economic policy – lower tax rates on higher incomes, higher tax burdens on workers, and labour legislation to redress the power of unions vis-à-vis management.[1] Although exports have not fallen over 1980–3, despite a world recession and declining price competitiveness, and although output per worker has risen as employment falls faster than output, there is as yet no evidence that British industry has fundamentally improved either the volume or the flexibility of its supply.

We must also ask some questions about profitability. In the long run, we expect the supply of exports to be related to the difference between export prices and costs. Most empirical work, on the other hand, relates it to the difference between export and home price indices. This gives us some hint that increasing true profitability would help exports, but it is far from certain. Neither is the direct evidence very convincing. For example, Gribbin (1971) found that UK exports were on average less profitable than home sales, but neither he nor Oppenheimer *et al.* (1978) found strong evidence that this seriously harmed exports.

Probably more important is Britain's poor productivity record. This does not necessarily show up in lower profitability if wages are sufficiently low or if investment projects that would have been profitable with higher productivity are in fact ignored. That productivity is low in Britain is beyond doubt. For example, Pratten (1976) found that, on average, UK branches of multinational companies were 50 per cent less efficient than North American branches and around 20 per cent less efficient than European branches, while the Central Policy Review Staff (1975) found productivity in Britain 30 per cent or more below that in West Germany on identical plant in the vehicles industry. Possible explanations are many: low investment, short production runs, restrictive practices and labour unrest, too much 'down-time' on assembly lines, inadequate stocks of spare parts for machinery, poorly qualified and insufficient skilled workers, and so on. However, even after allowing for everything that can be measured, Britain still

207

appears to have inexplicably low productivity. As Caves (1980) rather despairingly noted, the 'productivity problem originates deep within the social structure'. It seems, then, that we can replace Britain's enigma in trade performance only with another more basic one concerning productivity.

Design and sales effort

The other two sets of explanations for poor trade performance take us into non-price competitiveness proper. The first concerns product design – including factors like technical specification, reliability, servicing arrangements, and aesthetics – and the second concerns the process of selling – including the number and type of outlets, the size and quality of the sales staffs, and the extent of advertising. Many of these factors are very difficult to quantify, and as a result much of our evidence is impressionistic; nevertheless, there are good reasons for believing that both elements are important.

Several surveys have asked traders to rank by importance various factors affecting their behaviour. All suggest that non-price factors are at least as important as prices, especially in engineering-based industries. For example, the National Economic Development Council (1965) asked UK investors the main cause of their buying foreign machine-tools: price was mentioned by 5 per cent, but it was dominated by technical superiority (30 per cent), the absence of a British alternative (21 per cent), better delivery terms (20 per cent), and a willingness to meet special requirements (8 per cent). Similarly, in a sample of twenty-six large successful US exporters, 28 per cent attributed their success to prices, 25 per cent to technical factors, 12 per cent to after-sales service and 10 per cent to unique product design (Kravis and Lipsey, 1971). Finally, the Mechanical Engineering Economic Development Committee (1968), surveying over 200 UK engineering firms, found that marketing techniques were a more important explanation of changes in exports (28 per cent of the reasons offered) than product specification (14 per cent) or any other reason. Among marketing techniques were mentioned the quality of marketing staff, the frequency of customer visits, attendance at trade fairs, and advertising. Interestingly, both large and successful exporters found it better to administer their export sales themselves than to entrust them to agents, although for small and new exporters the latter is probably unavoidable.

The problem with survey material is the doubt about whether respondents are being truthful or whether indeed they actually understand the process they are describing. However, we also have some evidence on non-price competitiveness from other sources. For example, a detailed study of the British motorcar industry (Central Policy Review Staff, 1975) atributed the stagnant exports and rapidly rising import penetration in Britain to a lack of economies of scale, inefficiency, poor quality, inappropriate product ranges, poor delivery times and reliability, and inadequate distribution networks. These results are largely confirmed in an econometric study by Leach and Cubbin (1978).

Research and development

An important determinant of technical design is research and development effort. We have seen in Chapter 4 how this affects the composition of international trade. Can it, then, explain Britain's poor trade performance?

By now, the UK's research and development effort is proportionately well below that of many countries, but during the 1950s and 1960s, when her trade performance was already strongly in decline, Britain was second only to the USA. However, in a sense that was the very problem. The sectoral break-down of UK research and development was almost identical to that of the USA, whereas her competitors, especially West Germany and Japan, had a completely different structure (Freeman, 1979). While the latter concentrated on 'commercial' sectors, by far the largest expenditure in the Anglo-Saxon countries was on aircraft, much of it military (see Table 18.5). Hence Britain failed in certain sectors almost by default. But neither did she get very far in her favoured field. Research and development is like the Cup Final – coming second is not much use. The USA with its huge resources captured most of the advances, and reaped great economies of scale from its large domestic market. Furthermore, UK research and development tended to be concentrated on a few very large projects – for instance, Concorde and the advanced gas-cooled nuclear reactor – which bore little or no commercial return (see Henderson, 1977).

Table 18.5 The industrial structure of R&D in 1962–3 (percentage of total)

	UK (1962)	USA (1962)	W. Germany (1963)	Japan (1963)
Aircraft	35.4	36.3	—	—
Vehicles and machinery	10.3	15.6	19.2	12.7
Electrical machinery and instruments	24.0	25.5	33.8	28.0
Chemicals	11.6	12.6	32.9	28.3
Metals	4.1	2.6	6.6	9.7

Sources: Freeman and Young (1965), quoted in Freeman (1979).

It has even been argued that, because of its pattern, UK research and development has had a perverse effect on trade performance. By creaming off the best brains to these esoteric enterprises, research and development has denuded the production aspects of industry of qualified manpower. Hence, while nearly all West German managers hold engineering qualifications, few British managers do: Ray (1979) quoted the percentages of qualified engineers in the metal working industries in 1974 – Sweden 6.6, Germany 5.7, France 5.3 and Britain 1.8.

Quality and the exchange rate

The arguments about research and development treat technical quality as if it were entirely discretionary. This is obviously not entirely true, but, to the extent that it is, we must ask what determines the quality chosen. This is a complex area of economic theory and we shall not investigate it here, but before leaving the area we look at one international aspect of the choice of quality.

A depreciation tends to reduce export prices in foreign currency and/or raise them in local currency. With no change in the quality of goods, this allows exporters to sell more units abroad and/or earn higher profits per unit of exports. In other words, it reduces the pressure on them, allowing them to sell the same old designs for a little longer. An appreciation, on the other hand, worsens price competitiveness and reduces profitability, forcing exporters to innovate if they are to stay in business. Hence, runs the argument, appreciation enhances quality and this eventually boosts export performance.

Two assumptions underlie this hypothesis. First, it assumes that firms are satisficers not maximisers. If opportunities exist to raise profits by quality change, maximisers will take them even at lower exchange rates; only satisficers must be forced into it by appreciation. Second, it presupposes that 'poor' goods compete on price, while 'superior' goods compete on quality. In other words, at the bottom of the range, quality is not necessary to sell your goods provided their price is low enough, whereas, at the top, high prices are not a deterrent to selling quality goods.

In order to investigate these hypotheses about quality we need a measure of it. One possible candidate is the unit value of trade. Above we interpreted unit values as proxying prices: a rise in Britain's unit value relative to competitors' was bad for competitiveness. Now, however, we turn this on its head and argue that price might reflect quality. If the composition of trade within a trade heading shifts towards more expensive varieties of the good, the unit value rises and, if the higher-priced varieties are also better, we have an indicator of quality. Hence rising unit values indicate improving (non-price) competitiveness. Without detailed studies we cannot arbitrate between these two interpretations of the unit value series, but let us for now accept the quality interpretation.

On this interpretation, the evidence is convincing that Britain has been gradually moving 'down market' relative to her competitors. For example, the National Economic Development Office (1977) considered thirty-five industrial sectors and it found that, over 1970–4, West Germany increased her share of world trade in thirty-one of them and Britain in only three, despite the fact that the German unit values exceeded the British ones in twenty-nine cases. Similarly, it found that, for Britain, the unit value of imports exceeded that of exports in twenty-five sectors while the same was true for only nine German sectors. Connell (1979) considered time-series of unit values for exports of non-electrical machinery (20 per cent of UK exports), and found a declining UK world share along with a declining unit value relative to France and Germany.

Turning to the link with the exchange rate, Brech and Stout (1981) offered interesting evidence on the British engineering industry. They constructed a unit value based index of export quality over the 1970s, and related it to the exchange rate, world income and time. They found that product quality rises with world income (richer people buy better goods), declines through time, and is positively related to the exchange rate – depreciation being associated with reductions in quality.

Unfortunately, we cannot immediately jump to the policy conclusion that appreciation is good for exports. Brech and Stout's sample contained only about six quarters of appreciation, so the improvements they observe may be only short-run effects. In the long run, even exporters in the top end of the range may feel that the low profits engendered by the high exchange rates make exporting not worthwhile. Also Brech and Stout were looking at the average quality of exports. The average can rise either by increasing the number of high-quality exports or by decreasing the number of low-quality exports. Their results might just show that appreciation drives out low-quality exporters without stimulating any high-quality ones. Nevertheless, this is an interesting and important study.

Conclusion

Non-price competitiveness encompasses a wide range of effects that might plausibly affect trade performances. They range from delivery lags (which we examined in Chapter 17) to product design and sales effort. Since we cannot explain Britain's poor trade performance with prices or incomes, we must conclude that non-price competitiveness is important, but so far measurement problems have precluded our identifying precisely which aspects are dominant. The causal chains from these non-price variables to export performance are usually rather vague, and furthermore many of the apparently significant variables are not amenable to policy-induced improvements. Hence we should beware of trying to draw too firm a set of policy conclusions from this chapter. Rather, we should learn the negative lessons that certain economic policies, desirable from other standpoints, may have untoward trade effects via their influence on non-price competitiveness.

On the intellectual front, the interesting feature of non-price competitiveness is the doubt it must cast on our simple economic models. The manipulation of price with a view to profit maximisation looks excessively simple-minded when confronted with the evidence of sales effort, research and development, and exchange rate induced quality change. This is not to dismiss such models, merely to caution the reader against their seductive elegance and simplicity. Prices are important, but if this subsection teaches us anything it is that they are but one aspect of economic performance in the real world.

FURTHER READING

The elasticities approach is surveyed in *Lindert and Kindleberger* (1982) and *Stern* (1973), and an interesting early reference is *Haberler* (1949). *McKinnon* (1981) also offers some useful insight. The empirical literature is huge, but is more suited to the specialist than to the average student: *Magee* (1975) and *Thirlwall* (1980) survey the field, while *Stern, Francis and Schumacher* (1976) list many results. More details may be found in the text references. On currencies of invoice see *Magee* (1973a) and *Page* (1977).

In addition to *Thirlwall*, probably the best introduction to non-price competitiveness is *Ray* (1966). For a more recent analysis, as well as a survey of price and non-price effects, see National Economic Development Office (1977) and *Armington*'s (1977) review of it. On export unit values and marketing, *Connell* (1979) is excellent, while on research and development and technical manpower see *Freeman* (1979) and *Ray* (1979). An insightful early analysis of both price and non-price influences on British exports is *Wells* (1964). *Kravis and Lipsey* (1971) is a seminal study of trade, especially price aspects, but it is too long for any but the keenest students.

NOTE

1 J. K. Galbraith has characterised 'supply-side' policy as stemming from the belief that the rich do not work because they are paid too little, while the poor do not work because they are paid too much (*The Observer*, 5 September 1982).

211

19 Macro-economics and the Current Account

This chapter continues our discussion of devaluation by looking at macro-economic models of the balance of payments. These approaches see the foreign account as just one more element of the macro-economic balance of an economy and they show how the current account is intimately connected with developments in other sectors.

We start with the 'absorption approach', which expresses the trade balance as the difference between national output and expenditure. This illustrates that, unless these macro-variables are affected, no balance of payments policy can be effective. The next section specialises this model to look at a small, open economy, in which the prices of traded goods are entirely determined by world prices, but in which non-traded goods are explicitly considered. We then consider the role of wage rigidities in balance of payments policy and the effect of devaluation on local prices: these sections involve some empirical evidence. Finally we consider certain alternative policies to devaluation – in particular tariffs.

This chapter still assumes a fixed exchange rate regime and concentrates exclusively on the current balance. However, because of its macro-economic orientation, it attends more closely to income changes than did the previous chapter. Indeed, here we begin to see the interaction between price and income effects.

19.1 DEVALUATION: THE ABSORPTION APPROACH

To meet the criticism of the elasticities approach's partial equilibrium nature we now consider a simple but more general model. It is not a complete general equilibrium model because it largely ignores assets and inter-temporal questions, but at least it covers all goods markets. This approach takes us back to the links between income and foreign trade and to the accounting identities of section 16.1.

The fundamental equation

National income (Y) is defined as the sum of all final demands less the part of them that is met from imports (M). If we define total domestic final expenditure (consumption, investment and government expenditure) as A (for absorption) we have

$$Y = A + X - M, \qquad (19.1)$$

where X is final demand stemming from abroad, namely exports. From this we can derive the fundamental equation of balance of payments theory

$$B = Y - A, \qquad (19.2)$$

where B is the balance of payments on current account. This equation states that the current balance is merely the difference between total income (output) and total absorption (expenditure). It is easiest to think of (19.2) in real (constant price)

212

terms, although occasionally this causes difficulties if the relative prices of exports and imports change. Such occasions will be noted below.

Actually (19.2) may be viewed in two ways. Interpreted *ex ante*, that is, in terms of intended values, it specifies an equilibrium condition: if you intend to spend more than you earn you must be prepared to run a deficit. On the other hand, interpreted *ex post*, it is an accounting identity: given the way we construct the national accounts, it must apply in terms of actual outcomes to any economy. The strength of identities in economic analysis is that they cannot be violated – they constrain the set of feasible solutions, helping to limit the cases that need to be considered. Their great weakness is that alone they cannot tell us anything about causation. Hence, if we observe a deficit, i.e. $B < 0$, we know that income falls short of spending, i.e. $Y < A$, but we do not know why. Without further input we do not know whether economic policy should be directed at Y or A or both.

For balance of payments policy, (19.2) has one simple message. If you wish to manipulate B, your policy must affect either income or expenditure. Thus, the elasticities approach, which concentrates solely on the left-hand side of the equation, is deficient in that it says nothing about whether devaluation will raise Y or cut A.

On this basis we can divide balance of payments policies into *expenditure-reducing* and *expenditure-switching* policies. The former, fairly obviously, aim to change A, leaving Y unchanged in the first instance. The latter act initially on Y, leaving A unchanged. (The term 'switching' arises because you can raise Y for a given level of A only by switching some of A from foreign goods to your own goods.) Most actual policies have direct impacts on both elements of the account, and obviously all do so eventually because income and expenditure are linked through the circular flow of income.

The effect of these types of policy on the current balance may be easily seen. In terms of changes, (19.2) may be written

$$dB = dY - dA. \qquad (19.3)$$

However, the change in absorption will comprise a direct part (dA_D) and also an indirect part stemming from changes in income (dA_I). If we let the marginal propensity to absorb be α, the latter component will be

$$dA_I = \alpha dY \qquad (19.4)$$

so that

$$dB = (1 - \alpha) dY - dA_D. \qquad (19.5)$$

We now examine the three elements of this equation.

The marginal propensity to absorb (α)

The marginal propensity to absorb is the sum of the marginal propensities to consume, invest and undertake government expenditure. In general, we would expect it to be below unity, but it is possible that an investment boom could raise it above temporarily. For example, the growth of output could generate accelerator effects, or devaluation make investment by multinationals very attractive. (A multinational seeking to expand, and financing its expansion with foreign currency, gets more for its money after devaluation. Its investment will be the greater if it believes that the devaluation is temporary, because then, while the exchange rate is low, it is buying local resources at what it believes to be an unsustainably low price – McKinnon, 1980.)

213

The direct income effects of devaluation (dY)

Devaluation can have any of three main direct effects on income. First, the idle resources effect: the price effects of devaluation will stimulate the production of importables and exportables; if there are spare resources, this expansion will not be entirely at the expense of non-traded goods, and so income may rise directly. Second, there is the terms of trade effect. The terms of trade report the rate at which we can transform a unit of exports into a unit of imports – thus they determine how favourably national product can be converted into national income; given production, a deterioration in the terms of trade directly reduces income. The third effect is a real resources effect. If the exchange rate has been overvalued prior to devaluation this may have distorted the production sector of the economy – in particular reducing the output of tradables relative to non-tradables. By correcting this distortion, devaluation raises real output.

There is one special case to note here. If the economy is at full employment, income cannot rise; that is $dY = 0$. Hence, to be successful, devaluation must either reduce absorption directly or be accompanied by other expenditure-reducing policies. We turn now to the first of these possibilities.

The direct absorption effects of devaluation (dA$_D$)

We have seen that devaluation tends to raise the domestic currency prices of tradables and that non-tradables' prices might also rise. This may reduce absorption directly through any of several mechanisms.

Money illusion may cause people to reduce real expenditure when prices rise, even though their incomes have risen in line; this may reflect mistakes, or lags between price and income changes, or a reaction to the uncertainty that price and income changes engender.

Income distribution may also be affected by devaluation. First, devaluation raises prices, and so, if wages do not rise, there is a redistribution towards profits. If profit earners save more than wage earners, this may reduce overall absorption. Second, income may be redistributed between sectors. A common case is where a primary goods sector exports at a fixed world price, while manufacturing industry, with specialist output, faces a steep demand curve. In local currency terms, the former increases its prices proportionately to devaluation while the latter increases them by less. The result is redistribution towards the primary sector, which, especially if rurally situated, is likely to have a lower marginal propensity to absorb. Lindert and Kindleberger (1982) suggested that these factors accompanied the Argentinian devaluation of the peso in 1958. Third, most direct tax systems are progressive, but in terms of nominal not real incomes. Hence, inflation tends to push people into higher tax brackets and so reduce post-tax real income. Devaluation could obviously initiate this process, which is known as fiscal drag. Finally, however, on the other hand if wages increase more than certain prices, real incomes will rise. This may particularly apply to rents, which are frequently fixed by law. In these cases, wage earners (spenders) gain income at the expense of rentiers (savers).

If we introduce assets, there are further direct absorption effects. If people hold stocks of money, rising prices reduce the real value of these cash balances. This so-called *real balance* effect argues that, given real income, society has some optimal level of real balances. If these balances are reduced through the price rises associated with devaluation, people will replenish them by saving additional amounts. While this is going on, absorption will be reduced although, once real balances have regained their desired level, absorption too will return to its original rate. Finally, if we also introduce bonds, there may well be *interest rate* effects from devaluation. These could go either way, however, and we shall leave them to be examined later.

214

There is one further point to be mentioned here concerning the valuation of imports and exports. It is not easily incorporated into our formal analysis but the intuition is quite straightforward. Imagine a small country that devalues: in local currency, both imports and export prices rise in proportion to the devaluation. Suppose further that there are no quantity effects, so that export revenue and import expenditure both rise by the extent of the devaluation. If trade was initially balanced, the two rises cancel out, but if, as is usual with devaluations, import expenditure exceeds export revenue, the burden of higher import prices outweighs the benefit of higher export prices. The net result is that real absorption must be reduced in order to balance income and expenditure. The effect is like a terms of trade effect, but it arises not because relative import and export prices change but because the price of a good that the country is a net buyer of (tradables) has risen, hence reducing real income relative to real demand.

Expansion vs. contraction

The conventional wisdom is that devaluation is expansionary. If there are idle resources this shows up as rising incomes and employment, while if the economy is at full employment it appears as rising prices. (Traded goods producers, trying to obtain the extra factors with which to expand, bid up factor prices, and non-traded producers facing excess demand raise their output prices.) We have tended towards that position too, but it is not inevitable: the direct contraction of absorption could reduce output further than the direct income effects raise it. Krugman and Taylor (1978) argued that the valuation problem of the previous paragraph and the redistribution of income from wages to profits and from private to government hands tend to make devaluation contractionary in many developing countries.

Monetary aspects of the absorption approach

The real balance effect is not the only monetary aspect of the absorption approach. Just as, if an individual spends more than he earns during a period, he has to dip into his stocks of money, so too does a country. If Britain is buying more from abroad than she is earning and she has to pay in foreign cash, this must involve running down the foreign exchange reserves (we are still ignoring the capital accounts). Hence the deficit can persist only while the authorities have the exchange with which to finance it. Once this is exhausted, the exchange rate can no longer be supported, and it will fall, presumably far enough to balance future payments.

There is also a domestic dimension to this. The difference between UK income and expenditure is just the sum of the differences between income and expenditure for each of its residents. Hence a national deficit implies private deficits among its residents, and so private cash balances must also be declining. Unless these balances are replenished, the deficit must eventually stop, because the balances will eventually reach some minimum acceptable level. The only constraint on this automatic process is whether the government has sufficient foreign exchange to finance the deficit while it works. However, the fact that letting real balances fall works, does not make it optimal. Even if a deficit could be financed for long enough, this may be a very painful and inefficient way of curing it. Similarly, just because the deficit involves running down cash balances it does not mean that excessive liquidity was the cause of the deficit. However, more of this when we look at the monetary approach to the balance of payments.

The monetary aspects of the absorption analysis also illustrate the distinction between stock and flow disequilibria (Johnson, 1958). A stock disequilibrium arises if residents wish to alter their stocks of assets. For example, if the rate of inflation is expected to rise, holding money becomes less desirable, and if people run down their cash balances by increasing absorption there will be a current account deficit. Alternatively, as an economy is about to expand, manufacturers often wish to build up their stocks of raw materials. This too leads to a temporary deficit. The important feature of the stock disequilibrium is that it is temporary: once stocks have adjusted, the disequilibrium disappears. The only problem it presents is a financing one.

Contrast this with a flow deficit. If in the inflation example in the previous paragraph the government kept replenishing residents' cash balances, the deficit would persist. In this case, given government behaviour, there would be no natural end to the disequilibrium and some economic policy changes would be required. The obvious candidate might be to stop increasing the supply of domestic cash, but other expenditure-reducing policies would also suffice.

We seem to have reached the conclusion that flow deficits are the fundamental disequilibria and that stock deficits are mere temporary storms that have to be weathered. That is true in a sense, but it is worth remarking that economic crises are almost all of the stock variety.

Take, for example, the floating of sterling in June 1972. The UK current account was in record surplus during 1971, and although, by 1972, it was declining, it was still healthy by historical standards: £214m. surplus over the first half of the year. Furthermore, the foreign exchange reserves were also strong: over $8b. at the end of 1971. Nevertheless, the aggressive expansion of the economy, coupled with the threat of a dock strike and a comment by the Shadow Chancellor of the Exchequer that he expected a devaluation soon, led to a huge loss of confidence. Anyone who could, changed his stocks of sterling into other currencies. The result was that over three days nearly one-third of the exchange reserves was spent supporting the pound! This was a 'mere' stock deficit – temporarily sterling looked unattractive so people moved out of it – but the result was a strong bout of expenditure-switching. The pound was cut free and within a year had depreciated by over 20 per cent.

This episode also illustrates another aspect of the absorption approach to the balance of payments. The depreciation of sterling might have been expected to improve the trade balance, but in fact the opposite happened: 1973 showed a record visible trade deficit. This was partly because of the lags in the responses of trade to depreciation, but largely because the government accompanied it with no expenditure-reducing policies. The British government believed that by floating the exchange rate it could free domestic growth from foreign constraints, because any incipient deficit would be corrected by further depreciation. Hence, until mid-1973 it encouraged absorption to rise even though the economy was rapidly running out of capacity. The result of ignoring the simple accounting identity $B = Y - A$ was a huge deficit, accelerating inflation and, at the end of 1973, a viciously deflationary emergency budget.

The application of the absorption approach

The elasticities analysis was criticised because the relevant (total) elasticities were virtually impossible to measure. Unfortunately, the absorption approach is as bad, because the marginal propensity to absorb and the various direct effects are all likely to vary substantially between different episodes. Hence, as a predictive tool, equation (19.5) is not much use alone. Its importance, however, is that it leads us to ask the right questions and that it highlights the necessary concomitant changes to any shift in the balance of trade. It shows that high elasticities are not sufficient for devaluation to improve the current account, and that any policy that achieves that end must raise income or reduce absorption. Except for the terms of trade and resource reallocation effects, that amounts to saying that we cannot improve the balance of trade without someone producing more and/or consuming less. That is

a fundamental insight into the balance of payments and it captures immediately
the basic problem of balance of payments policy.

19.2 NON-TRADED GOODS – THE SMALL, OPEN ECONOMY

Non-traded goods have slipped into our analysis in several places already: in
Chapter 18 they provided a buffer between the traded goods output and domestic
incomes, while in Chapter 17 and section 19.1 they have comprised that section of
consumption that was not imported. We now take a detailed look at their role in
current account adjustment.

**The small,
open economy**

For simplicity, we consider a small country proper, with no influence over its terms
of trade. These are fixed by world prices, which we assume constant. This allows us
to combine all importables and exportables into a single aggregate called
tradables. The bundle of tradables produced will contain more exportables than
the bundle consumed (the difference being exports), but we ignore this for now:
international trade consists solely of swapping one tradable for another.

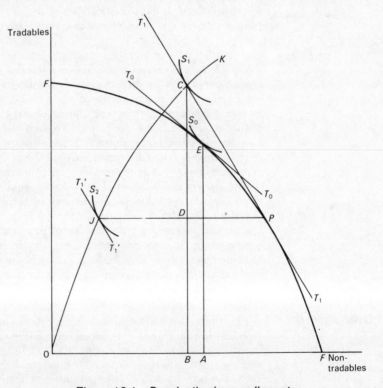

Figure 19.1 *Devaluation in a small country*

We are now back in a two-good model, but instead of exports and imports we
have tradables and non-tradables. We can represent this economy diagrammatically in a manner very similar to that used in Part I of this book. In Figure 19.1,
FF represents the production possibility frontier – assuming, as before, full
employment, flexible wages, mobile capital, etc. – and the curves marked S

represent social indifference curves. The position E represents a complete equilibrium: consumption and production of non-tradables (which must be equal) are OA, while production and consumption of tradables are AE. The equilibrium price ratio is given by the slope of T_0T_0, and the consumption frontier (the maximum consumption combinations allowed by production at E coupled with unlimited trade at the given price ratio) is given by the line T_0T_0.

Now suppose that for some reason the economy actually had a relatively lower price for tradables – T_1T_1, say. This would entail disequilibrium, because at those prices producers produce more non-tradables and fewer tradables by moving to P, while consumers, moving along the new consumption frontier, do the opposite by moving to C. Hence there is an excess supply of non-tradables (DP) and an excess demand for tradables (DC). The latter can be met by a trade deficit – we merely import more than we export – but the former will be reflected in growing stocks of non-tradables if production stays at P or unemployment if non-tradables cut back to D. (In this case we assume that the government maintains the consumption frontier at T_1T_1 by some sort of income supplement.)

The excess supply of non-tradables results in pressure to reduce their prices, but suppose that for some reason this is impossible. Similarly, while the government maintains the exchange rate, tradable prices cannot be raised, because world prices are fixed. What then becomes of the disequilibrium? Since we have ruled out the automatic adjustment mechanisms, we have to appeal to economic policy.

The policy solution

The first alternative is expenditure reduction – i.e. deflation – maintaining the disequilibrium terms of trade. As expenditure is reduced, by say taxation, the consumption frontier shrinks inwards parallel to T_1T_1. The income expansion line (or Engel curve) for that terms of trade is OK; it shows the consumption points chosen at prices T_1T_1 for each level of expenditure. Clearly, if expenditure reduction is to balance the foreign account it must reduce absorption until the consumption frontier becomes $T_1'T_1'$, at which point (J) the demand for and supply of tradables are equal. However, this is at the price of even greater excess supply of non-tradables (JP) and presumably greater unemployment.

The second policy alternative is devaluation to restore the equilibrium price ratio T_0T_0. (Devaluation raises tradable prices, boosting production and cutting consumption.) This is an expenditure-switching policy and in this instance it alone is sufficient to restore both balance of payments equilibrium and domestic full employment. It does not require support from expenditure-reducing policies because it is implemented in the presence of unemployment and also because the correction of the price distortion permits the movement of production from inside the transformation curve to a point on it.

Over-absorption

A similar analysis can be pursued where the cause of the current account deficit is over-absorption rather than incorrect relative prices. In this case the temporary consumption frontier is parallel to T_0T_0 but further out, and the deficit is accompanied by excess demand for non-tradables, as well as for tradables. Clearly, then, the policy solution is expenditure reduction, dragging the economy back to E.

It is possible, however, that the excess demand for non-tradables would bid up their price, so that in time the economy would be characterised by both excess absorption and incorrect relative prices. This is the most common predicament for deficit countries, and our analysis shows that, in these circumstances, attaining equilibrium requires both expenditure switching and expenditure reduction.

This model, as well as illustrating some of the points made in the previous section, shows how devaluation works without affecting the terms of trade – namely by altering the relative prices of tradables and non-tradables. Many economists feel that this is a far more important channel of effect than the terms of trade, and it underlies much modern theory. Even if the extreme assumptions of the model are not satisfied, the insight that it gives us into the role of non-traded goods in the adjustment process is very important.

Price flexibility

Before leaving this section we should reiterate the important assumptions that we made about prices. If non-tradable prices were perfectly flexible, it would be impossible to deviate from E, because the disequilibrium forces would always return relative prices to the level T_0T_0. For example, suppose we revalue from E, trying to attain prices T_1T_1. Tradable prices fall and this leads to an excess demand for tradables and excess supply of non-tradables. The latter would drive down the price of non-tradables until the excess supply was eliminated – i.e. until the economy returned to E. Hence the perfectly flexible economy does not need devaluation at all, and indeed, except for brief transitional periods while prices are adjusting, does not even suffer balance of payments difficulties. Left to itself such an economy will always settle at E.

In a simple barter model like ours, this automatic adjustment would be quite painless: the net result of any revaluation would be a lower price level but no real changes at all. In the real world, however, there may well be problems, because falling prices destroy confidence, increase the real value of nominal debt, and affect the distribution of income. For this reason, even if prices were flexible in the long run, an economy finding itself producing at P and consuming at C may prefer to devalue, hence raising tradables prices to attain T_0T_0, rather than let the market reduce non-tradables prices. The only difference in the long run would be in the final price level, which would be higher with devaluation. The case for devaluation (or any other form of intervention), then, depends largely on the adjustment costs of policy compared with those of the free market. There is not yet much evidence on this matter, and disagreements about such costs lie at the heart of the controversy between what might loosely be described as the 'Keynesian' and 'monetarist' schools of economic policy.

19.3 DEVALUATION AND WAGE RIGIDITY

So far we have not paid much attention to wages – we have assumed that they adjust passively to validate our conclusions. However, even the slightest acquaintance with the real world will convince the reader that wage formation is one of the most contentious parts of economic life; it is necessary to ask, therefore, what the consequences of less than passive adjustment are. First, however, we should ask how devaluation will affect wages.

**Devaluation
and income
distribution**

The precise effects of devaluation on income distribution depend critically on the assumptions made about the productive side of the economy. We shall not pursue this matter in detail but rather try to draw some broad conclusions.

The fundamental equation (19.2) suggests that to cure a deficit someone has either to work harder for the same consumption or to consume less for the same output.[1] The latter certainly suggests a decline in real post-tax incomes and the former also suggests some decline in welfare unless all the extra output stems from people who were previously involuntarily unemployed. Furthermore, since in Britain wages and salaries account for around 70 per cent of income before tax, and 60 per cent after direct taxes, any cut in real incomes seems very likely to impinge on wages.

This may also be seen from the model of the previous section. Assuming that non-tradables are relatively labour-intensive – they contain most services – the Stolper–Samuelson result of Chapter 13 states that a reduction in the relative price of non-tradables will reduce real wages. This is so whether the reduction occurs through falling money prices or through devaluation.

Finally, and perhaps most directly, devaluation raises tradables' prices and also possibly non-tradables' prices. If money wages are sticky, this will reduce real wages. Hence, there are several grounds for believing that, at least temporarily, devaluation will cut real wages.

Real wage rigidity

Now suppose that labour is able to resist the pressure on real wages. Imagine that at some historically determined level of wages and profits, the economy finds itself at a point like C in Figure 19.1, with tradables relatively under-priced and consumption at unsustainably high levels.

If the government now attempts a devaluation to achieve equilibrium, we may observe the following sequence of events. First, devaluation raises tradables' prices, but, we assume, does not affect non-tradables prices. At the original money wage this increases real profits in tradables, reduces them in non-tradables, and reduces real wages everywhere. However, if labour can resist the real wage cut by raising money wages, profits will fall in both industries relative to the first stage.

Now, if it were possible to cut profits to these levels without reducing output – i.e. if the money wage rise induced no further price rises – it would be possible to reach full equilibrium, because devaluation would have produced the correct price ratio, and profits in tradables would have risen relative to those in non-tradables, encouraging the shift in resources towards tradables. In this way, real wages would have been maintained in the face of devaluation at the expense of profits, particularly in the non-traded sector.

Much more likely, however, is that rising money wages drive up prices in the non-tradable sector (tradable prices cannot rise further because they are constrained by world prices). This could occur because profits were already at a minimum through competition, or because firms set prices as a straight mark-up over costs. Either way the rise in non-tradable prices reduces the real wage further, and, when this is matched by further money wage increase, non-tradable prices have to rise again, and so on. If neither profit margins nor real wages can be squeezed at all, we can attain equilibrium only after non-tradable prices have risen in line with tradable prices. But of course this new equilibrium has precisely the same relative prices as we started with. In other words, wage and profit rigidity frustrate any real effects of devaluation, merely converting an x per cent devaluation into an x per cent general price rise. Thus, eventually income and output must be contracted to balance the foreign account, resulting in a point like J in Figure 19.1.

The money supply

There is, in fact, one feature that may prevent us from getting back to precisely the same position as we started from – the money supply. If the total value of spending were related to the money supply and if the money supply were held fixed even though prices had risen, the real value of spending would fall after a devaluation. This, of course, is just the real balance effect mentioned above, but, with the stronger inflation entailed by rigid wages and profits, it would be stronger in this case.

220

Expectations　A further complication is the formation of price expectations. In this model, devaluation causes an equi-proportionate rise in the price level. This is not inflation proper because, once the new price level is achieved, price rises stop. However, it is possible that observing these price changes will lead people to expect further price increases in later years. This will lead to even greater money wage demands, validating the expectations and possibly leading to an even worse real squeeze. This could be an important consideration in avoiding, or at least postponing, a devaluation in the real world.

Money wage rigidity　Money wage rigidity is not normally such a problem in economic policy-making, because the real wage can still be reduced by price rises. It would, however, be equivalent to real wage rigidity in circumstances where one was wanting prices to fall – e.g. after a revaluation, or in section 19.2, where devaluation would be preferred to solve the economic problem in Figure 19.1 rather than allowing the excess supply of non-tradables to drive down their price.

The costs of wage rigidity　Real wage rigidity makes economic management very difficult. In our simple model, if it is impossible to alter real wages, and therefore impossible to alter the relative prices of tradables and non-tradables, the economy will eventually have to settle at J, with social welfare at level S_2. Since with flexibility we could achieve S_0, the cost of rigidity must be (S_0-S_2) – although of course this is quite unmeasurable.

Why, then, does such rigidity persist? There are many reasons, but most ultimately come down to distribution. First, if I resist my cut in real wages while everybody else accepts his, the economy will be in equilibrium (because one individual is infinitesimal compared with the whole economy), and yet I shall be consuming my higher, disequilibrium, amounts. Hence the problem is partly one of coordination: each waits to see others making sacrifices before he makes his own, and as a result nothing happens. Second, the bulk of any sacrifice is borne by a relatively small group of people – the unemployed. Since these are often the weakest members of society and are concentrated geographically (usually away from the country's capital city), it is very difficult for them to alter the rigidity that harms them. They have little political muscle and more often than not they are concentrated in the wrong areas and wrong trades to be able to take work at below the prevailing wage rate. Mobility is hindered by the vagaries of the housing market, by its considerable cost, and by the uncertainty of finding work anywhere if unemployment is widespread. Besides, even when the unemployed are prepared to undercut existing workers, employers valuing a quiet life and their own investments in their current workforce are often unwilling to take them on (Okun, 1981). In short, wage rigidities are not necessarily irrational for the individual, or even for individual employers, and eliminating them would require wide-ranging social and political measures that no government has yet shown the will to take.

Some estimates　It is obviously critical to our view of devaluation – or, indeed, of any economic policy – whether or not real wages are rigid. Unfortunately this has proved difficult to assess, because no one has yet discovered an econometrically satisfactory equation to explain wages. Equations that seem fine on one sample period are quite hopeless on another. Among the best references on this subject is Henry, Sawyer and Smith (1976). They examined several models of wage formation and found Sargan's the most satisfactory: this related the rate of wage increase in the UK to the rate of inflation, unemployment and real post-tax earnings. Over 1948–74, unemployment had little effect, but wages made up 60 per cent of the previous year's inflation, and were raised by 1 per cent for every 10 per cent reduction in real post-tax earnings. The latter suggests some degree of rigidity – past frustrations in real pay result in large claims to catch up. However, neither this nor the inflation effect amounts to full rigidity: together they imply that a 1 per cent rise in last year's prices will raise this year's wages by about 0.7 per cent.

Similar results stem from estimates of the other popular form of wage equation – the expectations-augmented Phillips curve – which relates wages to unemployment and expected prices. In general, inflation (past or anticipated) is not entirely made up in wage claims, while the coefficient on unemployment is small enough that a devaluation would have to be hugely expansionary before it would produce an equivalent wage rise through this mechanism – see, for example, Levačić and Rebmann (1982). Finally, in a direct study of wage flexibility in the USA, UK and Japan, Gordon (1982) found substantial evidence that in the latter two countries real wages can be cut.

To summarise, wages do react to price rises, and also probably to excess demand. However, they are not so sensitive as to prevent the reduction of real wages, although a cut of 1 per cent probably requires an average price rise of around 5 per cent.

19.4   PRICES AND DEVALUATION

It is clear that the behaviour of internal prices in the face of devaluation is an important issue, and we take a little time off now to consider some evidence on this issue. We shall see that, in a relatively large country like the UK, devaluation raises prices by raising costs and by cutting import competition. However, for all but the most open sectors, prices rise by less than the percentage of devaluation.

Material costs   Devaluation will raise the cost of imported material inputs for British industry. The importance of this varies over industries, depending on the share of such inputs in total costs (both directly and indirectly via inputs bought from other industries). For example, Barker (1968) estimated that in 1967 the sterling devaluation of 16.7 per cent raised British costs by 2.7 per cent on average (3.3 per cent in manufacturing), ranging from 13.1 per cent in petrol refining to 0.6 per cent in miscellaneous services.

Prices   That manufactured prices respond to costs is almost universally accepted among economists. More contentious is whether or not other factors are also involved – that is, whether the mark-up over costs is rigid or responds to economic conditions. We wish to know, in particular, whether prices respond to changes in demand, either in aggregate or for specific goods.

Prominent among those claiming the insensitivity of prices to demand are Coutts, Godley and Nordhaus (1978). They argued that prices are a fixed mark-up over costs, the latter defined at some normal level of output – the 'normal costs' hypothesis. They constructed such an index of costs for each of six branches of UK industry and then examined the deviation of actual prices from these indices. In particular they claimed that the deviations were unrelated to either the pressure of aggregate demand or import prices (which could affect the specific demand for each good). Unfortunately, however, most of their aggregate demand variables are not relevant to the question posed, and they cannot satisfactorily explain the secular decline in the mark-up or why cost changes are not completely reflected in prices. In short, their evidence is shaky.

On the other hand, the evidence that aggregate demand matters is pretty shaky

222

too. Typical, for instance, is Bain and Evans (1973) whose main argument is that, based on company accounts, companies say that demand matters. There is, however, rather stronger evidence that imports or import prices affect local prices. For example, Pagoulatos and Sorensen (1976) found that higher imports were correlated with lower domestic profit margins in several countries, while Bloch (1974) found that higher tariffs tended to raise both prices and costs in Canadian manufacturing industry.

The previous paragraph suggests that foreign prices in sterling terms affect British prices. This does not mean, however, that they entirely determine British prices, as would be implied by the so-called 'law of one price' (the LOOP). This asserts that, apart from known and exogenous factors like tariffs, British prices must equal the world prices for identical goods. The LOOP does not specify any particular chain of causation – for instance, equality could arise from competition in perfect markets, or because British costs adjust to bring cost-determined prices into line with world prices – it merely asserts that the equality holds.

To the extent that identical goods can be observed emanating from different countries (and if they cannot the theory is entirely vacuous), all the best evidence refutes the LOOP. Although a little support can be found at the level of aggregate price indices, if we are to accept the LOOP as something other than mere coincidence, the same sort of equality must hold for individual goods. While there are goods that roughly satisfy the equality (e.g. plywood, paper products), the majority do not. For example, Isard (1977), comparing West German export prices and USA domestic prices over the early 1970s, found massive divergences that were systematically related to exchange rate changes. In Figure 19.2, the LOOP would imply that the broken lines – the ratios of German to US prices in dollars – should fluctuate about a constant level, regardless of what happened to the exchange rate (the continuous line). In fact, they move almost identically with the latter, indicating that goods prices are fixed in local currency and that competitiveness (the ratio of prices in common currency) is mainly determined by the exchange rate. As time proceeds, the relative price of paper begins to fall back to its original level, suggesting a tendency for local currency prices to adjust as indicated by the LOOP, but even after four years the adjustment is incomplete. The apparel price relativity shows no tendency at all to compensate for the exchange rate shock.

The two goods illustrated are fairly typical, as may be seen by consulting the original article. Further evidence – possibly more damning for the LOOP because it refers to small countries – may be found in Richardson (1978) and Marsden and Hollander (1983). The former found no case out of twenty-eight examined where Canadian prices precisely followed American prices, while the latter found evidence of large and long-lived divergencies between Australian and world prices.

In terms of Britain, this evidence suggests strongly that, although devaluation will raise British prices, it will not do so uniformly or by the full extent of devaluation. This means that it can have real effects on the economy and hence that it is potentially a useful tool of economic policy.

The causes and consequences of refuting the LOOP

The LOOP fails because of market imperfections. A perfectly homogeneous good sold by many suppliers in a single market – e.g. foreign exchange – can have only one price. In world trade, however, different markets are isolated (e.g. through transport costs, tariffs, culture and linguistic barriers); some goods effectively have few suppliers (e.g. refined oil, large aeroplanes); and most goods are differentiated. The upshot is that sellers have much discretion over their prices, and although

223

market forces may generate some tendency towards one price the process is rarely completed. Hence, we observe throughout international trade substantial and sustained differences in the prices of similar goods from different countries.

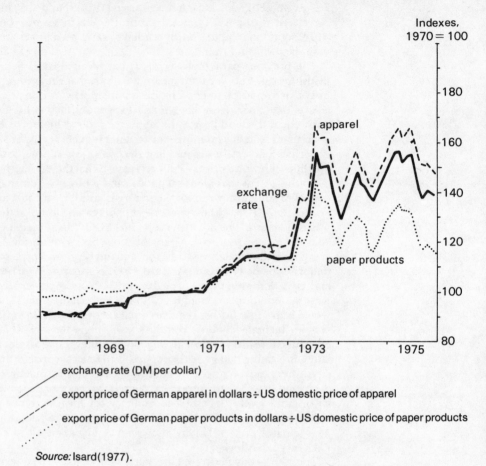

exchange rate (DM per dollar)

export price of German apparel in dollars ÷ US domestic price of apparel

export price of German paper products in dollars ÷ US domestic price of paper products

Source: Isard (1977).

Figure 19.2 *Relative prices and the exchange rate*

Much of our theory depends on the LOOP (the small country assumption), however, so we must ask where its failure leaves us. For some issues the failure has serious implications: for example, the failure of the LOOP implies that the demand curves for British exports are not horizontal, and hence that price competitiveness matters and that the exchange rate is an important tool of macro-economic policy. It also implies that free trade may not be nationally optimal. On the other hand, in many circumstances the LOOP is adopted as a simplifying rather than a critical assumption, and in these cases its loss complicates the analysis without invalidating the main insights. Examples include the analyses of non-traded goods above and that of effective protection (Chapter 6). Even in these cases, however, losing the LOOP invalidates the simple bold conclusions that so often seduce economists. For instance, with the LOOP, an *x* per cent monetary expansion in the small economy model merely raises prices by *x* per cent, but, without it, prices do not necessarily rise uniformly by *x* per cent, and so we can no longer rule out real effects.

224

An alternative to devaluation for switching expenditure may be tariffs and related policies. In fact, an *x* per cent subsidy to all exports and an *x* per cent tariff on all imports is equivalent to an *x* per cent devaluation: just as devaluation raises the local price of imports by *x* per cent, so would tariffs, and similarly both devaluation and subsidy lower foreign currency export prices. Hence, if devaluation were impossible, a uniform tariff-cum-subsidy would do just as well. We saw in Chapter 9 how Keynes (1931) recommended it as an alternative to devaluation, and how the Cambridge Economic Policy Group (*Cambridge Economic Policy Review*, 1978) recommended tariffs in circumstances where, they felt, devaluation would not work.

Import quotas and other non-tariff barriers will also have balance of payments consequences, although they will probably have different fiscal implications from tariffs. Financial disincentives to importing may be imposed, such as requiring importers to deposit funds at the central bank for six months to cover their imports; this amounts to a tariff equal to the interest forgone on these funds. Dual or split exchange rates may exist, whereby traders in one sort of good face a different exchange rate from traders in another. Most common is to have a fixed exchange rate for visible trade and services and a floating rate for other transactions. If we view the latter as 'the true exchange rate' (not necessarily a reasonable assumption, because only a small proportion of transactions may pass through it), then this amounts to the tariff–subsidy solution, with imports being taxed if the 'trade' rate is below the 'true' rate and subsidised if it is above.

Although all these switching policies differ in detail, we should never forget that none of them can break the identity $B = Y - A$. In other words, no policy can be effective unless it raises output, given absorption, or reduces absorption, given output.

FURTHER READING

The absorption approach was initiated in *Alexander* (1952); the other classic reference is *Johnson* (1958). *Thirlwall* (1980) gives a more thorough analysis than ours, and is particularly good on the history of the UK balance of payments; this is also surveyed in *Dornbusch and Fischer* (1980) from a more monetarist viewpoint. Both this reference and *McKinnon* (1980), who uses the absorption approach interestingly, will be more accessible after you have read the next chapter. *Cooper* (1971) offers a sensible analysis of devaluation in developing countries, along with some evidence of its effectiveness, while *Krueger* (1983a) offers a concise summary of the whole field.

Corden (1977) is a straightforward reference on the small open economy and on wage rigidities. The former model was introduced by *Salter* (1959), while *Corden and Jones* (1976) were among the theoretical pioneers on the latter problem. *Dornbusch* (1975b) extends the tradables/non-tradables distinction to large countries and provides interesting insight on devaluation, as does *Dornbusch* (1980a, part 2). *Pearce* (1961, 1970) integrates non-tradables into the standard model.

For the empirical work on wage and price formation, consult the references in the text, although some are econometrically difficult. *Brown, Enoch and Mortimer-Lee* (1980) summarise recent UK results. On the law of one price the *Journal of International Economics* (1978, no. 2) provides a useful symposium, while *Kreinin and Officer* (1978) offers a brief survey. *Winters* (1983a) uses the theory of this chapter to examine the case for a sterling depreciation in 1982. A fuller list of alternatives to devaluation appears in *Caves and Jones* (1981).

Finally, much of the ground in this chapter was covered by *Meade* (1951) thirty years ago!

NOTE

1   The immediate cut in absorption may occur in investment or government expenditure as well as directly in consumption, but ultimately these feed back into falling consumption.

20 Money and the Balance of Payments

Money has led a shadowy existence over the last few chapters. It certainly existed, for we spoke extensively of the price of different monies (the exchange rate), nominal wages and even real balance effects. However, it received little attention directly, and now, in view of the great resurgence of interest in monetary economics since 1970, we rectify this. The monetary approach to the balance of payments, which emphasises money above all else, takes us from a Keynesian world of fixed prices to a neo-classical one of perfectly flexible prices and wages, and consequently full employment.

The second part of this chapter reviews the various balance of payments theories within the same accounting framework. This shows their differences and similarities as well as giving the student a chance to review his/her understanding of each.

20.1 THE SIMPLE MONETARY THEORY OF THE BALANCE OF PAYMENTS

We start with a very stark and simple model of the balance of payments that not only concentrates on money, but does so to the exclusion of everything else of interest. It requires a fierce set of assumptions and bears little relationship to the real world; it nevertheless illustrates the monetarists' insights very well.

Frenkel and Johnson (1976) said that the balance of payments is a monetary phenomenon. They were referring to the official settlements balance, which is monetary in the sense that it can only be non-zero if residents (including the government, but excluding the central bank) are either accumulating or decumulating money. Let the official settlements balance be denoted B, and let R_f be total receipts from abroad (from all transactions) and P_f be total payments abroad. As we saw in Chapter 16,

$$B = R_f - P_f. \tag{20.1}$$

Now define R_d as total receipts of residents from residents, which obviously equals P_d, total payments by residents to residents, and we see that

$$B = R_f + R_d - P_f - P_d = R - P, \tag{20.2}$$

where $R = R_f + R_d$ and $P = P_f + P_d$. The difference between total receipts and payments is net accumulation of money and (20.2) shows this to equal the official settlements balance.

Viewed backwards, (20.2) shows that official settlements surpluses and deficits must be reflected in hoarding and dishoarding respectively. Hence a surplus serves to increase the stock of money held in the economy, i.e. raise the supply of money, while a deficit serves to reduce it. (The mechanism is that the excess of dollars earned over those spent is deposited in the foreign exchange reserves in return for sterling, which is then held by residents.) In this way, residents can vary the stock of money in the economy regardless of what the central bank does, because any money created that they do not wish to hold can be disposed of by spending it abroad – i.e. running a deficit. The only constraint on this is that money spent abroad has to be converted into dollars and so the process requires sufficient reserves to finance the desired outflow. For surpluses, there is no constraint as long as the authorities are willing to accumulate reserves indefinitely.

This process is the basis of the monetary approach to the balance of payments. To isolate it, however, and to obtain concrete results many other assumptions are necessary. We shall list these, then discuss the mechanism in more detail, and finally return to assess the roles of the assumptions again.

The assumptions

(i) The demand for money is a stable function of a few known exogenous variables – usually incomes, interest rates and prices, demand being proportional to prices. Residents hold only local currency.

(ii) The exchange rate is fixed.

(iii) The country is small; it is therefore a price-taker on world markets (including capital markets), so prices and interest rates are fixed exogenously. Its money supply is small relative to the world's.

(iv) Wages are perfectly flexible and are determined competitively – hence there is full employment.

(v) Product and asset markets are competitive and have perfect information.

(vi) Changes in reserves are not sterilised. This means that the central bank does not try to prevent changes in reserves from affecting the money supply by adopting offsetting open market operations. Hence the money supply is endogenous.

These assumptions – especially (iv) and (v) – guarantee the independence of the real economy from all monetary phenomena. The composition of output, factor rewards, relative prices and asset portfolios are determined as in standard general equilibrium models without money, by reference to marginal utilities, marginal productivities and so on. Given its composition, the level of output is fixed by the fact that full employment rules. In fact, the real economy is taken to be in long-run equilibrium at all times, so that, for instance, all unemployment is voluntary. This is precisely the economy described at the end of section 19.2, where economic policy is unnecessary because nothing ever goes wrong.

The mechanism

This dichotomy between real and monetary effects is well known in closed economy monetarist models, where the money supply determines the price level but nothing else. In our model, however, domestic prices are fixed by world prices, and monetary policy is isolated from the real economy by another mechanism. Imagine an economy, of the type described, in full equilibrium and in a perfectly static world. Equilibrium would cover both flows, such as income equalling expenditure, and stocks, so that all assets were willingly held at the prevailing prices. In particular, the demand for money would equal the supply. Now suppose that the central bank injected some extra money. With no change in income, prices or interest rates, people would not wish to hold this cash and so would seek to dispose of it by spending it on goods or assets. To the extent that residents buy from one another, the excess cash is shuffled around, always remaining surplus to national demand. If, however, it is spent abroad it disappears from the domestic economy and, in view of our country's smallness, is painlessly absorbed elsewhere. Hence the balance of payments provides a drain through which any excess money can be poured, subject always to there being sufficient reserves to effect the transfer.

During the process of adjustment the country runs a deficit, but, once the excess money has been drained off, the deficit ceases and the economy regains its former equilibrium. The cumulated deficit and hence the overall loss of reserves just equal the initial cash injection. Thus the only lasting effect of the injection is to change the composition of the (unchanged) money stock: the amount backed by domestic instruments rises, while the amount backed by foreign assets (the reserves) falls correspondingly. The whole process is like a huge national stock adjustment, switching from foreign to national assets, and the deficit is a stock deficit.

The only way that this model could generate anything like a flow deficit would be if the authorities persistently tried to supply too much money. This might occur if, for example, they constantly printed money to finance a budget deficit. Even this, however, is best thought of as a series of stock deficits, and a little thought will convince you that it is hardly surprising that a model in which economic behaviour is primarily defined in terms of stocks (as in the money demand equation) can generate only stock deficits.

Equation (20.2) is really just an accounting identity (think how it was derived), so it does not tell us that every deficit is *caused* by excessive money creation, but merely that each is *accompanied* by dishoarding. Deficits may arise as residents tide themselves over a bad harvest, say, or because misinformation leads people not to associate their consumption with declining cash balances elsewhere. The theory tells us that such deficits *could* be cured by cutting the money supply to match demand, or, if time and reserves permit, merely letting it fall to this level. This simple model also suggests that such a course would be optimal, but this most certainly does not generalise to the real world with all its rigidities and imperfections. One need only observe Britain since 1980 to see the agonies of cutting the rate of growth of the money supply, let alone the money supply itself.

Devaluation

Devaluation is not necessary in this model, but suppose it occurs. For a small country, an x per cent devaluation raises all tradable prices by x per cent; furthermore, since relative prices are determined by (unchanged) real factors, all other prices must also rise by x per cent. The uniform rise in prices increases the demand for money by x per cent, and, since supply is not affected initially, this demand can only be met from abroad. As residents cut expenditure in an effort to reconstitute their cash balances the country runs an official settlements surplus and cash flows in. This can only be temporary, however: once cash balances have reached the desired level the old equilibrium is restored. The only long-run difference that devaluation makes, therefore, is to raise all prices and the money supply equi-proportionately, and to raise the reserves by the amount of the extra money supply.

Assumptions again

These bold and simple results require that the *only* way money demand and supply can be equated is via the balance of payments; and this is where the bulk of the assumptions fit in. The stock demand for money depends on prices, interest rates and income; if these are constant then so too is money demand. If, on the other hand, increasing the money supply raised prices or incomes or lowered the rate of interest, then some of the additional cash would be held by residents and the payments deficit would not equal the money injection. Hence assumptions (iii)–(v) – namely, the independence of the real economy and the exogeneity of prices – are merely ways of blocking up alternative escape routes for the excess money. The remaining two assumptions define the stock behaviour that drives the model: excluding sterilisation ensures that the money stock is endogenous only through the balance of payments, while the demand for money function, which is the behavioural cornerstone of the theory, is assumed stable just because theories cannot cope with arbitrary changes in behaviour.

Assessment

The basic insights of the monetary approach are two: first, it brings out the real balance effect more strongly than other approaches; second, it emphasises that we must take account of the monetary (or rather asset-stock) implications of balance of payments disequilibria. Although these should be important factors in any theorising or empirical application, they will be the predominant influences only under a relatively special set of circumstances. Building a general theory around them is usually justified in terms of strategic simplification: 'by ignoring other (realistic) complications', runs the argument, 'we get a simple and accurate explanation of an important phenomenon.' There are several counter-arguments to this, however.

First, it is not clear that the monetary approach is an accurate explanation. The basic relationship is an accounting identity – any consistent set of data satisfies it – so it cannot separate one hypothesis from another. We therefore have to test the theory indirectly. There are considerable technical difficulties in this, which we cannot explore here, but overall the results are mixed. One approach is to test whether monetary expansions or contractions are completely offset by balance of payments flows – in general they are not. An alternative is to consider the balance of payments implications of economic growth: the Keynesian theories predict a deficit (via rising absorption and imports) whereas monetary theory predicts a surplus (via rising demand for money). Here the monetary theory is probably better supported than the Keynesian, but this is not conclusive because (a) both could be true, since they refer to different balances of payments, and (b) in the most striking cases of high growth and positive trade balances (Japan, West Germany) one suspects that the causation runs from trade performance to growth and not vice versa as payments theory assumes. A third test concerns the permanence of the balance of payments improvements induced by devaluation. Miles (1979), considering fourteen devaluations, suggested strongly that the gains were only temporary, which supports the monetary view. However, his model of the monetary and fiscal policy accompanying devaluation is very simple, and his results are at variance with detailed studies in the Keynesian mould, such as Artus (1975), who found the British current account £1.3b. stronger in 1971 as a result of the 1967 'devaluation package'. In short, empirical evidence has not yet permitted the rejection of one of the rival approaches in favour of the other.

Second, the level of the official settlements balance is not often a crucial economic question. It is if reserve exhaustion is the problem, but for most questions of economic policy – including that of how to *avoid* reserve exhaustion – it is necessary to have more detail of where the deficit arises. The monetary approach requires supplementing for these questions. For example, it does not determine whether a deficit arises from excessive absorption or from residents increasing their stocks of foreign bonds. (Indeed it ignores the fact that desired stocks of bonds might be subject to economic forces just as the desired stock of money is.) Similarly, in its simple form, it assumes away the problems of unemployment and terms of trade changes, which are clearly issues of great importance. Thus its simplicity and directness are bought at a high price in terms of relevance.

Third, there are problems of the internal consistency. Assumptions (iii)–(v) guarantee that a real equilibrium that exists at one money supply would also be available if the money supply were twice as large. They do not, however, guarantee that actually doubling the money supply will not disturb the real economy, because economists have yet to prove either the uniqueness or the stability of such equilibria. In other words, the process of adjusting to money supply changes may cause the economy to settle at a new, different, real equilibrium. This is especially likely if we recognise the existence of physical capital that is not instantly and costlessly transferable between uses. Furthermore, periods long enough to allow the real economy to attain equilibrium after a shock may well be too long for the supposed stability of the demand for money.

Fourth, there may be difficulties over the money demand equation. The equation relating demand to income implies a transaction demand for money – money to spend – but the emphasis in the analysis on money balances implies an asset demand – money to hold. During the course of a year people might both demand more money to hold, but then actually spend it, which, in the statistics, would disturb the assumed mutual exclusiveness of holding money and spending on goods. This is essentially saying that, if people are not in equilibrium, the attempt to build up cash balances does not necessarily imply a willingness to forgo goods.

Summary   The model presented here is the simplest of the monetary models, and few professional economists, even among those sympathetic to monetarist analysis, would claim much for its realism. Current research stresses the uncertain and variable lags in the adjustment of the economy to monetary shocks, and the role of real changes over this transitional period. This has its costs in terms of the simplicity and certitude of the policy prescriptions, but regrettably one still encounters the stark conclusions of the simple model in public debate, despite its theoretical shortcomings and the uncertainty over the time-scale to which it applies. It is wrong to believe that every deficit is caused by monetary disturbances just because each is accompanied by them. Similarly, just because a monetary contraction would eventually cure any deficit, it does not follow that contraction would be the optimum policy in all, or even any, circumstances. Therefore it is not sensible to work with models that admit only monetary solutions.

The importance of the monetary theory lies not in its identifying the fundamental determinants of the balance of payments – it has not – but in its reminding economists that any theory must satisfy certain monetary identities. Just as any balance of trade policy must affect income or absorption, so any balance of payments policy must bring the demand and supply of money into balance.

20.2   THE BALANCE OF PAYMENTS THEORIES COMPARED

We have presented three balance of payments theories. Our explanations have implied various similarities and differences but these have not been emphasised. We therefore complete our discussion of this area by bringing the theories together under one framework in order to compare and contrast them.

Let us aggregate the economy into three sectors: a private sector – all firms and individuals; an official sector – the government and the central bank; and a foreign sector – to record all transactions with foreigners. Let us also distinguish three markets: goods and services; bonds – which includes all financial instruments; and money. We can then draw up a social accounting matrix that records each sector's net transactions in each market. This is shown in Table 20.1. Now, since all bonds sold must be bought, the three net acquisitions of bonds must sum to zero, and likewise for goods and money. Similarly, because the acquisition of goods must be

231

matched by the disacquisition of something else (the means of payments), so each sector's net acquisitions sum to zero.

Table 20.1 Social accounting matrix

Net acquisition of:	Private		Official		Foreign		Total
				Sector			
Goods	$(I-S)$		$(G-T)$	+	$(X-M)$	=	0
	+		+		+		
Bonds	ΔD	+	ΔB	+	ΔF	=	0
	+		+		+		
Money	ΔM	+	ΔC	+	$-\Delta R$	=	0
	‖		‖		‖		
Total	0		0		0		

The matrix is quite easy to interpret. Consider the first row: private net acquisition of goods is expenditure (consumption, C, plus investment, I) minus income (consumption plus savings, S), which is just $(C+I)-(C+S)=I-S$; official net acquisitions are government expenditures (G) less those goods and services granted to it via taxation (T); and foreign net acquisition of goods is just exports (X) less imports (M). In the second row, D, B and F are net holdings of bonds by the private, official and foreign sectors, respectively, and the Δs denote changes. For example, ΔB represents the change in official net holdings of bonds; if, as is usual, the public sector issues more of its own bonds than it buys from other sectors, ΔB is negative. In the last row, ΔM represents private accumulations of money, ΔC official accumulations – usually negative because the central bank issues cash – and ΔR accumulations by the foreign sector. (To effect a cash transfer abroad our residents have to convert local currency into foreign currency, which runs down our foreign exchange reserves, R; hence the negative sign.) From this it is obvious that the last column measures the balance of payments: the current account, the capital account and the compensating reserve movements. For example, a deficit in the current account, $X - M < 0$, must be reflected either in borrowing from abroad (increasing foreign bond holdings, $\Delta F > 0$) or by running down the reserves, $\Delta R < 0$, so $-\Delta R > 0$.

The relationships between the entries in the matrix may be viewed either as *ex post* accounting identities, which must hold in any consistent set of data, or as *ex ante* equilibrium conditions. Either way they do not define causation – that is the job of economic theory – and we now turn to see how the various theories move from their postulates about behaviour in one part of the economy through to the balance of payments.

The elasticities approach
This looks at the current account, dealing with X and M directly. The matrix shows, however, that it must assume compensating changes elsewhere in the goods market if it is to explain the balance of payments.

The absorption approach
This also deals with the current account, and is just a rewritten version of the top row. The absorption equation is

$$B = Y - A, \tag{20.3}$$

and if we break up income by its various uses – consumption (C), savings (S) and taxes (T) – and absorption into its various components – consumption, investment (I) and government expenditure (G) – we have

$$B = X - M = (S - I) + (T - G). \qquad (20.4)$$

Hence any improvement in the trade balance must involve a smaller net acquisition of goods by the private sector (reducing $I - S$) or the government sector (reducing $G - T$).

The matrix also illustrates a special case of the absorption approach pioneered by certain Cambridge economists – Cripps, Godley and Fetherston (1974). They assumed that the private net acquisition of financial assets (NAFA) is fixed exogenously, i.e. that $\Delta D + \Delta M$ cannot change. The second and third rows of the matrix then tell us that changes in official NAFA ($\Delta B + \Delta C$) must be balanced by changes in foreign NAFA ($\Delta F - \Delta R$). But the second and third columns show that changes in official NAFA must be balanced by changes in the government budget deficit ($G - T$) and changes in foreign NAFA by changes in the current account ($X - M$). Hence, Cambridge concluded, the main determinant of changes in the current account is the government's budgetary stance. But this of course follows immediately from equation (20.4) once we realise that fixing $\Delta D + \Delta M$ also fixes $I - S$. Hence, with $\Delta(I - S) = 0$, $\Delta(G - T) = -\Delta(X - M)$.

The Cambridge view is interesting partly because it makes the special assumption that the marginal propensity to absorb is unity (with $I - S$ fixed, any extra income must be spent), but mainly because it shows how asset portfolio behaviour can drive absorption-type theories. Unfortunately, however, recent evidence has belied their simple portfolio assumption, so their approach represents more a mode of thought than a predictive tool.

The monetary approach
This is similar to the Cambridge view, but it combines the first two rows of the matrix instead of the last two. The monetarists claim that M (and therefore ΔM) is determined by incomes, etc., and that ΔC is determined by policy. Any discrepancy between ΔM and ΔC shows up as ΔR and this, via the last column, has implications for the official settlements balance ($X - M + \Delta F$).

Each theory discussed comprises behavioural assumptions about one cell (or groups of cells) of the matrix (e.g. the monetarists claim to know ΔM) and 'convenience' assumptions (constancy or accommodating changes) about others. A theory will be better, the more predictable are the former and the more plausible are the latter. In fact, it is not necessary to limit theory to a single behavioural cell. It is possible to have independent behaviour for any two cells out of each row and column without violating the consistency of the matrix. Hence, for example, Stern (1973) examined models with independent behaviour in the goods and money markets and in the goods and bonds market. The drawback of this, of course, is the complexity: the models are difficult to analyse and rarely produce the clear-cut results that we have found. Nevertheless, professional economists should recognise that the world is a complex place and should be less willing than they usually are to purchase elegance and simplicity at the expense of realism and accuracy.

233

FURTHER READING

The principal references for the monetary theory are *Frenkel and Johnson* (1976), and *Whitman* (1975). *Batchelor and Horne* (1979) is also useful. Critical commentaries are *Thirlwall* (1980), and *Hahn* (1977), which is difficult but worthwhile. The empirical literature is summarised in *Kreinin and Officer* (1978) and discussed in *Magee* (1976); the references to *Miles* (1979) and *Artus* (1975) are also useful.

Section 20.2 is based on *Winters* (1978), which offers some further simple analysis.

21 The Determinants of Exchange Rates

We now move from a world of fixed but movable exchange rates to one of perfectly flexible rates. This has consequences for economic policy that we shall examine in Chapter 22, but for the present we concentrate just on the factors determining the exchange rate. Fortunately we do not have to rework all the analysis of the previous four chapters because there is a very simple relationship between the balance of payments and the exchange rate. Under a perfectly flexible exchange rate the central bank does not intervene in the foreign exchange market at all. Hence any tendency towards deficit is met not by disbursements from the reserves but by a decline in the exchange rate. A deficit shows that more dollars are demanded for purchases abroad than are supplied by sales abroad. Under fixed rates the reserves make up the difference, whereas under flexible rates the price of dollars is allowed to rise, that is, the value of sterling falls. Hence any factor that at a fixed exchange rate would worsen the balance of payments tends, under flexible rates, to depreciate the currency.

Of course the exchange rate responds to any excess supply or demand for foreign exchange, so the relevant balance of payments concept is the balance on official settlements. In the absence of official intervention this must constantly be zero, and the exchange rate will adjust to bring this about. Hence we must look at the capital account as well as the current account, especially in the short run during which short-term capital flows can swamp any development on the basic balance. One result of the absence of intervention, and the consequent absence of reserve movements, is that the domestic money supply is perfectly insulated from the foreign sector.

This chapter describes the structure and participants of the foreign exchange market. It then considers the purchasing power parity theory of exchange rates: this is the oldest and simplest of exchange rate theories, but it is found seriously wanting in today's circumstances. We then examine the impact of asset markets on exchange rates. Several channels of possible influence are identified; these are incorporated into specific models of exchange rate behaviour in the last section. This section also examines the concept of 'overshooting' and looks at recent empirical evidence.

21.1 THE FOREIGN EXCHANGE MARKET

This section describes the foreign exchange market and the types of transaction that occur within it.

The foreign exchange market

Unlike the Stock Exchange or the London Metal Exchange, the foreign exchange market is not a physical institution where traders meet. It operates in the same way, but transactions are made by telephone and computer rather than face-to-face. Although anyone in Britain can now hold foreign currency, the London foreign exchange market itself is still the preserve of about a hundred specialised dealers. These firms, with their accumulated skills and world-wide communications, conduct wholesale transactions between themselves and with their foreign counterparts. 'Retail' foreign exchange transactions – such as buying currency to pay for a foreign holiday – all have to be effected ultimately through these main dealers.

Trading in the exchange market is extremely rapid and involves huge sums: the turnover of a large dealer can amount to £3b. per day, although by the end of the day its net purchases of foreign currency may be very small. Profits are made by constantly buying and selling on small margins as the price fluctuates through the day. Of course, only a small fraction of exchange deals give rise to physical transfers of cash. In the main, traders are merely swapping the ownership of deposits of cash in some bank. The newspaper article reproduced on p. 237 gives a flavour of life in the exchange markets.

During the week, foreign exchange can be traded twenty-four hours a day because, when London is closed, Tokyo or Singapore is trading, and so on. Furthermore, it is possible to trade in almost any currency in the big financial centres. It is not necessary, for instance, to go to Paris to trade francs – banks, the world over, are willing to deal in them. Rates are equalised in the various centres by *arbitrage*. If Frankfurt were offering $2.00 per £1.00 and London $1.90 per £1.00, it would be profitable to buy pounds in London for sale in Frankfurt, which would rapidly bring rates into line. Arbitrage also ensures that the many different rates of exchange are consistent. For example, if $1 US will buy $1 Australian and $1 Canadian, $1 Australian must also buy $1 Canadian; if not, profit opportunities exist. (Imagine $1.5 A = $1 C, how would you make money?)

Although you can buy most currencies in London, you cannot effect direct swaps between any arbitrary pair of currencies. To convert Greek drachma into Colombian peso, for instance, you would trade drachma for dollars and dollars for pesos. Just as trading shoes for mutton is smoothed by the existence of money, which removes the need for the double coincidence of wants, so trading drachmas for pesos is smoothed by the existence of an international money like the dollar. Without it, dealers would have either to have matched requirements or to hold stocks of every single currency. With a common *vehicle currency* in which to trade, however, these balances can be replaced by a single dollar balance and a knowledge of where each other currency can be swapped for dollars in the rare event of it showing up (the issuing central bank). Even so, the costs of trading in small currencies can be relatively high, so trade between small countries is often conducted entirely in terms of one of the vehicle currencies.

Spot and forward exchange rates

When we talk of 'the exchange rate' we almost always mean the price of dollars, say, if we bought *and received* them now. This is the *spot rate* and it corresponds to most other prices in the economy. It is not necessary, however, to complete the deal now. It would be possible, as say when reserving a hotel room, to agree now that we will buy so many dollars at a particular price at some specified time in the future. This would be a forward transaction, and its price the *forward exchange rate*. The price and the maturity are set now, but both sides of the transaction are effected in the future. The possible advantages of this will become apparent soon.

The forward exchange rate is determined by supply and demand in the foreign exchange market, just as is the spot rate. There are, however, large markets only for certain standard maturities: thirty and ninety days, six months, a year, and, for the main currencies, two years. Other time-spans are possible but tend to involve high transactions costs. Obviously the spot and forward rates can differ: we refer to the percentage excess of the latter over the former as the *forward premium*. Sterling is at a forward premium if it takes more dollars to buy one pound forward than spot. A negative premium is known as a *discount*.

The great money-go-round

by LINDSAY VINCENT

WHEN the pound sank into what a City economist termed 'the black hole' on Far Eastern markets last Tuesday, one of Britain's clearing banks pulled it out.

'The "black hole" price ($1.51.2) was there for a few seconds,' said a leading dealer in the bank's foreign exchange department. 'We took it. We bought £7 million. The bank who sold had to buy it back at around $1.54.'

Since the ending of fixed-rate parities, he said, money has become a commodity to be traded 'like cocoa.'

'Tuesday was a hell of a day. We had a turnover of over half-a-billion dollars. And by the end of the day, we had an exposed position of only a few million.

'Sure, we've made money

this week. Maybe six or seven other banks did, too. But the 50 or so others operating in London certainly didn't,' he added.

Buying and selling half-a-billion dollars worth of currencies in just one day may be beyond the comprehension of most of us, but such are now the sums in the foreign exchange numbers game.

An authoritative US banking journal recently estimated that in a 'normal' day, no less than $200 billion worth of currencies are traded round the world, round the clock, each day.

Of this, only $10 billion is related to trade and investment in currencies by institutions. The rest—95 per cent of a day's business — is straightforward speculation.

While no precise figures for daily currency volume are available, the Bank of Eng-

land on Friday confirmed that the ratio of 95.5 of speculation-v-genuine demand was 'about right.'

The great majority of this speculation is done by the banks themselves under strict limits imposed by respective central bank authorities. Multinationals, like General Motors, IBM and the oil majors, are themselves no novices when it

comes to gambling in money. But the sums they play with are relatively small.

'Perhaps our speculation does mean that daily fluctuations are sharper than they used to be. But the short-term trend is dictated not by us, but by capital movements,' said the London dealers.

'We read each day that currencies move for this or that reason. The truth is that we don't know for weeks after why there are prolonged movements one way or another.

'Peter Shore's 30 per cent devaluation cry has been blamed for this latest setback, but that's trine. He said it ages ago. The momentum behind sterling's latest slide was a very large selling order by a pension fund who sold pounds to buy yen.'

The pound

BELGIUM : 73.20 francs.
CANADA : $C1.9880.
FRANCE : 10.58½ francs.
GERMANY : 3.73½ marks.
HOLLAND : 4.10½ guilders.
ITALY : 2.151 lire.
JAPAN : 363 yen.
SPAIN : 198.30 pesetas.
SWITZERLAND : 3.05½ francs.
UNITED STATES : $1.5360.

The trade-weighted index of the pound fell from 82.8 to 80.9 on the week.

Reprinted from *The Observer*, Business Section, 30 January 1983.

With its relatively large number of dealers, nearly perfect communication and nearly costless transactions, the foreign exchange market is as perfect a market as exists. The price of foreign exchange is merely the price that equates the sum of all demands to the sum of all supplies. We now turn to these demands and supplies by looking at the various types of transaction in the market.

Trade

The most obvious transaction in foreign exchange is the purchase of foreign currency for spending on imports or the sale of currency arising from exports. The extent of these demands and supplies depends on the value of international trade, which, in part, depends on the exchange rate itself. A rise in the exchange rate (measured in dollars per pound) will tend to increase the supply of sterling and the demand for dollars. Typically traders deal in the spot market, and this mechanism relates the exchange rate to the current account.

Hedging

The lag between ordering and paying for an import involves one or other of the parties in exchange risk. Suppose a British exporter is interested only in his receipts in sterling terms, but that he prices his goods in dollars. Between agreeing a price and receiving payment he bears exchange risk, because a change in the exchange rate will alter his sterling returns from a given dollar sale. He might find this uncertainty inconvenient or unpleasant, and hence seek to avoid it by hedging. The most obvious way to do this is to sell the dollars forward. He knows how many dollars he will receive in, say, three months, and the forward market allows him *now* to fix the price at which they will convert into sterling. This mechanism, designed solely to avoid risk, relates the forward rate to trading behaviour.

Arbitrage

Arbitrage is the process of buying in one place (or time) and selling in another with a view to making profits. If there are several markets selling the same commodity, arbitrageurs are likely to equalise the prices, for they will buy cheap and sell dear. The important thing about arbitrage is that it involves no risks: both buying and selling prices are known before the transactions take place.

As well as equalising exchange rates across different markets, arbitrage also links the spot and forward rates. Suppose I have £1 to invest for a year. I could invest it in London at interest rate i_k and receive $£(1 + i_k)$ after a year. Alternatively, I could convert it into $\$S$ at spot rate S, invest it in New York at interest rate i_s to receive $\$S(1 + i_s)$ after a year, and agree *now* to sell the dollars forward at rate F, finally collecting $£[S(1 + i_s)/F]$. Both chains involve only information that is available *now*, so neither involves uncertainty. Hence, provided plenty of funds exist to exploit any arbitrage opportunities, the two rates of return should be equalised. That is

$$(1+i_k)=S(1+i_s)/F \qquad (21.1)$$

which is known as the *interest arbitrage condition*.

Suppose that, given the two interest rates, the spot rate were too high relative to the forward rate for (21.1) to hold. Arbitrageurs would immediately sell pounds spot and buy them forward: this would reduce S (the spot price of pounds) and raise F, thus restoring the equality. Also, since no one would be investing in London, i_k would probably also rise and this would further help re-establish (21.1). In fact, the only thing that can prevent the interest arbitrage condition from holding is transactions costs (including legal constraints) and default risks. For large stable countries, therefore, where default is almost inconceivable, (21.1) holds almost exactly.

238

The interest arbitrage condition can also be written in terms of the forward premium (p), the proportionate difference between forward and spot rates:

$$p = \frac{F-S}{S} = \frac{i_s - i_k}{1 + i_k}, \qquad (21.2)$$

which, when i_k is small (e.g. for short loans), may be approximated by

$$p = i_s - i_k. \qquad (21.3)$$

Note that interest arbitrage alone is not a theory of the exchange rate; it is more an equilibrium condition that any other theory must satisfy. This is because any or all of the four variables it relates could adjust to bring it about.

Speculation

The transactions considered so far have sought to avoid the uncertainty of exchange markets. Speculators, on the other hand, seek it and aim to benefit from it. Speculation consists of taking an 'open position' in something – namely, having unequal assets and liabilities in it. Hence a speculator, expecting the dollar to appreciate next week, will seek to hold more claims on dollars then than he has liabilities. If he achieves this, and is right in his prediction, he will become wealthier, because something of which he is a net holder will have risen in value.

The essence of speculation is expectations – in the present circumstances, expectations about the future exchange rate. In the simplest case, suppose one expects the spot rate in a year to be below the present forward rate for that maturity. One would sell pounds forward now and plan to buy them back at the then ruling spot rate, expecting to make $\$ (F - \hat{S}_1)$ on each pound, where $\hat{S}_1$ is the expected spot rate one year hence. Obviously the actual unit profit will be $\$ (F - S_1)$, where S_1 is the actual spot rate in one year, which could be positive or negative. Notice that this transaction involves no commitment of cash until the settlement date: any profit arises solely from the speculator's willingness to take risks.

The obvious effect of speculation is to bring today's forward rate towards the expected future spot rate, and if there is widespread agreement about that future rate this effect can be very strong. It also, of course, affects the current spot rate, because that is linked to the forward rate by interest arbitrage.

Speculation could also occur directly in the spot market. If one expected a fall in sterling $(\hat{S}_1 < S)$, it would pay to sell sterling now and buy back later. If one also took interest rates into account one would compare £1 invested in London, to yield $(1 + i_k)$, with £1 converted spot, invested in New York and converted back *at the expected rate* in one year; i.e. with $S (1 + i_s)/\hat{S}_1$. One would sell sterling now if the latter dominated. This, of course, is just the interest arbitrage condition with $\hat{S}_1$ replacing F. In fact, if interest arbitrage holds, the two types of speculation are equivalent. Either serves to relate the current spot rate to the expected future spot rate – an important feature in the theory of flexible exchange rates.

Speculation might appear to tie the forward rate rigidly to the expected future spot rate, but this is not necessarily true. Speculation involves risk and this must be compensated by higher returns. Speculators will operate only if F and $\hat{S}_1$ diverge by enough to pay transactions costs and reward risk. Furthermore, if they are not certain of their estimate of $\hat{S}_1$, they may be unwilling to bet heavily on it, hence there may be insufficient speculation to force F all the way to $\hat{S}_1$.

Speculation is often thought to be anti-social. It is true that speculative flows can be very disruptive of the real economy – e.g. Britain in 1972, see p. 216 above – but in general they merely speed up an inevitable change in the exchange rate.

239

Without any speculation, exchange markets would be very inefficient, because if no one were willing to take open positions in foreign currency every trader selling pounds would have to find another who wished to buy them. This would be more difficult than the present requirement of finding someone who is willing to hold pounds temporarily. Indeed it would be impossible unless trade were balanced! Looked at alternatively, if no one were willing to bear uncertainty, only riskless transactions could be effected, and this is surely a very small subset of what we actually observe today.

The authorities

The transactions just described are undertaken, often simultaneously, by a variety of market participants. However, our last class of transaction is defined by its executor – namely, official transactions.

Under a fixed exchange rate regime the Bank of England fixes a parity rate, say $2.40. It then sells pounds to prevent the rate moving above, say, $2.42, and buys them to prevent it falling below $2.38, but between these limits keeps out of the market. At the other extreme, under a perfectly flexible exchange rate regime, the central bank would never intervene in the market, although of course it may conduct commercial activities on behalf of the government or other customers. In between lies the 'dirty float', where the Bank intervenes but not around any pre-announced target. It may aim just to smooth out day-to-day fluctuations or to influence the rate significantly. Intervention may occur in the forward market as well as the spot market, although exchange rate targets and commitments invariably refer to the latter. We shall consider different intervention regimes later; for the rest of this chapter we imagine a clean float, or perfectly flexible rate.

21.2 PURCHASING POWER PARITY

Purchasing power parity is the oldest and simplest of theories about the exchange rate. It is implicit in the work of certain nineteenth-century economists, and was formalised by Cassel around 1920. In one form it involves only the market for goods and services, but at a more sophisticated level it also takes account of the money market.

The exchange rate and the goods market

At its simplest, purchasing power parity (PPP) is really the same as the law of one price, which we have already met. If there were no imperfections in world markets and all goods were traded, the price of any good would be the same regardless of its origin. Imagine some typical basket of American goods valued at $100. If the value of an identical basket originating in Britain were £50, the only equilibrium exchange rate possible would be $2.00:£1.00, equating the price of the basket in the two countries. If, for example, the rate were $1.90:£1.00, everyone would buy from Britain: starting with $100, one could buy £52.63 on the exchange market and hence get the basket of goods plus £2.63 by buying British. The resultant increased demand for pounds would drive up their price towards $2.00. This theory is known as the absolute version of PPP.

Various restrictions to trade such as transport costs and tariffs and the existence of non-tradable goods combine to frustrate absolute PPP, and this has led to a more sophisticated version of the theory – relative PPP. Suppose that our typical American basket were, in fact, worth $110 in America and £50 in Britain, but that because of these imperfections the exchange rate of $2.00:£1.00 were an equilibrium. Relative PPP asserts that, if British prices doubled, the exchange rate would halve: in other words, the original price relativity between British and

American goods would be preserved; despite the inflationary shock, American goods would still be 10 per cent more expensive than British goods. The justification for this is the dichotomy between the real and nominal economies that we encountered in section 20.1 above. The relative price of American and British goods is a real phenomenon so, provided no real changes accompanied the assumed inflation, it would be unaffected.

A monetary approach

So far we have considered only the goods market, but many economists argue that PPP also has a monetary dimension. To explore this we return to the monetary model of Chapter 20, repeating all the assumptions but assuming a perfectly flexible rather than a perfectly fixed exchange rate. Previously the domestic money supply varied with the foreign exchange reserves; any excess money created flowed out of the economy via an official settlements deficit. Now, however, the money cannot escape, because by not intervening in the exchange market the central bank prevents any movements in the reserves. Since it also controls domestic credit, the bank now has complete control of the money supply under flexible exchange rates.

What then happens to excess money? By assumption, nothing real can change, so as people attempt to rid themselves of excess cash they bid up local currency prices. Previously this had been prevented by fixed world prices and a fixed exchange rate, but under floating rates domestic inflation is consistent with given world prices provided that the exchange rate falls equi-proportionately.

In the simple monetarist model starting from equilibrium, a 1 per cent increase in the money supply raises prices by 1 per cent; to preserve PPP (or the LOOP) the exchange rate must fall by 1 per cent (strictly by 100/101 per cent), leaving the real economy entirely unaffected. In terms of PPP, the monetarists add to the theory by offering an explanation of the price level, which had previously just been assumed.

Some difficulties with PPP

Before PPP can be of practical use in explaining or predicting the exchange rate, it must be implemented empirically. This raises a number of difficulties, which we examine before passing onto the empirical evidence.

The price index. Which basket of goods should PPP refer to, or more practically which price index numbers are to be used? If the index is dominated by tradable primary goods (e.g. wheat, metals) we appear to have PPP, but in fact have reverse causation. Homogeneous goods like these tend to satisfy the LOOP, hence whatever the exchange rate local currency prices adjust to ensure equality with world prices in a common currency. This does not invalidate PPP, but it does preclude its being a theory of the exchange rate. For that, we require exogenous prices with the exchange rate adjusting. Consequently economists prefer to test PPP on indices containing more manufactures and non-traded goods. Of course, if one holds the monetarist interpretation of PPP, the index should be the one that appears in the money demand equation, because it is the latter that drives that model. Both these arguments lead us to prefer consumer price indices or GDP deflators to the more commonly used wholesale price indices.

Ultimately the exchange rate adjusts to clear the foreign exchange market. The special assumptions of PPP are made in order that the exchange market respond only to the aggregate price level. This might be disturbed in real life, however, in a number of ways.

Capital flows. Either short-run flows seeking interest rate advantages (see next section) or long-run direct investment could be important. Imbalances in the latter can be very long-lived – for example, the USA had a capital account surplus for about sixty years during the nineteenth century.

241

Income changes. The monetarists believe that growth will stimulate a foreign surplus, appreciating the exchange rate, whereas Keynesians hold that it will generate a deficit and depreciation via imports. Also world growth could be significant if different countries' exports face different income elasticities. If Britain's exports have low income elasticities, we would expect a gradual depreciation of sterling to offset the deleterious income effects.

Non-traded goods. Suppose the LOOP applies to all traded goods. In rich, high-productivity countries, these world prices can support high wages, but in low-productivity countries they can support only low wages. Now suppose that there is also a non-traded sector, in which productivity is the same in all countries (e.g. haircuts). In rich countries, with high wages, these goods and services will be expensive, but in poor, low-wage economies they will be cheap. When we combine traded and non-traded sectors, therefore, average prices will be higher in rich than in poor countries. Hence if the exchange rate is really determined by tradables but we apply the general indices, PPP will appear to be violated: rich countries will appear to have overvalued exchange rates (see Balassa, 1964).

Structural change. Change of a more random nature, for example the discovery of oil, can also be significant.

Impediments to trade. Changes in transport costs, tariffs or trading institutions could upset PPP by making balance of payments equilibrium possible at different price levels.

Empirical evidence

We have seen how PPP's close cousin the LOOP fails to stand up to the evidence on individual prices. We now briefly confront PPP with the evidence of aggregate price indices. As virtually no data exist on absolute prices (price indices report price changes since a base year), all of these tests refer to the relative version of PPP.

The story behind PPP is essentially a monetary one and so one would expect PPP to perform best for extreme monetary shocks. The German hyper-inflation of 1921–3 is an excellent example of this. The Reichbank largely financed reparations to the allies by printing money. Between August 1922 and November 1923, the money supply and prices rose by 10,000 million times! Frenkel (1976) related the spot exchange rate to various price indices. His equations explained over 99 per cent of the variation in exchange rates and showed a close proportionality between prices and the exchange rate, although there was still some evidence of other systematic factors at work.

Under more normal circumstances, when real factors are relatively more significant, PPP fares worse. For each of eleven industrial countries over the period 1950–70, Kravis and Lipsey (1978) compared changes in the GDP deflator in dollars with changes in the US GDP deflator. If PPP held, the two would be identical, but actually strong deviations emerge. Even over short periods like two years, changes in the national deflators differed from those in the US deflator by more than 5 per cent in 26 per cent of the cases observed. For changes over ten years, 86 per cent of the differences exceeded 5 per cent.

These results refer to a period of fixed but adjustable exchange rates, but PPP does not fare any better on more recent floating rate data. For example, Genberg (1978) found that floating increased both the extent and the duration of deviations from PPP, the average quarterly deviation after 1973 being 4.1 per cent and the average duration more than three years. Frenkel (1981) examined the USA, France, West Germany and the UK over 1973–9. He found PPP rejected for all exchange rates except the pound–DM rate, arguing that only the last rate is not disturbed by real changes in one or other of the economies. This is supported by

242

Branson (1981), who identified a strong downward trend in the USA's equilibrium exchange rate relative to PPP after the early 1970s.

PPP – a summary

Purchasing power parity is a simple and bold theory of the exchange rate. Such theories are easy to knock down because they make such uncompromising predictions, and this has been the fate of PPP. However, while it is quite inadequate in itself – except under very rare circumstances – it clearly has some role in exchange rate theory. One could no more claim that exchange rates were independent of prices than that they were completely dependent on them. A satisfactory exchange rate theory must take account of real as well as monetary factors. Many of the real determinants of exchange rates have been encountered above under our balance of payments theory. To these must be added asset considerations and expectations, to which we turn next. It is hardly surprising that a single variable – relative prices – is insufficient to represent such a wide range of causes.

21.3   ASSETS AND EXCHANGE RATES

The previous section considered how goods and money affect the exchange rate. We now introduce a third factor, which is important both in its own right and through its interactions with these others. It is wealth. We assume that wealth is held either as domestic money or as Treasury bills issued either by the domestic government or abroad. This does not do justice to the menu of financial assets actually available, but it suffices for our purposes. (We use short-term bills as our non-monetary asset in order to avoid the difficulty that the capital values of long-run instruments vary with the interest rate.)

**Portfolio
equilibrium**

How do people allocate their wealth over these three assets? Two factors are important: the rate of return on each asset and the extent of risk. We shall not say much about the latter, save to note that risk can normally be reduced by diversification. In a diversified portfolio the assets that are doing badly are at least partly compensated for by those that are doing well; in a concentrated one you may do very well, but you may do very badly if you choose wrongly. Hence, if people are risk averse, they will hold assets with returns lower than the maximum available, just in order to be more secure. That is, they will trade off returns against security. If the risk properties of an asset change, people may well rearrange their portfolio because the terms of this trade-off will have altered.

The rate of return on an asset has several dimensions. Most obvious is the rate of interest. Just as important, however, is any capital gain it makes, and against both must be set the transactions costs of liquidating it. The ease and certainty with which money can be converted into other things is one of its major attractions as an asset. We shall assume that this is sufficient to ensure a demand for money no matter how high the rate of interest. Capital gains enter our discussion via the exchange rate, changes in which affect the relative worth of domestic and foreign assets. Specifically, we shall define the rate of return on foreign bills as the rate of interest less the proportionate change in the exchange rate $(i_f - \dot{r})$; an appreciation of the pound, i.e. a depreciation of the dollar, reduces the worth of Britain's dollar assets.

Risk and the rate of return determine how a given stock of wealth is allocated

243

over assets, but changes in wealth are also important. First, some assets may be 'luxury assets' whose share of a portfolio grows with wealth, while others may do the opposite. Second, if wealth is growing we have something like a flow demand for assets, because 'new' wealth must be allocated across assets. Under these circumstances, a rise in the attractiveness of an asset raises its share not only in present wealth but also in future increments, and hence leads to a permanently increasing demand for it. Third, wealth can get revalued; a depreciation immediately raises the domestic value of foreign assets. This could unbalance the relationship between wealth and income or the division of the portfolio between home and foreign assets. Fourth, if wealth is redistributed from one country to another (e.g. from OECD to OPEC during the 1970s), and if these countries have different asset demands, the overall demand for different assets will change.

Equilibrium and adjustment with asset markets

Given total wealth, and the rates of return and risks on all the various assets, residents have some preferred portfolio; they know in what proportions they wish to hold the alternative assets. Hence the demand for assets is known. It is, however, a *stock demand*: we know how many of each asset people are willing to hold, not immediately how many they will buy in any period. Since the supply of assets is also a stock phenomenon (namely, how many bonds exist), equilibrium in asset markets is a *stock equilibrium*. We define it as being when all existing assets are willingly held.

The exchange rate is involved in these stock processes in two basic ways. First, the adjustment of asset portfolios may require current account changes, and these are normally achieved by exchange rate changes. For example, we know that foreign investment – a current account surplus – is one way of accumulating extra wealth; if we exclude real capital and if the government will not issue any more bonds, it is the only way. If rising income increases desired wealth or stimulates the demand for foreign assets, this could be met by depreciating the exchange rate and running a current surplus. On the other hand, a higher stock of foreign assets means more income from abroad. Hence, once the accumulation has occurred, we will then require a smaller surplus from trade to achieve current balance, which means that the exchange rate could eventually appreciate.

Second, anticipated changes in the exchange rate influence relative rates of return, and thus impinge on the asset markets. Conversely, therefore, asset equilibrium could influence the current exchange rate, given expectations. This occurs through the stock adjustments associated with interest arbitrage and speculation. It is most easily seen in speculation. If domestic and foreign bills are perfect substitutes, if speculators are risk neutral (do not require compensating for bearing risk) and if there are no transactions costs, then the returns on all bills are equal, so $i_d = i_f - \dot{r}$. Now, if the expected exchange range at the maturity of these bills is $\hat{S}_1$, the expected change in the rate ($\dot{r}$), is $(\hat{S}_1 - S)/S$, and if i_d, i_f and $\hat{S}_1$ are fixed, only one value of S can ensure equilibrium. Once we relax the assumptions, the uniqueness goes, but the principle remains. For example, if speculators require higher returns to compensate for risk, holders of sterling will require $i_f - \dot{r} > i_d$ before speculating, while dollar speculators will require $i_d + \dot{r} > i_f$. Hence, there will exist some feasible band for S given the other variables.

Arbitrage and speculation do not actually have to occur to bring these relationships about. Merely the threat of them is sufficient: no one will offer to trade at prices that do not roughly reflect interest arbitrage because he would be overwhelmed. Hence prices are constrained even though no actual trade may occur. An important corollary of this is that exchange rates can jump from one value to another. Changed conditions can be reflected immediately in a discrete

change in the exchange rate. This is in stark contrast to variables such as the stock
of bills that can evolve only gradually.

Rational expectations

Obviously expectations are crucial to the process just described. How, then, are
they formed?

There are two main approaches in economic theory. First, there are auto-
regressive expectations – basically those formed from previous and current values
of the variable concerned. These may be simple – for instance that tomorrow's
exchange rate will be the same as today's – or much more complex, involving the
extrapolation of rates of change, or even the rate of change of rates of change. The
difficulty with this approach is that it uses very little information: it is easy to
construct examples where expectations are always wrong, and also where
expectations feed back onto themselves in an explosive manner. The main
advantage of the approach is its simplicity.

The second expectational mechanism is so-called rational expectations. These
were first introduced in 1961, but have become fashionable only since about the
mid-1970s. The idea is that *all* existing information is used optimally to make
forecasts. In particular it is assumed that operators in the market know all that
economists know, so that if *we* know the true mechanism of the exchange rate
determination so does the market. Hence models have an element of self-
reference in them that makes testing them very difficult: one is looking for a
process which, *if* it explained expectations, could also explain reality, and there is
rarely an assurance that only one such process exists.

This problem is compounded by the fact that, since expectations cannot be
observed, the rational expectations hypothesis may only be tested in the context of
an overall model of the exchange market. This necessarily involves other
assumptions – e.g. that speculators are risk neutral – and if the model is rejected it
can never be unambiguously determined whether it is these or rational
expectations that are at fault.

An implication of rational expectations (embedded in the right model, of
course) is that expectations are unbiased: that is, they are not consistently in error
in any particular fashion. If that were not the case, they could not be rational
because they would be ignoring the information embodied in the consistency of
the errors. The corollary of this is that future actual rates are unbiased estimates of
the expectations, so that in applications it is sometimes possible to substitute actual
outcomes for forecasts. If we then ignore the random errors – as is often done –
rational expectations take us back to perfect foresight, dissolving the need for
expectations mechanisms anyway!

A further implication of rational expectations is that 'news' is very important. If
markets are efficient (they use all available information optimally to estimate
future exchange rates), the only shocks to the system must be unanticipated – i.e.
depend on news. If news changes expectations significantly it can have a strong
and immediate effect on exchange rates. A policy implication of this is that, for
stable exchange rates, governments should seek to make available as much
information as possible and operate themselves according to known rules.

The strengths of rational expectations are, first, that they reflect the fact that
forecasts are made using diverse sources of information and an analytical framework, and, second, that they have an internal consistency, in that the model cannot
be correct if expectations are consistently falsified. Against these must be set their
empirical difficulties and their assumption of an implausible degree of
sophistication on the part of most operators. They have proved theoretically
fruitful over the last decade, but, as yet, their empirical relevance is not established:

245

as we shall see below, there are no entirely successful models of exchange rates, whether with rational expectations or not.

21.4   EXCHANGE RATE THEORIES AND OVERSHOOTING

This section applies the arguments of the previous sections to specific models. It concentrates on the dynamics of adjustment as much as on equilibrium levels of the exchange rate, and it examines some evidence on exchange rate determination.

Equilibrium and overshooting

The equilibrium exchange rate is one that is under no pressure to change. This in turn implies that it must produce balance on official settlements. During the short run, this implies that deficits on basic balance must be matched by short-term capital surpluses, and vice versa. Over the longer run, short-term flows must roughly balance out, so the long-run equilibrium exchange rate is determined by the basic balance, of which the predominant element is generally the current account.

Overshooting occurs if a variable has to adjust in the long run, but actually adjusts by more than the required amount in the short run. The idea is unique to neither exchange rate theory nor the last ten years. The easiest example is Marshall's 'market period', during which quantities are quite inflexible. Imagine a fish market that, from equilibrium, experiences an unforeseen jump in demand. While supplies are rigid, price shoots up, but if, after a day, supply is able to increase, the final price will be higher than originally but lower than immediately after the demand surge.[1] This overshooting is caused by the different speeds of adjustment of different parts of the market, and the same applies to some exchange rate overshooting. However, the latter can also occur without differential speeds of adjustment if there are fixed nominal magnitudes in the economy, such as the supply of money. Either way the basic cause is that, in the short run, only part of the economy adjusts. As Friedman (1953, p. 183) wrote, introducing the idea of exchange rate overshooting,

> It is clear that the initial change in exchange rates will be greater than the ultimate change required, for, to begin with, all the adjustment will have to be borne in those directions in which prompt adjustment is possible and relatively easy. As time passes, the slower-moving adjustments will take over part of the burden, permitting exchange rates to rebound toward a final position which is between the position prior to the external change and the position shortly thereafter. This is, of course, a highly oversimplified picture: the actual path of adjustment may involve repeated overshooting and under-shooting of the final position. . .

Interest in exchange rate overshooting revived in the 1970s because flexible exchange rates proved much more volatile than had been predicted. This could of course have been due to the volatility of events exogenous to exchange rate determination, but it raised the question of whether the volatility might not be inherent. For example, during 1973 the dollar first fell by around 20 per cent against the DM and then recovered to end nearly 20 per cent above its original level. Similarly, sterling covered a range of around 40 per cent over 1976 and 1977. Batchelor (1979) found that the mean monthly deviation of sterling about its trend over 1973–8 was nearly 7 per cent, while the figures for DM and francs were around 5 per cent. Finally, it is quite common to find daily changes of 3 per cent in a currency's value and 6 per cent is not unknown. It is difficult to see how such variability could reflect only the real economic environment.

**Simple asset
theories**

The simplest asset approach to the exchange rate is, in fact, the monetarist model that we have already examined. Residents have stock demands for money and the exchange rate adjusts to bring these into line with the exogenous supply of money. Above we assumed that all the adjustment had to be borne directly by goods prices and the exchange rate, but now, with bills in the picture, we can be more sophisticated, following Dornbusch (1976).

Imagine that, in the long run, PPP holds perfectly. In the short run, however, nothing can change in the goods market, but asset markets are perfectly flexible, and hence bear all immediate adjustment. Suppose that equilibrium is disturbed by an x per cent increase in the money supply. Goods prices cannot adjust, but domestic interest rates (i_d) fall immediately. This reduces the attractiveness of domestic assets, and so a capital outflow threatens to depreciate the exchange rate. How far will it fall? Our long-run assumptions suggest x per cent, and with rational expectations people know this. But in the short run this is not far enough, because at this long-run exchange rate no further change is anticipated; hence the return on foreign bills (i_f) still exceeds the reduced i_d, and a depreciation of x per cent is insufficient to stem the capital outflow. That can be done only when the net returns on foreign and domestic bills are equalised, i.e. when the lower domestic interest rate is supplemented by an anticipated appreciation. This requires the exchange rate to fall below its equilibrium level, so that its return to that level gives the required appreciation. Frankel (1979) has estimated that the dollar–DM exchange rate falls by 1.23 per cent in the very short run for every unanticipated 1 per cent increase in the US money supply.

The basic insight of this model – that overshooting occurs despite the final equilibrium exchange rate being known – is very important, but there are many objections to the details of this simple form. It is very short run, because it admits no real adjustment nor any change in the level of wealth. It is inconsistent, in that residents know and react to the fact that exchange rate movements alter returns on foreign bills, but apparently do not see that local currency price increases (such as are implied by assuming PPP) affect returns on local currency savings. Its assumption of infinite speeds of adjustment in asset markets is inappropriate, as are its assumptions that investors are risk neutral and that domestic and foreign bills are perfect substitutes (i.e. that $i_d = (i_f + \dot{r})$ holds precisely).

A second simple model that corrects the last problem is found in Niehans (1980). Abandoning perfect substitutability allows the domestic interest rate to be determined jointly with the exchange rate. Let there be four assets: domestic and foreign money and domestic and foreign bills. Freezing the foreign interest rate and the long-run equilibrium exchange rate, we relate the demand for domestic bills and money to the domestic interest rate (i_d) and the exchange rate (r). Figure 21.1 plots combinations of i_d and r that maintain equilibrium in the money market (MM) and the bill market (BB). Consider the money market: the money supply is fixed, so any rise in the interest rate, which cuts money demand, must be offset by a fall in the exchange rate, which, by promising an appreciation, increases demand. Hence MM slopes downwards. Note also that an increase in the exogenous money supply shifts MM inwards, because more money will be held only at lower interest rates. The bill market reacts in the opposite fashion. Higher interest rates, which raise demand, must be offset by a higher exchange rate promising a capital loss; an increased supply of bills shifts BB to the right since it will be held only at higher rates of interest.

247

We now use Figure 21.1 to explore various shocks to the asset markets. First, increasing the foreign exchange reserves – that is, official purchases of foreign money. This does not appear explicitly in the figure, but the issue of domestic money to effect the purchase shifts MM inwards, moving equilibrium from E to F, and reducing both r and i_d. Second, a reduction in the supply of domestic bills. This shifts BB leftwards and produces a new equilibrium at G, raising r and lowering i_d. Finally, an open market operation buying bills; this shifts MM in and BB up. The net result is equilibrium at Q, where i_d has fallen but r could have risen or fallen. Obviously the effect on r depends on the asset demand behaviour, which determines the relative shifts in MM and BB.

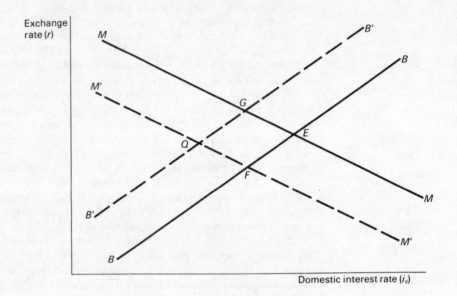

Figure 21.1 *Equilibria in asset markets*

The longer run

In the longer run, expectational mechanisms are gradually displaced by real and asset-accumulation effects on the exchange rate. For example, a money supply increase produces a depreciation, as we have just seen, which will be worsened by any J-curve effect from the real economy. In time, however, the depreciation will generate a current surplus, and if this outweighs the J-curve (which is likely) it will cause the net accumulation of wealth in terms of foreign assets. This will affect interest receipts and consumption behaviour, and possibly also the accumulation of real capital. The first two will affect income and absorption while the last could influence relative costs and prices since investment is the means of improving technology. Thus, in the long run, the exchange rate cannot be treated in isolation from the real economy because even nominal shocks may have real effects.

Empirical estimates

As so often happens, economic theory has outstripped our ability to test it. Consequently, many of the more complex ideas presented above are currently without any but the most casual empirical application.

The monetary theory assumes PPP, so one might take the rejection of the latter to imply the rejection of the former. Nevertheless there have been many direct tests of it. Writing the demand for money as a function of real income, prices and interest rates, the exchange rate between two countries' currencies can be written as a function of their relative incomes, interest rates and money supplies. Estimating such equations has proved adequate for the hyper-inflations of the 1920s (Frenkel, 1976), but thoroughly unsuccessful for the 1970s: exchange rates have deviated from PPP by up to 30 per cent, and frequently the current exchange rate seems quite independent of the money supplies. There is now overwhelming evidence that the monetary theory alone is not sufficient.

Turning to the asset theories, much less empirical evidence exists, not least because the theories are much less precise. A useful general exploration is by Hacche and Townend (1981), who examined the effective exchange rates of eight major currencies over 1972–80. They calculated only the simplest of summary statistics and reached the following conclusions. PPP had almost nothing to contribute, even over long periods. Interest rates affected exchange rates but sometimes positively (as above) and sometimes negatively if interest rate rises were interpreted as indicating an attempt by the central bank to support the exchange rate above its equilibrium level. Portfolio diversification was significant over the late 1970s: world wealth moved towards OPEC, which caused a substitution of other currencies for the dollar. There was a marked positive relationship between current balances and exchange rates: in part this may reflect the J-curve (falling exchange rates reduce the current surplus temporarily), but mainly it reflects the influence of current balances on exchange rate expectations. Countries with current deficits seem likely to have to depreciate sometime.

The relevance of the current balance was also explored by Dornbusch (1980b). Assuming the efficiency of exchange markets (i.e. that they use all current information effectively), Dornbusch related unanticipated exchange rate changes to 'news' about the current account, output and interest rates. Unanticipated exchange rate changes were defined as actual exchange rate changes less the interest rate differential, which, assuming perfect asset substitutability, measures expected changes (remember $i_d = i_f - \dot{r}$, p. 244 above). 'News' was defined as the difference between the actual current balance and output and the values predicted six months earlier by OECD, and for the interest rates as the actual rate minus that predicted by an estimating equation. The results suggested strongly that unforeseen US current surpluses induced dollar appreciation; for example, a surplus of \$1b. over six months induced a $\frac{1}{4}-\frac{1}{2}$ per cent appreciation in the effective exchange rate. Interest rate shocks also had a role – rises usually inducing depreciation – as did output shocks – an unforeseen expansion in GDP of 1 per cent inducing a 1–2 per cent depreciation. These results reinforce the view that expectations are important.

The problem with Dornbusch's approach is the assumption of efficient exchange markets. Several very technical studies have challenged this assumption, but we can consider a more humble calculation. Hacche and Townend (1981) estimated that during 1972–80 unanticipated exchange rate changes (in Dornbusch's sense) accounted for the following proportions of actual exchange rate changes: USA 44 per cent; UK 77 per cent; France 94 per cent; Japan 128 per cent; and West Germany 177 per cent. In the last two cases the implication is that more often than not the so-called anticipations were of the wrong sign! Even excluding these cases, it is difficult to believe that such shocks so heavily dominate the foreseen changes in the economy.

Perhaps the crowning ignominy for exchange rate models is the work of Meese and Rogoff (1983). They tested the predictions of four simple exchange rate models over the late 1970s: the monetary model, the Dornbusch (1976) model, an asset model adding current account factors to the Dornbusch model, and a model

249

stating that next period's exchange rate will equal this period's. For the dollar's effective exchange rate, the prediction errors of the best-performing model averaged 2 per cent for one-month forecasts and 9 per cent for twelve-month forecasts, with larger errors on various bilateral exchange rates. These figures suggest considerable ignorance about exchange rate determination, and this is confirmed when we discover that the best performing model is the one assuming that next period's rate equals this period's! In other words, for general forecasting purposes (i.e. in the absence of identifiable special economic factors), the theories we have to hand appear to add nothing to our understanding. At least part of the failure must be due to the empirical implementation of the theories, rather than the theories themselves. It is, after all, difficult to believe that wealth and expectations do not influence the exchange rate at all. Nevertheless, if ever there was an issue about which economists should be humble, this is surely it.

FURTHER READING

The anatomy of the exchange market is presented well in *Yeager* (1976), *Cohen* (1969) and *McKinnon* (1979). Purchasing power parity has an enormous literature: *Officer* (1976a) and *Katseli-Papaefstratiou* (1979) provide useful surveys and the *Journal of International Economics* (1978, no. 2) covers empirical applications. *Frenkel* (1981) extends the evidence to the late 1970s, and *Branson* (1981) offers an excellent alternative analysis of his evidence. The monetary theory is surveyed in *Kreinin and Officer* (1978), *Frenkel and Johnson* (1978) and *Laidler* (1981).

More general studies of exchange rates include *Isard* (1978), *Niehans* (1980) and *Hacche and Townend* (1981), all of which are excellent. *Dornbusch* (1978; 1980b) provides an interesting excursion from the monetary theory to the portfolio theories, the latter complemented by an excellent comment by *Branson* (1980), who also provides a clear (though mathematical) exposition of a simple portfolio model in *Branson* (1977) and *Branson, Halttunen and Masson* (1977). *Dornbusch* (1980a) offers an advanced analysis of many of the problems of this chapter. For the sterling exchange rate *Batchelor* (1977) is useful, and on overshooting see *Schadler* (1977) and *Frenkel and Rodriguez* (1982). *Krueger* (1983b) provides a recent survey of exchange rate theory.

Note: Most studies measure the exchange rate as the price in local currency terms of one dollar, not as the dollar price of one local currency unit as we do. Hence the signs of exchange rate effects tend to be reversed.

NOTE

1   In the accompanying figure, when demand increases from D to D', price at first rises from p_e to p_m, while supplies are fixed at q_e, and then falls part-way back (to p_a) as supplies expand.

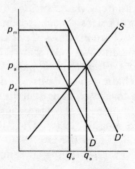

22 Macro-economic Policy in the Open Economy

So far we have considered what determines the balance of payments and the exchange rate, but have not explicitly asked whether such factors can be used for the purposes of economic policy. Neither have we asked how the openness of the economy affects the use of other instruments of policy to achieve other targets, e.g. full employment. This chapter extends our discussion in these directions. We first consider the achievement of internal and external balance in the open economy, and then consider the ways in which the exchange rate regime and the degree of capital mobility influence the effectiveness of monetary and fiscal policies as instruments for internal balance. Finally we briefly examine empirical work on the degree of capital mobility and financial integration.

22.1 POLICIES FOR INTERNAL AND EXTERNAL BALANCE

Targets and instruments

The purpose of economics, at least as a prescriptive science, is to increase (economic) welfare. This is too vague a target for policy purposes, however, so economists set themselves various intermediate goals. In the long run, these include items such as raising economic growth and improving the distribution of income; over the shorter run, however, the most prominent has been *internal balance*. This broadly means the achievement of full employment and price stability. The two elements are linked together because, although each may have some independent existence, there are strong grounds for treating them as opposite ends of the same measure: high unemployment is likely to reduce price inflation, while over-full employment will exacerbate it. We shall assume that internal balance has just one dimension, but the interested student will be able to see how to generalise the principles, if not the practice, to the broader case.

The other principal target is *external balance*; for this, read balance of payments equilibrium. Unlike internal balance, external balance has no direct implications for welfare; it is, rather, a constraint that any feasible economic policy package must satisfy, because one cannot run deficits or surpluses indefinitely. Hence, for short-term macro-economic policy we assume that governments are simultaneously trying to achieve full employment and payments equilibrium.

Before considering specific policies, there is an important principle to note: to achieve n independent targets requires at least n independent policy instruments (Tinbergen, 1952). Imagine driving a car about an airfield. To reach any particular spot of longitude and latitude you need two controls – a forward–back control and a left–right control. Now imagine flying an aeroplane to any particular location: the target is defined by three dimensions, longitude, latitude and height, and in general you will require three controls. Similarly, if we are to achieve the two independent economic goals of internal and external equilibrium, we shall require at least two independent policy instruments. If there are fewer, the complete attainment of both targets will be precluded, and the policy-maker will have to trade off one objective against the other. Such a trade-off may also be necessary when there are constraints or costs on the use of certain instruments. For example, you cannot change the standard rate of income tax every week, so it may prove impossible to achieve joint internal and external balance at all points of

251

time. Our formal analysis ignores both this latter problem and the difficulties arising from uncertainty over how the policies affect the targets. Both of these considerations are important in practice, and both make it advantageous to have more instruments than targets.

Policy in a Keynesian economy

To illustrate these principles of economic policy we return to a very simple model of the open economy. We assume a Keynesian world, with fixed local currency prices and a fixed, but adjustable, exchange rate. The government has available both expenditure-switching and expenditure-reducing policies – say, the exchange rate and government expenditure. How can it then achieve internal and external balance? The first step is to discover – from economic theory – how each policy affects each target. An increase in government expenditure raises income and employment, but, through that, worsens the balance of payments; a devaluation improves the balance of payments, and through that raises income and employment. We can show these results diagrammatically in Figure 22.1. The line YY plots those combinations of government expenditure (G) and the exchange rate (r) that produce internal equilibrium. Starting from point A on YY, suppose G is increased; this increases employment and, to bring it back to equilibrium along YY, a rise in the exchange rate is necessary; hence YY slopes upward. Conversely, BB, the locus of points ensuring balance of payments equilibrium, slopes downwards. Starting from C, an increase in G produces a deficit and this must be counteracted by a depreciation to restore balance.

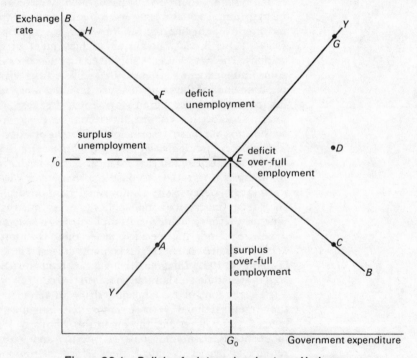

Figure 22.1   *Policies for internal and external balance*

It is plain from Figure 22.1 that, if YY gives all combinations of G and r for internal equilibrium, and BB gives those for external equilibrium, the only policy combination that ensures both is (G_0, r_0), i.e. point E. This is the heart of the policy problem. Provided the government knows the locations of *BB* and *YY* – that is, provided it knows both the nature and the parameters of economic behaviour – it can calculate their intersection, impose (G_0, r_0), and all is well.

Unfortunately, life is not so simple, not least because the government does not know the precise locations of *BB* and *YY*. Even so, it can make some progress as follows. The loci *BB* and *YY* divide the graph into what Swan (1955), the originator of this analysis, called four zones of 'economic unhappiness'. Any point above and to the right of *BB* involves a balance of payments deficit (starting on *BB*, either an appreciation or a rise in government spending will cause a deficit), while any point below or left of it involves a surplus. Similarly, any point above or left of *YY* involves unemployment (consider government contraction from a point on *YY*), while any point below or right involves over-full employment. There are, thus, four possible zones, which are marked in the diagram; merely by observing the state of the economy, the government knows which applies. Furthermore, in each zone the direction of change for one policy instrument is known: for instance, whenever we have a deficit and unemployment we know the exchange rate should fall. We do not know by how much, nor do we know what to do about government expenditure, so there is still a role for econometricians in establishing the positions of the loci. Nevertheless, even without full information, some qualitative guidance is available.

The assignment problem

Another approach to our ignorance of the precise locations of *BB* and *YY* would be trial and error. Just jumping about the graph randomly would not be very helpful, especially if there were costs to changing policies; but some economists have suggested allocating each policy to a separate target, and then changing each in turn. For example, suppose the economy started at point *D* in Figure 22.1 and that the exchange rate had been allocated external balance and government expenditure internal balance. From *D*, observing the deficit, we would devalue by sufficient to induce external balance; on the diagram, we fall vertically from *D* to the *BB* line, arriving at *C*. We would then alter government spending to achieve internal balance, moving horizontally to the *YY* line at *A*. From there the exchange rate would be altered to reach the *BB* line at *F*, and so on until we gradually converged in a cobweb to the joint equilibrium point *E*.

There are several objections to such an approach. First, it requires the correct assignment of instruments to targets. Suppose the opposite assignment had been chosen. Starting from *D*, the iterations would have taken us outwards along the cobweb to *G* and *H*, rather than inwards to *C* and so on. Hence the assignment would have been divergent. Roughly speaking, to get convergence, the instruments must be assigned to the target on which they have relatively greatest influence; thus some information is required in order to make the assignment. Second, even if we have a convergent path, it involves considerable variability of both instruments and targets. This is expensive in terms of transition costs and in introducing greater uncertainty into the economy. Much of the variability could be avoided by using the policies in conjunction. Third, unless we know the locations of *BB* and *YY* it is impossible to know by how much to move the policy instruments, so there is further variability and time loss as this is discovered experimentally.

Hence, 'one-to-one' assignment does not reduce the need for information; it merely shows that independently controlled instruments *could* be assigned objectives such that the final outcome was acceptable. However, except where institutional factors entirely preclude cooperation between the controllers of the two policy instruments, a much better solution is likely to be the joint use of both instruments for both targets.

253

The prime conclusion of all this is that, although each instrument affects each target, achieving n targets requires n independent instruments. We also showed that an essential ingredient of successful policy-making is knowledge of how the economy works. The simple model used here has been subject to many refinements in earlier chapters, but the same rule applies to all models. If we wish to control n endogenous variables, we need both n policy instruments and a knowledge of how the system works.

Internal and external balance with a fixed exchange rate

If the exchange rate were no longer available to us, how could we then achieve external and internal balance? Mundell (1962) suggested a short-run solution involving monetary and fiscal policy and recognising the role of capital flows. Consider expanding national income by x per cent, using either fiscal or monetary policy. Although each policy worsens the current account by the same amount (dependent on x), each has different implications for the capital account. Both policies raise the demand for money by raising income, but, whereas this is met by an increasing supply of money with monetary policy, it is not accommodated in the case of fiscal policy. As a result, fiscal expansion entails a higher interest rate than monetary expansion, and hence attracts an inflow of capital to offset the current account deficit. (The inflow may exceed or fall short of the current deficit.) Overall, therefore, for a given income effect, fiscal policy has less impact on the total balance of payments than monetary policy.

Monetary and fiscal policy could, therefore, be used to improve the external balance without altering the level of income: a monetary contraction would lower income and produce an external surplus, while a fiscal expansion would return income to its previous level and, although worsening the balance of payments, would not entirely offset the beneficial effect of the monetary policy. This policy combination was pursued by the USA over the early 1960s and also by Britain during the stop–go policy of the 1950s and 1960s. High interest rates were used to defend the balance of payments from the consequences of fiscal (vote-catching) expansion. It is, however, only a short-term palliative rather than a solution of the policy problem: high interest rates may have harmful domestic effects; nothing occurs to cure the current account deficit – the capital inflow merely finances it; one cannot borrow for ever because eventually lenders' confidence collapses; and high interest payments abroad reduce the level of domestic consumption supported by any given level of output.

A similar situation arose in the early 1980s in the USA. Tight monetary policy (designed to cure inflation), coupled with an expansionary fiscal stance (a huge budget deficit), generated very high interest rates and strong upward pressure on the dollar.

22.2 DOMESTIC POLICY AND THE EXCHANGE RATE

We now turn to the second of the questions raised in the introduction: how does the openness of the economy influence the effectiveness of domestic economic policy? In particular we examine the influence of international capital mobility and exchange rate flexibility on the operation of monetary and fiscal policies. Throughout, we shall take national income as the variable to be controlled.

The IS–LM model

As a preliminary we introduce a slightly different method of analysing the economy. Much closed-economy macro-economic analysis uses the *IS–LM* framework, and we now adapt this to the open economy. The present exposition is very cryptic and the student is advised to seek further information in standard macro textbooks for the basic model, and in Stern (1973) or Argy (1981) on the open-economy variant.

The *IS–LM* model analyses a fixed-price Keynesian economy with goods, bonds and money markets. It is best explored by means of a diagram with the interest rate (i) and national income (Y) on the axes, (see Figure 22.2). The *IS* curve connects combinations of i and Y that ensure the equality of the supply and demand for goods and services; that is

$$Y = C + I + G + X - M, \qquad (22.1)$$

where Y is income, C consumption, I investment, G government expenditure, X exports and M imports. The *IS* curve slopes downwards because lower interest rates stimulate higher investment and hence require higher income/output to equate supply and demand. If the exchange rate falls, exports rise and/or imports fall; hence, with constant interest rates, demand rises and the *IS* curve moves outwards. Similarly, expansionary fiscal policy shifts *IS* outwards.

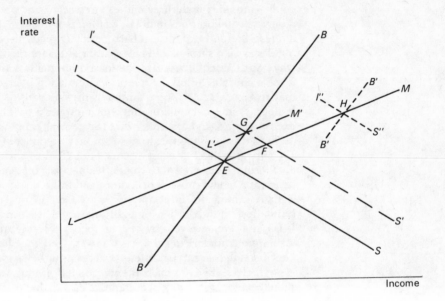

Figure 22.2   *Equilibrium in the open* IS–LM *model*

The *LM* curve plots combinations of i and Y that ensure equilibrium in the money market. The supply of money is assumed exogenous in nominal terms, but the demand depends on both interest rates and income. Income affects demand positively through the transactions demand: the more income you have, the more cash you require for spending. Interest rates have a negative effect by affecting the costs of holding cash: the higher the interest rate, the more the interest forgone by holding money instead of bonds. Hence a higher income must be offset by a higher rate of interest if demand is to equal a given supply, and so *LM* slopes up. (We ignore any horizontal segment of *LM* arising from the liquidity trap.) Money demand also depends on prices. Income and interest rates determine the real demand for cash, and this must be multiplied by the price level to find the nominal demand to be equated with the nominal supply. When prices rise, *LM* shifts up and to the left because, with given nominal supply, real demand must fall if equality is to continue.

The third locus in Figure 22.2 is *BB*, which plots levels of interest rates and incomes consistent with external balance, recognising both capital and current accounts. Higher income worsens the current account and so must be offset along *BB* by a rise in interest rates. The slope of *BB* depends on the degree of capital mobility, which in turn depends on the degree of substitutability between foreign and domestic assets in desired portfolios, and on the extent of transactions costs. If assets are entirely non-substitutable, or if transactions costs are prohibitively high, *BB* is vertical – that is, external equilibrium depends only on the current account, and thus, given income, is quite independent of the rate of interest. If, on the other hand, substitutability is perfect and transactions costs minimal, *BB* is horizontal – any deviation between world and domestic interest rates generates an infinite inflow or outflow of capital. A fall in the exchange rate shifts *BB* to the right: the improved competitiveness must be offset by higher incomes, given the interest rate, if balance is to be maintained.

The intersection of *LM* and *IS* defines internal equilibrium, but we can have full equilibrium only if all three curves intersect at one point. If not, we assume that domestic equilibrium is maintained (that is, *LM* and *IS* determine income and the interest rate) and that there is balance of payments disequilibrium. Above and left of *BB* there is a surplus, and below and right a deficit. (Check that you understand why.) Such disequilibria are, at least eventually, self-correcting, because they involve constant accumulation or decumulation of assets. For example, suppose that, in Figure 22.2, *IS* were shifted by fiscal expansion to *I'S'*. Point *F* defines the temporary internal equilibrium, which implies a payments deficit. Under a fixed exchange rate, and assuming that the central bank does not try to sterilise the outflow, this contracts the domestic money supply (see Chapter 20), and thus shifts *LM* leftwards. This process occurs until *LM* has shrunk back to *L'M'* and full equilibrium is restored at *G*. Under flexible exchange rates, on the other hand, the deficit at *F* would cause depreciation and this would push both *I'S'* and *BB* to the right. Assuming, for now, that prices are fixed in local currency terms, *LM* would be unaffected, and the final equilibrium would be given by a point such as *H*.

Do not be deceived by the simplicity of this analysis. There are many assumptions underlying the basic model; and the shapes of the curves, which depend on the various parameters of economic behaviour, could be very complex. Nevertheless, this approach is very popular among macro-economists and you should explore some more examples to ensure that you are familiar with it. (Try, in particular, the case where *LM* is steeper than *BB*.) We now use the model to develop some further results on economic policy.

The Mundell–Fleming analysis

An influential piece of analysis from the early 1960s – Fleming (1962) and Mundell (1963) – considered the effectiveness of monetary and fiscal policy as controllers of income. Making the crucial assumption that international capital flows were perfectly mobile, Mundell and Fleming concluded that monetary policy was effective only under flexible exchange rates, and that fiscal policy was effective only under fixed rates. Their model was a neo-Keynesian one, and the nature of their results is simply explored in the *IS–LM* framework. Perfect capital mobility makes the *BB* curve horizontal at the ruling world rate of interest. Any other interest rate would lead to an infinite inflow or outflow of capital, preventing equilibrium.

256

We consider first the fixed exchange rate case, shown in Figure 22.3. Starting
from complete equilibrium at *E*, imagine a fiscal expansion, shifting *IS* to *I'S'*. The
potential domestic equilibrium would be at *F*, with a higher interest rate and
income. The higher interest rate would not, however, be sustainable, because it
would immediately cause a huge capital inflow (balance of payments surplus),
which would expand the money supply and push out the *LM* curve. Only when *LM*
had reached *L'M'* would equilibrium be re-established in all three markets. At the
new equilibrium, income would have risen and the balance of payments would
show a current account deficit balanced by a capital account surplus. (Higher
income generates higher imports, and these are paid for by borrowing at the
world rate of interest.)

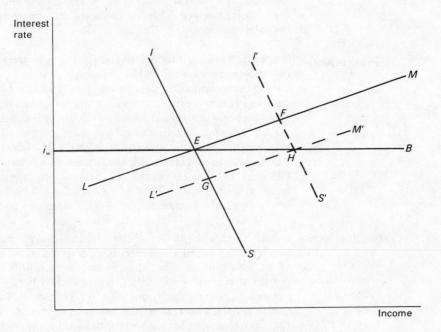

Figure 22.3   *Monetary and fiscal policy with capital mobility*

Now consider a monetary expansion. *LM* shifts out to *L'M'*, implying domestic
equilibrium *G*. This entails a large foreign deficit (capital flowing out because of the
fall in interest rates), and this serves to drag *L'M'* back. Only when it has reached
LM again does the process stop. This is just the result of Chapter 20: with fixed
exchange rates, governments cannot control their money supplies, hence
monetary policy is useless.

Turning to flexible exchange rates, we again start from *E*, and let fiscal policy
shift *IS* to *I'S'*. Again we have a potential domestic equilibrium at *F*, but now the
capital inflow appreciates the currency and brings *I'S'* back towards *IS* as exports
fall and imports rise. Ultimately, equilibrium re-emerges at *E*, where a balance of
payments current deficit is balanced by a capital surplus. This is a case of complete
'crowding-out': raising government expenditure merely results in an equivalent
worsening of the trade balance. Monetary policy, on the other hand, would be
highly effective – and for essentially the same reason. Expanding the money supply
to shift *LM* to *L'M'* produces a payments deficit and thereby a depreciation. This

shifts *IS* out to *I'S'* and produces equilibrium at *H*, where income has risen and a current surplus is balanced by a capital deficit. Hence, shifting from fixed to flexible exchange rates completely reverses the comparative advantages of monetary and fiscal policy.

These are stark results and they do not accord entirely with reality. Under fixed rates governments certainly did exercise some monetary policy, and under flexible rates we still find some use of fiscal policy. What then is wrong with the model? An obvious candidate is the assumption of perfect capital mobility, but from Figure 22.3 it is plain that a slight relaxation of this (a slight tilting of *BB*) does not change the relative rankings of the two policies. We shall look at the drastic alteration of this assumption below, but first we examine certain other refine-ments of the *IS–LM* model. They are introduced in the Mundell–Fleming framework, but are perfectly applicable to the general model with imperfect capital mobility.

Price effects

The basic Keynesian model assumes that prices are fixed in the producer's local currency and are unaffected by depreciation. If, however, as we found in Chapter 19, depreciation raises local prices, there will be two additional effects in the flexible exchange rate case. First, *IS* will move less in response to exchange rate changes, because competitiveness will alter by less. Second, depreciation will shift the *LM* curve leftwards because, by raising prices, it reduces the real money supply. Consider, for example, an expansionary fiscal policy. The potential equilibrium at *F* induces an appreciation; this reduces internal prices, hence *LM* shifts right while *I'S'* does not shrink completely back to its original position. The resulting equilibrium lies somewhere to the right of *E*. In other words, fiscal policy now works. By similar analysis we can see that monetary policy is less effective.

Wealth effects

As specified, the *BB* line refers to the overall balance of payments, being indifferent to whether a current deficit is balanced by a capital surplus or vice versa. This may be acceptable in the short run, but not in the longer run. A persistent current account deficit, financed by borrowing, reduces the country's net wealth, and ultimately this will affect behaviour. Specifically, as net worth falls, the *IS* curve falls back, as savings rise to try to reconstitute wealth holdings, and the *LM* curve shifts out because, as the demand for money declines, higher income is required to absorb the given money supply. Hence the final points described above are not long-run equilibria because they involve the accumulation or decumulation of assets. Full equilibrium is possible only where the current account is in balance. In terms of the *IS–LM* model, the locus of current balance equilibrium is a vertical line, since the current balance is independent of the domestic interest rate. It will shift to the right with depreciation, and to the left as the *accumulated* value of foreign debt rises, because higher debt involves higher interest payments abroad. For full equilibrium, the other loci must all intersect on this vertical line.

We illustrate these features for fiscal policy under fixed exchange rates. At *H* in Figure 22.3, the point previously called an equilibrium, there is a current deficit; hence over time, *I'S'* falls back and *L'M'* tries to move right. This, however, produces downward pressure on the interest rate causing a capital outflow and an immediate drawing back of *L'M'*. Indeed, the capital mobility assumption ensures that the money supply is always fixed at just the level that causes *LM* to intersect *IS* along *BB*. Hence, as *I'S'* moves back, *L'M'* comes with it. Suppose both curves contract back to their original positions – does this now restore complete equilibrium? The answer is 'no', because the accumulated current account deficit during the adjustment period has reduced net interest receipts from abroad, thus lowering the level of income consistent with current account balance. The contraction, therefore, has to continue further, ending somewhere to the left of E. Indeed, it may not stop there, but proceed even further left, to a position of temporary current surplus, so that net wealth can be recouped. If asset behaviour is entirely unaffected by these disequilibria, the accumulated surpluses will balance the previously accumulated deficits, eventually making E re-attainable as a full equilibrium. In such an economy, policy may have temporary effects, but long-run control is impossible.

Under flexible rates there is a third wealth effect to consider. To the extent that prices are determined in local currency, and domestic wealth holders intend to spend their wealth locally, the exchange rate affects total real wealth, because a depreciation will raise the value of assets denominated in foreign currency. If domestic residents are net holders of foreign assets, this will raise domestic wealth, raising money demand and pulling the LM curve back to the left, whereas if residents are net debtors the opposite happens. This is an immediate effect, and initially it will dominate the LM shift arising from changing stocks of assets.

Imagine a fiscal stimulus under flexible exchange rates. The Mundell–Fleming analysis of the temporary equilibrium implies no change in income but a current account deficit brought about by an appreciation. Assuming that residents are neither net borrowers nor lenders of foreign assets, we can ignore valuation effects on foreign assets and assert that, from the 'Mundell–Fleming' point E, IS will shift left and LM shift right. This implies downward pressure on the exchange rate, which tends to reverse the shift in IS and raise the level of income consistent with current balance. If we ignore the price effects of depreciation on the LM curve, there is nothing to reverse its gradual outward drift, hence the final equilibrium (if there be one) must be to the right of E; that is, fiscal policy recovers some effect on income. Similar reasoning suggests that wealth effects reduce the effectiveness of monetary policy under flexible rates.

The wealth effects reverse the exchange rate implications of the original policy measures. For example, with monetary policy the temporary equilibrium involves a lower exchange rate and a current surplus, but from there the exchange rate gradually appreciates to its long-run position. This is a form of overshooting. In the short term the level of wealth is fixed, so all adjustment is borne by the exchange rate, but gradually wealth does adjust, thus relaxing the pressure on the exchange rate.

Expectations

Implicit in the Mundell–Fleming analysis is the assumption that people never expect any change in the exchange rate from its present position. Under a firmly controlled fixed-rate system this may be reasonable, but not under flexible rates. We therefore now introduce expectations into the model, assuming, for simplicity, rational expectations. Coupled with the assumed absence of uncertainty, this amounts to assuming perfect foresight.

Anticipated changes in the exchange rate alter the relationship between the domestic and the foreign rates of interest. Capital mobility equates the net return on bills, but the return on home bills bought by foreigners is the home rate of interest plus any appreciation. Thus, if appreciation is expected (known to be coming), the domestic interest rate will have to fall below the world rate if capital flows are to be avoided (see section 21.1).

We now add expectations to a model that already includes wealth and price effects. Under flexible exchange rates, but without expectations, monetary policy shifts the economy from E to H in Figure 22.4. (Unlike in Figure 22.3, we assume that H involves some allowance for price changes.) At H the exchange rate has depreciated and there is a current account surplus. This will, in time, appreciate the exchange rate, leading to a new equilibrium as described above. Now suppose this appreciation is foreseen: to gain from it, people will start buying domestic currency, so H cannot be considered even a temporary equilibrium. Indeed, even before the economy had reached H, people would have started buying in anticipation, with the result that, under rational expectations, the exchange rate will not fall as far as without expectations. Hence our 'expectations-ridden' IS curve lies to the left of the one through H and the LM curve to the right of its position through H – say, $I"S"$ and $L"M"$ respectively.

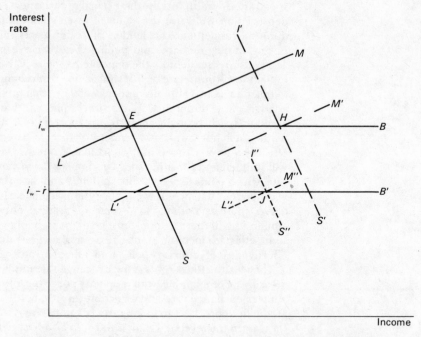

Figure 22.4   *Monetary policy with flexible rates and rational expectations*

The anticipated appreciation (call it $\dot{r}$) also has another effect. By raising the return on domestic bonds it reduces the domestic rate of interest consistent with capital equilibrium from i_w to $(i_w - \dot{r})$; i.e. it lowers the external balance line B to B'. For equilibrium under rational expectations, $I"S"$ and $L"M"$ must intersect at this lower rate of interest – at J, say. Without further information we cannot locate J precisely: it depends on the extent and the speed of the expected appreciation ($\dot{r}$ is measured as percentage change *per year*, to be compatible with i_w), which, in turn, depends on how strongly expectations mitigate the original decline. As before, the wealth effects will gradually shift the economy back from J, and as the appreciation occurs there will be less to expect, so B' will gradually return to B.

A similar analysis can be conducted for fiscal policy under floating rates. The current deficit that would apply at the temporary equilibrium without expectations would cause a depreciation. The anticipation of this mitigates the original appreciation, and prevents IS from shrinking right back to its original position. It also means that the domestic interest rate must rise to equate the net return on domestic bills with the world rate of interest.

260

This analysis can all be repeated with the opposite assumption to Mundell and Fleming's – namely, complete capital immobility. This renders the balance of payments locus vertical, because only the current account would exist, and that would depend only on income. It quite transforms the results – at least in the simplest cases.

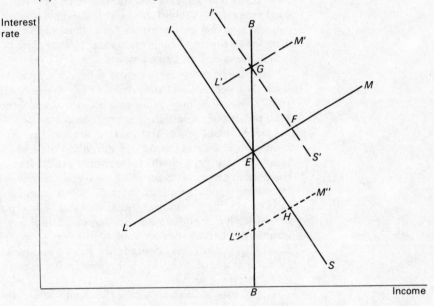

(A)   *With fixed exchange rates*

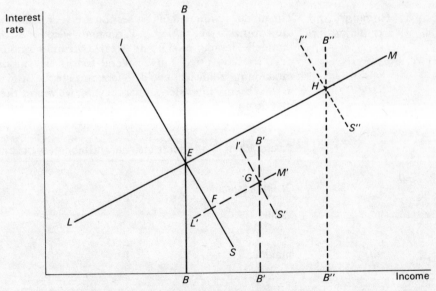

(B)   *With flexible exchange rates*

Figure 22.5   *Economic policy with capital immobile (A) With fixed exchange rates.
(B) With flexible exchange rates.*

261

Consider a regime of fixed exchange rates. In Figure 22.5(A), fiscal policy would shift *IS* out to *I'S'*. In temporary equilibrium there is a current deficit, for nothing has happened to shift *BB*, and this will continue until either the deficit has depleted the money stock sufficiently to shift *LM* back to *L'M'*, or the government has run out of reserves and reversed its fiscal stance. In the former case, the new equilibrium would be *G*, and in the latter it would revert back to *E*; in neither case, however, would any increase in income be possible. This is because the need for current account equilibrium dictates the level of income, and no policy available can change that relationship. Note that, unlike the mobile capital case, the progress to the new equilibrium takes a finite time because *L'M'* can shrink back only at the rate of the current deficit.

The case of monetary policy is similarly simple. An expansion of *LM* to *L"M"* leads to a deficit (at *H*) and, again, either to the gradual run-down of the money supply, re-establishing *LM*, or to a policy reversal. Hence again income cannot be manipulated because of the external constraint.

Under flexible rates the current account/income relationship is no longer rigidly fixed: a depreciation will shift *BB* to the right. Consider monetary policy – illustrated in Figure 22.5(B). *LM* is shifted to *L'M'*, leading temporarily to *F*, at which there is a deficit. The resulting depreciation shifts both *IS* and *BB* outwards, producing a new equilibrium at *G*. Hence monetary policy is effective under flexible rate even without capital mobility. Fiscal policy, on the other hand, is dramatically dependent on the degree of mobility: with capital mobility it is impotent, whereas with immobility it is very powerful. A fiscal expansion taking *IS* to *I'S'* generates a payments deficit and a consequent depreciation. This shifts *BB* rightwards and also enhances the shift in *IS* out to *I"S"*. The final equilibrium is given by a point such as *H*.

These cases are also subject to the qualifications about price and wealth effects discussed above, but the details are left to the student, as is the case where imperfect capital mobility makes *BB* upward-sloping. Of course, with no capital flows, exchange rate expectations are of hardly any interest.

Summary and qualification

The models examined in this section are very definite in their conclusions. These are summarised in Table 22.1 in terms of 'weak' or 'strong'. Although in the simple Mundell–Fleming model, the 'weak' outcomes amount to complete ineffectiveness, we have listed above several factors that moderate this extreme. These moderating influences could, in fact, reverse the original rankings of policies, but, in the absence of evidence that they do, we report the more likely outcome that they do not.

Table 22.1 The effects of fiscal and monetary policy[a]

| | Exchange rate regime | |
Capital assumption	Fixed	Flexible
Mobile	strong *weak*	weak *strong*
Immobile	weak *weak*	very strong *strong*

Note:
[a] Fiscal policy is described in roman print, monetary policy in italics.
Source: text.

The table speaks for itself, but before adopting it as fact we should review certain qualifications to the exercise from which it was derived. First, we compared rigidly fixed exchange rates with perfectly flexible ones, whereas nearly every country in the world has some sort of intermediate regime. In particular, we normally view fixed rates as being occasionally movable. This would have entirely changed the analysis of fixed rates under capital immobility because, with a devaluation, it would have been possible to shift *BB* to the right. Obviously, the exchange rate could not be moved with every change in fiscal or monetary policy, but occasional changes could avoid the worst limitations on policy.

Second, there are difficulties over the timing of the responses we have reported. Capital flows adjust rapidly, but the adjustment of money demand, and particularly of real demand, takes some time. Hence strictly we should not assume that the economy jumps easily from, say, *E* to *H* in Figure 22.3. However, as soon as we acknowledge that transition takes time, there is a need for compensatory capital flows, and expectations become involved. One particular case occurs if depreciation initially worsens the balance of trade (the J-curve). Now, an initial trade deficit, instead of being self-correcting through depreciation, is self-exacerbating, so that payments equilibrium is possible only if the exchange rate falls sufficiently to generate a counterbalancing capital inflow on the strength of an anticipated appreciation. This is another case of overshooting, and it seems unfortunately realistic.

Third, one may question the Keynesian framework. We admitted above that depreciation may affect prices, but if it does so proportionately, thus allowing no control over the degree of competitiveness, all the flexible exchange rate results change. If, furthermore, we adopt the other monetarist assumption of full employment, there is no role for policy anyway. Hence the whole exercise is futile!

Fourth, we could argue that any degree of policy effectiveness is sufficient to control the economy, provided we are willing to pull the levers on the less effective policies sufficiently hard. This is logically correct, but it ignores the costs of large policy changes, such as the increased variability in interest rates and profits, and the increased transition costs borne privately as people adjust.

Fifth, even in the regimes described, the fluctuations required for effective policy may be too great. Specifically, monetary policy under flexible rates works through exchange rate changes, and over the 1970s there was obvious conflict between maintaining monetary policy and choosing the exchange rate. Once we recognise the possibility of exchange rate overshooting in response to policy changes, governments may prefer some loss of monetary independence to the devastation of the real economy that an incorrect, or sharply fluctuating exchange rate could cause. In other words, although under flexible rates monetary policy is an effective macro-economic policy, it may be that its detailed effects are too severe to permit governments to exploit that effectiveness.

Sixth, one might question whether the assumed degree of capital mobility is desirable. Some international capital flows are obviously useful in smoothing out the day-to-day fluctuations in the current account, although this could as well be achieved by official intervention in the exchange market. However, the mass migration of funds in search of capital gains – and the consequent distortions of interest rates they produce – serves little social purpose, especially if expectations are poorly formed. There may thus be a strong case for limiting the mobility of short-term capital. While this would involve administrative costs and some loss of speculators' profits, it may well enhance the control and the stability of the economy, by preventing excessive exchange rate fluctuations and permitting greater freedom in the choice of interest rates.

263

22.3   THE EVIDENCE ON FINANCIAL INTEGRATION

The degree of capital mobility – or rather the extent of international financial integration – is clearly an important consideration in the choice of economic policy tools and exchange rate regime. It also intimately affects the behaviour of the exchange rate and foreign exchange reserves, as we have seen in earlier chapters. This section, therefore, examines the empirical evidence on financial integration.

Some difficulties

Before looking at the econometric results, we should consider certain empirical and theoretical difficulties. In the former group fall problems of measurement and of causation. It is almost impossible to measure gross capital flows because they change direction so rapidly, but some data on net positions are possible. More serious is our inability to measure net wealth satisfactorily or expectations at all. The more dramatic shifts in international capital occur because of expectations, but more often than not such episodes are omitted from empirical work because no measure is available for 'speculative sentiment'.

The problems over causation are even greater. First, it is rarely clear whether the authorities are pursuing their monetary policy despite, or because of, the movements in capital flows, interest rates and exchange rates. Second, although the interest parity relationship is known to hold well, we do not know which variable adjusts to bring it about (see section 21.1). These problems can cause bias in econometric estimates (simultaneity bias) and considerably reduce the confidence we can place in them.

The major theoretical difficulty concerns the practical definition of financial integration. Complete integration would involve the loss of all national control over the interest rate and either the money supply (under fixed rates) or the exchange rate (under flexible rates). It could occur, however, without our actually observing any capital flows at all – the mere threat of huge inflows or outflows would prevent the domestic interest rate from deviating from the world rate. We should, therefore, concentrate on the interest rate rather than on capital flows themselves. We then have to decide whether to examine the 'covered' or 'uncovered' interest differential between countries. The uncovered differential is just the difference between rates in, say, London and Paris, whereas the covered differential adjusts the crude difference for the expected change in the pound–franc exchange rate (see section 21.1). For assessing international capital mobility, covered rates are relevant because that is what most capital responds to, but for domestic policy purposes local uncovered rates are required. Remember, however, that, if covered differentials are zero, the uncovered interest differential must equal the forward premium. That is, interest rate autonomy is bought at the price of compensating expected changes in the exchange rate.

A further complication arises over whether to use Euro-market or national interest rates. We look at the Euro-market in Chapter 28 below; here we need merely note that it comprises deposits (loans) placed (raised) in banks in a currency other than that of the country where the bank is situated (e.g. dollars lent in London, pounds lent in Paris). This reduces the chances that the loan will become subject to exchange restrictions, because the sovereign power where the loan is placed has no interest in another country's currency, while the issuer of the currency has no power over the loan. The Euro-market is also subject to many fewer legal and administrative restrictions than are national banking systems. For these reasons we do not expect equality between, say, the Euro-sterling and London sterling rates of interest. Thus, although interest parity holds almost perfectly between the various Euro-currencies, imperfections between them and

the national centres allows some scope for covered differentials between the
latter.

The evidence   There are four approaches to measuring the degree of financial integration. First
we can just compare interest rates across countries: if they are similar and move
similarly we have found *prima facie* evidence for international integration. This
approach avoids the problems over causation, but of course, by ducking that issue,
it can give us no indication of how to manipulate interest rates if there is any scope
for doing so. A recent study in this tradition is Nellis (1982). He considered covered
and uncovered interest rates in France, West Germany, the UK, Canada and the
USA under both fixed exchange rates (1962–71) and floating (1973–80). His
technique was to seek, statistically, a common factor that explained the evolution
of all five interest rates. Under fixed rates, he found a factor to explain 71 per cent
of the variance in uncovered rates and one to explain 72 per cent of that in covered
rates, whereas with flexible rates the figures were 49 per cent and 75 per cent
respectively. These figures indicate that, while interest rates do move together
internationally, there is still an independent component. This is strongest for
uncovered rates under floating, which suggests that floating has allowed greater
(although far from complete) financial autonomy. The contrast with the results for
covered rates – where floating has not changed the degree of integration – shows
that the extra freedom over interest rates has been offset by a stronger degree of
determination of forward premia and thus of exchange rates.

Once we recognise the possibility of interest rate independence, we need to ask
what determines interest rates. This leads to the second approach to measuring
integration, namely the estimation of equations explaining interest rates. A recent
study of the UK over the 1970s (when exchange controls still existed) is Briault and
Howson (1982). They used an asset markets approach to the exchange rate, and
determined the London sterling rate, the Euro-sterling rate and the exchange rate
simultaneously. They found strong evidence of imperfect substitutability between
London and Euro-sterling markets, and also that, as before, financial independence comes at the expense of control of the exchange rate. Overall, a 1 percentage point increase in Euro-dollar rate generated a 0.4 percentage point
increase in London rates, while a £1b. rise in the UK's net foreign assets would
have increased London rates by 0.19 percentage points. A problem not considered
by Briault and Howson is the authorities' role in capital markets. Herring and
Marston (1977) argued that UK interest rates are determined directly by the
government, but that the government is constrained in its choice by factors such as
the balance of payments and foreign interest rates. They estimated (on data over
1961–71) that, in the long run, a 1 percentage point increase in the Euro-dollar rate
raises London rates by 0.45–0.65 percentage points.

We now briefly consider direct studies of capital flows. If there is not perfect
mobility we can consider capital flows as a function of interest rates. If, as we have
argued, capital flows are a means of reallocating wealth over assets, and if the
desired portfolio (stock) of assets is a function, *inter alia*, of relative interest rates,
then capital *flows* should be related to *changes* in interest rates. Many researchers,
however, relate them to the level of interest rates, implying that the accumulation
of assets could continue indefinitely. For short-run purposes the difference hardly
matters, but it should be borne in mind for longer-term work. Typical estimates of
the effects on UK capital inflows of a 1 per cent rise in the covered interest
differential are £300m. (Beenstock and Bell, 1979) and £475m. (Hodjera, 1971).
These are considerably reduced if we look at uncovered differentials (£48m. and
£100m. respectively), suggesting a strong compensatory movement in the forward

265

premium as interest rates change. These estimates refer to the 1960s when total current credits were only around £6–£10b.; hence the inflows are relatively important, and one can only presume that increasing financial sophistication, and the abolition of exchange controls, increased their sensitivity to interest rates during the 1970s.

An alternative way of explaining capital flows eschews interest rates, and looks directly at the extent to which private capital flows offset domestic monetary changes and the extent to which the authorities sterilise reserve changes. Both offsets and sterilisation lead to a negative relationship between the domestic and foreign components of the money supply, and they are virtually impossible to tell apart. Kouri and Porter (1974) estimated offset coefficients of 40–80 per cent for certain European countries, whilst Argy and Kouri (1974) suggested similar or greater sterilisation coefficients. The estimates vary considerably over studies, and, of course, apply only if the authorities are intervening in the exchange markets; as with all the other approaches, however, they suggest substantial but incomplete integration.

The evidence suggests that international short-term capital is mobile – especially through covered arbitrage transactions; that countries still have some monetary autonomy via the restrictions and risks of their own markets; and that if they are not concerned to manage their exchange rates they could have considerably more control under floating rates than under fixed rates, via movements in the forward premium.

FURTHER READING

The use of simple policy models was pioneered by *Meade* (1951) and *Tinbergen* (1952), and first applied in our specific cases by *Swan* (1955) and *Mundell* (1962). Interesting recent extensions are *Meade* (1978) and *Argy* (1981, Part Six), both of whom consider the current situation.

The *IS–LM* model is expounded in many textbooks: *Stern* (1973) is useful for the basic model, while both *Argy* (1981) and *Llewellyn* (1981) consider some variants. The developments in the text are taken mainly from *Branson and Buiter* (1982), but *Argy and Porter* (1972) were the first to introduce expectations into the model. *Llewellyn* (1981) considers the question of financial integration in depth from both theoretical and empirical standpoints, while *Hodjera* (1973) offers a survey of work on capital mobility until about 1972. *Goldstein* (1980) is a useful survey of flexible exchange rates and macro-economic policy.

23 Economic Adjustment – The Case of Oil

We now apply the models of the last few chapters to a specific issue – the oil shocks of the 1970s. There were two: the large rises in the price of oil in 1973–4 and 1979–80, which affected the whole world, and the discovery and exploitation of oil that affected the UK. These problems are important in their own right, but they will also help to cement our understanding of the theory that we have just covered.

The chapter starts with a simple model of the oil price rise; it then considers separately the impact of booming oil production on the rest of the economy. Finally it combines the two to examine the developments in the British economy over the 1970s.

23.1 THE PRICE OF OIL

Pure theory   We start with some simple trade theory, using a static, full employment and flexible-price model to explore the effects of an oil price rise. We compare the world economy at full equilibrium under two sets of circumstances differing only in the assumed price of oil. Imagine a world comprising just a group of oil producers (OPEC) and a group of oil importers (OECD). The oil importers use oil to produce both traded and non-traded goods, some of the former being exported to OPEC in return for oil. For simplicity we assume that OPEC has no non-traded sector. Imagine also that the world is in full equilibrium at some given price of oil and that suddenly and quite exogenously that price rises. (We shall not debate which price, if either, is the 'correct price' – although most Western economists discussing the 1970s presume that the earlier, lower, price was correct and the later, higher, one an unjustified distortion to free trade.)

Assume that OECD's demand for oil is insensitive to price, and that OPEC always spends all its income on tradables. The price rise is then just equivalent to a transfer of income from OECD to OPEC (see Chapter 14). OECD reduces its expenditure and OPEC increases its by the same amount. However, the composition of their expenditure differs: OECD will cut back on both tradables and non-tradables, whereas OPEC will, by assumption, spend only on the former. The result is excess demand for tradables and excess supply of non-tradables. This will be eliminated by higher relative prices for tradables, and, assuming some mobility of factors of production between sectors, a shift in output away from non-tradables and towards tradables. If we identify tradables as manufactures and non-tradables as services, OECD is forced to *industrialise* to pay for the higher-priced oil.

Further price effects could arise if tradables and non-tradables use different amounts of oil: the oil-intensive good will rise in price relatively, which may either reinforce or reduce the original income effects. Also, if the demand for oil is price sensitive, the extent of the transfer would be reduced. Indeed, if demand for oil were price elastic, total OECD expenditure on oil would be reduced by the price rise, and, although OECD would suffer from having to find substitutes for oil, OPEC would also suffer, so there would be no simply identified transfer.

The oil price rise represents a deterioration in OECD's terms of trade, which cuts its national income. This will not necessarily cut everybody's income, however, because relative factor rewards will be affected both via the factor intensities in tradable and non-tradable sectors (a Stolper–Samuelson result), and also via the substitutability of each factor for oil. For example, British coal miners almost certainly benefited from the higher price of oil.

Some Keynesian considerations

We now extend the simple model to account for various rigidities in the process of adjustment. First, suppose that OPEC cannot spend all its extra income immediately. The price rise then transfers income from spenders (OECD) to savers (OPEC) and the result is a fall in demand. If prices are rigid – a Keynesian world – this has multiplier effects and reduces income, output and employment by a larger amount. It also, of course, has balance of payments consequences. OECD's exports no longer balance its imports, so it runs a current account deficit, whereas OPEC has an equal surplus. These imbalances can be financed only by corresponding capital flows. At first these may involve accumulating or decumulating reserves (national cash balances), but eventually they must involve OPEC lending its excess savings to OECD. This mitigates the decline in world demand and in OECD consumption, but only at the expense of substantial shifts in world wealth. Furthermore, such a situation cannot last indefinitely – the deficits and wealth transfer must eventually be corrected. Nevertheless, capital flows prolong and ease the period of adjustment.

The reduction in world income and the surplus of savings will probably combine to reduce the (real) rate of interest. This should encourage investment in OECD – especially in oil-substituting activities. It is most unlikely, however, given the fall in output and the general uncertainty surrounding an oil price rise, that such investment would approach the original loss of consumption in magnitude. This conclusion is reinforced once we observe that investment requires long-term finance whereas, over 1974–80, much of OPEC's lending was of a short-term nature.

A further complication involves adjustment within OECD countries. If wages and prices are rigid downwards, the required changes in relative prices can come about only through price rises. If there is additionally some element of real wage resistance – for instance, indexing money wages to compensate for price rises – adjustment would set off an inflationary spiral. Under these circumstances economic policy becomes important. If the government refuses to expand domestic demand to compensate for the demand lost through the transfer, and refuses to expand the money supply to validate the price rises in adjustment, the economy is doubly squeezed. There would be little inflation but a deep recession, although adjustment would be rapid. Alternatively, if the government pursued both compensating fiscal and monetary policy, this would postpone the decline in income but at the expense of inflation, a current deficit and prolonged disequilibrium. Roughly at these opposite poles were West Germany and Britain in 1974–5. The former adjusted quickly whereas the latter expanded her budget deficit and allowed the money supply to rise. Over 1974 Britain appeared to be weathering the OPEC storm better than most OECD countries, but by 1976 adjustment was forced on the country. Unfortunate though Britain's recent economic history may have been, however, we cannot be sure that a harsher response to the oil price rise would have improved it. There is, however, widespread agreement that the 1973 index-linking of incomes (which was introduced before the oil price rise) substantially hindered economic management over the period.

Many countries

So far we have treated OECD as a single country. Once we relax this assumption, there are several further complications. First, although OPEC is forced to lend its

268

surplus to OECD, it is not forced to lend it to any particular OECD country. Hence, while for OECD as a whole the current deficit is balanced by a capital account surplus, this need not be so for every country. In fact, the countries with the worst deficits are likely to receive least OPEC funds. To some extent this is avoidable by 'recycling' OPEC funds among OECD countries; the burdens of adjustment will none the less fall with different speeds and severity on different OECD countries. Some capital-importing countries may even find themselves with appreciating exchange rates despite their long-run need for depreciation to stimulate industrialisation.

A related difficulty concerns the portfolio of assets chosen by OPEC. As wealth is transferred from QECD to OPEC it is shifted from OECD-preferred assets to OPEC-preferred assets. In 1974–5, this almost certainly appreciated sterling and depreciated the dollar relative to what they would have been. Possibly more serious is the relatively greater mobility of OPEC-owned funds. OPEC chose to lend on rather short maturities, which were easily switched between centres. The result was an increase in the potential volatility of exchange rates, which, even if it had never materialised, constrained governments in their policy-making.

Third, as OECD countries adjusted to their current deficits they reduced imports from each other as well as from OPEC; hence each country shifted some of its burden onto its fellow OECD members. The net result was a multiple contraction among OECD (see p. 183 above). This is a very strong argument for coordinating economic policy within OECD along the lines of the convoy or locomotive theories.

To conclude, therefore, an oil price rise involves a long-run process of industrialisation in OECD countries. The adjustment path is likely to be painful, involving recession and inflation, and is significantly complicated by the inter-actions between OECD countries.

23.2 THE DISCOVERY OF OIL

We now turn to the second oil shock experienced by Britain in the 1970s – the discovery and exploitation of North Sea oil. Although this was a boon, increasing incomes in Britain significantly, it was not without its attendant difficulties, most importantly the change it required in the structure of the economy. We concentrate on the British case, but it is not unique: similar natural resource discoveries have affected Australia (minerals), Holland (natural gas), Norway, Indonesia and Mexico (oil). We start, as before, with a simple trade model and gradually broaden out to a more realistic view.

Pure theory   The most obvious theoretical approach to this problem is to apply the Rybczynski theorem (section 14.1 above). If we have two tradable sectors – oil and non-oil – an influx of the factors of production intensive in oil production (namely oil-fields) would indicate an expansion of oil and an absolute contraction of non-oil. This, however, is too simple and simple-minded. It requires that all prices are fixed by world trade, and it implies that non-oil must contract because it loses factors of production to oil. Since oil production requires few local factors, this is not a plausible view.

A more fruitful approach explicitly introduces demand, and recognises the role of the non-tradable sector as well as oil and non-oil tradables. The simplest model is from Forsyth and Kay (1980), on which the following example is based. Imagine a small, open economy with full employment, perfect competition, perfect

269

information and a perfectly static environment. We examine it first with a small primary goods sector, and then with a large one, representing higher oil production. The economy's demand, supply and trade in the former case are described in part (A) of Table 23.1: a deficit (excess demand) in primary goods is balanced by a surplus (excess supply) in manufacturing; services are assumed to be entirely non-traded and therefore must have demand equal to supply.

Table 23.1 The effects of higher oil production

Actual income

	(A) *Without oil*			(B) *With oil*		
	Demand	Supply	Trade	Demand	Supply	Trade
Primary	10	5	−5	12	25	+13
Manufacturing	40	45	+5	48	35	−13
Services	50	50	0	60	60	0
Total	100	100	0	120	120	0

Permanent income

	(C) *Before/after oil*			(D) *During oil boom*		
	Demand	Supply	Trade	Demand	Supply	Trade
Primary	11	5	−6	11	25	+14
Manufacturing	44	40	−4	44	40	−4
Services	55	55	0	55	55	0
Total	110	100	−10	110	120	+10

Assume now that the net output of primaries rises by 20 units to 25. Assume also that the extra income is all spent and is allocated *pro rata* over the demand categories. The resulting demands are given in part (B) of Table 23.1. We can also immediately write in the output of primaries (25, by assumption), and the trade balances in primaries, services (zero by definition) and overall (zero because income and expenditure increase by equal amounts). Hence, we may simply deduce the trade balance in manufactures, and thence output in manufacturing and services. Services production must expand in line with demand, but that of manufactures declines, shifting that sector from surplus to deficit on the foreign account.

The mechanism by which these adjustments are achieved in a small, open economy is almost certainly via exchange rate appreciation. This reduces the relative price of tradable to non-tradable output. Depending on one's model of production, one can deduce from this the effects on factor rewards. In a Heckscher–Ohlin world, with manufactures as the labour-intensive good, real wages fall. In a factor-specific world, the rewards of factors tied to manufacturing fall by more than the price of manufactures, but the effects on the mobile factors are ambiguous. In either case, however, if wages are rigid, the fall in rewards tends to be reflected in a fall in employment.

Forsyth and Kay (1980) presented considerably more detail and derived their figures from the UK economy, but this simple comparative static exercise is the basis of their assertion that 'the contraction of manufacturing . . . [is] the only way [to] benefit from the North Sea'. However, while there is much force in their argument it is not unassailable.

The most significant criticism of the Forsyth and Kay argument is its static nature. By comparing two equilibria, they entirely ignored the feasibility and costs of moving from one to another. These are important in all analyses, but for Britain and North Sea oil they are doubly so. Britain's period as a major oil producer will last, perhaps, thirty years. Hence, transition from equilibrium (A) to equilibrium (B) will inevitably be followed by transition back again – i.e. de-industrialisation followed by re-industrialisation. Such adjustment is costly: de-industrialisation causes substantial hardship, and many would argue that re-industrialisation after twenty years of declining industrial output will be virtually impossible, because Britain will no longer have the skills or the technological infrastructure to compete. Hence, what may be sensible given perpetual oil production, may not be so for Britain.

One answer to this, which is consistent with Forsyth and Kay's analysis, is that we should not consume all the income from oil, but rather should invest it and consume only the interest. That is, we should look at the permanent income from oil, namely the increase in consumption that oil permits us to maintain for ever. Assuming the oil lasts twenty-five years and that a real rate of return of 3 per cent per annum is available on investment, the increase in permanent income is about half the annual increase in actual income while the oil flows. Looking at our illustrative economy, the situations with and without oil are given in parts (C) and (D) of Table 23.1. Consumption is now the same in the two cases, but of course production varies. Assume that the discovery of oil was entirely unexpected: the economy starts from the position (A) in Table 23.1 with a manufacturing surplus financing a primary deficit; it then evolves to (D), where oil exports finance both a manufacturing deficit and an outflow of investment abroad (the overall balance of trade surplus); finally it settles at (C), where the primary and manufacturing deficits are met by earnings on the earlier investment abroad. Compared with the previous scenario this pattern involves substantially less adjustment, although manufacturing still contracts somewhat.

In fact, of course, the oil and its contribution to permanent income will be anticipated, and so the economy will tend to shift from (A) to (C) prior to oil's coming on stream. In this case, borrowing is necessary to finance the payments deficit, but it is forthcoming given the collateral of future oil. In addition, the exchange rate starts to appreciate and manufacturing starts to decline even before the oil is physically available. There are strong reasons to believe that such anticipations affected Norway and Britain after 1975.

The picture just painted involves investing the oil revenues abroad. This helps to keep the exchange rate down while the oil is flowing, and provides the foreign exchange with which to maintain consumption afterwards. Forsyth and Kay preferred this policy to domestic investment in either non-tradables or tradables. To be invested at home, the oil needs to be converted into goods and services, and to the extent that these are non-traded this increases the squeeze on tradables. Furthermore, they argued, given its contraction, the returns on investment in the tradable manufacturing sector will be unreasonably low. However, although the private returns to foreign investment may exceed those of domestic investment, this is not necessarily so for the social returns. For example, private returns are reduced by taxes on profits, the risk of appropriation, externalities through raised employment and externalities from the dynamic effects of investment; however, whereas with foreign investment all these are lost to the investing nation, with home investment they accrue to it as social benefits (see p. 158 above). Hence it may pay Britain to invest her oil revenue in the expansion of the manufacturing sector: while the oil flows, manufacturing will be importing capital goods and probably making losses, but, when the oil has gone, the maintained manufacturing sector will still be healthy enough to earn the surplus necessary to finance the

271

higher permanent consumption. Clearly the trade-off between foreign and domestic investment depends on the difference between private and social returns, the size of the transition costs in adjusting manufactures, and the extent to which local investment requires non-traded goods. Thus it is not possible to reject home investment *a priori* as Forsyth and Kay did.

This section has argued that, if the benefits of an oil discovery are to be enjoyed, the revenue has to be spent, and this will inevitably lead to some structural change. We have analysed a very simple example of this change and shown that manufacturing must contract. This conclusion arises from nearly every analysis of this problem. Nevertheless, we have also argued that the extent and pattern of structural change is amenable to policy control, and that there may well be cases where it is beneficial to keep adjustment below the level implied by the free market.

Macro-economic adjustment

We now turn briefly to the macro-economics of adjustment to an oil discovery (following Eastwood and Venables, 1982). We take as given that the oil raises domestic demand, and that in the long run the relative price and output of non-tradables must rise. We shall assume that this implies an exchange rate appreciation. With perfect markets, flexible prices and rational expectations, adjustment would be instantaneous, but once we allow for sticky prices and wages there is a period of disequilibrium. We analyse this in the framework of a 'Dornbusch' economy assuming perfect capital mobility. With rational expectations, an oil discovery would lead to an immediate jump in demand to its new permanent income level and also to an immediate appreciation. This appreciation would not, however, reach the long-run equilibrium exchange rate or eliminate all the excess demand for domestic output; these are achieved only later, through further gradual appreciation. The reason for this undershooting is that the initial appreciation lowers import prices, which, by reducing the demand for money, lowers the domestic interest rate. This is consistent with foreign balance only if an anticipated appreciation equates the net return on domestic bills to the world rate of interest.

With rational expectations, the immediate jump in demand more than offsets the deflationary effects of the exchange rate appreciation, meaning that discovery is followed by excess, not deficient, demand for domestic output. However, if we assume that demand does not rise until residents actually receive the extra income, then there is a contraction, because the appreciation now reduces demand from the level that just matched pre-oil supply. Such a situation seems quite plausible. Most residents reap the benefits of an oil discovery only through tax cuts, and they are unlikely to be able to borrow or to reduce their savings by a corresponding amount just on the strength of expected future tax cuts. Hence, unless the government finances immediate tax cuts through its own borrowing, there will be a time lag between the oil discovery and the increase in demand. The result will be an exchange rate led depression, concentrated on the tradable goods sector.

Apart from government action, the only other possible relief of the depression is that the investment programme to extract the oil raises demand. However, this is unlikely to offset the effects of appreciation entirely. In fact, if the programme were largely financed from abroad, it could exacerbate the appreciation, because, even if all physical equipment were imported, investment would still raise the demand for local goods and services such as construction. In addition, compared with domestic finance, foreign finance of the investment would reduce the long-term value of the exchange rate, because it would reduce local incomes and generate an outflow of profits. It seems possible, then, that under such circumstances some overshooting could occur.

There is one final consideration on the exchange rate. There has been great uncertainty surrounding the future price of oil, especially over the 1970s. Rises in the price hit industrial economies hard, and oil self-sufficiency reduces the impact of such shocks. This affects the risk properties of a self-sufficient country's currency, which will rise when 'oil-importer' currencies fall. Hence oil self-sufficiency provides an excellent hedge against oil price rises, and such 'portfolio' demand could lead to further appreciation. Few major currencies are 'backed by' oil self-sufficiency, so this may have been a major factor in the demand for sterling since the late 1970s.

23.3   THE BRITISH EXPERIENCE

We have examined separately the two oil shocks of the 1970s – a huge price rise and the discovery of substantial oil reserves. We now combine our analyses to look at Britain in the late 1970s. We ask whether Britain gained from the combined oil shocks; what, if any, structural change is required; and whether the high exchange rate and falling output were the inevitable consequence of North Sea oil, rather than the result of the tight monetary policy.

Some history

Figure 23.1 illustrates the evolution of the British economy of the 1970s with respect to the 'real' exchange rate (the exchange rate adjusted for relative prices), the change in the real money supply (M3), the level of manufacturing production, the world real price of oil (i.e. relative to manufactures), and British production of crude oil and gas.

The exchange rate is adjusted by wholesale prices in Britain relative to competitors; it amounts to no more than British prices relative to competitors' prices in a common currency. It shows a sharp fall over 1972–3 – the Heath–Barber boom – and an equally sharp and more far-reaching appreciation after 1977. The middle period is one of gradual increase punctuated by a crisis in 1976. The fortunes of manufacturing output mirror the exchange rate fairly closely, with an early boom followed by relative stagnation and a huge decline. Of course, such coincidence does not prove causality, but given our theory it is hard to reject it. The main purpose of this section, however, is to consider whether the pattern of the real exchange rate can be partly or entirely explained by the 'oil events' of the 1970s – namely, the oil price rises and the discovery of North Sea oil. The obverse of that is whether or not monetary policy was important.

One important variable not shown in the figure is known oil reserves. With rational expectations the discovery of profitable oil reserves will stimulate the exchange rate immediately. The big discoveries in the North Sea occurred between 1971 and 1973, but no appreciation is evident then. This is because, at that time, the oil reserves were not very profitable (Bank of England, *Quarterly Economic Review*, March 1982). It was only after the 1978 rise that the world price exceeded North Sea production costs significantly, and at that point sterling did appreciate. The effect of actual production on the exchange rate is not clear theoretically and, although the recovery of sterling runs reasonably closely with production, it would be unwise to postulate a formal link.

The second graph refers to changes in the real money supply – total M3 deflated by the GDP deflator at factor cost.[1] The large movements occurred in the early and mid-1970s – the Heath–Barber boom and its aftermath. After 1976 this measure of

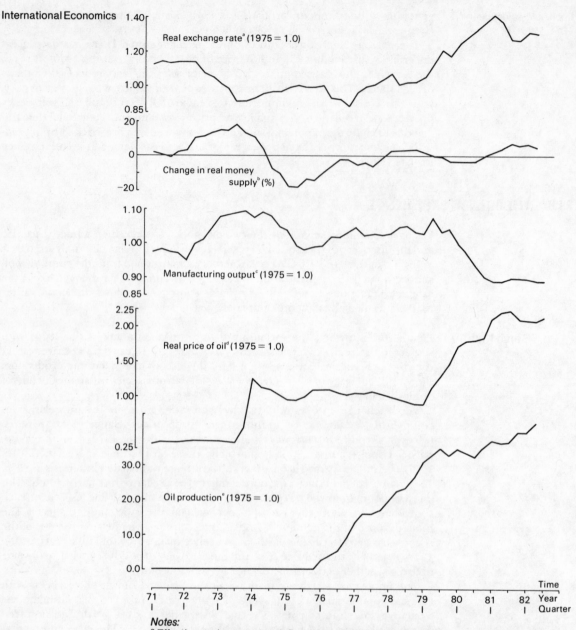

Real exchange rate[a] (1975 = 1.0)

Change in real money supply[b] (%)

Manufacturing output[c] (1975 = 1.0)

Real price of oil[d] (1975 = 1.0)

Oil production[e] (1975 = 1.0)

Notes:

[a] Effective exchange rates deflated by 'relative wholesale price' in *Economic Trends.*

[b] Total M3 (Bank of England *Quarterly Economic Review*), deflated by GDP (factor cost) deflator (*Economic Trends*). Percentage change over same quarter in previous year.

[d] Price of crude oil deflated by unit value of manufactured exports from major exporters, both measured in US dollars. Crude oil price from *National Institute Economic Review* from 1978, and from United Nations, *Monthly Bulletin of Statistics* Table 59, previously: deflator from UN, *Monthly Bulletin of Statistics*, special tables.

[e] *National Economic Review* and Central Statistical Office, *Monthly Digest of Statistics.*

Figure 23.1   *British economic indicators since 1971. Real exchange rate (1975 = 1.0). Change in real money supply (%). Manufacturing output (1975 = 1.0). Real price of oil (1975 = 1.0). Oil production (1965 = 1.0).*

the real money supply was roughly constant, with a slight tightening through 1979–80. In fact, the monetary squeeze in the UK over 1979–80 was much stronger than is indicated here: the rise in indirect taxes in the 1979 budget (VAT increased from 8 per cent to 15 per cent) raised transaction prices, and hence the demand for money (probably by about 3 per cent); M3 gives too liberal a view of the money supply – other monetary aggregates rose by less, while M3 growth was distorted upwards by the removal of 'the corset'; and, finally, the government announced plans to cut future money supply growth considerably, acting aggressively enough to make such control seem plausible. Buiter and Miller (1981) discussed this period in depth and concluded that monetary factors explain much of the spurt in sterling in 1979–80.

The analysis

Possibly the best-known estimate of the effects of North Sea oil on the UK economy is Forsyth and Kay (1980). We have already examined their theoretical approach, and we now briefly consider their estimates. Recall that they dealt with an oil discovery rather than both oil shocks, although subsequently (Forsyth and Kay, 1981) they sought to incorporate the oil price rise into their analysis. Their argument was simple: at 1980 prices the advent of oil raised value-added in the primary sector by about £10b. – doubling that sector's size and directly adding 5.5 per cent to GDP. The trade balance in manufactures had to deteriorate by about £22b. (in gross output terms), of which about £9b. would arise directly from the increase in income. The remaining £13b., about 20 per cent of exports, had to be shed through losses of competitiveness, and, using estimated price elasticities, Forsyth and Kay suggested that a decline in competitiveness of about 12–15 per cent was required. This required an appreciation of around 20–25 per cent, and since this is roughly what occurred in nominal terms between the years Forsyth and Kay compared (1976 and 1980), they concluded that oil explains the appreciation of sterling. They also estimated the gains to Britain from North Sea oil at around 10 per cent of national income, split about equally between the direct contribution of oil and the indirect terms of trade effects stemming from appreciation.

Forsyth and Kay's calculations were challenged on a number of grounds. The gross contribution of oil was said to be exaggerated (especially given the likely repatriation of foreign-owned profits), the actual appreciation understated, and the elasticities used too pessimistic. A higher income elasticity for imports and higher price elasticities on imports and exports would all serve to reduce the exchange rate changes resulting from oil. Professor John Williamson, in a letter to the *Guardian* (July 1980), suggested that an appreciation of only about 10 per cent arose from oil, leaving some 10–15 per cent to be explained by economic policy.

A more forceful argument arose from the Bank of England (*Quarterly Economic Review*, December 1980 and March 1982) and Eastwood and Venables (1983). This attacked not the logic of Forsyth and Kay's analysis but rather its relevance. While an oil discovery may cause a substantial appreciation compared with what would have happened, it did not explain the sterling appreciation of the late 1970s, because discovery was superimposed on the depreciation arising from the rise in oil prices.

Eastwood and Venables assessed the change in Britain's permanent income that accrued from the 'oil events' of the 1970s, and from this deduced the exchange rate effects. They identified four 'oil events':

- the discovery of North Sea oil,
- the 1973–4 price rise,

- the 1978–9 price rise, and
- revisions in expectations about the relative price of oil after 1980.

They calculated the effects of these events under two assumptions about expectations in 1970. Under 'perfect foresight', both oil price rises were assumed to be anticipated, hence perceived permanent income was already low in 1970 because people took into account the future high cost of oil. Under 'myopia', however, neither price rise was expected, and so permanent income was high in 1970 because people expected to continue consuming at the 1970 rate indefinitely. The oil price rises then came as a nasty surprise that cut perceived permanent income substantially.

The oil discovery, on the other hand, was assumed to be unexpected under both scenarios. It raised permanent income. With perfect foresight this was from a low base, whereas with myopia its positive impact was set against the permanent income loss that was incurred through the price rises. (Despite having local supplies, Britain still had to adjust to the new higher prices for oil.) Comparing 1970 and 1980, Eastwood and Venables tentatively suggested that, with perfect foresight, 'oil events' raised permanent income by $4\frac{1}{2}$ per cent, whereas with myopia they lowered it by 2 per cent. The latter result does not imply that Britain did not gain from North Sea oil, but merely that its unexpected benefits were more than offset by the unexpected loss from the price rises. Eastwood and Venables also suggested that the myopic view is the more nearly correct,[2] and hence rejected Forsyth and Kay's analysis, which is akin to the perfect foresight case (a straight injection of income).

The next step was to calculate the indirect income gains accruing through the change in the terms of trade of non-oil goods. Since Britain's non-oil trade was largely with other oil importers (OECD), the question concerned the impacts of the shocks on Britain relative to the rest of OECD. Eastwood and Venables argued that the oil price rises hit both equally, hence only the oil discovery could change the terms of trade between them. The resources devoted to oil were lost to other activities, and the authors estimated that the opportunity cost of oil was a loss of non-oil production of about 2 per cent of GDP. North Sea oil contributed about $4\frac{1}{2}$ per cent to GDP directly and this increased demand for local output by about 3 per cent of GDP. The fall in supply coupled with the rise in demand raised the relative price of UK non-oil goods. Assuming an infinite price elasticity of supply for imports, price elasticities of demand of $-2/3$ and $-4/3$ for imports and exports respectively, and an import/GDP ratio of $1/3$, the price elasticity of demand for UK output was $1/3$.[3] Assuming a zero price elasticity of supply for UK output, a 5 per cent cut in demand needed terms of trade change of 15 per cent, and this indirectly raised permanent income by a further 5 per cent of GDP.

Combining the direct and indirect benefits, Eastwood and Venables suggested a net gain in permanent income between 1970 and 1980 of about 7–9 per cent under perfect foresight and of around 0–2 per cent under myopia. The structural implications of these income and relative price effects are that the perfect foresight case suggests considerable growth of non-traded output and decline in manufacturing (cf. Forsyth and Kay), whereas the myopia case suggests little change or even a growth of manufacturing. Since the latter appears more realistic, there was probably little need for structural change between 1970 and 1980. On the other hand, appreciation was still necessary under myopia because the rest of OECD had to increase its volume of exports in response to the price rise, while the UK did not. In other words, the UK had to maintain her volume of exports while the rest of OECD expanded theirs; this still required a loss in Britain's share of world trade, but not the contraction of British manufacturing. The exchange rate change necessary to bring this about is not precisely estimable, but the evidence suggests it is considerably below the catastrophic levels reached in 1980 and 1981.

Summary

We have applied some elementary economic theory and quantification to the very real problem of the oil shocks of the 1970s. The conclusions are as follows:

(i)   The oil price rise substantially reduced OECD's real permanent income.
(ii) Britain is richer for having North Sea oil. But
(iii) the benefits of North Sea oil only just, if at all, outweigh the costs of the higher oil price. 'Oil events' overall did little to boost income between 1970 and 1980.
(iv) If (i) had been anticipated and adjusted to by 1970, then (ii) would have required considerable readjustment: spending would have had to rise and non-traded sectors expand at the expense of traded good sectors. If, alternatively, (i) were not anticipated, the combination of (i) and (ii) would leave little room for a boom or structural change. The evidence suggests that the latter was the case.
(v)   The discovery of North Sea oil significantly improved Britain's terms of trade. This involved appreciation, but probably not by the extent observed by the early 1980s. Thus the latter must be explained by monetary policy as well as by oil.

FURTHER READING

Corden (1977) provides a simple analysis of the oil price rises of the 1970s. More formal approaches to oil as an intermediate good are *Dornbusch* (1980a) and *Findlay and Rodriguez* (1977) who consider the macro-economic implications. For a treatment of resource discoveries in the abstract, see *Corden and Neary* (1982) on trade theory, and *Eastwood and Venables* (1982) on macro-economics. *Corden* (1981) tackles the theoretical untangling of monetary policy and resource booms. Specific analyses of resource booms stretch back to *Gregory* (1976) – on Australia – and *Ellman* (1977) – on Holland; more recently they include – on Britain – *Forsyth and Kay* (1980, 1981), *Bank of England* (*Quarterly Economic Review*, December 1980 and March 1982) and *Eastwood and Venables* (1983). The later Bank of England report is extremely clear and offers a thorough analysis of the costs of North Sea oil. *McCormick* (1982) provides some novel analysis for the UK, whilst *Barker and Brailovsky* (1981) offers a detailed and Keynesian approach to resource discovery in several countries.

NOTES

1   M3 includes notes and coin plus all bank deposits.
2   Their evidence comes from various pre-1973 writings, and the fact that the largest appreciation of sterling coincided with the 1978 oil price rise.
3   The calculation involves totally differentiating $Y = Q + pM$ and $S = Q + X$ holding $dY = 0$, where Y is income, Q local sales, M imports, X exports and p the price of foreign goods in terms of UK goods. S represents the demand for domestic output, the variable of interest.

24 Flexible Exchange Rates and Optimum Currency Areas

So far we have examined the determinants of flexible exchange rates and their impact on economic policy. We now extend the discussion to see, first, whether fixed and flexible rates behave differently in the face of economic shocks (section 24.1) and second, when one regime might be preferable to the other (sections 24.2 and 24.3). In the latter exercise, we contrast flexible (or floating) rates with the realistic alternative of fixed but adjustable rates: we consider rigidly fixed rates only when we examine optimum currency areas – areas that share a single currency – in section 24.4.

24.1 TRANSMISSION AND INSULATION

In this section we ask which exchange rate regime offers the domestic economy most insulation from unwanted economic shocks. The latter may be of either domestic or foreign origin – they are deemed equally undesirable.

The simplest transmission mechanism for economic shocks is the international trade multiplier of Chapter 17. Assuming fixed exchange rates and ignoring all capital flows, it shows that economic activity in one country spills over (positively) to another via the trade balance. For example, an investment boom in France stimulates demand for both French and British output and causes expansion in both. Under fixed rates, therefore, British income is sensitive to activity in France. Now repeat the exercise with flexible rates. If the exchange rate always adjusts to keep the trade balance at zero, it would seem that Britain is insulated from France. Moreover, since Britain can no longer provide net resources to France (because trade is always balanced), all the extra investment must be supplied locally and so the expansion of French income will be correspondingly greater. Thus flexible rates, it seems, reduce the impact of foreign demand shocks and increase the effects of local demand shocks.

This result is broadly true, but the analysis is really too simple to be acceptable. The change in the exchange rate necessary to balance trade alters relative prices (because, in this Keynesian model, prices are fixed in local currency terms), and at the very least this should be taken into account. In the previous example, the French boom depreciates the franc and thus worsens the French terms of trade. Conversely, of course, it improves Britain's terms of trade, and consequently makes her better off for any given level of output. Higher income normally entails higher savings, and since money income has not risen, higher savings involves lower money expenditure. Since the price of British output has not changed either, lower money expenditure means lower demand and output. Hence with flexibility a French boom reduces British output (though not her real income). This is known as the Lausen–Metzler effect (1950; and Behnke, 1980).

Even this is too simple, however, and we now turn to the full open *IS–LM* model to examine the impact of various shocks. The analysis is formally like that of Chapter 22, where we examined the effect of economic policy; however, there we asked whether (policy) shocks could shift income/output, whereas now we ask which regimes prevent shocks from influencing income. It could be argued that concern with insulation is misplaced, since shocks could always be met by countervailing policy shocks. This is forceful in theory, but not wholly convincing in practice, because it ignores the information and execution problems of conducting policy so precisely. In other words, an automatically stable regime is likely to save time, effort and mistakes.

Domestic expenditure shocks – e.g. investment booms – are precisely equivalent to fiscal policy in Chapter 22. With capital mobility, flexible rates offer more stability; in the simple model, flexible rates prevent any fiscal impact, but even in subtler models we would expect less than under fixed rates. With no capital mobility, however, fixed rates are more stable. Similarly, domestic monetary shocks are akin to monetary policy, and hence fixed rates are preferable regardless of the degree of capital mobility.

Consider now a foreign expenditure shock, raising the demand for local goods. This raises output and creates a current account surplus. Under flexible exchange rates, this surplus generates an appreciation that tends to offset the initial shock. Under fixed exchange rates, the surplus raises the money supply and this validates the output rise. Hence, flexible rates are more stable. A foreign monetary shock lowers the world rate of interest. Without capital mobility this presents no shock, but under perfect mobility it generates a huge potential inflow of funds. Under fixed rates, this expands the money supply (pushing the *LM* curve out) and raises income. With flexible rates, on the other hand, it produces an appreciation, dragging the *IS* curve back and reducing income. These two outcomes cannot strictly be ranked in terms of stability, but, since foreign monetary expansion is likely to be coupled with a foreign demand stimulus, it is likely that flexible rates result in less change in local incomes.

These simple exercises are not unambiguous, but they tend to confirm the earlier result that for foreign shocks flexible rates probably offer most insulation, whereas for domestic shocks fixed rates do. Intuitively, flexible rates bottle-up a disturbance in its country of origin, whereas fixed rates spread it around the world economy. Empirically, therefore, we would expect floating to be reflected in a weakening of the synchronisation of trade cycles around the world. In fact, synchronisation has increased since 1973 (Ripley, 1978), although this may well be due to economies experiencing common shocks (e.g. oil) rather than to causal links between them. Alternatively it may be that the exchange rate fluctuations necessary to ensure complete insulation were larger than governments could tolerate, and hence that only incomplete insulation was permitted. Recall from Chapters 17 and 18 how income effects tend to dominate short-term balance of payments behaviour. Hence, even relatively modest fluctuations in incomes may need very large exchange rate changes to offset them.

Note finally that this section refers to income insulation; price insulation involves different issues. In particular, a flexible rate may allow a country to avoid importing inflation, via either the rising import prices or the pressures to cure payments surpluses that arise under fixed rates. On the other hand, the translation of random exchange rate fluctuations into local prices could increase the price variability associated with floating.

24.2 FLEXIBLE EXCHANGE RATES AND SPECULATION

We have encountered speculators several times already in this book. Here we ask whether speculation will tend to stabilise or de-stabilise the exchange rate, and (which is not quite the same thing) whether flexible rates are necessarily fluctuating rates. This is a critical matter in the argument over flexible exchange rates, because many of the objections to flexibility amount to a dislike of excess variation. We start by briefly considering speculation under fixed exchange rates.

Speculation can be profitable only if a change in the exchange rate occurs. Under a fixed rate system, the rate can fluctuate between the intervention points but not normally beyond. Provided the intervention points are close to parity, there is little scope for speculators because the size of any gain will be relatively small. The result is that a fixed rate system normally experiences little speculation, and the rate is stabilised by modest levels of official intervention. Occasionally, however, changes in the parity may be required – for instance, after a long period of inflation or the discovery of mineral resources. Then the speculators can have a field-day. The direction of change is obvious; the only uncertainty concerns the timing and the extent of the change. Suppose sterling is expected to depreciate: no one willingly holds sterling, and so the exchange rate falls to the lower inter-vention point. Here the Bank of England has to sell dollars to buy any sterling offered. This can go on only so long as the Bank has dollars to sell; when they run out, the exchange rate falls. The costs to speculators of backing such an outcome are very small. There is no prospect of an appreciation, so the only possible cost is the interest differential between holding dollars and sterling. If this were, say, 5 per cent per annum ($i_£ = i_$ + 5\%$), it would still be profitable to speculate so long as sterling falls by 5 per cent within a year. Speculators face an almost sure thing. The pressure they put on the exchange rates can be massive and the costs of resisting it huge in terms of deflation and interest payments.

Under fixed rates, then, there is generally little speculation, but occasional periods of intense and destructive pressure. Under flexible rates on the other hand, there is always the prospect of significant changes in the rate and so speculation occurs most of the time; however, the fact that the rate responds to any pressure prevents the huge build-up of pressure. We now ask whether perpetual speculation could cause undue variability in exchange rates.

In the absence of speculation, the exchange rate would still fluctuate around its equilibrium path because, for example, trade may not be balanced every day. Would the addition of speculators to this market be stabilising, in the sense of moving the actual rate towards the equilibrium rate, or de-stabilising, moving it away? In terms of Figure 24.1, would speculation produce pattern (A) or pattern (B)?

The usual argument (due to Friedman, 1953) is that, if speculators push the rate out to (B), they will lose money, because they have to buy when the price is high (e.g. at T_1) and sell when it is low (T_2). Since people will not (indeed cannot) act persistently to make losses, Friedman argued, the great bulk of speculation must be stabilising. Within the context of a smoothly evolving equilibrium rate and a fixed group of speculators, this argument has never been satisfactorily refuted. However, this is not really the relevant framework for exchange rates. First, anyone making a foreign transaction can speculate merely by slightly re-timing his payment, so the group of speculators is fluctuating. Second, it is not difficult to speculate when the equilibrium value is obvious; the difficulty and scope for error arise when the equilibrium changes. This is especially likely when there is only incomplete information (often only rumour) on which speculators can base their estimates. In such circumstances it is easy to envisage speculation pulling the actual rate away from the true equilibrium rate. Third, the eventual elimination of unprofitable speculators says nothing about the damage they can do as they make their losses. For instance, the profitability criterion did not prevent the Wall Street crash of 1929!

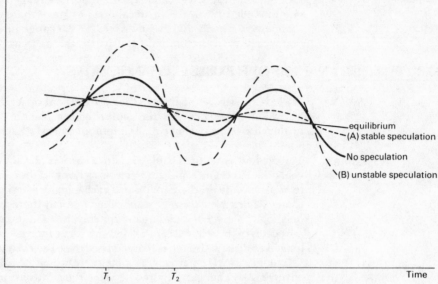

Figure 24.1   *Speculation and the exchange rate*

In the end, then, this is an empirical issue, and one that can be answered only by reference to actual exchange rate markets. The critical factor is the formation and precision of expectations. It is frequently argued that speculators, as professionals, will be better at this than other market participants. This is probably true, except compared with the central bank. It is hard to maintain that the bank could not out-predict speculators, for it has access to all the information they have plus some more. The issue then becomes whether or not the central bank would intervene only in the form that speculators would – to make profits – or whether it would use its position to try to exert a more far-reaching influence. If it did only the former – and this was obvious publicly – the exchange market would be more stable with bank intervention than with speculation. None of this argues that speculation is not normally stabilising – it probably is – or that an exchange market with no intervention and no speculation would not be highly unstable. It merely says that, of the two, official intervention is probably more stable than speculation.

Consider, finally, a market with both speculation and intervention. The latter could obviously displace the former, but if there is a suspicion that the bank has objectives other than profit, or if it regularly forms different expectations from the speculators, then there is scope for trouble. With no intervention, private speculation is constrained by the possibility that the exchange rate could move in the direction opposite to that expected, producing large losses. If, however, the bank is in the market, and if the bank always gets its way over the rate (by virtue of its huge resources), then speculators who can second-guess the bank have nearly the 'sure-thing' found under fixed rates. In such circumstances the volume of speculation forthcoming could be huge and intervention a difficult and costly process. This so-called 'dirty float' – with intervention to influence the rate, but not around any announced parity – could be less desirable than either of the more extreme regimes.

There is virtually no empirical evidence on speculation alone, because it is impossible to disentangle it from other determinants of exchange rates. It clearly cannot be de-stabilising in all circumstances since there are plenty of examples of

281

stable flexible rates, e.g. Canada in the 1950s (see Yeager, 1976). On the other hand, one has only to read the financial press to know that speculative sentiment can change very rapidly and greatly affect the exchange rate. It is difficult to believe that such jitters do not sometimes drive the rate away from equilibrium.

24.3 FURTHER ANALYSIS OF FLEXIBLE EXCHANGE RATES

We have now examined two of the pros and cons of flexible exchange rates – their insulation properties and the nature of speculation. We now consider some further, less technical but equally important issues.

Adjustment

The obvious case for flexible exchange rates is that they ease the adjustment to economic shocks affecting foreign transactions. Rather than the authorities having to identify shifts in the equilibrium exchange rate and bring about the required change, a flexible exchange rate will find its way there automatically, responding only to the supply of and demand for currencies in the market. According to the advocates of flexible exchange rates, this is cheaper, more reliable, and avoids the long-lived disequilibria that characterised the fixed exchange rate period.

If all prices were perfectly flexible there would be no need for exchange rate changes. Any changes required between the relative prices of tradables and non-tradables could be achieved by changes in local currency prices. However, in practice this is actually a long and painful process (if it is possible at all), and it may be avoided by changing the exchange rate. As Friedman (1953) observed, it is more efficient to change the single price of foreign currency than to reprice every single good an economy produces, just as during British summertime it is more efficient to alter the clocks to save daylight than to reschedule every activity by an hour.

This argument is, however, more a case against rigidly fixed rates than in favour of perfectly flexible rates. Provided governments do not persist too long with unrealistic rates, its main force may be accommodated by fixed but adjustable parities. Flexible exchange rates do not remove the external constraint; they merely translate it from a quantity dimension (balance of payments deficits) to a price dimension (depreciation). In fact, since 1973, disequilibria appear to have been just as persistent as before. West Germany and Switzerland, for instance, still show a strong tendency towards surplus and appreciation, while the USA shows the opposite.

Discipline

Related to the previous paragraph are fears that only the discipline of fixed rates prevents governments from pursuing profligate policies of monetary expansion. This is a silly argument – it supposes that deficits provide greater discipline than depreciations – and it is readily dismissed by reference to the vicious deflations of 1980–2, e.g. in Britain, West Germany and the USA.

Inflation and vicious circles

A more plausible ground for concern is the possibility that asymmetries in adjustment give a system of flexible rates an inflationary bias. If prices can adjust only upwards, a depreciation will raise the local currency prices of tradables, while the ensuing appreciation will raise the price of non-tradables. Either the government accommodates these price rises by expanding the money supply or it resists them and runs the risk of a depression as adjustment is thrown onto the quantity side of the economy. The latter is particularly likely if wages are inflexible downwards. If an appreciation reduces local currency tradable prices, but not labour costs, profits will be squeezed and this will eventually have repercussions on investment and output. This complaint against flexible rates is strengthened by comparison with the asymmetries of the fixed rate system. Since reserves are bounded below by zero, but not above, it is usually felt that fixed rates place greater burdens of adjustment on deficit countries than on surplus countries. Since the latter are obliged to pursue domestic deflation and anti-inflation policies, the system as a whole has a deflationary bias.

There has also been a fear of the development of vicious circles of inflation and depreciation. If some exogenous shock required a depreciation of the currency, but this led to an equal amount of inflation via real wage and profit inflexibility coupled with an accommodating monetary policy, then one could envisage a vicious cycle. Each round of inflation would be offset by further depreciation, but this would generate further inflation, and so on. The process could be accelerated by expectations, which could cause depreciations to precede the inflation round that causes them. Such a process is sometimes thought to have characterised Britain over 1973–5, when the indexation of wages and a loose monetary policy made adjustment to the oil crisis very inflationary.

This scenario is logically possible if the economy is homogeneous in all prices, and wages and prices react very quickly to each other. In most economies, however, there are lags in the adjustment of wages and only incomplete compensation for past inflation (as in Britain's 1973–4 indexation scheme). Furthermore, most tax systems exhibit fiscal drag, increasing their real tax-take in response to inflation, and most governments do not allow monetary policy to accommodate past price rises entirely. The result is that the inflation–depreciation cycle gradually squeezes real incomes and hence eventually collapses. Nevertheless, a shock requiring, say, a 5 per cent 'real' depreciation may involve a nominal depreciation of around 15–20 per cent.

This objection to flexible rates finds favour particularly with staunch monetarists like Mundell and Laffer. They argue that, since economies are homogeneous in prices and domestic prices are perfectly flexible, exchange rate flexibility is unnecessary, and that, as it can exacerbate inflationary shocks, it is to be deplored.

The evidence on inflation from the 1970s is ambiguous. That the level and dispersion of inflation rates have increased with floating is undeniable, but of itself this does not prove causation. Many would argue that the fixed exchange rate regime was abandoned *because* of the dispersion of inflation rates. Furthermore, even if flexible rates did exacerbate inflation levels and differences between countries, one cannot draw immediate welfare conclusions. In adjusting to the oil shocks, the ability of different economies to select different paths could have been beneficial.

Overall, flexible rates do seem to allow countries greater scope for inflation, but whether governments choose to exercise this freedom and whether such freedom is a 'bad thing', has not yet been determined.

Reserves

Perfect flexibility entails no official intervention in the exchange market. Apart from balances to fund official 'commercial' transactions, therefore, floating removes the need for foreign exchange reserves. Since reserves earn lower returns than longer-term investments (because of their greater liquidity), this represents a potential increase in income.

In practice, however, these savings are likely to be very small: earning, say, 2 per cent extra on 80 per cent of UK reserves in 1980 (the peak year) would have raised GNP by 0.1 per cent. Furthermore, there is doubt about whether floating has significantly reduced the use of (and demand for) foreign exchange reserves. The 1970s were a turbulent period and, of course, were mostly characterised by managed, rather than free floating; but Heller and Khan (1978) estimated that industrial countries (excluding the USA) reduced their reserve holdings by only 10–15 per cent relative to the pre-1972 era, while non-oil developing countries actually increased their holdings after 1972, probably reflecting their difficulties in pegging their exchange rates to major currencies that were themselves fluctuating.

Uncertainty

Before the advent of floating it was frequently maintained that flexible exchange rates would increase the uncertainty involved in international economic transactions, and hence, by reducing them, harm international specialisation. There are several replies to this.

First, it was denied on the grounds that taking forward cover allowed traders to avoid this risk. This is only part of the answer, however, because forward markets are costly and incomplete. The cost is reflected by the spread between buying and selling prices that rewards forward dealers for their risk. Both spreads and forward risk – the average difference between the forward rate for delivery at a date and the spot rate at that date – have increased substantially since floating (Aliber, 1976; Crockett and Goldstein, 1976). Such costs, however, are so small absolutely (around 0.5 per cent of price in 1981 – International Monetary Fund, *Annual Report*, 1982) that they can hardly affect trade strongly.

A second reply is that flexible exchange rates, while increasing exchange rate risk, may reduce other risks – especially on long-term transactions. For example, if one is contemplating direct investment, one is concerned about future costs in the host nation relative to the rest of the world. Flexible exchange rates may prevent the large discrepancies that could arise under fixed rates, because the exchange rate would move to offset differences in local currency inflation. Also, govern-ments sometimes adopt policies such as tariffs and exchange controls to defend fixed exchange rates; if flexible rates obviate the need for these, they further reduce uncertainty to private traders. In fact, neither of these arguments carries much conviction: since 1973 real exchange rate variability has increased rather than declined (International Monetary Fund, *Annual Report*, 1982), and trade restrictions have multiplied.

The third reply is empirical. No one has yet found convincing evidence that trade has suffered significantly from floating. Hooper and Kolhagen (1978) related trade volumes and prices to several measures of exchange variability, and found virtually no relationship at all. It is too early to be certain, but this seems to reject the possibility of large effects from uncertainty.

A closely related issue is the ability of flexible rates to generate required structural change. A fluctuating exchange rate is constantly signalling the need for structural readjustment – towards tradables as the rate falls, and back again when it rises. Entrepreneurs obviously cannot follow each of these signals, and so they may, in fact, be rather slow to detect genuine indications for change. We do not, however, know of any evidence on this matter.

Stability

It is frequently argued by advocates of flexible rates that instabilities in the exchange rate can only reflect instabilities in the economies they connect, and that it is better to let these instabilities work themselves out in the exchange rate rather than elsewhere. For massive disequilibria, this statement is probably true (think how distorted East European economies have become by eschewing the price mechanism), but for smaller, week-to-week, fluctuations there is no such presumption. For example, nearly all firms hold stocks of goods to smooth out demand fluctuations without resort to price changes, and there is no sound reason for denying such behaviour to countries in managing their foreign trade.

More significant still are the conclusions of section 21.3. Price rigidities, volatile expectations and asset considerations combine to magnify real instabilities in the exchange market. Hence, although a perfectly stable environment may generate perfectly stable rates, ordinary economic fluctuations may generate great exchange rate volatility. Empirically, however, this has yet to be established, for the huge oil price rises, the massive monetary injection, and the conversion of many major governments to monetarism (and back?) of the 1970s hardly constituted 'ordinary' economic fluctuations.

Table 24.1 reports two measures of exchange rate stability over the fixed and floating periods. The first refers to monthly fluctuations in effective exchange rates. These understate the degree of bilateral variability, but show clearly that floating has increased short-term fluctuation by around 50 per cent. Later data (International Monetary Fund, *Annual Reports*) show that stability has not improved since 1978. The second reports annual fluctuations about an approximation to the effective rate. It shows that longer-term variability has also increased since 1973, both absolutely and relative to trend movements in exchange rates. This probably indicates that floating involves long-lived disturbances as well as short-term fluctuations, but, as noted above, one cannot refute the alternative view that the 1970s just saw unusually large exogenous shocks.

Table 24.1 Exchange rate fluctuations under fixed and floating exchange rate regimes

(A) *Short-term*[a]

	January 1967–March 1973	April 1973–December 1978
Developed countries	1.127	1.680
Industrial	0.875	1.320
Other	1.567	2.311
Less developed countries	1.705	2.411

(B) *Long-term*[b]

	1953–71	1972–82
Ten industrial countries		
(i) absolutely	1.5	7.0
(ii) relative to trend	1.5	6.2

Notes:
[a] Variability is measured by the standard deviation of monthly percentage changes in the effective exchange rate.

[b] For each year the percentage change in the mean annual rate against the dollar is calculated for ten currencies: Belgian franc, Canadian dollar, French franc, Deutsche Mark, lira, yen, guilder, Swiss franc, sterling and US dollar. (The last obviously has a change of 0 per cent.) Let these be X_{it} (currency i, year t), and let $\bar{X}_t = \frac{1}{10} \sum_{i=1}^{10} X_{it}$. Figure (i) is then $\sqrt{\frac{1}{9} \sum_i (X_{it} - \bar{X}_t)^2}$ averaged over 1953–71 and 1972–82. Let $\bar{X}_i = \frac{1}{T} \sum_t X_{it}$; figure (ii) is then $\sqrt{\frac{1}{T-1} \sum_t (X_{it} - \bar{X}_i)^2}$, where the summation and $\bar{X}_i$ are calculated over 1953–71 and 1972–82 respectively.

Sources: (A) International Monetary Fund, *Annual Report* (1979); (B) data supplied privately by John Black.

24.4   OPTIMUM CURRENCY AREAS

The previous sections have presented several strong arguments in favour of flexible exchange rates, and many economists are entirely convinced by them. However, if it is desirable for the UK to have a flexible exchange rate, why should Wales not have one, or Birmingham, or even Edgbaston within Birmingham? Clearly, as areas become smaller there is an increasing presumption that they will tie their currency to a larger neighbour's, and this section asks why. For simplicity's sake we compare a system of entirely flexible rates with a system of immutably fixed rates – indeed, rates fixed so firmly that the two currencies involved merge into one.

Adjustment   Suppose that Birmingham runs a deficit with the rest of the UK. Under flexible rates this would cause a depreciation of the Birmingham pound. As a small area, depreciation would not alter Birmingham's terms of trade, but rather alter the relative prices of tradable and non-tradable goods; for adjustment, resources would have to flow from non-tradables to tradable industries, and real absorption would have to decrease. But the non-traded sector in Birmingham is very small – in small-enough areas even hair-cuts become tradable (!) – and so, to generate a sufficient transfer of resources, a large exchange rate change would be necessary. However, if nearly all consumption is imported and if wages are fixed in local currency, exchange rate changes involve large switches in real incomes; such fluctuations are generally deemed undesirable, and more often than not they are resisted. The money illusion that allows depreciation to cut real incomes in larger economies is less likely to apply in smaller ones where the real income consequences are so obvious. Thus, unless the terms of trade can be changed, attempting to cure Birmingham's deficit by depreciation is likely to result in excessive fluctuations in prices and/or incomes.

Now contrast this with adjustment when the Birmingham pound is immutably tied to sterling, as in reality. To finance the deficit, private wealth has to be transferred from Birmingham to the rest of the UK. Since both areas use the same currency this is relatively straightforward and is, in fact, effected largely automatically through the banking system. When Birmingham residents' wealth has declined sufficiently, they will reduce their absorption. If Birmingham had an official institution responsible for managing the deficit, it would also probably help this process along with some expenditure-reducing policy. The more open the economy, the more effective (or less costly) is expenditure reduction as a method curing deficits: the higher the marginal propensity to import, the smaller the proportion of any expenditure cut that falls on domestic production and causes contraction via the multiplier. In the limit, a completely open economy (all consumption imported) needs to reduce consumption by only £1 for every £1 fall in imports required.

The decline in local absorption will reduce demand for such non-tradable output as there is. This may reduce wages, improving competitiveness in tradables and hence taking the economy back to equilibrium. As we have observed many times already, if local currency prices are flexible there is no balance of payments problem. More likely, however, is that falling demand leads to unemployment. This will be alleviated, as will the deficit, if the unemployed move from Birmingham to the rest of the UK. To be sure, this is expensive both personally (financial and psychic costs) and socially (under-used infrastructure), but it is probably preferable to persistent unemployment. Hence another aid to adjustment under fixed rates is factor mobility.

286

Factor mobility cannot avoid all the consequences of depression in regions linked by a common currency, and within most countries a further element of adjustment (or finance) is introduced by government transfers. These may take the form of labour and investment subsidies to the regions or straightforward income transfers through unemployment benefits, etc. Hence, the willingness to transfer income between regions of a currency area is also an important part of its working.

To conclude, the exchange rate is less effective as an equilibrating mechanism in very open economies, whereas expenditure reduction is more effective. Adjustment under fixed rates is eased by the willingness to swap private assets, to move factors and to transfer income between different parts of a currency union. This suggests that regions/countries that have considerable mutual trade, compatible private and political institutions, and close cultural connections could benefit from forming a currency area.

Monetary factors

So far we have considered the real factors determining optimum currency areas, but there are also monetary considerations. First, the price fluctuations produced by exchange flexibility in a small, very open economy may reduce the 'moneyness' of the currency. Money is used as a store of value and a unit of deferred payment; to be effective it must be relatively stable in terms of the transactions it is used for. Flexible rates basically fix the price level in terms of domestic output, whereas fixed rates fix it in terms of foreign goods. Now, if consumers buy mostly foreign goods they will prefer to hold an asset and do their accounting in terms of foreign goods. Hence, domestic money will be unattractive unless there is a fixed exchange rate. In the limit, an attempt to float the rate may be greeted by a refusal to hold domestic currency and its displacement in internal circulation by the currency of a major supplier of imports. This argument is due to McKinnon (1963).

Clearly this argument is stronger the more open the economy. Clearly, also, it presupposes that the shocks that alter the exchange rate are domestic. If the foreign price level is fluctuating, a flexible rate may insulate domestic currency holdings by opposing movements, and render them more stable (in terms of foreign goods) than foreign currency. This counter has led many economists to reject McKinnon's (1963) argument, but it is not invincible. While fixing your currency to an unstable partner currency may not ensure stability, it is likely that, provided that that partner is a large and diversified economy, fluctuations in its price level will be smaller and less variable than the shocks that can hit a small economy. This is especially so if the latter's production is concentrated on a few primary products.

A second monetary factor concerns monetary policy. Obviously with only one money there can be only one monetary policy. Each region therefore loses the ability to pursue a monetary policy geared to its own aims. All that can be set against this is that, in a small, very open economy, monetary policy is unlikely to achieve much anyway, because of the absence of money illusion. An independent fiscal policy is still feasible – although it is hard work because of the high leakage into 'imports'. For example, in the early 1980s Sheffield City Council raised employment by stimulating local business through fiscal incentives.

In loose monetary unions where countries keep their separate currencies but are strongly committed to particular rates of exchange, independent monetary policy is conceivable, but not very useful. If the union allows fairly free capital movement, any money created in one partner will rapidly flow out (as in Chapter 20), and the government will merely lose reserves as it fights to maintain the exchange rate.

This brings us to a third monetary factor. If two countries have substantial mutual trade and they elect to keep a fixed rate between their currencies, this rate has to be defended. If they then combined to have a single currency they would save on reserves. They may even find that the combined currency would be sufficiently attractive to third countries that they could earn seignorage by issuing it abroad. (Seignorage is the gain from creating and 'selling' money for goods – see Chapter 26.) In view of the comments above, the gains from reducing official reserves are likely to be small, although we have no estimate of the private gains from the corresponding reduction in private transaction balances.

Political factors

A currency area allows its participants to benefit from fixed exchange rates (certainty, etc.) on their mutual trade. Against this must be set the loss of exchange rate and monetary policies as means of adjustment. These costs will be minimised if there is agreement between the participants on the conduct and use of monetary policy and on making inter-partner transfers of incomes. On the former, for example, a tight money regime and an inflation-prone regime (e.g. West Germany and the UK in the 1970s) are unlikely to make happy bed-fellows. Of course, if there are intentions of political integration, or even just of further economic integration involving tax harmonisation, etc., these will be very much more easily achieved with currency union than without. Indeed, once one gets above some relatively small minimum size it seems that the main advantages of currency union are political. This minimum size is contentious but almost certainly most European countries exceed it.

Some evidence

Table 24.2 shows the exchange rate regimes ruling in mid-1983. The majority of countries pegged their rates to major partners' currencies or some basket of currencies for the reasons we have discussed. Many of the others had only limited flexibility, and indeed only eight admitted to independent floating. Despite this, however, 80 per cent of world trade takes place across a floating exchange rate (Emminger, 1979); for instance, Panamanian imports from Ireland cross a floating rate because the dollar, to which Panama pegs, floats against the European currency unit to which Ireland (loosely) pegs.

Table 24.2 Exchange rate arrangements (30 June 1983)[a]

Pegged currencies:		Examples
to US dollar	36	Barbados, Egypt
French franc	13	Congo, Mali
Other single currency	5	Bhutan (Indian rupee), The Gambia (sterling)
SDR	14	Jordan, Zambia
Other basket	25	Algeria, Sweden
Restricted flexibility:		
EMS	8	France, West Germany
Relating to US dollar	9	Guyana, Saudi Arabia
Flexible currencies:		
Independent	8	UK, USA
Adjusted by indicator	5	Brazil, Portugal
Other managed	22	Australia, India
	145	

Note:
[a] Excludes Democratic Kampuchea.
Source: International Monetary Fund, Annual Report (1983).

288

Monetary unions stretch from immutable combinations (e.g. the states in the USA), through dominant/follower relationships (as the UK and Ireland were before 1979 when the Irish broke loose from sterling), to very loose associations seeking some exchange rate stability (the European Monetary System). We conclude by briefly examining this weakest of approaches.

The European Monetary System

Monetary integration has always been one of the main aims of the 'European integrationists'. The customs union was merely the first step towards further integration of laws, taxes, institutions and money. Indeed, it was planned in the Werner Report of 1971 that monetary integration should occur hand-in-hand with the other measures and be complete by 1980. The first step was the so-called 'snake in the tunnel' of 1972–8. This restricted movements between European currencies to tighter limits (the snake) than those permitted by the Smithsonian Agreement against other currencies (the tunnel). This was more wishful thinking than anything else. No steps were taken to bring the stability about and, in particular, each country had complete freedom over its own macro-economic policy. The more independent nations rapidly dropped out – notably France and Britain – and the snake really became a Deutsche Mark area, comprising West Germany and her smaller dependent neighbours.

Monetary integration dropped quietly from view with all the other problems of the mid-1970s, but it was revived in 1978 as the European Monetary System (EMS) – an altogether more robust creature than the snake. It realistically aimed for margins around parities of $\pm 2\frac{1}{4}$ per cent (± 6 per cent for Italy) – considerably greater than the 1 per cent of Bretton Woods – and formally allowed for parity changes. It obliged partners to conduct macro-economic policy in conformity with their parity exchange rates, with the need for action being publicly indicated by a 'divergence indicator'. It invented a European currency unit (ECU) – a basket of currencies – against which parities are measured, which is used for intra-EEC accounting and which is backed by reserve deposits by member nations. Finally, it made provision for short- and medium-term loans to ease adjustment problems. All countries save the UK joined, the smaller deficit countries being attracted by the adjustment assistance.

The EMS covers a considerable slice of each members' trade, hence there are gains to be had from stabilisation (Page, 1982). Day-to-day fluctuations have been smoothed out, but it is doubtful whether any longer-term stability has arisen. Between March 1979 and September 1982 there were six parity changes, and the interval between them has been falling. Furthermore, there is little sign that policy has been coordinated or that inflation or growth rates have converged among EMS members. Page (1982) considered that its survival to 1983 was rather a matter of luck and that its future was not rosy. Nevertheless, she argued that the consultation and slight cooperation that it had produced would be beneficial in future. In truth, the EMS was designed to achieve little by way of economic integration and has achieved even less. Its main aim was political, and it is only as a tentative first step towards something else that it has any significance.

FURTHER READING

Argy (1981) provides more detail on the material in this chapter, including recent controversies. Tower and Willett (1976) adds further analysis on the transmission of disturbances, while the arguments over speculation are summarised by Stern (1973) and Lindert and Kindleberger (1982). On flexible exchange rates Artus and Young (1979) provides an excellent and balanced survey including recent empirical evidence, and *Yeager* (1976) gives a detailed account of the traditional case, along with historical case studies. Classic references on this subject are *Friedman* (1953) and *Meade* (1955). Further details of recent empirical evidence should be sought in the text references. Statistical data and commentary on recent events may be found in International Monetary Fund, *Annual Reports*.

The literature on monetary integration and currency unions is huge. *Corden* (1972a) gives a balanced view, and *McKinnon* (1963) is a thought-provoking article. More thorough and analytical is *Tower and Willett* (1976). On the EMS, *Page* (1982) summarises progress so far, while *HM Treasury* (1978) – the official document on Britain's attitude – sheds an interesting light on currency areas and balance of payments policy in practice.

Part III

25 The Demand for International Reserves

Part II of this book dealt with macro-economic aspects of the open economy from the viewpoint of a single country. We considered the determinants of a country's balance of payments and/or exchange rate largely taking the rest of the world as given. We now examine the interactions of countries within the world economic system. The real aspects of this question are parallel to the single country results and were dealt with in Part II (e.g. the international multiplier, the transmission of fluctuations), but the monetary aspects raise new problems. These are the subject of this part of the book.

This chapter introduces the idea of the world as a single economic system. It considers what constitutes 'world money' and then discusses the public and private demand for that money. The next two chapters consider the supply of world money. They take a historical approach, describing the evolution of the world economy from a gold standard through to the present 'non-system' of payments. In the course of the history, however, the theoretical issues become perfectly plain. The final chapter deals briefly with an important institution of the current monetary scene – the Euro-currency market.

25.1 WORLD MONEY AND THE WORLD ECONOMIC SYSTEM

Until we discover life elsewhere in the universe, the world is just a large, closed economy. All goods sold must be bought, and all paper money must be 'inside' money, i.e. must constitute a liability somewhere within the system as well as an asset.

The $(n-1)$ problem Since it is closed, the world economy as a whole cannot run a balance of payments deficit or surplus. Thus one country's surplus *must* contribute to another's deficit and the sum of all countries' net payments positions *must* be zero. Therefore, if, out of n countries in the world, $(n-1)$ have determined their balances of payments, that of the nth is determined automatically as minus the sum of the others. In other words, if all countries have payments objectives, the adding-up constraint implies that, except by chance, only $(n-1)$ of them can possibly be successful. Exactly the same constraint applies to countries' stocks of assets. If the stock of assets is fixed and if $(n-1)$ countries have determined their holdings, the nth is willy-nilly left with the remainder. Similarly with exchange rates: the exchange rate is the price of one money relative to another, but with n currencies there can be only $(n-1)$ independent relative prices.

There are several ways of coping with the '$(n-1)$ problem'. At one extreme, one large country could agree to forgo any objectives over its balance of payments, assets and exchange rate, pursuing a policy of 'benign neglect'. (The nth country must be large enough to bear the surplus or deficit demanded by the other $(n-1)$, however. For example, Chad's benign neglect would not grant OECD complete freedom over its balance of payments objectives.) At the other extreme, all countries could surrender a little sovereignty by agreeing to operate according to some rule that ensured that their objectives were consistent with adding-up. In

Chapters 26 and 27 we shall see how different institutional frameworks imply different solutions to this problem.

'World money' and international reserves

We are often told 'money is what money does'; although not very precise, this captures satisfactorily the notion that whatever fulfils the functions of money *is* money. Hence, anything that is used as a means of payment and a store of value in the international sphere might be called 'world money'. Official balances of 'world money' are known as international reserves.

Precise definitions vary, but most economists would treat holdings of the following as world money: gold, convertible foreign currencies, reserve positions with the International Monetary Fund (IMF), and holdings of Special Drawing Rights (SDRs). The latter pair are available only to official holders, and private gold is normally treated as non-money, but there are both private and official holdings of convertible currency.

The criteria that make these assets attractive to central bankers as reserves are their liquidity and their unconditional availability. Gold is always readily saleable. Foreign currencies are termed convertible if they may be exchanged on demand for gold or other currencies at their issuing central bank. We include officially held sight deposits, time deposits and short-term bills (e.g. Treasury bills) as part of reserves. IMF positions refer to potential borrowings from the IMF that are available automatically to the central bank. Beyond these, other credit is available but only on increasingly tight conditions. SDRs are basically an international paper money issued by the IMF. (Valued initially at SDR 1 = $1.00, their value in December 1983 was SDR 1 = $1.042; see section 27.1 for further discussion of SDRs.)

Figure 25.1(A) illustrates the growth of these four components of world reserves between 1951 and 1981. Gold is valued throughout at SDR35 per ounce. This was its value to central banks until 1974, but since then banks have been able to sell gold on the private market at substantially higher prices. At these prices, gold reserves amounted to SDR524 billion at end-1980, which would more than double world reserves; however, any attempt to sell any but the slightest proportion of official gold would cause the price to collapse, so this is not a realistic estimate of world liquidity.

The figure illustrates the gradually increasing role of foreign currencies until 1970, after which holdings increased rapidly. IMF positions and SDRs contributed only slightly to world liquidity, while gold switched from a predominant to a subsidiary role.

Fierce though the increase in reserves over the 1970s appears, it did not keep pace with the value of world trade (see Figure 25.1(B)). In 1951, world reserves were around 60 per cent of annual imports, but this fell to 50 per cent in 1960, 31 per cent by 1970 and 14 per cent by 1980. This reflects great improvements in the efficiency with which international money was used and also the declining role of official reserves under floating exchange rates. Private balances of foreign currencies compensated partially, growing significantly relative to trade over this period, although measurement difficulties preclude their precise quantification.

Table 25.1 gives the composition of foreign currency reserves. The dollar is completely dominant, with the Deutsche Mark gradually replacing sterling as the second currency. The period from 1950 to 1970 (for which comparable data are not available) was characterised by the rise of the dollar and the decline of sterling as reserve currencies. In 1950, sterling reserves were twice the size of dollar reserves, although restrictions on their use imposed by the British government limited their liquidity.

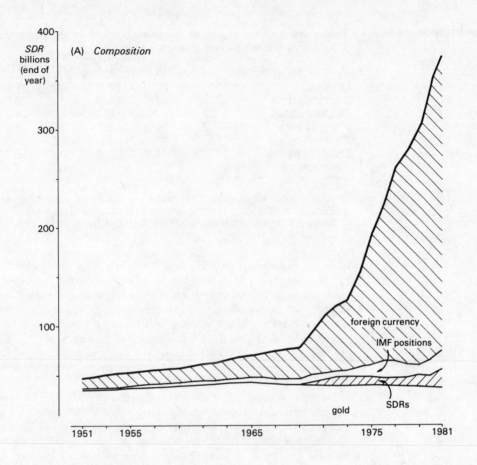

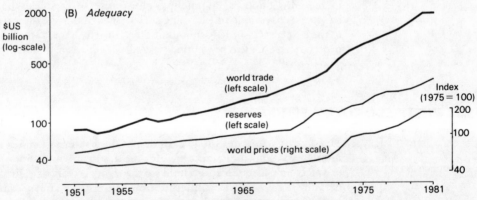

Source: International Monetary Fund, *International Financial Statistics*, Yearbook, 1981 and October 1982.

Figure 25.1 *World reserves, 1951–81. (A) Composition. (B) Adequacy.*

Supply and demand
A single small country's reserves are determined in level and composition by its demand for reserves. For the world as a whole, however, reserves are mainly determined by supply. In the short term, the supply of gold is virtually fixed in

Table 25.1 The share of national currencies in world foreign exchange reserves[a] (percentage, end of year)

	1970	1973[b]	1976	1979	1980	1981
US dollar	83.3	84.5	86.7	78.9	73.1	73.9
Pound sterling	8.8	5.9	2.1	2.0	3.0	2.5
Deutsche Mark	2.1	6.7	7.3	11.3	14.0	13.8
French franc	0.1	1.2	1.0	1.0	1.3	1.2
Swiss franc		1.4	1.6	3.2	4.1	3.2
Dutch guilder	5.7	0.4	0.5	0.7	0.9	1.1
Japanese yen		—	0.7	2.8	3.7	4.3

Notes:
[a] All currencies measured in SDR; ignoring translation of certain EMS reserves into ECUs.
[b] End March 1973.
Sources: International Monetary Fund, *Annual Report* (1981, 1982); Heller and Knight (1978) for 1970.

quantity, and until recently in price. So too are IMF positions and SDR quotas. With foreign currencies, demand holds some sway if central banks will exchange their currency for other non-currency assets; then selling, say, sterling to the Bank of England for gold reduces the amount of sterling circulating (the supply of sterling), but merely redistributes holdings of gold. At present, however, one currency is convertible on demand only into another currency. Hence, the total level of currency reserves is basically supply determined, although their is scope for shifting currencies between official and private portfolios. By and large, however, the figures in Figure 25.1 reflect supply.

Foreign exchange reserves are created (supplied) by deficits on the basic balance of payments of reserve-currency countries. The USA may finance a deficit by either running down her assets (reserves) or increasing her liabilities. The latter involves creating a deposit of dollars in the name of the foreign country at a US bank. The foreign country now has more money and the world's supply of dollars has increased. Countries demanding more reserves acquire them by running a balance of payments surplus. The surfeit of currency they so earn is merely added to the reserves in some form or another. Clearly there is another face of the $(n-1)$ problem here. Unless new money is created, net acquisitions of reserve assets must sum to zero.

25.2 THE DEMAND FOR RESERVES

This section examines the overall demand for international reserves by national monetary authorities, ignoring, for now, their composition and the role of privately held assets. Nations hold stocks of money for basically the same reason as do individuals – to allow different time patterns for income and expenditure. If income and expenditure had to balance at each point of time, transactions would degenerate virtually to barter, but with money one can buy on one day and sell on another. This is especially necessary if there is uncertainty about the value or timing of transactions.

Finance and adjustment

Imagine an economy in perfect equilibrium that suddenly loses part of its income. In the absence of reserves it has immediately to undertake some form of adjustment. Either it must cut expenditure to balance income or it must run down its net worth by selling assets. The latter may be straightforward, but if its assets are illiquid the necessary rush may be expensive in terms of the price earned. The former – as we saw above – is likely to be painful. Now, if the loss of income were known to be permanent there would be a case for immediate adjustment – although economists frequently hold that adjustment costs rise with the speed as well as the extent of adjustment. If, on the other hand, the income loss were temporary there would be little case at all for adjustment, so long as it cost anything. An adequate stock of reserves allows a country to avoid real adjustment in response to temporary shocks, and to postpone – and thereby ease – adjustment in the case of permanent changes. Postponement could be overdone, but some will nearly always be desirable.

Clearly, then, one determinant of the demand for reserves is the cost of adjusting to external shocks. If this is small, few reserves are necessary, whereas if it is large, more are. For real adjustment, three broad alternatives exist: one can cure a balance of payments deficit by deflation, depreciation or trade controls. For a given deficit, the costs of deflation decline relatively as the marginal propensity to import rises, because more of any expenditure reduction falls directly on imports. The costs of depreciation and trade controls probably increase with openness, because a proportionately greater switch of resources out of non-tradables production is necessary and this involves a greater shift in the terms of trade.

Which of the adjustment mechanisms is dominant – especially for relatively small and short-lived fluctuations – depends mainly on the exchange rate regime in operation. Fixed rates emphasise expenditure reduction, and floating rates expenditure switching via depreciation. We might therefore, expect that, *ceteris paribus*, fixed rates would entail less open economies requiring relatively more reserves, while floating would entail the contrary. In fact the evidence is very mixed, probably because researchers tend to use the average rather than the marginal propensity to import to measure openness, and this could influence reserves through another channel (see p. 298 below). Heller and Khan (1978), for example, found that their negative relationship between reserves and openness became more negative on floating, whereas Frenkel (1978b) found a positive relationship under fixed rates and a negative one under floating!

As well as possibly affecting the relationship between reserve demand and openness, the exchange rate regime has a more direct effect. Under fixed rates the authorities are obliged to intervene in the market to finance temporary disequilibria, and adjustment is discretionary. Under floating rates no obligation exists – indeed intervention may be prohibited – and adjustment is at least partly automatic. Hence reserve demands are likely to fall with the advent of floating. Heller and Khan and Frenkel confirmed this for developed countries since 1973, but not for non-oil developing countries. This is because the latter still pegged to the major currencies, a job made considerably more difficult by the disturbances of the 1970s.

Reserves are also influenced by the speed of adjustment: faster adjustment entails fewer reserves. We know of no empirical work on this question, however, although Clark (1970) has evidence of the equally plausible reverse relationship that countries with higher reserves can (and do) adjust more slowly.

Disturbances

Our discussion of adjustment obviously presupposed the existence of economic shocks requiring finance or adjustment. If some finance is desirable, the amount depends on the size of the shock. Countries facing large and frequent payments shocks require greater reserves than more stable ones.

There are two sorts of shocks to consider. The first are temporary, reversible imbalances, i.e. the variability of net demands for foreign currency. Such random shocks are clear candidates for finance rater than adjustment, and the object must be to hold sufficient reserves to minimise the possibility of running out and having to adjust. Provided that the shocks really are random, the reserves will receive on average as many injections (via surpluses) as withdrawals; but this does not preclude there being a series of consecutive withdrawals. Clearly, the more reserves one has, the lower the probability of such a series exhausting them but, by the same token, the lower the probability of actually having to use the last unit of reserves. Hence the expected benefit of the marginal unit of reserves falls as the reserves grow, so, provided there is a cost to reserve holding, reserves will not be indefinitely high.

Just as obvious is that, if one can tolerate a given probability of reserve exhaustion, the greater the size of these random shocks, the greater the level of reserves required. There are many methods of measuring the variability of the balance of payments, but all confirm the theoretical result. Very roughly, a 10 per cent increase in the standard error of the shocks increases reserve holding by about 5–8 per cent under fixed rates and slightly less under floating rates.

A more contentious sort of shock is the permanent shock – for instance, the loss of an export market. Here adjustment is inevitable and finance can be justified only in terms of reducing costs by allowing a longer adjustment period. Again, the more likely and the larger these shocks, the greater the level of reserves required. It is obviously difficult to gauge the expected exposure to such shocks, but one measure of a country's vulnerability to foreign shocks is its average propensity to import. This argument predicts a positive relationship between reserves and the average propensity and clearly conflicts with the negative relationship predicted by the costs of adjustment argument. In general, the positive effect appears to dominate empirically.

Reserves and trade

An important motive for individual cash holdings is the transactions motive – holding money to spend. Similarly with nations: the greater the volume of international trade, the greater the amount of reserves necessary to finance it. There are, however, economies of scale in cash use and so reserves appear to grow less than proportionately with trade. Estimates vary, but, for every 10 per cent rise in a country's imports, reserve demand probably increases by between 5–8 per cent.

Wealth

Foreign exchange reserves are part of a nation's net wealth. They are unlikely to be inferior assets (in the technical sense) and so we would expect them to rise with wealth. This appears to be so empirically (Hipple, 1974), although the close relationship between wealth and imports makes it difficult to distinguish this and the previous explanation for reserve holdings.

Expectations

In the face of a permanent shock, the decision to phase adjustment over several years represents an inter-temporal decision. Reserves expended this year are not available next year, and by using them now the government is implicitly stating that they are worth more now than later. This clearly involves a judgement about the future – i.e. expectations. These are impossible to measure, but governments expecting large future adverse shocks or increased future variability are likely to hold higher reserves.

Alternatives to reserves

Owned reserves are often referred to as *unconditional liquidity*: there are no constraints at all on their use. A partial alternative is *conditional liquidity*, by which is meant certain borrowing from the IMF and other banks. It is conditional because increased resources are available only in return for promises, and eventually action, to implement an approved programme of recovery. These (often onerous) conditions and the time required for their negotiation clearly differentiate potential borrowing from reserves, but there is probably some degree of substitutability between them. Hence, a world system guaranteeing such borrowing would reduce reserve demand.

It is also possible to borrow from private capital markets. Increasingly over the 1970s, developing countries borrowed on the Euro-markets, and, as we saw in Chapter 16, the UK also visited this fount of beneficence, although mainly through the intermediation of various public non-monetary authorities. Although such finance is usually more expensive and of shorter maturity than official borrowing, at least for relatively small amounts it is unconditional. Sometimes, however, private bankers will not lend until the borrower has borrowed also from the IMF. This reflects not a lack of funds but a wish to impose some conditionality, and also the belief that countries with the 'IMF seal of approval' will not default on their other debts.

One final alternative for 'banker' countries is to issue their own debt. Instead of running down assets, they finance deficits by increasing liabilities; that is, they issue their own currency abroad in return for goods and assets. The USA and the UK have done this extensively in the past – hence the world's large holdings of their currencies. The rest of the world is willing to hold such currency so long as it pays a suitable rate of interest, is not likely to be devalued, and can obviously be converted into other currencies on demand. While this continues, such *liability settlement* is a profitable way of running an economy, since it permits deficits in excess of reserve (asset) levels. The problem arises, however, when there is doubt over the desirability of the currency; then the holders rush to convert it into other currencies and the reserves are instantly under pressure. Hence, issuing debt is an alternative to reserve holding, but, as liabilities rise, reserves must partly follow in order to maintain confidence in that debt.

The cost of reserves

All the previous points concern the benefits of reserve holding. There is also an opportunity cost, however, because wealth held as reserves cannot be invested in real capital or long-term financial assets. Most foreign currency reserves are, in fact, short-term deposits, so the opportunity cost is the difference between long- and short-term rates of return. One should make some allowance for the higher variability of capital values on currency compared with real capital – especially since the latter may be invested at home – and also for the fact that gold earns no interest, but, all told, the opportunity costs of reserve holding are probably rather small.

The optimal reserve holding

Combining all the above arguments would allow us to calculate an optimal level of reserves for any country. It would, of course, be such that the marginal benefit of the last unit of reserves just equalled the marginal cost. No empirical work has successfully identified all the effects mentioned, but fairly typical equations are Heller and Khan's (1978), for the fixed-rate period 1964–72. For industrial countries (excluding the USA – the principal banker),

$$\log R_t = 1.38 + 0.44 \log m_t + 0.68 \log M_t + 0.66 \log \sigma_t \qquad (25.1)$$

and, for developing countries,

$$\log R_t = -1.86 - 0.61 \log m_t + 1.33 \log M_t + 0.33 \log \sigma_t \qquad (25.2)$$

299

where R_t is reserves in quarter t, M_t imports, m_t the average propensity to import and σ_t a measure of variability. The coefficients are all statistically significant at 5 per cent, except for those on m_t in (25.1) and σ_t in (25.2), and they largely accord with the arguments above.

Heller and Khan also estimated the speed with which actual reserves were adjusted towards their optimal level. Developed countries took up about 30 per cent of the discrepancy per year and developing countries about 90 per cent. This probably indicates that poorer countries hold much smaller reserves relative to their shocks than rich countries. Bilson and Frenkel (1979), with very different methodology, found both groups adjusted by about 50 per cent of the discrepancy per year. Both sets of estimates imply rapid adjustment, which suggests that the equations above do represent some kind of desired long-run position.

The arguments so far refer to countries' own assessments of their reserve needs. The interrelationships of the world economy, however, also give countries interests in each other's holdings. For example, a country may have strong views about the appropriate level of reserves for countries owing it money; alternatively, if country A fears country B's deflation, it will wish B to have high reserves to induce a 'more responsible' domestic policy. The net effect of such interests is uncertain, but they illustrate that (a) the optimum level of world reserves is not necessarily just the sum of countries' own individually optimal levels, and (b) the optimum level of world reserves has a cosmopolitan as well as a nationalistic dimension.

25.3   PRIVATE vs. PUBLIC RESERVES

Exactly analogous arguments apply to private holdings of foreign exchange as to official reserves. Precise quantification is impossible, not least because it is so difficult to disentangle the figures for the Euro-dollar market (see Chapter 28), but it is beyond dispute that private balances have expanded rapidly, especially since the demise of the Bretton Woods system in 1971. The following figures probably define the minimum levels of private foreign exchange reserves. The Bank of England (*Quarterly Economic Review*, December 1982, 'Monetary Statistics') estimated that in March 1982 British private sector non-bank foreign currency deposits were £14.3b. (of which £11b. were with UK banks), compared with official reserves of £12b. in foreign currency and £7b. in other assets. Deutsche Bundesbank (*Monthly Review*, November 1982) estimated private balances at DM 14.1b. compared with reserves of DM 76.7b. at end 1981.

Since the incentives to hold cash are largely private, one may ask why official reserves are required at all. There are several explanations, of differing degrees of conviction. First, it is argued that pooling individual balances into a single holding yields economies of scale. This is certainly true, because balances grow less than proportionately with transactions and there will also be some offsetting between one person's surplus and another's deficit. Hence the combined reserves could be substantially smaller than the sum of the individual balances they replaced. However, if the economies of scale are so significant we would expect pooling to occur even in the absence of the monetary authority.

The second explanation of official reserves is as a 'war chest'. This amounts to their being no more than the government's own precautionary cash balance.

Third, reserves are the necessary concomitant of a fixed exchange rate. The government can maintain the exchange rate between narrow bands only if it has a means of buying and selling foreign exchange at the intervention prices. This is possible only if it owns some. Under a perfectly floating rate, intervention would not occur, so this explanation would not suffice. In the present managed float, reserves are required for management, and although they may not be used extensively their existence lends authority to the government's view of the correct exchange rate. Clearly there is no private substitute for this role for the reserves.

The fourth reason concerns power. One of the principal activities (if not functions) of governments is to define and enforce legal tender. This accords the government considerable power, and allows it to earn the seignorage from issuing its own money. If its money were displaced by foreign currency it would lose that income. It is, therefore, in the government's interest to prevent residents from using foreign money internally and this is most easily achieved by preventing them from holding it. Residents are required to deposit their foreign exchange at the central bank in return for domestic currency, and can withdraw it only in order to make transactions abroad. These deposits constitute the foreign exchange reserves.

Many countries have exchange regulations of this kind, and often they are supplemented by restrictions on the purposes and extent to which withdrawals are possible. This is one way of trying to suppress an incipient deficit, and was pursued with increasing vigour in the UK until the mid-1970s. In 1979 exchange control was abolished. This presumably transferred some currency holdings from official to private hands. At the same time, however, by increasing the ease with which money could be shifted out of the country, it increased the size of the possible shocks that could hit the British economy. This increased the government's desire for reserves, thus offsetting the first effect.

25.4   THE COMPOSITION OF RESERVES

Section 25.2 discussed the costs and benefits of holding reserves in total. We now consider the composition of the reserves, and, since we argue that countries choose their portfolios to maximise the benefit from the reserves at least cost, we consider much the same factors as before.

Transactions costs and vehicle currencies

Suppose the only purpose of reserves were to finance the purchase of imports, and that the value and country of origin of all imports were known at the outset of the year. By matching the currencies in its reserves to the pattern of forthcoming transactions a country could (a) avoid the transactions costs of converting one currency to another during the year and (b) avoid any uncertainty about how many imports it could buy. Similarly, suppose the reserves comprised only the receipts from the previous year's exports: they would then comprise the currencies of a country's trading partners. Obviously the real world is more complex than this, but we do nevertheless find a strong relationship between the geographical composition of a country's trade and the currency composition of its reserves.

This argument suggests that countries will hold many currencies in their reserves. In fact, though, there are economies from concentrating on relatively few. First, concentration allows smaller overall holdings: since reserves rise less than proportionately with the trade they finance, covering several countries' trade with the same currency will save reserves. For example, suppose we have 10 units of trade with countries A and B, and that to finance them we need 5 units of each currency in the reserves. If both were financed in A-currency, however, we would need no B-currency, but, from our estimate in section 25.2, doubling the trade denominated in A-currency would raise holdings of it by only 50–80 per cent. Hence, rather than hold 10 units of reserves we could manage with $7\frac{1}{2}$–9 units.

Second, holding currency involves the risk of exchange rate changes. If we hold fewer currencies, there are fewer for which information and forecasts are required. Third, and closely related, the markets for the rarer currencies are rather thin – there are few buyers and sellers. Thus, their prices fluctuate more and any attempt to sell a significant amount could easily produce a price fall. Consequently, holding these rare currencies is riskier than holding others, and transacting in them more expensive. It was for this reason, we argued in Chapter 21, that trade between small economies is frequently conducted in a third or vehicle currency. The arguments about holding currencies reinforce this tendency towards a few world currencies. Furthermore, given the link between currency holding and trade, and given that a currency is in a sense backed by the output of the country where it is legal tender, the vehicle currencies will tend to be those of the major economies. Such factors obviously contribute to the dominance of the dollar and the Deutsche Mark in reserve portfolios.

Financing trade is not the only function of foreign exchange reserves. They are also used to settle deficits, or, equivalently, support the exchange rate. Indeed, given the rough balance between export and import flows with particular trading partners and the fact that most trade is financed privately, one might consider this the principal role for exchange reserves. Hence, the dominant transaction may well be exchange market intervention, and so the reserves will be heavily biased towards the intervention currency. For floating currencies this is not formally specified, but most countries intervene mainly in dollars. Where one currency is pegged to another, however, intervention almost always occurs in the latter. Holding reserves primarily in this currency not only avoids transaction costs but also avoids any uncertainty about the value of the reserves in terms of intervention.

Risk and return

Whatever their function, reserves represent a stock of wealth. We therefore expect that, consistent with fulfilling their purpose, they would be subject to the normal portfolio considerations of risk and return. For any degree of risk, reserve managers would maximise returns, and for any level of returns they would minimise risk. As we saw in section 21.1, the expected return from holding a short-term asset is the rate of interest plus the annual rate of change of capital value. The risks arise almost entirely from the latter – the value of foreign currencies (the exchange rate) cannot be perfectly foreseen. Central banks are probably more constrained in their portfolio management than private speculators, but nevertheless within limits these factors will be relevant.

The first prediction of this view is that, *ceteris paribus*, countries will prefer reserve assets paying higher rates of interest. The second is that very volatile currencies (or those expected to be volatile) will not be popular – another argument against holding 'minor' currencies. Third, currencies whose values are negatively correlated will be chosen together, because the risk of losses on one is offset by the chance of gains on the other. Fourth, and most important, if exchange rate changes are anticipated, central banks as well as private speculators will seek to move out of the currency whose depreciation is expected.

Constraints on reserve composition

If all countries were suddenly to try to liquidate their holdings of dollars, the price of dollars would slump and a huge crisis would emerge as the value of assets was slashed. To avoid this, some constraint on the freedom to swap between reserve assets is required. This is usually exercised by the major countries of the world by means of political agreement. It involves them in some loss of wealth or return, but is deemed to be worthwhile for the sake of preserving the system. Smaller

302

countries, whose asset holdings are relatively small, are not normally party to such agreements. Political arrangements have in the past benefited both the UK and USA by stemming sales of their currencies, and at present operate to limit EMS countries from holding too many reserves of each other's currencies.

The evidence

Evidence on the determinants of the composition of reserves is hard to find because central banks are so coy about revealing their portfolios.

Chrystal (1977) examined total (private and official) holdings of dollars, sterling, Deutsche Marks and francs over the 1960s by looking at the issuing countries' liabilities. He found strong evidence that holdings were influenced by rates of interest, some evidence that expected depreciation reduced holdings, and some evidence that currency holdings were related to the extent of the issuer's international trade.

Heller and Knight (1978) concentrated only on official reserves, looking at seventy-seven countries' reserves over 1973–6. They, too, found a link between currency holdings and trade, but they also found that countries pegging to sterling and the franc held more of those currencies than other countries. The shares of sterling and francs rose by 25 and 74 percentage points respectively.

Using the same data, Ben-Bassat (1980) calculated an optimal basket of reserve currencies for both developed and developing countries. Optimality encompassed the return and risks of the reserve portfolio in terms of their purchasing power over countries' normal baskets of imports. For example, countries importing half from the USA and half from Britain were assumed to seek maximum returns in terms of a composite basket comprising half dollars and half sterling. He found that for developing countries the actual and predicted reserve portfolios matched fairly closely, whereas for developed countries they did not. This suggests that portfolio considerations and international trade patterns do determine reserve composition, but that developed countries have additional objectives and face constraints on the adjustment of their portfolios. Ben-Bassat also showed that, to reduce risk, portfolios should include substantial shares of both dollars and the European currencies since their fluctuations tend to be in opposite directions.

Gold and SDRs

Until relatively recently, gold was the predominant reserve asset. It is still held widely today, despite paying no rate of interest and despite no country being on a gold standard. Its sole attraction is the belief that it is a more secure store of value than paper currencies – that, while paper currencies depend on governments for their value, gold's almost universal acceptance guarantees its value under all circumstances. Gold is demanded particularly at times of general uncertainty – such as political crises – when the whole future of paper money may be questioned, but also as a refuge for funds removed from the dollar when the latter is under pressure. Its security is seen as compensation for its lack of earning power.

Over the 1960s, gold became very attractive relative to sterling and the dollar and it was only strong political pressure to avoid a crisis that prevented the wholesale conversion of currency balances (see section 26.3 below). One consequence of this incipient 'gold rush' was the introduction of a new reserve asset – the Special Drawing Right (SDR). Its value was defined in terms of gold, and guaranteed by the IMF, but by also paying a small rate of interest it was intended to be more attractive than gold. Since then it has been redefined in terms of a basket of five major currencies in both its value and its rate of interest. With its different characteristics from gold and currency, the SDR clearly has some role in diversified reserve portfolios. Indeed, Murphy and von Furstenberg (1981) found some evidence that non-oil LDCs find it a preferable asset to foreign exchange.

303

FURTHER READING

General references on the international monetary system include *Williamson* (1973), *Grubel* (1977), *Crockett* (1976), *McKinnon* (1979) and *Argy* (1981). Detailed accounts of the system in practice are available in International Monetary Fund, *Annual Reports*.

On the specific issues of this chapter, *Grubel* (1977) provides a more detailed introduction, and *Williamson* (1973) an excellent survey of older work. *Hipple* (1974) gives a thorough discussion of modelling the demand for reserves, while *Frenkel* (1978b) and *Heller and Khan* (1978) provide more recent estimates. *Clark* (1970) provides a formal model linking reserves to income, disturbances and the speed of adjustment.

The composition of currency reserves is best discussed in *Heller and Knight* (1978) and *Ben-Bassat* (1980), while *Williamson* (1973) considers the gold/SDR/currency decision.

26 The Supply of International Money: (A) The Past

This chapter starts our analysis of the supply of international money. We take a historical approach, starting with the gold standard of the late nineteenth century, at which time gold was the only source of international money. The gold standard was suspended during the First World War. It was reintroduced in the mid-1920s, but in the changed circumstances it proved inadequate and had collapsed by 1931, giving rise to a period of monetary disorder until 1939.

After the Second World War, the Western world, led by the USA, instituted a gold exchange standard where both gold and foreign exchange were used as world monies. We examine the negotiations over the new system culminating in the Bretton Woods Treaty establishing the International Monetary Fund. We then trace the history of the IMF and the Bretton Woods system until the latter's collapse in 1971. Over its lifetime the gold exchange standard was revealed to have critical shortcomings in both theory and practice; these are examined below. The history and analysis of the period since 1971 are reserved for Chapter 27.

26.1 GOLD AND THE GOLD STANDARD

The oldest form of money – international or domestic – is gold. Its attributes as money are well known: limited supply, durability, portability and, above all, almost universal acceptability. For centuries, gold tokens or coins circulated freely without regard to national boundaries – monarchs stamped the coins of their realms more to indicate purity than to claim jurisdiction. Provided none tried to debase or adulterate his coinage, the only difficulty of accepting another's coins was the inconvenience of different denominations. Gradually coins were supplemented by paper notes that indicated a claim over gold, but provided repayment was guaranteed such notes were 'as good as gold'. At least this was so domestically, because the notes could easily be presented to their issuer, but holding foreign notes was less secure because the costs of presenting them were higher.

Hence, notes were not so mobile internationally, and it became normal to convert from one country's paper to another as one crossed national borders. Such conversion was quite simple, however, since each currency was fixed in terms of gold; with a little more expense one could always change pounds into gold and gold into francs, say, instead of converting pounds directly into francs. Thus the pound–franc exchange rate was determined by the currencies' gold values. In time, gold coinage became less popular but paper monies remained convertible into gold bars and so the principles of the system remained the same.

To illustrate the workings of the gold standard, consider a world economy of two countries operating with the circulation of gold coins but no other money. Starting from perfect equilibrium, suppose country A's aggregate demand rises. If output is fixed, A's absorption exceeds its income and it runs a balance of payments deficit. The excess expenditure is effected by buying goods in B *for gold coin*. Hence A's money supply decreases and B's rises. This could have any of three consequences: A's prices might fall, its income (and hence absorption) might fall, or its interest rate might rise. The first two cure the current account deficit, while the last finances it by an inflow of capital from abroad. Obviously B, whose money supply has risen, experiences the opposite effects.

The story of the previous paragraph is basically Hume's 'Specie Flow Mechanism'.[1] It provides the intellectual basis of the monetary approach to the balance of payments: deficits lead to an outflow of cash and hence automatically correct themselves. It also schematically describes the operation of the gold standard. Provided that countries (i) maintain rigid links between their currencies and gold, (ii) allow gold to flow freely between themselves, and (iii) allow their money supplies to rise and fall with their stocks of gold, the same story applies whether gold or paper circulates domestically and whether or not domestic paper is fully or just partially backed by gold.

Observe in all this how the world supply of money – the stock of gold – is assumed exogenous. Applying the same principles to the world economy as to national economies, if gold supplies rise relative to demands, prices and/or incomes will rise and interest rates fall, whereas if they fall, prices and incomes will tend to fall or interest rates rise. Indeed, to the extent that the money supply affects anything, that thing will be beyond policy control under a gold standard.

Some history

Between 1880 and 1914 the industrialised world operated a gold standard satisfying the three conditions enumerated above. Although output was rather stagnant over the first part of the period (known as the Great Depression, until the 1930s outdid it), the gold standard was judged a success on the basis of this experience. It is not clear, however, that it was really tested. Economic and political conditions were very stable over the period, supplies of monetary gold were expanding, hence avoiding any deflationary strain, and economic management was very conservative. Furthermore, Britain – the centre of the world's financial system at that time – was persistently in current account surplus, so her only policy problem was to tailor her foreign investment to match her surplus. This was done via the interest rate and it obviated the need for more fundamental domestic policy changes. Such behaviour suited Britain and the other industrialised countries well, but it caused some instability in the Empire and other 'peripheral' developing countries, as their sources of short-term finance periodically dried up as Britain cut back.

The second period of gold standard management was quite different. Gold convertibility was suspended during the First World War. The economic devastation prevented its immediate restoration in 1918, but its eventual re-establishment became an object of policy. Unfortunately, it was also held in Britain that it should be restored at pre-war exchange rates, and this involved undoing much of the inflation of the war and post-war boom. The result was vigorous deflation over the early 1920s, with prices and wages falling by up to 50 per cent. Even so, when Churchill restored convertibility in 1925 at the pre-war parity, Britain was still very uncompetitive, and the slump predicted by Keynes (1925) duly occurred. Most other major countries had followed Britain back to gold by 1927, but within five years the whole system had collapsed.

Several reasons have been advanced for this. First, it has been suggested that wages and prices had become less flexible since the war and hence that adjustment laid more burden on incomes. This is not incontrovertible, but doubtless the General Strike of 1925 and its aftermath worsened the political environment for wage flexibility. Second, gold was unevenly distributed: France and the USA had excessive stocks, while the UK had too little. Coupled with the UK's relative economic weakening since 1913, her overvalued exchange rate and the amount of sterling held abroad, there was constant doubt about the ability of Britain to honour her debts in gold. The result was greater speculation than had previously been experienced and persistently tight domestic policies.

306

Third, whereas before 1913 Britain had acted as world banker, essentially running the gold standard via her interest rate policy, by 1926 she no longer had the economic power or the monopoly of financial expertise required to do so. Both New York and Paris challenged London's supremacy, but neither France nor the USA recognised any international role; besides, even if they had, it is not clear that three 'central banks' is a viable alternative to one. In other words, no country was willing or able to police the international monetary system for the common good.

Fourth, economic and political conditions were harsher than before the war. The reparations paid by Germany to her former enemies still distorted current account positions and contaminated the political atmosphere against cooperation. Business cycles were less synchronised and hence greater payments adjustment was necessary. There was a huge financial crisis in 1929–30, which destroyed both wealth and employment. This, in particular, turned countries inwards and heralded a decade of competitive depreciations and protectionism – 'beggar-my-neighbour' policies. The cycles and the slump may, of course, have been caused by the inappropriate restoration of the gold standard – it is impossible to be sure; either way they certainly highlighted the system's shortcomings.

26.2   THE GOLD EXCHANGE STANDARD – THE PLANS

The gold exchange standard had its hey-day from the end of the Second World War to around 1970. Thus it has become closely identified with the *Bretton Woods system*, but in fact the latter is just one (important) practical application of the general principle. We start by briefly examining the principle and then go on to look at the plans and practice of Bretton Woods.

Gold and paper money

Gold may have desirable properties as money, but its overriding disadvantage is its cost. Real resources are expended in mining and refining it, only for it eventually to be locked away underground again in the vaults of central banks. If a cheaper but equally desirable money could be found, these resources could be used productively. This is where paper currencies come in. We have already noted that paper replaced gold in circulation, and we know from domestic banking theory that paper need not be wholly backed by gold to be acceptable. So long as one is sure that if one tried to encash one's own paper it would be honoured, paper is acceptable; and, so long as everyone feels like that, the issuing central bank knows that not all its paper will be presented at once. Hence, it need hold gold only up to some fraction of its paper liabilities.

The gold exchange standard proper exists when central banks around the world are willing to hold some other central bank's paper (debt) instead of gold. Hence, paper not only circulates but enters asset portfolios. Obviously the system is unstable if every central bank issues its own debt, which is held by other central banks who then issue more of their own paper on the strength of it; but such circularity would quickly be recognised and rejected. However, if only one or two central banks with substantial reserves of gold issue paper, then the system may prove workable. Before 1913, some sterling was held in world reserves, backed by the gold and economic strength of the UK. After the First World War, exchange holdings rose at first, but after the instabilities reported above fell substantially. After the Second World War, the role of exchange reserves was recognised and formalised by the Bretton Woods agreement, and the US dollar became the principal asset.

307

Seignorage

If paper money saves resources, who benefits? This depends on the interest rate paid on paper money. In the domestic economy no interest is paid on cash and the whole of the benefit of creating cash accrues to the central bank, which lends it to the government. Assuming it costs virtually nothing to create paper money, the government benefits by £1 of resources for every £1 created. If that £1 were invested, it would earn, say, i per cent per annum, so £i/100 represents the income flow generated by creating £1. If the government had to pay i per cent per annum on its created cash in order to persuade people to hold it, the government would gain nothing and the resources saved by using paper money would accrue entirely to the holders.

In the international monetary system, governments do pay interest on their debts, but, because these debts are short term and highly liquid, it is usually below the long-run rate of return on investment. If the latter is i_L per cent, but the government pays i per cent on its money debts, resources of i per cent accrue to the holders of foreign currencies and $(i_L - i)$ per cent to the issuers. Of course, both i_L and i must be measured as real rates of interest.

Seignorage is the term for the real resources that accrue to the issuers of money. In the case just discussed, this would be the present value of the income flow £$(i_L - i)$/100 per annum for every £1 issued.

Bretton Woods

Over the 1930s the USA maintained her traditional isolationist view of the world, but the Second World War made her realise that if the non-communist world was to be successful and prosperous she would have to play a much more prominent part. Consequently, even as early as 1941 officials in both the UK and the USA were thinking about the shape of the post-war economy. There was general agreement that the flexible exchange rates and beggar-my-neighbour policies of the inter-war period were unacceptable. Beyond that however, Britain, facing huge debts but still having an Empire, sought a liberal financial system offering plenty of credit but was less concerned with free trade. The USA, on the other hand, as the potential provider of credit, favoured a tighter financial system but more open trade and capital movements.

Britain's aspirations were embodied in the 'Keynes Plan'. This suggested the establishment of a world 'clearing union' at which all countries would hold accounts. These accounts would be denominated in a common unit – the 'bancor' – in terms of which exchange rates would be fixed; international imbalances would be settled by shifting bancor from one country's account to another. The extent to which balances could deviate from zero was to be limited, with both surplus and deficit (positive and negative balance) countries being obliged to adjust. Prominent among the methods of adjustment would be exchange rate changes. The limits on the bancor balances defined the extent of international credit, and this would be determined by the union to alleviate business cycles and promote world expansion.

The Keynes Plan was not a gold exchange system. Gold was not necessary and in general countries would not hold dollars or sterling; all reserves would be in terms of the new international paper money – the bancor. The world's money supply would be under international control, and used as a policy instrument. In fact, the system would closely mirror the domestic banking system, with a controllable paper money and a single central bank (the clearing union) at which separate money-issuing commercial banks (the national central banks) would hold deposits.

The actual outcome of the Bretton Woods Conference owed more to the American 'White Plan' than to the Keynes Plan – reflecting the USA's greater power and influence. In terms of international monetary economics the most

308

important institution established was the International Monetary Fund, which opened its doors in 1946 with thirty-five member countries. Each member was accorded a quota that determined its rights, obligations and voting powers. The quotas roughly reflected the members' levels of GNP and international trade, and voting was virtually in proportion to quotas.

Each country subscribed to the Fund reserves equal to its quota, 25 per cent in gold and 75 per cent in its own currency. In return it could borrow foreign currencies from the Fund up to 100 per cent of its quota. The first slice, or *tranche*, of 25 per cent corresponded to the country's gold subscription, and was available automatically. The remaining three tranches of 25 per cent, however, were to be available only on increasingly firm commitments to pursue policies to cure the balance of payments deficit. They also involved increasing service and interest charges. There were certain obligations on surplus countries, but since these were never implemented in practice, the Bretton Woods system placed all the adjustment burden on the borrowing, deficit countries.

The whole of the country's quota cannot be counted in its reserves because it is not available unconditionally (see Chapter 25), but, clearly, the larger the quotas the greater world liquidity. (Note (a) to Table 26.1 defines precisely what is counted as reserves.) The IMF started with modest quotas ($8.8b. compared with Keynes' suggested $25b.); its articles made no recommendation for future growth, although quotas were to be reviewed at least every five years. It was generally expected that gold would provide for increases in world liquidity, and any general increase in quotas required an 80 per cent majority of votes.

The 80 per cent rule applied to virtually all issues at the Fund and it ensured that either the USA or the major European powers acting together could veto any

Table 26.1 The IMF and world liquidity (SDR billions, end of year)

	1946	1960	1965	1970	1975	1980	1981	1984[f]
Total reserves	n.a.	60.0	71.2	93.3	194.4	354.5	376.1	n.a.
of which: IMF reserve positions[a]	n.a.	3.6	5.4	7.7	12.6	16.8	21.3	n.a.
borrowing from IMF[b]	n.a.	0.4	3.0	3.2	7.4	8.5	13.4	n.a.
IMF statistics:								
Quotas[c]	7.5	14.7	16.0	28.4	29.2	59.6	60.7	90.0
SDRs allocations	—	—	—	3.4	9.3	17.4	21.4	n.a.
Other facilities[d]	—	0.4	6.7	5.8	11.5	25.0	34.1	n.a.
Shares of IMF quotas[e] (per cent):								
USA	36.8	28.1	25.8	23.6	22.9	21.2	20.8	19.9
UK	17.4	13.3	12.2	9.9	9.6	7.4	7.2	6.9
France	7.0	5.4	4.9	5.3	5.1	4.8	4.7	5.0
West Germany	—	5.4	4.9	5.6	5.5	5.4	5.3	6.0
Japan	—	3.4	3.1	4.2	4.1	4.2	4.1	4.7
Saudi Arabia	—	0.04	0.05	0.05	0.05	1.7	3.5	3.6

Notes:
[a]That part of IMF quotas and 'regular' borrowing counted as reserves. For any country this comprises its *gold* or *reserve tranche* (the first, unconditional, 25 per cent of its quota) plus total IMF lendings of its currency.
[b]Under all schemes except SDR facilities.
[c]Excluding quota of $1.3b. allocated to the USSR but never taken up.
[d]Total IMF resources under General Arrangement to Borrow, Oil Facility, Supplementary Financing Facility, Stand-by, Extended Arrangements and Medium Term Borrowing.
[e]A country's votes are calculated as 250 plus 1 for each SDR 100,000 of its quota.
[f] As proposed in Eighth General Review of Quotas, 1982.

Sources: 1960–81 – International Monetary Fund, *International Financial Statistics* (1982), Supplement No. 3; 1946 – IMF, *Report of the First Meeting of the Board of Governors;* 1984 – *IMF Survey,* 5 December 1983.

change. This recognised the politics of the international economy, and, although frustrating to other nations, it has at least allowed the establishment and continuance of the institution itself. The Seventh General Review of Quotas in 1977 reduced the USA's share of votes below 20 per cent for the first time, and she agreed to accept the Review only on condition that the majority required for most proposals be raised from 80 per cent to 85 per cent, thus maintaining her veto.

Table 26.1 traces the evolution of quotas, showing, first, the slightness of their contribution to world liquidity and, second, the relative power of the various economies. Through time, the USA and the UK have lost influence, in keeping with their declining relative economic importance, displaced first by other industrial countries and latterly by OPEC countries such as Saudi Arabia. It also shows how various other IMF facilities have grown up in response to specific shortages of funds or adjustment.

The other major obligation of members of the IMF was to maintain their exchange rates within 1 per cent of their declared parity levels by means of intervention. Parities were declared relative to gold, but only the USA traded currency for gold; all other countries traded national currency for dollars. Hence, as the intervention and *de facto* peg currency, the dollar was given a unique and pivotal role. Although exchange rates were not immutably fixed, they were to be changed only in circumstances of '*fundamental disequilibrium*', and even then only after consultation or permission from the IMF. Fundamental disequilibrium was never defined, but it is clear that the Americans envisaged much less exchange rate flexibility than did Keynes.

The IMF also imposed obligations on members to abolish exchange controls on current account transactions (but not on capital transactions), to abolish any discrimination between trading partners, and to consult regularly. Over the years, several of the IMF's provisions have changed (see section 26.3 below), but the consultation has persisted and for this alone the IMF has been significant.

26.3   BRETTON WOODS IN PRACTICE

As we have seen, the Bretton Woods Agreement favoured the more conservative American approach of a credit fund over Keynes' more radical banking solution. We now see how it performed, distinguishing three broad periods of history.

A quiet start, 1947–58

For the first eleven years of its life the IMF contributed little to world economic performance. Initially, its quotas were small and it interpreted conditionality very fiercely. (In fact, at first even gold tranche borrowings were conditional.) It also refused to make loans for reconstruction, which were seen as the province of the International Bank for Reconstruction and Development (IBRD) – the World Bank. As a result there was little borrowing.

This did not reflect a surplus of reserves, however. After the war the European economies were very weak and greatly in debt to the much stronger USA, who ran huge current account surpluses. Indeed, the problem was beyond the IMF and so, in order to stimulate European development, the USA instituted a system of unilateral transfers in 1948 – Marshall Aid. Over four years, nearly $12b. was transferred, plus $2b. in loans. This greatly helped the European economies and allowed the USA huge influence in the evolution of economic institutions in Europe and the world.

After 1950, however, the position changed. The exchange rate realignments in 1949 and the recovery programme stimulated European growth and competitiveness, and with increasing military expenditure abroad the US balance of payments slipped into deficit. This was financed by borrowing: the European nations took ownership of dollar deposits in New York. This was the start of the gold exchange standard, and it suited everybody well at first. The USA had no need to adjust and earned seignorage, spending it abroad in the form of her current deficit; meanwhile the emerging European economies were able to increase their low level of reserves. The dollars were fully backed and so commanded complete confidence: the ratio of US gold to official short-term dollar liabilities was 7.3 in 1949 and 2.1 in 1958. Over most of this period 'the' international monetary problem was generally perceived to be a shortage of liquidity (reserves), although by 1958 it was beginning to shift from being primarily a shortage of any liquidity towards being a shortage of liquidity with which to back the increasing stock of dollar debts.

Emerging problems, 1959–67

The IMF became of age in 1956 when as a result of the Suez débâcle the UK was obliged to seek assistance, followed by France in 1957 and 1958.[2] Also in 1958, negotiations nearly doubled the effective level of quotas, and introduced convertibility for the major currencies. By this time, however, serious problems were beginning to emerge.

Most important was the issue of *confidence*. The US dollar had, in the absence of alternatives, become a major reserve asset abroad, but the USA's persistent and growing deficits were pushing the world to a state where dollar liabilities exceeded gold reserves. (This occurred in 1958 for total short-term liabilities and in 1964 for official short-term liabilities.) This raised questions of whether the fixed price of dollars in terms of gold could be maintained. Provided central banks abroad did not *all* try to cash in their dollars for gold, marginal transactions could be made at the official price, but a run on the dollar would be catastrophic. The European countries and Japan faced an impossible dilemma. Either they accepted poorly backed dollars or they cashed their dollars in, and, by causing a devaluation, brought about the very situation they feared. To quote a popular American saying, 'if a man owes you a thousand dollars, that's bad news for him; if he owes you a million dollars, that's bad news for you'.

The only solution to this was to substitute 'faith' for gold as the backing for the dollars, and accept them merely as paper money whose worth depended entirely on being able to pass them on to someone else. The problem then was how to stop the USA from just creating more dollars by running further deficits and absorbing real resources (the seignorage) in return. If one could not exercise the financial rein, only political agreement remained; that was of only limited effectiveness, however.

A closely related problem concerned *liquidity*. Since dollars were the only way of increasing world reserves, if the rest of the world desired more reserves it had to allow the USA's deficit, pay the seignorage and suffer the confidence problem that that entailed. If, on the other hand, it insisted on the USA curing her deficit, the resulting deflation or devaluation of the dollar would curtail the demand for its own goods and would be compounded by a shortage of international liquidity. Triffin (1960) first identified the horns of this dilemma: the world could cure its liquidity problem at the expense of its confidence problem, or its confidence problem at the expense of its liquidity problem – but not both together.

A further, and possibly more basic, problem was that of *adjustment*. Even for non-banker countries, exchange rate changes in either direction had not proved popular. Appreciation hit the tradables sector while depreciation hit incomes. Hence, balance of payments disequilibria tended to be persistent and foreign considerations dominated domestic policy-making. For example, the West

311

Germans persistently ran surpluses and accumulated reserves (hence withdrawing liquidity from countries that required it), and faced almost constant pressure to inflate domestically to cure the situation. Conversely, the UK showed persistent deficits, reserve crises and domestic deflation.

For the banker country the situation was even more difficult. Few people favoured devaluing the dollar in terms of gold (see below), so there was nothing the USA could do about her exchange rate. Her trading partners, however, were constantly urging deflationary policy at home in order to cure the deficits for the sake of monetary stability abroad. This was resented in the USA, because it entirely subordinated domestic economic management to foreign considerations, when less than 10 per cent of GNP was traded. Besides, the USA argued with some justification, as the owner of the peg currency she was the nth country (see section 25.1). Hence her deficits owed more to her partners' desire to acquire reserves than to her own profligacy; they should adjust, not she.

These problems were highlighted by a series of crises. In 1959–60 the US deficit had risen alarmingly and domestic measures were taken to reduce it. There was also a run on the dollar: as private holders switched into gold its price rose to $40 per ounce – well above the official price of $35. This was met by an agreement between major countries to form the 'Gold Pool', which sold (and could conceivably buy) official gold on the private market to maintain the price at $35.

Meanwhile, West Germany experienced the opposite trouble. With a strong balance of payments position she had accumulated substantial reserves. However, the domestic economy was already overheated so she rejected the possibility of reflation, and indeed pursued moderately deflationary policies over 1960–1. This raised interest rates and led to large inflows of capital, despite several policies designed to discourage or penalise foreign deposits. Eventually, the pressure became too great and to preserve her monetary autonomy Germany revalued the Mark by $4\frac{1}{2}$ per cent in March 1961.

Over this period Britain faced repeated sterling crises. The current account showed persistent weakness and official liabilities far outweighed liquid reserves. In 1964 the election of a Labour government led to an outflow of capital and, despite three years of increasing deflation, sterling had to be devalued in November 1967. During sterling crises, liquid funds migrated to New York and supported the dollar, but in general the USA's difficulties continued, and over 1962–7 increasingly strong measures were taken to reduce the dollar outflow and to maintain confidence in the dollar. These included strong political pressure on creditor nations not to convert dollars into gold – honoured by all major countries but France – and the raising of foreign loans denominated in foreign currency rather than dollars (known as Roosa Bonds, after a US official).

Some solutions

The problems of the international monetary system were a great preoccupation for economists – both official and academic – over this period. Many solutions were proposed and a few palliatives were adopted.

The price of gold was a major consideration. It was argued that raising it substantially (that is devaluing the dollar) would instantaneously cure the confidence and liquidity problems. World liquidity would rise as the gold component became more valuable, and the ratio of US liabilities (in dollars) to its assets (gold) would immediately be restored to a satisfactory level. Furthermore, the higher price would increase the supply of monetary gold in future both from private dishoarding and increased production; hence, it was said, liquidity would never be a problem again. Solving these two problems would also allow time and scope for fundamental adjustment to occur.

The counter-arguments were strong, however. The inefficiency of having to expend resources producing world money was noted. In addition, once confidence had been restored in the dollar it would (temporarily) be a more attractive asset than gold, because, by saving resources, it would be able to pay interest. Hence dollar debts would increase again, until suddenly confidence snapped and the crisis repeated itself. In other words, raising the gold price would not cure the fundamental instability of the gold exchange system. Furthermore, showing the gold price to be flexible would only exacerbate speculation in future, and the uncertainty of periodic jumps in its price would be very disruptive. Politically, it was felt, a price rise would mean the USA reneging on her promises to maintain the price and would also reward some very unpopular countries – South Africa and the USSR (the major producers), and France (the major hoarder), who had continued converting dollars into gold despite that fact that doing so weakened the backing of everybody else's dollars.

A second set of proposals suggested enhancing the IMF into something approaching a world central bank, along the lines of the Keynes Plan. This would involve converting gold and currency reserves into bancor. With the USA no longer responsible for providing liquidity, the monetary consequences of her curing her deficit would be ameliorated (although not the ensuing reduction of demand for other countries' exports). Equally radical – at least at the time – were proposals for flexible exchange rates. Advocates of this course argued that adjustment would become automatic and liquidity and confidence irrelevant since no one would require reserves. As we have now discovered, this was rather too simple a view.

A fourth solution to the liquidity problem was to allow other major currencies a reserve role. This would share the benefits of seignorage and break the world's dependence on the US deficit. However, in such a simple form it would probably create more confidence crises than before, because reserve holders could (and would) switch from one currency to another. To avoid this, some people suggested creating a composite reserve unit as a fixed bundle of major currencies, backed by deposits of those currencies at the IMF. This is similar to the way Special Drawing Rights (SDRs) have turned out, so we postpone discussion of it until the next chapter.

None of the above came about, but a final set of proposals did bear fruit: *extending IMF facilities*. In fact, the IMF had extended its facilities to members over the 1950s in two directions. First, it introduced *stand-by credits* in 1952. These were equivalent to overdraft facilities at the bank: countries negotiated the right to certain credit at the IMF but did not actually receive the money until they drew it. Stand-bys were still subject to conditionality and to the same limits as ordinary drawings, but their attraction was that they could instil confidence in the currency concerned without involving the interest charges of an actual loan. For the IMF, they supported members but used less resources than ordinary loans. Stand-bys have proved popular ever since – not least with Britain who had several over the 1960s and 1970s. By 1981, 475 stand-bys had been negotiated, involving SDR 36b., compared with SDR 56b. of ordinary loans, and at end-1981 existing stand-bys totalled SDR 6.5b., of which SDR 2.8b. had been drawn.

The second extension was the *General Arrangement to Borrow* (GAB), established in 1962. These are arrangements for mutual lending between the ten richest nations of the world – The Group of Ten. The Group decide the conditions and availability of their loans themselves, but the loans are administered by the IMF and any member of the Group who has made such a loan can, if needs be, borrow an equivalent amount from the IMF. The GAB was established with a view to

313

supporting the US dollar, but in fact over 1964–6 Britain was the first and main beneficiary.

In 1963 a further development occurred – the *Compensatory Financing Facility* (CFF) – to allow countries to borrow if their export earnings fell below some 'normal' level through no fault of their own. Designed basically for primary producers, this at first merely defined the circumstances in which members could draw on their credit tranches unconditionally, and was limited to 25 per cent of quotas. By 1966, however, it had been extended to 50 per cent of quotas and was available additionally to normal borrowing. These arrangements were further modified over the 1970s (see Chapter 27). On a similar level was the *Buffer Stock Facility* under which the IMF would lend up to an additional 50 per cent of quota for the establishment of buffer stocks in critical primary export goods. This was introduced in 1969.

The final extension was the most radical – the introduction of *Special Drawing Rights* (SDRs), agreed in 1967 and implemented in 1970. SDRs were an unbacked international paper money. However, they were introduced too late and too cautiously to save the Bretton Woods system. We return to examine them in detail in Chapter 27.

Collapse, 1967–71

The devaluation of sterling in November 1967 heralded the demise of the gold exchange standard. After a huge speculative attack, and despite a slight improvement in the current account, sterling was devalued by 14.3 per cent. This showed the power of capital movements and the fallibility of reserve currencies, and thus encouraged later speculation. Immediately after sterling, the dollar came under pressure. This was partly from European and Japanese governments, frustrated at the growing US deficits (especially military expenditure and long-term capital outflows) and the inflationary pressure they induced abroad, but mainly from private conversions into gold. Between September 1967 and March 1968, Gold Pool sales were $3.5b., of which $2.4b. came from the USA (nearly 20 per cent of her overall reserves). Eventually, therefore, the Gold Pool was abandoned, the private price cut free and agreement reached that official transactions would take place only at the official price of $35 per ounce. This essentially demonetised gold: no government would part with gold at $35 per ounce when the private price exceeded $150.

Next the European countries suffered pressure and hot money movements. France experienced outflows and eventual devaluation as a result of the political crisis of 1968, while Germany again faced domestic overheating and strong surpluses. The latter resulted in huge capital inflows – up to $4b. over three days in May 1969 – and eventually appreciation by 9.5 per cent in October.

During 1969, international capital migrated to the USA in response to tight monetary conditions and high rates of interest, but in 1970, as the US policy stance reversed, it flowed out again. By now the US trade balance had worsened significantly and military expenditure abroad continued unabated, with the result that US reserve liabilities rose by $7.5b. in 1970 and $27.5b. in 1971. As may be seen from Figure 25.1, these debts expanded world reserves massively (9.5 per cent and 30 per cent respectively), building up strong inflationary pressures throughout the international economy. By 1971, US gold reserves had fallen to $11.1b. – just 21 per cent of official liabilities and 16 per cent of total liquid liabilities.

In May 1971, West Germany, who was still facing overheating and huge capital inflows, finally gave up trying to sterilise or prevent the latter and floated the DM. The US deficit showed no sign of improving meanwhile, so on 15 August 1971 a new approach was unveiled: a domestic price freeze was announced, coupled with

314

a 10 per cent import surcharge (tariff), export stimuli and controls on investment outflows. Most important formally, however, was the official suspension of dollar convertibility into gold. The world had had a *de facto* dollar system for several years – certainly since the two-tier gold market started in 1968 and really rather longer, because convertibility had been effectively ruled out since the mid-1960s. Now it was official. Over the next few weeks, as short-term capital rushed around the world, most countries abandoned their parities and floated their currencies.

The new policy was accompanied by US demands that other countries finance more of NATO's military expenditure abroad, liberalise their imports and, above all, revalue their currencies. The US object was to improve her current balance by about $13b. – about 25 per cent of total current credits! That substantial adjustment was necessary was universally agreed, but there was argument about how it should be achieved. The Europeans and Japanese argued that the dollar must be devalued, partly to increase the liquidity value of their gold (they expected to re-monetise gold sometime) and partly as a sign of some political contrition on the USA's part. The USA, on the other hand, wanted everyone else to revalue!

After six months the Smithsonian Agreement was signed in December 1971. This re-established fixed exchange rates, with an 8 per cent dollar devaluation relative to gold and revaluations of most other currencies relative to the dollar. Despite President Nixon's calling it 'the most significant monetary agreement in the history of the world', however, the Smithsonian arrangements had collapsed within fifteen months, leaving the world with the managed floating 'non-system' it has today.

The lessons

The lessons of the period 1950–71 are several.

First, an international monetary system must promote smooth adjustment.

Second, the optimum number of assets in a system is one: any more and there is scope for destabilising switching. The force of this is seen by considering recent domestic monetary history. Over 1973–7 sterling depreciated by 50 per cent in terms of goods, and yet there was no wholesale flight from domestic cash. Quite simply, there was nowhere to flee to. If there were only one international asset, the confidence problem would hardly exist.

Third, a system based on a key currency is viable only if there is the political will to make it work. This can come about by all countries pooling their sovereignty and agreeing to abide by a set of rules that might not always be immediately beneficial nationally. It is more likely, however, to be associated with the political hegemony of the key currency country. In this case, the key country seems some benefit in constraining its behaviour to maintain the system healthily, while the other countries lack the power to 'rock the boat'. Monetary difficulties have correlated perfectly with periods of political strain over the past century (1925–39, 1970–83), during which no single country has been able to unify the 'free world'.

FURTHER READING

For useful textbook treatments of the history of the international monetary system, see the first edition of this book, *Yeager* (1976), *Grubel* (1977, 1981), and *Argy* (1981). On post-war history alone, see also *MacBean and Snowden* (1981). Classic references include *Triffin* (1964) on the gold standard and *Keynes* (1980) on the establishment of the IMF. The latter gives a wealth of insight into both technicalities and politics, leaving strong impressions of Keynes' remarkable foresight and the enduring nature of economic problems. The analytical aspects of the gold exchange standard are covered in *Triffin* (1960), *Johnson* (1967a) and *Williamson* (1973), while *Strange* (1971, especially ch. 1) treats political aspects of international money.

Finally, details of the IMF's role are published in International Monetary Fund's *Annual Reports* and *IMF Survey*, and discussed in many articles in the *IMF Staff Papers* – see the general index, November 1981.

NOTES

1   Hume emphasised equilibration through prices.
2   The Suez crisis was an ill-advised and ill-executed attempt by the UK and France to invade Egypt to prevent the nationalisation of the Suez Canal. It resulted in a run on both currencies and a withdrawal of economic cooperation by the USA.

27 The Supply of International Money: (B) The Present

The 1970s were a turbulent period for international monetary arrangements. The huge injections of liquidity in 1970–2 (see Figure 25.1) and the generally expansionary domestic policies caused unprecedented levels of inflation. This was exacerbated by a quadrupling of the price of oil, which placed great adjustment and financing burdens on all countries. The recycling of OPEC surpluses to the oil-deficit countries further raised liquidity and inflation in general, while different speeds of adjustment led to large divergencies between national inflation rates. Fixed exchange rates could not survive in these conditions so the major currencies floated, and, as we have seen, fluctuated considerably.

Meanwhile, the IMF tried to adapt itself to the new circumstances. Unable to institute a fixed exchange rate system, it established rules for floating currencies and sought to smooth adjustment paths by providing new sources of finance. Most of these were aimed at developing countries, and provided extended credit for restructuring. In 1978–9 the price of oil rose again, plunging the world into another bout of inflation and stagnation, from which, perhaps, it began to emerge in 1983.

This chapter looks at the history of this period – examining particularly the evolution of the institutions of the international monetary system. It starts, however, by examining Special Drawing Rights and concludes by considering the less developed countries' position in the international monetary system.

27.1 SPECIAL DRAWING RIGHTS

Over the 1960s there was considerable debate – especially among the rich countries of the Group of Ten – about the problems of the international monetary system. Increasingly, the European nations objected to the flow of dollars into the world economy, but, as we saw in Chapter 26, the only way that they could force adjustment on the USA without causing themselves a liquidity crisis was by replacing the dollar as the only expanding source of international reserves – that is, by finding a new asset. The USA also had some interest in a new asset for she hoped that it would supplement her gold reserves, thus alleviating the confidence problem. Discussions finally ended in 1967 with a proposal that the IMF should offer additional reserves to its members by means of *Special Drawing Rights* (SDRs).

Paper gold Special Drawing Rights are quite unlike any other asset: they are an internationally created, unbacked, inconvertible paper money. Their value was initially defined as 1/35th of an ounce of gold – equivalent to US$1.00 – but they could not be encashed for gold. After agreeing on the extent of an SDR issue, each country receives SDRs in proportion to its IMF quota. They are unconditional reserves, but were (and are) subject to strict limitations on their usage. Countries receive (pay) interest on the excess (deficit) of their holdings over their SDR quota, but originally the interest rate was only $1\frac{1}{2}$ per cent per annum. SDRs can be created within the IMF's SDR accounts once every five years starting from 1967. They are then distributed to members over the following five years when they have been 'activated' by decision of the IMF. This decision must take account of (a) the need for additional reserves, (b) the improvement of balance of payments dis-equilibrium since 1967 (the world refused merely to finance US deficits indefinitely), and (c) the likelihood of extra SDRs aiding the adjustment process.

SDRs were invented as a substitute for gold rather than for dollars – hence the gold valuation and the low rate of interest. Their seignorage accrues mainly to the *users*. The IMF gives SDRs away and so gets nothing; neither does the country holding just its quota. The main gainers are countries that run down their SDR reserves in return for real goods and assets, because they can earn, say, i_L per cent per annum with these but pay only $1\frac{1}{2}$ per cent on their spending. SDR issues increment members' reserves but, unless explicit action is taken, not their internal money supply. This differs from 'earned' reserve increments, where the internal money supply rises in line with reserves unless policy action is taken. The quantity of SDRs is entirely within the control of the international community.

The issue of a new money is a risky business: one cannot tell whethèr it will be too popular, and hence drop out of circulation into national hoards (reserves), or unpopular, and hence circulate very fast as holders vie with each other to get rid of it. It was this uncertainty that led to the restrictions on SDR use. SDRs could be used only for transactions between official bodies, and then only for balance of payments settlement or in the light of a country's overall reserve policy; they were not available for shifting the composition of reserves between assets. Further-more, each member was committed to hold an average of 30–300 per cent of its SDR issue over any quarter. When a country wished to use SDRs within the confines of these rules, it could ask the IMF to 'designate' a country that would swap SDRs for foreign currency. Designation was made with a view to the designatee's balance of payments, reserves and SDR holdings.

Between 1968 and 1969 the IMF studied the case for activation. The ratio of reserves to both imports and trade imbalances had been falling steadily over the 1950s and 1960s, and although these are not ideal indicators of reserve need – see Chapter 25 – this does suggest some tightening of liquidity. In addition, by this time the US deficit had contracted, both suggesting better adjustment and reducing reserve growth. Finally, there was evidence of increasing resort to restrictions on international transactions and requests for international financial support. Hence it was concluded that some increase in liquidity was required.

Deciding the amount of SDRs to issue was complex, however; while overall reserve demand might be estimable, the increase in the supply of other assets was not. The final decision was that reserve need would expand by $4–5b. per annum, while other reserves would grow at $1–1.5b. per annum – $0.5b. in gold and Fund reserve positions and the remainder in US dollars. It was therefore decided to issue $3.5b. in 1970 and $3b. in each of 1971 and 1972 (the last year that SDRs created in 1967 could be issued). In the event, the predictions proved woefully wrong and the SDR issue just contributed to a glut of world liquidity: world reserves increased by $14.5b. (18.4 per cent) in 1970, $30.0b. (32.2 per cent) in 1971 and $23.6b. (19.2 per cent) in 1972. In the second quinquennium starting in 1972, therefore, no SDRs were created. In retrospect, it is clear that controlling just one source of reserves is useless if the requirement is to control liquidity.

Paper money? After 1971 there was little about international money that was systematic; exchange rates fluctuated violently and the gold market remained split, with the official price still a small fraction of the private price. It became increasingly anachronistic to value the SDR in terms of gold. In July 1974, therefore, the SDR was redefined to transform it more into a currency substitute than a gold substitute. Its value was fixed by a basket of the currencies of the sixteen countries

318

with more than 1 per cent of world trade over 1968–72. The weights of this basket, which reflected each country's financial and commercial importance, are given in Table 27.1. The rate of interest was also raised – to 60 per cent of the average of the rates on the five major currencies. This increased SDR's attractiveness as an asset, but still left net holders subsidising net users.

Table 27.1 The value of the SDR

Date of basket currency	July 1974		June 1978		January 1981	
	Units	% weight	Units	% weight	Units	% weight
US dollar[a]	0.40	33	0.40	33	0.54	42
Deutsche Mark[a]	0.38	$12\frac{1}{2}$	0.32	$12\frac{1}{2}$	0.46	19
Pound sterling[a]	0.045	9	0.050	$7\frac{1}{2}$	0.071	13
French franc[a]	0.44	$7\frac{1}{2}$	0.42	$7\frac{1}{2}$	0.74	13
Japanese yen[a]	26.00	$7\frac{1}{2}$	21.00	$7\frac{1}{2}$	34.00	13
Canadian dollar	0.071	6	0.070	5	—	—
Italian lira	47.00	6	52.00	5	—	—
Dutch guilder	0.14	$4\frac{1}{2}$	0.14	5	—	—
Belgian franc	1.60	$3\frac{1}{2}$	1.60	4	—	—
Swedish krona	0.13	$2\frac{2}{3}$	0.11	2	—	—
Australian dollar	0.012	$1\frac{1}{2}$	0.17	$1\frac{1}{2}$	—	—
Danish krone	0.11	$1\frac{1}{2}$	—	—	—	—
Norwegian krone	0.099	$1\frac{1}{2}$	0.10	$1\frac{1}{2}$	—	—
Spanish peseta	1.10	$1\frac{1}{2}$	0.15	$1\frac{1}{2}$	—	—
Austrian schilling	0.22	1	0.28	$1\frac{1}{2}$	—	—
South African rand	0.0082	1	—	—	—	—
Saudi Arabian riyal	—	—	0.13	3	—	—
Iranian rial	—	—	1.70	2	—	—

Note:
[a]The SDR interest rate is some fraction of the weighted average of short-term rates on these currencies in their issuing countries. The weights are proportional to the weights of the basket.
Sources: International Monetary Fund *Annual Reports*; Bank of England, *Quarterly Economic Review*, September 1974 and June 1979.

The next stage in the SDR's development came with the Jamaica Agreement of 1976. This endorsed the Second Amendment to the IMF Articles, which became operational in March 1978. It legitimised the SDR as a peg for countries to define their exchange rates by, and reduced the restrictions on its use. In particular, the minimum holding was reduced from 30 per cent to 15 per cent of quota, the interest rate was raised to 80 per cent of the average in the big five currencies, and permission was given for authorities to use SDRs for any transactions among themselves without IMF designation. These moves considerably enhanced the 'moneyness' of SDRs; they were supplemented by a redefinition of the basket in June 1978 based on trade statistics over 1972–6. SDRs took over many of the roles gold had played in transactions with the Fund – e.g. in depositing the first 25 per cent of the IMF quota and as a unit of account – and members reaffirmed their intention that the SDR should become the world's principal reserve asset. Finally, in each of 1979, 1980 and 1981 SDR 4b. were issued.

Development continued in 1981 with the abolition of the minimum holding, the extension of the list of official institutions accepting SDRs and a rise in the rate of interest to 100 per cent of the average in the big five currencies. The valuation calculation was also simplified to cover just the five major currencies (see Table 27.1), with provision made for reconsideration of the basket every five years. In 1983, discussions commenced on whether to create more SDRs during the fourth quinquennium, which had started in 1982.

The future of the SDR

Gold has finally dropped out of the international monetary scene, and the SDR is now firmly established as a money substitute. For official institutions it serves as a store of value, a unit of account and a medium of transaction. Unfortunately, however, it is not unique, or even predominant, in these roles, and there are reasons for believing that in its present form it never will be. That is, unless changes are made, we shall continue to live in a world of multiple reserve assets, with all its destabilising portfolio shifts and lack of control of international liquidity.

The interest rate on SDRs is now a market rate, so on that score it rivals and could displace currencies. Its value, too, is fixed as the average of several currencies, but this in fact is a mixed blessing. The SDR's value fluctuates with each of its five component currencies, although obviously only in proportion to that currency's weight in the basket. Consequently, its value is more stable in terms of goods than that of the most variable currency in the basket, but necessarily less stable than that of the least variable one. Hence, at any one time there will always be at least one more stable haven for funds than SDRs; if this one currency changes through time (e.g. sterling one year, dollars the next), the SDR may be acceptable on average, but there is a danger of destabilisation as reserve holders seek the currency that is expected to rise faster over the near future. If, on the other hand, one currency is persistently more stable than the SDR, it will displace the SDR as a store of wealth. The only ways around these problems are either to raise the SDR rate of interest above the market rate or to enact some self-denying ordinance by which authorities do not hold significant quantities of currency.

One could not ban all currency holding, however, because the SDR is not a universal money – in particular it is not used privately. (Some private transactions are now denominated in SDRs, but all settlement has to be effected in a national currency.) This highlights a further difficulty with SDRs – they usually have to be exchanged into currency before use, and this entails a cost. Furthermore, this cost is avoidable if, instead of holding SDRs, monetary authorities hold reserves of dollars, marks, francs, yen and sterling in just the proportions of the SDR basket. This portfolio would have just the same value and rate of interest as SDRs but would be freely and instantaneously usable in private markets. The obvious solution to this is to allow SDRs to be used in private settlements. In that case, however, since one could not prevent private transactors from also holding currency, there would be scope for private speculation against SDR–currency parities.

These problems are serious. Until the political will exists to make the SDR the true centre of the system, further developments are unlikely. Such will involves sacrificing the short-term national benefits of being able to switch assets in the reserve portfolio to the long-term cosmopolitan aim of a universal stable world money.

27.2   INTERNATIONAL MONEY SINCE 1972

The Committee of Twenty

The most lasting feature of the Smithsonian Agreement was the Committee of Twenty (C20) – the group set up to advise on the repair or replacement of the

Bretton Woods system. It comprised representatives of the Group of Ten plus ten from the rest of the world. The less developed countries (LDCs) were better represented than ever before in monetary discussions, largely at the instigation of the USA, who was anxious to dilute the wrath of Europe and Japan.

There was general agreement in C20 that liberal world trading and financial arrangements were desirable; that excessive capital movements were undesirable; that world liquidity should be controllable and controlled; and that excessive exchange rate movements (especially competitive ones) were to be avoided. Beyond that, however, there were differences. The USA advocated a system very like the Keynes Plan of 1944: symmetrical adjustment by deficit and surplus countries; exchange rate flexibility and restricted convertibility of dollars for gold. She was reluctant, however, to see the dollar displaced as a reserve asset, and opposed any moves towards compulsory asset settlement – that is, financing her deficit by selling reserve assets rather than by issuing dollar liabilities.

Europe and Japan, on the other hand, had a much more conservative approach. They favoured less exchange rate flexibility and stressed the role of 'responsible' internal policy as a means of producing adjustment. They were anxious to impose asset settlement on the USA (after all, everybody else already had it) and to dethrone the dollar as principal reserve asset. For this they suggested a 'substitution account' whereby the IMF converted dollar liabilities into SDRs and the USA gradually bought the dollars back from the IMF with SDRs earned from a balance of payments surplus. By 1974, however, the 'dollar overhang' of outstanding short-term liabilities exceeded one year's total current credits, so such repayments would have required a huge rise in US competitiveness over Europe and Japan. Besides, as we saw above, the SDR was most unlikely to have been an effective substitute for the dollar anyway. All told, it was probably a good thing that the substitution account was never born.

The third group – the LDCs – supported fixed exchange rates (although, some commentators think, mistakenly), freedom over reserve composition, and an 'aid link' for SDRs (see p. 328 below).

While C20 worked towards a redesigned par value system, the world went the other way. In mid-1972, sterling and the French franc floated and by early 1973 all the major currencies had floated. With simultaneous upswings in most major countries, inflation rates grew alarmingly and their dispersion across countries increased, making fixed exchange rates quite infeasible. C20 reported in June 1974 with only minor repercussions on the world system. They recommended their own continuation as part of the IMF system – known as the Interim Committee – which is important for the politics of the IMF; they redefined the SDR (see p. 318 above); and they produced some rules for floating exchange rates. These were designed to prevent changes contrary to the requirements of orderly adjustment, and to encourage the smoothing of day-to-day fluctuations.

The oil price shock

C20's reform plans were entirely swamped by the consequences of the rise in the price of oil. Between late 1973 and late 1974 the dollar price of crude oil quadrupled. We have discussed the real consequences of that already, but we now briefly consider its financial implications. Suddenly the OPEC oil producers found themselves with huge liquid resources – way beyond their spending capacity – while OECD and the non-oil LDCs faced huge current account deficits requiring both short-term finance and medium-term adjustment. The extent of the current account and terms of trade changes are reported in Table 27.2

The industrial countries' net payments for oil (oil payments less exports to OPEC) increased by about $55b. in 1974 (Organization for Economic Co-operation

321

Table 27.2 Current accounts, terms of trade and world prices, 1973–82

	1973	1974	1975	1976	1977	1978	1979	1980	1981	1982
Current account balances:										*$US billions*
Industrial countries	20.3	−10.8	19.8	0.5	−2.2	32.7	−5.5	−40.2	−0.3	−3.6
Seven larger countries	14.8	−2.7	24.9	10.1	10.4	36.2	6.9	−13.6	15.4	10.5
Other industrial countries	5.5	−8.1	−5.1	−9.6	−12.6	−3.5	−12.4	−26.6	−15.7	−14.1
Developing countries										
Oil-exporting countries	6.7	68.3	35.4	40.3	30.2	2.2	68.6	114.3	65.0	−2.2
Non-oil developing countries	−11.3	−37.0	−46.3	−32.6	−28.9	−41.3	−61.0	−89.0	−107.7	−86.8
Total[a]	15.7	20.5	8.9	8.2	−0.9	−6.4	2.1	−14.9	−43.0	−92.6
Terms of trade:								*Percentage change since previous year*		
Industrial countries	−1.8	−10.6	2.5	−1.0	−1.1	2.7	−2.4	−7.4	−0.8	2.5
Developing countries										
Oil-exporting countries	13.3	140.0	−5.1	5.8	0.8	−10.4	29.1	41.5	11.1	−1.3
Non-oil developing countries	5.3	−5.9	−8.5	5.9	5.9	−3.7	−0.3	−6.2	−3.9	−2.7
World trade prices (in US dollar terms) for major commodity groups:										
Manufactures	17.7	21.8	12.3	1.0	9.0	14.7	15.3	10.5	−5.1	−2.0
Oil	40.0	225.8	5.1	6.3	9.3	0.1	48.7	62.0	10.1	−4.6
Non-oil primary commodities (market prices)	53.2	28.0	−18.2	13.3	20.7	−4.7	16.5	9.7	−14.8	−12.1

Note:
[a]Reflects errors, omissions and asymmetries in reported balance of payments statistics on current account, plus balance of listed groups with other countries (mainly the USSR and other non-IMF countries of Eastern Europe and, for years prior to 1977, China).
Source: International Monetary Fund, *Annual Report* (1983).

and Development, *Economic Outlook*, December 1978), but their combined current account worsened by only $32b. in 1974 and not at all in 1975 relative to 1973. Much of their adjustment fell on imports, which shifted the burden of the OPEC surpluses onto the non-oil LDCs, whose combined current account deficits exceeded that of 1973 by $20–35b. in each of the succeeding five years. This partly reflected rising oil payments but mainly falling exports and primary export prices, caused by the sharp recession that the oil crisis induced in OECD. The LDCs' response to this was partly real adjustment (output growth fell somewhat) but mainly to borrow extensively.

Borrowing was not difficult in 1974, because OPEC's profits were kept largely in liquid form in the international banking centres and the Euro-currency markets. For example, of its $55b. financial surplus in 1974,[1] OPEC deposited $23b. on the Euro-markets, $15b. in US and UK short-term assets, and $4b. with the IMF and World Bank (Argy, 1981). These funds were *recycled* to the LDCs partly through increased official bilateral loans and aid from OECD and OPEC, and mostly through increased commercial loans – mainly from the Euro-markets – and export credit. The Euro-markets were also important for certain OECD countries. For example, the UK raised $5.7b., France $3.2b., and Italy $2.2b. in 1974. Japan, on the other hand, borrowed extensively in US domestic markets.

The contribution of official financial institutions to the alleviation of the oil crisis was modest but significant. The IMF's existing facilities were extensively used and two new facilities were developed. First, the *Extended Fund Facility* offered LDCs assistance to cure longer-run balance of payments problems. It involved both longer and larger loans than existing facilities (up to 140 per cent of quota over three years) and, although still conditional, it represented a step towards development or reconstruction finance. The second – the *Oil Facility* – was explicitly short term: for two years from May 1974 countries could borrow to finance balance of payments difficulties due to the oil price rise. This was additional to other facilities and there was no further conditionality. The loans lasted for three–seven years. To finance these loans the IMF borrowed from surplus countries – mainly OPEC – but, of course, it was able to do so more cheaply that the LDC clients to which it re-lent the money, because it was itself underwriting the loans. As an addition to this scheme, certain rich donors agreed to subsidise the loans to the very poorest borrowers.

Figure 27.1 shows the use that was made of IMF facilities over 1972–81. Part (A) reports the drawings in each year – showing the sharp rise in the use of Fund credit and the roles of the Extended Facility (which is included under 'ordinary') and the Oil Facility. Over its short life-time the latter transferred about SDR 7b. from seventeen lenders to fifty-five borrowers.

The Second Amendment

The oil crisis dominated the international scene for several years. With countries seeking to adjust at different rates, the dispersion of inflation rates grew and there was no prospect of restoring a fixed-rate system. Besides, with widespread and deep recession, attention was focused primarily on providing stimulus and liquidity. The Interim Committee continued C20's deliberations and presented its proposals at a summit meeting in Jamaica in early 1976; these were adopted as the Second Amendment to the IMF Articles, to become operative in March 1978. Broadly speaking, the amendment legitimised floating, officially demonetised gold, increased Fund resources, and redesigned the SDR.

The Second Amendment allows currencies either to float or to peg to any numeraire except gold. Members are obliged to foster exchange stability by appropriate domestic policies, and to this end are subject to Fund *surveillance* and must consult the Fund over exchange rate policies. Surveillance requires members to provide the IMF with information to ensure that exchange rate policy meets three basic rules: (a) manipulation must not prevent effective adjustment or be directed at gaining competitive advantages; (b) intervention is required to counteract disorderly market fluctuations; and (c) policies must take account of other members' interests. The IMF may institute discussions if a member appears to be in contravention of these rules, although in the end it has no sanction until the member seeks assistance.

The Second Amendment abolished the official price of *gold*. This completed the unfreezing of countries' gold reserves, which had begun in 1973 with permission to sell gold on the private market and continued in 1974 by allowing gold to be valued at private prices when it was used as collateral for official loans. More important, however, were the elimination of members' obligations to use gold in certain Fund transactions, and the decision to sell one-third of the IMF's gold. One-sixth was sold to members in proportion to their quotas at the old official price, while the other sixth was sold on the free market and the proceeds distributed to member LDCs. This latter was one of the LDCs' *quid pro quos* for agreeing the rest of the package (given the 80 per cent rule, LDCs as a group had a blocking vote over the amendment).

323

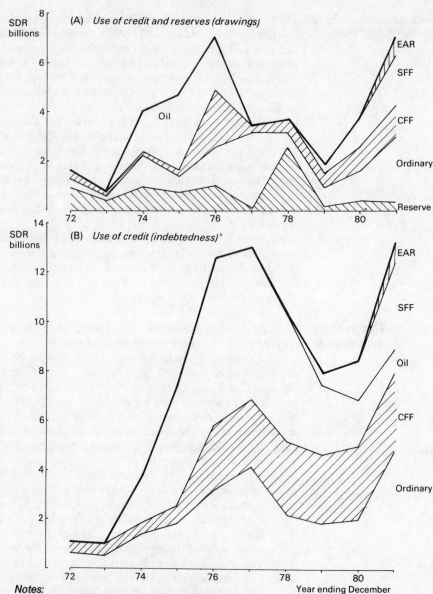

Notes:
^a Excludes Buffer Stock Facility. Other facilities are:
EAR   Enlarged Access Resources (on both Credit Tranche and Extended Facility).
SFF   Supplementary Financing Facility (on both Credit Tranche and Extended Facility).
Oil   Oil Facility.
CFF   Compensatory Financing Facility.
Ordinary   Credit Tranche and Extended Facility from ordinary (non-borrowed) resources.
Reserve   Reserve Tranche Drawings.
^b At year end. Reserve Tranche Drawings are excluded, because they represent the recovery of a deposit rather than a credit facility.
Source: International Monetary Fund, *International Financial Statistics* (1982), Supplement No. 3.

Figure 27.1   *The use of IMF facilities, 1972–81. (A) Use of credit and reserves (drawings). (B) Use of credit (indebtedness).*

The Jamaica Agreement was accompanied by the Sixth General Review of Quotas. Rises of about 35 per cent were agreed, but until these could be formally ratified (in 1978) the IMF agreed to raise all its borrowing limits correspondingly. The Compensatory Financing Facility was also liberalised. Both concessions were actively used (see Figure 27.1(A)), making an immediate contribution to world liquidity, and when the new quotas were ratified in 1978 there was a further surge in Reserve Tranche (unconditional) borrowing.

Despite this activity, however, IMF resources had still contracted as a proportion of total liquidity since the 1950s and 1960s (see Table 26.1). The LDCs and deficit countries perceived this as a weakness, arguing that recovery from the post-oil slump could be thwarted by tight credit conditions, but a number of commentators viewed inflation as the major problem and advocated contractionary domestic policies and a reduction of world liquidity (e.g. Halm, 1977).

1977–83

By 1977 OPEC and OECD had largely re-established current account equilibrium. OPEC's surplus had been whittled away by strong increases in imports, a falling real price of oil and a fall in demand as non-OPEC sources of oil expanded and (minor) conservation measures occurred. The world economy began to expand and apart from rather large exchange rate fluctuations things seemed fairly healthy.

In 1978, however, revolution occurred in Iran, oil supplies fell and between 1978 and 1980 the price of oil rose by a further 150 per cent. This raised exactly the same problems as the previous oil crisis, but this time the LDCs were already substantially in debt, and domestic policy in several OECD countries was less expansionary. The resulting recession was less deep but longer lived than 1974–5, with lower inflation but higher real and nominal interest rates. This last feature hit the LDCs particularly hard and their combined current account deficits worsened by $20b. in each of 1979, 1980 and 1981. The deficit of $107b. in 1981 represented about 30 per cent of their total exports of goods and services and about 170 per cent of their foreign exchange reserves. By 1982, borrowing had become substantially more difficult as creditors worried about countries' ability to repay, and so adjustment was forced on these countries. Their annual deficit fell to about $90b., while OECD had regained overall surplus.

The response of the international community was also much as before, emphasising finance rather than adjustment. The existing facilities of the IMF were heavily drawn upon and further facilities introduced. A *Supplementary Financing Facility* was introduced in 1979. It was available only under Stand-by and Extended Arrangements, and like the Oil Facility was financed by borrowing from OECD and OPEC surplus countries. The IMF would lend up to 140 per cent of quota (conditionally), but the total facility was limited to SDR 7.6b., all of which was committed by March 1981. It was replaced by an *Enlarged Access* provision on similar terms, which offered borrowed and ordinary facilities up to 450 per cent of quota over three years. The *Compensatory Financing Facility* was also extended to cover rising import prices on cereals and expanded to 125 per cent of quota. Excluding Compensatory, Buffer Stock and Oil Finance, access is, however, generally limited to 600 per cent of quota. Finally, SDR issues were continued: the fourth quinquennium saw activation of SDR 4b. in each of 1979, 1980 and 1981.

The extension of IMF liquidity is still continuing. In January 1983, the Interim Committee proposed a general increase in quotas of 50 per cent, which was effected by the end of that year. It also proposed a significant extension in the General Agreement to Borrow – more than doubling its limit to SDR 17b., and allowing all members (rather than just the Group of Ten) to draw from it. In this respect it has become like the Supplementary Financing and Enlarged Access facilities. Negotiations on the fifth SDR issue opened early in 1984. Most member states of the IMF advocated a positive issue, but a blocking minority (notably the USA) frustrated this. Talks are currently in abeyance (and therefore no issue is possible), but the matter was to be re-opened at the IMF Annual Meeting in September 1984.

The menu of IMF facilities in 1983 is summarised in Figure 27.2. To maximise access to Fund credit, a nation should be a cereal-importing, primary-producing deficit country, trying to establish an export buffer stock, undertaking long-term structural adjustment, and willing to cooperate with the Fund over policies to improve its balance of payments. Among the largest borrowers at the end of 1981 were: Korea (435 per cent of quota), Turkey (400 per cent) and Jamaica (380 per cent).

27.3   THE INTERNATIONAL MONETARY SYSTEM AND THE LESS DEVELOPED COUNTRIES

Different objectives   In most respects the LDCs' requirements of an international monetary system are similar to those of the developed countries: both wish smooth adjustment,

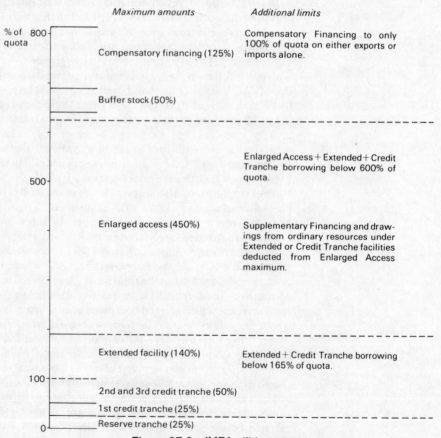

Figure 27.2   *IMF facilities, 1983*

326

adequate economic activity and overall stability. However, within these broad objectives emphases differ. Like any poor person the LDCs tend to hold relatively little by way of liquid reserves: any spare cash is quickly spent on the myriad pressing economic problems they face. Hence, in general LDCs place less weight on money as a store of value than the rich. Conversely, of course, starting from a lower base, the LDCs place a much greater emphasis on income growth.

The LDCs feel a greater need for adjustment finance than the developed countries, because holding relatively low reserves means that exogenous shocks impinge more readily on their domestic economies. If finance is not available, LDCs are more frequently obliged to pursue domestic adjustment even in the face of clearly temporary deficits. Besides, since they are more heavily specialised in primary goods, whose production and prices are less stable than those of manufactures, the LDCs suffer more shocks anyway. They also seek official adjustment finance more than developed countries because they frequently do not have satisfactory access to private capital markets. This may be because of a lack of means to pay commercial rates of interest or because private markets, rightly or wrongly, suspect their creditworthiness.

The result of these different emphases is that LDCs are persistently more expansionary in their international monetary aspirations than their richer partners, and typically keener to see surplus countries obliged to bear some of the adjustment burden.

International transfers

The major difference of opinion between the developed and developing world, however, is one of substance not emphasis. The LDCs hold that the international monetary system should be used to transfer resources from rich nations to poor. The reply from 'the North' – the developed world – is that, although redistribution might be desirable, it would be wrong to confuse it with the logically separate issue of monetary control. For example, in Britain both controlling the money supply and providing social security payments are aims of policy, but the two are kept administratively separate. To establish their case the LDCs have to show either that transfers through the monetary system would be more efficient, or that monetary affairs frustrate other transfers.

The main instrument of transfer at present is international aid flows. These take the form of grants or concessionary loans and may be either bilateral (i.e. between two specific countries) or intermediated by one of the international agencies. The latter receive or raise money in the rich countries and distribute it to the poor. Generally, aid is granted for specific developmental purposes, but emergency food aid and large amounts of bilateral military aid also occur. In 1980, total receipts of aid by all LDCs were $21.7b. (World Bank, *World Development Report*, 1981). This compared with direct investment inflows of $8.6b., private long-term loans of $36.9b. and official (non-concessional) long-term loans of $8.1b. Hence, aid amounted to 29 per cent of the long-term capital inflow. OECD countries contributed $26.6b. in aid and official loans (0.37 per cent of their GDP) and OPEC a further $7.0b. (1.36 per cent of GDP). It is difficult to get comparable figures, but short-term (non-concessional) loans to LDCs probably amounted to $25b. in 1980 (International Monetary Fund, *Annual Report*, 1982), so aid comprised 22 per cent of total inflows.

The main multilateral aid agency is the World Bank, which raises capital on world markets for lending to LDCs. Its loans are mostly for project investment (only 10 per cent may be devoted to the less precisely specified programme development), which must satisfy the Bank's criteria for commercial viability and social need. Interest rates are generally below market rates because the Bank is a

327

less risky borrower than an individual LDC, but the grant element is not great. The Bank established the International Development Association (IDA) in 1962 to make 'soft loans'. These are financed from donations by the rich countries and, while not having looser criteria than ordinary Bank loans, are aimed at the poorest countries, which cannot afford regular interest rates. In 1982 the Bank lent $10.3b. and the IDA $2.7b. (World Bank, *Annual Report*, 1982).

International aid has grown rather slowly since 1980, and will probably continue to do so: witness, for example, the USA's reduction of her grant to IDA from 1984. None the less, aid is still a significant source of resources for developing countries. Private borrowing has, however, taken over as the primary source of long- and medium-term finance. This is not strictly part of the international monetary system, however, and we now turn to the LDCs' relations with the international monetary system proper.

The LDCs and the IMF

With IMF votes proportional to quotas and quotas proportional to economic size, the IMF is quite clearly controlled by the rich countries of 'the North'. It has not ignored the LDCs, however; most of its borrowers are LDCs and it has gradually introduced measures to meet their requirements. Nevertheless, the LDCs feel that it has been less beneficent than it might have been, criticising it on two major issues: the size and distribution of resources and conditionality.

LDCs have persistently called for greater Fund resources. They have also argued that rather than expand every country's borrowing rights roughly proportionately, as has tended to happen, new resources should be concentrated on those most in need – the poor deficit countries. At first the LDCs protested in vain, but in 1973 the success of OPEC encouraged LDCs to act in concert and this considerably increased their political effectiveness. The LDCs were well represented on the Committee of Twenty – nine out of twenty places – and held a blocking minority of votes on the IMF Board. Thus they could effectively frustrate any plans the North might form, so their agreement was necessary for the Second Amendment.

The issue the LDCs fought most vigorously was the *SDR–aid link*. This suggested that SDRs should be issued solely to LDCs, which, by spending them, would rapidly put them into general circulation. Provided the rate of interest was below commercial rates (as applied to the LDCs) this would grant the LDCs seignorage – a form of painless (and invisible?) aid. The North objected on many grounds: not confusing money creation and aid; that 'the link' would encourage the over-creation of SDRs and hence inflation; that it would freeze the interest rate below market rates; and that if aid were given via SDRs it would just be withdrawn from other channels. Also, one suspects, a mere unwillingness to give away resources was present. In the event the link was squashed.

In compensation, however, the LDCs were granted several other concessions. Resources – especially the special funds – were expanded and the proceeds of the gold sales were distributed to the LDCs. Special arrangements are also now being made for countries with small quotas.

Conditionality

The need for conditionality of some sort is rarely questioned. The IMF exists to provide short-term circulating balance of payments finance; it therefore needs to ensure that repayments will be made on time so that resources are always available for new borrowers. Compensatory, Buffer Stock and First Credit Tranche finance are available on uncontentious 'low conditionality': borrowers are requested to take reasonable steps to balance their payments. Upper Credit Tranches, Extended and Enlarged facilities, on the other hand, require agreement with the IMF over macro-economic performance. These are enshrined in a 'letter of intent', and credit, which is always paid in instalments, is available only if the conditions are met. It is these conditions that are contentious.

Bird (1982b) identified eight areas of complaint and reply over conditionality:

- The IMF is hard-line and doctrinaire, considering only monetary solutions and ignoring structural elements of LDCs' balance of payments problems. This is denied, the Fund claiming to be pragmatic and pointing to the Extended Facility as evidence of its concern for structural adjustment.
- The IMF emphasises short-term balance of payments correction at the expense of longer-run development. This is justified by the Fund, arguing that its Articles oblige it to act only for short-term finance; nevertheless, lending periods have recently been extended.
- The IMF assumes that payments difficulties always arise from internal mismanagement rather than from external shock. The Fund, however, claims that the causes of a disequilibrium are of secondary importance; if it is permanent, balance of payments adjustment must occur and this usually involves domestic policy regardless of cause.
- The IMF is inflexible in its choice of performance criteria. This is denied, mainly on the grounds that the few broad criteria chosen cover very many different specific indicators.
- Conditions far exceed those necessary to guarantee the repayment of the small amounts of IMF lending. This is explained by (a) the fact that application to the Fund is often postponed until a crisis has arisen, and hence urgent action is actually necessary; and (b) Fund conditions are often necessary to attract the additional private finance needed for adjustment.
- The Fund frequently ignores domestic political and institutional constraints. This is denied – the 1979 Guidelines on Conditionality expressly enjoin the Fund to take these into account.
- The Fund is biased: it favours the rich – especially banker – countries and, among the others, free market economies. This is countered by pointing to the Fund's successful relationship with certain socialist states.
- Conditionality achieves little success. Balance of payments positions may be improved, but inflation, economic growth and income inequalities are often worsened. This is denied: the Fund argues that most of the shortfall between the conditions and the actual outcome is due to external shocks and/or a lack of political commitment to cure the problems.

Bird then analysed ten IMF recovery programmes in each of the periods 1964–9, 1970–3 and 1974–9. His principal conclusions were:

- The IMF must encourage and coordinate private finance. Its own resources are inadequate to the LDCs' needs.
- The IMF does emphasise credit control – nineteen out of twenty arrangements since 1970 involved credit ceilings. However, different parts of credit are specified for different countries to control, allowing considerable tailoring of conditionality to individual countries' circumstances.
- The IMF is not doctrinally committed to the monetary theory of the balance of payments. Many of its conditions – e.g. devaluation – are contrary to the prescriptions of these theories.
- The IMF does not insist unduly on devaluation. Only about one-quarter to one-third of all arrangements involve devaluation. Trade liberalisation figures about as frequently.
- The IMF does tend to emphasise demand over supply considerations, but given its short time-horizon an alternative approach is not obvious.

329

- The IMF is not even-handed in its treatment of borrowers; it is subject to political influences, especially via the nationally appointed Executive Directors. However, it is not overtly anti-socialist.
- The IMF has had mixed success with its programmes.

Donovan (1982), a Fund staff member, however, claimed considerable success when looking at a wider range of programmes than Bird; in particular, he said, IMF programmes improve the balance of payments and usually cut inflation, but not at the expense of significant falls in consumption or GDP growth.

To conclude, there is clearly some room for LDC dissatisfaction with the IMF. It is not, however, nearly as clear-cut as some critics claim. Given the IMF's role as a world monetary institution rather than a development agency, it would be unrealistic to expect it to funnel large amounts of low-condition finance to the LDCs. Moreover, the LDCs do not always capitalise on their moral case for increased transfers. Too frequently, resources are devoted to expensive military or prestige programmes rather than to unglamorous but basic economic development, and donors frequently express concern about the honesty and efficiency with which LDCs' domestic policies are administered. While these views often amount to the pot calling the kettle black, there is no doubt that they contribute to a reluctance by the North to transfer resources to the South, be it through aid or by redesigning the IMF.

Debt and the LDCs

Finally in this section we consider a current and most pressing problem – the debt burden on LDCs. Over the 1970s, the LDCs were forced to borrow heavily from the OECD and OPEC countries to finance their rising oil bills and falling export receipts. Most of this was intermediated through private banks and involved either short maturities or variable rates of interest. After 1979, most major Western countries pursued anti-inflationary policies, which caused real rates of interest to rise viciously, and many LDCs found it quite impossible to finance their debts. By 1982, average LDC interest payments on long-term debt accounted for $8\frac{1}{2}$ per cent of exports, and total servicing (interest plus capital repayments) for $22\frac{1}{2}$ per cent (International Monetary Fund, *World Economic Outlook*, 1982). Including short-term debt considerably raises these figures, and, of course, the burden is not evenly spread: current estimates put Latin America's debt service to exports ratio at 125 per cent in 1982 and 117 per cent in 1983 (*Financial Times* survey, 14 March 1983).

The uneven incidence of debt also has serious implications for lenders. The banks were keen to lend to LDC – especially the more advanced resource-rich Latin American countries – and did so with little concern for the risks involved. Consequently, debts have become very concentrated: in early 1983 about 40 per cent of bank lending to LDCs was to Argentina, Brazil and Mexico, and these countries' total debts amounted to around $40b., $80b., and $80b. respectively! With persisting high interest rates and low primary export prices (especially in Mexico's case, with a sharply falling oil price in 1983), there was no prospect of the short-term loans being repaid on time. This has caused the banks severe liquidity problems (they have to repay their depositors), and since the suspect debts often exceed the bank's capital assets there has even been thought of bank failures. Furthermore, since the banks lend extensively to each other, one failure could have very far-reaching consequences.

This raises difficult policy issues. If the LDC debts are taken over by international agencies, or covered by creations of IMF liquidity, the banks get away with their careless lending scot-free. They have earned handsome interest on them and society bears the cost of non-repayment via either reduced lending elsewhere or world inflation; but at least a banking crisis is avoided. Alternatively, if the authorities do not step in, the banks suffer the consequences of their profligacy but so too does everyone else, because either there is a major collapse, or the banks just cut back on lending for a long period. The situation is made more complex morally by a suspicion that the banks were relying on society bailing them out if they got into trouble, and hence consciously emphasised return over risk.[2]

Overall, we would favour some sort of socialisation of the debts, because the consequences of a crash would be horrendous; and, although private banks probably over-lent, they were at least partly compensating for the deficiencies of a world monetary system that created too little liquidity over the 1970s. On the other hand, the banks should be required to pay considerably for the extent to which they have brought these problems on themselves, not least to discourage a repeat performance. (The Federal Reserve Board's rescue of the Continental Bank of Illinois in mid-1984 resulted in the removal of the top management and considerable losses to shareholders, while preserving all deposits intact. In our judgement this was a nearly optimal outcome, certainly better than permitting a crash.)

So far these problems have not been resolved. The IMF has been active in negotiating emergency finance, the rescheduling of debt repayments and severe recovery programmes. One innovation has been that it has refused to enter a rescue until the private banks involved have agreed to continue their lending over the adjustment period and to reschedule their debts. This penalises the banks, which would like to cut and run, and also spreads the IMF's limited resources more widely. Indeed, demands on the IMF are so great that there is concern that it will run dry even with the increased quotas available in 1984. The packages being constructed by the IMF involve fierce adjustment over tight time-schedules and entail considerable deflation in the affected economies.

By the end of 1983, Mexico had rescheduled her debts, considerably reined in her economy, and achieved some measure of stability. Brazil also signed an agreement with the IMF in 1983 but, finding its conditions too onerous, repudiated it and lost all but the first tranche of borrowing it provided. This led to a frantic series of re-negotiations, domestic political friction and brinkmanship, culminating with a renewal of the agreement on slightly weaker terms. It is not yet clear whether this can actually be made to stick: some commentators argued that it would involve a cut in Brazilian GDP of up to 13 per cent in 1984. Meanwhile, Argentina's newly elected civilian government has insisted that its debts must be rescheduled (or worse), the Philippines has been revealed to be unable to honour her debts, and some thirty other countries have sought arrangements with their creditors.

The question of LDC debt is of the highest importance. However it is resolved, we can anticipate either a major crisis through a crash, or a long period of austerity as the banks slowly rebuild their positions. We see again how the absence of a single powerful central monetary institution, like the Bank of England in domestic monetary affairs, has allowed the international monetary system to slip into chaos.

FURTHER READING

For general discussions of recent monetary history, see the references to Chapter 26. *Williamson* (1977) gives a thorough and interesting account of the negotiations over the early 1970s, and the reasons for their failure, while *Bernstein et al.* (1976), *Kafka* (1976), and *Halm* (1977) explore the Jamaica Agreement. In fact, the *Princeton Essays in International Finance*, of which these are three, provide a useful and timely commentary on international financial matters in general.

On the SDR, *Chrystal* (1978) is stimulating (but slightly dated), and *Byrne* (1982) and *Coats* (1982) informative. Various issues of the International Monetary Fund's *Annual Reports* and the *Bank of England Quarterly Economic Review* provides details of the evolution of the SDR. The former also describe fully the various IMF facilities, but a useful summary is International Monetary Fund, *International Financial Statistics, Supplement (No. 3) on Fund Accounts* (1982).

The special position of the LDCs in world monetary affairs is examined by *Bird* (1982a,b). *Nowzad* (1981) considers the IMF's general position, while *Donovan* (1981, 1982) examines the success of IMF recovery programmes. *Hayter* (1971) and *Payer* (1974) provide radical critiques of the IMF with respect to the LDCs. The issue of LDC debt is considered in *House of Commons* (1983), and its attendent evidence.

NOTES

1   The financial surplus is the current account less export credits granted on oil.
2   This argument figured prominently in the USA during the (nearly successful) campaign to block the extension of IMF quotas. Additional quotas, it was said, would just rescue the banks from their own irresponsibility. Subsequently, however, the Federal Reserve Bank had to rescue the Continental Bank of Illinois, and in the process implicitly promised to underwrite all commercial bank deposits. It is hoped (in August 1984) that this salutary experience may lead the USA to adopt a rather more accommodating line on international liquidity.

28 The Euro-Currency Markets

We examined the causes and consequences of international capital mobility in Part II. We now turn to one important institutional aspect of the means by which capital moves – the Euro-currency markets. This chapter defines Euro-currencies and describes the mechanism by which they are created. It then considers the quantitative significance of the markets and the causes of their rapid growth since 1960. It considers whether they have had profound effects on the world liquidity and, finally, whether they should be subject to control.

On any measure the Euro-markets have grown prodigiously over the last twenty years. This has been partly due to a series of 'happy accidents' and partly due to the improvements they introduced in the efficiency of borrowing and lending money. The rate of improvement has now probably declined, however, and we would anticipate slower growth in future. Certainly there is unlikely to be much internally generated credit expansion.

28.1 THE STRUCTURE OF THE EURO-MARKETS

A definition
The original Euro-currency was the *Euro-dollar*, which was a deposit (loan) of US dollars made at (by) a European bank. Since then, the definition has broadened to cover any deposit or loan made by a bank in a currency other than that of its country of residence. Most major currencies now have Euro-markets and significant markets exist in, for example, Singapore, Hong Kong, Rio de Janeiro and New York, as well as in European centres. Euro-banking should not be confused with multinational banking *per se*, which is merely banks owned in one country operating like local banks in another. While many actual banks fall into both categories, the two are logically distinct.

Recently a Euro-bond market has also developed. This is similar to the Euro-currency market except that it deals in longer-term paper. It is now possible for large companies and official bodies to issue bonds in any of a number of currencies and in any of a number of centres. However, our discussion considers Euro-bonds only to the extent that Euro-banks subscribe to them.

Some features of Euro-banking
Euro-banks accept deposits and make loans in a variety of currencies independently of their physical location. There are no formal restrictions on entry into Euro-banking, so many banks are involved and the market is highly competitive. Most major banks are involved to some extent. Transactions take the form of large sums ($1m. and upwards) lent or borrowed for fixed periods of time. This 'wholesale' nature makes for great efficiency because the fixed costs of a transaction are spread over a large quantity of funds. The fixed time-periods mean that Euro-deposits are not primarily used for transactions balances, although obviously their existence allows such balances in domestic banks to be kept to a minimum. The geographical spread of the market is very wide. Over 1975–80, three-quarters of the business involved one non-European partner. As we saw in section 27.2, the Euro-market is important in global intermediation – especially recycling OPEC surpluses to deficit countries. On the other hand, for European and American residents the Euro-market provides an alternative to the domestic

banks for large transactions. In this way its existence handicaps monetary policy, which depends primarily on government control of the domestic banking system.

Apart from the banks themselves, the principal agents in the Euro-markets are multinationals and the central banks of the less developed countries. Both have extensive balances to be managed and the Euro-markets allow these to be invested at relatively high rates of interest, while still maintaining considerable liquidity and flexibility over their currencies of denomination.

An important feature of the Euro-system is the prevalence of inter-bank lending. About 70 per cent of gross transactions occur *between* banks. This provides an efficient 'invisible hand' to shift money from net lenders to net borrowers. The bank receiving a deposit does not itself have to know of a potential borrower, it merely re-lends to one that does. In fact, the typical Euro-loan has passed through several banks since it was originally deposited in the system. This phenomenon makes measuring the Euro-market very difficult, for one cannot just add all banks' balance sheets. It also means that, if banks can arbitrage between domestic and Euro-business, Euro interest rates are primarily determined by banks' behaviour rather than directly by the supply and demand for money by non-banks in the Euro-market. Finally, extensive inter-bank lending implies that difficulties for one Euro-bank could rapidly spread through the system and entail difficulties for many.

At the start of the era of floating exchange rates, several banks took open positions in currencies and a number suffered for it. In 1974, Lloyds Bank announced exchange losses of £33m. and Franklin National Bank, New York's largest commercial bank, also reported large losses. Most significant, however, the West German bank Herstatt went into liquidation owing over DM 2b. in deposits. This had several results. First, money flooded back from the Euro-markets to the domestic banks – although only temporarily. Second, Euro-banks were much more discriminating about potential bank borrowers, charging smaller and less well-known banks substantial premia. Third, considerable concern was expressed over the security of the Euro-market. Facing virtually no regulations, Euro-banks held few reserves and little capital and thus were vulnerable to default. Furthermore, since no overseeing body was responsible for the market, no lender of last resort was obvious. The Bank for International Settlements – a sort of central banks' bank situated in Basle – coordinated rescue-lending by national central banks in 1974, and drew up a rather weak agreement about future responsibilities.

Finally, these bad experiences made banks much more cautious, and as a result they typically keep virtually closed positions in all currencies. That is, their assets and liabilities in each currency virtually match. This matching does not extend into maturities, however. Banks make money by borrowing short and lending long, since long-term interest rates generally exceed short. Table 28.1 shows the assets and liabilities of the London Euro-banks. It illustrates several points. First, London is a net borrower from non-banks and a net lender to the rest of the banking world. This largely reflects the UK's current surplus over 1981/2; it was not always the case. Second, Euro-banks are heavily concentrated in the short maturities. Third, while maturities with other banks are fairly well matched (the excess of long loans over deposits is proportionately great but quantitatively unimportant), considerable maturity transformation occurs with non-bank organisations. This suggests that the inter-bank market is merely a circulation of deposits looking for lending opportunities, whereas non-bank loans represent the *raison d'être* of the market.

334

Table 28.1 The assets and liabilities of London-based Euro-banks
(US$ billions)

Maturity	Total Liabilities	Total Assets	Inter-bank Liabilities	Inter-bank Assets	Non-bank Liabilities	Non-bank Assets
	\multicolumn{6}{c}{Position at 18 August 1982}					
< 8 days	122.4	94.3	89.1	79.7	33.3	14.6
8 days ≤ < 1 month	112.5	93.9	74.5	79.5	38.0	14.4
1 month ≤ < 3 months	177.4	146.2	120.3	128.0	57.1	18.2
3 months ≤ < 6 months	128.8	107.8	90.5	95.0	38.3	12.7
6 months ≤ < 1 year	35.8	36.2	25.7	27.1	10.1	9.1
1 year ≤ < 3 years	15.8	36.5	8.5	16.8	7.2	19.6
3 years ≤	11.7	78.3	4.9	21.4	6.8	56.9
Total	604.4	593.2	413.5	447.5	190.9	145.5

Note: Figures may not sum because of rounding.
Source: Bank of England, *Quarterly Economic Review* (December 1982).

28.2   THE GROWTH OF THE EURO-CURRENCY MARKETS

Several different estimates exist of the size of the Euro-currency markets. The most popular is the Bank for International Settlement's *net* concept. This considers only banks physically situated in Europe, but nets out their inter-bank transactions. Since 1970 this has tended to understate expansion, however, because the non-European markets, especially those of the Far East, have tended to grow faster. Table 28.2 reports, therefore, both the BIS measure and a broader measure that allows for these other markets but cannot net out inter-bank transactions. Both measures, however, show clearly that the Euro-markets have grown prodigiously since the early 1960s, and it is to this that we now turn.

In asking why the Euro-currency markets have grown we are essentially asking (a) why non-Americans wish to hold dollars and not their own local currencies, and (b) why holders of dollars wish to deposit them outside America. Analogous

Table 28.2   The growth of the Euro-currency markets ($US billions)

Year	Net narrow[a]	Gross broad[b]	World imports	Year	Net narrow[a]	Gross broad[b]	World imports
1964	9	20	163	1973	132	315	540
1965	12	24	177	1974	177	396	790
1966	15	29	195	1975	205	483	819
1967	18	36	205	1976	247	595	928
1968	25	50	228	1977	300	740	1,067
1969	44	85	259	1978	375	949	1,238
1970	57	115	298	1979	475	1,233	1,560
1971	71	150	334	1980	575	1,524	1,923
1972	92	208	391				

Notes:
[a]European Reporting Area: Group of Ten plus Switzerland until 1977; plus Austria, Denmark and Ireland since 1978. Net of inter-bank lending *within* reporting area.
[b]Liabilities of banks in major European countries, the Bahamas, Cayman Islands, Netherlands Antilles, Panama, Canada, Japan, Hong Kong and Singapore.
Sources: col. 1 – Bank for International Settlements, *Annual Reports*;
col. 2 – supplied privately by the Morgan Guaranty Trust Company;
col. 3 – International Monetary Fund, *International Financial Statistics* (1982), Supplement No. 4.

questions may be posed about borrowers, although in general it has been pressure from lenders that has stimulated growth. The simple answer is, of course, that the Euro-markets offer a better combination of risk and return than local markets. But why? We should distinguish two classes of causes: natural economic advantages, and policy-induced and political factors.

Politics and policy

The origin of the Euro-dollar market is usually attributed to politics. During the early 1960s the Russians sold substantial amounts of gold for dollars. For reasons of ideological purity and fearing the possible confiscation of their assets, however, they wished to keep them outside the USA. Hence they deposited dollars in Europe – especially with the London banks. The banks found they could readily re-lend these dollars to the European and Japanese economies where rapid growth and tight money combined to produce credit shortages. In general, the dollars were converted to local currency and invested domestically.

Growth was further stimulated by a piece of American legislation. During the late 1960s Regulation Q restricted the rate of interest US banks could pay on deposits. The British banks could easily out-bid this and so funds flowed into London. The resulting American credit shortage forced borrowers to Europe also, and this reverse flow rapidly became institutionalised as US banks established London branches to funnel funds back to New York.

A final political stimulus was the OPEC surpluses of 1974. OPEC too feared possible confiscation, but its surpluses were so huge that any means of recycling them to deficit countries would have been used. The Euro-markets, in fact, proved very efficient in this respect (see the following sub-section) and so underwent very considerable growth as OPEC prospered.

Related to these explanations is that of 'potential policy'. Many countries have established exchange controls at some time or another; these affect the terms on which money may be deposited in the country with respect to interest payments or the repatriation of capital. The attraction of the Euro-markets is that, say, sterling deposited in Paris is beyond the reach of the British authorities, while the French authorities have little interest in trying to control it since it has no implications for their currency. Hence Euro-markets allow depositors and borrowers to avoid one source of risk – namely, the possibility of restrictive action by the government in whose currency they are dealing.

Economic advantages

These special factors undoubtedly stimulated the growth of the Euro-currency market, but, having been born, a number of sound economic reasons can be adduced as to why it has continued to thrive. These explain why it can handle funds more cheaply than domestic banking systems. 'Cheapness' involves lower dealing margins; that is, a lower spread between lending and borrowing rates of interest. Euro-deposit rates almost invariably lie above those of their corresponding domestic markets, whereas Euro-borrowing rates lie below.

The first economic consideration concerns *key currencies*. We have argued above that there are economies in both transactions and information costs if just a few currencies are used for international commerce. Coupled to this, companies benefit from dealing with *local banks*. A Belgian firm, for instance, is likely to wish to hold dollars in Belgium, and thus a Euro-market is born. In fact this argument suggests that Euro-markets would exist even if they had larger spreads than domestic markets. Nevertheless, the fact that they have smaller spreads is probably of some significance.

The second advantage the Euro-markets have is that of being free of the restrictive practices of domestic banking. It is difficult to avoid the conclusion that

336

domestic banking systems are *oligopolistic*: there are generally few major banks, entry to the market is restricted (usually by legislation) and prices (rates of interest) are uniform across banks, although substantial non-price competition occurs. Hence, domestic margins tend to exceed the minimum required to survive, and there is room for a competitive institution – the Euro-market – to undercut local systems. This is especially so if it can bid away a section of business that is particularly cheap to service. In domestic banking, most customers pay an average charge, so that 'cheap' customers subsidise 'expensive' ones. By concentrating on large transactions, the Euro-market can service large 'cheap' customers at *their* marginal cost.

Allied to the lack of competition is the plethora of *controls* that domestic banks face. They are often obliged by the authorities to undertake particular types of business (e.g. rescuing ailing companies or financing exports) that are not in their immediate commercial interest, and they are subject to rigid restrictions on their balance sheets. To ensure the security and stability of the banking system, domestic banks in Britain are obliged to hold some minimum proportion of their deposits in non-interest-bearing central bank reserve assets (see Griffiths, 1981). This cuts the proportion they can lend commercially and hence raises their prices (spreads). The Euro-banks are generally free from these restrictions and so can undercut local banks.

The reason that competition from off-shore banks suddenly blew up in the early 1960s is probably the huge improvements in communications technology. The Euro-markets are not physical institutions; rather they comprise separate bodies linked by telex and computer. Hence communication is a necessary condition for their existence.

A fourth advantage of the Euro-markets has already been mentioned. By restricting themselves to *wholesale transactions* the Euro-banks avoid providing expensive retail services (counter services, savings accounts, etc.), and are able to spread the fixed costs of transactions over large sums of money. Frequently, loans are too large for a single bank to cover alone, so consortia are formed. One bank conducts all the negotiations, receiving a fee, but the loan is then subscribed by several banks at the arranged rate of interest. The attraction to the banks of this procedure is that it allows a large loan to be issued without it dominating the balance sheet of any particular bank. As we saw above, a diversified portfolio is less risky than a concentrated one because it is highly unlikely that all borrowers will default at once. Hence, consortia reconcile large loans with risk spreading.

A final advantage for the Euro-system concerns *information*, as was noted by Niehans and Hewson (1976). Suppose a US bank has surplus funds and a Japanese bank has a potential borrower. If these two are to be matched without any mediation, the US bank has to know the Japanese bank and trust it enough to accept its assurances about its own and its client's creditworthiness. On a national level, if every US bank had to 'know' every Japanese bank the information requirement would be overwhelming. Now, however, introduce mediation by the Euro-banks. The Japanese Euro-banks know their local colleagues, as do US banks, but the Japanese and US Euro-banks also 'know' each other, if not directly then through a chain of other Euro-banks. Through this chain each bank need deal only with banks it knows, yet final borrowers and lenders quite unknown to each other can be put into contact. The system works because at each stage the Euro-bank borrows in its own name – thus guaranteeing its creditor repayment whether or not the ultimate borrower pays up. Hence, trust need never extend over more than one link of the chain.

Thus the Euro-market is an intermediary making money by economising on information. Each bank needs only relatively few contacts inside and outside the Euro-system, but through their mutual links the Euro-banks are able to connect final borrowers to final lenders. The mutual links are the inter-bank transactions, which are thus seen to be an essential part of the system. Notice that, in this role, no maturity transformation need occur at all. The whole string of loans would probably be liquidated at the same time.

28.3   THE CREATION OF LIQUIDITY

The ability of the Euro-markets to create international liquidity has been fiercely debated. There are basically two schools of thought: first, those who believe the Euro-system is analogous to the domestic banking system and that it could therefore create significant amounts of liquidity, and, second, those who believe it is merely an example of non-bank financial intermediation, with the power to raise the velocity of circulation modestly but little else. The former view generates a multiplier analysis of the market, while the latter produces a portfolio general equilibrium approach. Our own preference is for the latter.

A multiplier analysis This approach to Euro-markets is based on the analogy with a domestic banking system, so we start by briefly rehearsing a simple version of that analysis. Commercial banks are obliged to hold a proportion, r, of their deposits as reserves of non-interest-bearing cash. The remainder they lend out to the non-bank sector at positive rates of interest. Suppose we start from equilibrium, with total bank deposits (D) and reserves (R), where

$$R = rD. \tag{28.1}$$

Now suppose some additional cash (A) is deposited in the banking system (say via a balance of payments surplus). The banks keep rA of this as backing for A, but re-lend the remaining $(1-r)A$. The people who borrow this will spend it (assume at home) and the recipients will place most of what they receive back in their bank accounts in the commercial banking system: say they re-deposit proportion d, then $d(1-r)A$ will flow back to the banks. But this just provides more cash to the banks, so they keep r of it ($rd(1-r)A$ in all) and lend out the remaining $d(1-r)^2 A$ of which $d^2(1-r)^2 A$ returns, and so on. The total increase in money supply (M) from this process is the sum of all the increments to deposits: namely,

$$\Delta M = A + d(1-r)A + d^2(1-r)^2 A + \ldots = \frac{1}{1 - d(1-r)}A. \tag{28.2}[1]$$

Hence the domestic money multiplier relating the increase in money supply to the initial impact is $1/[1 - d(1-r)]$. Clearly it is higher, the higher is d and the lower is r.

Now let us reinterpret this model in terms of Euro-currencies – specifically Euro-dollars. The reserves of the Euro-currency system are dollar deposits in New York; the analogue of the deposits above (the money supply) is Euro-deposits. The Euro-banks receive a deposit of A and lend out $\$(1-r)A$, keeping $\$rA$ back in reserves. Of the $\$(1-r)A$, $\$d(1-r)A$ is re-deposited in the Euro-system, and the story is just as before. The effect of the Euro-markets on world liquidity, therefore, seems to depend crucially on the reserve ratio (r) and the re-deposit ratio (d). We have already seen that Euro-bank reserves are very small: r is certainly below 0.05 and probably around only 0.01. Taken alone, the low r and the huge potential reserves (the whole of the domestic bank deposits in the US) would suggest an almost unlimited ability to create liquidity.

Now, however, consider the re-deposit ratio (d). Generally this is fairly low, because the Euro-loan is probably for transactions purposes (i.e. to spend) and Euro-markets are not designed primarily for holding that kind of balance. Hence the borrower is likely to keep the Euro-loan in a transactions account in some domestic banking system, as is the recipient of the money when it is spent. If this transaction account is in dollars in New York, nearly all the original dollar deposit (A) is passed from the Euro-market back to the US commercial system and no further Euro-creation occurs.

The alternative place to keep transaction balances is in local currency at non-US domestic banks. This involves swapping the dollars for local currency, which will normally entail their either returning to the USA (as above) or entering some country's official reserves. Since these, too, are generally held in American domestic banks, further Euro-dollar creation is stopped in this case too. If, however, central banks were to re-deposit their reserves on the Euro-markets, then d could rise substantially and multiple credit-creation could occur. This danger was recognised in the early 1970s when the Group of Ten agreed not to re-deposit, but it is still fairly significant today among LDCs. In 1981, 30 per cent of official foreign exchange reserves were in Euro-currencies (International Monetary Fund, *Annual Report*, 1982).

The *average* propensity to deposit on the Euro-markets is under 0.05 because Euro-deposits account for less than 5 per cent of world money supply (Johnston, 1983, p. 51). The *marginal* propensity is certainly higher, not least because much of the world money supply is not internationally mobile (because of exchange restrictions), so Euro-currencies account for a higher proportion of what is circulating freely in the international economy. Nevertheless, it is unlikely that d exceeds 0.20. Coupled with a minimum value of r of 0.01, the maximum multiplier is probably only 1.25.

Before leaving this analysis we should note that even with a relatively low multiplier the Euro-system could significantly raise the world money supply. The reserves for the Euro-system are deposits in the domestic banking systems of the Euro-currencies. Hence huge amounts are potentially available. Moreover, since the domestic deposits backing, say, Euro-dollars never leave the US banking system, the US money supply is not reduced by a shift into Euro-deposits, so any multiple Euro-creation represents a net gain in the world money supply.[2]

Portfolio analysis

The multiplier analysis just outlined depends on two crucial assumptions: (a) that whenever banks receive additional cash they wish to lend out as much as possible of it, and (b) that they can actually find borrowers at the ruling rate of interest. The latter is somewhat dubious even in a domestic system. The former, however, is ensured at home by the existence of legal reserve requirements in excess of those the banks would naturally choose, and the fact that reserves earn very low or even zero rates of interest. In the Euro-dollar market neither of these conditions holds: reserves are held at commercial short-term rates, and banks are entirely free to choose their own portfolios. Hence, at any set of ruling interest rates we must assume that the Euro-banks are content with their mix of reserves and commercial loans. Similarly, because there is no government 'advice' about whom banks may lend to, as there often tends to be at home, we might presume that all potential borrowers at the ruling rate of interest are actually satisfied. In other words, in the absence of any restrictions, the Euro-market is in competitive equilibrium, with the interest rate just balancing the supply of and demand for Euro-loans.

339

Let us represent the Euro-market in Figure 28.1. Ignoring the banks' spread between borrowing and lending rates, DD represents the (non-bank) demand for Euro-loans, while SS represents the (non-bank) supply of deposits to the Euro-market. Equilibrium is initially at (q_0, i_0), but suppose it is disturbed by a shift in the supply of deposits. Imagine this just represents a change in preferences such that, at any rate of interest, $q_0 q_2$, extra deposits are offered to the Euro-banks. The net result, of course, is a fall in the rate of interest and a net expansion of Euro-business by $q_0 q_1$; the 'multiplier' is $q_0 q_1 / q_0 q_2$, which is necessarily below unity.

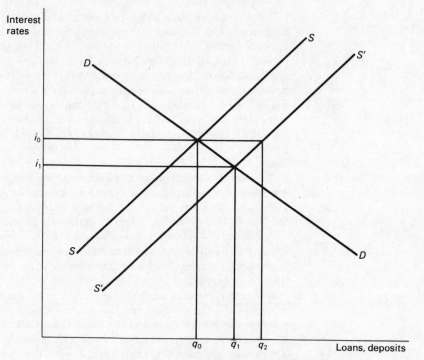

Figure 28.1   *The Euro-dollar market in portfolio equilibrium*

The story behind Figure 28.1 is as follows. The Euro-banks, having received extra deposits, try to lend them out, but since at i_0 all demand has been met, this is only possible with a fall in the rate. The fall in the rate, however, makes re-lending less attractive relative to holding reserves – assuming that the reserve rate of interest remains unchanged – so only a fraction of the new deposits is lent out. Similarly, the falling rate of interest makes Euro-deposits less attractive to lenders relative to other assets, and so some deposits are withdrawn from the market. Hence, if the market is initially in full equilibrium, any change in deposits must be accompanied by interest rate changes, and these reduce the final increment to the Euro-market's total deposits below the size of the initial impact.

This model is simple but not fundamentally misleading. It is possible to add the national banking systems or differing maturities of loans to the general equilibrium system without altering the basic result (see, for instance, Freedman, 1977a, and Johnston, 1981). The result could be upset, however, by central bank re-depositing if this occurred independently of interest rates, but we have already seen that this is not prevalent among the major banks.

Liquidity creation in the portfolio model

The portfolio model just described treats Euro-banks as non-monetary financial intermediaries. It suggests that they cannot create credit (liquidity) because, given a stable demand and supply of deposits, their expansion is likely to be balanced by a contraction elsewhere. Although this is largely true at any one time, it is not true through time, however, because intermediaries are able to influence the scope of the market.

First, Euro-markets shift money from people who want to save to people who want to spend. Hence, they raise the velocity of circulation of any given money stock. Second, they may overcome restrictions and/or restrictive practices in other parts of the financial system, and hence increase the *effective* demand and/or supply of deposits overall. Third, and closely related, by competition they may improve the efficiency of the rest of the system, hence increasing its effectiveness and overall business.

These reasons suggest that even on the portfolio view Euro-markets may have added to the world money supply as they introduced new borrowing opportunities. For instance, they have probably increased the general efficiency of banking, they have almost certainly found customers who could not borrow on national systems (e.g. the LDCs), and they have shifted funds from countries where banks' reserves are excessive (surplus countries) to those where reserve shortage has constrained bank credit (deficit countries). However, not all Euro-business contributes additional liquidity – some of it merely displaces other national business. Furthermore, any such expansion is of a one-off nature. The market expands as the Euro-banks innovate but, once the supply of new customers is exhausted, growth is constrained by the rate at which existing customers raise their demand, which is normally much below that which can be achieved by broadening the market. In other words, the fact that the Euro-banks have found new borrowers for their deposits and hence raised world liquidity in the past does not guarantee that they will be able to do so for any future injection of funds.

'Net' vs. 'gross' liquidity

If all loans had the same maturity, financial institutions would be able to raise only the velocity of circulation. Someone who did not want his money for, say, three months would lend it to someone who did. The money would 'work harder', but little would be gained in terms of liquidity because the second person's (temporary) gain of purchasing power would be roughly balanced by the first's (equally temporary) loss. Thus, if Euro-banks' loans had identical maturity structure to their deposits, they would create little 'useful' or 'net' liquidity, regardless of the value of the multiplier.

Returning to Table 28.1, however, we see that Euro-banks do transform maturities and hence do create 'useful' liquidity. The lender of an eight-day deposit feels quite liquid – he will get his money back in a week – but so does the borrower of a three-year loan – he can spend extra cash over the next three years. The exact increase in 'net' liquidity depends on how we trade off one maturity against another; Johnston (1983) discussed two possible approaches, but we shall do no more than note that maturity transformation creates 'net' liquidity.

28.4 CONTROLLING THE EURO-MARKETS

Several arguments have been forwarded for controlling the Euro-markets. First, their ability to increase the velocity of circulation and (possibly) their ability to create credit have both been blamed for inflation. The former has occurred and may have raised inflation historically but, unless more financial innovations are

341

forthcoming, velocity, and therefore inflation, will not rise in future. Credit-creation has already been discussed and we have argued that the Euro-markets have little power to create credit themselves.

Second, there have been 'prudential' concerns. This argument states that unregulated banks tend to over-lend, and that they are consequently liable to crash. When this occurs they impose costs not only on themselves but also on depositors and the economy in general as economic activity slumps. Hence, it states, banks should be forced to keep larger reserve ratios and to behave in a 'responsible' way. This argument moves in and out of fashion. In 1974 and early 1983 it was popular because crashes seemed likely, but when times are easier most people are pleased to benefit from the economic stimulus that liberal lending induces. Our own view is that some measure of external supervision would be beneficial in the longer run.

A third argument for control has been antipathy towards international capital mobility. Capital mobility frustrates monetary policy and almost certainly exacerbates exchange rate variability (see Chapter 22). Since it is difficult to believe that short-term private mobility has many social benefits, it is argued, there would be net gains from reducing it; and since the Euro-markets have certainly permitted greater capital mobility, one way of achieving this would be to control them. We sympathise with the aim of this argument, but it would be useless to control the Euro-banks without also controlling other channels of capital mobility.

Even if one accepts the case for control, it is not clear what controls should be enforced or how. The most obvious candidate is the enforcement of reserve ratios similar to domestic ones. This would reduce any multiplier and raise the Euro-banks' interest rate spreads, thus curtailing their level of operation and their power to generate expansion internally. Obviously, however, all countries would have to enforce the same ratio or banks would migrate to the 'lower-ratio' countries. Equally obvious are the incentives for countries to cheat.

A further difficulty is where the reserves would be held. In domestic systems the central bank controls monetary policy and receives the reserves as subsidised loans. In return, it acts as lender of last resort, which involves periodically taking on commercially undesirable loans. On a world scale this role should ideally fall to some international institution, but one doubts the political feasibility of concentrating such power in any one place – *vide* the IMF's laboured procedures. All told it will require much greater political will than is presently evident to exercise effective control of the Euro-markets.

FURTHER READING

The literature on the Euro-markets is massive. *Crockett* (1977), *McKinnon* (1979), *Llewellyn* (1980) and *Grubel* (1981) provide alternative textbook treatments. *Johnston* (1983) provides a recent book-length introduction, while *Freedman* (1977b) describes the growth of the Euro-markets in terms of a series of happy accidents, and surveys some early references. On modelling the Euro-markets, *Niehans and Hewson* (1976) is excellent. *Crockett* (1976), *Johnston* (1981) and *Grabbe* (1981) also discuss the relationship between the multiplier and portfolio approaches, while *Hewson and Sakikabara* (1974), *Freedman* (1977a) and *Grabbe* (1981) present full general equilibrium models.

NOTES

1   The sum of an infinite series $1+x+x^2+\ldots$ is $\frac{1}{1-x}$, provided $x < 1$.

2   This statement is rather over-simplified but it is nearly true. Of course, we have yet to conclude that multiple creation does actually occur.

Bibliography

Ahmed, J. (1978), 'Tokyo Rounds of trade negotiations and the Generalized System of Preferences', *Economic Journal*, vol. 88, pp. 285–297.

Aitken, N. D. (1973), 'The effects of the EEC and EFTA on European trade: A temporal cross-section analysis', *American Economic Review*, vol. 63, pp. 881–892.

Aitken, N. D. and Obutelewicz, R. S. (1976), 'A cross-sectional study of EEC trade with the Association of Africa Countries', *Review of Economics and Statistics*, vol. 88, pp. 425–433.

Alexander, S. S. (1952), 'The effects of devaluation on a trade balance', *IMF Staff Papers*, vol. 2, pp. 263–278; also in Caves and Johnson (1968).

Alexander, S. S. (1959), 'The effects of devaluation: a simplified synthesis of elasticities and absorption approaches', *American Economic Review*, vol. 49, pp. 21–42.

Aliber, R. Z. (1976), 'The firm under pegged and floating exchange rates', *Scandinavian Journal of Economics*, vol. 78, pp. 309–322.

Aquino, A. (1981), 'Changes over time in the pattern of comparative advantage in manufactured goods', *European Economic Review*, vol. 15, pp. 41–62.

Argy, V. (1981), *The Postwar International Money Crisis*, Allen & Unwin, London.

Argy, V. and Kouri, P. (1974), 'Sterilization policies and the volatility in international reserves', in R. Z. Aliber (ed.), *National Monetary Policies and the International Financial System*, Chicago University Press, Chicago, Ill., pp. 209–230.

Argy, V. and Porter, M. G. (1972), 'The forward exchange market and the effects of domestic and external disturbances under alternative exchange rate regimes', *IMF Staff Papers*, vol. 19, pp. 503–528.

Armington, P. S. (1977), 'The role of "non-price competitiveness" in exporting', *The Banker*, August, pp. 39–43.

Artus, J. R. (1970), 'The short-run effects of domestic demand pressure on British export performance', *IMF Staff Papers*, vol. 17, pp. 247–274.

Artus, J. R. (1973), 'The short-run effects of domestic demand pressure on export delivery delays for machinery', *Journal of International Economics*, vol. 3, pp. 21–36.

Artus, J. R. (1975), 'The 1967 devaluation of the pound sterling', *IMF Staff Papers*, vol. 22, pp. 595–640.

Artus, J. R. and Rhomberg, R. R. (1973), 'A multi-lateral exchange rate model', *IMF Staff Papers*, vol. 20, pp. 591–611.

Artus, J. R. and Sosa, S. C. (1978), 'Relative price effects on export performance: the case of non-electrical machinery', *IMF Staff Papers*, vol. 25, pp. 25–47.

Artus, J. R. and Young, J. H. (1979), 'Fixed and flexible exchange rates: a renewal of the debate', *IMF Staff Papers*, vol. 26, pp. 654–698.

Bacon, R., Godley, W. A. H., McFarquhar, A. (1978), 'The direct costs to Britain of belonging to the EEC', *Cambridge Economic Policy Review*, No. 4, 1978, pp. 44–49.

Bain, A. D. and Evans, J. D. (1973), 'Price formation and profits: explanatory and forecasting models of manufacturing industry profits in the UK', *Oxford Bulletin of Economics and Statistics*, vol. 35, pp. 295–308.

Balassa, B. (1964), 'The purchasing power parity doctrine: a reappraisal', *Journal of Political Economy*, vol. 72, pp. 584–596.

Balassa, B. (1971), *The Structure of Protection in Developing Countries*, Johns Hopkins Press, Baltimore, Md.

Balassa, B. (1975), *European Economic Integration*, North Holland, Amsterdam.

Balassa, B. (1978), 'Exports and economic growth: further evidence', *Journal of Development Economics*, vol. 5, pp. 181–189.

Balassa, B. (1979), 'A "Stages" approach to comparative advantage', in I. Adelman (ed.), *Economic Growth and Resources*, vol. 4, Macmillan, London, pp. 121–136.

Balassa, B. (1981), 'Adjustment to external shocks in developing countries', World Bank Staff Working Paper, No. 472, World Bank, Washington, DC.

Baldwin, R. E. (1969), 'The case against infant industry tariff protection', *Journal of Political Economy*, vol. 77, pp. 295–305.

Baldwin, R. E. (1970), *Non-Tariff Distortions of International Trade*, Allen & Unwin, London.

Baldwin, R. E. (1971), 'Determinants of the commodity structure of US trade', *American Economic Review*, vol. 61, pp. 126–146.

Baldwin, R. E. (1976), 'Trade and employment effects in the US multilateral tariff reductions', *American Economic Review*, vol. 66, pp. 142–148.

Baldwin, R. E. (1971), 'Determinants of the commodity structure of US trade', *American Economic Review*, vol. 61, pp. 126–146.

Baldwin, R. E. (1982), 'The political economy of protectionism', in Bhagwati (1982), pp. 263–286.

Baldwin, R. E. and Murray, T. (1977), 'MFN tariff reductions and LDC benefits under the GSP', *Economic Journal*, vol. 87, pp. 30–46.

Bale, M. D. and Lutz, E. (1981), 'Price distortions in agriculture and their effects: an international comparison', *American Journal of Agricultural Economics*, vol. 63, pp. 7–22.

Balogh, T. (1963), *Unequal Partners*, Basil Blackwell, Oxford.

Balogh, T. and Streeten, P. (1960), 'Domestic versus foreign investment', *Bulletin of the Oxford Institute of Economics and Statistics*, vol. 22, pp. 213–224.

Bank for International Settlements, *Annual Report*, BIS, Basle.

Bank of England, *Quarterly Economic Review*, Bank of England, London, quarterly.

Barker, T. S. (1968), 'Devaluation and the rise in UK prices', *Bulletin of the Oxford University Institute of Economics and Statistics*, vol. 30, pp. 129–141.

Barker, T. S. (1970), *The Determinants of Britain's Visible Imports 1949–66*, no. 10 of J. R. N. Stone (ed.), *A Programme for Growth*, Chapman & Hall, London.

Barker, T. S. (1977), 'International trade and economic growth: an alternative to the neo-classical approach', *Cambridge Journal of Economics*, vol. 1, pp. 153–172.

Barker, T. S. (1979), 'The identification of activity effects, trends and cycles in import demand', *Oxford Bulletin of Economics and Statistics*, vol. 41, pp. 63–68.

Barker, T. S. and Brailovsky, V. (1981), *Oil or Industry*, Academic Press, New York.

Batchelor, R. A. (1977), 'Sterling exchange rates 1951–1976: a Casselian analysis', *National Institute Economic Review*, no. 81, pp. 45–66.

Batchelor, R. A. (1979), 'Must floating exchange rates be unstable', *Annual Monetary Review*, no. 1, City University, London, pp. 51–58.

Batchelor, R. and Horne, J. (1979), 'Money, the balance of payments, and the exchange rate', *Annual Monetary Review*, no. 1, City University, London, pp. 19–27.

Batchelor, R. and Minford, A. P. (1977), 'Import controls and devaluation as medium-term policies', in H. Corbett *et al.*, *On how to Cope with Britain's Trade Position*, Thames Essay No. 8, Trade Policy Research Centre, London, pp. 44–72.

Bator, F. M. (1957), 'The simple analytics of welfare maximisation', *American Economic Review*, vol. 47, pp. 22–59.

Beckerman, W. (1974), *In Defence of Economic Growth*, Jonathan Cape, London.

Beenstock, M. and Bell, S. (1979), 'A quarterly econometric model of the capital account in the UK balance of payments', *Manchester School*, vol. 47, pp. 33–62.

Behnke, E. A. (1980), 'International transmission of business cycles – the Sohmen–Lausen–Metzler effect', in Chipman and Kindleberger (1980), pp. 257–266.

Ben-Bassat, A. (1980), 'The optimal composition of foreign exchange reserves', *Journal of International Economics*, vol. 10, pp. 285–296.

Bernstein, E. M. *et al.* (1976), *Reflections on Jamaica*, Princeton Essay in International Finance, No. 115, Princeton University Press, Princeton, NJ.

Bhagwati, J. N. (1964), 'The pure theory of international trade: A survey', *Economic Journal*, vol. 74, pp. 1–84; also in Royal Economic Society, *Surveys of Economic Theory*, vol. 2, and Bhagwati (1969b).

Bhagwati, J. N. (1968), *The Theory and Practice of Commercial Policy: Departures from Unified Exchange Rates*, Special Paper in International Economics, No. 8, Princeton University Press, Princeton, NJ.

344

Bibliography

Bhagwati, J. N. (1969a), *International Trade: Selected Readings*, Penguin, Harmondsworth, Middx.

Bhagwati, J. N. (1969b), *Trade, Tariffs and Growth*, Weidenfeld & Nicholson, London.

Bhagwati, J. N. (1971), 'The generalized theory of distortions and welfare', in J. N. Bhagwati *et al.*, *Trade, Balance of Payments and Growth*, North Holland, Amsterdam, pp. 69–90; also in Bhagwati (1981).

Bhagwati, J. N. (1978), *Foreign Trade Regimes and Economic Development: Anatomy and Consequences of Exchange Control Regimes*, Ballinger Publishing Co., Cambridge, Mass.

Bhagwati, J. N. (1981), *International Trade: Selected Readings*, MIT Press, Cambridge, Mass.

Bhagwati, J. N. (1982), *Impact Competition and Response*, National Bureau of Economic Research, New York.

Bhagwati, J. N. and Ramaswami, V. K. (1963), 'Domestic distortions, tariffs and the theory of optimum subsidy', *Journal of Political Economy*, vol. 72, pp. 44–50; also in Caves and Johnson (1968).

Bhagwati, J. N., Ramaswami, V. K. and Srinivasan, T. N. (1969), 'Domestic distortions, tariffs and the theory of optimum subsidy: some further results', *Journal of Political Economy*, vol. 77, pp. 1005–1010.

Bilson, J. F. O. and Frenkel, J. A. (1979), 'International reserves: adjustment dynamics', *Economics Letters*, vol. 4, pp. 267–270.

Bird, G. (1982a), *The International Monetary System and the Less Developed Countries*, 2nd edition, Macmillan, London.

Bird, G. (1982b), 'The International Monetary Fund and developing countries: retrospect and prospect', mimeo.

Black, J. and Winters, L. A. (1983), *Policy and Performance in International Trade*, Macmillan, London.

Blaug, M. (1980), *The Methodology of Economics*, Cambridge University Press, Cambridge.

Bloch, H. (1974), 'Prices, costs and profits in Canadian manufacturing: the influence of tariffs and concentration', *Canadian Journal of Economics*, vol. 7, pp. 594–610.

Bond, M. E. (1979), 'The world trade model: invisibles', *IMF Staff Papers*, vol. 26, pp. 257–333.

Branson, W. H. (1977), 'Current markets and relative prices in exchange rate determination', *Sozialwissenschaftliche Annalen*, vol. 1, pp. 69–89; also reprinted as Princeton Reprint in International Finance, No. 20, Princeton University, Princeton, NJ (1981).

Branson, W. H. (1980), 'Comment' (on Dornbusch, 1980b), *Brookings Papers in Economic Activity*, vol. 10, no. 1, pp. 187–194.

Branson, W. H. (1981), 'Comment', *European Economic Review*, vol. 16, pp. 167–171.

Branson, W. H. and Buiter, W. H. (1982), 'Monetary and fiscal policy with flexible exchange rates', in J. Bhandari and B. Putnam (eds), *The International Transmission of Economic Disturbances*, MIT University Press, Cambridge, Mass.

Branson, W. H., Halttunen, H. and Masson, P. (1977), 'Exchange rates in the short-run, the dollar–deutschmark rate', *European Economic Review*, vol. 10, pp. 303–324.

Brech, M. J. and Stout, D. K. (1981), 'The rate of exchange and non-price competitiveness: a provisional study within UK manufactured exports', *Oxford Economic Papers*, vol. 33, Supplement, pp. 268–281; also published as Ellis and Sinclair (1981).

Brecher, R. A. and Bhagwati, J. N. (1981), 'Foreign ownership and the theory of trade and welfare', *Journal of Political Economy*, vol. 89, pp. 497–511.

Brecher, R. A. and Bhagwati, J. N. (1982), 'Immiserising transfers from abroad', *Journal of International Economics*, vol. 13, pp. 353–364.

Brechling, F. and Wolfe, J. N. (1965), 'The end of stop–go', *Lloyds Bank Review*, No. 75, pp. 23–30.

Briault, C. B. and Howson, S. K. (1982), *A Portfolio Model of Domestic and External Financial Markets*, Discussion Paper No. 20, Bank of England, London.

Brock, W. A. and Magee, S. P. (1978), 'The economics of special interest politics: the case of the tariff', *American Economic Review, Papers and Proceedings*, vol. 68, pp. 246–250.

Brooman, F. S. (1970), *Macroeconomics*, 3rd edition, Allen & Unwin, London.

Brown, R. N., Enoch, C. A. and Mortimer-Lee, P. D. (1980), *The Interrelationships between Costs and Prices in the United Kingdom*, Discussion Paper No. 8, Bank of England, London.

Buiter, W. H. and Miller, M. (1981), 'The Thatcher experiment: the first two years', *Brookings Papers in Economic Activity*, vol. 11, pp. 315–379.

345

Business Statistics Office, 'Import penetration and export sales ratios for manufacturing industry', *Business Monitor*, MQ12, HMSO, London, quarterly.

Business Statistics Office, *Report on the Census of Production*, HMSO, London.

Byrne, W. J. (1982), 'Evolution of the SDR, 1974–81', *Finance and Development*, vol. 19, no. 3, September, pp. 31–35.

Calvo, G. A. and Rodriguez, C. A. (1977), 'A model of exchange rate determination under currency substitution and rational expectations', *Journal of Political Economy*, vol. 85, pp. 617–625.

Cambridge Economic Policy Group, *Cambridge Economic Policy Review*, Gower Press, Aldershot, Hants, periodical.

Capie, F. (1983), 'Tariff protection and economic performance in the nineteenth century', in Black and Winters (1983), pp. 1–24.

Carse, S., Williamson, J. and Wood, G. E. (1980), *The Financing Procedure of British Foreign Trade*, Cambridge University Press, London.

Caves, R. E. (1974a), 'The causes of direct investment: foreign firms' shares in Canadian and U.K. manufacturing industry', *Review of Economics and Statistics*, vol. 56, pp. 279–293.

Caves, R. E. (1974b), 'Multinational firms, competition, and productivity in host country markets', *Economica*, vol. 41, pp. 176–193.

Caves, R. E. (1976), 'Economic models of political choice: Canada's tariff structure', *Canadian Journal of Economics*, vol. 9, pp. 278–300.

Caves, R. E. (1980), 'Productivity differences among industries', in R. E. Caves and L. B. Krause (eds), *Britain's Economic Performance*, The Brookings Institution, Washington, DC, pp. 135–192.

Caves, R. E. (1981), 'Intra-industry trade and market structure in the industrial countries', *Oxford Economic Papers*, vol. 33, pp. 203–223.

Caves, R. E. (1983), *Multinational Enterprise and Economic Analysis*, Cambridge University Press, Cambridge.

Caves, R. E. *et al.*, (1980), *Competition in the Open Economy*, Harvard University Press, Cambridge, Mass.

Caves, R. E. and Johnson, H. G. (1968), *Readings in International Economics*, Allen & Unwin, London.

Caves, R. E. and Jones, R. W. (1981), *World Trade and Payments*, 3rd edition, Little Brown, Boston, Mass.

Central Policy Review Staff (1975), *The Future of the British Car Industry*, HMSO, London.

Central Statistical Office, *United Kingdom Balance of Payments* (The Pink Book), HMSO, London, annual.

Central Statistical Office, *Economic Trends*, HMSO, London, monthly.

Central Statistical Office, *Monthly Digest of Statistics*, HMSO, London, monthly.

Chacholiades, M. (1981), *Principles of International Economics*, McGraw-Hill, New York.

Cheh, J. (1974), 'United States concessions in the Kennedy Round and short-run labour adjustment costs', *Journal of International Economics*, vol. 4, pp. 323–340.

Chipman, J. S. (1965), 'A survey of the theory of international trade', *Econometrica*, Part I 'The Classical theory', vol. 33, pp. 477–519; Part II 'The neo-classical theory', vol. 33, pp. 685–760; Part III 'The modern theory', vol. 34 (1966), pp. 18–76.

Chipman, J. S. and Kindleberger, C. P. (1980), *Flexible Exchange Rates and the Balance of Payments*, Essays in Memory of Egon Sohmen, Studies in International Economics, No. 7, North Holland, Amsterdam.

Chrystal, K. A. (1977), 'Demand for international media of exchange', *American Economic Review*, vol. 67, pp. 840–850.

Chrystal, K. A. (1978), *International Money and the Future of the SDR*, Princeton Essay in International Finance, No. 128, Princeton University Press, Princeton, NJ.

Clark, P. B. (1970), 'Demand for international reserves: a cross-country analysis', *Canadian Journal of Economics*, vol. 3, pp. 577–594.

Cline, W. *et al.* (1978), *Trade Negotiations in the Tokyo Round: A Quantitative Assessment*, Brookings Institution, Washington, DC.

Coase, R. H. (1937), 'The nature of the firm', *Economica*, vol. 4, pp. 386–405.

Coats, W. L., Jr (1982), 'The SDR as a means of payments', *IMF Staff Papers*, vol. 29, pp. 422–436.

Cohen, B. J. (1969), *Balance of Payments Policy*, Penguin, Harmondsworth, Middx.

Connell, D. (1979), *The UK's Performance in Export Markets – Some Evidence from International Trade Data*, National Economic Development Office, London.

Consumers' Association (1979), *The Price of Protection*, Consumers' Association, London.

Cooper, C. A. and Massell, B. F. (1965a), 'Towards a general theory of customs unions for developing countries', *Journal of Political Economy*, vol. 73, pp. 461–476.

Cooper, C. A. and Massell, B. F. (1965b), 'A new look at custom's union theory', *Economic Journal*, vol. 75, pp. 742–747; also in Robson (1971).

Cooper, R. N. (1969), *International Finance*, Penguin, Harmondsworth, Middx.

Cooper, R. N. (1971), *Currency Devaluation and Developing Countries*, Princeton Essay in International Finance, No. 86, Princeton University Press, Princeton, NJ.

Corbet, H. (1979), 'Importance of being earnest about further GATT negotiations', *The World Economy*, vol. 3, pp. 319–342.

Corden, W. M. (1957), 'Tariffs, subsidies and the terms of trade', *Economica*, vol. 24, p. 235–242.

Corden, W. M. (1960), 'The geometric representation of policies to attain internal and external balance', *Review of Economic Studies*, vol. 28, pp. 1–22.

Corden, W. M. (1966), 'The structure of a tariff system and effective protective rate', *Journal of Political Economy*, vol. 74, pp. 221–237; also in Bhagwati (1969a, 1981).

Corden, W. M. (1971), *The Theory of Protection*, Oxford University Press, Oxford.

Corden, W. M. (1972a), 'Economies of scale and customs union theory', *Journal of Political Economy*, vol. 80, pp. 465–475.

Corden, W. M. (1972b), *Monetary Integration*, Princeton Essay in International Finance, No. 93, Princeton University Press, Princeton, NJ.

Corden, W. M. (1974), *Trade Policy and Economic Welfare*, Oxford University Press, Oxford.

Corden, W. M. (1977), *Inflation, Exchange Rates and the World Economy*, Oxford University Press, Oxford.

Corden, W. M. (1981), 'The exchange rate, monetary policy and North Sea oil: the economic theory of the squeeze on tradeables', *Oxford Economic Papers*, vol. 33, Supplement, pp. 23–46; also published as Ellis and Sinclair (1981).

Corden, W. M. and Fels, G. (1976), *Public Assistance to Industry*, Macmillan, London.

Corden, W. M. and Jones, R. W. (1976), 'Devaluation, non-flexible prices, and the trade balance for a small country', *Canadian Journal of Economics*, vol. 9, pp. 150–161.

Corden, W. M. and Neary, J. P. (1982), 'Booming sector and de-industrialisation in a small open economy', *Economic Journal*, vol. 92, pp. 825–848.

Cornwall, J. (1977), *Modern Capitalism*, Martin Robertson, Oxford.

Coutts, K., Godley, W. A. H. and Nordhaus, W. (1978), *Industrial Pricing in the United Kingdom*, Cambridge University Press, London.

Cripps, T. F., Godley, W. A. H. and Fetherston, M. J. (1974), *Evidence to the Select Committee on Public Expenditure*, 9th Report, HC 328.

Crockett, A. D. (1976), 'The Euro-currency market: an attempt to clarify some basic issues', *IMF Staff Papers*, vol. 23, pp. 375–386.

Crockett, A. D. (1977), *International Money: Issues and Analysis*, Nelson, London.

Crockett, A. D. and Goldstein, M. (1976), 'Inflation under fixed and flexible exchange rates', *IMF Staff Papers*, vol. 23, pp. 509–544.

Customs and Excise, *Overseas Trade Statistics of the United Kingdom*, HMSO, London, monthly.

Customs and Excise, *Guide to the Classification for Overseas Trade Statistics*, HMSO, London, annual.

Deardorff, A. V. (1979), 'Weak links in the theory of comparative advantage', *Journal of International Economics*, vol. 9, pp. 197–210; also in Bhagwati (1981).

Deardorff, A. V. (1980), 'The general validity of the law of comparative advantage', *Journal of Political Economy*, vol. 88, pp. 941–957.

Deardorff, A. V. (1982), 'The general validity of the Heckscher–Ohlin Theorem', *American Economic Review*, vol. 72, pp. 683–694.

347

Deardorff, A. V. (1983), 'Testing trade theories and predicting trade flows', Chapter 10 of R. W. Jones and P. B. Kenen (eds), *Handbook of International Economics, vol. I, International Trade Theory*, North Holland, Amsterdam.

Deardorff, A. V. and Stern, R. M. (1983a), 'The effects of domestic tax/subsidies and import tariffs on the structure of protection in the United States, United Kingdom and Japan', in Black and Winters (1983), pp. 43–64.

Deardorff, A. V. and Stern, R. M. (1983b), 'Economic effects of the Tokyo Round', *Southern Economic Journal*, vol. 49, pp. 605–624.

Deardorff, A. V. and Stern, R. M. (1984), 'The economic effects of complete elimination of post-Tokyo Round tariffs on the major industrialised and developing countries', in *Trade Policy in the Eighties*, Institute for International Economics, Washington, DC.

de Marchi, N. B. (1976), 'Anomaly and the development of economics: the case of the Leontief paradox', in S. J. Latsis (ed.), *Method and Appraisal in Economics*, Cambridge University Press, Cambridge, pp. 109–127.

Department of Commerce, *Survey of Current Business*, US Department of Commerce, Washington, DC, monthly.

Department of Employment Gazette, HMSO, London, monthly.

Department of Trade and Industry (1983), 'Memorandum', in House of Lords, *7th Report of the Select Committee on the European Communities: The United Kingdom's Changing Trade Patterns Subsequent to Membership of the European Community*, HMSO, London, pp. 1–41.

Department of Trade and Industry, *British Business* (formerly *Trade and Industry* and *The Board of Trade Journal*), HMSO, London, weekly.

Deutsche Bundesbank, *Monthly Review*, Bonn, monthly.

de V. Graaff, J. (1957), *Theoretical Welfare Economics*, Cambridge University Press, Cambridge.

Diaz Alejandro, C. F. (1975), 'Trade policies and economic development', in Kenen (1975), pp. 93–150.

Dixit, A. K. and Norman, V. (1980), *Theory of International Trade*, Nisbet/Cambridge University Press, London.

Dixit, A. K. and Woodland, A. (1982), 'The relationship between factor endowments and commodity trade', *Journal of International Economics*, vol. 13, pp. 201–214.

Donovan, D. J. (1981), 'Real responses associated with exchange rate action in selected upper credit tranche stabilisation programs', *IMF Staff Papers*, vol. 28, pp. 697–727.

Donovan, D. J. (1982), 'Macro-economic performance and adjustment under Fund-supported programs: the experience of the seventies', *IMF Staff Papers*, vol. 29, pp. 171–203.

Dore, R. P. (1982), 'Adjustment in process: a Lancashire town', in Bhagwati (1982), pp. 295–317.

Dornbusch, R. (1975a), 'Exchange rates and fiscal policy in a popular model of international trade', *American Economic Review*, vol. 65, pp. 859–871.

Dornbusch, R. (1975b), 'Alternative price stabilization rules and the effects of exchange rate changes', *Manchester School*, vol. 43, pp. 275–297.

Dornbusch, R. (1976), 'Expectations and exchange rate dynamics', *Journal of Political Economy*, vol. 84, pp. 1161–1176.

Dornbusch, R. (1978), 'Monetary policy under exchange rate flexibility', in *Managed Exchange Rate Flexibility*, Conference Series No. 20, Federal Reserve Bank of Boston, Boston, Mass.

Dornbusch, R. (1980a), *Open Economy Macro-Economics*, Basic Books, New York.

Dornbusch, R. (1980b), 'Exchange rate economics: where do we stand?' *Brookings Papers in Economic Activity*, vol. 10, no. 1, pp. 143–185.

Dornbusch, R. and Fischer, S. (1980), 'Sterling and external balance', in R. E. Caves and L. B. Krause (eds), *Britain's Economic Performance*, The Brookings Institution, Washington, DC, pp. 21–71.

Dunning, J. H. (1972), *International Investment*, Penguin, Harmondsworth, Middx.

Dunning, J. H. (1974), *Economic Analysis and the Multinational Enterprise*, Allen & Unwin, London.

Dunning, J. H. (1979), 'Explaining changing patterns of international investment: in defence of the eclectic theory', *Oxford Bulletin of Economics and Statistics*, vol. 41, pp. 269–296.

Dunning, J. H. (1982), 'Explaining the international direct investment position of countries: towards a dynamic or developmental approach', in J. Black and J. H. Dunning, *International Capital Movements*, Macmillan, London, pp. 84–121.

Dunning, J. H. and Pearce, R. D. (1981), *The World's Largest Industrial Enterprises*, Gower, Farnborough, Hants.

Eastwood, R. K. and Venables, A. J. (1982), 'The macro-economic implications of a resource discovery in an open economy', *Economic Journal*, vol. 92, pp. 285–299.

Eastwood, R. K. and Venables, A. J. (1983), 'Oil sector shocks and the UK economy 1970–80: A macro-economic appraisal', mimeo, University of Sussex.

Eaton, J. and Panagariya, A. (1982), 'Growth and welfare in a small open economy', *Economica*, vol. 49, pp. 409–419.

Ellis, H. S. and Metzler, L. A. (1950), *Readings in the Theory of International Trade*, Allen & Unwin, London.

Ellis, W. A. and Sinclair, P. J. N. (1981), *The Money Supply and the Exchange Rate*, Oxford University Press, Oxford.

Ellman, M. (1977), 'Report from Holland: the economics of North Sea hydrocarbons', *Cambridge Journal of Economics*, vol. 1, pp. 281–290.

Emminger, O. (1979), 'The exchange rate as an instrument of policy', *Lloyds Bank Review*, no. 133, July, pp. 1–22.

Falvey, R. E. (1981), 'Commercial policy and intra-industry trade', *Journal of International Economics*, vol. 11, pp. 495–512.

Feder, G. (1983), 'On exports and economic growth', *Journal of Development Economics*, vol. 12, pp. 59–74.

Feinstein, C. H. (1972), *National Income, Expenditure and Output of the United Kingdom, 1855–1955*, No. 6 of Studies in the National Income and Expenditure of the United Kingdom, Cambridge University Press, London.

Feinstein, C. H. and Reddaway, W. B. (1978), 'Opec surpluses, the world recession and the UK economy', *Midland Bank Review*, Spring, pp. 7–19.

Findlay, R. (1970a), *Trade and Specialization*, Penguin, Harmondsworth, Middx.

Findlay, R. (1970b), 'Factor proportions and comparative advantage in the long-run', *Journal of Political Economy*, vol. 78, pp. 27–34.

Findlay, R. and Rodriguez, C. A. (1977), 'Intermediate imports and macro-economic policy under flexible exchange rates', *Canadian Journal of Economics*, vol. 10, pp. 208–217.

Finger, J. M. (1975), 'Trade overlap and intra-industry trade', *Economic Inquiry*, vol. 13, pp. 581–589.

Finger, J. M. (1981), 'Policy research', *Journal of Political Economy*, vol. 89, pp. 1270–1272.

Finger, J. M., Hall, H. K. and Nelson, D. R. (1982), 'The political economy of administered protection', *American Economic Review*, vol. 72, pp. 452–466.

Fleming, J. M. (1962), 'Domestic financial policies under fixed and under floating exchange rates', *IMF Staff Papers*, vol. 9, pp. 369–379.

Foreman-Peck, J. S. (1979), 'Tariff protection and economies of scale: the British motor industry before 1939', *Oxford Economic Papers*, vol. 31, pp. 237–257.

Forsyth, P. J. and Kay, J. A. (1980), 'The economic implications of North Sea oil revenues', *Fiscal Studies*, vol. 1, July, pp. 1–28.

Forsyth, P. J. and Kay, J. A. (1981), 'Oil revenues and manufacturing output', *Fiscal Studies*, vol. 2, July, pp. 9–17.

Frankel, J. A. (1979), 'On the Mark: a theory of floating exchange rates based on real interest differentials', *American Economic Review*, vol. 69, pp. 610–622.

Freedman, C. (1977a), 'A model of the Eurodollar market', *Journal of Monetary Economics*, vol. 3, pp. 139–161.

Freedman, C. (1977b), 'The Euro-dollar market: a review of five recent studies', *Journal of Monetary Economics*, vol. 3, pp. 467–478.

Freeman, C. (1979), 'Technical innovation and British trade performance', in F. Blackaby (ed.), *De-Industrialisation*, Heinemann, London, pp. 56–73.

Freeman, C. and Young, A. (1965), *The Research and Development Effort in Western Europe, North America and the Soviet Union*, OECD, Paris.

349

Frenkel, J. A. (1976), 'A monetary approach to the exchange rate: doctrinal aspects and empirical evidence', *Scandinavian Journal of Economics*, vol. 78, pp. 200–224; also in Frenkel and Johnson (1978).

Frenkel, J. A. (1978a), 'Purchasing power parity: doctrinal perspective and evidence from the 1920s', *Journal of International Economics*, vol. 8, pp. 169–192.

Frenkel, J. A. (1978b), 'International reserves: pegged exchange rates and managed float', in K. Brunner and A. H. Meltzer (eds), 'Economic Policies in Open Economies', No. 9 of the Carnegie–Rochester Conference Series on Public Policy, supplement to the *Journal of Monetary Economics*, pp. 111–140.

Frenkel, J. A. (1981), 'The collapse of purchasing power parities during the 1970's', *European Economic Review*, vol. 16, pp. 145–165.

Frenkel, J. A. and Johnson, H. G. (1976), *The Monetary Approach to the Balance of Payments*, Allen & Unwin, London.

Frenkel, J. A. and Johnson, H. G. (1978), *The Economics of Exchange Rates*, Addison-Wesley, Reading, Mass.

Frenkel, J. A. and Rodriguez, C. A. (1982), 'Exchange rate dynamics and the overshooting hypothesis', *IMF Staff Papers*, vol. 29, pp. 1–30.

Friedman, M. (1953), 'The case for flexible exchange rates', in *Essays in Positive Economics*, University of Chicago Press, Chicago, pp. 157–203; also abridged in Caves and Johnson (1968).

Fukuda, H. (1973), *Britain in Europe: Impact on the Third World*, Macmillan, London.

Gard, L. M. and Riedel, J. (1980), 'Safeguard protection of industry in developed countries: assessment of the implications for developing countries', *Weltwirtschaftliches Archiv*, vol. 116, pp. 471–491.

Genberg, H. (1978), 'Purchasing power parity under fixed and flexible exchange rates', *Journal of International Economics*, vol. 8, pp. 247–276.

General Agreement on Tariffs and Trade (1979), *The Tokyo Round of Multilateral Trade Negotiations*, Report by the Director General, GATT, Geneva.

Giersch, H. (1974), *The International Division of Labour: Problems and Prospects*, J. C. B. Mohr, Tübingen.

Goldstein, M. (1980), *Have Flexible Exchange Rates Handicapped Macroeconomic Policy?* Special Paper in International Economics No. 14, Princeton University, Princeton, NJ.

Goldstein, M. and Khan, M. S. (1976), 'Large versus small price changes and the demand for imports', *IMF Staff Papers*, vol. 23, pp. 200–225.

Goldstein, M. and Khan, M. S. (1978), 'The supply and demand for exports: a simultaneous approach', *Review of Economics and Statistics*, vol. 60, pp. 275–286.

Gordon, R. J. (1982), 'Why US wage and employment behaviour differs from that in Britain and Japan', *Economic Journal*, vol. 92, pp. 13–44.

Grabbe, J. O. (1981), 'Liquidity creation and maturity transformation in the Euro-dollar markets', *Journal of Monetary Economics*, vol. 10, pp. 39–72.

Greenaway, D. (1983), *International Trade Policy: From Tariffs to the New Protectionism*, Macmillan, London.

Greenaway, D. and Milner, C. R. (1983), 'On the measurement of intra-industry trade', *Economic Journal*, vol. 93, pp. 900–908.

Greene, M. L. (1975), *Waiting Time: A Factor in Export Demand for Manufactures*, Study in International Finance, No. 37, Princeton University Press, Princeton, NJ.

Gregory, R. G. (1976), 'Some implications of the growth of the mineral sector', *Australian Journal of Agricultural Economics*, vol. 20, pp. 71–91.

Gribbin, J. D. (1971), *The profitability of UK exports*, Government Economic Service Occasional Paper, No. 1, HMSO, London.

Griffiths, B. (1981), 'The new monetary control procedures in the UK', *Annual Monetary Review*, no. 5, The City University, London.

Grubel, H. G. (1977), *The International Monetary System*, 3rd edition, Penguin, Harmondsworth, Middx.

Grubel, H. G. (1981), *International Economics*, 2nd edition, Irwin, Homewood, Ill.

Grubel, H. G. and Lloyd, P. J. (1975), *Intra-Industry Trade: The Theory and Measurement of International Trade in Differentiated Products*, Macmillan, London.

Haberler, G. (1936), *The Theory of International Trade with its Applications to Commercial Policy*, W. Hodge and Co., London.

Haberler, G. (1949), 'The market for foreign exchange and the stability of the balance of payments: a theoretical analysis', *Kyklos*, vol. 3, pp. 193–218; also in Cooper (1969).

Haberler, G. (1950), 'Some problems in the pure theory of international trade', *Economic Journal*, vol. 60, pp. 223–240; also in Caves and Johnson (1968).

Hacche, G. and Townend, J. (1981), 'A broad look at exchange rate movements for eight currencies 1972–80', *Bank of England Quarterly Review*, vol. 21, pp. 489–507.

Hahn, F. H. (1977), 'The monetary approach to the balance of payments', *Journal of International Economics*, vol. 7, pp. 231–250.

Halm, G. N. (1977), *Jamaica and the Par-Value System*, Princeton Essay in International Finance, No. 120, Princeton University, Princeton, NJ.

Hamilton, A. (1790), *Report on Manufactures 1790*; reprinted in S. McKee, *Papers on Public Credit, Commerce and Finance by Alexander Hamilton*, Columbia University Press, New York (1934).

Hamilton, C. (1981), 'A new approach to estimation of the effects of non-tariff barriers to trade: an application to the Swedish textile and clothing industry', *Weltwirtschaftliches Archiv*, vol. 117, pp. 298–324.

Havrylyshyn, O. (1984), 'The direction of developing country trade: empirical evidence of differences between South–South and South–North trade', in *South–South or North–South Trade*, World Bank Conference Series, The World Bank, Washington, DC.

Havrylyshyn, O. and Civan, E. (1983), 'Intra-industry trade and the stage of development', in P. K. M. Tharakan (ed.), *The Economics of Intra-Industry Trade*, North Holland, Amsterdam, pp. 111–140.

Hawkins, C. and McKenzie, G. (1982), *The British Economy: What Will Our Children Think?* Macmillan, London.

Hayter, T. (1971), *Aid as Imperialism*, Penguin, Harmondsworth, Middx.

Helleiner, G. K. (1973), 'Manufactured exports from less developed countries and multinational firms', *Economic Journal*, vol. 83, pp. 21–47.

Helleiner, G. K. (1977), 'Transnational enterprises and the new political economy of U.S. trade policy', *Oxford Economic Papers*, vol. 29, pp. 102–116.

Heller, H. R. and Khan, M. S. (1978), 'The demand for international reserves under fixed and floating exchange rates', *IMF Staff Papers*, vol. 25, pp. 623–649.

Heller, H. R. and Knight, M. (1978), *Reserve Currency Preferences of Central Banks*, Princeton Essay in International Finance, No. 131, Princeton University, Princeton, NJ.

Heller, P. S. (1976), 'Factor endowment change and comparative advantage: the case of Japan, 1956–1969', *Review of Economics and Statistics*, vol. 58, pp. 283–292.

Helpman, E. (1981), 'International trade in the presence of product differentiation, economies of scale and monopolistic competition: a Chamberlin–Heckscher–Ohlin approach', *Journal of International Economics*, vol. 11, pp. 305–340.

Henderson, P. D. (1977), 'Two British errors: their probable size and some possible lessons', *Oxford Economic Papers*, vol. 29, pp. 159–205.

Henry, G. B. (1970), 'Domestic demand pressure and short-run export fluctuations', *Yale Economic Essays*, vol. 10, pp. 43–81.

Henry, S. G. B., Sawyer, M. C. and Smith, P. (1976), 'Models of inflation in the United Kingdom', *National Institute Economic Review*, No. 77, pp. 60–71.

Herring, R. J. and Marston, R. C. (1977), *National Monetary Policies and International Financial Markets*, North Holland, Amsterdam.

Hesse, H. (1974), 'Hypotheses for the explanation of trade between industrial countries, 1953–1970', in Giersch (1974), pp. 39–59.

Hewson, J. and Sakikabara, E. (1974), 'The Euro-dollar deposit multiplier: a portfolio approach', *IMF Staff Papers*, vol. 21, pp. 307–328.

Hindley, B. (1980), 'Voluntary export restraints and Article XIX of the GATT', in J. Black and B. Hindley, *Current Issues in Commercial Policy and Diplomacy*, Macmillan, London, pp. 52–72.

Hindley, B. (1983), 'Trade policy, economic performance, and Britain's economic problems', in Black and Winters (1983), pp. 25–42.

Hipple, F. S. (1974), *The Disturbances Approach to the Demand for International Reserves*, Study in International Finance, No. 35, Princeton University, Princeton, NJ.

Hirsch, S. (1967), *Location of Industry of International Competitiveness*, Oxford University Press, Oxford.

Hirsch, S. (1974), 'Hypotheses regarding trade between developing and industrial countries', in Giersch (1974), pp. 65–82.

Hirsch, S. (1975), 'The product cycle model of international trade – a multi-country cross section', *Oxford Bulletin of Economics and Statistics*, vol. 37, pp. 305–317.

Hirsch, S. (1976), 'An international trade and investment theory of the firm', *Oxford Economic Papers*, vol. 28, pp. 258–270.

HM Treasury (1978), *The European Monetary System*, Cmnd 7405, HMSO, London.

Hocking, R. D. (1980), 'Trade in motor cars between the major European producers', *Economic Journal*, vol. 90, pp. 504–525.

Hodjera, Z. (1971), 'Short-term capital movements of the United Kingdom 1963–1967', *Journal of Political Economy*, vol. 79, pp. 739–775.

Hodjera, Z. (1973), 'International short term capital movements: a survey of theory and empirical analysis', *IMF Staff Papers*, vol. 20, pp. 683–740.

Hood, N. and Young, S. (1979), *The Economics of Multinational Enterprise*, Longman, London.

Hooper, P. and Kolhagen, S. W. (1978), 'The effect of exchange rate uncertainty on the prices and volume of international trade', *Journal of International Economics*, vol. 8, pp. 483–511.

Horst, T. (1972), 'Firm and industry determinants of the decision to invest abroad: an empirical study', *Review of Economics and Statistics*, vol. 54, pp. 258–266.

House of Commons (1983), *International Monetary Arrangements: International Lending by Banks*, Fourth Report of the Treasury and Civil Service Committee, House of Commons Paper 21, Session 1982–83.

Hufbauer, G. C. (1970), 'The impact of national characteristics and technology on the commodity composition of trade in manufactured goods', in Vernon (1970), pp. 145–232.

Hufbauer, G. C. and Chilas, J. G. (1974), 'Specialisation by industrial countries: extent and consequences', in Giersch (1974), pp. 3–38.

Hughes, J. J. and Thirlwall, A. P. (1977), 'Trends and cycles in import penetration in the UK', *Oxford Bulletin of Economics and Statistics*, vol. 39, pp. 301–318.

Hughes, K. S. (1983), 'Exports and innovation: a simultaneous model', University of Bristol Discussion Paper No. 83/141, mimeo.

Hymer, S. H. (1979), *The Multinational Corporation: A Radical Approach*, Cambridge University Press, Cambridge.

Imlah, A. H. (1958), *Economic Elements in the Pax Britannica*, Harvard University Press, Cambridge, Mass.

International Monetary Fund, *Annual Report*, IMF, Washington, DC, annual.

International Monetary Fund, *International Financial Statistics*, IMF, Washington, DC, monthly, plus Yearbook and occasional supplements.

International Monetary Fund, *IMF Survey*, IMF, Washington, DC, twice monthly.

International Monetary Fund, *World Economic Outlook*, IMF, Washington, DC, annual.

Isard, P. (1977), 'How far can we push the law of one price?' *American Economic Review*, vol. 67, pp. 942–948.

Isard, P. (1978), *Exchange Rate Determination: A Survey of Popular Views and Recent Models*, Princeton Study in International Finance, No. 42, Princeton University, Princeton, NJ.

Johnson, H. G. (1953–4), 'Optimum tariffs and retaliation', *Review of Economic Studies*, vol. 22, pp. 142–153; also in H. G. Johnson, *International Trade and Economic Growth*, Allen & Unwin, London (1958).

Johnson, H. G. (1958), 'Towards a general theory of the balance of payments', in *International Trade and Economic Growth*, Allen & Unwin, London, pp. 153–158; also in Caves and Johnson (1968), Cooper (1969), and Frenkel and Johnson (1976).

Johnson, H. G. (1965a), 'Optimal trade intervention in the presence of domestic distortions', in R. E. Baldwin *et al.*, *Trade, Growth and the Balance of Payments*, North Holland, Amsterdam, pp. 3–34; also in Bhagwati (1969a) and Johnson (1971).

Johnson, H. G. (1965b), 'An economic theory of protectionism, tariff bargaining and the formation of customs unions', *Journal of Political Economy*, vol. 73, pp. 256–283; also in Robson (1972).

Johnson, H. G. (1967a), *Economic Policies towards Less Developed Countries*, Allen & Unwin, London.

Johnson, H. G. (1967b), 'Theoretical problems of the international monetary system', *Pakistan Development Review*, vol. 7, pp. 1–28; also in Cooper (1969).

Johnson, H. G. (1971), *Aspects of the Theory of Tariffs*, Allen & Unwin, London.

Johnston, R. B. (1981), *Theories of the Growth of the Euro-Currency Market: A Review of the Euro-currency Deport Multiplier*, BIS Economic Paper No. 4, Bank for International Settlements, Basle.

Johnston, R. B. (1983), *The Economics of the Euro-Market: History, Theory and Policy*, Macmillan, London.

Jones, R. W. (1956–7), 'Factor proportions and the Heckscher–Ohlin Theorem', *Review of Economic Studies*, vol. 24, pp. 1–10; also in Bhagwati (1969a) and Jones (1979).

Jones, R. W. (1971), 'A three factor model in theory, trade and history', in J. Bhagwati *et al.*, *Trade, Balance of Payments and Growth*, North Holland, Amsterdam; also in Jones (1979).

Jones, R. W. (1974), 'The small country in a many-commodity world', *Australian Economic Papers*, vol. 13, pp. 225–236; also in Jones (1979).

Jones, R. W. (1975), 'Presumption and the transfer problem', *Journal of International Economics*, vol. 5, pp. 263–274.

Jones, R. W. (1976), *'Two-ness in Trade Theory: Costs and Benefits'*, Princeton Special Paper in International Economics, No. 12, Princeton University Press, Princeton, NJ.; also in Jones (1979).

Jones, R. W. (1979), *International Trade: Essays in Theory*, North Holland, Amsterdam.

Kafka, A. (1976), *The International Monetary Fund; Reform with Reconstruction?* Princeton Essay in International Finance, No. 118, Princeton University Press, Princeton, NJ.

Katrak, H. (1973), 'Human skills, R. and D. and scale economies in the exports of the United Kingdom and the United States', *Oxford Economic Papers*, vol. 25, pp. 337–360.

Katrak, H. (1982), 'Labour skills, R and D and capital requirements in the international trade and investment of the United Kingdom, 1968–78', *National Institute Economic Review*, No. 101, pp. 38–47.

Katseli-Papaefstratiou, L. T. (1979), *The Re-emergence of the Purchasing Power Parity Doctrine in the 1970s*, Princeton Special Papers in International Finance, No. 13, Princeton University, Princeton, NJ.

Keesing, D. B. and Wolf, M. H. (1980), *Textile Quotas against Developing Countries*, Thames Essay No. 23, Trade Policy Research Centre, London.

Kemp, M. C. and Wan, H. (1976), 'An elementary proposition concerning the formation of customs unions', in M. C. Kemp, *Three Topics in the Theory of International Trade: Distribution, Welfare and Uncertainty*, North Holland, Amsterdam; also in Bhagwati (1981).

Kenen, P. B. (ed.) (1975), *International Trade and Finance*, Cambridge University Press, London.

Keynes, J. M. (1925), *The Economic Consequences of Mr. Churchill*, Hogarth Press, London; abridged in *Essays in Persuasion*, in *Collected Writings*, vol. IX, Macmillan, London (1972).

Keynes, J. M. (1929), 'The German transfer problem', *Economic Journal*, vol. 39, pp. 1–7; reprinted in Ellis and Metzler (1950).

Keynes, J. M. (1931), 'Mitigation by tariff', in *Essays in Persuasion*, Macmillan, London, pp. 271–287; also in *Collected Writings*, vol. IX, Macmillan, London (1972).

Keynes, J. M. (1980), *Collected Writings, Activities; Shaping the Post War World, vol. XXV, The Clearing Union, and vol. XXVI, Bretton Woods and Reparations*, ed. D. Moggridge, Macmillan, London.

Khan, M. S. and Ross, K. Z. (1975), 'Cyclical and secular income elasticities of the demand for imports', *Review of Economics and Statistics*, vol. 59, pp. 357–361.

Kleiman, E. (1976), 'Trade and the decline of colonialism', *Economic Journal*, vol. 86, pp. 459–480.

Komiya, R. (1980), 'Is international co-ordination of national economic policies necessary?', in Oppenheimer (1980), pp. 16–33.

Kopits, G. F. (1976), 'Intra-firm royalties crossing frontiers and transfer pricing behaviour', *Economic Journal*, vol. 86, pp. 781–805.

Kouri, P. and Porter, M. (1974), 'International capital flows and portfolio equilibrium', *Journal of Political Economy*, vol. 82, pp. 443–467.

Krause, M. B. (1972), 'Recent developments in customs union theory: an interpretive survey', *Journal of Economic Literature*, vol. 10, pp. 413–436.

Kravis, I. B. and Lipsey, R. E. (1971), *Price Competitiveness in World Trade*, National Bureau of Economic Research, New York.

Kravis, I. B. and Lipsey, R. E. (1978), 'Price behavior in the light of balance of payments theories', *Journal of International Economics*, vol. 8, pp. 193–246.

Kravis, I. B. and Lipsey, R. E. (1982), 'Prices and market shares in international machinery trade', *Review of Economics and Statistics*, vol. 64, pp. 110–116.

Kreinin, M. E. and Officer, L. H. (1978), *The Monetary Approach to the Balance of Payments*, Princeton Studies in International Finance, No. 43, Princeton University, Princeton, NJ.

Krueger, A. O. (1974), 'The political economy of the rent-seeking society', *American Economic Review*, vol. 64, pp. 291–303.

Krueger, A. O. (1978), *Liberalisation: Attempts and Consequences*, Ballinger, Cambridge, Mass.

Krueger, A. O. (1983a), 'The effects of trade strategies on growth', *Finance and Development*, vol. 20, no. 2, pp. 6–8.

Krueger, A. O. (1983b), *Exchange Rate Determination*, Cambridge University Press, Cambridge.

Krueger, A. O. and Tuncer, B. (1982), 'An empirical test of the infant industry argument', *American Economic Review*, vol. 72, pp 1142–1152.

Krugman, P. R. (1979), 'Increasing returns, monopolistic competition, and international trade', *Journal of International Economics*, vol. 9, pp. 469–479; also in Bhagwati (1981).

Krugman, P. R. (1980), 'Scale economies, product differentiation and the pattern of trade', *American Economic Review*, vol. 70, pp. 950–959.

Krugman, P. R. (1981), 'Intra-industry specialisation and the gains from trade', *Journal of Political Economy*, vol. 89, pp. 959–973.

Krugman, P. R. and Taylor, L. (1978), 'Contractionary effects of devaluation', *Journal of International Economics*, vol. 8, pp. 445–456.

Laidler, D. (1981), 'Some policy implications of the monetary approach to the balance of payments and exchange rate analysis', *Oxford Economic Papers*, vol. 33, Supplement, pp. 70–84; also published as Ellis and Sinclair (1981).

Lall, S. (1973), 'Transfer pricing by multi-national manufacturing firms', *Oxford Bulletin of Economics and Statistics*, vol. 35, pp. 173–195.

Lall, S. (1980), 'Monopolistic advantages and foreign investment by US manufacturing industry', *Oxford Economic Papers*, vol. 32, pp. 102–122.

Lall, S. and Streeten, P. (1977), *Foreign Investment, Transnationals and Developing Countries*, Macmillan, London.

Lancaster, K. (1957), 'The Heckscher–Ohlin trade model: a geometric treatment', *Economica*, vol. 24, pp. 19–39; also in Bhagwati (1969a).

Lancaster, K. (1969), *Introduction to Modern Micro-economics*, Rand McNally, Chicago, Ill.

Lancaster, K. (1980), 'Intra-industry trade under perfect monopolistic competition', *Journal of International Economics*, vol. 10, pp. 151–175.

Lancaster, K. (1982), 'Comment' (on Krugman), in Bhagwati (1982), pp. 208–216.

Lausen, S. and Metzler, L. A. (1950), 'Flexible exchange rates and the theory of employment', *Review of Economics and Statistics*, vol. 32, pp. 281–299.

Layard, P. R. S. and Walters, A. A. (1978), *Micro-economic Theory*, McGraw-Hill, New York.

Leach, D. and Cubbin, J. (1978), 'Import penetration in the UK passenger car market: a cross-section study', *Applied Economics*, vol. 10, pp. 289–303.

Leamer, E. E. (1974), 'The commodity composition of international trade in manufactures: an empirical analysis', *Oxford Economic Papers*, vol. 26, pp. 350–374.

Leamer, E. E. (1980), 'The Leontief paradox reconsidered', *Journal of Political Economy*, vol. 88, pp. 495–503.

Leibenstein, H. (1966), 'Allocative efficiency v. X-efficiency', *American Economic Review*, vol. 56, pp. 392–415.

Leontief, W. A. (1954), 'Domestic production and foreign trade: the American capital position re-examined', *Economia Internazionale*, vol. 7, pp. 3–32; also in Caves and Johnson (1968).

Lerner, A. (1936), 'The symmetry between import and export taxes', *Economica*, vol. 3, pp. 306–313; also in Caves and Johnson (1968).

Levăcić, R. and Rebmann, A. (1982), *Macro-economics, An Introduction to Keynesian and Neo-Classical Controversies*, 2nd edition, Macmillan, London.

Lewis, W. A. (1954), *The Theory of Economic Growth*, Allen & Unwin, London.

Lim, D. (1976), 'Export instability and economic growth: a return to fundamentals', *Oxford Bulletin of Economics and Statistics*, vol. 38, pp. 311–322.

Linder, S. B. (1961), *An Essay on Trade and Transformation*, John Wiley & Sons, New York.

Lindert, P. H. and Kindleberger, C. P. (1982), *International Economics*, 7th edition, Irwin, Homewood, Ill.

Lipsey, R. E. and Weiss, M. Y. (1981), 'Foreign production and exports in manufacturing industries', *Review of Economics and Statistics*, vol. 63, pp. 488–494.

Lipsey, R. G. (1960), 'The theory of customs unions: a general survey', *Economic Journal*, vol. 70, pp. 496–513; also in Bhagwati (1969a, 1981).

Lipsey, R. G. and Lancaster, K. (1956–7), 'The general theory of second-best', *Review of Economic Studies*, vol. 24, pp. 11–32.

List, E. (1841), *The National System of Political Economy*; reprinted by Longmans Green, New York (1904).

Little, I. M. D. (1957), *A Critique of Welfare Economics*, Oxford University Press, Oxford.

Little, I., Scitovsky, T. and Scott, M. (1970), *Industry and Trade in Some Developing Countries: A Comparative Study*, Oxford University Press, Oxford.

Llewellyn, D. T. (1980), *International Financial Integration: The Limits of Sovereignty*, Macmillan, London.

Lloyd, P. J. (1982), '3 × 3 theory of customs unions', *Journal of International Economics*, vol. 12, pp. 41–64.

Loertscher, R. and Wolter, F. (1980), 'Determinants of intra-industry trade: among countries and across industries', *Weltwirtschaftliches Archiv*, vol. 116, pp. 280–293.

Lund, P. J. and Miner, D. A. (1973), *An Econometric Study of the Machine-Tool Industry*, Government Economic Service Occasional Paper No. 4, HMSO, London.

Lyons, B. (1981), 'Price cost margins, market structure, and international trade', in D. Currie, D. Peel and W. Peters, *Microeconomic Analysis*, Croom Helm, London, pp. 276–295.

MacBean, A. I. (1966), *Export Instability and Economic Development*, Allen & Unwin, London.

MacBean, A. I. and Snowden, P. N. (1981), *International Institutions in Trade and Finance*, Allen & Unwin, London.

McCormick, B. (1982), 'North Sea oil: What will our children think?', in Hawkins and McKenzie (1982), pp. 187–212.

McCracken, P. *et al.* (1977), *Towards Full Employment and Price Stability*, OECD, Paris.

MacDougall, G. D. A. (1951), 'British and American exports: a study suggested by the theory of comparative costs', *Economic Journal*, Part I, vol. 61, pp. 697–724; Part II, vol. 62, pp. 487–521; Part I also in Caves and Johnson (1968).

Machlup, F. (1943), *International Trade and the National Income Multiplier*, Blakiston, Philadelphia.

Machlup, F. (1966), *International Monetary Economics*, Allen & Unwin, London.

McKinnon, R. I. (1963), 'Optimum currency areas', *American Economic Review*, vol. 53, pp. 717–724; also in Cooper (1969).

McKinnon, R. I. (1979), *Money in International Exchange*, Oxford University Press, Oxford.

McKinnon, R. I. (1980), 'Exchange-rate instability, trade imbalances and monetary policies in Japan and the United States', in Oppenheimer (1980), pp. 225–250.

McKinnon, R. I. (1981), 'The exchange rate and macro-economic policy: changing postwar perceptions', *Journal of Economic Literature*, vol. 19, pp. 531–557.

Magee, S. P. (1972), 'Welfare effects of restrictions on U.S. trade', *Brookings Papers in Economic Activity*, vol. 2, pp. 645–701.

Magee, S. P. (1973a), 'Factor market distortions, production and trade: a survey', *Oxford Economic Papers*, vol. 25, pp. 1–43.

Magee, S. P. (1973b), 'Currency contracts, pass-through and devaluation', *Brookings Papers on Economic Activity*, vol. 3, pp. 303–323.

Magee, S. P. (1975), 'Prices, incomes and foreign trade', in Kenen (1975), pp. 175–253.

Magee, S. P. (1976), 'The empirical evidence on the monetary approach to the balance of payments and exchange rates', *American Economic Review, Papers and Proceedings*, vol. 66, pp. 163–170.

Magee, S. P. (1980), 'Three simple tests of the Stolper–Samuelson theorem', in Oppenheimer (1980), pp. 138–153.

Maizels, A. (1965), *Industrial Growth and World Trade*, Cambridge University Press, London.

Mansell, K. (1980), 'UK visible trade in the post-war years', *Economic Trends*, October, pp. 135–150.

Markusen, J. R. and Melvin, J. R. (1981), 'Trade, factor prices and the gains from trade with increasing returns to scale', *Canadian Journal of Economics*, vol. 14, pp. 450–469.

Marsden, J. S. and Hollander, G. (1983), 'Floating exchange rates, inflation and selective protectionism: their effects on the competitiveness of Australian industry', in Black and Winters (1983), pp. 92–129.

Mayer, W. (1974), 'Short-run and long-run equilibrium for a small open economy', *Journal of Political Economy*, vol. 82, pp. 955–968.

Mayes, D. G. (1978), 'The effects of economic integration on trade', *Journal of Common Market Studies*, vol. 17, pp. 1–25.

Meade, J. E. (1951), *The Theory of International Economic Policy, Volume 1: The Balance of Payments*, Oxford University Press, Oxford.

Meade, J. E. (1955), 'The case for variable exchange rates', *Three Banks Review*, No. 27, September, pp. 3–28.

Meade, J. E. (1978), 'The meaning of "internal balance"', *Economic Journal*, vol. 88, pp. 423–435.

Mechanical Engineering Economic Development Committee (1968), *Market – The World*, National Economic Development Office, London.

Meese, R. A. and Rogoff, K. (1983), 'Empirical exchange rate models of the seventies: do they fit out of sample?', *Journal of International Economics*, vol. 14, pp. 3–24.

Melvin, J. R. (1969), 'Increasing returns to scale as a determinant of trade', *Canadian Journal of Economics*, vol. 3, pp. 389–402.

Metzler, L. A. (1950), 'A multiple region theory of income and trade', *Econometrica*, vol. 18, pp. 329–354.

Metzler, L. A. (1951), 'A multiple country theory of income transfers', *Journal of Political Economy*, vol. 59, pp. 14–29.

Miles, M. A. (1979), 'The effects of devaluation on the trade balance and the balance of payments: some new results', *Journal of Political Economy*, vol. 87, pp. 600–620.

Miller, M. H. (1971), 'Estimates of the static balance of payments and welfare costs of United Kingdom entry into the Common Market', *National Institute Economic Review*, no. 57, pp. 69–83.

Miller, M. H. and Spencer, J. E. (1977), 'The static economic effects of the UK joining the EEC: a general equilibrium approach', *Review of Economic Studies*, vol. 44, pp. 71–93.

Minhas, B. S. (1963), *An International Comparison of Factor Costs and Factor Use*, North Holland, Amsterdam.

Mishan, E. J. (1967), *The Costs of Economic Growth*, Staples Press, London.

Morgan Guaranty Trust Company, *World Financial Markets*, New York, monthly.

Morton, K. and Tulloch, P. (1977), *Trade and Developing Countries*, Croom Helm, London.

Mundell, R. A. (1957), 'International trade and factor mobility', *American Economic Review*, vol. 47, pp. 321–335; also in Bhagwati (1981).

Mundell, R. A. (1960), 'The pure theory of international trade', *American Economic Review*, vol. 50, pp. 67–110.

Mundell, R. A. (1962), 'The appropriate use of monetary and fiscal policy for internal and external balance', *IMF Staff Papers*, vol. 9, pp. 70–79.

Mundell, R. A. (1963), 'Capital mobility and stabilization policy under fixed and flexible exchange rates', *Canadian Journal of Economics and Political Science*, vol. 29, pp. 475–485; also in Caves and Johnson (1968).

Mundell, R. A. (1964), 'Tariff preferences and the terms of trade', *Manchester School of Economic and Social Studies*, vol. 32, pp. 1–13; also in Robson (1971).

Murphy, R. G. and von Furstenberg, G. M. (1981), 'An analysis of factors influencing the level of SDR holdings in non-oil developing countries', *IMF Staff Papers*, vol. 28, pp. 310–337.

Murray, T. (1977), *Trade Preferences for Developing Countries*, Macmillan, London.

Mussa, M. (1979), 'The two-sector model in terms of its dual: a geometric exposition', *Journal of International Economics*, vol. 9, pp. 513–526; also in Bhagwati (1981).

National Economic Development Council (1965), *Investment in Machine Tools: A Survey by the Management Consultants Association*, HMSO, London.

National Economic Development Office (1977), *International Price Competitiveness, Non-Price Factors and Export Performance*, NEDO, London.

National Institute (1971), 'Entry into the EEC: a comment on some of the economic issues', *National Institute Economic Review*, no. 57, pp. 35–61.

National Institute Economic Review, National Institute of Economic and Social Research, London, quarterly.

Neary, J. P. (1978), 'Short-run capital specificity and the pure theory of international trade', *Economic Journal*, vol. 88, pp. 488–510.

Nellis, J. G. (1982), 'A principal components analysis of international financial integration under fixed and floating exchange rate regimes', *Applied Economics*, vol. 14, pp. 339–354.

Newlyn, W. (1965), 'Gains and losses in the East African Common Market', *Yorkshire Bulletin*, vol. 17, pp. 130–138; also in Robson (1971).

Niehans, J. (1980), 'Purchasing power parity under flexible rates', in Oppenheimer (1980), pp. 255–272.

Niehans, J. and Hewson, J. (1976), 'The Euro-dollar market and monetary theory', *Journal of Money, Credit and Banking*, vol. 1, pp. 1–27.

Nowzad, B. (1981), *The IMF and its Critics*, Princeton Essay in International Finance, No. 146, Princeton University, Princeton, NJ.

Officer, L. H. (1976a), 'The purchasing power parity theory of exchange rate: a review article', *IMF Staff Papers*, vol. 23, pp. 1–60.

Officer, L. H. (1976b), 'The productivity bias in purchasing power parity: an econometric investigation', *IMF Staff Papers*, vol. 23, pp. 545–579.

Ohlin, B. (1929), 'The reparations problem: a discussion', *Economic Journal*, vol. 39, pp. 172–173; also in Ellis and Metzler (1950).

Ohlin, B. (1933), *Interregional and International Trade*, Harvard University Press, Cambridge, Mass.

Okun, A. M. (1981), *Prices and Quantities: a Macro-Economic Analysis*, Basil Blackwell, Oxford.

Oppenheimer, P. (1980), *Issues in International Economics*, Oriel Press, London.

Oppenheimer, P. *et al.* (1978), *Business Views on Exchange Rate Policy*, Confederation of British Industry, London.

Orcutt, G. H. (1950), 'Measurement of price elasticities in international trade', *Review of Economics and Statistics*, vol. 32, pp. 117–132.

Organization for Economic Co-operation and Development, *Economic Outlook*, OECD, Paris, semi-annual.

Organization for Economic Co-operation and Development (1979), *The OECD Linkage Model*, OECD Economic Outlook Occasional Papers, January.

Organization for Economic Co-operation and Development (1981), *International Investment and Multinational Enterprises, Recent International Direct Investment Trends*, OECD, Paris.

Oulton, N. (1976), 'Effective protection of British industry', in Corden and Fels (1976), pp. 46–90.

Page, S. A. B. (1977), 'Currency of invoicing in merchandise trade', *National Institute Economic Review*, no. 81, pp. 77–81.

Page, S. A. B. (1979), 'The management of international trade', in R. L. Major, *Britain's Trade and Exchange-Rate Policy*, Heinemann, London, pp. 164–199.

Page, S. A. B. (1981), 'The revival of protectionism and its consequences for Europe', *Journal of Common Market Studies*, vol. 20, pp. 17–40.

357

Page, S. A. B. (1982), 'The development of the EMS', *National Institute Economic Review*, no. 102, December, pp. 52–62.

Pagoulatos, E. and Sorensen, R. (1976), 'Foreign trade, concentration and profitability in open economies', *European Economic Review*, vol. 8, pp. 255–267.

Panagariya, A. (1980), 'Variable returns to scale in general equilibrium theory once again', *Journal of International Economics*, vol. 10, pp. 499–525.

Panić, M. (1975), 'Why the UK's propensity to import is high', *Lloyds Bank Review*, no. 115, January, pp. 1–12.

Panić, M. and Joyce, P. L. (1980), 'UK manufacturing industry: international integration and trade performance', *Bank of England Quarterly Review*, no. 1, pp. 42–55.

Panić, M. and Rajan, A. H. (1971), *Product Changes in Industrial Countries' Trade: 1955–68*, National Economic Development Office, London.

Payer, C. (1974), *The Debt Trap*, Penguin, Harmondsworth, Middx.

Pearce, I. F. (1961), 'The problem of the balance of payments', *International Economic Review*, vol. 1, pp. 1–21.

Pearce, I. F. (1970), *International Trade*, Macmillan, London.

Pelcovits, M. D. (1976), 'Quotas versus tariffs', *Journal of International Economics*, vol. 8, pp. 363–370.

Pincus, J. J. (1975), 'Pressure groups and the pattern of tariffs', *Journal of Political Economy*, vol. 85, pp. 757–778.

Posner, M. V. (1961), 'International trade and technical change', *Oxford Economic Papers*, vol. 13, pp. 323–341.

Pratten, C. F. (1971), *Economies of Scale in Manufacturing Industry*, Cambridge University Press, London.

Pratten, C. F. (1976), *Labour Productivity Differentials within International Companies*, Cambridge University Press, Cambridge.

Preeg, E. H. (1970), *Traders and Diplomats*, Brookings Institution, Washington, DC.

Ray, E. J. (1981), 'Tariff and non-tariff barriers to trade in the United States and abroad', *Review of Economics and Statistics*, vol. 63, pp. 161–168.

Ray, G. F. (1966), *The Competitiveness of British Industrial Products: a Round-Up*, Woolwich Economic Papers, No. 10, London.

Ray, G. F. (1979), 'Comment', in F. Blackaby (ed.), *De-industrialisation*, Heinemann, London, pp. 73–77.

Reddaway, W. B. (1968), *Effects of United Kingdom Direct Investment Overseas*, Cambridge University Press, Cambridge.

Rees, R. D. and Layard, P. R. G. (1972), *The Determinants of UK Imports*, Government Economic Service Occasional Paper, No. 3, HMSO, London.

Ricardo, D. (1817), *Principles of Political Economy*; reprinted as vol. 1 of P. Sraffa (ed.), *The Works and Correspondence of David Ricardo*, Cambridge University Press, London (1951).

Richardson, J. D. (1978), 'Some empirical evidence of commodity arbitrage and the law of one price', *Journal of International Economics*, vol. 8, pp. 341–352.

Riedel, J. (1977), 'Tariff concessions in the Kennedy Round and the structure of protection in West Germany: an econometric assessment', *Journal of International Economics*, vol. 7, pp. 133–144.

Ripley, D. M. (1978), 'The transmission of fluctuations in economic activity: some recent evidence', in *Managed Exchange-Rate Flexibility*, Conference Series No. 20, Federal Reserve Bank of Boston, Boston, Mass.

Robinson, J. (1937), 'The foreign exchanges', in *Essays in the Theory of Employment*, Basil Blackwell, Oxford, pp. 134–155.

Robson, P. (1971), *International Economic Integration*, Penguin, Harmondsworth, Middx.

Robson, P. (1984), *The Economics of International Integration*, 2nd edn, Allen & Unwin, London.

Rodriguez, C. A. (1974), 'The non-equivalence of tariffs and quotas under retaliation', *Journal of International Economics*, vol. 4, pp. 295–298.

Roningen, V. and Yeats, A. J. (1976), 'Non-tariff distortions of international trade: some preliminary empirical evidence', *Weltwirtschaftliches Archiv*, vol. 112, pp. 613–623.

Rothwell, R. (1980), 'Innovation: textile machinery', in K. Pavitt (ed.), *Technical Innovation and British Economic Performance*, Macmillan, London, pp. 125–141.

Bibliography

Russell, R. R. and Wilkinson, M. (1979), *Microeconomics: A Synthesis of Modern and Neo-Classical Analysis*, John Wiley, New York.

Rybczynski, T. (1955), 'Factor endowments and relative commodity prices', *Economica*, vol. 22, pp. 336–341; also in Caves and Johnson (1968).

Salter, W. E. G. (1959), 'Internal and external balance: the role of price and expenditure effects', *Economic Record*, vol. 35, pp. 226–258.

Sampson, G. P. and Snape, R. H. (1980), 'Effects of the EEC's variable import levies', *Journal of Political Economy*, vol. 88, pp. 1026–1040.

Samuelson, P. A. (1948), 'International trade and the equalisation of factor prices', *Economic Journal*, vol. 58, pp. 163–184.

Samuelson, P. A. (1949), 'International factor-price equalisation once again', *Economic Journal*, vol. 59, pp. 181–187; also in Caves and Johnson (1968) and Bhagwati (1981).

Samuelson, P. A. (1952), 'The transfer problem and transport costs: the terms of trade when impediments are absent', *Economic Journal*, vol. 62, pp. 278–304; also in Caves and Johnson (1968).

Samuelson, P. A. (1954), 'The transfer problem and transport costs, II: analysis of effects of trade impediments', *Economic Journal*, vol. 64, pp. 264–289; also in Caves and Johnson (1968).

Samuelson, P. A. (1962), 'The gains from trade once again', *Economic Journal*, vol. 72, pp. 820–829; also in Bhagwati (1969a, 1981).

Samuelson, P. A. (1981), 'Bertil Ohlin 1899–1979', *Journal of International Economics*, vol. 11, pp. 147–164.

Sapir, A. and Lutz, E. (1981), *Trade in Services: Economic Determinants and Development-Related Issues*, World Bank Staff Working Paper, No. 480, The World Bank, Washington, DC.

Schadler, S. (1977), 'Sources of exchange rate variability: theory and empirical evidence', *IMF Staff Papers*, vol. 24, pp. 253–296.

Smallwood, C. (1975), 'Economic growth and the pure theory of international trade', *Scottish Journal of Political Economy*, vol. 22, pp. 135–159.

Smith, A. (1776), *An Inquiry into the Nature and Causes of Wealth of Nations*; reprinted by Methuen, London (1961), ed. E. Cannon.

Smith, M. A. M. (1982), 'Some simple results on the gains from trade, from growth and from public production', *Journal of International Economics*, vol. 13, pp. 215–230.

Smith, S. R. *et al.* (1983), *UK Trade in Manufacturing: The Pattern of Specialisation during the 1970s*, Government Economic Service Working Paper, HMSO, London.

Snape, R. H. (1963), 'Some effects of protection in the world sugar industry', *Economica*, vol. 30, pp. 63–73.

Soete, L. L. G. (1981), 'A general test of technological gap trade theory', *Weltwirtschaftliches Archiv*, vol. 117, pp. 638–660.

Solomon, R. F. and Ingham, K. P. D. (1977), 'Discriminating between MNC subsidiaries and indigenous companies: a comparative analysis of British mechanical engineering', *Oxford Bulletin of Economics and Statistics*, vol. 39, pp. 127–138.

Spraos, J. (1980), 'The statistical debate on the net barter terms of trade between primary commodities and manufactures', *Economic Journal*, vol. 90, pp. 107–128.

Stern, R. M. (1973), *The Balance of Payments: Theory and Economic Policy*, Macmillan, London.

Stern, R. M. (1975), 'Testing trade theories', in Kenen (1975), pp. 3–49.

Stern, R. M. and Maskus, K. E. (1981), 'Determinants of the structure of US foreign trade, 1958–76', *Journal of International Economics*, vol. 11, pp. 207–224.

Stern, R. M., Francis, J. and Schumacher, B. (1976), *Price Elasticities in International Trade*, Macmillan, London.

Stern, R. M. *et al.* (1977), *The Presentation of the U.S. Balance of Payments: A Symposium*, Essay in International Finance, No. 123, Princeton University, Princeton, NJ.

Steuer, M. D. (1973), *The Impact of Foreign Direct Investment on the United Kingdom*, HMSO, London.

Steuer, M. D., Ball, R. J. and Eaton, J. R. (1966), 'The effect of waiting times on foreign orders for machine tools', *Economica*, vol. 33, pp. 387–403.

Stolper, W. F. and Samuelson, P. A. (1941), 'Protection and real wages', *Review of Economic Studies*, vol. 9, pp. 58–73; also in Ellis and Metzler (1950).

359

Strange, S. (1971), *Sterling and British Policy*, Oxford University Press, London.

Swan, T. W. (1955), 'Longer-run problems of the balance of payments', Paper to the Congress of the Australian and New Zealand Association for the Advancement of Science; also in Caves and Johnson (1968).

Swann, D. (1978), *The Economics of the Common Market*, 4th edition, Penguin, Harmondsworth, Middx.

Takacs, W. E. (1978), 'The non-equivalence of tariffs, import quotas and the voluntary export restraints', *Journal of International Economics*, vol. 8, pp. 565–574.

Takacs, W. E. (1981), 'Pressures for protectionism: an empirical analysis', *Economic Inquiry*, vol. 19, pp. 687–693.

Taplin, G. R. (1973), 'A model of world trade', in R. J. Ball (ed.), *The International Linkage of National Economic Models*, North Holland, Amsterdam, pp. 177–223.

Tarr, D. G. (1979), 'Cyclical dumping: the case of steel products', *Journal of International Economics*, vol. 9, pp. 57–64.

Thirlwall, A. P. (1979), 'The balance of payments constraint as an explanation of international growth rate differences', *Banca Nazionale del Lavoro Quarterly Review*, no. 128, pp. 45–54.

Thirlwall, A. P. (1980), *Balance of Payments Theory and the United Kingdom Experience*, Macmillan, London.

Tilton, J. F. (1971), *International Diffusion of Technology: The Case of Semi-conductors*, The Brookings Institute, Washington, DC.

Tinbergen, J. (1952), *On the Theory of Economic Policy*, North Holland, Amsterdam.

Tower, E. and Willett, T. D. (1976), *The Theory of Optimum Currency Areas and Exchange-Rate Flexibility*, Special Paper in International Economics, No. 11, Princeton University, Princeton, NJ.

Trades Union Congress, *Economic Review*, TUC, London, annual.

Triffin, R. (1960), *Gold and the Dollar Crisis*, Yale University Press, New Haven, Conn.

Triffin, R. (1964), *The Evolution of the International Monetary System: Historical Reappraisal and Future Perspectives*, Princeton Study in International Finance, No. 12, Princeton University, Princeton, NJ.; also in Cooper (1969).

Truman, E. V. (1975), 'The effects of European economic integration on the production and trade of manufactured product', in Balassa (1975), pp. 3–40.

Tsoukalis, L. (1977), *The Politics and Economics of European Monetary Integration*, Allen & Unwin, London.

Tyler, W. G. (1981), 'Growth and export expansion in developing countries; some empirical evidence', *Journal of Development Economics*, vol. 9, pp. 121–130.

United Nations, *Monthly Bulletin of Statistics*, United Nations, New York, monthly.

United Nations (1978), *Transnational Corporations in World Development*, Commission on Transnational Corporations, E/C.10/38, UN, New York.

United Nations (1981), *Commodity Indexes for the Standard International Trade Classification, Revision 2*, Statistical Paper Series M., No. 38/Rev., UN, New York.

United Nations Conference on Trade and Development, *General Report on the Implementation of the Generalized System of Preferences*, UNCTAD, Geneva, periodical.

United Nations Conference on Trade and Development, *Handbook of International Trade and Development Statistics*, UNCTAD, Geneva, annual.

Utton, M. A. and Morgan, A. D. (1983), *Concentration and Foreign Trade*, Cambridge University Press, Cambridge.

Vaitsos, C. V. (1976), 'Power, knowledge and development policy', in G. K. Helleiner, *A World Divided*, Cambridge University Press, Cambridge, pp. 113–146.

Vaitsos, C. V. (1974), *Intercountry Income Distribution and Transnational Enterprises*, Oxford University Press, Oxford.

Vanek, J. (1959), 'The natural resource content of foreign trade, 1870–1955, and the relative abundance of natural resources in the United States', *Review of Economics and Statistics*, vol. 41, pp. 146–153.

Bibliography

Vernon, R. (1966), 'International investment and international trade in the product cycle', *Quarterly Journal of Economics*, vol. 80, pp. 190–207.

Vernon, R. (1970), *The Technology Factor in International Trade*, National Bureau of Economic Research, New York.

Viner, J. (1937), *Studies in the Theory of International Trade*, Allen & Unwin, London.

Viner, J. (1950), *The Customs Union Issue*, Carnegie Endowment for International Peace, New York.

Walker, W. B. (1979), *Industrial Innovation and International Trade Performance*, J.A.I. Press, Greenwich, Conn.

Wells, J. D. and Imber, J. C. (1977), 'The home and export performance of UK industries', *Economic Trends*, August, pp. 78–89.

Wells, L. T. (1969), 'Test of a product cycle model of international trade: U.S. exports of consumer durables', *Quarterly Journal of Economics*, vol. 82, pp. 152–162.

Wells, S. J. (1964), *British Export Performance: A Comparative Study*, Cambridge University Press, London.

Weston, A. (1981), 'Who is more preferred? An analysis of the new Generalized System of Preferences', in C. Stevens, *The EEC and the Third World: A Survey*, Volume 2, ODI/IDS, London, pp. 73–86.

Whitley, J. D. (1979), 'Imports of finished manufactures: the effects of prices, demand, and capacity', *Manchester School*, vol. 47, pp. 325–348.

Whitley, J. D. and Wilson, R. A. (1979), 'Trends and cycles in import penetration in the UK: A comment', *Oxford Bulletin of Economics and Statistics*, vol. 41, pp. 68–77.

Whitman, M. von (1975), 'Global monetarism and the monetary approach to the balance of payments', *Brookings Papers in Economic Activity*, vol. 5, pp. 491–536.

Williamson, J. H. (1971), *On Estimating the Income Effects of British Entry to the EEC*, Surrey Papers in Economics, No. 6, Surrey University Press, Guildford, Surrey.

Williamson, J. H. (1973), 'International liquidity: a survey', *Economic Journal*, vol. 83, pp. 685–746; also in Royal Economic Society, *Surveys of Applied Economics, vol. II*, Macmillan, London.

Williamson, J. H. (1977), *The Failure of World Monetary Reform, 1971–74*, Nelson, Sunbury-on-Thames, Surrey.

Williamson, J. H. and Bottrill, A. (1969), 'The impact of customs unions on trade in manufactures', *Oxford Economic Papers*, vol. 23, pp. 323–351.

Winch, D. M. (1971), *Analytical Welfare Economics*, Penguin, Harmondsworth, Middx.

Winters, L. A. (1974), 'United Kingdom exports and the pressure of demand: a note', *Economic Journal*, vol. 84, pp. 623–628.

Winters, L. A. (1978), 'The accounting framework of certain balance of payments theories: a didactic note', *Journal of Economic Studies*, vol. 5, pp. 31–36.

Winters, L. A. (1981), *An Econometric Model of the Export Sector: UK Visible Exports and their Prices, 1955–1973*, No. 4 of Cambridge Studies in Applied Econometrics, Cambridge University Press, London.

Winters, L. A. (1983a), 'The consequences of devaluing sterling', in *International Monetary Arrangements*, Fourth Report of the Treasury and Civil Service Committee of the House of Commons, Volume III, House of Commons Paper 21-III, Session 1982–83, pp. 96–136.

Winters, L. A. (1983b), 'Memorandum', in House of Lords, *7th Report of the Select Committee on the European Communities: The United Kingdom's Changing Trade Patterns Subsequent to Membership of the European Community*, HMSO, London, pp. 369–387.

Winters, L. A. (1984a), 'British imports of manufactures and the Common Market', *Oxford Economic Papers*, vol. 36, pp. 103–118.

Winters, L. A. (1984b), 'Britain's trade patterns since joining the Common Market', *British Review of Economic Issues*.

Winters, L. A. (1984c), 'The patterns of international trade 1950–1980', *The Economic Review*, vol. 1, no. 4, pp. 33–38.

Wolf, B. M. (1977), 'Industrial diversification and internationalisation: some empirical evidence', *Journal of Industrial Economics*, vol. 26, pp. 177–191.

Wonnacott, P. and Wonnacott, R. (1981), 'Is unilateral tariff reduction preferable to a customs union? The curious case of the missing foreign tariffs', *American Economic Review*, vol. 71, pp. 704–714.

World Bank, *World Development Report*, Oxford University Press, Oxford, annual.

World Bank, *Annual Report*, IBRD, Washington, DC, annual.

Yeager, L. B. (1976), *International Monetary Relations: Theory, History and Policy*, 2nd edition, Harper & Row, New York.

Yeats, A. J. (1979), *Trade Barriers Facing Developing Countries*, Macmillan, London.

Yeomans, K. A. (1968), *Applied Statistics, Volume Two*, Penguin, Harmondsworth, Middx.

Author Index

Subject Index